SHOOT THEM DOWN!

The Flying Saucer Air Wars Of 1952

By Frank C. Feschino, Jr.

Shoot Them Down!
The Flying Saucer Air Wars Of 1952

Copyright 2007, Frank C. Feschino, Jr.

All Rights reserved. No part of this book may be used or reproduced by any means, graphic, electronic, or mechanical, including photocopying, recording, taping or by any information retrieval system without the written permission of the author.

Cover Illustration by Frank C. Feschino, Jr.
Interior Illustrations by Frank C. Feschino, Jr.

Photographers: Robert Tabasky, Douglas Gokey, Shona Feschino, Fred May and Frank C. Feschino, Jr.

Format and Graphic art designs by Nathan P. Carlson
Front and back cover designs by Nathan P. Carlson

ISBN: 978-0-6151-5553-1

Books may be ordered by contacting:

Lulu Enterprises
http://www.lulu.com
http://www.lulu.com/flatwoodsmonster

For more information go to:
http://www.flatwoodsmonster.com

Printed in the United States of America.

DEDICATION

Dedicated to the brave American fighter pilots and flyers who scrambled into the skies after UFOs to "shoot them down," and never returned home.

Chasing a flying saucer in a plane in January, 1948, Capt. Thomas Mantell, Jr., of Louisville crashed, died in this wreckage.

THE COURIER-JOURNAL MAGAZINE, APRIL 25, 1954

Oh, what a tangled web we weave, when first we practice to deceive!

— Sir Walter Scott, Lochinvar, 1808

CONTENTS

Foreword..	iii
Introduction...	vii
Acknowledgements..	ix
Chapter 1- June 1952- The "Space Ships" of Summer.................	1
Chapter 2– July Heats Up...	17
Chapter 3- The July 19 Washington Sightings............................	28
Chapter 4- The July 1952 Saucer Pursuits..................................	35
Chapter 5 – July 26, 1952-The Saucers Return To Washington....	42
Chapter 6 – "Shoot Down Flying Discs".....................................	49
Chapter 7 - The Flying Saucer Physicist....................................	60
Chapter 8 – Starfires and Sabre Jets...	70
Chapter 9 – August 5, 1952-Westover and Washington.............	75
Chapter 10- August Heats Up..	99
Chapter 11- The Space Ships Return...	108
Chapter 12 – Sanctuary..	120
Chapter 13 - Knight-Fall...	126
Chapter 14 - The Air Force Enters...	130
Chapter 15 - Air Force Intelligence!..	138
Chapter 16 - Double Jeopardy...	148
Chapter 17- Triple Threat..	160
Chapter 18 – "Shot Down"..	168
Chapter 19 - Case #2078-Was Astronomical.............................	177
Chapter 20 - Keyhoe Speaks Out...	185
Chapter 21 - The Air Force Fighters..	197
Chapter 22 - The Air Force Speaks...	203
Chapter 23 – Forgotten..	213
Chapter 24 - The Truth?..	217
Chapter 25 - With Out a Trace..	239
Chapter 26 – "Shoot Them Down"..	260
Chapter 27 - Descending Guardians..	277
Chapter 28 - Exit...	290
Chapter 29 – Ceased..	293
Chapter 30 - The Reptilians..	297
Chapter 31 – The Summer Ends..	314
Chapter 32 – Autumn Explanations...	320
Chapter 33 – Yesteryear and Today...	328
Chapter 34 – The Six Deadly Years..	332
Epilogue..	358
Selected Sources...	363
About the Author..	370

Foreword

Several years ago, I met Frank Feschino, Jr. at a UFO Conference in Gulf Breeze, Florida. We talked briefly about his investigation of the Flatwoods, West Virginia "monster" story. I wished him well having read just enough about the case to think it was probably worth pursuing. It was only after Frank telephoned in 2002 to invite me to participate in a 50th Anniversary Celebration of the event in Flatwoods on September 12, 2002, that I decided I had better review the case more carefully. I did and agreed to attend at the expense of Frank and an associate. It was a fascinating experience.

Most importantly, I had a chance to meet with Mrs. May and her two sons, who were among the most important first hand witnesses. I also met the mayor of Flatwoods, Mayor Clise, and to my surprise, she had been a witness to a UFO that flew over Flatwoods that night. Frank led a group of people attending the anniversary celebration in a trek to the actual locations on the farm where the incident occurred. I had the opportunity to see the flat mountaintop pasture where the craft had landed, the gully down below to which it had moved and the remains of the tree from behind which "the monster" emerged. We were all there on the farm exactly 50 years to the minute after the event took place. As soon as I was on the site, I realized I could add some new information. For example, once I saw the mountaintop location on the farm where the object landed, it was clear that it was the highest flat empty pasture in the area and a natural place for any pilot in trouble to try to land. One pilot I spoke with explained, "Look for a flat place and avoid mountains and trees."

I was particularly intrigued to find that Frank's persistence and hard work had involved important and unique resources including first time-videotaped interviews with key witnesses. He interviewed Colonel Dale Leavitt, the West Virginia National Guard commander who led his troops out onto the farm in Flatwoods, in secret, on September 12, 1952, gathering evidence, which was shipped off. He received no feedback. Also interviewed was A. Lee Stewart Jr., a local newspaper publisher and reporter, who was "Johnny-on-the-spot" with interviews with the main witnesses' right after the event. From my experience and my investigations of the Roswell Incident since the mid 1970s, I know how much work it takes to find people and then convince them to talk. Frank did it. Both Leavitt and Stewart are now dead, but Frank, fortunately won those races with the undertaker. Their testimony (backed by video) is included in this book.

It is well known that 1952 was a very big year for UFO sightings. Project Blue Book noted more sightings in 1952 than in any other year. Summaries of important cases often include that Nash-Fortenberry airliner observation over Chesapeake Bay on July 14, 1952, which is included in detail in this book. During a radio show a few years ago, the host and I were talking about the famous July 1952 Washington area sightings. Observations of UFOs were made by pilots and radar operators over Washington, DC, including certain areas that had forbidden flying zones above them such as the White House. As part of that radio show, a man called in saying he had been stationed at Andrews Air Force Base just outside Washington in 1952. He said there were frequent scrambles of Air Force jets after UFOs over the next year. He was particularly impressed with a case where two fighter jets went up and only one came back. The caller, with whom I spoke later, said that the pilot who did come back kept repeating, "It went straight up." Weeks later there was a newspaper article indicating that that particular plane had been "lost at sea." Frank had also noted and investigated a documented incident involving a Air Force jet interceptor that simply vanished at sea on September 12, 1952, shortly before the "Flatwoods Monster" incident occurred.

When the above information was made public, there were those who complained that the Public Relations material made it sound as though there had been dogfights between UFOs and military interceptors. One researcher said he was sure there hadn't been. He also demanded signed sworn investigative reports about the supposed disappearance of aircraft chasing UFOs *as though such highly classified material would be available.* This led Frank and I to dig much deeper into files of 1952. With the very welcome assistance of researchers Dr. David Rudiak, Barry Greenwood, and Daniel Wilson we discovered, to our surprise that the situation was much more complex than we had known. Barry Greenwood, who possesses a huge collection of scrapbooks of newspaper clippings about sightings, also, found at my request a number of UFO related articles from that era.

There was unambiguous evidence revealed in July of 1952 that military pilots had been ordered to "shoot down" UFOs who failed to land when instructed to do so including an Air Force Major General who said, "interceptor planes" were scrambled "several hundred times" after them. We also found an abundance of information in old out of print books and periodicals about such related events as told by past researchers. It was also clear that there were very many crashes of military fighter aircraft during that time, most over the United States. In three instances pilots, each with over hundred missions in Korea, fighting off MIGs, had come back to the USA and then crashed. Accident records were quite incomplete or missing at the National Archives. Words such as "disappeared" and "disintegrated" appeared in brief news accounts of such events. *It is clear that there was a real battle going on, unheralded in the press, between UFOs and our aircraft.* Why such orders and activities, if UFOs were not considered a threat to the security of the United States?

Frank spent years researching this subject and gathered up information that was scattered in a shotgun pattern. He reviewed 1952 Blue Book cases, researched declassified USAF accident reports involving fighter planes and examined *The New York Times* for fighter accidents as well. Frank also went to Glastonbury, Ct. to investigate a peculiar fighter crash that occurred there back in 1952 during a day of UFO activity. Throughout this time, we corresponded and also met at several UFO conferences around the country and went over much of the material. With all this information at hand, Frank analyzed it, reviewed several fighter cases with me including fighter crash statistics, and then put all the information in this book, which follows Project Blue Book through the summer of 1952.

I also reviewed what was happening in 1952 that might have led to an upsurge in activity. I started from the assumption that just as the United States and Russia considered that investigation and analysis of each other's activities with regard to all things military – especially their weapons delivery systems and electronic sensing systems for monitoring each others over flights – to be of great importance, so too would aliens wish to monitor these same capabilities. Both the US and the Soviet Union had quietly sent aircraft to near, and sometimes over, the other country's borders to see how well and rapidly airborne and electronic defense systems responded. Each side shot down a number of the other side's aircraft...all in secret until decades later. See, for example, James Bamford's "Body of Secrets."

An important book by William Burrows titled, *By Any Means Necessary*, (2001), details the loss of 166 crewmembers in reconnaissance missions near or over the Soviet Union, China, and North Korea, mostly in the 1940s and 1950s. The families of the lost airmen and the public were told nothing about what they had been doing leading to their unfortunate deaths as they crashed into oceans. Only in 2001 at a government-sponsored gathering, were the families given medals and information about the deaths of their loved ones, in some cases more than 50 years earlier. These incidents, and many other examples, exist of the government being willing and able to keep secrets most of which the Soviets had been aware of.

For example, in 1995 the Naval Research Laboratory finally noted that it had launched a series of Corona Electronic Intelligence spy satellites. The first success, after 12 hidden failures had taken place in 1960, 35 years earlier and obtained more information about Soviet electronic and radar installations than all the U-2 flights that had preceded it. The U-2 Spy Plane was developed in secret for the CIA in an attempt to fly much higher (above the range of Soviet aircraft and missiles) over the USSR to obtain electronic and military base information. The Soviet Union and the inner circle of the US government were both aware of these flights. Neither spoke out until Gary Powers was shot down in 1960 and he and his cameras paraded before the world.

I also recalled that at the Truman Library I had read a hair-raising comment in the declassified minutes of a National Security Council Meeting in 1951. It stated that the Soviets had made more progress in the development of nuclear weapons and systems for delivering them in the past 18 months than had been expected for the next 5 years. There was obviously great concern. Many, probably legitimately, expected Stalin to attack. Perhaps fortunately, he died March 3, 1953.

I had also already obtained information about Air Defense Command radar installations in 1947 in connection with my research on the Roswell Incident as reported, for example, in my book *Crash at Corona* with Don Berliner. I was then able to obtain more information about those and newer ADC radar installations in 1952. As it happens, many new and more sophisticated radar installations were being added along the US boundaries. Many were in the areas in the Eastern part of the US where Frank's research had demonstrated that there were large numbers of UFO sightings during the summer of 1952.

It also seemed reasonable to me that just as the US and Soviet military organizations would want to keep tabs on the development of electronic defense systems and new weapons technology, the alien visitors would be equally concerned about such matters. There indeed were important new developments taking place. US jet fighters were being fitted with new weapons control systems for electronically controlling the flight of air-to-air missiles rather than merely aiming the aircraft at a target. These would be of interest to any intruding airborne vehicles, whether Soviet or alien. Radar systems were also being improved and refined. In addition, there was a lot of testing of new and better nuclear weapons...and in new locations besides the Southwestern United States and islands in the Pacific. The first Soviet Nuclear Weapon, Joe 1, was tested August 29, 1949. Joe 2 was much more powerful and was tested October 3, 1951. Joe 3 was even more powerful (40 Kilotons) and was tested on October 22, 1951.

Obviously, there were now two countries testing more and more powerful nuclear weapons. Great Britain tested its first Atomic Bomb near Australia on October 3, 1952. If aliens were concerned about new aircraft and new radar, imagine the splash as seen from above when the first H-bomb with its three-mile wide fireball was tested at Eniwetok on November 1, 1952. The rating was 10.4 megatons (10.4 Million tons of TNT equivalent) compared to Hiroshima's "mere" 15 kilotons (15 thousand tons of TNT equivalent). Thinking of UFOs as alien spy satellites, one should note that the preparations took months and involved 242 Navy ships and 156 aircraft out in the middle of nowhere.

Equally impressive to alien visitors and closer in time would have been Operation Mainbrace, the NATO Naval exercise, which began on Sept. 13, 1952, near Norway and Denmark with headquarters in Scotland. It was the largest NATO military maneuver up to that time, involved 80,000 men, 1000 aircraft and 200 ships, and lasted 12 days. Contingents were present from nine countries and obviously would have been heading that way for the week preceding the Flatwoods event on Sept. 12. Furthermore, several UFOs were sighted during the Operation Mainbrace maneuvers, which are all well documented.

An important aspect of the Flatwoods case besides the US government's endeavor to cover-up this incident, is the attempt by UFO debunkers to try to explain away this astounding and important event. Particularly persistent in his negative attack has been Dr. Joe Nickell, a full time employee of the Committee for the Scientific Investigation of Claims of the Paranormal. Dr. Nickell, whose three degrees are in English, not in science, has worked as *a stage magician*. One can see some situations where this expertise might come in handy, but with a case like Flatwoods? On a daylong investigation, Nickell did visit Flatwoods, but did not talk to the Mays and did not visit the actual site. His explanations of a 6-foot tall barn owl and a meteor crash seem absurd on their face. There were a number of witnesses who saw a slowly moving large object land. There was no crater, no meteorite fragments in the ground, no shock wave and no meteor shower at the time. Astronomy experts have provided Frank with the fact that there are only three instances on record in West Virginia of recovered meteorites. A six-foot owl that puts out a noxious vapor, has never been reported before or since, and certainly sounds like trying to fit a square peg into a round hole... especially when there were no reports of moving wings. All the eyewitness testimonies of the so-called "monster," actually indicate it was a mechanical device about 12 feet tall. Having taken on other so-called skeptics, I was anxious to do battle with the likes of Nickell and add a word about the "Committee for the Scientific Investigation of Claims of the Paranormal."

Frankly, as somebody who has worked on the space program, it is hard for me to imagine why anyone would consider flying saucers (truly unidentified flying objects) as paranormal phenomena. After all, with our own short history, we earthlings have learned to fly a wide variety of airborne and space borne vehicles. We have flown huge rockets and broken the gravitational bonds of Earth. Considering that there are sun-like stars in our local galactic neighborhood (less than 40 light years away) that are one billion years older than the sun, it seems perfectly normal to me that there are visitors somewhat more technologically advanced than are we. Given our obvious status as a primitive society whose major activity is tribal warfare, why would one expect them to treat us as equals? What is paranormal about advanced vehicles capable of flying around in our atmosphere and being able to both probe and avoid our defense systems? Technological seems far more appropriate than "paranormal."

With all the multiple witness radar visual cases, more than 5,000 physical trace cases from 95 countries, the testimony of more than 4,000 pilots about manufactured airborne vehicles behaving in ways Earthling technology cannot yet duplicate (often involving radar), what is paranormal? Within the context of rapidly expanding and important US and Soviet technological advances that may well have interested advanced interstellar civilizations, we have Flatwoods. As a nuclear physicist, who has been professionally interested in UFOs since 1958, and who has lectured ("Flying Saucers ARE Real") in all 50 states, 9 provinces and 16 other countries, I am convinced by the evidence, as collected by Frank Feschino, that the "Flatwoods Monster" case was a truly outstanding and important event. There were multiple witnesses, physical effects, government cover-up and, thankfully, truly extraordinary investigative work by Frank. I expect that some of the people reading this book will have new information to provide and perhaps even a piece of the wreckage that was recovered at the site.

Furthermore, it is interesting to see the many indications of fighter plane and UFO encounters that appeared in print years ago that are out there. For example, we recently found in the 1970 book *Flying Saucers Have Arrived* (Edited by Jay David for World Publishing Company) there is a chapter by Tom Comella "Have UFOs Swallowed Our Aircraft?" about fighter plane disappearances in the 1950s. Surely, what has been found so far is just the tip of the iceberg of attempted military intercepts of UFOs and intercepts of our planes by UFOs. We are racing the undertaker to get more first hand testimony about these events involving fighter planes and UFOs.

Pilots or persons who know of any such incidents can call me toll free at **1-877-457-0232**. My email is: **fsphys@rogers.com**. My website address is: **www.stantonfriedman.com**. My mailing address is PO. Box 958, Houlton, ME 04730-0958. *Names won't be used without permission.*

Stanton T. Friedman

Stanton T. Friedman

ACKNOWLEDGEMENTS

This book, *Shoot Them Down! - The Flying Saucer Air Wars Of 1952*, is the result of a tremendous team effort by several persons who assisted me throughout the years. It was made possible because of their dedication and support. Among my supporters, I would like to thank my parents Frank Sr. and Shona, and my entire family for their help and encouragement. A very special thank you to my dear friend Rob Tabasky and his family for their continued support over the years. I extend a sincere thank you to Stanton T. Friedman and the many researchers who assisted me with their information and knowledge. A special thank you to Kathleen May, Freddie May and the entire May family for their help and patience. Special thank you to writer Anthony Sica who worked countless hours with me and helped make this book possible. A sincere thank you to Scott Hall for his assistance and for bringing my research and story together in this book.

I would like to thank my assistant Don Hobar and video technician Marcos Torres for all of their outstanding work and support. A very special thank you to Mr. Rogelio Farinas for his support and knowledge over the years…"It was only a weather balloon!" I would especially like to thank all the American military veterans who assisted me throughout the years. Their knowledge and help has been priceless. I would like to thank computer technician Nathan P. Carlson for his help and for putting this entire book together, I am grateful. Very special thanks to my friend Larry Bailey for believing in this project. I wish to thank my entire team for their help and guidance, their support has been invaluable. I am proud of them all.

Introduction

Only fifty-five years ago, worried Americans were anticipating a potential Soviet nuclear aerial strike against the United States. The eyes of a jittery America were glued to the skies and ready to report Russian bomber planes as new technologically advanced rocket-bearing fighter jets stood by on alert to scramble at a moments notice. Air Force fighters were also implemented in massive air defense exercises across the country that mocked soviet aerial assaults. Schoolchildren and citizens alike were drilled on a regular basis in the event of an A-bomb attack and air raid sirens blared throughout the country reminiscent of World War II Europe. America was involved in the Cold War.

When the first months of 1952 passed by with no signs of Soviet bombers, another problem had arisen over the skies of the United States. Another type of aerial intruder plagued the skies and panicked Americans; the Air Force referred to them as UFOs but they were commonly known as "flying saucers."

Throughout the 1952 summer, Americans reported a record amount of UFO sightings to Project Blue Book, the Air Force group responsible for investigating unidentified flying objects. The United States was in the midst of a major UFO wave as concerned citizens and military installations reported "flying saucers" and unconventional-looking aircraft flying over America's airspace on a daily basis. My research involves a detailed account of the Project Blue Book "Unknown" cases that happened that summer.

This book encompasses the summer of 1952 and America's overwhelming UFO problem during that time. My primary focus, the numerous aerial encounters that occurred between United States fighter planes and UFOs over the United States, a shadowy topic not widely discussed. On July 28, 1952, an Air Force information officer, spoke briefly on the subject. He stated, "The jet pilots are, and have been under orders to investigate unidentified objects and to shoot them down if they can't talk them down." The July 29, 1952 edition of the San Francisco Examiner newspaper reported, "The Air Force revealed today that jet pilots have been placed on twenty-four-hour nationwide 'alert' against 'flying saucers' with orders to 'shoot them down' if they refuse to land.' "

Appropriately, I have titled this book, *Shoot Them Down! - The Flying Saucer Air Wars Of 1952*; an in depth historical account that involves the fighter jet and UFO confrontations that occurred during the summer of 1952. With the assistance of UFO researcher and nuclear physicist Stanton T. Friedman and others, we have finally put some light on this very dark and seedy subject, long overdue in the history books. A lost piece of military history has finally been found. I give a detailed account of the July jet scrambles over Washington D.C. on consecutive weekends when flying saucers actually flew over the restricted air space of the capitol. These brazen maneuvers shook up the military, worried the nation, and made world headlines overnight. Throughout that summer, unconventional and strange-looking craft continued to plague the skies over America and fighter jet scrambles after these unidentified flying aircraft became relentless. Yet, none of the UFOs reported were identified as Soviet bombers. Russia never launched their nuclear aerial assault, which prompted many to believe that these UFOs were not of this world.

On July 30, 1952, the day after a large flying saucer news conference was held at the Pentagon, the press reported, "Maj. Gen. Roger Ramey, deputy Chief of the Air Force Staff of Operations, told the news conference that interceptor planes have raced aloft several hundred times as a result of reported sightings of unidentified objects. He said that was just standard procedure." With this information at hand, Mr. Friedman and I obtained recently declassified Air Force aircraft accident statistics and official reports from the summer of 1952. Official statistical documentation reveals a staggering amount of fighter planes accidents occurred during that era when saucers roamed the skies over America. I also reviewed several declassified Air Force aircraft accident reports, dissected them and extensively analyzed their contents. I was flabbergasted by the irrational stories, erroneous timelines, flawed documentation and poor explanations as set forth by the Air Force.

Among the numerous other UFO cases that I researched were the numerous saucer sightings that occurred over Chicago, Illinois and its neighboring towns during that summer. In 1952, O'Hare Airport was also a Sabre Jet base and frequently scrambled after flying saucers. More than a half century later, the flying saucer sightings continue over O'Hare Airport, tracking a long history of sightings over that vicinity.

My latest on-scene investigation involves the mysterious fighter jet crash of a Westover AFB F-86 Sabre Jet in Glastonbury, Connecticut on August 5, 1952. On that same day, UFOs were sighted over Westover and various other states throughout the east coast. These events climaxed when fighter jets were scrambled after unidentified objects over Washington D.C. that night. I discuss this case in explicit detail and reveal the numerous inconsistencies that I discovered in the government's official accident report when compared to the original media coverage of the incident. The discrepancies in this case are overwhelming...a big cover-up.

The month of September ended the very hot and long summer of 1952. On September 12, the summer of saucer sightings culminated into a horrific encounter. On that night, a group of local Flatwoods, WV residents sighted a flaming UFO land in their town. Shortly after, a curious group of boys led by an adult, Mrs. Kathleen May, confronted the occupant of this downed object. The occupant, a huge 12-foot tall being called the "Flatwoods Monster" frightened the group who fled in terror. In this book, for the first time you will read the *unedited* and *accurate* version of this incident. I have been given the opportunity to tell the *complete and uncut story* of the "Flatwoods Monster" incident which includes the *precise* documentation of 18 ½ hours of UFO sightings, that also occurred that day. Furthermore, I disclose information about a fighter jet that mysteriously vanished on September 12 and report on the major "Aircraft Accident" case files that are missing for that very same day.

Throughout my investigation, I wondered how many American fighter pilots died in aerial battles with UFOs after being scrambled after them during the 1950's. On the record, the U.S. government has never admitted to any, but there is a very long and guarded paper trail. Fighter planes were going after UFOs throughout the 50s and the government took them seriously. An aerial war was also going on during that era and it wasn't over MIG alley over Korea. An aerial war was going on over the United States between American fighters and UFOs and certain authorities within the Air Force were doing everything possible to explain the saucers and overwhelming number of jet accidents away. Their excuses, illogical stories, and cover-ups worked in certain cases, but not all of them. Today, the cover-up is now unraveling.

In 1952 pioneer UFO researcher Donald Keyhoe stated, "Week after week, jet fighters are 'scrambled' at points around the country for 'saucer chases.'" Former 1952 Project Blue Book Chief Captain Edward J. Ruppelt wrote, "In the summer of 1952 a United States Air Force F-86 interceptor shot at a flying saucer." In reference to UFO encounters that involved fighter planes and UFOs that were thought to be peaceful Ruppelt stated, *"There have been other and more lurid 'duels of death.'"* Fueled by Keyhoe and Ruppelt's statements, I researched *The New York Times* archives for fighter accident stories released to the press. I discovered a staggering amount of fighter pilots including veteran fighters that died in strange and mysterious accidents or simply vanished into thin air between 1951 and 1956. I found more than 200 reported fighter plane accidents during those six years, which represent only a fraction of the true amount of fighter accidents that occurred.

I was shocked to learn that the majority of these more than 200 accidents and disappearances occurred over the United States. One such fighter accident story states, "4 Jets Crash in Formation Dive, Killing Pilots in Georgia Mystery," and informs, "Officials at Dobbins Base said all the men were experienced jet pilots and they knew of no reasons for the crashes." I then researched the dates of known UFO incidents and was actually able to cross-reference some of them to areas of fighter accidents. This book lifts the lid on the UFO cover up and recognizes the heroic aviators who scrambled after UFOs to "shoot them down" and never returned home.

SHOOT THEM DOWN!
The Flying Saucer Air Wars Of 1952

Fighter pilots of the 142nd Fighter Interceptor Squadron based at New Castle County Airport, Delaware.

JUNE 1952 - THE "SPACE SHIPS" OF SUMMER

Inside the immense gray and red building of the Air Technical Intelligence Center at Wright Patterson AFB, in Dayton, Ohio, the tension in one particular office was intensifying. This brightly lit 15 x 30 foot room was filled with large metal filing cabinets, bookshelves and various world maps attached to its walls. Stuck in these maps were countless pin location markers that resembled a shotgun pattern sprayed into a wall.

Large rotary clocks on either sides of the room overlooked the four desks and office furnishings that were piled with documents, reports and books that held them down. A few scraps of paper and documents were strewn about the floor, from the breeze made by the whirling ceiling fans. This was the office at Project Blue Book, the name of the Air Force's newest 1952 unit in charge with the investigation and evaluation of UFO reports in the United States, and its worldwide properties.

The June heat of 52' took its toll on the understaffed workers in Blue Book's office, which was getting more hectic by the minute. Airman 1st Class Max Futch was patiently sorting out a mountain of reports and telegrams piled around him as a nearby telephone was ringing off the hook.

Lt. Kerry Rothstein picked up the phone and frantically started writing notes, as he talked to an Air Force base commander reporting a flying saucer sighting. Another officer, Lt. Andy Flues walked over to Rothstein, laid down a long teletype on his desk, and weighted it down with a book. Shortly after, Lt. Rothstein hung up the phone and reread his notes. He then collaborated with Flues about this sighting over Michigan; a flying saucer had flown over Selfridge Air Force Base again.

Airman Futch handed Lt. Flues a finished case report and then went back to his paperwork. Lt. Rothstein joined Lt. Flues, walked over to the United States map, and stood in front of it. Flues, while shaking his head, pointed to New Mexico on the map then handed Rothstein the report. They turned, looked at each other then Rothstein walked to a nearby desk and picked up a pin from a box. He walked back to the map and stuck it in the city of Albuquerque amongst the other pins that designated UFO sightings throughout the state.

Lt. Flues looked on, muttered a few words, and they both walked back to Rothstein's desk. Flues then picked up the book weighing down the recent teletype, lifted it and began to read the message aloud as Lt. Rothstein listened on. The saucers were back over Illinois once more, over the Chicago area.

The inundated office of Project Blue Book headquarters in June of that year was not accustomed to the flurry of saucer reports that they were receiving. The phones continued to ring, the teletypes kept rolling in and the officer's tensions continued to rise. Concerned American citizens across the country were contacting the Air Force in increasing numbers to report UFO sightings, as did military bases around the world.

Standing over his desk and talking on the phone with a firm look on his face was Captain Edward J. Ruppelt, the officer in charge of Project Blue Book. Ruppelt was a 29-year-old WWII combat veteran who had returned to active duty during the Korean War. The Intelligence officer, who held a degree in aeronautical engineering, was assigned to ATIC and worked there doing aeronautical analysis of the Russian fighter jet, the MIG-15. In October of 1951, Ruppelt was assigned to the government's UFO project, named Project Grudge, which was later renamed Blue Book in March of 1952.

Skilled at handling demands and dealing with people, Ruppelt leaned on his desk while maintaining his composure and continued to talk to a worried saucer witness on the phone. The Captain calmed the witness, nonchalantly jotted some notes, hung up the phone, and casually walked over to a teletype machine and tore off the incoming message. He looked at it, turned away and then walked back toward his desk with a very disarming look on his face. Another sighting had occurred in the northeast United States, this time over Boston, Massachusetts, it was a multiple sighting.

Lt. Flues walked across the room with another teletype in his hand then stood in front of another map, the world map. He began to study it as Ruppelt walked by him and answered another phone call. Rothstein then joined Flues, said a few words about this sighting and they looked upon the Far East region of the map. Lt. Flues picked up a marker pin, aimed it, and stuck it into the already crowded country of Korea, to designate yet another military UFO sighting.

Shortly after, the two men consulted with Ruppelt as he hung up the phone from Lt. Robert Olsson, who had just reported in on his field investigation from Virginia. Captain Ruppelt read the teletype, picked up some papers, walked across the room to Max Futch and put them down on a pile of papers on his already cluttered desk. In passing, he uttered a few words to Futch and without breaking stride, proceeded to the door on the other end of the room at a moderate pace.

Captain Ruppelt then walked out of the office, went down the hallway and through the double doors leading outside to get a breath of fresh air. The officer stood in front of the huge building, took a deep breath and looked out across the massive base of Wright Patterson, then exhaled. A thundering noise heard out in the distance passed overhead moments later as a fighter jet soared over the ATIC building. As Ruppelt looked up at it, sweat began to trickle down his brow and over his face. He hurriedly grabbed his handkerchief, wiped his face and continued to watch the jet as it ascended into the sky and diminished in size. Captain Ruppelt took another deep breath, exhaled and then took another moment to compose.

He then turned around, and began to walk back toward the building when another jet soared overhead in the same direction as the previous jet. Without flinching, Ruppelt continued toward the entrance and glanced up at a large sign bolted to the building and located just above the double doors. Captain Ruppelt paused, read the sign, walked underneath it, and then went back inside the building. The sign read, "AIR TECHNICAL INTELLIGENCE CENTER-HQ 1125th FIELD ACTIVITIES GP-1126 th AIR INTELLIGENCE SERVICES SQ.," This was Ruppelt's domain, this is where he would spend much of his time during 1952. The United States Air Force explained Project Blue Book; "The United States Air Force has the responsibility under the Department of Defense for the investigation of unidentified flying objects (UFOs). The name of this program, which has been in operation since 1948, is Project Blue Book. It has been identified in the past as Project Sign and Project Grudge." The Air Force also explained the objectives of this project; "The objectives of Project Blue Book are two-fold: first, to determine whether UFOs pose a threat to the security of the United States; and, second, to determine whether UFOs exhibit any unique scientific information or advanced technology which could contribute to scientific or technical research. In the course of accomplishing these objectives, Project Blue Book strives to identify and explain all UFO sightings to the Air Force."

Captain Ruppelt proceeded back down the hallway to his office, stopped, glanced back down the hallway, opened the door and walked in to one of the busiest Air Force offices in the country that year. Welcome to Project Blue Book. The flying saucer reports that swamped the Project Blue Book office during 1952 made for a long and trying year for Captain Ruppelt and his staff. With summer around the corner, it would be longest and most trying time of Ruppelt's career as the saucer wave of 1952 was about to begin.

Captain Ruppelt was the Chief of Project Blue Book from November 1951 until September 1953. After Ruppelt retired from the Air Force, he wrote a book titled, *The Report On Unidentified Flying Objects*. In his 1956 book, he spoke about the history of the Air Forces involvement with UFOs from 1947 through his tenure ship at Project Blue Book and shortly after. Ruppelt's book was only a partial history of that era though. When he wrote his book, numerous cases and events he reported on had not been declassified. In many cases, Ruppelt was unable to reveal the contents of his subject matter to the public and his stories were not complete. However, there were other major UFO related news stories and events that Ruppelt did not mention or barely touched on in his book that occurred in 1952. That year had the largest amount of UFO sightings reported to Project Blue Book in its seventeen-year existence. There was 1,501-reported UFO cases, 303 were not explained, the "Unknowns." The summer of 1952 also had more reported UFO sightings than any other three-month period in Blue Book's 17-year history yet major pieces of history are missing from Edward Ruppelt's book concerning that time.

News stories that Ruppelt did not write about in his book concerned the fighter aircraft events that had occurred during that era. Ruppelt does not mention a major *International News Service* wire story out of Washington D.C. nor the follow up story that ensued with negative public repercussions. The "INS" wire story was carried by a few American newspapers on July 29, 1952 and informs on July 28, "The Air Force refused to confirm this but Lt. Col. Moncel Monts, information officer stated :'The jet pilots are, and have been under orders to investigate unidentified objects and to shoot them down if they can't talk them down.'"

After this shoot down order against UFOs appeared in newspapers, it prompted an alarming public disapproval in America. On July 29, Robert Farnsworth, president of the United States Rocket Society, sent a telegram to President Truman, the Secretary of Defense, the Secretary of the Navy, and the Secretary of the Army concerning this statement. In part, he suggested, "no offensive action be taken against the objects reported as unidentified which have been sighted over our nation. Should they be extraterrestrial such action might result in the gravest consequences." On July 30, the *Associated Press* and *United Press* wire services released the telegram story. Several newspapers carried the story, one such headline read, "Don't Shoot." Edward Ruppelt does not mention either one of these major July UFO news stories in his book.

Furthermore, during 1952, an overwhelming amount of United States military fighter jet scrambles after UFOs occurred over America. In his book, Ruppelt does talk about several jet scrambles after UFOs but does not give any indication of how many. On July 30, 1952, *The Louisville Courier Journal* newspaper reported a news story that did not receive much coverage. It actually gave an indication of how many times jets were scrambled after UFOs. It reported, "Maj. Gen. Roger Ramey, deputy chief of the Air Force staff for operations, told the news conference that interceptor planes have raced aloft several hundred times as a result of reported sightings of unidentified objects. He said that was just standard procedure." This important and revealing jet news story was not mentioned in Ruppelt's book either. Was the subject matter too sensitive to put in his book?

Moreover, in 1952 an outstanding amount of mysterious fighter jet accidents also occurred over America that involved devastating crashes. Fighter jets were dropping out of the sky over America in frightening numbers, especially during the summer of 1952. Yet, Ruppelt makes no mention at all about these fighter aircraft accidents, even though numerous newspapers including *The New York Times* reported several of them. Why did Ruppelt neglect to talk about all of the jet crashes that occurred during 1952? Did the Air Force warn Ruppelt against writing about all the mysterious jet accidents that occurred over the United States during that 1952 "shoot them down" era?

In his book, *The Report on Unidentified Flying Objects*, Edward Ruppelt did not give an entire picture of the UFO and military news events of 1952, although in some instances, he did write and leave us some clues to a much bigger picture. There was much more going on in 1952 than meets the eye, which we will explore in this book. Was Edward Ruppelt's book censored by the United States Air Force? Yes, I believe so.

In Edward Ruppelt's book, he states, "In early June 1952 the Air Force was unknowingly in the initial stages of a flap- a flying saucer flap-the flying saucer flap of 1952." Ruppelt stated, "If you can pin down a date that the Big Flap started, it would probably be about June 1." According to the Air Force, a "flap" is considered a condition, a situation, or a state of being of a group of persons characterized by an advanced degree of confusion that has not quite reached panic proportions.

One definition of a "UFO" is, "The stimulus for a report made by one or more individuals of something seen in the sky which the observer could not identify as having an ordinary natural origin, and which seemed to him sufficiently puzzling that he undertook to make a report of it." An Air Force definition, "The Air Force defines an unidentified flying object as any aerial object which the observer is unable to identify." The Air Force also explained the following, "Reports of unfamiliar objects in the sky are submitted to the Air Force from many sources. These sources include military and civilian pilots, weather observers, amateur astronomers, business and professional men and woman, and housewives."

During that era when a person witnessed a UFO, they could contact the Air Force by telephone to report their sighting. An intelligence officer would try to obtain as much data on the sighting for a case report. In some instances, witnesses would also send letters or telegrams to report their UFO sightings. A witness who volunteered to give more information was sent a "Tentative Observers Questionnaire," a standard eight-page form that consisted of 68 questions to describe their sighting. Ruppelt stated, "From this standard questionnaire the project worked up two more specialized types. One dealt with radar sightings of UFO's, the other with sightings made from airplanes." Cooperative witness would fill out the question form, which included detailing every aspect of the UFO sighting, including sections to draw pictures of the object and illustrate its movements. Captain Ruppelt said that the "questionnaire" contained questions that "were booby-trapped in a couple places to give us a cross check on the reliability of the reporter as an observer."

The UFO witness would then mail the questionnaire back to the Air Force for Project Blue Book to review. When received, the questionnaire would be reviewed and evaluated and then a summary card, a "Project 10073 Record Card," would be filled out. This card listed the data in several sections concerning the UFO sighting that included the location, time, number of observers, and comments, to name a few. The sections would either be filled out by checking one of the multiple choice blank boxes in each section or writing in an answer in the indicated sections where required. The "Conclusion" section was the final section to be filled out on the card. The following eleven categories were listed as the choices and had a blank box next to each one to check off. They are listed below:

1. Was a Balloon
2. Probably Balloon
3. Possibly Balloon
4. Was Aircraft
5. Probably Aircraft
6. Possibly Aircraft
7. Was Astronomical
8. Possibly Astronomical
9. Other _____
10. Insufficient Data for Evaluation
11. Unknown

During 1952, a UFO case that was evaluated as unidentified was referred to as an "Unknown." Captain Ruppelt stated, "When a report came through our screening process and still had the 'Unknown' tag on it, it went into the MO ["movement orders"] file, where we checked it against other reports." He added, "When a report came out with the final conclusion, 'Unknown,' we were sure that it was an unknown."

An individual who assisted the Blue Book staff as a scientific advisor on UFO matters was astrophysicist Dr. J. Allen Hynek. Hynek taught astronomy at Ohio State University and was the director of their McMillan Observatory. In 1952, Hynek was appointed the chief scientific consultant to Project Blue Book and remained until 1969 when Blue Book was disbanded. No stranger to the military, Hynek worked on several important military projects for the government during World War 2 before being secured by Ruppelt for Blue Book.

As the scientific consultant of Blue Book, Hynek helped separate cases of astronomical phenomena such as meteors, planets and stars from the UFOs or as the Air Force referred to them, "Aerial Phenomena." However, Project Blue Book was not an accurate and complete record of all the UFO events that occurred during their 17-

year study of the, "Aerial Phenomena" problem.

Over the years, several UFO witnesses including military personnel did follow through with the reporting procedure of a UFO. Considering this point, how many witnesses never bothered to call the Air Force to report a UFO sighting thus resulting in undocumented cases? More over, how many witnesses, upon calling the Air Force and receiving the eight-page questionnaire never bothered to fill it out and send it back? Numerous UFO sightings were not documented at all and never reached the public. Several UFO incidents were documented publicly through newspapers and magazines but were not recorded in any official capacity.

How many good cases went cold because the staff at Blue Book did not investigate them or were unable to investigate them within a reasonable period? Furthermore, how many good and legitimate UFO sightings did Project Blue Book write off and incorrectly evaluate? Several Blue Book cases contained questionable conclusions.

J. Allen Hynek made the following statements about Project Blue Book in his 1972 book, *THE UFO EXPERIENCE*:

A.) "The popular impression through the years was that the Blue Book was a full-fledged, serious operation. The public perhaps envisioned a spacious, well-staffed office with rows of file cabinets, a computer terminal for querying the UFO data bank, and a group of scientists quietly studying reports, attended by a staff of assistants. The actual situation was unfortunately the opposite…This was not exactly a first-line, high priority operation."

B.) "The program did not change through the years. Reports came in and were handled in a completely routine manner, always on the assumption that they had been spawned by untutored people unable to identify perfectly natural occurrences."

C.) "Since the reported actions of UFOs clearly didn't fit this world picture, they simply had to be figments of the imagination produced in one way or another. All my association with Blue Book showed clearly that the project rarely exhibited any scientific interest in the UFO problem."

D.) "The statistical methods employed by Blue Book are nothing less than a travesty."

E.) "In reviewing cases that had come in the previous month, I often asked that additional often crucial information on a case be obtained. The results at best were minimal."

F.) "Blue Book was a 'cover-up' to the extent that the assigned problem was glossed over for one reason or another. In my many years' association with Blue Book, I do not recall even one serious discussion of methodology, of improving the process of data gathering or of techniques of comprehensive interrogation of witnesses."

Blue Book reported a steady increase in their UFO cases during the early months of 1952, which escalated into the most famous wave of UFO sightings in American history. The Press called them called, "flying saucers," some called them "space ships," while others claimed they were, "natural phenomena," and "hallucinations." Nevertheless, whatever they were called, and no matter how well these UFOs were investigated, they were seen in overpowering numbers that year.

On Sunday morning June 1, the flying saucer flap of 1952 started over the United States. In California, radar technicians of the "Hughes Aircraft Company," of Los Angeles were testing a new radar system. Throughout the morning, they had tracked several military and civilian planes flying over the area. Later that morning, they tracked a target thought to be a DC-3 commercial airliner at first, which flew north of them and over the San Gabriel Mountains. They were wrong.

As the technicians continued to track the blip on their scope, they discovered that their target did not display the characteristics of a conventional aircraft. The technicians tracked the speed of the object at a 180 MPH as it flew at an altitude of 11,000 feet. The UFO then ascended, picked up speed and soared into the sky at a speed of 550 MPH, leveled off and continued to climb. The object then soared into the heavens and passed the 55,000-foot ceiling mark on a southeast trajectory, dove and then leveled off as the engineers watched their scope in amazement.

The radar set was repeatedly checked for a malfunction and the engineers were certain the radar was in fine working order. Shortly after, one of the test engineers who had tracked the object called ATIC at Wright Patterson AFB. He spoke to Blue Book Chief Edward Ruppelt about the incident. The engineer told Captain Ruppelt that he had just contacted Edwards Air Force Base to find out if they were testing any experimental aircraft in the area. One of the Flight Operations personnel at Edwards AFB told the inquiring engineer that they were not testing any craft. The object that the engineers tracked on that Sunday morning was never explained.

There were other June 1 UFO sightings that were reported to Project Blue Book as well. The reports evaluated as "Unknown" cases were received from Rapid City, South Dakota, Walla, Washington and Soap Lake, Washington. The South Dakota UFO sighting was listed as Case 1243, the Walla, Washington case was listed as case number 1245 and the Soap Lake, Washington incident was listed as Case 1246.

During June, the team at Project Blue Book evaluated and classified thirty-nine of the, "148" UFO reports received as "Unknown" cases. Twenty-five of those unexplained cases were attributed to military sightings, which accounted for the majority of the June "Unknowns." Nine of those unexplained military cases, directly involved Air Force installations and base sightings, they are as follows:

1. Case 1257. June 5, 1952. Offut AFB, NE
2. *Missing*. June 6, 1952. Kimpo AB, Japan
3. Case 1285. June 15, 1952. Standiford AFB, KY
4. Case 1295. June 16, 1952. Walker AFB, NM
5. Case 1298. June 17, 1952. Mc Chord AFB, WA
6. Case 1308. June 19, 1952. Goose AFB, Canada
7. Case 1319. June 21, 1952. Kelly AFB, TX
8. Case 1332. June 23, 1952. Mc Chord AFB, WA
9. Case 1364. June 29, 1952. O'Hare Airport, IL

During the first half of June, several UFO sightings did not make the Project Blue Book "Unknown" list but are considered worth mentioning. One of these cases is documented in Project Blue Book and occurred on June 11, 1952, just northeast of Chicago, Illinois. An "Air Intelligence Information Report" dated, "4 July 52" gave the details of the sighting. An official at the Headquarters of the "4706 Defense Wing, Chicago, Illinois", wrote this report. This defense wing was actually located at O'Hare Airport in Chicago. This airport provided certain facilities for the United States Air Force and was home for F-86 Sabre Jets of the 4706th Fighter Interceptor Wing. Captain Neil McLaghian wrote the following in the Intelligence report:

Two globular objects, dark blue with grey centers, appearing six inches in diameter, at an estimated 6,000 feet, were observed in hazy outline without visible trail or sound. Objects passed in trail southwest to northwest at estimated 500 miles per hour. Number two [object] assumed lead after passing number one [object] to the left before disappearing.

Edward Ruppelt stated that, "In June the Air Force was taking the UFO problem seriously." During April and May, he reported that Project Blue Book received, "178 reports…not counting the thousand or so that we'd received directly from the public." Ruppelt then talked about what occurred after May of 1952. He stated, "In June the big flap hit – they began to deliver clippings in big cardboard cartons."

During the UFO flap of 1952, civilians were not the only witnesses to have sighted and reported saucers across the United States and the world. Military personnel also sighted them as well and in overwhelming numbers. "Flying saucers" were being sighted over and near key military installations throughout the world including; Air Force bases, air bases, Naval bases and Marine Corp air stations.

The saucers were also sighted over sensitive government locations including atomic energy plants, rocket-testing bases, and testing grounds. The UFOs were frequently seen over several major American cities, most with a high concentration of defense industries. Chicago, Boston, and Washington D.C. were among the top visited areas.

In addition to the typical "flying saucer," and disc-shaped objects being sighted, there were also several other types of UFOs being seen. During this era, oval, round, and cigar-shaped objects were readily sighted around the world, especially over the United States. Several other varieties of odd looking and unconventional type-flying objects were also being reported, all which proved very alarming to the United States government.

During this era, the United States was involved in the Korean War as the Cold War heightened across the world. The Soviet Union had moved their military into the jet age and prioritized their resources on gaining air superiority. The Russians had also made astonishing advancements in their nuclear weapons program and President Truman feared the threat of a compromising nuclear air strike. In 1952, it was estimated that the United States could not completely ward off an initial Soviet atomic bomb attack, but probably had sufficient air defense to cut down a concentrated attack. Furthermore, because of this threat, Washington officials were concerned that the channels of communications being clogged by irrelevant UFO reports could compromise the United States if an actual Soviet aerial assault occurred. The reporting of false alarm UFO sightings worried the military, especially the Air Defense Command, who were constantly scrambling fighter jets.

In the event of a nuclear assault, concerned American citizens exercised cover-protection techniques at home while schools drilled children in safety procedures in classrooms. Across America, the unnerving cries of air-raid sirens being routinely tested were reminiscent of war-torn Europe during the Second World War. The eyes of the United States were focused on the skies of the country in anticipation of Soviet bombers and another potential enemy that was flying over the skies of the United States, the flying saucers.

The first half of June 1952, June 1-June 15, accounted for fifteen "Unknown" cases of thirty-nine unknowns listed by Project Blue Book for the month. The remaining twenty-four "Unknown" June cases were listed from June 16 until June 29, 1952, which indicates there was a steady incline in the "Unknown" UFO reports.

A particular Blue Book "Unknown" case that occurred at the mid point of June involved an odd-looking UFO that passed near Standiford AFB in Louisville, Kentucky. Details of Case 1285 appear in an "Air Intelligence Information Report. Intelligence Section, 108th Ftr. Standiford AFB" document, dated, "15 June 52." It reported that the witness, Edward Duke, an ex-United States Navy radar technician, first saw the UFO when it appeared a quarter mile from Standiford field at an altitude of "5,000 feet" at approximately 12:00 a.m.

Mr. Duke told Intelligence officer Major Hefling the following information, which appeared in the report. He stated, "A cigar-shaped object, size of large aircraft fuselage, blunt at the front end, appeared to be lighted at both sides, had a reddish hue on the stern end; one object sighted, estimated speed was 400 to 500 miles per hour, no audible sound, maneuvered leisurely in area for fifteen minutes - - turned due west, then South and then disappeared to the Northeast."

This cigar-shaped type of flying object had been seen in the late 1940's and was continually sighted throughout the summer of 1952. Most of the cigar-shaped UFOs that were seen during 1952 were described as quite large and predominantly red in color. Some often displayed flames being emitted from the aft end of the craft during flight. Witnesses never reported any type of wings or appendages on these cigar-shaped objects.

According to Ruppelt, other UFO sightings were reported on June 15, 1952 and caused quite a commotion. On that afternoon and into early evening UFO reports poured in from central Virginia that prompted several fighter jets to be scrambled. The story unfolded at 4: 20 p.m. that afternoon over Gordonsville, Virginia. Ruppelt reported a "round, shiny object," was sighted over Gordonsville then five minutes later, a "silver sphere" was reported over Richmond by the crew of a commercial airliner.

Eight minutes after the Richmond sighting, a Marine fighter jet was in the air after being scrambled from the Quantico Marine Corps Air Station in Virginia. At 4:43 p.m., the fighter was guided to its target area just south of Gordonsville and "tried to intercept" the UFO, described as a "round shiny sphere." This intercept attempt failed and the jet returned to its base shortly after. During this time, fighters were constantly being scrambled after these intruders in the skies over America, commonly referred to as, "flying saucers." The United States military was now taking the UFO situation very seriously.

One hour later at 5:43 p.m., the Air Force stepped into the picture and took over. One of their fighter jets, "tried to intercept" the same UFO, south of Gordonsville. Witnesses also described the object as a, "shiny sphere." The fighter pilot attempted to intercept the object but upon reaching the, "35,000" foot level; he realized his target was far beyond him. The intercept attempt was unsuccessful and the jet was ordered back to base. About two hours later at 7:35 p.m., a UFO was reported approximately 80 miles south of Gordonsville, over, "Blackstone, Virginia." Once again, witnesses described an object as a, "round, shiny object." Additional information said it emanated a "gold" colored glow. This UFO was obviously the same object sighted previously. Ruppelt reported that its "progress" across the sky was being reported by, "radio commentators," as witnesses over central Virginia monitored the object.

Just before 8:00 p.m., the Air Force stepped into the picture again. Langley AFB fighter jets at Hampton, Virginia were scrambled after the object that so brazenly moved across the skies of Blackstone. By the time, the fighters arrived into the area to attempt an intercept on the object it had "disappeared," the time, 8:05 p.m.

On the following day, June 16, a news wire story from "NEW YORK," quoted a statement made by General Hoyt. S. Vandenberg, the Air Force Chief of Staff. It concerned the flying saucer topic. Vandenberg who was always cautious to speak out on the saucers stated the following. In part, it states:

HXR127. GENERAL HOYT VANDENBERG --- AIR FORCE CHIEF OF STAFF---SAYS THE AIR FORCE HAS LAUNCHED A SECRET RESEARCH FOR "FLYING SAUCERS." SAID VANDENBERG: 'THE AIR FORCE IS INTERESTED IN ANYTHING THAT TAKES PLACE IN THE AIR.' AND HE ADDED: 'WITH THE PRESENT WORLD UNREST, WE CAN [SIC] ANNOT [CANNOT] AFFORD TO BE COMPLACENT.'

THE NEW HUNT FOR FLYING SAUCER IS REPORTEDLY BEING CARRIED OUT BY THE AIR TECHNICAL INTELLIGENCE COMMAND. ONE HIGH-PLACED INTELLIGENCE OFFICER IS QUOTED AS SAYING: 'OUR JOB IS TO DETECT ANY WEAPON THAT MIGHT BE USED AGAINST THE UNITED STATES. IN THE FUTURE A WEAPON THAT "PROBABLY WAS A METEOR" MAY PROVE TO BE A GLOBAL ROCKET.'

In closing this news wire states, "THE AIR FORCE INVESTIGATION IS DESIGNED TO PROVE WHETHER THE AIR PHENOMENA AND MISINTERPRETATIONS OF BALLOONS OR JET PLANES…WHETHER THEY ARE REFLECTED LIGHT FROM EARTH…OR WHETHER THEY ARE MAN-MADE OR SPACE SHIPS AND INTER-PLANETARY MISSILES."

The Air Force was taking the UFO problem seriously and especially concerned with the possibility that "SPACE SHIPS," were flying in the air space over the United States. The military's apprehension included several intercepts to investigate these unknown objects and learn more about them…and they did, relentlessly.

On June 17, 1952, a United States Air Force fighter jet had a direct encounter with a UFO. This encounter was documented in Project Blue Book as case #1299 and was evaluated as an "Unknown." This hair-raising encounter occurred over the vicinity of Cape Cod, Massachusetts at 1:28 a.m. The witness who filed this report was the fighter pilot involved in the incident. He reported that he was flying an F-94 Starfire at the time of his encounter. The pilot claimed he saw a UFO that resembled a brilliant "light like a bright star." As he continued on his flight, the UFO headed toward his jet from the side. The object flew in his direction, proceeded toward the Starfire and then "crossed" the nose of the aircraft at blinding speed. The pilot said he observed the UFO for "fifteen seconds" during the time of his encounter before it disappeared.

On June 24, 1952, *The New York Times* reported a UFO story that occurred the previous week on June 19.

The headline read, "'Flying Saucers' Sighted" and stated, "Several 'round and silver shaped flying saucers' and 'cigar-shaped' objects have been reported flying over Jersey shore, Pa., an Air Force officer said today. Capt. Arthur S. Loyd of Olmsted Air Force Base here said Army Capt. Harold Hermann and his wife reported seeing a 'round and silver saucer-like object flying fast across the heavens about 6 P.M. last Thursday [June 19].' Two other persons saw flying saucers."

A Project Blue Book Memorandum also reported a UFO sighting that occurred over Trenton, New Jersey on June 19, 1952. This documents title is "Unidentified Flying Objects –Summary of Information Covering the Period of 19 June 52." It reported that a former ground crew member in the Army-Air Force during WW II, saw what he thought might be a "flying saucer." In addition, it appeared to have a "swirling motion" as he watched it from the back yard of his home at 9:50 p.m. The sightings of odd–shaped crafts as well as saucer-shaped objects had started to increase over the northeast United States.

The summer 1976 issue of *Canadian UFO Report* Volume 3, # 8, talks about three UFO sightings that occurred over Goose Bay AFB, in Goose Bay, Labrador, Canada in 1952. The first reference involves a June 19, 1952 incident. It reads, "The presence of a glowing disc was confirmed by radar and ground personnel at Goose Bay Air Force Base (Labrador). The same or a similar disc, which returned to the base on the nights of November 26 and December 15, easily eluded jets." This base turned out to be a hot bed for sightings throughout the early 1950s. The June 19, 1952 incident reported to Project Blue Book and evaluated as an "Unknown" was Case 1308, from Goose Air Force Base. This base was actually was involved in four UFO incidents that were recorded as Blue Book "Unknown" cases. These unexplained cases are listed below:

1. Case 969. September 13, 1951.
2. Case 1308. June 19, 1952.
3. Case 2555. May 1, 1953.
4. Case 2601. June 22, 1953.

Why were the UFOs constantly visiting this large Canadian air base during the early 1950s? On June 19, 1952, the objects dropped in over another Air Force Base that they frequently visited, McChord AFB, located in Tacoma, Washington. On June 20, a Tacoma newspaper, *The REPORTER*, reported the story. In part, it stated, "Four Mysterious silver objects were sighted by many Tacomans at approximately 1:30 p.m. Thursday and for the second time in three days the McChord Air Force Base switchboard was flooded with calls. Observers claimed that the objects were round and silver, traveling swiftly at a high altitude and making no noise. McChord officials declined comment, but had earlier reported they were taking names and addresses of those who sighted the four 'fireballs' Tuesday night."

It was reported that, "Unofficial sources said that the four objects sighted Tuesday night, apparently noticed by hundreds of Tacomans, had shown up on military radar screens. There were also unofficial reports that McChord jet planes had unsuccessfully pursued the lights."

It was also stated that, "The McChord public information office said the matter was being investigated by Air Force intelligence." The overwhelming UFO sightings near McChord AFB prompted Air Force officials to send a priority message to following Air Force Branches:

1.) Air Force Headquarters at the Pentagon, Washington D.C. 2.) The ADC Headquarters, Ent AFB, Colorado Springs, Colorado. 3.) Project Blue Book at ATIC, Wright Patterson AFB, Dayton, Ohio.

During the summer of 1952, Project Blue Book recorded and evaluated three McChord AFB UFO incidents as "Unknowns." However, the June 19, 1952 incident was not included on that list. The following three "Unknowns" involved McChord AFB:

1. Case 1298. June 17, 1952. 2. Case 1332. June 23, 1952. 3. Case 1708. July 28, 1952.

At ATIC, Edward Ruppelt responded to the McChord AFB Priority message and went to the base on June 27, 1952. A McChord AFB Flight Service Center document titled, "MEMORANDUM FOR RECORD" stated, "Trip to McChord AFB and Fairchild AFB Washington," and explained the trip. Ruppelt visited the base for four days, Between June 27 and June 30, 1952 and spoke to McChord's 4704 Air Defense Wing Intelligence officer, Captain Harnaway. Ruppelt was told about the earlier June sightings in detail. Harnaway told Ruppelt that the witnesses said the UFOs were always sighted in the northern sky and the majority of the sightings occurred at 8:00 p.m. Furthermore, the sightings that occurred on June 17, 19, and 23, all occurred within a 20 - mile radius of the base. During one sighting, McChord AFB scrambled Jets after the UFOs without success. Moreover, Ruppelt was actually at McChord AFB when the July 28 incident occurred but no mention was made about him seeing the UFOs.

Ruppelt interviewed several civilian witnesses in the area and was told, "The objects would seem to stop short, and go in level flight and then come to a stop and make a turn." Ruppelt then discovered that the 25th Air Division did not keep records of their radar tracks when he made an inquiry to them. Moreover and oddly enough, no one recalled any strange targets on the nights in question! In contrast, though, when Ruppelt met with an Intelligence officer, Major Goldman, of the "97th Bomber Wing," based at McChord, he was told that the Spokane sightings were not "officially" reported because of lack of work force. Ruppelt replied and told him a teletypewriter called a "TWX," would be adequate and could be used during an "emergency" in the future.

Why did the UFOs visit this area over McChord AFB, in Tacoma, on a regular basis during June and July of 1952? Why was this Air Force base being reconnoitered? The unknown objects continued to concentrate their reconnaissance of military installations and major cities and in several cases were quite brazen in their appearances. These bold actions prompted the military to continue to scramble interceptors over the United States and from their foreign bases. Captain Edward Ruppelt and his staff at ATIC had noticed by the end of June, the best UFO reports were coming in from the eastern United States. He stated, "In Massachusetts, New Jersey, and Maryland jet fighters had been scrambled nightly for almost a week." The month of June was only a prelude for what was about to happen during the month of July. The UFO activity over the United States was increasing and only beginning to heat up and the Air Force continued in their relentless pursuit of the unknown objects.

Researcher and author Major Donald Keyhoe, U.S. Marine Corps retired, was a prominent figure and pioneer investigator during the early days of flying saucers. He had an ongoing relationship with the Air Force and corresponded with them over the years. Keyhoe was often privy to Blue Book UFO reports that were considered classified at the time and wrote about these cases in his books and magazine articles. He strongly believed that the saucers were probably extraterrestrial spacecraft or as he put it, "real machines under intelligent control." Harold Wilkins, a British author began investigating, what he stated "crudely named 'flying saucers,' in all their many shapes and sizes shortly after WWII." His landmark book, *Flying Saucers on the Attack* was published in 1954.

According to these authors, in January 1948, an F-51 Mustang pilot, Captain Thomas Mantell, Jr., died while chasing a UFO near Franklin, KY. In October 1948, Lt. George Gorman, an F-51 pilot with the North Dakota ANG survived an aerial dogfight with a UFO. Edward Ruppelt, in his 1956 book, *The Report on Unidentified Flying Objects*, names Keyhoe and Wilkins as historians in reference to the 1948 Mantell and Gorman cases. In regards to other historian writers, Ruppelt states, "Other assorted historians point out that normally the UFOs are peaceful, Gorman and Mantell just got too inquisitive, 'they' just weren't ready to be observed closely. *If the Air Force hadn't slapped down the security lid, these writers might not have reached this conclusion. There have been other and more lurid 'duels of death.'"* A major clue. It is obvious that Ruppelt was trying to leaves us a small but powerful message in this particular statement that seems to have been overlooked over the years. Here, Ruppelt actually wrote about fighter aircraft encounters with UFOs, which led to death that were covered by security. Hence, relating to some of the fighter accidents that occurred during that era, especially during the summer of 1952 at the height of the UFO flap over the United States.

Edward Ruppelt also made the following statement in his 1956 book that reveals the truth behind the scene, of how jet scrambles after UFOs are financially written off as a "training cost." Ruppelt stated, "The matter of scrambling interceptors has been a sore point with the UFO business for a long time. Many people believe that the mere fact the Air Force will send up two, three or even four aircraft that cost $2000 an hour to fly is proof positive that the Air Force doesn't believe its own story that UFOs don't exist. The official answer you will get, if you ask the Air Force, is that they scramble against any unknown target as a matter of defense. But over coffee, you get a different answer. They write the UFO scrambles off as training cost. Each pilot has to get so much flying time and simulating intercepts against an unidentified light is more interesting than merely 'burning holes in the air.' If appropriations are ever cut to the point where training must be curtailed, and heaven forbid, there will be no more scrambles after flying saucers. And the colonel who told me this was emphatic." Another clue to the fighter jet mystery left by Ruppelt. Through my research, I discovered that an overwhelming amount of mysterious jet accidents during 1952 occurred while on, *"routine training missions."*

In February of 1952, Captain Ruppelt met with the Commanding General of the Air Defense Command, General Benjamin Chidlaw, at the ADC Headquarter in Colorado Springs, Colorado. Ruppelt presented a plan to Chidlaw and his staff that concerned how the Air Defense Command could assist the Air Technical Intelligence in obtaining better data on UFOs. During this briefing, the ADC concurred that they would set forth a directive to their units that would clarify the state of affairs concerning the UFOs. The ADC also told Ruppelt that they would also explain to their units, the specifics of how to handle a UFO sighting when a situation arose.

The ADC UFO directive would call for their radarscope equipped radar units to photograph UFO targets. They would also be required to submit them to the Air Technical Intelligence Center along with a detailed account of the incident filled out in a questionnaire form. Captain Ruppelt stated that, "The Air Defense Command UFO directive would also clarify the scrambling of fighters to intercept a UFO." In 1952, it was standard policy for the Air Defense Command to establish an unidentified target's identity. Ruppelt stated, "There were no special orders issued for scrambling fighters to try to identify reported UFOs. A UFO was something unknown and automatically called for a scramble."

Many controllers though, had been hesitant about sending up fighters when their radarscopes clearly indicated that a target was unconventional and not a plane. The directive stated that it was within the range of existing regulations for controllers to scramble fighter planes into the air when unconventional radar targets where tracked on radar. Ruppelt explained them as "radar targets that were plotted as traveling too fast or to slow to be conventional airplanes." The decision to scramble fighter jets was actually up to the discretion of the controller. Ruppelt said, "Scrambling on UFO's would be a second or third priority."

Captain Ruppelt also talked about another aspect of the directive that was not clear. He stated, "The Air Defense Command UFO directive did not mention shooting at a UFO. This question came up during our planning meeting at Colorado Springs, but, like the authority to scramble, the authority to shoot at any thing in the air had been established long ago. Every ADC pilot knows the rules for engagement; the rules tell him when he can shoot the loaded guns that he always carries. If anything over the United States commits any act that is covered by the rules for engagement, the pilot has the authority to open fire." Ruppelt's statement here, is a roundabout rewording of Moncel Monts July 28 statement carried by the INS. "The Air Force refused to confirm this but Lt. Col. Moncel Monts, information officer stated :'The jet pilots are, and have been under orders to investigate unidentified objects and to shoot them down if they can't talk them down.'" Ruppelt actually did confirm the orders in his book but did not mention the article, the article revealed a contradicting statement, *"The Air Force refused to confirm this..."* More clues to the dark fighter aircraft events of that era.

In 1952, Donald Keyhoe stated the following, "Unless an object attacks our planes, or is obviously a threat to this country, the decision is left up to our pilots." This included anything identified as an enemy aircraft or an aerial object that was deemed as potentially hostile or threatening to the United States. This also included flying saucers and any other unconventional looking aircraft. In the official GOC magazine, *The Aircraft Flash,* Vol. 1, No. 1, General Chidlaw stated, "Within seconds after notification of enemy planes approaching, ever-ready interceptors of the ADC would be in the air and on their way to shoot down as many [enemy aircraft] as possible. Meanwhile, Civil Defense Organizations in target areas would have been alerted as a result of the early detection and would have an opportunity to prepare for an attack."

In 1955, UFO investigator Robert Gardner met with UFO researcher Leonard H. Stringfield. Mr. Stringfeld stated in his 1977 book, *Situation Red, The UFO Siege!* that "Gardner reiterated his concern about 'our losing aircraft to the UFO'. He described several cases in detail." Gardner's research had an impact on Stringfeld, which prompted Stringfeld to get a "Written statement" from him. Len Stringfield published Robert Gardner's statement in an issue of "Orbit" dated November 1955. He states in full, "In the latter part of February 1953, I carried a letter of introduction and recommendation from a New York official in charge of our Eastern Air Defense to General Benjamin Chidlaw, then in charge of our Continental Air Defense at Ent Air Force Base in Colorado. The letter concerned a plan I had which the Eastern Air Defense considered important to our National Defense. Out of courtesy to General Chidlaw, who has since retired, I have withheld until now the vitally important information…revealed. In the course of the half hour private interview the General mentioned, among many interesting items the following, 'We have stacks of reports about flying saucers. We take them seriously when you consider we have lost many men and planes trying to intercept them."

At this time I ask; how many American fighter planes were lost in 1952 because of "scrambles after flying saucers" and written off as training accidents? How much information in Ruppelt's book was censored by the Air Force?

I reviewed all of the Project Blue Book "Unknown" cases for the year 1952. I searched for cases that reported involvements of UFOs and United States Air Force fighter jets. I discovered that Project Blue Book reported 15 unknown cases that involved a direct interaction between either an AF fighter and UFO, or AF fighter pilots being in the area of a UFO who reported a sighting. The following is a list of those cases:

1. Case 1076- March 23, 1952
2. Case 1082- March 29, 1952
3. Case 1299- June 17, 1952
4. Case 1556- July 22, 1952
5. Case 1572- July 22, 1952
6. Case # unknown – June 23, 1952
7. Case 1554- July 23, 1952
8. Case 1567- July 23, 1952
9. Case 1731- July 29, 1952
10. Case 1827- August 5, 1952
11. Case 1889- August 13, 1952
12. Case 1961- August 24, 1952
13. Case 2142- October 1, 1952
14. Case 2266- December 8, 1952
15. Case 2267- December 9, 1952

The month of June only accounted for one of these "Unknown," UFO and fighter jet incidents. In July, six of the fourteen "Unknown" cases involved USAF fighter jets and UFOs. In addition, there were other 1952 "Unknown" cases involving non-Air Force fighters and UFOs. These UFO reports were received from the Far East.

Edward Ruppelt stated that, "In June the Air Force was taking the UFO problem seriously. One of the reasons was that there were a lot of good UFO reports coming in from Korea. Fighter pilots reported seeing silver colored spheres or disks on several occasions, and radar in Japan, Okinawa, and in Korea had tracked unidentified targets." Blue Book documented the two following "Unknown" UFO incidents from the Far East, which involved United States Marine Corps jets.

1. Case 1313. Four "Marine Corps" fighters saw a UFO over Korea on June 20, 1952.

2. Case 1189. A "Marine Corps" fighter attempted an intercept on a UFO over Japan on August 13, 1952.

Blue Book Case 1313, an "Unknown," occurred over central Korea on June 20, and involved a formation of fighter planes. Four Marine Corps pilots were flying F4U-4B Corsair fighters at an altitude of 5,000 feet on a bombing mission when they sighted a UFO flying below them as they were about to begin their bombing run.

An "Air Intelligence Report," from the "1st Marine Air Wing, Marine Air Group," gave the details of this incident. At "1503/1" [3:03 p.m. local time], one pilot, Captain McDonald, stated, "I observed an unidentified object at position one mile southeast of target-coordinates CT 091129. It appeared to be a white object, circular or oval in shape and about 10 feet in diameter." Another pilot in the formation, Captain Francisco stated, "The object was below me at least 5,000 feet and was traveling at a very fast speed and appeared to be white or silver in color…I was unable to tell the shape too well but it appeared to be round." Pilot Captain Foster stated, "I estimate the object was 10 to 12 feet in diameter. Bomb craters on the ground were about 3 or 4 times as large as the object and I later estimated the bomb craters to be 40 to 50 feet in diameter." He then said, "This object made a 630 degree turn [circled area twice] and was in sight at all times. It made approximately a 4 mile circle."

Fighter pilot Foster deemed the UFO a potentially hostile enemy aircraft and chose to go after it. He broke away and attempted to intercept the unknown craft flying below him. The fourth pilot Captain Pittman stated, "Captain Foster made a run at the object." Foster then put his jet into a dive and attempted to go after it, and descended to, 4,000 feet, only 1,000 feet above the ground.

Captain Bobbie Foster stated the following information that describes his intercept attempt in an Intelligence report, "REPORT OF CAPTAIN BOBBIE FOSTER 024474/7302, USMC." He said, "It [UFO] circled our target and retired east. I started a dive on the object and at an indicated speed of 250 knots at 4,000 feet the object went out of sight still low on the ground (below 1,000') estimated 1,000 MPH or 4 times mine." Captain Pittman said the following about the object, "It pulled away from him." Captain Foster explained what occurred after the intercept attempt, "I pulled back in to flight and we continued our Close Air Support flight."

Far East Air Force Intelligence officers rated these pilots reliability as "A-1," in their report. This object was obviously an intelligently controlled craft that was maneuvering below these jets and actually escaped one of them during an intercept attempt. The team at Project Blue Book was very impressed with this military report because it involved multiple witnesses; four highly trained Marine combat fighter pilots, thus evaluating it as an "Unknown."

June 21, was the first day of summer and would prove to be one of the longest summers in history for the United States Air Force. Blue Book received more UFO reports during those three summer months in 1952, June 21 through September 21 than any other three consecutive months in history.

Captain Ruppelt stated, "To anyone who had anything to do with flying saucers, the summer of 1952 was just one big swirl of UFO reports." During 1952, the American public had sighted UFOs and flying saucers across the United States at an alarming rate. Concerned citizens throughout the country continued to work their way into a panic and reported these strange objects in record numbers.

On June 21, the UFO nightmare of that summer started over the United States. Two UFO incidents were reported to ATIC that day and both involved very small objects. Ed Ruppelt wrote about one of them in his book and the other incident was recorded as Project Blue Book case 1319, and was evaluated as an "Unknown."

The two small objects sighted in both incidents were actually air visual sightings made from Air Force aircraft. Moreover, both of these objects seem to have been some type of controlled reconnaissance vehicles.

At 10:58 p.m., an aerial dogfight occurred over the prohibited airspace of the Oak Ridge National Laboratory, located in Oak Ridge Tennessee. A small light was sighted by the local Ground Observers Corps and was picked-up on radar as well. Shortly after, the UFO passed over the ORNL no-fly zone. When the object penetrated this air space, a patrolling aircraft attempted to intercept it. Ruppelt explained what happened, "An F-47 Aircraft on combat air patrol in the area was vectored in visually, spotted a light, and closed on it. They fought from 10,000 to 27,000 feet, and sometimes the object made what seemed to be ramming attacks. The light was described as, white, 6 to 8 inches in diameter, and blinking until it put on power. The pilot could see no silhouette around the light."

It is interesting to note the definition of a "combat patrol," as defined by the USAF, "Combat air patrol. (CAP) An air patrol over any area or force for the purpose of intercepting and attacking hostile aircraft before they reach their objective." During this episode, the F-47 plane was on a combat air patrol in anticipation of the object described as a white light therefore this object was considered the, "attacking hostile aircraft," according to definition. It is also interesting to note that this incident was not considered an "Unknown." If it had been then UFOs would have consequently been considered hostile! Luckily, for the fighter pilot, this aerial duel did not end in death.

At 12:30 p.m., another small type object that resembled a small vehicle was sighted flying over Texas. This incident was recorded by Blue Book as Case 1319 and evaluated as an "Unknown." An "Air Intelligence Information Report," from the "3510th Fly. Tng. Wing, Kelly AFB," and dated "21 July 52" gave the details. During this episode, an Air Force witness saw more than a light in the sky, he actually saw the definite shape of an object as it passed near his aircraft.

Witness Sergeant Howard Davis, a "flight engineer," flying a board a Kelly AFB "B-29 bomber," saw the small strange-looking object. While flying at an altitude of "8,000 ft.," the witness saw a bright UFO. Sergeant Davis said the UFO "dove" by the aircraft at a distance of only "500 ft." away. He described the object as being "flat," and approximately three and one-half by three and one-half feet in dimension. The witness also drew a detailed picture of the object and described its colors. The front part of the UFO was triangular-shaped with the point facing forward and the aft part of the UFO was rounded. From the aft end, a protrusion was described with an apparent "opening."

The witness labeled the drawing of the UFO and described its colors and some details. The center part of the flat side of the object displayed a, "DARK-BLUE LIGHT." An aura of "WHITE LIGHT," surrounded the dark-blue light. A "REDDISH LIGHT," surrounded the white light out to the edges of the object.

The rear part of the object emitted, "REDDISH SPARKS AND STREAKS OF LIGHT. (APPROX. 15' LONG)." The witness labeled this exhaust as being visible and starting three feet back as it trailed behind the body. The small size of this UFO indicates that it was probably not occupied. Its small size would indicate that it was probably a controlled vehicle and since it passed within such a close proximity of the plane, it could have been on a reconnaissance mission. The UFO sightings at the start of the 52 summer were off to a big start as the UFO reports started to pile into ATIC at a record rate.

On June 22, 1952, the UFO reports continued to come in from the Far East and another was received from Korea. This military UFO sighting occurred over Pyunthek, Korea and once again, a small type UFO was sighted. This UFO incident is documented in Project Blue Book as Case 1323. This Far East UFO incident was evaluated as an "Unknown," and was reported by two Marine Corps Sergeants who saw the object over their base. An Intelligence report sent to ATIC reported the incident that involved this small and odd-looking UFO.

The report stated that it was, "approximately four feet in diameter and orange in color." This peculiar looking craft was seen "at 10:45 p.m. just above the K-6 airstrip." Shortly after the two men spotted the UFO, they said, "The object went into a vertical dive and suddenly leveled off at a point approximately one hundred feet above the west of the airstrip." When the object was in its vertical dive the two Sergeants saw, "a trail of bright flame extending from two to five feet in length." The object then ascended back up into the sky and then made a "180 degree turn to the right, spending about forty-five to sixty seconds in the turn." The object then "emitted a bright flash," and headed east and emitted a "second bright flash," then disappeared.

It is uncanny that a small UFO was sighted over Korea the day before that was also trailing a long red flame and displayed the same characteristics. These two small objects seemed to have been some type of surveillance craft that were on reconnoitering missions. Was this actually the same UFO seen over both of those areas?

On the following day, June 23, the UFO sightings flared up across the United States once again and the Blue Book staff was inundated with reports. Project Blue Book recorded five "Unknown" cases that occurred over the United States that day. June 23 had the highest amount of recorded "Unknown" cases for a single day in June: 1. Case 1331-Spokane, Washington. 2. Case 1332-Tacoma, Washington. Mc Chord AFB. 3. Case 1333- Kirksville, Missouri (Case Missing). 4. Case 1334- Oak Ridge, Tennessee. 5. Case 1335-Owensboro, Kentucky.

The first UFO sighting that day occurred over Oak Ridge, Tennessee at 3:30 a.m. The witness was secretary, Ms. Martha Milligan. On that early morning, she saw a strange UFO streak across the sky above her. Ms. Milligan described the object as looking "bullet-shaped" and it emitted a "burnt-orange exhaust" as it flew straight and level. The startled witness said that she observed the UFO for somewhere between "30-60 seconds." An interesting point to this story is this sighting occurred in Oak Ridge, home of the "Oak Ridge National Laboratory." Only two days before an aerial dogfight occurred over the prohibited airspace of the Oak Ridge National Laboratory between an F-47 fighter plane and a strange light.

At 10:00 a.m. in the Owensboro area of Kentucky, a National Guardsman sighted two very strange-looking objects. Lt. Col. Depp described these UFOs as looking like "giant soap bubbles" as they passed through the sky. These two objects were reported to be "reflecting yellow and lavender colors." The witness said that the UFOs "flew in trail for five seconds" until they disappeared from sight.

The next two sightings on June 23 occurred over the state of Washington. On that afternoon, a great report came from an "airport weather observer" at Spokane at 4:05 p.m. The witness, Rex Thompson reported seeing a large UFO that he described as a "round disc" that displayed a "metallic shine." The witness said that he observed the disc for approximately "5-7 minutes." During that time, Mr. Thompson said the disc "flashed" and "fluttered" in the sky. He also said that it looked like a "flipped coin." Reports such as this one, where the witness was a trained weather observer were hard for the Blue book staff to dismiss as a known aerial object or a misidentification... "Unknown." The second sighting that occurred over Washington that day was a military sighting and occurred over Tacoma Washington. Witness 2nd Lt. K. Thompson at McChord Air Force Base reported that he saw a UFO at 9:00 p.m. that evening. The witness stated that he saw a "very large light" and said that it "flew straight and level" across the sky. Thompson said that he watched the UFO for "ten minutes" as it passed near the base. Once again, this sighting was another one that was hard to dismiss, such as a weather balloon, a meteor, or a temperature inversion... "Unknown."

The Kirksville, Missouri Unknown report for June 23, 1952 is missing from the Project Blue Book files. The final "Unknown" sighting on June 23, 1952 had no case number. It was a military sighting, came to the United States via Japan, and involved an Air Force fighter plane. The exact location was undisclosed in the report but it came from a Japanese Headquarters designated "CV 4359." At "6:08 A.M." local time it was reported that a USAF fighter pilot of the "18th Fighter-Bomber Group reported a UFO. The fighter pilot stated the UFO was "black" in color, was shaped like a "coin." He said the object was about "15-20 feet in diameter." The fighter pilot said, as he watched the black object, it made an "irregular descent" through the sky.

There were eight more unexplained cases between June 25 and June 29, 1952. They are as follows:
1. Case 1340 – Tokyo, Japan. June 25. (Case Missing from Files).
2. Case 1344 – Chicago, Illinois. June 25.
3. Case 1347 – Japan/Korea region. June 25.
4. Case 1348 – Terre Haute, Indiana. June 26.
5. Case 1351 – Pottstown, Pennsylvania. June 26.
6. Case 1355 – Topeka, Kansas. June 27.
7. Case 1361 – Lake Kishkonoug, Wisconsin. June 28
8. Case 1364 – Chicago, Illinois- O' Hare Airport. June 29.

The military continued to report UFO sightings from Korea and Japan during the month. Meanwhile, in the United States, and for some unknown reason, the UFO sightings were increasing over Chicago, Illinois. A Blue Book "Unknown" case, Case 1344 reported that on June 25, two witnesses in Chicago had a long UFO sighting. The report states that Mrs. Norbury and Mr. Matheis saw a "bright yellow-white" UFO. The couple described it as an "egg-shaped object." At times, it was said to have "had a red tail," according to the witnesses. They also said that during the course of the "1-1/2" hours that they watched this object, it made "seven circles," in the sky.

Four days later, on June 29, the UFOs were back over Chicago, Illinois. Project Blue Book recorded this incident as "Unknown" Case 1364. Blue Book states that this sighting occurred near the area of "O'Hare Airport," home of the 4706th Fighter Interceptor Wing.

At 5:45 p.m., three Air Force police officers of the 83rd Air Base Squadron sighted a UFO as it hovered over a pair of radio towers about seven miles away from their post. The officers described the UFO as a "flat oval object." They said that it was "bright silver" in color, and it appeared to be approximately, "30 feet in diameter." The military records report that after the UFO was first spotted, it was said to have moved. After that point, the sighting continued for another "45-minutes." An "Air Intelligence Information Report. HQ 4706 Defense Wing, Truax AFB, Illinois" by Captain Neil Mac Lachlan and dated, "3 July 52," states the following,

"During the next 45 minutes the object traveled to the southwest and then back north to approximately its original position. It also moved to some extent in the vertical plane. Its acceleration during these movements was practically instantaneous to a speed which appeared to be much faster than any jet fighter At times, the object moved slowly and during the time it hovered, it appeared to rock on its longitudinal axis. When the object rocked or turned into a vertical plane its shape was easily discernable as oval and when in a horizontal position it appeared to be flat or thin and was difficult to see at this time. At all times during the first 25-30 minutes of the observation, the object was encircled by a blue circle of white haze."

Once again, this military sighting of a UFO was hard to dismiss, especially when the sighting of this unconventional aerial object lasted more than 45 minutes. Why did these saucers continue to reconnoiter the city of Chicago and O'Hare Airport during that time in 1952? Early in the summer of 1952, Air Force officials and Civil Defense directors from 46 states and 4 territories met to review current efforts to defend the United States from an enemy attack. *Air Force—The Magazine of American Air Power* stated in its December 1952 issue that during this meeting it was said that, "Despite a $300,000,000 radar fence around the nation's perimeter, gaps exist through which enemy aircraft could penetrate our defenses undetected... The only practical means of filling the gaps in our defenses is through a 24-hour operation by civilian volunteers." America's radar network was not sufficient. During this era, radar gaps existed because ground radar stations were not always able to spot planes flying under 5,000 feet.

The governments plan was to utilize civilian volunteers to observe the skies over the United States to fill the low-level gaps. These volunteers would staff government stations and visually scan the skies over America to look for unknown aircraft. These volunteers, who were to work with the Air Force, were the men and women of the Ground Observer Corps (GOC). This new government operation was named "Skywatch" and would be put into action in July of 1952. During this time though, the threat of Soviet bombers invading the skies over America was not the only problem. The month of June was a hot month for UFO sightings and tensions continued to rise in the Blue Book office at ATIC. In Washington D.C., government officials kept a close watch on the situation and were concerned with the overwhelming amount of UFO sightings over America. As the reports, continued pile in they were put into the UFO pressure cooker but the lid on this UFO cover-up became harder to keep down. The UFOs continued to turn up the heat over America with their constant blatant appearances, which caused the secret contents in UFO pressure cooker to boil. This started the lid on the United States government's UFO cover-up to wobble as Washington officials tried to hold it down.

JULY HEATS UP

In early July, flying saucers and other strange looking crafts continued to appear over the United States and throughout the world. In the United States, military officials in Intelligence were alarmed at the growing rate of the sightings that were reported that summer and the military continued to scramble interceptors.

On July 1, 1952, Air Force fighter jets were scrambled back into the air in hot pursuit of a UFO over Massachusetts. This case involved two F-94 Starfire interceptors, which were sent aloft after a UFO that was sighted over the Boston area at approximately 7:25 a.m. According to Edward Ruppelt, the first witnesses reported seeing two fighter jets attempting to intercept a "cigar-shaped object" over Boston. Shortly after another witness, an Air Force captain, saw the same object 15 miles northwest of Boston over Bedford, Massachusetts. The captain described the UFO as a "silvery cigar-shaped object," as it passed through Bedford's sky. These cigar-shaped objects frequented the skies over America throughout the summer of 1952.

Ruppelt also stated, "By July 1 we were completely snowed under with reports." UFO reports came in from "Fort Monmouth, New Jersey" as well as "Washington D.C." that day. Over New Jersey, two objects hovered near Fort Monmouth "for about five minutes." Another witness reported that he saw a UFO descend over Washington D.C. According to Ruppelt, a "George Washington University physics professor" saw the object that was seen over the Capitol. The professor described the UFO as a, "dull, gray smoky-colored" object and claimed to have watched it "for eight minutes." He said the UFO descended and "steadily dropped lower and lower until buildings in downtown Washington blocked off the view." The UFOs were getting bolder in their actions as was evident in this particular incident when the object actually descended low over Washington.

The "cigar-shaped object," sighted over Massachusetts on July 1, 1952, was definitely not a conventional-type aircraft. Moreover, the two UFOs that "hovered" over Fort Monmouth, New Jersey and the descending object over D.C. did not display the flight characteristics of conventional aircraft, yet on that day; Project Blue Book did not record any "Unknown" UFO cases.

On the following day, July 2, a brilliant formation of 10 or 12 lights was filmed over Tremonton, Utah. A Navy photographer, Warrant Officer Delbert C. Newhouse, took them. He shot 40 feet of film with his hand held 16 mm "Bell and Howell Automaster" camera that had a telephoto lens attached and captured the objects maneuvering throughout the sky. This incident is one of the most important and valuable pieces of UFO evidence recorded in the early years of UFO history. The photographer's testimony appears in the book, "Scientific Study of Unidentified Flying Objects" by Edward Condon. In part, it states, "Toward the end one of the objects reversed course and proceeded away from the main group. I held the camera still and allowed this single one to cross the field of view, picking it up again and repeating for three or four such passes. By this time all the objects had disappeared." Later it was stated that Newhouse, "described them as 'gun metal colored objects shaped like two saucers, one inverted on top of the other.'"

Officer Newhouse graduated from naval photographic school and had been in the Navy for 19 years at the time he recorded the UFOs. He had over one thousand hours of aerial photography missions that included 2,200 hours logged as chief photographer. The film was sent to Project Blue Book for analysis and evaluation and was studied for three months by the "Photo Reconnaissance Laboratory" in Dayton, Ohio. Investigator Hartman who reviewed the case stated, "It is believed [he] could be classified as an expert photographer." USAF public representative Albert Chop later stated that, "Fraud was completely ruled out. They tried every trick and method to duplicate the film but it couldn't be done."

Blue Book recorded an "Unknown" case on July 3, 1952, that involved a spectacular UFO sighting near an Air Force base in Michigan. At 6:15 a.m. CST, Selfridge AFB, near Mt. Clements received a UFO report from a witness on the Manitou Beach Highway near Rome Center. An official at Selfridge AFB then sent a teletype to "The Director of Intelligence, USAF" in Washington D.C. The teletype reported that two, "circular shaped lights" said to be approximately "20 feet in diameter," had passed only a few hundred feet above the terrain. The witness described the UFOs as moving, "HORIZONTALLY AT A TREMENDOUS SPEED."

On July 3, 1952, the UFOs were back over the windy city of Chicago. Once again, the UFOs involved in this incident were reported to Project Blue Book. Furthermore, this episode was evaluated as an "Unknown." This was the third UFO sighting over Chicago that Blue Book evaluated as an "Unknown" in 10 days. Project Blue Book recorded this sighting as Case 1382 and stated the event occurred over Chicago, Illinois at 11:50 p.m. CST. The witness, Mrs. J.D. Arbuckle said that her UFO sighting lasted about "six seconds." During that time, she saw "two discs" that she said were a "bright pastel green color." The observer reported the pair of discs "flew very fast, straight and level" as they passed across the sky before disappearing. The following three "Unknown" cases describe the UFOs sighted over Chicago during that ten-day period:

1. June 25. Case 1344. Egg-shaped object. Bright yellow-white in color.
2. June 29. Case 1364. Flat-oval object. Bright silver in color.
3. July 3. Case 1382. Discs. Bright pastel green in color.

What was the attraction that continually drew these bright UFOs to the city of Chicago? Were the UFOs looking for something in Chicago?

Also on July 3, 1952, *The New York Times*, printed an article titled, "AIR FORCE'S NEW SUPERSONIC JET PLANE" This article states in part:

LOCKHEED F-94C STARFIRE

The military took some of the wraps off one of its most important shoreline defenses today, a high-flying supersonic jet warplane that automatically seeks out enemy bombers in any kind of weather. The new airplane is the Starfire F-94C, built for the Air Force by Lockheed Aircraft at Burbank, California.

It is the first fighting plane ever to have all-rocket armament, carrying twenty-four rockets, 2.75 inches in size, in a ring of firing tubes around the blunt nose. The plane carries a two-man crew.

Radar and specialized 'brain-like instruments enable the Starfire to spot the enemy miles away, lock onto the target, track, close, aim and open fire-all by itself, according to Hall L. Hubbard, Lockheed vice president and chief engineer."

This article also states, "The interceptor-type plane was designed specifically to knock out invading bombers." In July though, and the months to follow, the F-94C Starfire was primarily used by the Air Force to pursue UFOs over the United States. None of which proved to be enemy bombers, moreover, Soviet bombers.

Lockheed Aircraft Corporation built the Starfire aircraft. The USAF accepted the first C-Model Starfires during fiscal year 1953 (July 1, 1952 until June 30, 1953). On July 2, 1952, a Department of Defense release headline read: "Air Force Announces Production of New Aircraft": The Air Force has announced that the new Lockheed F-94C, 'Starfire', an all weather interceptor, is in production." The F-94C Starfire 50-966 was used as the publicity aircraft in the photograph press releases.

In the September 1952, issue of Flying Magazine, Lockheed Aircraft Corporation reported, "the 'C' was the third in the Starfire series and was now being delivered to the USAF to augment squadrons to F-94A's and F-94B's now on 24-hour duty protecting U.S. borders." The F-94C was a two-man fighter that carried a rear seat navigator/operator. This jet was capable of attaining speeds in excess of 600 mph. The C-model F-94 Starfire was the first two-seat straight-wing combat aircraft to break mach one in a dive. Primary armament for the F-94C consisted of rockets rather than fixed machine guns. The rockets had a greater range than conventional aircraft machine guns and were fitted with explosive warheads, which made them more deadly. There were 24 of these rockets grouped in four six-round compartments situated around the radar dome in the jet's nose. They were housed behind four retractable doors from which they could be salvoed. The F-94C Starfire also carried over 1,200 pounds of electronic equipment on board. The jet had an automatic pilot, which could be coupled with the radar for attack runs. This meant that once the autopilot was engaged and coupled with the radar, the jet would react automatically and center the steering dot on the pilot scope.

The rocket firing system was controlled automatically with a firing control system that combined radar tracking with a rocket-firing computer. This system enabled the Starfire to spot its target, lock on, approach, close, aim and fire automatically. The pilot and radar operator would principally act as monitors, although manual firing was available if needed or desired.

When these rockets were fired, they were stabilized by means of folding fins. The fins were opened by air pressure immediately after the rockets left the jet. Even though these propelled rockets were unguided, the spread they created would blanket a large area of sky in destruction. The F-94C Starfire was a prime example of a truly powerful modern-era combat jet. Its debut in July of 1952 could not have come at a better time as the UFO sightings during the summer of 1952 continued to escalate throughout the United States.

On July 4, 1952, O'Hare Airport was back in the news concerning Chicago's recent rash of flying saucer reports. The New York Times reported the following *United Press* information:

Chicago, July 3 (UP) – Air Force officers at O'Hare base said today "flying saucer" reports have stacked up lately. The public information office said it had received sixteen reports of mysterious objects in the sky in the Chicago vicinity this week." It was also reported that O'Hare, "Public Information officers said jet patrols normally are on alert 'twenty-four hours a day.'"

There were six more unexplained Project Blue Book cases between July 3 and July 13, 1952. All of these UFO incidents occurred over the United States. Two of these "Unknown" cases were outstanding sightings; one involved a State Patrol aircraft and the other incident was a military sighting that involved a pilot.

The first incident was Case 1390 and occurred on July 5, 1952. This UFO sighting happened over Norman, Oklahoma at 7:58 p.m. On that night, Oklahoma State Patrolman Hamilton was flying in a "State Patrol plane," over the vicinity of Norman. The sky was partly cloudy and Hamilton was flying at "cruising speed," when he noticed the UFOs. The pilot described them as "three dark discs" that were silhouetted against a cloud.

When the pilot first saw them, he said the "discs were hovering." Moments later, they accelerated and "then flew away," he said. Patrol officer Hamilton stated that the entire time of his UFO sighting lasted about "15 seconds." Shortly after landing, the pilot reported his sighting to the Oklahoma State Police Department. Hamilton's UFO report was then forwarded to the authorities at the Air Technical Intelligence Center, in Dayton, Ohio. Blue Book officials evaluated this case as an "Unknown," adding to that already long list of unexplained cases involving flying discs.

On July 9, 1952, another UFO incident was reported to ATIC from Colorado Springs, Colorado, home of Ent Air Force Base, Air Defense Command Headquarters. At 12:45 p.m., the witness, an Air Force pilot had sighted a very strange looking "luminous white" object. He described it as looking like an "air foil less its trailing edge." An airfoil is defined as, "a surface or body, as a wing, propeller blade, rudder, or the like."

For "12 minutes," the pilot reported that he watched the airfoil-shaped object fly throughout the sky. He said, "It moved slowly and erratically" during that time. Project Blue Book recorded this very unusual and unconventional looking aircraft in their files as "Unknown" Case 1405.

The flying saucer sightings across the United States continued and more UFOs were seen on the following day, July 10, 1952. *The Washington Daily News* reported on July 23, 1952, that a Marine pilot saw two UFOs on July 10, 1952. The paper reported, "A Marine pilot told the *United Press* he saw 'two green objects –like shooting stars without tails –shooting across the sky at terrific speed and a very high altitude over Quantico, Va., on the night of July 10." The Quantico Marine Corps Air Station is located in Quantico, Virginia.

Two nights later, another UFO sighting occurred over a major city and raised quite a commotion. Once again, the sighting took place over the windy city, Chicago! Edward Ruppelt wrote about this UFO sighting in his 1956 book. This incident occurred on Saturday night, July 12, 1952. It was a very hot night in Chicago, and Montrose Beach was the ideal place to seek relief and cool off, but the night only got hotter.

Ruppelt reported that there were approximately 400 people on the beach that evening; many of them were star watching. The excitement started at 9:42 p.m. when an object appeared in the sky. Witnesses described the object as a "large red light with small white lights on the side." The UFO came across the sky from the west north-west direction. Suddenly, it "made a 180 degree turn directly over their heads, and disappeared over their heads" according to Edward Ruppelt. The object was said to have, "changed to a single yellow light as it made its turn," according to other witnesses who saw it.

Ruppelt stated the following information about this sighting, "One of the people at the beach was the weather officer from O'Hare International Airport, an Air Force captain. He immediately called O'Hare. They checked on balloon flights and with radar, but both were negative; radar said that there had been no aircraft in the area of Montrose Beach for several hours. I sent an investigator to Chicago, and although he came back with a lot of data on the sighting, it didn't add up to anything known." It is interesting to note that even though the investigator had "a lot of data on the sighting it didn't add up to any thing known." Edward Ruppelt wrote about this Chicago incident in his book but did not report F-86 Sabre Jets from the 4706 Fighter Interceptor Wing based at O'Hare field had a UFO sighting that same day.

Project Blue Book records show a message was sent from the Air Force Office of Investigation, Washington D.C. to O'Hare Airport's Defense Wing concerning the incident. The message is dated "21 JULY 52" and was in response to a wire message sent earlier by Air Force officials at O'Hare Airport:

MESSAGE
TO: CO 4706 DEFENSE WING-O'HARE INTERNATIONAL AIRPORT- PARK RIDGE- ILLINOIS
FROM: AFOIN-ATTIA

The message reported that on "12 July 52," a pair of O' Hare F-86 Sabre Jets from the "4706 Fighter Interceptor Wing" were said to have be on a "routine training mission." The jets were flying northeast of O'Hare over the area of Arlington Heights. One of the Sabre Jet pilots was on a 240 degree heading at an altitude of "22, 000 feet" when he saw a UFO approximately "15 miles" away. The pilot flew in the direction of the UFO, got a good look at it and described the object as "oblong" and "yellow" in color. He said the UFO was emitting an "exhaust," and traveling at about "700 knots." During that time, the pilot's wing mate was out of position and did not see the object out in the distance. The fighter pilot continued toward the UFO, radioed ground control on the F channel, otherwise known as "Foxtrot", and began to chase the object. Meanwhile, the pilot's wing mate was listening in on the radio transmissions between the jet and the ground control operator.

The Sabre Jet pilot's intercept attempt lasted for approximately "20 seconds" before the UFO pulled away from him. As the pilot was about to break away and change course, a radio transmission came over the F-channel or "Foxtrot Channel." This message states the quiet F-channel was disrupted by an eerie voice that uttered the word, "C-A-S-E-Y." Both Sabre Jet pilots heard the strange radio transmission, and unbeknownst to them, it came from an unidentified source. This radio transmission did have some significance though; the intercepting pilot's name, none other than..."Casey." The "Office of Special Investigation" made a request to O'Hare Air Force officials to complete the appropriate forms according to protocol and stated the following:

INCLUDE DETAILS OF UNUSUAL RADIO TRANSMISSION MENTIONED IN SUBJECT WIRE.

The source of the radio transmission was never determined and is still unknown! Were the fighter pilots' radio transmissions being monitored by their target? Also on July 12, 1952, "Operation Skywatch" was officially put into action. The eyes of the Ground Observer Corp were focused on the skies and ready to alert the Air Force to scramble jet interceptors after any airborne intruders. On July 13, 1952, *The Springfield Union* of Massachusetts reported in part:

OPERATION SKYWATCH OPENS MONDAY

Washington [July 12]- President Truman made a bid Saturday for more volunteers to man-lookout stations which will go on a round-the-clock watch Monday against Air invaders…He added that the watchers will be helpful to prevent war. The first shifts of some 150,000 volunteers will take their posts Monday at about 6,000 stations in 27 states to scan the skies for any raiders who might slip through the radar screen for a sneak attack that could set off World War III.

During 1952, nearly 200,000 civilian sky watchers made up the GOC, but the Air Force still needed another 350,000 volunteers to watch the skies over America. Tensions mounted during the year concerning the possibility of a Soviet aerial nuclear attack. The Air Force trained the observers in different techniques and the procedures required to fulfill their jobs as part of the "Air Defense System." The duties and responsibilities of the Ground Observers included, "Aircraft Identification" and "Reporting Procedures."

In addition to the numerous GOC observation posts, there were other basic units of the defense system. According to information in an official *Ground Observers Guide*, they are as follows:

1. "'THE EARLY WARNING RADAR STATIONS'; they searched the skies for enemy planes by electrical means rather than visual means."
2. "'THE GROUND CONTROLLED INTERCEPT RADAR STATIONS'; they could follow the course of enemy aircraft by radar and then direct fighter aircraft to the proper position and altitude to attack them."
3. "'THE FIGHTER INTERCEPT AIRCRAFT BASES,' where fighter planes were stand ready to take off and attack approaching enemy aircraft."

This GOC guide also stated, "For the first time in our history, a potential enemy has the power to make sudden, devastating attacks on any part of our country…A single plane carrying an atomic bomb can wipe out an entire city. It is a dangerous situation…There is little probability of turning back an enemy air attack completely." The guide also explained how radar systems had a limited range and gaps in their networks and "lookouts" were needed. As part of being the "eyes of the country" it stated, "Your reports may constitute the first warning of an enemy approach. The Aircraft Flash message you send in may put into motion forces that will save a whole city from destruction."

The August 1952 issue of *Flying* featured an article about the Ground Observer Corps titled, "Defense of the Homeland," by C. L. Hamilton. An excerpt subtitled "Taking Saucers Seriously" appeared in the article and stated, "Another GOC activity, and one about which very little has been said, is its potential in observing 'flying saucers.' This is a matter, which the Air Force takes very seriously, regardless of any opinions to the contrary. Radar almost daily is tracking flights, which due to their speed and unknown origin could not conceivably be airplanes, as we know them. If the civilian Ground Observer Corps were fully organized and activated on a round-the-clock basis, it would provide constant visual observation of every mile of sky over some two-thirds of the United States. This fact has been recognized by the Air Force and provision made for reporting by civilian posts of objects which, lacking any better designation, are termed 'flying saucers.'"

Another piece of information that appeared in the article, "'OPERATION 'SKYWATCH' OPENS MONDAY" stated, "The start of 'Operation Skywatch' follows by a few weeks an Army announcement that antiaircraft men and their guns are now on continuous duty around key target areas across the country."

On August 1, 1952, a story appeared in *The Los Angeles Times* that reflected on this story. The title reads, "BY THE WAY with BILL HENRY." Mr. Henry, a writer, was also a radio celebrity on a nightly show on KHJ that aired Monday through Friday. In this article, he writes:

WASHINGTON- It's got so that when you come flying into this town of an evening you spend your time hoping, as you glide down out of the clouds, that some trigger-happy attack gunner won't make you famous as the first victim to be mistaken for a flying saucer rider and suddenly extinct. This town has the heebie jeebies! FLYING SAUCERS – It might not be particularly flattering to be mistaken for a saucer jockey, but chances are that such an error would at least be exciting.

Have you had a look around at your airports lately? I have not personally seen very much in the papers about it, or heard very much discussion, but there are antiaircraft batteries with long black guns located on the outskirts of nearly every city of any consequence that I have visited recently. It is no different from the days of 1941 except for the fact that, up to the moment, we have not yet had a repetition of the great 'Battle of Los Angeles.'

Were these antiaircraft guns stationed around the country prepared to fire upon Soviet bomber aircraft as well as the other UFOs as in reference to the "flying saucers?" To complicate matters, civilians were still reporting flying saucer sightings across the United States at an alarming rate...the country was panicked.

By mid July, the UFO sighting reports continued to pour into the ATIC. On the night of July 14, a spectacular "flying saucer" encounter occurred over Virginia when the crew of a Pan American Airlines DC-4 encountered a group of UFOs over Virginia. Edward Ruppelt gave a very vague account of this incident in his book, which achieved overnight recognition and became a classic flying saucer incident. In his one liner he stated, "On July 14 the crew of a Pan American airliner en route from New York to Miami reported eight UFOs near Newport News, Virginia, about 130 miles south of Washington." This incident was one of the biggest saucer stories of 1952 and was recorded as Project Blue Book "Case 1444," and then evaluated as an "Unknown." Why did Ruppelt reference this UFO sighting in short passing and only in a single line?

This is the story of one of the most important flying saucer incidents in American history. The crew of the DC-4 plane were, First Officer Captain Nash a Former Navy transport pilot and a pilot with Pan American for ten years, and Second Officer Captain William Fortenberry, a former United States Navy fighter pilot with Pan American Airlines since 1945.

In the 1950s, author Max Miller was President of the "Flying Saucers International," organization. He wrote a UFO book titled, *Flying Saucers-Fact Or Fiction* that was published in 1957. In Miller's book, William Nash gave a rare account of what occurred on that night. The story unfolded about one hour after sundown as Nash and Fortenberry were flying over the Chesapeake Bay in Virginia en route from New York to San Juan.

The night sky was clear, visibility was unlimited, and the plane was at cruising speed. At 8:12 p.m., Nash and Fortenberry were approaching Norfolk, about 20 miles ahead of them, when they noticed something very peculiar flying through the sky. Nash stated, "Suddenly a red brilliance appeared ahead of us and to our right, almost on the ground it seemed, and about ten miles beyond Newport News which lay 25 miles ahead and to the west of Norfolk." The words, "What the hell is that," echoed through the cabin of the DC-4, as both pilots simultaneously spotted something unusual. "Almost immediately we perceived that the brilliance consisted of six red objects streaking toward us at tremendous speed, and obviously well below us," Nash said. On July 16, 1952, *The Miami Herald* reported the incident in an article, "Miami Pilots Spot 8 Saucers." The pilots said the objects were, "glowing like hot coals." Miller reported the pilots stated, "They appeared to have the about twenty times the brightness of the city lights of Norfolk, over which they passed. Their shapes were clearly outlined and evidently circular. The edges were well defined, not phosphorescent or fuzzy in the least. Their red-orange color was uniform over the upper surface of each craft."

The pilot then described how their flight formation was arranged in levels above and below each other, Nash stated, "They were flying in what appeared to be a stepped-echelon formation." At that point, the objects were about halfway to the plane and were contrasted against the dark waters of the Bay below them. "The three front objects began to slide back and forth over each other, as though the leader had begun to decelerate and the second two apparently were not alerted, or –as pilots say – 'loused up formation,'" Nash stated.

According to the pilot, "They seemed to stay below 2000 feet as they shot into a position, slightly forward and below us." As they neared, Nash described the objects as, "coin-shaped," and said the diameter of each object appeared to be, "roughly 100 feet." He then stated, "Suddenly, as we thought they were going to pass beneath us, their glow diminished." Next, the six objects maneuvered and changed their positions as they neared the plane while the pilots watched in amazement. The Pan American pilot explained, "Together, they flipped on edge and reversed formation, sliding past one another to do so. When this formation was reversed the glow increased, and they shot away from us almost in the opposite direction." Nash also stated, "We agreed that when the 'things' were on edge, their thickness appeared to be about 15 to 20 percent of their diameters; or 15 to 20 feet thick if the crafts were 100 feet in diameter. The edges seemed unlit."

Immediately after the six objects redirected away from the plane, two additional objects passed under the wing of the DC-4. Nash stated, "They appeared to be higher than the others. They dived at the rear of the others on an apparent intercept heading." After the sixth and seventh objects joined formation, Nash exclaims, "Suddenly the original six blinked out-just as though someone had turned off an electric switch. And almost immediately the second two blinked out." Moments later, "They all blinked on again – all together in an in-line formation."

In a letter dated, "5 March 1970," from William Nash to Professor James E. McDonald, the pilot gave some further details of the incident. Nash explained, "The angle of elevation, relative to our visual horizon was about 45 degrees up when they blinked out. The blink-out was not in front to back order, but mixed order. Not a disappearance by perspective diminishment." When the UFOs lit back up and glowed, they were in a single file flight formation. Shortly after, they went into a climb. Nash stated the following, "The steep climb was after the objects re-lighted." He added, "The climb-out of the eight objects occurred after they had re-crossed Chesapeake Bay (after approaching our vicinity) and some of the land bordering the bay. Their angle was steep (about 45 degrees). They bobbed up and down as they climbed, as though very sensitive on the controls." The eight glowing discs then climbed above the flight level of the aircraft at an incredible speed. In Miller's book, Nash said, "Still low, they streaked across the western edge of Newport News, and to about ten miles beyond that." The objects continued to climb and ascended into the night sky over Virginia. The pilot explained what occurred next, "At some extreme altitude they seemed to blink out again, but separately in a mixed up fashion. I wondered later if this might indicate that they one-by-one were disappearing into a sort of carrier craft for the [eight] small craft." Nash stated, "We were stunned to say the least. We looked all around to see if there were possibly more, but there was nothing to be seen." The pilots then documented what they saw, Nash stated, "When we realized they were not coming back, we proceeded to compile some data while the weird experience was still fresh in our minds." He added, "Both of us have flown more than ten thousand hours, and this was our first experience with anything in the sky that we could not explain."

Donald Keyhoe stated, "The pilots radioed Norfolk and reported the sighting in detail." Edward Ruppelt explained what occurred next, in an unpublished draft for his book, "The report that the two men sent out through Norfolk radio reached ATIC about midnight and got me out of bed. As a routine matter I sent a TWX [message sent via a teletypewriter] to Miami to have the two pilots interrogated as soon as possible, but the sighting didn't mean too much because of a note at the bottom of the report, it said that five jet aircraft had been in the area at the time of the sighting and that the [Pan American] pilots had evidently mistaken them for the eight UFOs." The pilots continued on their flight and flew to Miami, Florida where they landed at Miami International Airport without any further incident.

At 7:00 a.m. the following morning, officials from the Office of Special Investigations telephoned William Nash and William Fortenberry and asked if they would meet with them for an interview. Donald Keyhoe said, "By the time Air Force Intelligence officers met them in Miami, the story was already on the news wires."

Five men, including one in uniform separated the two pilots into different rooms. Nash and Fortenberry were questioned for, "one hour and 45 minutes", and then were brought together and questioned together for, "half an hour." Nash explained, "When the special Air Force investigators interviewed us the next morning, they told Bill [Fortenberry] and I that seven other reports had come to them within thirty minutes after our sighting." He stated, "All from Norfolk describing six or eight red- orange objects making abrupt changes of direction in the sky." Nash also said, "We made sketches and drew the track of the objects on charts."

Back at ATIC in Dayton, Ohio, Ruppelt had a Blue Book officer attempt to track down the person responsible for writing the "five jet aircraft" postscript, on the previous night's report. He stated, "The next day, as a matter of course, Lt. Andy Flues followed up on the five jets but couldn't find anybody who would admit putting the 'P.S.' [post script] on the report. He checked with Langley AFB, the Norfolk Naval Air Station, Shaw AFB, and Marines at Quantico, and a dozen other bases within jet range of Newport News but no one had anything in the air around Newport News that." Who was the unknown person that wrote the postscript on this report, and what was their motive in doing so? Did this unknown person try to nip the Nash-Fortenberry incident in the bud and squash the story before it received any recognition?

The Miami Herald reported the following information in their July 16 article:

"We definitely saw them," Nash swore. "There is no doubt in our minds that we saw missiles of some kind operating under intelligent control. We feel, because of the way the missiles acted and because of all the other reports that have been heard, that they must be from some extra-terrestrial source." he added.

Keyhoe stated, "Both Nash and Fortenberry were convinced the discs were intelligently controlled machines from outer space." Keyhoe also read the Air Force's report and stated, "In the Intelligence report ATIC made no comment on the pilot's opinion. As usual, in unsolved cases, it ended with a terse: "Conclusion: Unknown."

Two days later another multiple UFO incident occurred, and this time they were photographed. This story involved a now famous photo taken on July 16, 1952. It showed a group of UFOs situated in the sky above a parking lot with a building to the left with smoke stacks. The photo was released and appeared in *The New York Times* on August 2, 1952. The headline states, "Mystery Photo, Jet Pilots' Report Added to Flying Saucer

Puzzle." The photo appears directly above the text of the article. It was taken at the Coast Guard air station in Salem, Massachusetts shows "four huge lights in the sky" in a "V' formation and was taken at "9:30 A.M."

The article states, "Coast Guard headquarters here [Washington] released the strange photograph taken from it's Salem air station…The picture released by the Coast Guard was taken by one of it's photographer, Shell R. Albert. Mr. Albert was quoted as saying the phenomenon was 'a quick flash.'"

Saucer researcher Major Donald Keyhoe stated, "During the first two weeks of July the saucers' reconnaissance of the earth was rapidly stepped up." Over the United States, "most of the saucers were operating at night, and they seemed to be focusing on defense bases, atomic plants, and military planes," he added. In his 1956 book, Captain Ruppelt also talked about the UFO situation during the first two weeks of July. He stated, "By mid-July we were getting about twenty reports a day plus frantic calls from intelligence officers all over the United States as every Air Force installation in the U.S. was being swamped with reports." This statement made by Ruppelt in his book, gives a much higher rate of received reports during mid-July than what was reported in a *United Press* story on July 17, 1952. *The New York Times* carried the following UP article that appeared on July 18, 1952:

    60 Flying 'Saucer Reports Fly at Air Force in 2 Weeks. By The United Press.

DAYTON, Ohio, July 17 – An Air Force spokesman said today some sixty reports had been received during the last two weeks. He could give no reason for the sudden increase. Captain E. J. Ruppelt of the Air Intelligence Center at Wright –Patterson Air Base said 'people are seeing unidentified objects in the sky at a rate almost double over last year. Captain Ruppelt, Project officer for the Air Force group that investigates unidentified aerial objects, said there was no connection between the saucer sighting increase and the recent inauguration of Operation Skywatch by the Ground Observer Corps.

The official Project Blue Book tabulation for "Unknown" sightings during the first half of July 1952, between July 3 and July 15, was only nine cases. During the first half of July 1952 there were only three cases listed as Military sightings evaluated as "Unknown" cases. Considering the amount of reports and frantic calls that Project Blue Book received during the first half of July the amount of cases they evaluated as "Unknown" cases is miniscule. During the first half of July, there were two days that had the most recorded "Unknown" cases in a single day, two. These two days were July 3 and July 9, 1952.

The second half of July was an entirely different story as the sightings continued to escalate. The staff at Blue Book was overwhelmed with reports and actually evaluated and listed 42 "Unknown" cases between July 15 and July 30, 1952. During the second half of July 1952, there was an amazing rise in Military sighting cases that were unexplained; between July 17 and July 29, 1952, Blue Book officials evaluated 19 "Unknown" Military UFO sightings.

On Friday, July 18, 1952, a Massachusetts newspaper, *The Lowell Sun* ran a story about Ruppelt and Project Blue Book. This *United Press* story is dated "DAYTON, O., July, 18th (UP)." The headline reads, "UNEXPLAINABLE OBJECTS TRACKED BY AIR FORCE." This article reports, "'we are convinced that persons making these reports actually see something in the sky,' Ruppelt said, 'but what they are is another question.'" This article also reported a very compelling quote made by Ruppelt that involved USAF jet interceptors, "Ruppelt said jet fighter equipped with the very latest radar have been sent aloft to 'make contact' with the phantom objects."

During the build up of UFO sightings that occurred in July of 1952, Ruppelt also made an interesting comment about the Ground Observer Corps. This comment appeared in *The New York Times* on July 18 and states, "Captain Ruppelt, project officer for the Air Force group that investigates unidentified aerial objects, said there was no connection between the saucer sighting increase and the recent inauguration of Operation

Skywatch and the Ground Observer Corps." This statement reflects the truth that even though there thousands of GOC observers watching the skies over the U.S., the alarming high rate of flying saucer sightings were also being reported from other sources.

The Sidney Morning Harold in Australia also carried Ruppelt's interceptor comment. Its July 18 headline read, "Flying Saucers Still a Mystery" and was datelined "New York, July 18 (A.A.P.)." This article states, "Jet fighters equipped with radar had been sent up, but none had yet made contact with a 'saucer' said Captain E. J. Ruppelt." *The United States Air Force Dictionary* defines the application of "contact," in sense four of the word. It states, "Contact...To be in contact or make contact: a. to be, or to get, close enough to an enemy as to see or strike him." It certainly seems that Captain Ruppelt and the United States Air Force did deem the flying saucers as their enemy and a threat to National Security during that time.

AT ONE OF the four desks in the small, 30-by-15-foot rooms, partitioned off from the rest of the Air Technical Intelligence center, Rothstein and Ruppelt check off one of the 1,000 sightings reported to their office in the past two years.

In Keyhoe's 1960 book, *Flying Saucers-TOP SECRET*, he wrote the following about the 1952 flying saucer flap, "1952. This year saw the greatest number of verified UFO sightings recorded." Keyhoe then supplied the following statement made by Ruppelt to the press in 1952, "Captain Ruppelt, at Project Blue Book, told the press, 'The flying saucers haven't struck yet. But that doesn't mean they are not a potential threat.'" Ruppelt's statement actually confirms that these UFOs were "flying saucers." Did Ruppelt's "lurid duels of death" statement come into play after the saucers "struck" back after being chased relentlessly and fired upon?

After mid-July of 1952, the Air Force received a steady stream of saucer reports from along the East coast of the country. The Air Force stated it was, "receiving flying saucer reports" during the summer of 1952, "at a rate higher than at any time since the initial flood of sightings in 1947."

On July 18, 1952, Project Blue Book evaluated three incidents as "Unknown" cases. One sighting involved an incident in Miami and two of them over two Air Force bases in the United States. The first UFO incident listed in the Blue Book Unknown reports is "Case 1482" and occurred over Lockbourne AFB, in Lockbourne, Ohio. At 9:00 p.m. witnesses, Airmen 3rd Class Jennings and Technical Sergeant Mahone sighted an "elliptically-shaped object" as it passed across the sky. The witnesses stated that the object was, "amber-colored" with "a small flame at the rear." The UFO moved at a high rate of speed and reportedly gave off a "resonant beating sound" and would increase in "brightness," during the duration of its flight. The Air Force witnesses said that they watched the object for "1-1/2 minutes" before it flew off and vanished. The UFO sightings continued to intensify that night.

The second "Unknown" Air Force base incident recorded on that same night is listed as "Case 1485." It involved one of the most spectacular UFO aerial displays over the United States that summer. The location of the sighting was made from the "base operations" center of Patrick Air Force Base in Cocoa Beach, Florida. The events on that evening unfolded at "10:45 P.M. EST," when two base officers at Patrick were outside and saw an odd light in the sky. They reported that they saw an "amber" colored light above the horizon line "to the west." One of the officers stated that it was, "quite a bit brighter than a star." At first, the two men thought it was "a balloon." The amber light then moved and flew across the sky and passed over the base and became stationary for "about one minute." The object started to move again; the officers said that it then turned and "headed north." A check with the base weather officer had revealed that there was a balloon in the air but not in their area and it was moving west according to the balloon-tracking team. Furthermore, it was reported, the light on the balloon was out. Meanwhile, several more officers and aviators had walked out side and had begun to watch the UFO aerial display out over the horizon.

Shortly after, a second light appeared in the same general area where the first light had made its appearance. It moved and proceeded north at a high rate of speed in the same direction as the first amber light. Moments later, the original light stopped and proceeded south and back over Patrick AFB and then turned away. A few minutes later a third light appeared from the west. It passed directly over the base proceeding east at a high rate of speed and flew out over the coastal waters of the Atlantic. This was definitely not the weather balloon. A fourth object then appeared out over the horizon to the west of Patrick AFB. It also proceeded east at a high rate of speed and also passed over the base then flew out over the Atlantic Ocean. This object then made a maneuver, very uncharacteristic of a weather balloon and turned 180 degrees and proceeded back to Patrick, passed over the base and continued west. Shortly after, a fifth light appeared in the west and followed the same pattern as the previous light before it vanished to the west.

The invasion of the saucers had begun over Florida…and in grand appearance as indicated by these brazen maneuvers over Patrick AFB that night. The UFOs were constantly reconnoitering selected United States Air Force bases and were frequently visiting the city of Chicago. Captain Ruppelt and the staff at Project Blue Book had their hands full as the sightings continued to escalate across the United States. The remaining days in July would prove to be a nightmare for the Air Force and the United States government.

On July 19, 1952, Project Blue Book evaluated two UFO incidents as "Unknown" cases, both occurred over the United States. The first incident is case 1492 that occurred over Williston, North Dakota and involved a civilian pilot. At 2:55 a.m., the witness, referred to as an "experienced pilot," reported that he observed a UFO for approximately "5 minutes." The pilot said that the UFO was an "elliptical-shaped" object that displayed a glowing fringe. The pilot added that the object made, "various maneuvers" during that five-minute sighting.

The second "Unknown" is recorded as Case 1494 and occurred over, Elkins Park, Pennsylvania. An USAF pilot, Captain Powley and his wife reported they watched two UFOs pass through the sky for approximately, "5-7 minutes." The witnesses said the pair of "star-like lights" hovered and maneuvered during the duration of their sighting then disappeared. They offered no explanation as to what the objects were.

On the night of July 19, 1952, the UFOs returned. They were sighted over Chicago and Elgin, Illinois. An Air Force Intelligence document titled, "SPOT INTELLIGENCE REPORT," and addressed, "343 South Dearborn, Chicago, Illinois," and written by Lieutenant Colonel Morgan, gave the details. It was reported, "Six luminous round objects, independently carting about the sky, 10:00 p.m.[CST/11:00 p.m. EST], July 19th over Chicago, were reported by a woman resident. She said they moved horizontally and then in a vertical matter."

This same document also noted an Elgin newspaper, *The Elgin Review News* that carried a short story about a single UFO sighting on July 20, 1952. It stated in part, "A 'mysterious and unidentified object' in the skies over Elgin was spotted by three persons who were on duty at the Ground Observers post atop the city hall."

Shortly after the UFOs visited the Chicago area, they were sighted over another one of their favorite cities, Washington D.C. These UFO sightings became one of the most well known UFO incidents in history, even though they did not make the Blue Book "Unknown" list. Starting on July 19, 1952, the UFOs continued to turn up the heat on America. The lid on the United States government's UFO cover-up was about to blow off. The secret contents contained in the UFO cover-up were heating up as if in a pressure cooker. These secrets were boiling and as the pressure continued to build up, they readied to explode. On July, 19 and 20 they almost did…right over the nation's capital, Washington D.C.

Chapter 3

THE JULY 19 WASHINGTON SIGHTINGS

Some of the most sensational events that occurred in July during the flying saucer flap of 1952 occurred over Washington D.C. on consecutive weekends. The first weekend of UFO sightings occurred on Saturday night July 19 and lasted until Sunday morning July 20. The drama unfolded at Washington National Airport, Washington D.C. on Saturday night at 11:40 p.m. EST/ 12:40 p.m. EDT. There were no clouds in the sky that evening and air traffic was light as usual for that time of night. Eight air traffic controllers at Washington National Airports Air Traffic Control Center were in command of the skies over the Washington area. The ARTC Center was a large converted hanger that contained a big windowless room that was dimly lit. This room contained two glowing radarscopes used by the radar controllers.

Located outside of the ARTC building was a large metal girder structure with a large parabolic radar antenna that slowly rotated and transmitted a rotating radio beam into the sky on the nearby property. A rotating streak swept around the scope six revolutions per minute in the radar room. The long-range transmitting radio beam would reflect off an aircraft or target up and back to the antenna station receiver.

The controllers in this room never saw the planes that they directed in to the airport. They used their main scope to track them. The main scope was a 24-inch diameter glass cathode-ray scope that was phosphor-coated and radiated with a violet glow. A pale violet colored dot or blip would then appear on the glass face of the scope that would indicate the targets position.

As an aircraft would move across the sky, a series of seven blips would remain on the screen until the first one faded. This series of blips formed a track that enabled the controller to plot the aircrafts course. The radar controller could also tell the speed of the aircraft by the ten-second interval of the sweep. The targeted aircrafts compass bearing, location and distance from the airport could be measured on the scope.

At 11:40 p.m. EST/12:40 p.m. EDT, one of the air traffic controllers Edward Nugent, stood over the twenty-four inch radarscope and saw seven purple blips appear on the face of it. Senior Air Traffic Controller Harry Barnes was called to the scope. Controllers James Copeland and James Ritchey stood nearby. Harry Barnes wrote a story that appeared in *The Washington Daily News* on July 29 titled "CAA Officials Own Story- How Radar Spotted Whatzits That Air Force Couldn't Find." He stated, "Our shift had been on duty about 40 minutes…Ed Nugent called me over to the radar scope and joked, 'Here's a fleet of flying saucers for you.'" Barnes stated that there were "seven pips clustered irregularly together in one corner." The position of the pips on the radar screen indicated that the objects were, "15 miles south southwest of Washington," according to Barnes. He also stated this about the objects, "We knew that the [radar scope] spots were not aircraft – at least, not identified and friendly aircraft." These objects moved between "100 and 130 miles per hour" over an area of about "nine miles in diameter," according to Harry Barnes. The Senior Air Traffic Controller also stated, "We tracked the seven pips for about 5 minutes" and "their movements were completely radical compared to those of ordinary aircraft." Harry Barnes placed small plastic triangular-shaped markers on the face of the scope and tracked them.

Harry Barnes concluded that these mysterious targets were one of three possibilities:
1. They were a group of "enemy aircraft."
2. They were a group of "unexplained flying objects."
3. "Something went wrong with the radar."

During the early stages of tracking the blips on the radarscope, the senior air traffic controller watched as the mysterious blips would disappear from the face of the scope at intervals. Barnes recalled watching the mysterious movements of the blips as they moved across the scope and disappeared. He stated, "Later I realized that if these objects had made any sudden burst of extremely high speed that would account for them disappearing from the scope temporarily." Barnes also stated the following about their radar system, "Our radar is only designed to track known types of aircraft or objects in the air at speeds known to all of us."

After watching the targets on the radarscope for about five minutes, Harry Barnes then consulted controllers James Ritchey and James Copeland to check their findings. Barnes stated, "They confirmed our findings." At ARTC, technicians checked Barnes radar set to be sure there were no malfunctions and it was working properly. He stated, "Our technicians had carefully checked the equipment to make certain that it was operating perfectly." Captain Edward Ruppelt confirmed this and stated, "The set was in perfect working order."

Barnes said, "Then I called the airport control tower [Tower Central] to see what the radar showed there." The control tower was located a quarter mile away from "hanger No. 6" where the Air Traffic Control Center was located. Harry Barnes explained, "Atop of the main terminal building Tower Central utilized a radar system known as short-range radar that was used to guide in aircraft for final approaches, landings, and takeoffs. The ARTC radar had a longer-range service." Barnes added, "The radar we were using scans a 70-mile radius." The Tower Central radar operator that Barnes called and spoke to was five-year CAA veteran Howard Cocklin, "The radar operator confirmed the same thing," Barnes said.

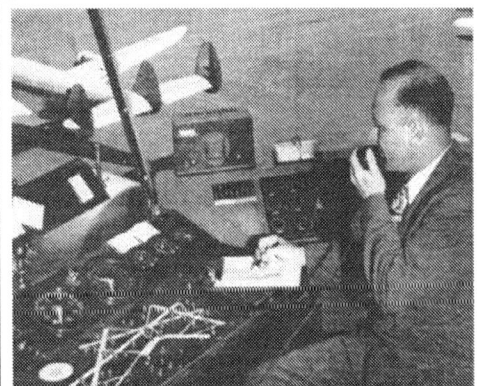

The Air Route Traffic Control tower at Washington National Airport circa 1952

A July 29 article by *The Washington Daily News* titled, "Laugh if you want to-But There They Were!" stated the following information about what occurred next. This article said, "When the center radar [ARTC] showed one of the unidentified objects in a low position in the northwest sky, the operators in the tower [Tower Central] were able to see it." Harry Barnes and his crew were unable to see the unidentified object because there were no windows in the Air Traffic Control Center. Furthermore, they could not leave the building, go outside, and check their own radar sightings visually. Howard Cocklin was one of the Tower Central witnesses who saw the UFO from the window of his control tower that overlooked Washington National Airport.

Donald Keyhoe explained what happened, "I can see one of the things. It's got a bright orange light-I can't tell what's behind it," Cocklin said. *The Washington Daily News* July 29 article gave further information about Cocklin's UFO sighting.

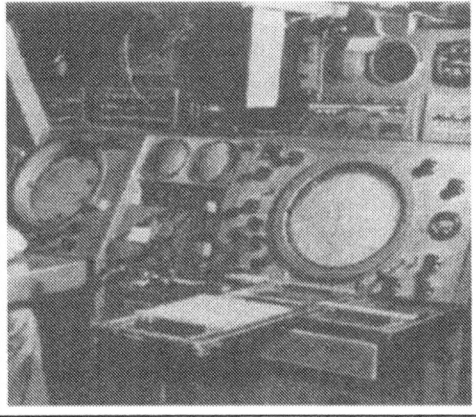

The witness in the tower stated, "It was a good-sized light, yellow to orange in color. At first, it looked like a great big star. Then it began to move in a manner, which made me realize it couldn't be a star. There was no unusual high speed about its movements and at times, it seemed to hover. We [other tower controllers] could see it moving around like that for about 15 minutes. It just disappeared."

Meanwhile, at Andrews AFB, another UFO sighting was made by Airman Second Class William Goodman. He was on tour of a guard post in Section A of the 1053rd Maintenance Squadron and called Airman First Class Brady in the Andrews tower to report his sighting. Brady explained what occurred in his own "STATEMENT-Andrews AFB," dated, "22 July 1952." Airman Brady stated, "Airman Goodman called the tower and reported he had seen objects in the air around Andrews, while we were discussing them he advised me to look to the south immediately. When I looked out there an object which appeared to be like an orange ball of fire, trailing a tail, it appeared to be about two miles south and one-half mile from the Andrews range. It was very bright and definite, and unlike anything, I had seen before. The position of something like this is hard to determine. It made kind of a circular motion." Brady then explained that the object, "took off at an unbelievable speed."

Shortly after, Captain S.C. Pierman, a Capitol Airlines pilot was sitting in the cockpit of his DC-4 plane on the runway at Washington National Airport. He was going over his preflight checklist and preparing for a 12:00 a.m. EST/ 1:00 a.m. EDT takeoff. *The Boston Globe* July 23 article, gave further information about the pilot and his flight, "Capt. S.C. Pierman of Detroit, [was] piloting Capitol Airlines Flight 807, southbound from National Airport." While Pierman was working on his checklist, he glanced up and over the dashboard and looked through the windshield. Something had caught his attention. Pierman looked over the horizon and saw a UFO streak across the horizon leaving a trail of fire. The pilot notified the control tower of his sighting, and then finished his preflight preparations. At 1:00 a.m. EDT, Pierman lifted off and moments later, the DC-4 ascended and climbed over the skies of Washington D.C.

During that time, UFOs were reported to be in the same air space of nearby planes and had actually passed near them. ARTC radar controllers were well aware of the entire situation as they simultaneously tracked all of them on their radarscopes. Harry Barnes and his controllers sent out an alert to airborne pilots to be on the look out for the UFOs. He stated the following information, "At the first opportunity, [ARTC Controller James] Ritchey contacted Capitol Airline pilot Capt. S.C. Pierman, a veteran of 17 years of flying. Shortly after takeoff, Ritchey asked Pierman to look out for the objects. He agreed to do this." Moments later, Captain Pierman radioed ARTC from the air and contacted Barnes. Pierman said, "There's one and there it goes."

The Washington News reported, "For about 14 minutes Pierman was in direct two-way communications with Barnes. And while he was with in radar range Pierman was able to see objects which showed up on the path indicated by the [ARTC] Center's radar. Pierman's sightings reported to Barnes coincided with the radar sightings exactly, Barnes reports." The newspaper added that Captain Pierman was "flying at normal cruising speed of 180 to 200 miles per hour" when he reported the group of objects.

The Boston Globe article gave further information about Pierman's commercial airline incident. It stated the pilot, "soon reported seeing seven objects between Washington and Martinsburg, W. Va. He said they changed pace, sometimes moving at tremendous speed. At other times hanging motionless" It was also said that Captain Pierman "was asked by the [Washington National] airport to keep an eye out for the objects when they showed upon radar screens."

Project Blue Book Files, "Roll No. 12 Case 1649" recorded an interview with Captain Pierman conducted by "Lt. George H. Janczewski." It was reported when Pierman's DC-4 reached an altitude of "6,000 Feet" over "Charles Town, Virginia," he and co-pilot then saw "a bluish-white light." The pilot said the light appeared and was descending "in a 25 degree dive" and was on a "north east to south west heading." Captain Pierman also stated that both he and his co-pilot then saw a "brilliant bluish-white flash pass from high over their left.

The pilot then said, "It disappeared in level flight dead ahead traveling at a tremendous speed." During the next seven minutes of Flight 807s journey, the two pilots sighted as many as seven more lights that were said to be mysterious.

The Washington Daily News article gave additional information about Captain Pierman's sighting. The pilot said, "Three flew in an approximate 25-degree dive at 'a substantial speed' and three more 'very, very high' on a horizontal plane…they traveled at 'tremendous vertical speed' and then changed pace and seemed to hang motionless." It was also reported, "He lost sight of them when they went into what he called 'a terrific power dive' near Martinsburg." The official USAF dictionary defines a power dive as, "A dive in an airplane, esp. a steep dive, with the engine or engines delivering considerable or full force"

Captain Pierman also said, "In my years of flying I've seen a lot of falling or shooting stars-whatever you call them-but these were much faster than anything like that I've seen before. They were moving too fast for that. They were about the same size as the brightest stars."

One week later, on July 29, *The Washington Daily News* reported, "Charles Watson, first officer on the flight with Pierman who has been flying for 12 years confirms Pierman's sightings." First Officer Watson stated, "Before the other night I always discounted alleged flying saucers as atmospheric phenomenon. But now I feel that I have actually seen some active strange objects which defy explanations." This article also reported, "A review has been written and officially recorded on the subject…It's the first time three separate radar sets have recorded identical sightings."

Edward Ruppelt explains what occurred next. He stated, "By now the targets had moved into every sector of the scope and had flown through the prohibited flying areas over the White House and the Capitol." Donald Keyhoe adds, "The unknown machines had separated. Two were over the White House, a third near the Capitol, both prohibited areas." A very concerned Harry Barnes stated, "They had been over the restricted areas of Washington." He then stated, "At this time I notified the Air Force about our observation. This is a regular procedure, but some parts of it are a secret. I am not at liberty to explain it in full detail." Harry Barnes then contacted Andrews Air Force Base located at Camp Springs, Maryland, about 10 miles east and asked for assistance.

Edward Ruppelt explains, "ARTC had called for jet interceptors to come in and look around. But they didn't show and finally ARTC called again – then again." *The Washington Daily News* reported what occurred next in an article "Jets Couldn't Find Them – Air Force after D.C. 'Saucers." This article dated July 23, 1952 stated, "An operations officer at Ana Costa Naval Air Base told the News that National Airport called on Andrews [AFB] to send up its radar-equipped, all-weather jets to intercept the visitors but that no jets were available. Andrews's officials told the News that the [Andrews AFB] 121st Fighter Interceptor Squadron has been moved temporarily to a base at New Castle, Del., while Andrews's runways are being repaired. They did not know whether the 121st was asked to swoosh down from Delaware to take a look." (Note, *The Air Force Dictionary* states the following: "New Castle County Airport. A Municipal airport in New Castle County, Delaware, named for the county, at which certain accommodations are provided for USAF units.")

This same newspaper article also reported the alleged reason for the Air Forces lack of information. It was said, "An Air Force press information man said the Air Force so far has only a preliminary, telephone report on the Sunday visitors." On July 23, *The Boston Globe* reported a "WASHINGTON, July 22 (AP)" news release in an article titled, "'Flying Saucers' Reported in Air Force's 'Backyard.'" It reported, "The flying saucers over the capital were reported late yesterday, about 36 hours after the incident occurred." This story also stated that the Air Force claimed they did not scramble jets after the UFOs that night. It reported:

The Air Force did not send up interceptor planes when notified of the Washington objects. Officers explained yesterday [Tuesday July 21] that this was because its own radar had not picked up the images and because the round-the-clock observer operation had not sent out any warnings.

According to Donald Keyhoe, he stated, "For several days officers denied that Andrews Field radar men had tracked the machines. One spokesman insisted the Control Center scope had been defective. Another officer, to prove the incident was unimportant, said that no fighters had been sent to the area. But their attempts to reduce public fear were in vain." The jet interceptor statement that was also given by the Air Force shortly after the UFO incident was false as well.

Keyhoe also gave the following information that contradicts the Air Forces July 21 radar/image statement. He stated, "Barnes called Andrews Field, across the Potomac [River] in Maryland. ' We're tracking them, too,' a worried radar man told him. 'We've got them the same place you have.'"

The USAF did indeed pick up the images on radar when notified of the Washington objects as Major Keyhoe stated. Edward Ruppelt also wrote about the Air Force picking up the Washington objects on radar that night. Ruppelt stated, "Once during the night all three radars, the two at Washington and the one at Andrews AFB, picked up a target three miles north of the Riverdale Radio beacon, north of Washington. For thirty seconds the three radar operators compared notes about the target over the intercom."

An "AIR INTELLIGENCE INFORMATION REPORT" dated, "22 July 1952" by Captain Benjamin Berkow, stated what happened next at 12:30 a.m. EST/1:30 a.m. EDT. The document states, "Targets remained on Washington Tower radar screen until 0030 during this time one target left a trace from west of Andrews to Riverdale, a distance of seven miles in four seconds." It was also stated, "There was also a visual sighting by the controllers of Washington National [Airport]. *They observed an orange disk about 3,000 feet at 360 degrees."* It is interesting to note that this Intelligence report quoted the shape of the UFO as a "disk."

The Washington Daily News July 23 article also reported the Navy's involvement that night. The Ana Costa Naval Air Station operations officer, revealed the following information to the paper, "The Navy sent up jets up from Norfolk when Andrews couldn't make it. But they failed to make contact with the mysterious objects the Navy man said." *The Washington Daily News* also contacted the Air Force and reported the following from an "Air Force information man." The News reported that, "He said the report that Navy jets went up from Norfolk 'is news to me.'" The UFO activity continued and by 1:00 a.m. EST/2:00 a.m. EDT, persons at Andrews Air Force Base in Maryland reported seeing more UFOs.

One witness, Air Force Staff Sergeant Davenport of the 1053rd Maintenance squadron saw a reddish-orange colored light that appeared to the south of Andrews Field. Contained in Bluebook is a statement made by Staff Sergeant Davenport and dated "22 July 52." In part it reads, "I saw a strange light south of Andrews AFB and traveling from east to west at a terrific rate of speed…At times it would appear it would appear to stand still then make an abrupt change of direction and altitude." Davenport then called Andrews AFB tower and asked the radar controllers if they had seen the light. He stated, "They finally saw it for a few seconds off runway 28, about that time it shot out of sight at terrific speed."

At the same time, Washington National Airport radar controllers picked up targets on their radarscopes near Bolling AFB and contacted them. Richard LaCanna, an airport operations dispatcher telephoned Bolling AFB and advised them to look at the sky near the base. Staff Sergeant Donald Wilson who answered the call looked. Wilson reported that he saw, "an unidentified roundish object drifting low in the sky about seven miles southeast of the base." He also stated the UFO "was about the intensity of a star and [a]white-amber color." He reported that it was, "visible for a few minutes." This UFO being tracked by Washington National Airport was actually a solid aerial object, which reflected their radar beam was also confirmed by a visual sighting.

About 30 minutes later, at 2:30 a.m. EDT, Airman Second Class William Goodman was finishing his tour at the guard post of the 1053rd Maintenance Squadron at Andrews when he reported another UFO sighting. He stated, "I noticed an object to the southwest of Andrews." Goodman said it was ball-shaped and "bright orange in color…it looked to be more round in shape than flat." The witness watched the object moving about the sky for nearly 20 minutes.

Contrary to the Air Force's July 21 statement that they did not send up interceptor planes when notified of the Washington objects, Major Donald E. Keyhoe discovered that the Air Force did indeed send up jets that night. Major Keyhoe reported, "It was almost 3 O'clock [3:00 a.m. EDT] when the Air Force jets reached Washington." Two F-94 Starfires were actually scrambled from the 142nd Fighter Interceptor Squadron at New Castle County Airport in Delaware and preceded toward the Washington area.

While en route to Washington, ARTC controller Harry Barnes actually directed the two jets on intercepts toward some UFOs sighted above Maryland, over the vicinity of Andrews AFB. Donald Keyhoe explains what happened, "Two or three times saucers darted away the instant he [Barnes] gave pilots directions for interception." Harry Barnes expressed that he had the distinct impression the UFOs were monitoring his radio transmissions. The UFOs disappeared as soon as he gave the fighter pilots their positions. Keyhoe stated, "Barnes had an eerie feeling that the mysterious visitors were listening to his radio calls."

The Starfire jets continued toward Washington D.C. to intercept the mysterious objects but shortly before they arrived, the UFOs disappeared. Major Keyhoe explains what happened next, "Five minutes after the jets left, the queer machines reappeared, swarming all over Washington. One of them, its shape hidden by a large white light followed a Capital airliner close to the [Washington National] airport." This incident actually occurred over Washington D.C. and involved a Capital Airliner on Flight 610 en route from Herndon, Virginia to Washington D.C. Harry Barnes described this incident. He stated, "One other commercial pilot did flatly confirm seeing a light off his left wing, which we [ARTC] saw as a pip on the scope. He was coming in for his landing and the tower scope [Tower Central] reported the same radar sighting. The light disappeared on our scope and from his view before he touched his wheels down."

Then at 3:30 a.m. EDT, Staff Sergeant Davenport of the 1053rd Maintenance Squadron at Andrews had another sighting while on patrol. The witness stated, "It was about tree-top level from where I was watching. It was very bright but not the same color [as previously sighted]. This was bluish silver. It was very erratic in motion as it moved from side to side. Its motion was very fast. Three times I saw a red object leave the object at a high rate of speed and move out of sight." Captain Ruppelt added the following information with reference to Andrews Air Force Base. He stated, "The clincher came in the wee hours of the morning, when an ARTC traffic controller called the control tower at Andrews and told the tower operators that ARTC had a target just south of their tower, directly over the Andrews Radio Range station. The tower operators looked and there was a 'huge fiery-orange sphere' hovering over the sky directly over their range radar."

Then during the early hours of dawn, a group of UFOs reappeared once again. *The Cumberland Times* of Maryland reported that a group of 10 unidentified lights appeared in the sky over the vicinity of Andrews Air Force Base in Maryland. These UFOs were also picked up on radar and confirmed as well. Shortly after, seven more UFOs passed over the area. They were also picked up on radar and appeared until 5:30 a.m. EDT.

At 5:30 a.m. EDT another visual sighting was reported over Washington D.C. Donald Keyhoe reported, "As the sky began to lighten, the saucers ended their five-hour survey of Washington. At least one witness distinctly saw the shape of the elusive machines. At about 5:30 [a.m. EDT] a radio engineer named E.W. Chamberlain was leaving the WRC transmitter station when he saw five huge discs circling in loose formation. As he watched, dumbfounded, the discs tilted upward and climb steeply into the sky."

The 3:00 a.m. intercept flight involved a pair of F-94 jets that were scrambled from New Castle County Airport in Delaware. In his book, Edward Ruppelt actually explained an intercept scramble that night that only involved a single fighter jet, an F-94 Starfire. He stated, "Finally, just about daylight, an F-94 arrived, but by that time they were gone. The F-94 crew searched the area for a few minutes but they couldn't find anything unusual so they returned to their base. So ended phase one of the Washington National sightings." Ruppelt does not state a pair of jets searched the area. He explains that a lone F-94 arrived "just about daylight." The hunt for the saucers was over…but that was only a temporary situation.

A Project Blue Book file contains an interesting document identified as, "Facility Operations Branch, 1-

547 Chief, Washington Center -9." The Subject of this document states, "UNIDENTIFIED TARGETS, JULY 20 1952," and gives a statement by senior radar controller Harry Barnes. He states, "I'm positive they were guided by some intelligence. If no planes were in the air, the things would fly over the most likely points of interest—Andrews Field, the aircraft plant at Riverdale, the (Washington) Monument, or the Capitol. One or two circled our radio beacons. But as soon as an airliner took off, several would dart off, several would dart across and start to follow, as if to look it over." Harry Barnes then told the press, "There is no other conclusion I can reach but that for six hours on the morning of the 20th of July there were at least 10 unidentifiable objects moving above Washington. They were not ordinary air craft."

Considering the magnitude of this UFO incident, Captain Ruppelt was not notified at his off base home in Dayton Ohio of the events that night and early Sunday morning. Furthermore, he was supposedly not aware of the UFO sightings at all during the entire day of Sunday.

Ruppelt flew to Washington D.C. Monday morning on a routine business trip. He was accompanied by Colonel Donald Bower and was supposedly still unaware of what occurred! On Monday, July 21, 1952, he landed in Washington and stated, "I heard about the sighting about ten o'clock Monday morning when Colonel Bower and I got off an airliner from Dayton and I bought a newspaper in the lobby of the Washington National Airport terminal building. I called the Pentagon from the airport and talked to Major Dewey Fournet, but all he knew was what he'd read in the papers." Ruppelt stated, "When reporters began to call intelligence and ask about the big sighting behind the headlines, 'INTERCEPTORS CHASE FLYING SAUCERS OVER WASHINGTON, D.C.,' they were told that no one had ever heard of such a sighting." He added, "Nobody bothered to tell Air Force Intelligence about the sighting." It seems strange that they claimed to have no knowledge about the UFO sightings until Monday morning, yet the press knew about the sightings!

The month of July was indeed a very hot month during the summer of 1952, especially throughout the eastern United States and it was about to get hotter as the UFOs continued to turn up the heat. The lid on the United States government's UFO cover-up had started to come off. Government officials desperately tried to keep the lid on the UFO pressure cooker down, but it was not easy.

Left, Controller Richard Thomas talks with Harry Barnes, center, while another controller looks on.

Chapter 4

THE JULY 1952 SAUCER PURSUITS

The U.S. Navy and U.S. Air Force were in an all out endeavor to "make contact" and intercept the unknown objects on the weekend of July 19/20th. Before this endeavor, US military jets had already been chasing UFOs for some time, and continued to pursue them. Several more incidents involving jet fighters and UFOs occurred in the wake of the July 19/20th Washington sightings.

On Tuesday, July 22, 1952, several UFOs were seen over the skies of Tampa, Florida as well as MacDill Air Force Base, located in that city. On July 23, *The Tampa Times* reported the following information in an article, "MacDill Mum On Saucers Here." It stated, "MacDill Air Force officials today are investigating reports from about 20 residents in the area that a formation of flying saucers was frolicking in the heavens last night. Officials at the field said telephone calls started coming in about 10 o'clock and continued until about three o'clock this morning, describing activities of the mysterious objects."

A Tampa witness, Mr. Kohlmeyer, watched two objects from his front porch and stated, "It was about 10:15 P.M. when I first saw them…There were two yellowish-orange colored discs traveling south over the city. They swept in an arc over MacDill Field and then sped away to the east." The witness said he saw another UFO about 10 minutes later, and watched it with his binoculars. He stated that, "It too hovered over the field and then darted off to the west."

The newspaper also reported, "Kohlmeyer said he called the field and was told by someone at base operations that they had picked up the objects on their radar screen." *The Tampa Times* also reported additional information that came from MacDill AFB public information officer Captain Paul Mitchell. The Times reported, "Mitchell said today three planes were dispatched to check the objects, but said he could not disclose their findings."

Why was the Air Force unable to disclose their findings about what they discovered that night? MacDill AFB was just another Air Force base added to the long list of bases being reconnoitered by the UFOs during the summer of 1952.

The UFOs also made appearances over New England that Tuesday night July 22 and were sighted over Massachusetts. On July 23, 1952, *The Boston Globe* reported:

MANY SEE FLYING SAUCERS'- MAKE DEBUT OVER BOSTON

The new crop of "flying saucers" that have been buzzing about the country recently, made their appearance over Boston last night and early yesterday morning according to four reports. Last night persons in South Boston, Dorchester and Jamaica Plain spotted the greenish-blue objects, three of them, making a great arc through the sky in the southwest and then disappearing. Then at 1:15 this morning, another greenish-blue glowing object "appeared to be hovering over Dorchester Bay rising slowly into the air."

These UFOs were also described in detail by the witnesses. One witness, Mr. Vejoda, stated, "He saw a single 'saucer' rising over South Boston at 1:15." It was reported that, Arthur Langolia, "a Jamaica Plain man spent much of yesterday trying to find out about a 'flying, flame–shooting shape' that terrified his wife and daughter as it dipped low over his home yesterday morning." The Langolia family was sitting on their front porch when they saw the nearby object. Langolia's 16 year old daughter, Donna, "described it as 'shaped like a squatty vase, shooting out sparks and flame from underneath and moving terrifically fast.'" Arthur Langolia said, "The sky around us lighted up and we heard hissing and spitting." The Globe also reported, "Their description tallied with many reports being received in Washington concerning a new crop of 'Flying saucers.'"

The Massachusetts newspaper, *The Lawrence Tribune*, reported an *Associated Press* story on Wednesday July 23, 1952 that involved UFO sightings on July 22 over Worcester. Worcester is located just southeast of Boston and 40 miles away. The headline of this article reads, "Strange Objects in Worcester Sky." This article states," A war time flight engineer with the Seventh Air Force in the Pacific said he saw three silvery objects whiz across the Worcester Sky shortly before 10 p.m. [EST] last night- 'like planes in attack formation.'"

This incident was reported by Mr. "Eubert T. White and was confirmed by his wife and another couple. The article states:

Out of the Southeast over Grafton [10 miles S.E. of Worcester] he said, flashed three objects flying in line toward the city. 'They were like planes in attack formation' he claimed. 'While I was calling my wife to see them the No. 2 objects circled to starboard toward Boylston [just N.E. of Worcester]. The leader came straight over the city... the third object' Wright said, 'broke formation shortly after the No. 2 had swerved off and turned back toward Grafton. The object that came over the city was really something to see. There was a bluish glow in front of it and a reddish tint-behind. The red wasn't that of a plane exhaust. It circled the city very rapidly and disappeared over Holden' [just N.W. of Worcester].

The article also stated that, "The other couple said they saw the objects from Lake Park, near Lake Quinsigamond, [borders Worcester to the East] and also saw one back toward Grafton."

During this era one of the primary air, weapons chosen to defend the United States were the F-94 Starfire fighter jets. The F-94 was used to defend the skies over Trenton, New Jersey on that Tuesday night, July 22, moreover, into early morning, July 23. Project Blue Book recorded this incident as "Unknown" Case #1572, which involved 13 visual UFO sightings made by fighter pilots and radar tracking, by one F-94 jet. The first UFO sighting occurred on Tuesday night at 10:50 p.m. The remaining reported sightings occurred between 10:50 and continued until "12:45."

Project Blue Book reported the following, "Crews of several USAF F-94 jet interceptors from Dover AFB, Del., made 13 visual sightings and one radar tracking of blue-white lights. White, green and blue lights were seen by Ground Observers and F-94 pilots, moving in arcs and blinking out suddenly. F-94 crew got radar lock-on at 30,000... object the size of an F-94, at 9,000 ft. away - The object made a right turn, suddenly dropped in height and disappeared. Other sightings in the Dover-Trenton area." Project Blue Book also evaluated and recorded four other "Unknown" cases for July 23, 1952. They are as follows:

    1. Case 1554. Pottstown, Pennsylvania
    2. Case 1556. Boston/Provincetown, Massachusetts.
    3. Case 1567. Altoona, Pennsylvania
    4. Case 1578. South Bend, Indiana

Later Wednesday morning the UFOs returned and sightings were reported across the country; Air Force fighter jets continued to be scrambled as well. July 23, 1952 was a very busy day for USAF fighter jets as the UFOs continued to plague the skies over the northeast United States.

Information from a Project Blue Book document informs us of an early morning UFO incident in which several jet fighters were scrambled over the northeast. This incident occurred over Jamestown, Rhode Island at

"7:36 a.m." This information states that the "USN TRACKED [a] HIGH SPEED TARGET HEADING NORTH AT 42,000 FT. AND CONFIRMED BY ADC [Air Defense Command] RADAR NEAR CAMP HERO NEW YORK. F-94's AND F-86's SCRAMBLED."

In this incident, F-94 jets were scrambled from the east of Jamestown by Otis AFB, located at Falmouth Massachusetts. The F-86 Sabre Jets were scrambled from Westover AFB, located at Chicopee Falls, Massachusetts. During 1952, the North American F-86 Sabre Jet was another primary USAF fighter jet used to defend the United States. It was the first sweptwing aircraft in the United States inventory of fighter jets. The F-86A, E, F and H, models were day fighters or fighter bombers and the F-86D, K, and F models were all weather interceptors. All models of these jets were rated in the 650 MPH category and had a service ceiling of over 45,000 feet. All of these jets were armed with guns except the D-model, which carried rockets.

Westover AFB is located northwest of Jamestown. Westover AFB was a subcommand of the Eastern Air Defense Wing, the 4707th Defense Wing, and 60th Fighter Interceptor Squadron. On July 23, 1952, Westover AFB officials recorded four different, "SPOT INTELLIGENCE REPORTS" of UFOs, reported by witnesses throughout Massachusetts. They also contacted the USAF Headquarters of the Air Defense Command at Ent AFB, located in Colorado Springs, Colorado to report their July 23 scramble after the UFOs over Jamestown, Rhode Island. The "COC," A/K/A., the "Air division combat operations center," at Ent AFB, sent a Flying Object Report to Air Force Headquarters at the Pentagon to report all of the scrambles:

FLYOBRPT.

23 JULY 1952
TO: JEP HQ/DIRECTOR OF INTELLIGENCE HQ USAF WASHINGTON 25 D.C.
FROM: COC ADC AFB COLORADO.

On that same morning, and shortly after, another incident involving fighter jets and UFOs occurred in nearby Pennsylvania. This incident was recorded as an "Unknown" Project Blue Book case; it was Case #1554. This incident occurred over Pottstown, Pennsylvania at "8:40 a.m." This incident lasted between "1-4 min." and involved F-94 Starfire all-weather jet interceptors as well.

The report states, "2-man crews [pilot and radar operator] of 3 USAF F-94 jet interceptors saw a large silver object, shaped like a long pear with 2-3 square beneath it, fly at 150-180 knots (170-210 MPH), while a smaller object, delta-shaped or swept back, flew around it at 1,000-1,500 knots (1,150-1,700 MPH)." These UFOs were definitely not weather balloons, swamp gas, canopy light reflections, meteors or temperature inversions. They were unexplained objects and the event was evaluated as an "Unknown," according to the men at ATIC.

Project Blue Book also recorded another unexplained incident that occurred on July 23 that involved jet interceptors; it was Case #1567. It also occurred over Pennsylvania. Once again, this UFO incident involved U.S. Air Force F-94 Starfires fighter jets.

This incident occurred over the afternoon skies of Altoona, Pennsylvania, at "12:50 p.m." and was said to have lasted for "20 min." This "Unknown" case reported the following, "2-man crews of 2 USAF F-94 jet interceptors at 35,000-46,000 ft. altitude saw 3 cylindrical objects in a vertical stack formation fly at an altitude of 50,000 – 80,000 ft." Once again, these objects were definitely not conventional aircraft by any stretch of the imagination. What they were and where they came from is another question; the military continued their relentless pursuit of the mysterious UFOs in search of answers.

July 23rd proved to be a hectic day for the United States Air Force. They sent up several jets to pursue UFOs during the morning and afternoon hours of that Wednesday and continued to scramble jets after the objects well into the evening hours.

Project Blue Book Case 1556 occurred later Wednesday July 23 near, "Braintree" Mass., which is located between "Boston and Provincetown." The city of Braintree, Massachusetts is located near the Massachusetts coastline. It is located about 9 miles south of Boston, nine miles southeast of Jamaica Plain, and seven miles southeast of Dorchester. UFOs appeared over these locations less than 24-hours before. Approximately 40 miles west of Braintree is the city of Worcester, Massachusetts where the three UFOs were also seen the night before in attack formation. UFOs flying over these heavily populated Boston areas and UFOs flying in an attack formation over Worcester prompted the Air Force to scramble fighter jets after these objects on July 23, 1952.

Two separate UFO episodes occurred over this area of Braintree, the first occurred at "10:20 P.M.," and the second encounter occurred at "10:47 P.M. EST." At 10:20 .p.m., the crew of an F-94B jet interceptor from "Otis AFB" was cruising along at an altitude of "25, 000 feet" when the pilot saw a UFO at about the same level as his jet. The UFO was described as a "large round spinning object" that was "throwing off a blue light." Suddenly, the object maneuvered and flew by the Starfire at a distance of approximately, "one mile." The Starfire pilot then made a "180 degree turn," engaged the afterburner, and pursued the large spinning object. The object responded by also making a 180-degree turn and surprisingly headed toward the jet. Moments later, on a collision course toward the jet, the object sped over the top of the Starfire and continued past it. The persistent fighter pilot then maneuvered the Starfire into a renversement and attempted to catch the object, which pulled away from the jet and ascended out of sight. Was it a coincidence this F-94 fighter jet, was flying near an Unidentified Flying Object when it was sighted at 10:20 or was it scrambled after the UFO? Moreover, was it in the air on a combat air patrol in anticipation of an attack?

Donald Keyhoe wrote about the second Otis jet and UFO encounter that occurred over the Braintree/Boston area that night in his 1953 book, *Flying Saucers from Outer Space*. He states, "On the night of July 23 a saucer showing a bluish-green light was seen over Boston. A few minutes later, it was picked up by GCI [Ground Control Intercept] radar. When Ground Control vectored an F-94 toward the saucer, he saw a weird light and locked onto the object with his own radar. But the jet was swiftly outdistanced." Project Blue Book explained the incident in a "FLYOBRPT" [Flying Object Report], dated, "23 July 1952."

Donald Keyhoe

At 10:47 p.m., three F-94 jets were flying at an altitude of, "15,000 feet, when their crews saw UFOs above them, at about 25,000 feet." The pilots radioed Otis AFB and described to them, "a flickering white light," and another UFO described as a, "Swishing, circling blue light." The report stated the blue UFO flew by like a, "bat out of hell." One Starfire pilot did manage to reach the altitude of one of the objects and attained a radar lock-on. An Otis AFB, "FLYOBRPT" dated "23 July 52" was sent to the, "DIRECTOR OF INTELLIGENCE, USAF" in Washington D.C. It stated the following:

Afterburner was lighted and the F-94 closed to within three thousand yards. At this time the object exceeded the limits of the scope and broke lock by what appeared on the scope as a hard break right and down. The RF return on the scope was approx. the same size as that of an F-94.

This statement closed by saying, "This was the second sighting by the crew on the same mission." In his 1956 book, Edward Ruppelt wrote about the jet intercept over Trenton New Jersey on July 22/23 as well as this July 23, Boston area jet intercept referenced by Keyhoe. Ruppelt stated, "In two night encounters, one in New Jersey and one in Massachusetts, F-94s tried unsuccessfully to intercept unidentified lights reported by the ground observer Corps. In both cases, the pilots of the radar-nosed jet interceptors saw a light; they closed in and their radar operators got a lock-on. But the lock-ons were broken in a few seconds, in both cases, as the light apparently took violent evasive maneuvers." How many incidents actually occurred that involved fighter pilots that did actually fire on these mysterious objects?

Over Los Angeles, California, UFO sightings had occurred on four consecutive nights from July 20 until July 23 and made headline news. On July 25, 1952, the *United Press* news released the story and *The New York Times* reported it. This article states:

'SAUCERS' VISIT ON COAST

LOS ANGELES, July 24 (UP)—An aircraft parts company owner said today that "audacious" flying saucers had been hovering over his neighborhood for the last four nights. Edwin C. Johnson said at least twenty-five persons had seen the objects, which showed up at the same time each night, between 7 and 8 p.m.

Javk Swinburn, one of Mr. Johnson's employees, two objects he saw looked like pulsating stars. "But they weren't stars," he added. "They stood still for a while, then shot off. They were being controlled by something."

According to *The New York Times*, yet another UFO incident involving fighter jets occurred on the night of July 23, 1952. The UFOs continued to make their blatant appearances over America throughout the night:

Columbus, Ohio, July 24 (AP) six armed jet planes thundered high over central Ohio last night [July 23], chasing a mysterious object they never did catch. Thousands on the ground thought they might be watching a flying saucer, but the Air Force decided it was only a weather-research balloon.

What prompted the USAF to scramble six fighter planes after this "mysterious object" said to be only a weather balloon? Why were they unaware of the balloon operations in that area? Why did the Air Force send up six fighters instead of two fighters, was it a very big balloon? The opening line in Edward Ruppelt's book states, "In the summer of 1952 a United States Air Force F-86 jet interceptor shot at a flying saucer." Ruppelt does not disclose the date, location, or the names of those involved in this flying saucer episode. He only states, "There is a fighter base in the United Stated which I used to visit frequently because, during 1951, 1952, and 1953, it got more than its share of good UFO reports. The commanding officer of the fighter group, a full colonel and command pilot, believed that UFOs were real… he had a lot of faith in his pilots-and they had chased UFOs in their F-86's. He had seen UFOs on the scopes of his radar sets, and he knew radar."

After the incident, Captain Ruppelt went to the undisclosed base where the fighter pilot was stationed and met with officials there. He discovered that an Intelligence officer at the base had written up a UFO report detailing the incident. Ruppelt reported, "But at the last minute, just before sending it [to ATIC], he was told to hold it back." Captain Ruppelt had a chance to read the last copy of the UFO report and stated, "The incident made up the most fascinating UFO report I'd ever seen." The Intelligence officer then told Ruppelt, "I can't give you the report, because Colonel [name with held] told me to destroy it. But I did think you should know about it." The Intelligence officer followed his commanding officers orders and then "Burned the report", according to Ruppelt. ATIC officials at Project Blue Book never received the UFO report.

Since the publication of Ruppelt's 1956 book more information has been obtained concerning the cover-up of this jet and UFO encounter. In 1998 Edward Ruppelt's widow sent a large collection of his original papers and notes to the Center for UFO Studies in Chicago, Illinois. One of Ruppelt's notes reveals the "Fighter base" in question as Kirkland Air Force Base in Albuquerque, New Mexico, home of the 34th Air Defense Division.

The unnamed intelligence officer was, "Lieutenant Glenn Parrish." The commanding officer who ordered the UFO report destroyed was commander "Colonel Methany." This information was disclosed in the following paper by Ruppelt. In part it reads, "**LT. GLENN PARRISH.** This officer fits into the UFO picture because he was the Intelligence Officer at the 34th Air Defense Division at Albuquerque, where Col. Methany was the C.O.

[Commanding Officer]. Parrish sent in some of the best reports [to Project Blue Book] that we had and he is the man who showed me the report *on the pilot who shot at the UFO*." Ruppelt claims, "We had most of our meetings in Parrish's, or Colonel Methany's Office at Kirtland AFB." Even though the UFO report was burned, Edward Ruppelt wrote a detailed account of the UFO encounter in his book.

This episode over New Mexico unfolded when a UFO was picked up on radar and the target was over the vicinity of Kirkland's airfield. Ruppelt was quoted as saying, "They [radar operators] reported the target, and F-86's were scrambled." Shortly after, the jets reached an altitude of 40,000 feet and began to search the skies but to no avail. The pilots received orders from the ground to descend in altitude and to continue their search for the UFO. One Sabre Jet let down to 20,000 feet and the other jet descended to 5,000 feet in a dive and began to pull out when he saw a light. Moments later, the pilot started to "flatten out of his dive a little" and proceeded toward the UFO.

He continued to descend and "closed" on the Unidentified Flying Object. Ruppelt explained, "He had built up a lot of speed in his dive and was now flying almost straight and level at 3,000 feet and was traveling 'at the mach'." The chase was on and at a closing distance of "1,000 yards," the fighter pilot got a good look at his target. It was said by Ruppelt "the pilot described it as being 'like a donut without a hole.'" The pilot tried to radio his wingman, "Two or three times" but received no answer. He was also unable to contact the controller in the tower then attempted to contact the other pilot once again… but failed. The pilot continued after object.

According to Ruppelt after a two-minute pursuit, the F-86 Sabre jet closed within "approximately 500 yards" of the object. The strange object slowly began to pull a way from the fighter jet. It then accelerated faster and "traveled out about 1,000 yards" from the F-86. This model Sabre Jet was armed with machine guns that fired .50 caliber bullets and moments later, the pursuing fighter pilot unleashed a barrage of cannon fire at the evading object. Ruppelt explained, "Quickly charging his guns he started shooting… a moment later the object pulled up into a climb and in a few seconds it was gone." Shortly after, the attacking pilot broke off his pursuit, ascended to 10,000 feet, and was then able to make radio contact with his wingman.

The two F-86 Sabre Jets then rendezvoused and proceeded back to Kirkland AFB. The two Sabre Jets landed shortly afterward and a report was written up. I ask, how many other combat episodes similar to this particular incident were covered up by the military and had official documentation destroyed?

In his 1953 book *Flying Saucers from Outer Space*, Donald Keyhoe talks about a conversation that he with a former USAF fighter pilot in reference to a UFO intercept procedure. His name was "Major S. Lewis Norman, Jr." the Air Force's radar expert, of the "Aircraft Control & Warning" branch, stationed at the Pentagon. During the conversation, Keyhoe said, "He had been telling me the final steps in a UFO interception." Major Norman stated, "First you prepare for combat-in case you're fired on. Then you try to ease in-at least I would-for a gun-camera shot."

Donald Keyhoe responded and asked, "Suppose you got close and saw some strange machine-I mean really close. Would you signal for it to land?

'How,' Major Norman replied." Keyhoe responded, "Blink your lights, if it didn't answer your radio. Or maybe fire maybe fire a burst to one side."

Keyhoe then stated, "Norman eyed me. I had a feeling he thought I wasn't too bright."

Major Norman responded," That's the last thing I would do; unless it [UFO] attacked me, cutting loose your guns could be suicide."

Before the release of his 1953 book, Keyhoe mentioned an excerpt of this conversation in the December 1952 issue of *True Magazine*, in an article, "What radar tells about Flying Saucers." In reference to shooting at UFOs Keyhoe said, "'Even if they weren't hostile,' another officer told me, 'barging in too close might scare them in to attacking.'" This is an interesting statement because it gives the saucer pilots' point of view.

Author and UFO researcher Leonard Stringfield wrote the following in his 1977 book, *Situation Red, The UFO Siege*. He stated that "Back in the early 1950s, when I knew of the jet scrambles that sometimes led to disaster; I agreed with Major Keyhoe's writings that in these we may know the intent of the UFO. I also agreed that 'losing our aircraft to the UFO' may have been the reason for official secrecy, fearing that the public would panic if they knew the whole truth." The saucer intercepts continued throughout the month of July and I wonder; how many fighter pilots became trigger happy while chasing UFOs across America and did cut their guns loose?

Project Blue Book listed two "Unknown" cases for July 24, 1952, none for July 25, and four for July 26, 1952. One of the July 26 cases is missing from the official files. These next six cases are as follows:

1. Case 1584- Carson Sink, Nevada. July 24.
2. Case 1588- Fairfield, California. Travis AFB. July 24.
3. Case 1628- Kansas City, Missouri. July 26.
4. Case 1637- Albuquerque, New Mexico. Kirtland, AFB. July 26.
5. *Case Missing*- Williams, California. July 26.
6. Case 1661- Washington D.C. July 26.

Even though there were not any "Unknown" cases recorded on July 25, 1952, there is an incident worth mentioning. In late 1952, General Joseph F. Carroll, the Director of the Air Force Office of Special Investigations, received a UFO investigative report from, Gilbert Levy, Chief of the Counter Intelligence Division of the Inspector General of the AFOSI. Contained in this report was a detailed account of a jet scramble after UFOs that occurred on July 25, 1952, over the Washington area. On that night, ARTC radar operators at Washington National Airport, began to track UFOs at 9:15 p.m. Gilbert Levy stated they "were described by radar operators as 'good sharp targets. They were observed in numbers from four to eight."

Mr. Levy explained the fighter jet incident that occurred at 11:20 p.m. that night. He wrote:

At 2320 hours, 25 July 1952, two (2) Air Force F-94's were dispatched from New Castle AFB, Delaware, to intercept objects which had been sighted by radar. One of the F-94's reportedly made visual contact with one of the objects and at first appeared to be gaining on it, but the object and the F-94 were observed on the radar scope and appeared to be traveling at the same approximate speed. However, when it attempted to overtake the object, the object disappeared from the pursuant aircraft and the radarscope. The pilot remarked of the "incredible speed of the object."

Even though the object disappeared, the UFO sightings continued after midnight until 12:10 a.m. The events that occurred on the night of the 25th and the early morning hours of the July 26 were only a prologue of what was to happen later that night. On the evening of July 26, 1952, the UFOs turned up the heat on the government and the pressure cooker nearly let loose. The lid on the United States government's UFO cover-up started to blow off right over Washington D.C. when the flying saucers returned. Luckily, for the government, they quickly slammed the lid back down before its contents were revealed to the American public. Blue Book Case 1661 recorded the UFO sightings that occurred over Washington D.C., which also included visitations over nearby Andrews AFB.

F-94C Starfire located at the New England Air Museum in Windsor Locks, CT.

Chapter 5

July 26, 1952 - THE SAUCERS RETURN TO WASHINGTON

On Saturday night July 26, 1952, the "flying saucers" returned to Washington D.C., and remained until 4:15 a.m. Sunday the 27. Washington National Airport radar controllers including Harry Barnes and the radar operators at Air Traffic Control Center tower were involved in this event. Edward Ruppelt stated, "When the second Washington National sighting came along, almost a week to the hour from the first one, by a stroke of luck things weren't too fouled up. The method of reporting the sighting didn't exactly follow the official reporting procedures…but it worked."

A declassified USAF Intelligence report released back in 1985 documented some of the events that occurred that night. This report is titled, "Washington D.C.-Night of 26/27 July 1952" and was originally classified "RESTRICTED." The events unfolded on Saturday night when ARTC radar operators led by senior controller Harry Barnes picked up "varying numbers (up to 12 simultaneously) of U/I [Unidentified targets]" on their 24 inch radarscope. CAA personnel "termed" the radar targets/blips as "generally solid returns" that were described as being "similar to a/c [aircraft] except slower."

A July 28 article in *The Washington Post*, "They're in the Sky Again- Radar Spots More Mystery Objects Here, Fliers Report Sighting Glowing Lights" reported, "Last nights visitors showed up first on the screen at 9:08 p.m. and remained for some time…radar operators plotted their speed at from 38 to 90 miles per hour."

Donald Keyhoe stated the following, "At 9:08 P.M., A formation of saucers descended on Washington…luckily, they were too high to be seen by most people in the city." The ARTC controllers and radar crew who worked at Washington National Airport that night are as follows:

1. Barnes, Harry
2. Biron, Jerome
3. Ceconi, Phillip
4. Copeland, James
5. Dawson, Stewart
6. Ritchey, James
7. Staff, Austin
8. Sankow, Mike
9. Sykes, Loyd

The radar operators at Tower Central:
1. Marinello, Salvatore
2. Woodahl, Lester

Meanwhile, several newspaper and magazine reporters accompanied by photographers caught wind of the breaking story and went straight to Washington National Airport to cover the story. A July 28 headline story in *The Washington Daily News* read, "Jets Ready to Chase Lights-24-Hour Alert Ordered after Second Appearance Here" It reported, "A CAA spokesman said CAA has two radar sets at the [Washington National] airport, one long–range and one short-range." The representative also stated that "the 'blips' showed up identically on both." It was reported that, "This proved there was not just a mechanical failure in the [radar] set and convinced one of our greatest skeptics."

Edward Ruppelt explains what occurred next after the targets were watched and plotted by the ARTC radar controllers. He said, "When all the targets had been carefully marked, one of the controllers called the tower and the radar station at Andrews AFB-they also had unknown targets." A document titled, "Transcription for the record at WNA-The Cupless Saucer," recorded the following at "2130 EDT" [9:30 p.m. EDT]:

Andrews: This is Andrews. Our radar tracking says he has got a big fat target out there northeast of Andrews.
He says he's got two more south of the field.
Washington Tower: Yes, well the Center has about four or five around the Andrews range Station. The Center is working a National Airliner – the Center is working and vectoring him around his target. He went around Andrews. He saw one of them – looks like a meteor (garbled)...went by him...or something. He said he has got one about three miles off his right wing now. There are so many targets around here it is hard to tell as they are not moving very fast.

Shortly after, at 9:30 p.m., Captain Ruppelt was phoned at his home in Dayton, Ohio and informed about the sightings over the Washington area. Oddly enough, the USAF did not tell Ruppelt about the UFO events that were unfolding. LIFE Magazine writer and saucer expert "Robert Ginna" actually contacted him that night, according to Ruppelt. Ginna heard about the breaking saucer incident from LIFE Magazine's "Washington News Bureau." In his book, Ruppelt does not state how Ginna systematically obtained his home telephone number.

In the meantime at Washington, "No definable pattern of maneuver except at [the] very beginning about 2150 EDT [9:50 p.m. EDT/8:50 p.m. EST]" was noted according to the Intelligence Report. The report also stated there were "4 targets in rough line abreast about 1 ½ mile spacing [that] moved slowly together…At the same time 8 targets were scattered throughout the scope."

In Dayton, after Ruppelt hung up with Robert Ginna, he stated, "I called the intelligence officer in the Pentagon and I was correct, intelligence hadn't heard about the sighting." Additional information in a Project Blue Book memorandum states the intelligence officer's name. It appears in a document titled, "SUBJECT: Report of Unidentified Aerial Objects…28 July 52." It informs that the intelligence officer was "Colonel Thomas" from the "Directorate of Intelligence" and the call was made at "10:00 p.m." Ruppelt then said, "I asked the duty officer to call Major Fournet and ask him to go out to the airport." Major Dewey Fournet, Jr. was the Pentagon liaison for Project Blue Book. According to the Intelligence Report it was also stated that, "ARTC checked Andrews Approach Control by telephone at 2200 EDT [10:00 p.m. EDT/9:00 p.m. EST] to verify the targets."

Meanwhile, another man in the UFO circle that was contacted was Albert M. Chop. He had spent one year with the Air Force at ATIC at Wright Patterson AFB, in Dayton Ohio before he became their public liaison who handled UFO inquiries at the Office of Public Information in Washington. An FAA officer telephoned Chop at his home that night by the name of Raymond Nathan. Chop then called Major Fournet at his home and told him that he was going out to Washington National Airport and would meet him there. Fournet then contacted an Intelligence officer by the name of Lieutenant Holcomb, a Navy electronics expert, and informed him about the incident. Fournet told him that he would pick him up at his home in route to the airport. Major Fournet then picked him up and both men proceeded to ARTC. Albert Chop arrived at Washington National Airport before midnight ahead of Major Fournet and Lieutenant Holcomb then immediately rushed to ARTC.

In a July 28 article "They're in the Sky Again," *The Washington Post* reported "The mysterious objects were reported to have been seen glowing in the sky within a 30- mile radius of the city." Edward Ruppelt named the locations and stated, "They were spread out in an arc around Washington from Herndon, Virginia to Andrews AFB." The unidentified aerial activity over the Washington area prompted officials to call for F-94 all-weather jet interceptors to intercept the unknown targets. The Intelligence report explains that "ARTC then called the Air Force Command Post at the Pentagon. At 2238 EDT-[10:38 p.m. EDT/ 9:38 p.m. EST], the USAF Command Post was notified of ARTC targets." In turn, Air force officials at the Pentagons "Command Post notified ADC [Air Defense Command] and KADF at 2245 [10:45 p.m. EDT/ 9:45 p.m. EST]."

The USAF Intelligence document states, "Some commercial pilots reported visuals ranging from 'cigarette glow' (red-yellow) to a 'light (as recorded from their conversations with ARTC controllers.)" The document adds the following information about another pilot. It states, "A CAA flight inspector, Mr. Bill Schreve, flying A/C #NC-12" had a sighting that he reported to ARTC Center Controllers. Mr. Schreve "reported at 2246 EDT [10:46 p.m. EDT/9:46 p.m. EST] that he had visually spotted 5 objects giving off a light glow ranging from orange to white; his altitude at the time was 2200." The Intelligence report explained what happened fourteen minutes later. It reported, "2 F-94s were scrambled from New Caste at 2300 EDT [11:00 p.m. EDT/10:00 p.m. EST]."

Fighter pilots Lt. William Patterson and Captain John McHugo piloted the two F-94 Starfires scrambled from New Castle Air Force Base. F-94 Starfire pilot Lt. Patterson, a Korean War Veteran led the way to Washington in hot pursuit of the intruders. At about this time, Air Force officials asked the press reporters and photographers to vacate the radar room at ARTC. The group departed the room and anxiously waited outside the building for breaking news on the events. Shortly after, the two Starfires soared toward Washington D.C.

The Combat Command Post at the Pentagon called Washington National Airport at "11:12" p.m. to see if the targets were still being tracked on their radar. ARTC was effectively tracking the targets and Pentagon Command Post officials granted Barnes permission to vector the incoming jets. As the two Starfires approached Washington, Harry Barnes and ARTC radar operators at Washington National Airport took over.

A Project Blue Book document identified as "Untitled ARTC log of 26 July 52" stated that the two F-94 jets were of the "Shirley" flight and Patterson's codename was "Red 1" and McHugo's was "Red 2." This ARTC log document stated the following information about Lt. Patterson. It states, "Shirley Red 1' at 20,000 feet was the first aircraft to ask Washington National for a vector…ARTC had something on its scopes at that very moment."

The USAF Intelligence report states that "ARTC controlled F-94s after arrival in Washington area with generally negative results (flew through a 'batch of radar returns' without spotting anything)" The report also states that, "however one pilot mentioned seeing 4 lights at one time and a second time as seeing a single light but unable to close whereupon light went out." Ruppelt also stated that "Lieutenant Patterson, said, I tried to make contact with the bogies below 1,000 ft…I saw several bright lights."

What could be called a fighter pilot's nightmare occurred during an intercept attempt that night; it was also deleted from the official government case files. It was not released to the press and was not written up by Edward Ruppelt in his 1956 book. Albert Chop did talk about the incident and described it in a tape-recorded interview held in the files of the National Investigation Committee on Aerial Phenomena, AKA., NICAP. Albert Chop was at the ARTC room that night. He heard the radio transmissions made by F-94 fighter pilot Lt. Patterson as they came across the ARTC intercom as this event unfolded.

Chop explained that a group of glowing objects surrounded Lt. Patterson's Starfire while he was flying over the vicinity of Andrews AFB. He said, "Lt. William Patterson was badly frightened when a group of glowing objects surrounded his interceptor. As the CAA radar operators watched the blips on the scope cluster around his plane, the pilot asked them in a scared voice what he should do. There was stunned silence...no one answered. After a tense moment the UFOs pulled away and left the scene." *The Washington Post* July 28 article reported, "At 11:33 p.m., one pilot [Lt. Patterson] observed four lights in the vicinity of Andrews Air Force Base. The lights were about 500 feet above him and about 10 miles away." Lt. Patterson stated that they were "really moving" and he was unable to close on them. Patterson eventually "lost sight of them two minutes later." At "11:55 p.m." Patterson contacted ARTC and notified them he was running low on fuel and was returning to New Castle AFB. F-94 pilot Capt. McHugo departed the Washington area shortly after at 12:04 am and returned to his base. *The Washington Post* reported, "One plane landed shortly before midnight and the other about 12:15 am," thus ending the first round of interception attempts that night.

Major Dewey Fournet, Jr. and Lt. Holcomb arrived at Washington National Airport shortly after the first two F-94 jets left the Washington area and missed the entire series of events. Ruppelt stated, "They drove to the ARTC radar room at National Airport and found Al Chop already there." The intelligence report recorded their arrival time, "Major Fournet (AFOIN-2A2) and Lt. Holcomb (USN, AFOIN-2C5) arrived at ARTC center about 27/0015 EDT [27 July/12:15 am EDT-11:15 p.m. EST]." Albert Chop, Major Fournet, and Lt, Holcomb observed the radar controllers tracking the targets on their radar screens. Holcomb then watched one of the scopes in solitaire and examined the targets in question.

Meanwhile, Andrews AFB radar controllers were getting sporadic strong returns until approximately 1:00 a.m. Lt. Holcomb checked with the National Weather Station concerning the altitude temperatures over the Washington area. Shortly after, he was contacted by phone and he received the information, he requested. According to the USAF Intelligence report log, there was only a "slight temperature inversion." The log also states that Holcomb "felt that the scope targets at the same time were not the results of an inversion and so advised the Command Post." The Intelligence report states, "Lt.Holcomb observed scopes and reported '7 good solid targets'...and advised the Pentagon Command Post with the suggestion that a second intercept flight be requested."

A call immediately went to New Castle AFB to scramble interceptors. In the words of Edward Ruppelt, he stated, "So at this performance the UFO's had an official audience." At "1:38 am", the "Redman" flight consisting of 2 F-94 Starfires headed toward Washington D.C. from Delaware. The call signs of the two jets, "Redman Blue" and "Redman Blue 2" proceeded toward the Washington area. *Time Magazine* reported this event in an article dated "August 4, 1952 and titled, "Blips on the scopes." Time stated, "Down from Delaware roared another flight of night fighters. This time the blips did not vanish. They stayed on the ground scopes, while jets screamed among them. But only one pilot saw a light; another saw a doubtful blip on his scope. It vanished before he could shoot." It is interesting to note that Time magazine wrote the intention of the jet pilot was to "shoot."

The two Starfires then flew over Washington's airspace at 1:47 am and descended from 19,000 feet to 10,000 feet. The interceptors circled over the area and awaited orders from the ground radar controllers concerning any potential UFO targets. The Starfires continued to patrol the airspace over Washington without incident until 2:10 a.m. For the next eleven minutes, ARTC vectored the pilots of "Redman Blue" flight toward the different targets they had on radar. The pilots found nothing and their intercept attempts were negative. The UFOs had finally left the skies over Washington. Shortly after, at 2:21 a.m. the Starfires were ordered back to their base at New Castle.

Throughout the night, several civilian pilots of private and commercial aircraft also reported strange glowing lights and UFOs. *The Washington Daily News* reported on July 28, "Mrs. Eleanor Randall, 2606 Wade Road, SE said she saw a white 'plate' over southeastern Washington between 2 and 3 a.m."

Another piece of information has become known concerning the night of July 26 when the saucers visited the Capital. On that night, Marine Lt. Colonel Marion "Black Mac" Magruder, a decorated World War 2 fighter pilot, received a phone call at his home in Washington. Shortly after, the highly respected combat veteran was escorted to the Pentagon in a black staff car, surrounded by a police motorcycle motorcade.

Magruder, a hardened marine veteran, was a legendary pilot and the leader of his Hellcat squadron known as "Black Mac's Killers," who fought the Japanese in the Pacific air wars. After the war, Magruder attended the "National Air War College" at Maxwell Field from July 1947 until June 1948.

On July 26, 1952, Lt. Col. Magruder was to bear witness to another kind of air war. Researcher and author William J. Birnes collaborated with Marion Magruder's two sons and discovered a phenomenal story as told to them by their father. Mark and Merritt Magruder told Mr. Birnes what occurred on the night of July 26, 1952, according to Lt. Col. Marion Magruder.

Mr. Birnes writes, "It was a night Mark Magruder remembers…It would be many years later before Mac told his sons what really happened that night. He said that we went to the Pentagon. A situation room."

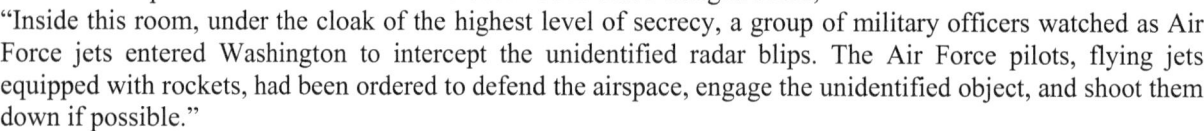

Birnes explains what was said to have occurred in that Pentagon room, "Inside this room, under the cloak of the highest level of secrecy, a group of military officers watched as Air Force jets entered Washington to intercept the unidentified radar blips. The Air Force pilots, flying jets equipped with rockets, had been ordered to defend the airspace, engage the unidentified object, and shoot them down if possible."

Birnes then reports on the chilling accounts of missing pilots that night, he states, "Magruder would tell his sons years later that at least one jet simply vanished from the radar screen. He told his sons that the Air Force lost pilots that night, pilots who'd been scrambled to intercept." Magruder also stated, "We lost aircraft that night of July 26th." Mr. Birnes also writes, "Amazingly, Mac Magruder reports that even while standing inside a Pentagon situation room in the presence of other military personnel looking at the blips on radar, he was unable to offer his opinion on what was happening." It was said that Magruder, "wasn't sure who had the clearance to hear what he had to say…Magruder could not tell anyone what he knew or even why he had been picked up and brought to the Pentagon."

It is interesting to note that the two jet intercept flights over Washington that night as described in the two official USAF documents do not coincide with the two intercept flights that Edward Ruppelt wrote about in his book. The Air Force Intelligence report, "Washington, DC-Night of July 26/27 July 52" states, "two flights of interceptors were dispatched from New Castle, Del." It reports the first flight, "2 F-94's were scrambled from New Castle at 2300 EDT [11:00 p.m. EDT]." They were the two F-94 jets of the "Shirley" flight led by Lt. Patterson and Caption McHugo. The Project Blue Book document "Untitled ARTC log of 26 July 52" stated Patterson's codename was "Red 1" and McHugo's was "Red 2."

Edward Ruppelt actually refers to two additional intercept flights not mentioned in the official Air Force documents. Ruppelt references the first scramble in his book and states, "By 11:30 P.M. four or five targets were being continually tracked at all times, *so once* again a call went out for interceptors. *Once again* there was some delay, but by midnight two F-94s from New Castle County AFB were airborne and headed south...but just as the two 'F-94's arrived in the area the targets disappeared from their radarscopes." The pilots then searched the area, did not see anything and were unable to find any targets on their radar systems. Ruppelt explains the jets then "left the Washington area." The first scramble occurred at "11:00 p.m." according to the Intelligence report. The second scramble as told by Ruppelt occurred well after that time, "by midnight two F-94's from New Castle County AFB were airborne and headed south." The Air Force "untitled ARTC log of 26 July 52," reported at "11:55 p.m.," Lt. Patterson of Shirley flight contacted ARTC and notified them he was running low on fuel and was returning to New Castle AFB. F-94 pilot Capt. McHugo departed the Washington area shortly after at "12:04 a.m." and returned to his base. *The Washington Post* also reported, "One plane landed shortly before midnight and the other about 12:15 a.m."

The Intelligence report then explains the next scramble, said to be the second intercept flight but was actually the third. They were the two F-94 Starfires of "Redman" flight that headed toward Washington D.C. from Delaware at "1:38 a.m." The call signs of the two jets, "Redman Blue" and "Redman Blue 2." The Air Force "untitled ARTC log of 26 July 52" document reported the "Redman" flight entered the airspace over Washington at "1:47" and returned to New Castle, AFB at "2:21 a.m." This was actually the third intercept flight that night, not the second intercept flight.

Ruppelt then explains yet another intercept flight that night. He writes, "At Washington the traffic controller again called Air Defense Command, and *once again* two F-94s soared south toward Washington…the controllers vectored the jets toward group after group of targets…all during the chase the radar operator in the F-94 was trying to get the target on his set but he had no luck. After staying in the area about twenty minutes the jets began to run low on fuel and returned to their base. Minutes later it began to get light, and when the sun came up all the targets were gone."

This sunrise scramble occurred well after the "Redman" flight entered the airspace over Washington at 1:47 a.m. and returned to New Castle, AFB at 2:21 a.m. By combining information from the Intelligence documents about the two official intercept flights with Ruppelt's other two accounts brings the total amount of intercept flights for July 26/27 up to four. Why did the second and fourth intercept flights not appear in any of the Air Force documents? Were any of the jets from the intercept flights that Ruppelt wrote about lost in action that night…jets that Lt. Col. Magruder mentioned? Once again, Ruppelt dropped yet another major clue into the mix for us to figure out years later.

Air Intelligence Officer Commander Boyd, USAF, made this statement in a FBI memorandum from V. P. Keay to H. Belmont dated July 29, 1952, referring to the sightings over Washington on the weekend of July 26, 1952. He stated, "The objects sighted may possibly be from another planet . . . the Air Force is attempting in each instance, to send up interceptor planes in order to obtain a better view of these objects."

On July 29, 1952, the front page of *The New York Times* printed the following headline, "Air Force Explains 2-Hour Delay In Chasing 'Objects' Over Capitol." The story states in part, "WASHINGTON, July 28 (AP). The Air Force said tonight [Monday, July 28] the current series of 'flying saucer' reports had brought no change in its twenty-four-hour-a-day program to challenge any unidentified and potentially hostile object in the sky." It adds, "An Air Force official tonight said its Air Defense Command had been ready for many months to challenge any unknown object aloft."

The article then explains the delay that occurred on the night of July 26/27 when UFOs were sighted over the Washington area. It states, "Actually the jet interceptors did not take off from their base near New Castle, Del., until nearly two hours after the radar watcher at Washington first had seen the unexplained objects on his radar screen. The Air Force explained today that the delay occurred when the report was sent to an Air Force flight center at Middletown, Pa., instead of through the Air Force command post in the Pentagon."

Another sighting also occurred on July 26, 1952, that shook up two Air Force pilots. According to Edward Ruppelt, this UFO incident occurred "on the same night as the second Washington sighting," and was considered a "good report from California." During this episode, an F-94C Starfire was scrambled after "a large, yellowish-orange light" according the crew that chased it. Later, Ruppelt talked to the pilot and radar observer of the Starfire and said, "They played tag with the UFO." Ruppelt also stated, " when I talked to the F-94 crew on the plane, the pilot said that they felt as if this were just a big aerial cat-and-mouse-game-and they didn't like it- at any moment they thought the cat might have pounced."

How many fighter pilots sitting behind .50 caliber and 20 mm cannons actually fired on the cat before it pounced on them, because they were tired of playing the game? How much longer would it be before the cat found out the new mouse in town was "Mighty Mouse?" This was the nickname of the 2.75 in. Aeromite rocket armaments carried by the new F-94C Starfire. The rules of the game were about to change.

On Sunday night July 27 the UFOs came back and were sighted over New York State. On July 29, 1952, *The New York Times* printed the following story:

'OBJECTS' SEEN OVER TARRYTOWN
Special to The New York Times

TARRYTOWN, N.Y., July 28—Streaks of light reportedly similar to those spotted over Washington Twice within the last week, were sighted in the sky above the Hudson River shortly before midnight last night [Sunday]. Eastern Air Defense Force officials are investigating. The flashes were reported in White Plains by Joseph Pulsoni, [GOC] post supervisor, and two ground force observers at a spotters post, atop an apartment house here. The report was relayed to an area radar station, according to Maj. F. B. Johnson, commanding the filter center.

Project Blue Book also listed three "Unknown" cases for July 27, 1952. On July 28, Project Blue Book received 43 UFO sighting reports that occurred on that day alone. This proved to be the most reports received by ATIC in Air Force History, yet only three were evaluated as "Unknown" cases. These July 27 and July 28 cases are as follows:

1. Case 1664- Wilmington, Delaware. July 27.
2. Case 1680- Mt. Clemens, Michigan. Selfridge AFB. July 27.
3. Case 1684- Wichita Falls, Texas. July 27.
4. Case 1700- Heidelberg, Germany. July 28.
5. Case 1707- Wrightson, New Jersey. McGuire AFB. July 28.
6. Case 1708- Tacoma, Washington. McChord AFB. July 28.

It is interesting to note that over the course of that two-day time span, three of the five UFO incidents over the United States involved Air Force bases, two on July 28. Shortly after 1:00 a.m., on July 28, 1952, the saucers made a grand appearance over Franklin, Indiana. This incident is interesting because it involved three UFOs that seemed to be engaged in an aerial "Dogfight" between them. *The Indianapolis News* reported the story on "MONDAY EVENING, JULY 28, 1952," in an article titled, "HUNDREDS IN STATE SEE 'FLYING SAUCERS'- Franklin 'Dogfight' Alerts State Troopers." In part it states, "Three 'flying saucers' were spotted by hundreds of Hoosiers, including police and military personnel, over South Central Indiana today. The objects appeared to have a 'dogfight' over Franklin and disappeared as dawn approached."

Just after 1:00 a.m., it was reported that "hundreds of motorists," sighted the three objects while driving along U.S. Highway 31. One motorist contacted the local police who in turn contacted the Civil Defense Director of Franklin, Mr. Robert Wolf. The three Objects were said to have flown across the sky from three different directions, the south, north and east. When they passed over Franklin, they engaged in what appeared to be a "dogfight." Wolf stated, "When they chased each other, they danced all over the sky."

He then contacted the Filter Station at South Bend, Indiana on two occasions. After the second call at 3:30 a.m., he was told the ADC was alerted but by 4:00 a.m., no fighter jets had arrived. Shortly after, the objects proceeded south and passed over nearby Attebury AFB, where several military sighted them. The last UFO sighting occurred at 5:00 a.m., when Indiana State Police sighted a UFO that passed over Franklin. The nearly four-hour aerial display had ended and yet no jets were scrambled after the UFOs. It may have been wise that the Air Force stayed out of this UFO aerial "Dogfight." Later on, that day would prove to be a big day in Washington D.C. for one particular flying saucer news story that shook the American public.

Chapter 6

"SHOOT DOWN FLYING DISCS"

On Monday, July 28, 1952, the lid on the "flying saucer" cover-up began to open up again at the nation's capitol. The July 28 edition of *The Washington Daily News* ran an article titled, "Jets Ready to Chase Lights - 24 - Hour Alert Ordered after Second Appearance Here." In part it states, "Jet interceptor planes of the Eastern Air Defense Command are on stand-by, round-the-clock orders today to take-off immediately if any more mysterious lights show up in the sky or on a radar screen." This article also states, "'We have no evidence they are flying saucers,' an Air Force representative said." He added, "Conversely we have no evidence they are not flying saucers. We don't know what they are."

A *United Press* news service story from Washington D.C., dated July 28 stated the following information in an article, "Air Force Alerts Jets to Chase 'Flying Saucers' Anywhere In U.S." In part it reads, "WASHINGTON, July 28 (UP)-The Air Defense Command alerted jet interceptor pilots Monday to take off instantly in pursuit of any 'flying saucers' sighted in the country…interceptor planes are ready to go aloft at any time." Further information states, "The Air Defense Command's mission is air defense of the United States and it is virtually interested in anything unidentified that flies in the air a spokesman said."

> Seattle *Post-Intelligencer*, July 29, 1952, p. 1
>
> # Air Force Orders Jet Pilots To Shoot Down Flying Saucers If They Refuse To Land

A staff correspondent for the International News Service, Larry Auldridge, wrote the following story that appeared in the *San Francisco Examiner*. Their July 29 headline stated, "Jets on 24-Hour Alert to Shoot Down Saucers." A portion of this article states, "WASHINGTON July 28 [INS] The Air Force revealed today that jet pilots have been placed on a 24 hour nationwide alert against 'flying saucers' with orders to 'shoot them down' if they refuse to land. It was learned that pilots have gone aloft on several occasions in an effort to shoot the mysterious objects to the ground but never came close enough to use their guns. The Air Force refused to confirm this, but Lt. Col. Moncel Monte, information officer stated, 'The jet pilots are, and have been, under orders to investigate unidentified objects and shoot them down if they can't talk them down.'" Further information states, "Disclosures of the 24-hour alert came as new reports continued to pour into the Pentagon of mysterious objects in the skies." Auldridge also stated, "Capt. Forest R. Shafer, commander of the Air Force Filter Center at South Bend, said reports of 'whirling discs' over Indiana have been increasing the past week. He stated, 'The disks seem to fall into two categories – red whirling objects like balls of fire and bluish – white disks that revolve and travel with tremendous speed.'"

On July 29, the Seattle *Post-Intelligencer* carried the International News Service story. Their headline read, "Air Force Orders Jet Pilots To Shoot Down Flying Saucers If They Refuse To Land." A portion of this article rephrased their headline, "WASHINGTON July 28 [INS] ...In Air Force parlance this means that if a 'flying saucer' refuses to obey an order to land jet planes are authorized to shoot them to earth if they can get close enough to do so."

Jets Told to Shoot Down Flying Discs

The Fall River Herald–News of Massachusetts also covered the story. Their headline read, "Jets Told to Shoot Down Flying Discs – Air Force Puzzled But No Longer Skeptical." Writer Darrell Garwood reported, "Jet pilots are operating under 24-hour nationwide 'alert' to chase the mysterious objects and to 'shoot them down' if they ignore orders to land. However, the Air Force confessed that none of its jets have come within shooting range of the blinking, enigmatic flying discs. Several pilots, according to the Air Force, have tried to shoot down the mysterious discs but the 'steady bright lights' in the sky have outflown the pilots..."

A writer from *The Washington Post*, John G. Norris also wrote about the July 28 Air Force jet stories. The Post's July 29 headline read, "Jets Poised for Pursuit; 'Saucer' Peril Discounted." In part, Norris reported, "Air Force interceptor planes are on alert to take off in chase of any further 'flying saucer' manifestations a spokesman said yesterday." Norris also reported, "Units of the Air Defense Command have no new or special orders to intercept 'saucers,' the spokesman said, but they will pursue any unexplained 'glowing lights' or radar 'blips' as part of their mission to protect the United States against any threat from the skies."

A July 28 "International News Service" story from Washington D.C. also spoke about the Air Forces "shoot down" order. It states, "Air Force Seeks Solution; Gives 'Shoot Down' Order...WASHINGTON-(INS)." The Tuesday, July 29, 1952, FINAL Edition of *The New York Daily News* also covered the same July 28 news story. They printed the following headline on their front page in bold print, "ALERT JETS TO HUNT 'SAUCERS.'"

On Monday July 28, the Air Force summoned "experts" from Wright Patterson Field in Dayton Ohio for a Press conference to be held at the Pentagon on Tuesday July 29. President Harry Truman wanted some answers about the sightings that had occurred over Washington, the public was in a panic. Edward J. Ruppelt and a team of fellow officers from Air Technical Intelligence Center, the flying saucer specialists of Project Blue book, left for Washington "late Monday." Ironically, the staff at Project Blue Book was inundated with UFO reports that Monday. They received "forty- three," UFO reports that actually occurred that day.

Those reports proved to be the highest amount of UFO sightings that were reported to Blue Book to date. The UFOs turned up the heat on July 28, 1952, but it was only a prelude of what was in store the following day.

The lid on the United States government's UFO cover-up had starting to wobble again. Once again, the cover-up lid started to lift off and was about to boil and reveal its contents. The government quickly attempted to turn the heat down so the UFO pressure cooker would not explode. Major General John A. Samford would attempt to keep the lid down on the cover-up at the July 29 press conference, to be held at the Pentagon.

Meanwhile, the Air Forces 24-hour-day alert to chase UFOs and mysterious lights if they showed up in the sky or on radar was evident. July 29, 1952, was the other day in July, besides July 23, that had the single most "Unknown" cases with five. The July 29 cases are listed below:

1. Case 1731- Osceola, Wisconsin. July 29.
2. Case 1732- Hampton, Virginia. Langley AFB. July 29.
3. Case 1738- Merced, California. July 29.
4. Case 1739- Wichita, Kansas. July 29.
5. Case 1747- Ennis, Montana. July 29.

Early Tuesday morning, on July 29, 1952, at "1:30 A.M." the UFOs swarmed over the skies of Osceola, Wisconsin in overwhelming numbers. This sighting was recorded as Case # 1731 by Project Blue Book and was evaluated as an "Unknown." At about 1:30 several targets were picked by ground radarscopes as radars scanned the nearby skies. Over the course of one hour, Ground radar operators tracked "several clusters of up to 10 small radar targets and one small target." They reported that the "small targets moved from Southeast to East at 50-60 knots (60-70 MPH) following each other." The largest target of the group was said to have flown at "600 knots (700 MPH). During this time, an F-51 Mustang interceptor plane flew into the area to check out the situation. It was reported that the pilot had a sighting and "confirmed one target" but was unable to overtake it.

The Air Force was prepared and on 24-hour alert to guard the skies over America as fighters continued to scramble after the unknown objects. There were also numerous UFO sightings throughout the United States that early morning as well and throughout the day. On Wednesday July 30, 1952, *The New York Times* reported the following information about UFO radar targets that were picked up over Washington D.C. on the morning of July 29, 1952:

Third Time in Ten Days

Three times in the last ten days, it was disclosed; the Capital area has reported flying objects, some stationary, others moving at various speeds. The latest report came today [Tuesday, July 29] from operators of the Civil Aeronautic Administration radar apparatus at [Washington] National Airport who said that their equipment had picked up numerous objects from 2:30 to 6 A.M. A spokesman said as many as twelve unidentified objects had appeared on the radar screen at the same time but that, "no visual sightings were made."

Consequently, he added, the near-by Andrews Air Force Base was not notified and no jet fighters were dispatched to investigate. General Samford's staff attempted to explain the supposedly moving objects of separate phenomena.

On July 30, 1952, *The Washington Post* also reported the early morning July 29 radar targets picked up over Washington D.C. by Washington National Airport. This article talked about the recent July 29 Washington D.C. radar targets and explained what the "separate phenomena" may have been that Samford's staff used "to explain the supposedly moving objects." The Post reported what occurred on that early Tuesday morning, July 29, "Ray Nathan, CAA information officer, said one to 12 of 'blips' appeared traveling at speeds of from 90 to 120 mph, in a northwest to southeast direction-from about Herndon to Andrews Air Base. They were not traveling downwind, indicating they were not balloons or 'window' (tinfoil released from bombers to confuse radar observers.)"

Additional information explains the tinfoil story, "Still another possible cause of the sightings under investigation by the Air Force was the discovery of large numbers of little strips of tinfoil at the Upper Marlboro Race track and in the streets of Marlboro." This article explains that the, " Samples of tinfoil were turned over to the Air Force by The Washington Post, and tentatively identified by Major Gen. Roger Ramey, USAF operations chief as 'window' or 'chaff.'" The Post wrapped up the July 29, radar sightings and said, " A check is being made to determine if the foil was dropped by Air Force bombers in current Air Defense maneuvers. Normally, however, such radar counter-measures clutter up the scope." The chance that tinfoil may have caused the radar targets is just another excuse added to the already long list of possible 'Saucer' explanations.

Several other UFO sightings occurred over the northeast United States on Tuesday July 29, 1952. They were reported by an *"Associated Press* Staff Writer," named "Saul Pett." He reported, "In the New York area, In Washington, D.C., in New England and Ohio, reports came in of strange aerial objects that defied immediate explanation. The Air Force said the volume of such reports was the heaviest it has been in five years." He also stated, "Other sightings, varying in descriptions, were reported from Burlington, Vermont, South Portland, Me., and New York City."

The New England and Washington UFO sightings were explained by Harvard astro-physicist Dr. Donald Menzel, a well-known debunker of UFOs. He talked about these sightings but did not bring up the tinfoil story reported by *The Washington Post*.

On July 30, 1952, *The Boston Globe* reported, "'Flying Saucers' Merely Light, Says noted Harvard Scientist-Air Force Agrees with Dr. Menzel." He explained, "Flying Saucers, which threw New England and the nation's capitol into a fresh tizzy yesterday [July 29], are nothing more than refractions and reflections of light from the upper atmosphere and certainly nothing to be alarmed about. That's what one of the most prominent astro-physicists, Prof. Donald H. Menzel of Harvard University, suggested from his Duxbury home last night."

Was Dr. Menzel aware that Project Blue Book had already recorded 141 unknown cases for 1952? These cases were recorded from January 16 until the time that he made his statement from his Duxbury home.

On Wednesday July 30, 1952, *The New York Times* also reported the July 29 UFO sightings in the northeast. The following article reported:

"SIGHTINGS" INCREASE HERE

WHITE PLAINS, N.Y., July 29 – The Air Raid Filter Center here, clearing house for information from observation posts [GOC] in twenty-six counties of the New York Area, reported an increase today [July 29] of "unidentified airborne objects" since the 139 posts of the area had gone on round-the-clock duty July 14.

Headquarters of the Eastern Air Defense Command near Newburgh, in command of this center and other, replied that strange objects in the air in the last twenty-four hours in southwestern Indiana, New Jersey, Plainfield, N.J. and Tarrytown. "In the normal performances of its assigned mission, the headquarters said, it sends fighter intercept aircraft aloft, whenever unknown aerial objects are detected in its area with sufficient definiteness to warrant attempted interception."

In Donald Keyhoe's book *Flying Saucers from Outer Space*, he states what occurred on that Tuesday only about fours hours before the UFO press conference, "By noon the Air Force had still another headache. The night before a story by *INS* had reported a new Air Force order — if saucers ignored orders to land, pilots were to open fire. At Washington, Frank Edwards had picked up the flash and repeated it on the mutual network. Telegrams protesting the order were coming in from all over the country."

Keyhoe stated, that the President of the US Rocket Society, Robert L. Farnsworth wired telegrams to the White House. Farnsworth also gave a copy to the *United Press*. The UP story reported these telegrams were sent to, "President Truman, Secretary of Defense Robert Lovett, Army Secretary Frank Pace, Jr., and Navy Secretary, Dan Kimball."

The following points of information appeared in that telegram:

1.) "Urgently request reconsideration by your order to destroy flying saucers."
2.) "Remarkably advanced aerodynamics indicate probably intercelestial origin. Interference without more cause, than saucers friendly curiosity could cause unbelievable suffering and death."
3.) "I respectfully suggest that no offensive action be taken against the objects reported as unidentified which have been sighted over our nation."
4.) "Should they be extra-terrestrial, such action might result in the gravest consequences, as well as alienating us from beings of far superior powers. Friendly contact should be sought as long as possible."
5.) "People much aroused and worried."

On that afternoon, the UFO press conference was held at the Pentagon at 4:00 p.m. General John Samford, Director of Air Force Intelligence and Major General Roger Ramey, Chief of the Air Defense Command led the July 29 press conference. General Samford's Press Conference was held in the Pentagon in Room 3E-869 and was the largest press conference held since World War II. It also proved to be the longest and lasted 80 minutes.

It is ironic that all of the sightings that occurred over Washington and New England were on the same day as the Washington D.C. flying saucer conference! Donald Keyhoe, who attended the news conference stated, "Their advisors spread out around the platform–an impressive group of colonels, majors, captains and civilian specialists."

The Air Force officials who participated in the July 29 press conference were:

1. Major General John A. Samford, Director of Intelligence, USAF.
2. Major General Roger Ramey, Director of Operations, USAF.
3. Captain Edward J. Ruppelt, Aerial Phenomenon Branch, ATIC. Project Blue Book Chief
4. Captain Roy L. James, Electronics Branch, ATIC
5. Colonel Donald L. Bower, Technical Analysis Division, ATIC
6. Burgoyne L. Griffing, Electronics Branch, ATIC

Standing: Captain R. L. Jones, Captain Edward J. Ruppelt, Colonel Donald Bower, B.L. Griffing.
Seated: Major General Roger Ramey, Major General John A. Samford.

The press was told that Samford and Ramey were the top flying saucer experts in the Air Force. General Samford talked about the UFO situation in his opening statement and stated the following, "The Air Force feels a very definite obligation to identify and analyze things that happen in the air that may that may have in them menace to the United States and, because of that feeling of obligation and our pursuit of that interest." Samford also gave a brief over view of the Air Force's involvement in the UFO field since 1947 and talked about the large amount of UFO sightings that were explained as:

1. Friendly aircraft erroneously recognized or reported.
2. Hoaxes.
3. Electronic phenomenon.
4. Meteorological phenomenon.
5. Light aberrations.
6. Many other things.

Major General Samford then stated, "However, there have remained a percentage of this total, in the order of twenty percent of the reports that have come from credible observers of relatively incredible things."

He then talked about the UFO reports they had received and then went into a confusing and long-winded story about how the Air Force needed to get the "measurement value" of them. At this point Donald Keyhoe described the scene in the room. He stated, "Several reporters looked at each other blankly. The man on my right leaned over me. 'If he's trying to befuddle us, he's already got me.' He whispered."

Samford continued to talk and then made the following statement of interest, "We can say, as of now, that there has been no pattern that reveals anything remotely like or remotely like consistency that we can in any way associate with menace to the United States." This comment floored Donald Keyhoe who stated, "Here, I knew Samford was skating on thin ice. Even before I saw all the ATIC evidence, I had enough reports that did show a definite pattern. *But it was the General's job to dispel public fear, and admitting a pattern would only have increased it.*" Samford then stated in part, "However, Our present dilemma of lack of measurement that can be turned to analysis and a complete lack of pattern in any of these things which any clue to possible purpose or possible use leaves us in dilemma as to what we can do about this remaining twenty percent of unidentified phenomena."

Samford also gave a brief history about UFOs dating back to the biblical times. He stated, "So, our present course of action is to continue on this problem with the best of our ability, giving to it the attention that we feel very definitely warrants in terms of identifying the growing or possible or disappearing, if it turns out to be that, menace to the United States to give it adequate attention but not frantic attention."

During the eighty-minute conference, Samford did most of the talking. He was very vague in his comments and answers to the questions from the press reporters. The press was confused with the doubletalk of Samford and Ramey as the two men attempted to debunk the sightings and quiet the flying saucer panic. At times, the scene in the room became chaotic as reporters questioned the Air Force officers and received round-about answers.

Edward Ruppelt made the following statement about Samford in reference to the July 19/20 and July 26/27 Washington sightings, "General Samford made an honest effort to straighten out the Washington National [Airport] sightings. He had to hedge on many answers to questions from the press because he didn't know the answers. This hedging gave the impression that he was trying to cover up something more than just the fact that his people had fouled up in not fully investigating the sightings." Moreover, Samford totally rebuffed the extraterrestrial theory. He explained that the flaps of "flying saucers" sighted over the Washington D.C. area were probably attributed to "natural phenomena." They came in the form of, temperature "inversions" or "reflections" from the ground and according to the Air Force, these occurrences appeared in humid and hot weather.

The final moments of the press conference involved the press asking Major General Ramey questions about the recent jet interceptions that had occurred over Washington D.C. It is quite interesting to note the uncertainty of Ramey's answers to the press, his lack of memory when he was asked a question, and his obvious tap dancing to avoid an issue. Considering Ramey's position as "Director of United States Air Force Operations," it is obvious that he avoided giving direct answers to the Press.

The following is a direct transcript between the Press and Major General Roger Ramey:

The Press: General [Samford], in connection to withholding information, I'd like to ask General Ramey a question. That is, how many times have fighter planes been brought down over the Washington area in the last couple weeks to investigate reports of flying objects?

Major General Ramey: That's a matter of record—three, I believe. I think two flights one night and one flight Saturday night. I don't remember the night the other two were up. I think there had been six sorties.

The Press: One fling the first Saturday night [July 19] and two flights— [Interrupted]

Major General Ramey: In this immediate area, yes. We have airplanes that investigate various reports all over the country or places where we have these fighters but- [Interrupted]

The Press: I thought the Air Force had said that it couldn't send up fighters because it didn't have them.
Major General Ramey: No, I don't believe it said that. [Andrews AFB, 121st FIS was at New Castle, Del.]
The Press: The first night. [July 19-20]
The Press: How about last night? [Actually 2:30 a.m. early morning July 29]
Major General Ramey: No, there were no fighters sent up last night.
The Press: Were their fighters sent in here from New Castle on both those Saturday nights in question?
Major General Ramey: That's right, yes."

Major Keyhoe stated, "As the conference broke up, I heard some of the newsmen's comments. 'Never heard so much and learned so little,' one man said acidly. His companion shrugged. 'What did you expect? Even if they knew the answer they wouldn't give it out now, with all this hysteria." Keyhoe also stated, "Ironically, even as the presses roared, Air Force jet pilots were chasing saucers over two Midwest states. One case, if it had been made public that [July 29] night, would have ruined the inversion answer and wrecked the debunking plan." Edward Ruppelt also talked about another jet incident that involved a chase after a UFO on the night of the conference. He wrote about this incident in his 1956 book, *The Report On Unidentified Flying Objects*. Ruppelt stated the incident occurred, "At nine-forty on the evening of the twenty –ninth," and was reported only a few hours after Samford's press conference. It involved the 61st Fighter Interceptor Squadron at Selfridge AFB, in Michigan.

Ruppelt stated, "An air Defense Command radar station in central Michigan started to get plots on a target that was coming straight south across Saginaw Bay on Lake Huron at 625 miles an hour. A quick check of flight plans on file showed it was an unidentified target."

An "Air Intelligence Information Report" dated "31 July 52," also gave first hand details of this intercept attempt. The radar operator of an F-94B Starfire told his story in a "STATEMENT," his name, First Lieutenant Victor Helfenstein. The preparing officer at the "61st Fighter –Interceptor Squadron" was "2nd Lt. Boscome T. Zilpha. The pilot of the F-94 Starfire was Captain Edward Slowinski. Edward Ruppelt also wrote about this incident in his 1956 book, and stated it occurred, "at nine forty on the evening of the twenty –ninth." Ruppelt continued, "An air Defense Command radar station in central Michigan started to get plots on a target that was coming straight south across Saginaw Bay on Lake Huron at 625 miles an hour. A quick check of flight plans on file showed it was an unidentified target."

On that night, it was reported that two Starfires were on a "routine training mission" and doing intercepts "on a B-36 bomber." After completing their last intercept of the training flight, Helfenstein and his pilot were at an altitude of "approximately 9,000 feet." Captain Slowinski put the jet into a climb, reached an altitude of 20,000 feet, and received a call from Ground Control Intercept. The flyers were asked if they could, "see a target at three o'clock low," but did not see any target. The GCI operator asked them to "look high." The following is a verbatim statement as told by the radar observer, Lieutenant Helfenstein:

My pilot Captain Edward J. Slowinski, then started a starboard turn, and as he did, I picked up the target on my scope at 60 degrees. I kept the pilot in a starboard turn until I had the target at 12 o'clock, 4 miles out, when I locked on the blip. I stayed locked on for 30 seconds when the blip jumped lock. However, in that short space of time, I was able to determine that it was an airborne target four miles ahead and level with us. On my visual observance, the target kept putting off what seemed like a changing light in definite sequences of white, red and bluish-green. This is the only means of identification we had. From a bombardier radar observer, and navigator, I have never experienced any sighting like this before.

Edward Ruppelt stated, "For ten minutes the ground radar followed the chase. At times, the unidentified target would slow down and the F-94 would start to close the gap, but always, just as the F-94 was getting within radar range, the target would put on a sudden burst of speed and pull away from the pursuing jet." The pursuit ended when the lock was broken and the UFO accelerated away. Captain Slowinski then radioed the GCI controller that the jet was running low on fuel and turned away. The UFO then decelerated when the jet had turned away from it. Ruppelt said, "It looked as if the target slowed down to 200 to 300 miles an hour as soon as the F-94 turned around." On "4 AUG 52", the Commander of the 61st FIS, 4708th Defense wing at Selfridge AFB, General Major Warren Patterson, Jr., issued a letter to the "Chief" of ATIC at Wright Patterson AFB. The officials at Blue Book were notified that the classification of this report had been upgraded to "SECRET" from its original "CONFIDENTIAL" status.

In his book, Ruppelt states, "What was it. It obviously wasn't a weather balloon or meteor." He then states the following, "A lot of people I knew were absolutely convinced this report was the key...These people believed that this report in itself was proof enough to officially accept the fact that UFOs were interplanetary spaceships. And when some people refused to believe even this report, the frustration was pitiful to see." Who were the people that Ruppelt spoke about here? Was Ruppelt trying to tell us something in the last line of this statement...*even this report*?

On Wednesday, July 30 the news media began "to grind out the conference story" according to Major Keyhoe. *The Louisville Courier Journal* newspaper article dated July 30 and titled, "Radar Spots 'Saucers' Over Washington Again," reported that "Maj. Gen. Roger Ramey, deputy chief of the Air Force staff for operations, told the news conference that interceptor planes have raced aloft several hundred times as a result of reported sightings of unidentified objects. He said that was just standard procedure." Donald Keyhoe recited this information in his 1953 book, *Flying Saucers from Outer Space*, and added a time as well. He said, "In the last two years, hundreds of fighters have been scrambled to intercept UFOs.

Before the release of this 1953 book, Keyhoe talked to the staff at *TRUE Magazine*, and wrote an article that appeared in their December 1952 issue, "What radar tells about Flying Saucers" by Donald Keyhoe." The introduction states, "In a new investigation of the flying saucer, *TRUE Magazine* has secured Air Force confirmation of these important facts...More than 300 times, Air Force interceptor planes have chased mysterious lights and unidentified objects revealed by radar scopes." All of this information truly reveals that the Air Force was in an all out effort to intercept the UFOs during that era. In reference to the Washington Press conference, Keyhoe stated, "I thought over the high points of the press conference. I was positive how it had been a cover-up, forced on the Air Intelligence men by the July crisis."

On Wednesday July 30, 1952, the front-page headline of *The New York Times* read, "Air Force Debunks 'Saucers' as Just 'Natural Phenomena.'" The subtitle headline read, "Intelligence Chief Denies a Menace Exists - 'Objects' Believed to be Reflections, but 'Adequate' Guard Will be Kept. WASHINGTON, July 29."

The majority of this article spoke about the flying saucer explanations stated at the press conference, "Air Force headquarters skimmed away into the broken dishware bin today the latest wave of 'flying saucers.' It called them 'natural phenomena' and announced through high-ranking general officers that henceforth the Air Force would treat reports with 'adequate but not frantic attention.'"

This article also stated, "Out of today's conference emerged a favorite theory, but one that experts conceded did not answer everything. It is in the kind of weather that has existed here-hot and humid-there is created something known as a temperature inversion." Also reported was the statement, "General Samford said that one reason for the 'saucer' flurries was undoubtedly the great increase in man-made activity in the air. He also cited 'jumpiness' because of war fears..."

On July 30, 1952, *The Washington Post* also reported the press conference. In this article, "Air Force Lays Saucer Blips Here to Heat," the story talks about press conference and the July 19/20 and July 26/27 "saucer" sightings. It states, "Air Force investigators disclosed yesterday they are satisfied the recent radar sightings of 'saucers' over Washington stem from natural causes – probably the long hot spell." It adds the following, "One theory said Samford is that these sightings are temperature 'inversions' or reflections from the ground in hot and humid weather. Edward Ruppelt summed up the result of the situation that involved the Press, the Air Force, and the UFOs at that July 29 Pentagon Press Conference. Ruppelt stated, "Some how out of this chaotic situation came exactly the result that was intended-the press got off our backs. Captain James' answers about the possibility of the radar targets' being caused by temperature inversions had been construed by the press to mean that this was the Air Force's answer, *even though today the twin sightings are still carried as unknowns."* Ruppelt made this statement in his 1956 book, but when the Project Blue Book case files were declassified, then released in 1976, the July 26/27 Washington D.C. case was listed as "Unknown" and the July 19/20 Washington D.C. case was not! The official Blue Book explanation for the July 19/20 sightings, "Temperature Inversions."

A "DEPARTMENT OF DEFENSE" document titled: "FACT SHEET" stamped with a date stating, "ISSUED ABOUT DECEMBER 1953," gives the following information. It explains, "Temperature inversion reflections can give a return on a radar scope that is as sharp as that received from an aircraft. Speeds of these objects reportedly range from zero to fantastic rates. The 'objects' also appear to move in all directions. Such sightings have resulted in many fruitless intercept efforts." Harry Barnes did not agree with this conclusion.

Major General Samford and his staff, helped close lid on the United States government's UFO cover-up at Washington D.C. The Air Force turned the heat down and kept the secret contents of the UFO pressure cooker to a simmer. Many were fooled by the Air Force's UFO explanations, but that was beside the point. People across the United States were still seeing the saucers and strange crafts flying through the skies over America. The government was constantly on guard as to not let the cover-up lid explode off forever. For now, the Air Force had a temporary control of the situation, by keeping the American public in the dark.

On July 30, 1952, *The Boston Globe* featured the following headline story, "'Flying Saucers' Merely Light, Says noted Harvard Scientist." It reported another scientists' flying saucer opinion:

Harvard astronomer Dr. Harlow Shapley offered this checklist last night on the origin of the saucers:
1) Results of anomalous refractions in the upper atmosphere of the earth where densities are anomalous.
2) Fireballs (bright meteors)
3) Meteorological test balloons
4) Search lights on broken cloud fields
5) Hallucinations

Dr. Shapley was probably not aware of the Project Blue Book "unknown" statistics either. A Dr. Menzel prediction also appeared in this article, "Two scientists agreed with General Samford that the recent Washington sightings were the result of the extremely hot weather. Dr. I. M. Levitt, director of the Fels Planetarium in Philadelphia and Dr. D. H. Menzel of Harvard, predicted that the sightings would disappear when the present hot spell is over." The opinions of these two men are very debatable as the UFO sightings continued in cool and cold weather.

I then reviewed the Blue Book Unexplained cases. Between October 1, 1952 and December 31, 1952, Project Blue Book recorded 23 "unknowns" that occurred over the United States. These UFO sightings had absolutely nothing to do with the hot weather. One of these unexplained incidents was Project Blue Book Case 2253. This unknown case involved an incident that occurred on November 30, 1952. It involved multiple unknown radar targets similar to those tracked over Washington D.C. July 26, four months earlier. This UFO incident occurred during cold weather. The location, none other than the capitol city, Washington D.C. and the same radar operators at Washington National Airport who tracked the UFOs in July, also tracked these unidentified targets. Dr. Levitt and Dr. Menzel's predictions were incorrect. The UFO sightings did not end when the "hot spell" was over. The last two sightings in July that Project Blue Book recorded as "Unknown" cases both occurred on July 30 in the Midwest United States:

1. Case 1755- Albuquerque, New Mexico. 2. Case 1758- San Antonio, Texas

Also on July 30, a flying saucer story came out of "New Castle Air Force Base, Del." A news headline reads, "Fighter Pilots at New Castle Stay Alert for More Saucer Reports." This story concerns the fighter pilots of the 121st FIS from Andrews AFB, who were temporarily stationed at New Castle AFB. In part, it states:

The Air Force may now consider those unidentified objects in the sky as natural phenomena, but if the Capital's favorite family of 'flying saucers' return, Washington fighter pilots at this base are all set to ferret them out. They are members of the 121st Fighter Interceptor Squadron using F-94 all-weather night fighters equipped with radar...The flyers are acting with the 142d Fighter Interceptor Squadron in maintaining a 24-hour alert, lately especially concerned with keeping strange things out of the sky over the Washington area...Last Sunday morning [July 27], after two pilots of the 142d went aloft on orders to find out what those now-famous things were over Andrews, two men of the 121st took over the early dawn patrol.

In this article, two fighter pilots of the 121st Fighter Interceptor Squadron made statements about how they would "re-act" in a situation concerning a hypothetical UFO intercept. The story continues and reports:

Most of them [fighter pilots] wonder how they'd re-act if they encountered an unidentified object while on a mission...First Lt. Mickey Jones 3313 Terrace Drive SE: "I'd try to get a picture, if possible, with my gun cameras. I'd use extreme caution. I'd report it to all Ground Control Intercept. From then on, it would depend on the circumstances." Captain Wayne Owens of 5408 Fifty-sixth place, East Riverdale, Md.: "First it would arouse my curiosity. I would then prepare for combat. I'd notify the authorities by radio. Then I'd proceed to investigate. I'd sure as hell not want to be caught flat-footed."

How many American fighter pilots engaged in combat with UFOs during intercept missions...because they did not want to be caught flat-footed? To reiterate a point, during the July 29 Pentagon news conference, it was stated that Major General Ramey, "told the news conference that interceptor planes have raced a loft several hundred times as a result of reported sightings of unidentified objects." How many American fighter aircraft and flyers were lost in combat while attempting to intercept unidentified objects?

Throughout the month of July 1952, jet fighters continued to scramble after UFOs in record numbers across the United States. Ruppelt reported, "As the end of July approached, there was a group of officers in Intelligence fighting hard to get the UFO 'recognized.' At ATIC, Project Blue Book was still trying to be impartial - but sometimes it was difficult."

On Thursday July 31, *The Lawrence Tribune* ran an *Associated Press* story dated Washington, July 30 (AP) that read, "Urges USAF Not to Shoot Saucers." A concerned individual wrote to the Air Force and stated the following in a telegram, "Urgently request reconsideration of your order to destroy flying saucers... people much arose and worried. An Air Force representative responded by stating, "That nobody is going around shooting at strange objects in the sky but that Air Defense planes would attempt to destroy any air craft or objects definitely identified as hostile and dangerous."

In 1952, Donald Keyhoe spoke with an Air Force jet fighter pilot who had recently returned home from the Korean War. This Captain was a veteran combat pilot who had earned the "Distinguished Flying Cross and Silver Star ribbons. Keyhoe spoke with this pilot, concerning Air Force fighter pilot intercepts against flying saucers. Reluctant to speak with Keyhoe at first, the pilot agreed to be interviewed when Keyhoe said, "I wouldn't quote you by name, Jim. But the public ought to know its serious business, chasing a saucer."

The following is part of that conversation; Captain Jim stated, "They [pilots] don't all feel the same. Some pilots never get very close." Keyhoe asked," What about the ones that do?" Captain Jim replied they're on edge-what the Hell do you think." The pilot continued and stated, "all right, I'll give you the picture, but it sounds kind of silly when you're on the ground good and safe… you're flying an F-94 jet, with a radar operator behind you. You're on a routine patrol. Ground Control Intercept calls you. They got an unknown on their radar, which is a surveillance type, with a longer range than yours [you're on board radar]. Their tracks show the unknown is making tight turns and speeds too high for any aircraft. So they give you the word-it's a UFO… right then, it stops being an ordinary intercept. Going after a MIG [Russian fighter jet], it's different. You know what you're up against. When you get him in your sights, you're ready to fire. With the saucers, you're on the spot. The orders are to intercept but not to shoot-unless you're sure they're hostile." Keyhoe stated, "I knew about that. Major General Roger Ramey, chief of the Air Defense Command, had told me about the instructions."

According to Donald Keyhoe, Captain Jim, "said harshly… 'How're you going to tell if they're hostile or not.'" The fighter pilot also stated, "All of a sudden, circling faster than any plane. Your radar picks it up, too, and you lock on, so you're automatically following the thing. About that time, Ground Control calls and says they got you both on their [radar] scope, and the UFO's right where your radar shows it. That does it. You know the things real-not a reflection or a set malfunction." Captain Jim then stated, "It's your job to get in close… so you open up and go in." He continued, "Then it makes a quick turn toward you. You know you have been spotted, and you start getting butterflies in your stomach-… sounds pretty dopey, Huh, a fighter pilot sitting behind 50-caliber guns and rockets and scared of a light in the sky. You watch the thing start a tight turn around you. Nobody on Earth could take all the gs [G-Force] in that turn. It's so fast you almost twist your neck off, trying to keep it in sight. Maybe you see a shape behind the light, maybe not. Even if you do, you can't tell its size- you don't know if the things close or a half a mile away… one thing sure, something with intelligence is in control of the thing, the way it maneuvers."

The fighter pilot then stated, "You'd give anything if it was suddenly daylight, so you could see exactly what the thing is. But all you really know is that you're a sitting duck, if whoever's watching you wants to let you have it." Shortly after Captain Jim told Donald Keyhoe, "You're right-people should know about all those UFOs intercepts." How many fighter pilots in hair-raising situations like this, actually felt like sitting ducks and did shoot? In *The Fall River Herald–News* article, "Jets Told to Shoot Down Flying Discs – Air Force Puzzled But No Longer Skeptical," Writer Darrell Garwood reported, "Several pilots, according to the Air Force, have tried to shoot down the mysterious discs." In fear for their lives, and the safety of their country, how many fighter pilots fired upon the discs and UFOs? Furthermore, on the other hand, how many UFOs have fired upon American fighter jet pilots?

Now I ask, has the Air Force ever admitted that fighter pilots have been lost, killed, or crashed because of these UFOs and flying saucer intercepts? The answer is no! The Air Force has never admitted any loss of aircraft or pilot life during an intercept with a saucer or an unconventional craft. Why, you may ask! In the forward of his book, *The Report On Unidentified Flying Objects*, Captain Edward Ruppelt sums it up best when he wrote, *"The report has been difficult to write because it involves something that doesn't officially exist."* In other words, since flying saucers and other unconventional-type crafts do not officially exist, then how could they be involved in aerial confrontations with military fighter aircraft?

In Tom Wolfe's classic 1979 best-selling book, titled *The Right Stuff*, the author referred to several Air Force pilots who died in fighter jet training. Wolfe stated, "In 1952 when Bridgeman [Bill Bridgeman, USAF test pilot] was flying at Edwards Air Force Base, sixty-two Air Force pilots died in the course of thirty-six weeks of training, an extraordinary rate of 1.7 per week. Those figures were for fighter-pilot trainees only; they did not include test pilots, Bridgeman's own confreres, who were dying quite regularly enough." Are these statistics for USAF fighter pilots who died in extraordinary numbers during jet training a true accounting? How many deaths in these statistics were fronts to cover-up pilots lost during UFO intercepts? The total amount of UFO reports that Project Blue Book received and recorded for the month of July was an outstanding 536 cases. There were 51 cases evaluated as "Unknown" cases that were listed for the dates between July 3 and July 30, 1952. Twenty-two of these "Unknown" sighting cases were reported by the United States Military.

THE FLYING SAUCER PHYSICIST

Nuclear physicist Stanton T. Friedman, raised the following question in the 1974 winter issue of *UFO Report* magazine, "The question must be asked if the purpose of jet interceptors is to protect the country and they mysteriously vanish; how can the Air Force persist in their stand that UFOs are not a threat to National Security?" When I spoke to Stanton Friedman about this statement, he also told me that usually, jets are not scrambled to go after unknowns in the sky to shoot them down unless they are considered a threat to National Security.

One such incident occurred on February 11, 1953 and involved a confrontation between a Marine fighter jet and a UFO. This event was documented by the UFO organization NICAP, which disclosed the name of the pilot as 1st Lieutenant Ed Balacco. When I read about this incident while doing research, I contacted Stanton Friedman and we talked about it. Shortly after, Friedman discovered the former fighter pilot was alive and well and resided in California. Shortly after Friedman contacted Mr. Balacco. They spoke about the incident in detail and then Stanton spoke to me about it. Marine fighter pilot 1st Lt. Edward Balacco was a Korean War combat veteran with 1,000 hours of flying time and had returned home to state side. On February 11, he was stationed at a small Marine Air Station located in Edenton, North Carolina, approximately 100 miles southwest of Norfolk, Virginia. At the time, the base was on a 24-hour intercept alert, only days before, UFOs were reported over the skies of Norfolk, Virginia, which stirred up a commotion.

At about 10:00 p.m. that night, a UFO had been tracked by Norfolk NAS radar and the alert siren was sounded at the Marine Air Station at Edenton. Balacco raced to his F9F Panther jet and minutes later was airborne and being guided to the Norfolk area in hot pursuit of the UFO. When he closed in on the area, the UFO disappeared off Norfolk's radar. Balacco did a visual search of the skies looking for the intruder, but to no avail. First Lt. Balacco then radioed Norfolk and informed them that the Panther was low on fuel and was granted permission to return to his station. The pilot then headed on a southern course along the coastline toward Edenton at an altitude of 20,000 feet with the Panther's running lights on.

While scanning the sky, Balacco suddenly noticed an object with red lights at an altitude far below him and just above the surface of the Atlantic Ocean. He glanced away for a few moments to look at his instruments and steadied the jet on a course for home. When Balacco looked back up, he was amazed to see that the object had maneuvered and climbed to his altitude, was in front of him, and only 2,000 feet away. The fighter pilot reset his heading on a course toward the UFO and the jet soared through the sky in excess of 500 MPH. As Balacco neared his target and got a closer look at it, he could plainly see it was a disk.

This unknown object was well within the Atlantic Air Defense Identification Zone and was deemed an enemy. Immediately, the fighter pilot pulled the trigger on his control stick to fire upon the disk and to his dismay, the distinct sound of machine gun fire was absent. The guns were not loaded with ammunition. The Panther soared toward the disk as Balacco continued to depress the trigger, but to no avail, the jet was completely unarmed. Moments later, the soaring jet came within 400 feet of the disk and passed near it. It was the color of white heat, had a red glow at the rear, and had two red flashing lights on its right side. Suddenly, the jet was engulfed in an intense bluish-white light that was emitted by the UFO. Bewildered, Balacco looked down at his trigger hand on the control stick and was shocked to see that he could see the bones in his hand through his leather glove. During that time, the pilot noted that everything seemed motionless and there was an eerie lack of sound. Furthermore, the roar of the engine's turbine was also nonexistent. Seconds later, the pilot saw a flash of light, the object flew away at a tremendous speed, and everything returned to normal. Balacco then redirected his Panther and returned to his station without any further encounters. During that time, another fighter pilot, Captain Thomas W. Riggs was scrambled in an attempt to intercept the UFO. Captain Riggs said he saw a low flying object in the vicinity of the North Carolina coastline but was unable to identify it.

When 1st Lieutenant Balacco returned to his station, he was taken to Marine Headquarters at Cherry Point, NC, interrogated and debriefed for several hours by numerous high- ranking officers. Edward Balacco was told to not to repeat the incident. Friedman stated, "The pilot and I agreed that probably the only reason that he is alive today and practicing law is that the guns weren't loaded."

As Friedman and I continued to talk about these jet encounters with UFOs, we wondered how many such cases occurred that the public did not know about. He asked, "I wonder, how many military aircraft either crashed or disappeared on alleged 'routine training missions' while chasing them [UFOs]." Stanton T. Friedman and I then began to look into the matter of lost and vanished planes during the 1950s era. The July 1952 era of UFO sightings seemed like a good starting point.

Stanton Friedman began to research this period. In early 2005, while at the National Archives, Friedman spent hours looking through declassified aircraft accident reports. He told me that he searched through numerous files and discovered that several of them were incomplete; several days and months worth of aircraft accidents were missing. In some instances, he discovered certain files were completely missing.

Friedman did obtain a recently "DECLASSIFIED" Air Force document that was dated "10 SEP 1952." It gives us an idea of how many major accidents occurred during June and July of 1952. This document stamped "CONFIDENTIAL" and "SECURITY INFORMATION" is a "MEMORANDUM FOR: Secretary of the Air Staff - SUBJECT: STAFF DIGEST ITEM" The name at the bottom of the document states," (AFCIS-3/Lt. Col. Myers/56948)." This memorandum is a tabulation of major accidents involving fighters, bombers, and cargo and trainer aircraft. In part, this document states:

(UNCLASSIFIED) THE AIRCRAFT ACCIDENT SITUATION IN JULY. Preliminary reports of USAF (Including ANG) major accidents in July indicate a 20 percent increase over June. Total flying hours increased by 6 percent…During July, jet fighter accidents increased one third over the June rate…Fighter fatalities increased 43 percent…Increases in major accidents occurred in USAFE, MATS, SAC, TAC and Headquarters Command. The following tabulation contains comparable accident statistics for June and July 1952…The following tabulation involves the fighter aircraft accidents for June and July.
June 1952. Fighter Major Accidents – 100. Fighter Fatalities–21. Fighter Aircraft Destroyed – 36.
July data are preliminary. **July 1952**. Fighter Major Accidents - 135. Fighter Fatalities-30.
Fighter Aircraft Destroyed - 58.

In June and July of 1952 there were 235 USAF fighters involved in major accidents, which resulted in 94 fighter aircraft destroyed and 51 fatalities. In June, there were 148 reports received by Blue Book and in July alone, there were 536 reports received. The two-month total of UFO reports received 684 reports. July 1952 also accounted for the highest amount of UFO reports received by Blue Book in its 17-year history!

At this point I will reiterate Edward Ruppelt's statement, "Other assorted historians point out that normally the UFOs are peaceful, Gorman and Mantell just got too inquisitive, 'they' just weren't ready to be observed closely. *If the Air Force hadn't slapped down the security lid, these writers might not have reached this conclusion. There have been other and more lurid 'duels of death.'"*

How many of these major accidents resulted from interceptor planes being involved in *"lurid duels of death'"* battles with UFOs? How many of these accidents occurred during alleged "routine training missions" that were written off? Now I ask *"If the Air Force hadn't slapped down the security lid,"* how many fighter pilot deaths would we know about today? Fifty-one years later, Captain Ruppelt's messages are now clear. Ruppelt definitely knew about the fighter aircraft situation during that time. His messages and clues were just waiting to be found.

The "Unknown" UFO cases from the files of Project Blue Book contained numerous fighter jet and UFO incidents. Between 1951 and 1960, I compiled twenty-five such "Unknown" incidents that involved fighters and UFOs. The year 1952 contained the most incidents with thirteen cases. They occurred between March 23 and Dec 9, 1952. The month of July had the highest amount of incidents with five "unknown" cases, accounting for one-fifth of these incidents over a nine-year period. These unexplained fighter jet /UFO incidents were among the "Unknown" cases, but I ask how many legitimate cases never made this list? How many legitimate UFO cases were written off and explained away to divert attention away from them?

Professor J. Allen Hynek, as astronomer and a consultant to Project Blue Book for twenty years, stated the following in his book, *The Hynek Report*. He stated, "Sometimes there was no astronomical explanation for the nocturnal lights they [military officers] perceived. Since Blue Book could find no justification for discounting the testimony of highly trained men, nocturnal Light cases were finally evaluated as 'Unidentified.' For some of these, however, the Air Force did try their hardest to come up with a natural explanation was simply not available, Blue Book resorted to the label 'insufficient information.' Anything but 'unidentified.'"

Another Air Force document also obtained by Friedman and dated "22 July 1952," has been recently "DECLASSIFIED" by the US government. This document is stamped "CONFIDENTIAL SECURITY INFORMATION" along the bottom of the page. This document, "AFCF5-4A" is a "MEMORANDUM FOR: GENERAL CRAIG - SUBJECT: (unclassified) Accident Record, First six Months 1952" from the "Office of The Inspector General, USAF Norton Air Force Base"

In Part it states, "USAF ACCIDENT EXPERIENCE FIRST SIX MONTHS 1952" and states "Measurable progress in aviation safety was achieved during the first six months of 1952. Although the sum total of accident losses was tremendous – 479 fatalities and over 1100 major accidents representing a net material loss of $126,000,000 – the occurrence of accidents, when equated against exposure (flying hours) showed detailed improvement over previous half-year periods…Improvement of the accident situation has taken place in spite of the large scale expansion of flying activity. Our experience in the present emergency is completely dissimilar to our experience in the period prior to and during the early part of World War II, when an alarming upswing in accident rates exceeded the increase in total flying activity."

Further documentation appearing in the September 1, 1952 issue of *American Aviation*, stated, "The USAF's flying safety rate promises to set a new record in 1952 if present trends continue. In the first six months of this year, the rate was 29 major accidents per 100,000 flying hours, nine percent under the 1951 record despite substantially higher activity. *Highest accident rate was in jet fighter category with 79 per 100,000 hours*, which nonetheless was down from 97 in the second half of 1951. Other rates included 66 for other (non-jet) type fighters, 10 for cargo aircraft, and 23 for trainers."

According to the General Craig Memo, even though there were 1,100 major USAF aircraft accidents that resulted in 479 deaths during the first 6 months of 1952, the Air Force stated, "Measurable progress in aviation safety was achieved." This aviation safety progress represented "a net material loss of $126,000,000" and that was only the first half of the year!

The Air Force also talks about their "present emergency" in this document. The USAF dictionary defines "emergency, n. (emerg). Any circumstances in which irretrievable loss or disaster threatens, and immediate action is called for." Was the Norton AFB comment about the Air Force's "Present emergency" in reference to their "tremendous" aircraft accident losses? It certainly seems so. During this time, the United States was involved in the Korean War in the Far East. Did all of 1,100 major accidents and 479 fatalities during the first six months of 1952 occur over Korea? The answer, no. During the first six months of 1952, were all of the jet fighters lost by the Air Force lost in the air war over Korea? No. During the entire year of 1952, were all of the jet fighters lost by the Air Force, Navy, and Marines lost in the Korean air war? No.

Did the United States military cover up cases that involved fighter planes, damaged or destroyed, during UFO intercept missions? Is it possible to cover up something this big for so many years? Yes, it is.

The next source of information that I used for my fighter aircraft research was *The New York Times*. I spent countless hours searching through this paper's 1952 index and microfilm rolls looking for major American fighter plane accidents.

I found forty-one articles from 1952 that reported forty-one fighter accident incidents; *in each incident, at least one fighter aircraft was destroyed*. They involved Air Force, Navy and Marine Corps fighter planes yet none of these accidents occurred in Korea or over its airspace. None of these jets was destroyed in the "MIG Alley" air battles. Two accidents occurred over the Pacific, one over Japan, one over Germany, one occurred over England and one near Norway during Operation Mainbrace. The remaining thirty –five major fighter accidents occurred over the United States and its coastal waters. Only two of those incidents over America involved mid air collisions, these occurred between fighter planes and other military aircraft. The remaining thirty-three "major fighter accidents" reported were single accidents involving one plane.

Of the thirty –five major fighter accidents that occurred over the United States and its coastal waters: the Air Force accounted for twenty-four accidents, the navy had eight and the Marine Corps had three. The Air Force, Navy and Marine Corps each had a fighter that vanished over America in 1952, which are included in these accident statistics.

During the first six months of 1952, there were 19 reported fighter plane accidents over America, 14 were Air Force, and four were Navy aircraft and one Marine Corps fighter. The second half of 1952 accounted for the remaining 16 accidents as reported in the Times articles. The Air Force accounted for 10 accidents, the Navy 4 and the Marine Corps 2. Even though these numbers only represent a fraction of the major fighter accidents as recorded by the Air Force, the information contained in these articles was valuable. American fighters were dropping out of the sky around the world, and the majority of the accidents occurred over the United States.

The New York Times reported that these fighter jets were, crashing to the ground, crashing into coastal waters, exploding in mid-air, and running into trouble. Several crashed over America while on "routine training missions." Other articles stated that some fighter pilots reported no problems with their jets shortly before crashing and being killed. Three fighter interceptors simply disappeared into thin air. Several accidents occurred under blatant mysterious circumstances. Why were so many American fighter aircraft falling out of the sky across the United States in 1952?

These forty-one *New York Times* articles represent a very small percentage of the jet fighter accidents that actually occurred in 1952. In 1952, Major General Ramey and the government knew the entire fighter accident situation and never told the press the truth, they were only fed a few morsels of information. How many more fighter jet accidents were never reported to the press in 1952? How many more fighters were lost over America during 1952 that we are don't know about? How many fighters were lost over America when they "raced aloft several hundred times as a result of reported sightings of unidentified objects"?

One night I was online doing research about the United States Air Force in 1952. While searching the internet I discovered that the Air Force had released their cases for Major "Aircraft Accidents of 1952." The "Directorate of Flight Safety Research –Norton Air Force Base, California," documented the cases. These unclassified cases were recorded on a 16 mm microfilm format. These microfilms were from the "Department of the Air Force – Air Force Historical Research Agency – Maxwell Air Force Base, Alabama." The Maxwell AFB Historical Research Agency previously stated, "More than 85 percent of the agency's pre-1955 holdings are declassified and the agency systematically reviews documents for downgrading or declassification." Finally, the 1952 documents were released.

I wanted to see if there were any mysterious fighter plane accidents possibly related to UFO sightings during the summer and fall of 1952. I quickly telephoned Stanton T. Friedman at his home and explained the information that I found and he offered to contact the individual responsible for the holdings. One of the microfilm reels I requested was reel # 34 that contained the major aircraft accident reports for July 26 and 27, 1952; the second week end of the Washington D.C. sightings. I gave Friedman the contact information he needed to obtain the microfilm reels that I was interested in seeing. Mr. Friedman made the contact and a few weeks later, he received the microfilms that I requested. He then mailed them to me and I reviewed them.

The release major accident reports have shed a new light on the history of the Air Forces aircraft activity and problems during that 1952 era. This was also the prime era when the Air Force was chasing flying saucers and UFOs.

The cases that I reviewed involving major fighter accidents did not refer to flying saucers or UFOs. No surprise there! That would have made it too easy to link the fighter accidents together with the UFO sightings during that time. I never expected to find any references to flying saucers in these reports. What I found were some strange and questionable episodes that involved fighter aircraft and I also discovered cases that were missing.

When I reviewed reel # 34 that contained the dates from July 24, 1952 until July 30 1952, I discovered there were four dates that stated, "MISSING FILE." The missing case files are listed below:

1. 52-7-24-3. [July 24, 1952. Case File #3]
2. 52-7-26-4. [July 26, 1952. Case File #4]
3. 52-7-28-1. [July 28, 1952. Case File #1]
4. 52-7-28-8. [July 28, 1952. Case File #8]

One of the many cases that involved fighter jet accidents that I did review occurred on July 27 under unusual circumstances. An F-94B pilot and radar operator from Tyndall AFB in Florida were deployed to O'Hare AFB in Chicago to participate in a special air mission designated "Operation Signpost." This operation was the first joint air defense test on the United States-Canada border. Jet fighters from both countries were involved in a mock warfare and went up against B-36 bombers who acted as a "Russian attack force."

On Sunday morning, July 27, twenty B-36 planes of the Strategic Air Command came out of Canada on their practice sneak attack and headed straight toward Detroit, Michigan. The bombers proceeded south on their mock mission and headed into the heart of the United States.

During this exercise, ADC units detected the invading bombers. The USAF scrambled fighter jets after the B-36s and intercepted them. On that Sunday, there were odd circumstances throughout the entire incident when UFOs were sighted near the planes during this mock warfare bombing-raid.

On July 28, 1952, *The Lansing State Journal* newspaper headline read, "Jet Bombers Bring 'Saucer' Reports." The paper reported that three Lansing residents saw UFOs from a hunting lodge near Onaway. A man, his wife, and their daughter, "reported seeing the 'cigar shaped discs' about 9:40 a.m. Sunday after being awakened twice by a noise which they thought might be bombers overhead. For more than 20 minutes, the trio watched them trail off into the distance in perfect formations, as if guarding a 'mothership' which brought up the rear." Onaway is located in the upper tip of Michigan. It is located just southeast of Cheboygan near Lake Huron where the United States borders Canada. Onaway was in the general flight path line where the B-36 bombers passed over coming out of Canada en route to Detroit. This was the first reported UFO sighting.

The article also stated, "Theirs was not the only reports of 'saucers.' Three persons in south central Michigan also said they saw 'flashing lights' in the sky." The next morning's sighting occurred over Ypsillanty, which is located just southeast of Detroit.

On July 28, *The Ypsillanty Press* newspaper in Michigan, also talked about the Sunday morning sightings that occurred over their town, in an article, "'Things' in Sky Here Sunday Appear like Flying Saucers." This story states the following, "Ypsillanty residents were 'seeing things' too, Sunday, adding to the accumulation of evidence that there are really flying saucers." *The Ypsillanty Press* reported the following incident:

Sunday morning at about 10:15, Warren Erlewine, 437 Owendale, was startled to see a silvery disc sweep over jet planes moving in an arc toward them, before moving away. It was cloudless at the time and he heard planes going south and saw their vapor. He estimated that the 'flying saucer' was between 200 and 300 feet across and faster in flight than [the] jets. The UFO was first noticed north of the jet planes and appeared to be circular. He saw it east to southeast of his residence, apparently in the vicinity of the air terminal.

The Lansing State Journal article also reported, "Descriptions of the 'things' varied from cigar shaped to looking like flying saucers. The Air Force at Selfridge field [Mt. Clemens] where some of the 'things' were reportedly seen refused to comment." I wonder why the Air Force made no public comment about the UFO sightings. Was the Air Force trying to hide something from the public that occurred that day? Obviously so, officials at Selfridge AFB, did report a UFO sighting to Project Blue Book on July 27, 1952. Furthermore, it was also evaluated as an "Unknown" incident, Case 1680!

The F-94B Starfire accident in question occurred during the "Operation Signpost" exercise on that Sunday morning. It was recorded by the Air Force in accident case # "52-7-27-3." The following story is how the Air Force explained the first of two scrambles that involved this fighter jet accident. The "Aircraft Flight Report" states the times of the scrambles and longevity of the flights in local time, CST. It reported the first flight started, "FROM-10:20" and lasted "TO-11:25." This report then states the total length of the mission; "MISSION-1:05" or one hour and five minutes from takeoff until landing.

In this accident case file, the "Medical Report of an Individual- Involved in AF Aircraft Accident" stated otherwise. It reported the pilot, Colonel William Jones and radar operator Captain Romeo Ferretti "flew on an interceptor mission in an F-94 lasting 1:30 hours" or one hour and thirty minutes. According to this same report it was then said, "Approximately 30 minutes after landing another scramble mission was called. Officer Jones ran approximately 150 yards to his aircraft. Accident occurred 15 minutes later."

There is a 25 minute time differential between these two reports. Why does one report state the mission as "lasting 1:30 hours" or one hour and thirty minutes and the other report states it lasted "1:05", or one hour and five minutes? The correct length of time of this mission was actually one hour and thirty minutes. Why does a 25-minute discrepancy appear between the reports? Twenty-five minutes is a long period to be unaccounted for while flying around in an interceptor jet. Was there a harmless mistake in the "Aircraft Flight Report" or was this actually part of a cover up to hide what Jones and Ferretti were doing during the unaccounted 25-minutes?

Jones and Feretti were actually scrambled five minutes after the 200-300 foot "flying saucer" was reported to have swept toward the jets in an arc over Ypsillanty and then moved away. Was this a coincidence or were Jones and Feretti scrambled on a UFO intercept mission that had nothing to do with "Operation Signpost"? Colonel Jones was a prime candidate. He was a "Senior Pilot" and was recorded as having a "total flying time of 3,400 hours." Jones was no rookie to fighter aircraft and had "75 hours" of flying time in the F-94 Starfire.

Then there was the second scramble, "Approximately 30 minutes after landing another scramble mission was called." During the second intercept scramble, the report states that, "eight F-94Bs were scrambled from O'Hare." The "Aircraft Flight Report" states the second flight started, "FROM-12:25" and lasted "TO-12:40." The total length of time of the "MISSION-15" or fifteen minutes. At the bottom of this document, it states, "ENTER TOTAL FLIGHT TIME ON REVERSE SIDE," yet that designated area, "TOTAL FLIGHT TIME" was left blank! The Medical Report stated, "Accident occurred 15 minutes later." Among the eight jets scrambled were flyers Jones and Feretti, they were scrambled by "Bolster" Ground Control Intercept. There was a five-minute inconsistency in the time that the second scramble was said to have occurred:

1. The "Aircraft Flight Report" states, "FROM-12:25."
2. The "REPORT OF AF ACCIDENT REPORT" states, "1230 CST."

Nevertheless, at this point, I ask the following:
1. Was this eight-jet scramble part of the "Operation Signpost" mock air war exercises, or
2. Was this an actual scramble alert against UFOs, or
3. Did these jets encounter UFOs in the air during their war exercise?
4. Were these jets armed when they were scrambled on those two occasions?

Minutes after takeoff, Jones and Feretti were approximately 30 miles west of O'Hare and climbing to an altitude of 14,000 feet. The report states, "The aircraft had reached 14,000 feet at climb power settings with the engine in afterburner." It was said that Colonel Jones stated, "Upon reaching approximately 14,000 feet the cockpit filled with smoke and I believed the cockpit to be on fire. The smoke smelled like an oil fire. I pulled the throttle out of afterburner and went back to idle position." Something very unusual also occurred during the time that the smoke filled the cockpit. According to the pilot, "The fire warning lights were not on nor were any other warning lights. The smoke thinned but kept coming in, with the throttle at idle. The engine started to vibrate."

The pilot then notified Ground Control of the problem and stated he was, "aborting and returning to O'Hare." Radar Operator Captain Ferretti stated, "I observed excessive smoke in the cockpit and also heard vibrations in the art section of the aircraft. Col. Jones alerted me to prepare for ejection in case this emergency situation became critical."

Major Ernest Biggs, one of the other Starfire pilots who was on this interceptor mission stated, "My call sign was Gleaner Orange…I heard Gleaner Block [Jones and Ferretti] call, 'May day, Bolster Control, smoke in the cockpit, what is your nearest base.' Bolster advised the vector to O'Hare was 90 degrees – but seemed hesitant to give [Jones and Ferretti] Instructions." Why did Ground Control Intercept hesitate to give instructions at this point? Where there other factors involved that were not disclosed? GCI radar controllers are highly skilled technicians whose quick split decisions can mean the difference between life and death. The circumstances of this entire event seem very odd .

At this point in flight pilot Major Biggs then, "maneuvered into very close formation and looked the aircraft over…he then called O'Hare and cleared runway 14 for his [Colonel Jones] landing." Biggs then followed the damaged and smoking jet back to O'Hare. Biggs actually observed the damaged Starfire make its emergency landing and crash as he flew over the base area. He stated the following, "I saw a wheel roll off the runway. At this time both myself and my radar operator observed a flash of fire from the nose section…I continued on my intercept mission."

Upon landing his damaged Starfire, Colonel Jones stated, "I had excessive speed, which I knew as the last time I saw the airspeed was 150 kilometers…The nose wheel came off on the third porpoise and the aircraft settled on the stub of the nose gear and came to a stop on the end of the runway." To make matters worse, once the jet finally stopped the cockpit canopy was malfunctioned. The pilot stated, "The canopy would not raise electronically." The two aviators had to manually open the canopy and "physically pushed upward to assist opening," according to the radar operator. The pilot of the damaged Starfire stated, "At this time, I do not know what caused the smoke or the vibration in the aft section."

In a letter dated July 31, 1952, a Field Service Representative for Allison Division, GMC, stated the following information after a preliminary investigation of the jet's engine:

After completing a preliminary investigation on the engine installed in the F-94, we have been unable to discover any cause for the smoke in the cockpit or the reported engine vibration. No evidence of oil leakage was found in the plenum chamber area, around the engine accessory mounting pads or on any of the external oil pads. However, our inspection was hampered by not being able to take the engine out of the aircraft. No doubt a more thorough and complete inspection can be made by the people at Tyndall AFB when they have the engine removed.

There is evidence of slight oil loss from the engine accessory case breather located on the bottom of the fuselage .This is the latest type ram vent installed with a 1" spacer for slight ram pressurization of the accessory case. I DO NOT BELIEVE THAT THE LEAKAGE HERE COULD HAVE CAUSED THE LOSS OF 2 QUARTS OF OIL IN A 15 MINUTE FLIGHT.

We motored the engine with the starter several times and could detect no roughness or unusual noise that might indicate that a bearing had failed. EACH TIME THE ENGINE COASTED SMOOTHLY TO A STOP. As nearly as we could determine there were no broken turbine buckets. SEVERAL BRIGHT SPOTS ON THE OUTER RING OF THE NOZZLE DIAPHRAGM AND ON THE TURBINE SHROUD SEGMENTS SHOULD BE CHECKED WHEN THE ENGINE IS REMOVED FROM THE AIRCRAFT.

Robert E. Wilson

A Tyndall AFB supervisor said that when the engine of the jet was removed by a maintenance crew at Tyndall AFB in Florida, it was "exceptionally clean and no evidence of overheating at any point of the engine or accessories."

He stated in a report that, "The turbine assembly for the Cabin Cooling system was removed. The bearing in this assembly had started to fail." The Supervisor also stated, "Five pieces of this assembly showed signs of heat and excessive wear. This condition would cause smoke in the cockpit and excessive vibration while the turbine was in operation." The "Engineering Officers Report" said that there was a "Defective air cooling Turbine assembly." There are questions in this incident to raise here:

1. Where did the two quarts of oil disappear to, as pointed out by the Allison engine field representative?
2. Why is there is no mention of the excessive oil loss problem by the Tyndall AFB supervisor?
3. What caused the jet to lose two quarts of during its 15-minute interception flight?
4. When the Allison engine field representative motored the engine several times he said there was "no roughness." Why didn't the engine vibrate during that point?
5. What were the "several bright spots" on the engine, that the Allison engine field representative wrote in the report? He said that they should be checked when the engine was removed. Why was he concerned with them? Where they radioactive?
6. Why is there no mention of the bright spots in the Tyndall AFB report?
7. The Senior Pilot flying the jet stated, "The fire warning lights were not on nor were any other warning Lights." Why did the warning lights fail to come on?
8. Why was the warning light system of the jet not working? The pilot raised the point, so why wasn't the point addressed anywhere in the accident report? Was there a problem with the on board electrical system of the Starfire?
9. When the jet came in for its landing, why did it come in at a very high excessive rate of speed?
10. When the Starfire landed, what caused the electrical system to malfunction and not open the canopy?

11. Did the group of eight F-94 jets attempt to intercept one or more UFOs?
12. Did these two airmen actually have an encounter with a UFO that caused their aircraft to have a mid-air malfunction?
13. Is it just another coincidence, that another fighter jet fell from the sky with a problem in the vicinity where UFOs were sighted? Other UFO sightings also occurred later that night. They are listed below:
  1.) Ionia Airport, Michigan. Witnesses: Two GOC watchers of "Operation Skywatch."
  2.) Battle Creek, Michigan. Witnesses: Several GOC watchers saw "football-shaped" objects.
  3.) Battle Creek, Michigan. Witness: A housewife saw "14 very bright objects, blurred at the edges."
  4.) Battle Creek, Michigan. Witness: An accountant "said it looked like a giant bulb."
  5.) Lyons, Michigan. Witness: A machinist saw "a brilliant white light hovering in the sky."
  6.) Detroit, Michigan. Witnesses: "Several citizens reported seeing 'yellowish-orange things' hovering in the sky.

Another incident occurred on July 27, 1952, that involved a jet and a UFO. This episode happened over Georgia. An Air Force pilot, Mr. Eugene R. Henderson, did not disclose his encounter until 17 years later when he wrote a personal letter about his encounter to NICAP. In his letter dated, "4 August 1969," he wrote about his aerial sighting that occurred while he was flying his T-33 jet over the area of Moody AFB, located in Valdosta, where he had just departed from. The pilot wrote the following:

I was about 20,000 feet when I saw an object in the right side of the windshield. I instinctually started to turn away either right or left. But my mind did not have enough information, i.e. was the object going from right to left or the reverse, or was it coming toward me or away. Upon analyzing the situation for a second or two, I found that its position wasn't changing much. Since it appeared circular, I assumed I was flying directly behind another jet aircraft. After observing it for several seconds, I could see no wings or horizontal or vertical stabilizer. The object started emitting thin smoke or vapor and suddenly started climbing, relatively slow at first, then incredibly fast. The initial acceleration was in a zigzag fashion, then straight. It was out of sight in a matter of a few seconds. I was in a T-33, climbing at about 230 mph.

This incident is not documented in any official Air Force records. How many other incidents involving jets and UFOs were not made public through military channels? On the following day, July 28, 1952, the UFOs were back over the northeast United States and sighted in large numbers over New Jersey. Blue book listed this case, Case 1707 as an "Unknown." At 6:00 a.m., McGuire AFB Control Tower operators, in New Jersey, tracked a "large cluster" of targets on their radarscopes, described as "very distinct blips." Several men were in the base Control Tower at the time of the incident, including the Ground Control Approach radar operator, "M/Sgt. W.F.Dees." The entire episode lasted for 55 minutes, and during that time, a visual observation was made as well. The UFOs were described as, "oblong objects" and had no appendages. It was also stated that they had "no wings" and "no tails." At one point during the visual observation, witnesses said the objects were "in echelon formation."

Later that morning at 10:30 a.m., it was said that an "F-51H Mustang" fighter plane on an "ANG Flight," had a mid-air explosion shortly after practicing "Ground Control Approaches" at McGuire AFB. This same Control Tower was also involved in tracking the UFOs earlier that morning.

The "Directorate of Flight Safety Research –Norton Air Force Base, California", documented this case, "52-7-28-5." This incident involved four F-51 Mustangs of the "139th FIGHTER INTERCEPTOR SQUADRON, WESTCHESTER COUNTY AIRPORT, WHITE PLAINS, NEW YORK."

The description of accident states the F-51 Mustang "was on an authorized routine training mission from Reading, Pennsylvania. After completing, a number of GCA [Ground Control Approach] runs at McGuire Air Force Base the aircraft rejoined his flight at approximately 6,000 feet and proceeded to clear out his engine at full power. During this procedure, an explosion was heard in engine section, and the engine acted very erratically, cutting in and out. Pilot tried all emergency procedures with no success. At 2,000 feet pilot abandoned aircraft. Aircraft crashed into a wooded area." The pilot "1st lt. John Jelke III" was said to have "successfully parachuted down." This "REPORT OF AIRCRAFT ACCIDENT" dated "5 Aug 52," is filled with inconsistencies and questionable procedures as handled by certain Air Force personnel. One such example was brought forth in a letter stamped and dated "13 NOV 52," and titled from the "HEADQUARTERS, FIRST AIR FORCE, Mitchel Air Force Base, New York."

The following letter was written by "H. M. Turner-Major General, USAF Commanding." and sent "TO: Commanding General, Continental Air Command, Mitchel Air Force Base, New York."

In part this letter states:

1. In general, this Report of Investigation is considered to be unsatisfactory.
2. The following irregularities were noted:
a. The report does not reveal whether or not a reasonable effort was made to determine the cause of engine failure prior to shipment to depot for disassembly.
b. Pilots statement does not provide a complete description of events prior to, and after, engine failure.
c. Form 54, "Unsatisfactory Report" pertaining to engine is not attached to AF form 14 C, Engineering Officers Report, as required by paragraph 47a, (7), AFR 62-14…
3. It is recommended that the Commanding Officer, 568th Air Base Group, McGuire AFB, Trenton, New Jersey, be advised of the irregularities contained in the Report of Investigation…
4. This headquarters was not informed of this accident thru normal reporting procedures (preliminary report) as required by Section V, AFR 62-14…
5. A letter will be sent to Headquarters, New York Air National Guard, New York, requesting that action be taken regarding this matter.

I will now raise the following points and questions:
1. Why was there a lack of information concerning the plane's engine inspection before it was sent away for disassembly?
2. Why did the pilot's statement not provide a description of the events leading to his accident?
3. Why were there so many irregularities contained in the Report of Investigation?
4. Why the "Continental Air Command" not notified of the accident after it occurred?
5. Why was the Report of Investigation vague in its details?
6. Were officials at McGuire AFB and Norton AFB hiding the truth?

The USAF later stated that the cause of the engine failure was "Failure of A-4 rear intake valve that is believed to have resulted from excessive seating velocity of intake valve allowed by excessive valve to tappet clearance. Excessive valve to tappet clearance occurred when the retaining nut became loose and subsequently allowed tappet to turn to extreme 'open' position. RECOMMENDATIONS- those maintenance personnel at all activities be informed of this crash which resulted from improper tightening of the camshaft rocker tappet nut."

7. Did this accident occur because of a nut being improperly tightened, or did the engine explode because the plane was involved in a UFO encounter?

The July nightmare had finally ended, but the month of August was a whole other story. Edward Ruppelt had stated, "I was anxious to start enlisting the aid of scientist, as General Samford had directed but before this could be done we had a backlog of UFO reports that had to be evaluated. During July, we had been swamped and had picked off only the best ones. Some of the reports we were working on during August had simple answers, but many were unknowns." How much valuable information was lost during this time?

Chapter 8

STARFIRES AND SABRE JETS

Project Blue Book received "326" reports for the month of August. They only evaluated 27 cases as "Unknown" for the month. Five of those unexplained cases directly involved UFOs and Air Force Base sightings. The following is a list of those cases:
1. Case 1783. August 2, 1952. Lake Charles AFB. Lake Charles, LA.
2. Case 1827. August 5, 1952. Haneda AFB, Japan. (Control Tower)
3. Case 1870. August 9, 1952. Lake Charles AFB. Lake Charles, LA.
4. Case 1979. August 25, 1952. Holloman AFB. Alamogordo, NM.
5. Case 2006. August 28, 1952. Brookley AFB. Mobile, AL & Chickasaw, LA

I also searched the August "Unknown" cases that reported incidents between UFOs and United States Air Force fighter jets. Project Blue Book reported three cases that involved a direct interaction between either a fighter and UFO, or a fighter pilot being in the area of a UFO who reported a sighting. They are as follows: 1. Case 1827. August 5, 1952. Haneda AFB, Japan 2. Case 1889. August 13, 1952. Tokyo, Japan. 3. Case 1961. August 24, 1952. Hermanas, NM.

In 1952, the primary fighter jets used by the USAF to protect the U.S. and its borders were the Lockheed F-94 Starfire, and the North American F-86 Sabre Jet. *The Unicorn Book of 1952 Outstanding Events of the Year* stated, "So fast and so intricate did new aircraft become that their human pilots were obsolescent [sic]. The Air Force unveiled semiautomatic interceptors such as the Lockheed F-94C Starfire, and the D model of the North American F-86 Sabre. Each fired 2.75-inch rockets rather than conventional but less lethal guns, and was laden with 1,000 odd pounds of electronic gear. This electronic brain, faster and surer than the human brain, picked up the enemy bomber, charted its course, guided the interceptor toward the target, and selected the instant to fire the rockets. Electronic gear on [the] plane picks the moment to fire rockets, each one of which could bring down (the) biggest bomber ever built."

The North American F-86 Sabre Jet was the first swept wing aircraft in the United States inventory of fighter jets. The F-86D version was an all-weather interceptor that had a top speed of 650 miles per hour. This jet was armed with twenty-four "Mighty Mouse" rockets that were carried in a retractable carriage in the fuselage. This carriage would lower on an elevator to fire the rockets and then retract back up into the body of the jet. The D-model featured a 35 degree swept back wing and tail and was designed with an under slung engine air-intake channel at the front of the fuselage for airflow.

This jet was equipped with aerodynamically actuated wing leading-edge slats that were used for high lift and a hydraulically power-operated irreversible controls system. These controls gave the jet an artificial feel for an all-movable tail, ailerons and its rudder. It had a service ceiling of more than 45,000 feet and had a range of about 1,000 statute miles. The F-86D Sabre Jet and the F-94C Starfire were the United States Air Forces top all-weather interceptor jets in their inventory during that time. Both were true examples of modern jet fighters.

On August 1, 1952, the Air Force was back in the skies in hot pursuit of the saucers once again. The following incident involved F-86 Sabre Jets on an interception mission. An August 2, 1952, *The New York Times* headline read, "Make Positive Statement. DAYTON, Ohio, Aug. 1 (AP)" It was stated, "Reports by interceptor pilots today marked the first time pilots checking on flying saucer reports here made such a positive statement." This article referenced "two interceptors" that were scrambled after they "had received five or six reports of 'flying saucers'" It was said, "The pilots, attached to the Ninety-seventh Fighter wing were Major James Smith and 1st Lt. Donald Hermer." ATIC officials at Wright –Patterson AFB, "immediately banned the two pilots from commenting further on their experiences and ordered a ban on pictures of the two."

North American F-86D Sabre Jet

Donald Keyhoe spoke about this incident in his 1953 book, *Flying Saucers from Outer Space*. Keyhoe had the Intelligence report for this incident cleared to him, which also included the ATIC analysis report. This was only one of several Intelligence case reports he was allowed to read. Keyhoe met with public liaison Albert Chop at the Pentagon on August 21. He was given all of the reports to review including this case. Keyhoe called it "The Bellefontaine sighting."

The incident unfolded at 10:51 a.m. in Ohio. Keyhoe stated, "The strange machine was seen from the ground by several civilians near Bellefontaine. It appeared to be round, with a shiny, metallic gleam." At 10:51 a.m., radar men at the 664th AC &W radar site near Bellefontaine had spotted "blips" that "came on the scope." Shortly after, two F-86 Sabre Jets were sent after the target in question. Upon reaching an altitude of 30,000 feet, the two pilots saw a UFO maneuvering above them. It was described as, "a bright, round, glowing object" by pilots Smith and Hermer.

The two Sabre Jets soared higher to an altitude of 40,000 feet in pursuit of the object. Major Smith was able to get gun-camera film footage of the UFO. Keyhoe Stated, "As he began the camera run, Smiths radar gun sight had caught the saucer for a moment." He went on and said, "From the range of his radar set, Major Smith knew the unknown device must be between 12,000 and 20,000 above him to cause such a weak blip." The UFO then accelerated and vanished.

Major Keyhoe stated, "For the first time a saucer had been photographed during simultaneous radar and visual sightings, with the camera also locked on by radar. It was absolute proof that this saucer was a solid object, a controlled, disc-shaped machine." He also stated that, "The intelligence report on this case which had been cleared for me, also included the ATIC analysis." The following information was from that Intelligence report in reference to the incident:

A.) "The Ground radar squadron established two facts: Reaffirmation that the UFO moved at 400 knots (480 land mph) and indications that the F-86s and the UFO appeared simultaneously on the GCI [Ground Control Intercept] scope. It is obvious that all eyes and antennas put a fix on the same object."

B.) "The object was obviously not a balloon, since the speed was too fast (a radiosonde balloon was released at 1500 zebra [10 a.m. Central Time] and moved off to the east. The object was sighted north-

northwest of the base.) "The object moved against the wind, its blip size that of a normal craft.

The object was not a known aircraft because the altitude was too high. It was not astronomical, as the dual radar returns eliminate this."

C.) "The electronic or visual image of meteorological phenomena is out of the question, as the radar set was high on the beam and both would not occur simultaneously in the same place. The sighting occurred above the weather. Conclusion: Unknown." Keyhoe stated, "I put down the report and looked at Chop.' You know of course what this does to the press conference story."

When Keyhoe wrote about this incident and it appeared in his 1953 book, *Flying Saucers from Outer Space*, the report stated that this case was evaluated as an "Unknown."

Before the release of this 1953 book, Keyhoe mentioned this incident in the December 1952 issue of "True" magazine, in an article, "What radar tells about Flying Saucers." Keyhoe had been working in collaboration with the Air Force and gathering information for this particular article. In this article, he states the following information about the case:

No final conclusion has been made by the ATIC in this case. That this might have been a balloon, as suggested, does not stand up, for two reasons. First, and most important, no balloon can hover, and suddenly race off, out distancing the jets. Second, ordinary weather balloons will not show on radarscopes…All weather balloon records are available to the ATIC and no radar target was available.

Edward Ruppelt also wrote about this same incident as well. Three years later, Edward Ruppelt said the following in his 1956 book, *The Report On Unidentified Flying Objects*. According to Ruppelt, Lieutenant Andy Flues, assigned this case, had reversed his unknown decision. Ruppelt said, "He talked to the two pilots a half dozen times and spent a day at the radar site at Bellefontaine before he reversed his 'Unknown' decision and came up with the answer. The unidentified target the radar had tracked across Ohio was a low flying jet. The jet was unidentified because there was a mix-up and the radar station didn't get its flight plan."

Ruppelt also talked about the balloon involved in the incident that was in the vicinity as well. It was said to be a "20-foot-diameter radiosonde weather balloon from Wright Patterson." He explained, "When the ground controller blended the two F-86s into the unidentified target, they were at 30,000 feet and were looking for the target at their altitude or higher so they missed the low flying jet-but they did see the balloon."

Ruppelt then stated, "The only part of the sighting that still wasn't explained was the radar pickup on the F-86s gun sight." He also explained this away, "The people in the photo lab made a few calculations and measurements, and came up with the answer, 'A 20-foot balloon photographed from 30,000 feet away would be the same size as the UFO in the gun camera photos."

Edward Ruppelt stated that Lieutenant Flues "wrote it off as an unknown but it still bothered him; that the balloon in the area was mighty suspicious." This supposedly prompted Flues to reinvestigate the case. I ask,

1. Was there really a "mix-up" in the incident as Ruppelt put it?
2. Did this report really bother Lieutenant Flues or the higher up Intelligence officials who
released the report to him?
3. Was there another reason the evaluation of this report was reversed?
4. Was Keyhoe set up by intelligence, because they knew they were going to reverse the case after he read it; thinking he would look foolish by writing about it in his book and then disclosing another story later?

Donald Keyhoe stated something interesting in his 1953 book in reference to the December 1952 article he wrote for *True Magazine*. He said that the article he had written for *True Magazine* was already finished when the "Bellefontaine sighting analysis" and other cases given to him at the Pentagon to review. These cases were "left out [of the *True Magazine* article] because of a last minute double-check on clearance." He stated, "When the final word came, True's presses were already rolling."

Albert Chop had asked Donald Keyhoe to come to the Pentagon just before the *True Magazine* article went to press. Chop stated to Keyhoe, "I've got an insert the Air Defense Command wants you to use." It was a statement from Major General Roger Ramey, Director of USAF Operations. The statement reads, "No orders have been issued to the Air Defense Command, or by the Air Defense Command, to its fighter units to fire on unidentified aerial phenomena. The Air Force, in compliance with its mission of air defense of the United States, must assume responsibility for investigation of any object or phenomena in the air over the United States. Fighter units have been instructed to investigate any object observed or established as existing by radar tracks, and to intercept any airborne object identified as hostile or showing hostile interest. This should not be interpreted to mean that Air Defense pilots have been instructed to fire haphazardly on anything that flies."

When the December issue of *True Magazine* appeared shortly after it gave the following edited version of Major General Ramey's statement, "No orders have been issued to the Air Defense Command or by the Air Defense Command, to its fighter units to fire on unidentified aerial phenomena."

This article also stated the following information, "In a new investigation of the flying saucer, *TRUE Magazine* has secured Air Force confirmation of these important facts:" Point Two on the facts list refers to the fighter scrambles after UFOs and states, *"More than 300 times, Air Force interceptor planes have chased mysterious lights and unidentified objects revealed by radar scopes."* Donald Keyhoe stated, "week after week, jet fighters are 'scrambled' at points around the country for 'saucer' chases."

On August 1, another jet fighter incident occurred. This sighting happened in the evening during an Air Force night flight mission. The story appeared in *The New York Times* on August 2, 1952. The headline states, "Mystery Photo, Jet Pilots' Report Added to Flying Saucer Puzzle." This WASHINGTON, Aug. 1. (AP) story explained, "A report from jet pilots on a night flight [stated] that an object they sighted was not a reflection, added new twists today to the 'flying saucer' puzzle." Further information states:

Sighted at 17,000 Feet

The pilots said that at an altitude of 17,000 feet they had watched an object having a bright red light for ten seconds. They said they deliberately maneuvered around to be sure it was not a light reflection. It hovered, they said, then disappeared at a high rate of speed.

The New York Times also reported that, "The new sighting report was turned in by the interceptor pilots at Wright-Patterson Air Force Base, in Ohio. This is the location of the Air Force's Air Technical Center which checks up on outlandish things aloft." This was the second fighter story to appear in this paper on that day.

On August 2, 1952, the *Associated Press* released a news story from the Air Defense Headquarters at Ent AFB in Colorado Springs, Colorado. On August 1, a Public Information Officer claimed how the Air Force was taking the current flap of UFO sightings across the country very seriously. He also explained that many of the UFO reports came through official government channels. The PIO also talked about how active the Air Force was during the flap and stated, "We've really been scrambling," but he refused to say a word about the results of the fighter interceptions.

An *Associated Press* news release from "Hamilton AFB" dated "3 August 1952," reported an incident that involved an intercept attempt in California the day before. At 5:45 p.m. that day, "eight silver-colored objects" passed Marin County, California. One of their pilots who saw them from his nearby home had contacted the 83rd Fighter Interceptor Squadron at Hamilton. The pilot called his base shortly after the eight UFOs passed over him and reported his sighting. Ground Control Intercept radar also tracked the targets on their scopes and GOC spotters also called in with reports. The UFOs flew at about "8,000 ft." and were heading west in an "irregular diamond formation." During their flight, the objects altered their "diamond formation" and then flew in a "single file" formation.

Moments later, a scramble alert went out and "three F-86" Sabre Jets took to the skies after the eight objects. By the time that the fighter jets got into the air and started their pursuit, the objects were too far ahead of them. The objects disappeared before the fighter jets reached their altitude.

This incident does not appear in the Project Blue Book "Unknown" cases. Shortly after the incident though, Donald Keyhoe went to the Pentagon, and met Albert Chop and read the "Air Technical Intelligence Center" report for this case. Keyhoe stated the name of the pilot who notified the base after watching the objects was, "Lieutenant D.A. Swimley." He actually observed the objects with a pair of binoculars, which prompted his call to Hamilton AFB. Keyhoe stated, "When an Intelligence officer questioned Swimley, he estimated the discs to be 60-100 feet in diameter. ' And don't tell me they were reflections,' he added. 'I know they were solid objects.'"

Earlier that day at Lake Charles AFB in Louisiana, a UFO sighting occurred over the vicinity of that base located in Charles Lake. This UFO sighting was evaluated as an "Unknown" case in the Project Blue Book records. Case 1783 states, at "3:00 A.M." a witness, "1st Lieutenant W. A. Theil" and another enlisted man saw an object in the sky. It was described as a "Ball with a blue flame tail" trailing behind it as it flew through the sky on a "straight and level" trajectory." The witnesses saw the UFO for an estimated "3 to 4 seconds."

"'Saucer Man' Doubts Disks Exist; Says Air Force Finds No Basis." This headline story appeared in *The New York Times* on August 4, 1952 and was date lined "Washington, August 3 (AP)." On August 3, Major General Roger Ramey was interviewed on the CBS television show *Man of the Week* in front of a national audience. During his interview, he spoke about the flying saucer situation over the country and had a few choice words to say. The Times reported what he had to say, "Maj. Gen. Roger M. Ramey, the Air Force 'saucer man,' said today that six years of flying saucer reports had 'reasonably well' convinced him there was no such thing." The article also reported, "Not one of some 1,500 saucer reports since 1947, General Ramey said, has offered solid evidence that anything material was involved."

Major General Ramey, the so-called "saucer man," made the following statements about the "Unidentified objects" on that same TV show:

1. "We are reasonably well convinced they are not material, solid objects"
2. "About 20 percent of the reports in Air Force hands remain to be unexplained"
3. "I can definitely say they (saucers) are not our own." [It is interesting to note here that the writer inserted the word "(saucers)" in authors' brackets]. Ramey was actually referring to the 20 percent of unexplained sightings, moreover, not referring to the saucers.
4. "I still believe they, are some phenomena that is not easily explained"
5. "The radar sightings have been sporadic. There has been no suggestive pattern established."
6. "Some people see things that aren't there. Some people describe things they haven't seen."

It is apparent that the government wanted to reach the masses of the public to debunk the saucers and calm the UFO situation. Major General Ramey was just the man to do the job…on national television.

The magazine, *Aviation Week* wrote about the flying saucers in their August 4, 1952 issue. They stated the following information in the "NEWS DIGEST" section of their periodical, "DOMESTIC." It reads, "Flying Saucer" reports are being received by the Air Force at the rate of 100 month and all are being investigated. Recent flurry of 'radar sightings' is attributed to radar's well- known habit of getting responses from rain, birds, weather fronts, and other natural phenomena. Only one-fifth of reports are from 'credible observers,' says USAF, and keeps being concerned about them." One thing was true; The USAF did continue to be concerned about "them"…the flying saucers and continued to scramble after them.

AUGUST 5, 1952 - WESTOVER AND WASHINGTON

August 5, 1952, was the halfway point of the summer of 1952 and UFO sightings continued to be reported throughout the United States. Author Max Miller, who was the President of the "Flying Saucers International," organization, said the following in the August issue of *MYSTIC MAGAZINE*, titled, WHAT ARE THE FLYING SAUCERS. He stated, "Elliot Rockmore, President of the Flying Saucer Researchers of Brooklyn, estimates that he received from four to six hundred flying saucer sightings from newspaper sources in mid-summer 1952, rivaling the Air Forces own files." August 5 was truly a banner day for UFO sightings across the United States that involved a series of events that actually culminated into another flap that occurred over Washington D.C.

This flap, not as well known as the twin July sightings, should actually be considered the third major UFO visitation to the Capitol during the summer of 1952. The UFO sightings on August 5 actually began early that morning just after midnight and continued into the early afternoon hours of the day. By mid afternoon, a Westover Air Force Base F-86 Sabre Jet from Massachusetts lay crashed and burning in the small town of South Glastonbury, Connecticut near Hartford. By evening, the UFOs were back over Washington D.C. and being chased by fighter jets.

The first early morning UFO sighting that occurred that day actually took place over Westover AFB, located in Chicopee Falls, Massachusetts. This base is located about 12 miles north of the Connecticut state border, 29 miles northeast of Hartford, CT and only about 42 miles due north of South Glastonbury.

Westover AFB was a major command of the Air Defense Command and a subcommand of the Eastern Air Defense Force and played a key role in the Korean War between 1950 and 1954. This base took part in major operations and transported freight, Air Force personnel and troops to the Far East during this time. Troop casualties were also brought back to the Westover Hospital, making this base one of the heaviest traveled AF bases over that four-year period.

The early morning UFO sighting at Westover AFB on August 5, was described in a "Air Intelligence Information Report," It was dated "11 Aug 52," and written by Lieutenant Colonel Robert Jones, and gave the details of the UFO incident that unfolded on "5 Aug 52."

At 12:25 a.m., it was reported that three UFOs flew in a "triangular formation" over Westover AFB at an estimated altitude of "5,000 feet." Ground personnel who saw the group of UFOs described them as brilliant white dots and the lead object was said to have looked like an automobile headlight. The witnesses stated that the UFOs were flying, "faster than jets" as they passed over the area. During the sighting, there was no jet activity recorded by Westover AFB officials.

Later that morning another unusual sighting occurred over Augusta Georgia at 7:30 a.m. that gained some attention. *The New York Times* reported the incident on August 6, 1952 in the following article:

'Shapeless Light' Sighted At Hydrogen Bomb Plant - By The Associated Press.

AUGUSTA, Ga., Aug. 5 – A "shapeless incandescent flash of light" was reported over the Atomic Energy Commissions billion-dollar hydrogen bomb project early today. Officials said, "Appropriate authorities have been notified." The brilliant flash was first reported by an official of the E.I. du Pont de Nemours Company, which is building the plant. They told *The Augusta Chronicle* the flash had been observed at 7:30 a.m. and "looked to me like a huge bulb in a flash camera." He added that "many persons" said they observed the unusual sight at the same time. Later in the day, an official of the A.E.C., who like the du Pont asked to remain anonymous, said he had no logical explanation.

The next sighting that day occurred in the early afternoon. It was reported from Baltimore, Maryland, according to the NICAP publication, "UFO Investigator." This publication dated 1958; "Volume I, #5" gave details of this daytime sighting. Donald Keyhoe also reported on this sighting in his 1960 book, *Flying Saucers Top Secret*.

The witness, Dr. James C. Bartlett, was a well-known Baltimore, MD astronomer and had written several scientific articles in various astronomy journals. Dr. Bartlett's UFO sightings occurred as "he was making a daylight observation of Venus" from his Baltimore location. His sightings lasted over an eight-minute time span between 12:12 p.m. and 12:20 p.m. EST/1:20 p.m. EDT. His first sighting involved two objects that he described as "copper" in color. Donald Keyhoe reported, "The two disc-shaped objects passed to the south of Baltimore, then turned east."

Shortly after, while watching the sky, Keyhoe reported that Bartlett said, "He saw two more discs overhead." The report stated that Dr. Bartlett said the middle portion of objects were "30 degrees of arc" in appearance. He described this feature as, "bump like." Keyhoe stated, "Like the dome UFOs frequently described." These flying saucer types were seen quite often during 1952 and throughout the 1950s.

In the northeast at 2:25 p.m. EST/3:25 p.m. EDT, an F-86E Sabre Jet from Westover AFB, in Chicopee Falls, Massachusetts, had crashed and burned in a wooded area on the outskirts of South Glastonbury. This incident interested me when I first read about it in an August 6, 1952, article in *The New York Times*:

PILOT TRAPPED IN FALLING JET

SOUTH GLASTONBURY, Conn. Aug. 5 (AP) – A Royal Air Force exchange pilot, trapped in a powerless F-86 Sabre jet, hammered his way out and parachuted to safety seconds before the plane crashed here today. A companion jet managed to land at nearby Rentschler Field. Both had been returning to Westover Field, Mass., when their planes ran out of fuel. The first pilot said he was in a heavy overcast when the engine failed. He pulled the button to open the canopy over the cockpit and eject him from the plane, but the mechanism jammed and he found himself trapped in a falling jet. He stood up and battered the canopy with his arms and helmet, he said, until it was opened. He was at 4,000 feet when he finally freed himself and jumped.

This article attracted my attention, as Westover AFB was certainly no stranger to the UFO. On the morning of this jet crash, August 5, 1952, three UFOs flew over Westover AFB. On July 23, 1952, only 13 days before, officials documented four "SPOT INTELLIGENCE REPORT" cases involving UFO activity. Furthermore, on July 23, Westover was also documented as being involved in a two-jet scramble after UFOs over Jamestown, Rhode Island. UFO Researcher Loren Gross supplied the following valuable information contained in the following Blue Book Intelligence reports. The following four UFO reports were received by Westover AFB on July 23, 1952:

1.) "SPOT INTELLIGENCE REPORT." Lt. Colonel Robert Jones. "DO #1 Westover AFB, Massachusetts. 29 July 52." Location: Nahant Coast Guard Station, Nahant, Massachusetts. 10 miles northeast of Boston. This report stated, "Two bluish lights…appearing as flat, disc shaped objects having

no aerodynamic features and moving without sound or exhaust trail…at an altitude of 1,000 to 2,000 feet."
2.) "SPOT INTELLIGENCE REPORT. Lt. Colonel Robert Jones. "DO #1 Westover AFB, Massachusetts 29 July 52." Office of Special Investigations Records. Location: Waltham, Massachusetts. 8 miles northeast of Boston. This report stated, "An orange light" made "large sweeping circles," for several hours. 3:00 a.m. report by Mr. Owens.
3.) "SPOT INTELLIGENCE REPORT." Lt. Colonel Robert Jones. "DO #1 Westover AFB, Massachusetts 31 July 52. OSI [Office of Special Investigations] Records." Location: Waltham, Massachusetts. 8 miles northeast of Boston. This report stated, the same "orange light" sighted earlier by Mr. Waltham, "climbed sharply and moved out of sight." 5:00 a.m. report by Mr. Owens.
4.) "SPOT INTELLIGENCE REPORT." Lt. Colonel Robert Jones. "DO #1 Westover AFB, Massachusetts 31 July 52." Location: Springfield, Massachusetts. 4 miles south of Westover AFB. This reported stated: "The object," was an "orange, oval glow." It remained stationary for about one minute then moved fast to the right. "When the object reached the extreme right hand movement, twinkling of its lights could be seen, then it would reverse its direction and return, very fast, to its original stationary point." The object repeated the pattern to the left, returned to its original position then dropped to the earth, and then rose again. The object repeated this T-pattern in the sky, "then disappeared by growing smaller and smaller until it could no longer be seen."
5.) "FLYOBRPT. 23 JULY 1952. TO: JEP HQ/DIRECTOR OF INTELLIGENCE HQ USAF WASHINGTON 25 D.C. FROM: COC ADC AFB COLORADO." Location: Jamestown, Rhode Island. This report stated, that a pair of "F-86" Sabre Jets were "SCRAMBLED" from the "4707 TH" Defense Wing at "WESTOVER AIR FORCE BASE," on "23 July 52."

In his 1953 book, *Flying Saucers from Outer Space*, Donald Keyhoe writes about a meeting he had with a friend, Jim Riordan, the fighter pilot who had just returned from Korea. From his research, Keyhoe had plotted points on a map that showed the main locations where UFO sightings had occurred across the country. These locations included Atomic energy plants, USAF bases, U.S. Naval bases, NAS locations and major cities. Donald Keyhoe showed this map to pilot Riordan.

Keyhoe stated, "Let's check the things the saucers seem most interested in. Maybe you'll spot some clue I've missed."

"Have you plotted any foreign sightings?" asked Riordan, as I spread out the United States map."

No but they show the same pattern." Riordan bent over the map, which showed the following key locations, "1. Atomic energy plants… 2. U. S. Air Force Bases…Westover, Massachusetts."

Westover AFB was actually one of the USAF bases that were plotted on the map by Keyhoe. After looking and discussing the plotted locations on the map, Keyhoe then said to Riordan, "Well, that's the general setup. Of course saucers have been seen at dozens of other places, but these are the ones where they've made repeat visits or shown special interest."

The South Glastonbury crash incident was documented by The "Directorate of Flight Safety Research – Norton Air Force Base, California", as case "52-8-5-5," and is 99 pages long. This incident involved four F-86 jets from the, 4707th Defense wing, 60th Fighter Interceptor Squadron at Westover AFB. At about 1:20 p.m. EST/2:20 EDT two flights of F-86 jets, consisting of two aircraft each were preparing for takeoff from Westover. Each flight had a different mission. The first flight consisted of flight leader Captain Leo Baca and his wing mate Captain Evan Rosencrans. This flight was scheduled for an, "air to air gunnery mission." When this flight taxied onto the runway for takeoff, Captain Rosencrans' jet was reported to have "developed a malfunction." An "oil leak," was said to have grounded him and forced him to park his aircraft. Captain Leo Baca, "then took off alone."

The second flight consisted of an Assistant Flight Leader by the name of Captain Fred Stevens and RAF exchange pilot Lt. James Dell, his wing mate. This second flight "was scheduled to accomplish formation training." The two jets took off at 1:22 p.m. EST/2:22 p.m. EDT. Shortly after takeoff, Captain Fred Stevens was said to have had a problem with his jet. Dell, who was following Stevens, informed him that he noticed his landing gear doors were still down. After "several unsuccessful attempts to raise them", he abandoned the sortie and proceeded back to the base. The RAF pilot, Lt. Dell continued into the sky. Dell stated, "Captain Stevens then contacted Captain Leo Baca who was also airborne at the time, and suggested that he (Captain Baca) should rendezvous with me and we should carry out some productive training." According to the report, Stevens had to land his jet because his "landing gear doors" supposedly "would not retract."

The two airborne pilots, Captain Leo C. Baca, and RAF pilot, Lt. James Dell were both actually on two separate flight missions. Now with their wing mates both grounded at Westover AFB, they were then said to have rendezvoused in mid air. Captain Stevens proceeded to land and Captain Rosencrans went to the base lounge. According to the "DESCRIPTION OF ACCIDENT" report, "a rendezvous was then affected and the two proceeded to the range for practice in air to air camera gunnery."

It was reported that the two pilots rendezvoused "at 1427 hours over Westover Air Force Base." While in flight, Captain Baca supposedly briefed Lt. Dell "for a camera gunnery mission." Dell stated, "I rendezvoused with Captain Baca at 1427 hours over Westover Air Force Base and he proceeded to brief me over the R/T [Radiotelephone] for a camera gun exercise."

It is interesting to note that another document in this file contradicts the type of mission that Lt. Dell was involved. The "MEDICAL REPORT OF AF AIRCRAFT ACCIDENT" states that Lt. Dell was on a "formation training flight." That mission was said to have changed to a "gun camera exercise" while in flight.

During their mission, the pilots allegedly carried out several gunnery passes on each other with the target aircraft towing at 165 knots. Lt. Dell was said to have turned with Captain Baca on a reciprocal heading and completed two more passes.

After their alleged "camera gunnery mission" the two pilots headed home to Westover AFB at about 2:50 p.m. EDT. A/1C Bergwater at Westover Approach Control stated, "At approximately 1350 EST [1:50 p.m. EST/2:50 p.m. EDT], Westover Tower advised me that two F-86's were calling Westover Approach Control for a letdown." Unbeknownst to them, the two pilots were heading into a thunderstorm over the area of the base. At the Board proceeding, Captain Rosencrans stated, "When Captain Baca first tried to contact AWA and GCA and the tower they seemed to give him no help except for standard GCA approach."

Approximately 28 to 30 minutes had passed since their takeoff and the jets had used 1,210 pounds of fuel of the "2790 pounds" that Lt. Baca stated he started with at takeoff. At the Board Proceeding Captain Baca was asked:

Q. When you took off on your mission, what was your fuel?
A. I had 2790 pounds
Q. How much fuel did you have left when you first started to head back to base for a landing?
A. We executed a 180-degree turn approximately 12 minutes away from the base and five minutes later approximately I asked Flight Lieutenant Dell for a fuel check. He had, at the time, around 1580 pounds and I had approximately the same.

During this same time, a flight call went out to Westover tower for a weather report but the tower only heard a weak transmission. A tower operator answered the pilots and gave them the latest weather update, but the pilots did not respond. The airwaves were silent.

Meanwhile, Westover AFB had received word that, "an aircraft was down in the vicinity of New Haven [Connecticut]." Two jet pilots were ordered to the area. One of the pilots was Captain Rosencrans. He was supposed to be Captain Baca's wing mate during the earlier mission. He was grounded though because his jet had an oil leak and never left the ground.

Captain Rosencrans' wing mate on this new mission was jet pilot Major Meyler. Rosencrans stated the following, "Major Meyler and I were told to take to take two aircraft and search the area to see if we could spot any wreckage."

The two pilots took to the runway and began to taxi out. Captain Rosencrans stated, "I had trouble contacting the tower and at the same time I noticed a large thunderstorm approaching the field. I was receiving the tower and receiving other aircraft but evidently, the control tower was not receiving me. At this time, I heard Captain Baca request landing instructions at Westover for a flight of two." This flight was the "SYLVIA BLACK" flight, of Captain Baca and Lt. Dell.

During this time, the mission was aborted. Captain Rosencrans and his wing mate parked their jets and began to assist in this emergency. The radio airwaves were met with severe interference for the next few minutes. Captain Baca had "considerable difficulty" in contacting Westover AFB, according to Rosencrans. He also said the following about the two airborne pilots, "Their transmissions were very garbled and hard to understand." Captain Baca stated that the following about the radio compasses in both jets at the time he tried to contact the tower, "Both radio compasses were indicating an extreme oscillation."

At about 3:00 p.m., the Westover Transport Control Duty officer reported, "the two (2) jets were in trouble due to local weather." During this time, the two pilots were contacted by the control tower. Captain Baca stated, "The tower finally got through and advised us the weather at base was 2500 feet broken ceiling with approximately five miles visibility. Baca also stated the following about his attempts to contact Lt. Dell, "I attempted to contact him but the static was quite heavy."

Shortly after, at about 3:05 the jets were over Springfield, Massachusetts and proceeded toward their base. The pilots called Westover for a Directional Find steer and received one. They began their letdowns and at 3:09 p.m., another steer was given, but the pilots did not respond.

At 3:10 p.m., the flight was now calling "MAYDAY." It was reported by 1st Lt. Meehan of Westover Approach Control stated, "I was informed that a Jet flight "Sylvia Black" was in the area attempting a letdown and the pickup controller, S Sgt Scanlon, informed me that we had no communication with the flight." He goes on to say, "At approximately 1410 EST [2:10 p.m. EST/3:10 p.m. EDT] one aircraft of the 'SYLVIA BLACK' flight called 'MAYDAY.'" Captain Rosencrans stated, "When Flight Lieutenant Dell transmitted in the blind the Dog channel [Emergency D-Channel], giving a 'May Day' transmission, no one answered it"

Captain Baca continued his letdown and penetrated a thunderstorm and at 3:11 p.m., he reached Westover AFB and circled over the base at approximately 250 feet. When he attempted to land at 3:13, it was reported that he, "successfully accomplished his letdown and made two passes at the field during the midst of the storm, each time he endeavored to accomplish a landing the runway was lost because of low visibility."

A/1C Norman Dean who was on duty at the Westover Control Tower stated, "After two passes at the runway the aircraft pulled up and away and transmitted on Channel 'D' to the D/F operator, that he lost contact with the field." He was instructed to climb, by the D/F operator and contact Westover Approach Control."

Meanwhile, Lt. Dell had lost Captain Baca in the clouds and separated from him and communications were temporarily lost. The Accident report stated he "Had accomplished a turn immediately upon losing sight of the lead ship in order that there would be no danger of collision and he immediately began to climb." Dell stated, "I moved in as close as I could to Captain Baca's aircraft and then I heard a rattling on the aircraft. Then Captain Baca's aircraft just disappeared. I made a motion to break away from him as I was afraid of a collision at this particular time."

After two unsuccessful landing attempts over Westover field, Captain Baca departed the area and flew back up into the clouds. Captain Rosencrans stated, "I saw that he overshot the final turn and he disappeared."

A/1C Norman Dean at the Westover Control Tower stated, "He was instructed to climb, by the D/F operator and contact Westover Approach Control." He also said, "There was no further contact after this transmission and no acknowledgement of same from the aircraft. The D/F operator continued to monitor channel 'D' and take fixes on the aircraft as it departed in a southerly direction. Three fixes were passed on to Westover Approach Control."

Lt. Dell attempted to contact Baca and Westover Tower, "But could not transmit or receive for several minutes as the radio static was very heavy," he stated. Finally, when Lt. Dell contacted Westover by a radio he was given a series of directional steers. Dell stated, "These steers were heading me back into the storm center, but as the tower had not said otherwise, I assumed that landing conditions were satisfactory at the base." He also stated, "They did not seem in the least way concerned about the weather and proceeded to give me two D/F [Directional Finding] steers back to the base."

Captain Rosencrans stated, "Flight Lieutenant Dell received either two or three steers but could not reach the field because of weather. About the same time, Captain Baca stated that he was over Memorial Bridge and coming toward the field. Flight Lieutenant Dell was continuing to get steers at this time." Lt. Dell did not make a landing attempt at Westover AFB during this time. Captain Rosencrans contacted both pilots a moment later while still transmitting from his jet on the ground.

Rosencrans said, "I realized it would be impossible for either craft to land there unless they flew a GCA [Ground Control Approach] all the way to touchdown. I asked for their fuel state and as I recall, they had been between 250 and 280 pounds." He instructed both pilots to tune in to "Hartford radio," and while in radio contact they kept Rosencrans informed on their fuel capacity. Captain Rosencrans stated, "I just kept repeating 190 and 329 kilocycles because there were two fields at Hartford and there is Barnsfield, directly west of Westover; Bradley Field, about half way between Westover and Hartford; any four they could have easily landed. The Duty Control Officer at Westover Approach Control, Captain James Wood, stated the following occurred at 3:15 p.m., "Boston ARTC was advised that 'SYLVIA BLACK' flight might be heading south toward Hartford at an unknown altitude."

During this time and until the end of the incident Westover Approach Control was said to have broadcasted "instructions in the blind on VHF channels D, H, G and on Chicopee range frequency (272 KCs)," according to witness 1st Lt. Daniel Meehan. Duty Control Officer Captain James Wood also stated, "My attempt to contact the pilots was unsuccessful. Westover Approach Control was advised that the current weather at Bradley Field, Windsor Locks, Connecticut, was ceiling two thousand five hundred feet in broken clouds, visibility was seven miles. For approximately six minutes, the following message was broadcast blind on channels D, H, and G and 272 KCs: 'Take up heading of 180 degrees and attempt to find Connecticut River. Fly south for approximately 15 miles. Bradley Field will be on your right. Weather at the station, twenty-five hundred broken, seven miles visibility."

Both fighter pilots continued to fly on a southern heading toward Connecticut in search of an alternate field. Their alternate landing fields are listed below:

A. Bradley Airport located in Windsor Locks; approximately 18 miles southwest of Westover AFB.

B. Rentschler Field located in East Hartford; approximately 28 miles south of Westover AFB.

C. Brainard Airport located in Hartford; approximately 32 miles southwest of Westover AFB.

Lt.Dell then stated the following information, "I made several attempts to contact the tower. I then heard Captain Rosencrans telling me to climb on a heading of 195 degrees and tune the radio compass to 329 KC's for Hartford. This I proceeded to do, he then told me to give a distress call for a steer to any nearby airfield that could hear me. This call, which I transmitted three (3) times, was greeted with silence."

A/2C Harry Mendelson who was on duty at Westover Control Tower stated, "I heard one pilot advise the other [Rosencrans to Dell] to monitor the Hartford range frequency 329 Kcs, and try to land at Bradley, using his radio compass." Westover Control Tower Chief M/Sgt. Holuk stated, "Conversation between the pilots of 'SYLVIA BLACK' flight indicated that both aircraft were on a southerly heading." According to Captain Orville Beardsley at the Base Transport Control, a "crash alert" call was placed at "1520"/3:20 p.m. EDT.

He coordinated the dispatch of a SA-16 Rescue plane and received "calls regarding status of both pilots and aircraft concerned." Lieutenant Dell continued to climb through the clouds to an altitude of 10,500 feet. He stated:

The cloud was well layered up to 10,500 feet, the height at which my engine cut through fuel starvation. On instructions from Captain Rosencrans I trimmed the aircraft to 175 knots. After some minutes I noticed that the radio compass needle was indicating 030 degrees so I immediately zeroed the needle. Captain Rosencrans in the meantime was still passing all the relevant information to me with instructions that if there was any doubt about getting the aircraft down safely by the time I reached 4,000 feet indicated, bail out. At 4,000 feet indicated I was still in cloud but broke out at approximately 3600 feet indicated. I executed a left turn to see if I could spot a possible landing area, as I could see no such area ahead. The result was negative, so I then decided that I would leave the aircraft, and then informed Captain Rosencrans of my decision…I estimate that I left the craft at 2500 feet indicated.

A/2C Harry Mendelson then stated, "By monitoring their conversation, Westover Control Tower found out that one pilot was bailing out and that the other was landing at Rentschler Field, East Hartford, Connecticut." Shortly after, Captain Baca was said to have run out of fuel first over the East Hartford, CT area while looking for an alternate landing field. He ran out of gas but was able to make a "dead stick" landing at Rentschler Field at 3:27 p.m. EDT with no complications.

Lt. Dell flew past all three Connecticut alternate landing fields and proceeded south over the area of South Glastonbury before he bailed out. He actually bypassed Bradley Airport by about 20 miles, Rentschler Field by about seven ½ miles and Brainard Airport by about 6 ½ miles. The pilot bailed out over the South Glastonbury town center at about 3:25 p.m. and the jet continued southeast and crashed just over a mile away on a farm. Between 2:50 p.m. EDT and 3:25 p.m., a time of 35 minutes, the jets used up 1,580 pounds of fuel!

I found several discrepancies contained within this 99-page report. On August 8, 1952, a "Proceedings of an Aircraft Accident Board" was held at Otis AFB, Headquarters for the 4707th Wing. During the proceeding it was said, "The purpose of this investigation is to determine all factors relating to the accident, and, in the interest of flying safety, to prevent similar accidents. It is not for the purpose of obtaining evidence for disciplinary action, for determining pecuniary liability or line of status or for revocation of commission or removal from the active list as covered by AFR 36-2." This investigation was very weak in determining all of the factors involved in the accident and was not thorough by any stretch of the imagination.

There were several factors relating to the accident that involved lies and inconsistencies. They were brought out in the proceeding as Air Force personnel were caught lying amongst themselves and in sworn "Statements." There were discrepancies between the pilots, Westover AFB officials, and members of the "Aircraft Accident Board," and a lot of finger pointing. This case is not a pretty picture and the events as reported by the Air Force in this accident report are very convoluted. It is a very complex incident filled with mystery with several major points that don't add up. The information in this story is not believable at all.

During the proceedings, the blame was abounded as to what parties were at fault with their radio communications during the incident. There were communication breakdowns that included, no radio communications at all, missed channel changes, missed messages, static disrupted radios, and jet compasses that were oscillating to an extreme degree. Throughout the entire incident, Westover AFB Tower had extreme difficulties with their communications system and problems keeping in contact with the two pilots. Yet, a statement by "1st Lt. Daniel Meehan" stated the following, " Excepting for a period of approximately three minutes from 1401 EST [2:01 EST/3:01 EDT] to 1404 EST [2:04 EST/3:04 EDT], the Chicopee Range was functioning normally and all VHF channels at Westover Approach Control, although intermittently bothered by lightning strikes, seemed to be operating normally." Officials at the Board Proceeding grounded Captain Baca and hung him out to dry, even though he was not the Flight leader in charge of the flight.

A major discrepancy in this incident involved the point as to whether the Westover Control tower had told the two jet pilots about the weather conditions involving the thunderstorm when they headed toward the base. A board member stated the following at the Accident Proceeding held on August 7, 1952:

Both Captain Baca and Flight Lieutenant Dell are pretty fairly convinced that had the Control Tower given them the information about the thunderstorm in time, the emergency could have been averted. We have two statements here, one by Captain C.F. Berry, Jr., who was preparing for departure on a local flight in a C-97 and the other by airman Third Class Bernard B. Saltzman, who had been acting as an observer in the tower during the incident. Form these statements we find two major discrepancies. In that Captain Berry states that he heard the Sylvia aircraft, Captain Baca, call the tower for the present weather conditions. The control tower advised the pilot that that the ceiling was 2500 feet visibility 5 miles with a thunderstorm south of the field. Captain Baca maintains that he heard nothing about a thunderstorm and Captain Berry said that the tower did not notify any local aircraft that the field was rapidly approaching IFR [Instrument Flight Rule] conditions. Then Airman Third Class Saltzman in his statement said that Westover Operations knew of the prevailing conditions, but had not informed the tower.

At the point when Lt. Dell took off on this flight, he had eight hours of flying time in an F-86 Sabre Jet, yet had "700 hrs" in other types of British fighters in the RAF. His record showed "550 hrs." of the 700 hours were in combat fighter jets and he flew Vampire and Meteor planes. Lt. Dell had "2009 hours" of "TOTAL 1st PILOT HOURS." Captain Baca had "completed the all-weather school," at Tyndall AFB, FL in August of 1951. He also had, "approximately 4 hours of thunderstorm penetration" training as well. Until this mission, Captain Baca had logged "235 hours" of flying time in the F-86 Sabre type jet.

According to pilot Captain Rosencrans, who guided the two pilots, "there were two fields at Hartford and there is Barnsfield, directly west of Westover; Bradley Field, about half way between Westover and Hartford; any four they could have easily landed." All four of these alternate fields were within a 32-mile area of Westover AFB.

The following "FINDINGS" were written in the "DESCRIPTION OF ACCIDENT" segment of the report. They illustrate either situations in this flight gone awry or a cover up story implemented to hide something of a much greater magnitude.

1. "That the flight Commander, Captain Baca, demonstrated questionable judgment in attempting to land at Westover AF Base despite the weather conditions."
2. "That the Flight commander, Captain Baca, violated AFR 60-16 by flying IFR on a VFR clearance."
3. "That there was supervisory error in that there was no mobile control in use to offer assistance even though the unit was in commission."
4. "That there was supervisory error in that there was no officer in the tower during the absence of the mobile control unit."
5. "That base operations at Westover AF Base was at fault for failing to advise the tower of the existing hazard to flight immediately upon ascertaining that the condition existed."
6. "That the tower did not advise the aircraft of the potential danger of the approaching storm when the pilot first contacted them for landing instructions."
7. "That the tower demonstrated poor technique by transmitting steers to the distressed aircraft even while the storm was centered over the base."
8. "That there was no coordination between W.A.C., G.C.A., and the tower in order to assure that one

central agency could transmit all available assistance."
9. "That there was excessive channel changing during this emergency."
10. "That because of poor radio reception the instructions to change to 'G for Golf' was misconstrued to be 'D for Dog', thus creating a delay in transmitting valuable information."

Also contained in the "Findings" section of this document were these interesting points that all concerned Flight Lieutenant Dell. They are as follows.

1. "That the original Flight Commander, Captain Stevens, failed to adequately brief Flight Lieutenant Dell."
2. "That Captain Stevens, Flight Lieutenant Dell's original Flight Leader, failed to acquaint himself with the capabilities of personnel in his flight and thereby failed to fully brief them."
3. "That there was supervisory error in that Flight Lieutenant Dell was inadequately briefed for the mission."
4. "That Flight Lieutenant Dell had only eight (8) hours in the F-86 and had never flown an American aircraft on instruments before."
5. "Flight Lieutenant Dell demonstrated exceptional flying ability and judgment, having been placed in a dangerous situation by his Flight Leader, by accomplishing flight through the thunderstorm under the circumstances and by his procedures in attempting to reorient himself."

Captain Stevens actually briefed Lieutenant Dell for a "formation training flight" not a "camera gun exercise," the mission was supposedly changed when Lt. Dell was airborne. Why did Lt. Dell fail to inform Captain Stevens that he only had eight hours of flying time in the F-86 and had never flown an American aircraft on instruments before?
As recorded by the Accident Board officials, it was said that Captain Baca was the flight Commander of Lt. Dell during the "camera gunnery flight." I would like to bring up the following points in the "FINDINGS" section of the "DESCRIPTION OF ACCIDENT" of the report.

1. "That the flight Commander, Captain Baca, demonstrated questionable judgment in attempting to land at Westover AF Base despite the weather conditions."
2. "That the Flight commander, Captain Baca, violated AFR 60-16 by flying IFR on a VFR clearance."
3. "Flight Lieutenant Dell demonstrated exceptional flying ability and judgment, having been placed in a dangerous situation by his Flight Leader, by accomplishing flight through the thunderstorm under the circumstances and by his procedures in attempting to reorient himself."

Was Lt. Dell, "placed in a dangerous situation by his Flight Leader" said to be Captain Baca or did Dell place himself in a dangerous situation by neglecting to inform Captain Baca of his F-86 experience?
During the Aircraft Accident Board Proceeding, Captain Baca made the following statement to the board:

I would also like to state at this time that I was not the designated flight leader on this particular flight; we were two aircraft on two separate flights and we did rendezvous for a camera gunnery mission after take-off and our return to base and letdown. I asked Flight Lt. Dell to join up on my wing in order to try and help him get back to base knowing that Flight Lieutenant Dell had not flown long with our organization.

An Otis AFB, 4707 Defense Wing document dated "5 SEP 1952" was sent to the Directorate of Flight Safety Research at Norton AFB, in California and stated, "Captain Baca, the flight leader in this case has been transferred out of the fighter squadron and is presently scheduled for FEB [Flying Evaluation Board] action." On that same day, Otis AFB was also sent to the Commanding General, EADF, at Stewart AFB, NY, and stated, "Captain Baca, F/L Dells element leader during this flight, has been transferred from the 60th Fighter-Interceptor Squadron and is grounded pending final action on Flying Evaluation Board recommendations."

Why did Captain Baca take all the blame for this accident? Why did the Air Force pin the accident on him? Even though Captain Stevens contacted Captain Baca and "suggested that he should rendezvous" with Lt.Dell, so they "could carry out some productive training," Captain Stevens nor Lt. Dell did not receive any disciplinary actions against them. Why was this mission carried out at that point and not aborted?

The following dialogue also transpired between Lt. Dell and a member of the board at the Aircraft Accident Board proceeding:

Q. On this particular mission you were briefed for a formation training flight. Is that correct?
A. Yes, sir.
Q. When your flight leader [Captain Stevens] briefed you for that flight, do you recall his using a briefing check list?
A. Yes, I think he ticked off the various items; he had a list in front of him which I had seen used on various flights.

The following points show the discrepancies between Lieutenant Dell and Captain Stevens answers.
POINT ONE. THE WEATHER FORECAST- LT. DELL
Q. Now being briefed for the flight, were you given a local weather forecast.
A. No, sir.
Q. You were not?
A. No Sir.
POINT TWO. NAVIGATIONAL AIDS-LT.DELL
Q. Were you briefed on navigational aids in the area?
A. Not in the area, sir. Captain Stevens asked me if I knew how to tune in the radio compass and I told him yes.
POINT THREE. LOCAL FREQUENCIES-LT. DELL
Q. Were you given any local frequencies for use with the radio compass?
A. No, sir.

The following dialogue transpired between Captain Stevens and a member of the board at the Aircraft Accident Board proceeding:
Q. You conducted briefings on Flight Lieutenant Dell?
A. Yes, sir.
Q. You used the Briefing Check List?
A. Yes, sir.

POINT ONE. THE WEATHER FORECAST- CAPTAIN STEVENS
Q. We are interested in determining whether you gave Flight Lieutenant Dell a local weather forecast?
A. I gave him the weather we had in Operations at the time and at the time there was no thunderstorm activity reported.
POINT TWO. NAVIGATIONAL AIDS-CAPTAIN STEVENS
Q. How about navigational Aids.
A. Yes sir, I briefed on Navigational Aids surrounding Westover and also I briefed on check radio compasses before takeoff.
POINT THREE. LOCAL FREQUENCIES-CAPTAIN STEVENS

Q. Did you give Flight Lieutenant Dell the frequencies of any of the local stations?
A. I gave him the Chicopee Range, that was the only one.

Why are there discrepancies between Lieutenant Dell and Captain Stevens answers? Was one of these men lying? Was there ever a mission briefing to start with or was there actually an emergency situation?
The following "FINDINGS" were written in the "DESCRIPTION OF ACCIDENT" segment of the report.
1. "That the original Flight Commander, Captain Stevens, failed to adequately brief Flight Lieutenant Dell."
2. "That Captain Stevens, Flight Lieutenant Dell's original Flight Leader, failed to acquaint himself with the capabilities of personnel in his flight and thereby failed to fully brief them."
3. "That there was supervisory error in that Flight Lieutenant Dell was inadequately briefed for the mission."
Why did the "FINDINGS" of the board pin the blame Captain Stevens for improperly briefing Lt. Dell?
In the Royal Air Force, Flight Lieutenant Dell had 700 hours of flying in British fighter aircraft. He flew 550 hours in combat fighter jets and he flew Vampire and Meteor planes. Lt. Dell had 2009 hours of "TOTAL 1st PILOT HOURS." Why was Lt. Dell not prepared when he took to the skies on August 5, 1952?
I would like to raise the following point that appeared in the "FINDINGS" section of the "DESCRIPTION OF ACCIDENT" of the report.
1. "That there was supervisory error in that there was no mobile control in use to offer assistance even though the unit was in commission."
In reference to the Mobile Control Unit used for radio transmissions, the following dialogue transpired between the Westover AFB Operations officer, Major James M. Jones, Jr. and a member of the board at the Aircraft Accident Board proceeding:

Q. Can you tell us whether the Mobile Control Unit was in place?
A. No, sir. The Mobile Unit was not in place.
Q. Can you tell us why it wasn't in place?
A. The assistant Operations officer told me the Mobile Control was out of commission.
Q. How long had the unit been out of commission?
A. Colonel. Mobile Control was in commission.
Q. In other words, your assistant Operations Officer told you that the unit was out of commission when it actually was in commission.
A. Yes, sir.
Q. Who is your Assistant Operations Officer?
A. Captain Banks.
Q. Did Captain Banks know this unit was in commission?
A. I asked Captain Banks was Mobile Control in place and he said, "No." I asked him why and he said, "It was out of commission." Before that Major Meyler [pilot] had told Captain Banks to check on the Mobile Control and get the thing in place, if it was in commission, and when the trouble started [Dell and Baca's flight] I asked Captain Banks if the Mobile Control was out there and he said it was out of commission. I told Colonel Gray that Mobile Control was out of commission over there the other day but it was not.
Q. At the time this conversation between you and Captain Banks took place had the emergency occurred?
A. Yes, sir. Shouldn't have been an emergency.

1. Why were there discrepancies between these men and why were they lying about the status of the Mobile Control unit?
2. Was there an ongoing cover up to hide something that occurred that day between these men?

3. What was the reason that the unit was not in place?
 The Colonel continued to question Major Jones, the base Operations Officer:

Q. Do you feel that this emergency could have been averted had the Mobile Control Unit been in place and operating?
A. No, Sir. I do not.
Q. Why not?
A. Because it was a vicious storm. We had the same radio set up in Operations - - or Communications which is just across the hall - - I got on that set. The Communications set, the one we use for scrambles, and for giving vectors, Etc. I tried to contact them and tell them to get away from the field that the thing would pass sooner or later and if they were short on fuel to go somewhere else but I couldn't get any answer.

 I ask:
1. Did Major Jones use the "Communications set," the one they "use for scrambles," because this mission was actually a scramble mission and not a camera gunnery exercise or formation flight mission?
 2. Is that the reason why the Mobile Control Unit was not in its proper location prior to the jets take offs?
 3. Did Major Jones scramble the jets after UFOs that afternoon by utilizing his "Communications set"?
   The base Operation Officer, Major Jones, then gave the questioning Colonel a possible reason that the Unit was not in place where it should have been. He stated, "They called the tower - - Captain Rosencrans [and Major Meyler who were both sitting on the base line in their jets and talking to Baca and Dell] and the Mobile Control was very weak, now that is possibly one reason why Captain Banks didn't put it out there. You can read it with conditions right, if you are right over the field or right over Mobile Control, but you can't get it any distance away from the field at all." He also explained the Rosencrans and Meylers role in this situation as they sat in their jets on the line, "They more or less acted as Mobile Control and were giving instructions to both Baca and Dell."
   The possible reason that Captain Banks did not put the Mobile Control Unit "out there" in place where it should have been, because it only works under the right conditions is absurd. The unit was supposed to have been out in place on the field at the time of takeoff but was not. Furthermore, the storm was not over the base at the time of takeoff, it moved in about 30 minutes later, so the weak signal factor would not have factored into the situation. Captain Baca stated, "I was briefed on the weather prevailing around the area and according to our weather people, the actual immediate area was VFR, and no activity was expected in the area for the time I was airborne."
 During the board proceeding, the following dialogue transpired between Captain Stevens and a board member. It is in reference to the weather forecast at the time of Steven's briefing, shortly before they took off:

Q. We are interested in determining whether you gave Flight Lieutenant Dell a local weather forecast?
A. I gave him the weather we had in operations at the time and at the time there was no thunderstorm activity reported.

   The questioning continued and another aspect of this convoluted story came into play. I would like to raise another point in the "FINDINGS" section of the "DESCRIPTION OF ACCIDENT" in the report. It concerns the lack of an officer/pilot in the control tower during the crisis. The FINDINGS document states, "That there was supervisory error in that there was no officer in the Tower during the absence of the mobile control unit."
The following dialogue transpired between the Westover AFB Operations officer, Major James M. Jones, Jr. and a member of the board at the Aircraft Accident Board proceeding. The questions continued:

Q. Since there was no Mobile Control Unit present in operation on the runway, did you have an officer in the tower?
A. No.
Q. Could you tell us why?
A. A series of events: (1) I had just gotten home about 40 or 45 minutes before this and I went straight to the office and started on reports. (2) I asked what the aircraft was when I went in and I didn't think that we had any aircraft scheduled to be flying. (3) I have no reason.
The questioning continued concerning the lack of a pilot in the tower.
Q. Was your Assistant Operations Officer aware of the fact that with the [Mobile Control] unit out of commission that the pilot should have been in the control tower until the unit was returned in commission?
A. Yes, sir. I am aware of it. We are all aware of it. The flight leaders too.

Why did Westover AFB Operations officer, Major James M. Jones, Jr. state, "I asked what the aircraft was when I went in and I didn't think that we had any aircraft scheduled to be flying." Did he make this statement because there were no aircraft scheduled to be flying? Were the jets that were up in the air on an unscheduled flight mission because they were scrambled on an intercept mission after UFOs? Is this the reason why this entire situation went awry?
 I now ask the following questions in reference to this segment of the case.
1. When airborne, why did Lt. Dell fail to inform Westover Base Operations, Captain Stevens and Captain Baca that he only had eight hours of flying experience in the F-86 type jet and never flown an F-86 on instruments?
2. Lt. Dell was originally supposed to be on a "formation training flight." Why did Lt. Dell and Captain Baca form another flight and continue with another type mission... a "camera gun exercise"?
3. Why did Westover base operations allow Lt. Dell and Captain Baca to rendezvous in the air then continue on another mission? Lt. Dell was not briefed for an "air gunnery mission" by his flight leader Captain Stevens; he was briefed for a "formation training flight." Lt. Dell said that Captain Baca briefed him for the camera gun exercise when they were airborne. Is that true? Was this airborne briefing adequate and did it follow procedure?
4. Why did base operations not scrub both missions when a plane from each flight was grounded because of mechanical failure?
5. Was there an undisclosed situation that arose which brought these two pilots together on another mission when they were airborne? Especially when there was adverse weather, conditions were all around them!
6. Why was there such a discrepancy as to whether the pilots were notified about the thunderstorm by Westover tower? If the weather conditions were so severe, then why were the two jet pilots not recalled sooner by their base controllers? Were they involved in another situation that delayed them?
7. Had all the Air Force parties involved in this mission gone awry? Were they negligent or were there other unknown factors involved? Why was there a discrepancy between the tower and the pilots concerning the weather?
8. Did the UFOs that flew over Westover AFB earlier that day come back to the base that afternoon?
9. Did the storm cause the radio transmitting and receiving problems at Westover AFB, or were they caused by another outside source that eradicated them? Why did the pilots have communication problems with their base tower during this situation but were able to communicate with Rosencrans who was sitting in his jet on the runway?
10. Did the storm cause the onboard radios of the jets to have transmitting and receiving problems or did another outside source affect them?

11. Did the weather cause the pilot's compasses to act erratically or was there another force that affected them?
12. Were Lt. Dell and Captain Baca on a camera gunnery mission or were they scrambled on a covert intercept mission after UFOs?
13. Were Captain Baca and Lt. Dell involved in an aerial confrontation with UFOs, which delayed them in getting back to their base and beating the storm?
14. Were the two pilots fleeing the area and being led back to their base and into the storm because they could not go south toward their alternate fields in Connecticut?
15. Were the radio and compass problems that arose with the onboard systems of the jets due to electromagnetic fields in the air? Were the radio communications actually jammed?
16. When Captain Baca passed over the field on two separate occasions; was he unable to land or did he change his mind and go back into the sky to look for his wing mate who needed assistance?
17. What were the two jets doing during the unaccounted times of the last 35 minutes of their flight? Were the pilots involved in another aerial confrontation?

In the following segment, I raise three points in the time line of events and then ask ten more questions.

A. Lt.Dell stated the following information, "I made several attempts to contact the tower. I then heard Captain Rosencrans telling me to climb on a heading of 195 degrees and tune the radio compass to 329 KC's for Hartford. This I proceeded to do, he then told me to give a distress call for a steer to any nearby airfield that could hear me. This call, which I transmitted three (3) times, was greeted with silence."

B. Westover Approach Duty Control Officer Captain Wood stated, "My attempt to contact the pilots was unsuccessful. Westover Approach Control was advised that the current weather at Bradley Field, Windsor Locks, Connecticut, was ceiling two thousand five hundred feet in broken clouds, visibility was seven miles. For approximately six minutes, the following message was broadcast blind on channels D, H, and G and 272 KCs: 'Take up heading of 180 degrees and attempt to find Connecticut River. Fly south for approximately 15 miles. Bradley Field will be on your right. Weather at the station, twenty-five hundred broken, seven miles visibility."

C. Lt. Dell flew then flew past all three Connecticut alternate landing fields and proceeded south over the area of South Glastonbury before he bailed out. He actually bypassed Bradley Airport by about 20 miles, Rentschler Field by about seven ½ miles and Brainard Airport by about 6 ½ miles.

1. Why was there no communication between Lt. Dell and Westover Tower? Why couldn't Dell contact the Westover tower?
2. Why was Westover Approach unsuccessful in contacting both Lt. Dell and Captain Baca?
3. Why were all three of the nearby Connecticut Fields unable to hear Lt. Dell's distress calls? Dell said that he "was greeted with silence."
4. When Rosencrans was in communication with Dell, why did he fail to advise him to look for the Connecticut River and follow it South to Bradley Field in Windsor Locks?
5. Why was Lt. Dell able to communicate with Captain Rosencrans who was sitting in his jet on the runway at Westover AFB yet he could not contact the high- powered communications tower at Westover?
6. Why was Lt. Dell "greeted with silence" when he transmitted three distress calls while over the Hartford, Connecticut area? What are we to believe in this situation?
7. The weather station at Bradley Field reported there were "broken clouds" over Windsor Locks and the "visibility was seven miles." Did Lt. Dell really miss Bradley Airport in Windsor Locks?
8. Why did this RAF pilot take to the air on his mission without knowing his alternate landing fields? A pilot with 700 hours of flying time in fighter aircraft that included 550 hours in jets should have known this!
9. Were the two jets actually damaged during a UFO intercept that was said to be a camera gun exercise?

10. Did the electrical system of Lt. Dell's jet become damaged on the mission and did it cause the ejection system to fail?

In his 1953 book, *Flying Saucers from Outer Space*, Donald Keyhoe talked about a Canadian scientist, Wilbur B. Smith from Ottawa, that he met and had spoke throughout the early 1950's. Smith was the originator of a special Canadian project named, "Project Magnet," that was authorized in December of 1950. This team of geometric engineers and scientists at the Department of Transport worked in the Telecommunications Division and started the project. According to author Max Miller, they used, "The Department's laboratory and field facilities in a study of unidentified flying objects and physical principals which might appear to be involved."

Wilbur Smith, an electronics expert, was the official in charge of broadcast monitoring. Keyhoe said, "He could direct his men to listen for any strange messages." Even though this research project was done in a Canadian government laboratory, it was unofficial at first. On the first occasion they met, Smith told Keyhoe, "We're government engineers and scientists, but we are working on our time."

Donald Keyhoe explained that Smith as a "geometric engineer, with a government laboratory at his disposal, could carry out research on certain propulsion theories. Through the official ionosphere observatories he could keep a radar check on saucers flying at extremely high altitudes." Smith told Keyhoe in 1950, "I'm convinced they're real-that they're machines of some kind."

Smith stated, "Our experiments indicate that the true discs, which are probably launched from large parent ships, utilize magnetic fields of force." He also informed him, "We know now it is possible to create current by a collapse of the earth's magnetic field. Eventually, I think we can achieve enough current to power a flying disc. And we plan to build such a disc." A revised report of Smith's "information" was sent to the Canadian Embassy in Washington and cleared for Keyhoe by the "Defense Research" at the "Canadian Joint Staff." It explained the scientists' recent investigations that pointed "the way to a new technology in magnetics." Their investigations talked about, "a ready-made explanation for many of the striking features which have been reported in connection with the sightings of flying saucers."

The two men continued to collaborate and on another occasion, they met in Washington in 1951. Keyhoe brought along a declassified copy of the final report on "Project Sign," the original saucer project that was operative from September 1947 until February 1949. The two men reviewed the report and analyzed one particular section, "Confidential Analysis of Intelligence Reports." Smith explained to Keyhoe that with the discs, "There is a possible danger." He explained that "two fairly large fields of magnetic force" would surround a saucer "while it was in operation." Smith explained that "eddy currents," would create a, "danger zone." Keyhoe asked Smith, "How close could a plane come without danger?" Smith stated, "If a pilot did fly into a region where a magnetic field was collapsing, it would produce eddy currents in his plane.

He continued and explained, "At a moderate distance it would merely throw off his directional finder and compass. If he were fairly close, it could effect his ignition and set up strong vibrations in his plane. It might even cause a fire. But the plane would have to be well within the danger zone."

Could this "danger zone," be a possible explanation as to why fighter aircraft were getting lost, having electrical problems and crashing as well? Where the problems that arose in this Westover AFB incident caused by the "danger zone" of a UFO which Captain Baca's forced landing and cause Lt. Dell to crash on August 5, 1952?

A major point and a most obvious one that I discovered in the accident report that differed from the New York Times article, was the pilots departure from the jet before it crashed. The article reported that Lt. Dell "stood up and battered the canopy with his arms and his helmet, he said until it opened. He was at 4,000 feet when he finally freed himself and jumped." This was the original report on the incident.

The 99-page report tells a completely different version of the incident. The "MEDICAL REPORT OF AF AIRCRAFT ACCIDENT" states the following, "Bailed out when aircraft went below 4000' on controlled glide. Ejection and parachute decent uncomplicated, except that canopy failed to jettison when canopy lever was pulled several times, until pilot leaned forward to test shoulder harness." This later version states that the pilot ejected from his seat and then parachuted to safety. Furthermore, it states "uncomplicated" and there is no mention about him standing up and battering the canopy and setting himself free and then jumping out of the falling jet.

The "DESCRIPTION OF ACCIDENT—SECTION 'O'" of the report, also describes the incident and states, "Still finding no suitable place he began his procedures for abandoning the aircraft. His procedures are quoted here: 'I carried out the SOP [Standard Operating Procedures] for seat ejection. Locking my safety harness and crouching forward, I then attempted to jettison the canopy. I pulled the appropriate jettison handle three (3) times but the canopy remained in position. I then leaned forward to check that my safety harness was locked, and as I did the canopy ejected. [The previous five words were hand-underlined in the report]. Having disconnected my oxygen tube and assumed the correct position in the seat, I then pulled the ejection lever.' The pilot landed in a field and sustained no injury." These official accident reports are a far cry from the New York Times report datelined "Aug. 5 (AP)," the same day that the accident occurred.

The following "STATEMENT" was made by "Flight Lieutenant James L. Dell, R.A.F." It appears in the accident report:

I carried out the S.O.P. for seat ejection. Locking my safety harness and crouching forward, I then attempted o jettison the canopy. I pulled the appropriate jettison handle three (3) times but the canopy remained in position. I then leaned forward to check that my safety harness was locked, and as I die so, the canopy ejected. Having disconnected my oxygen tube and assumed the correct position in the seat, I then operated the seat ejection lever.

As I left the craft I lost my helmet, and proceeded to somersault backwards. I estimate that I left the aircraft at 2500 feet indicated. Looking down, I placed my left hand on the parachute ripcord so that I could readily locate it when I had parted from my seat. I then released the safety harness with my right hand and attempted to kick away from the seat, but I had already parted company from the seat. Transferring my right hand to the parachute ripcord I waited a second or so to make certain of being clear of the ejection seat, and then pulled. The chute opened immediately.

On looking to the ground I noticed that I was drifting backwards so I attempted to turn face the direction of drift, with partial success. I assumed the standard landing position and touched down in a small field immediately behind the South Glastonbury Fire Station. The ejection seat landed approximately 300 yards away and the aircraft approximately 2 miles away.

I will now raise the following questions concerning Lt. Dell's departure from his aircraft.
1. Why is there such a discrepancy between the original *Associated Press* story and the official documents in the Aircraft Accident Report?
2. Why does Lieutenant Dell describe a near perfectly executed bail out in his ejection seat?
3. Why did the pilot's story change about the procedure that he used to bail out of his disabled craft?
4. It is obvious that Air Force officials told Lt. Dell to change his story and cover up what really occurred. Why was the story changed?
5. Did Lt. Dell's ejection system have an electrical problem caused by some external force?

There was a slip-up during the Aircraft Accident Board meeting that was overlooked. During Captain Evan W. Rosencrans interview by the board, he stated the following information that details what he told Lt. Dell over the radio during his bailout, "I asked him if he knew all his procedures for bailout and he stated he believed [that] he had them memorized. He reported going through 4000 feet and stated he had them memorized. His next transmission stated that he could not get the canopy off by using the ejection method. I instructed him to stay at 175 knots or below and roll the canopy open electrically and climb over the side."

The key words in this statement are Rosencrans instructed Lt. Dell to, **"Climb over the side."** Rosencrans actually instructed the pilot to climb over the side of the falling aircraft because he knew there was a major problem with the ejection system. This truth was that was not picked up by Air Force officials when the report was transcribed.

In mid-December 2006, I visited Connecticut, stayed until the first week of January 2007, and researched this incident. I visited different libraries in search of early accounts of the story as reported by the press for additional information. I also wanted to compare the first accounts of the story with the Air Force Aircraft Accident Reports' version.

I went to the Connecticut State Library located in Hartford near the state capitol building with my assistant Don Hobar. This library has massive archives of state records that include several major state newspapers on microfilm. During our day visit to the state library, we researched the jet story and actually found UFO articles as well as three newspaper articles about the South Glastonbury jet crash. These articles were found in the following newspapers, *The Hartford Courant*, *The New Haven Evening Register*, and *the Bridgeport Telegram.* The following articles involve the August 5, 1952 jet crash.

The Hartford Courant reported the crash on "WEDNESDAY MORNING AUGUST 6, 1952." The Courant's front-page headline reports, "RAF Pilot Fights Clear Of Crashing Jet, 'Chutes To Safety In South Glastonbury." The Hartford Courant covered the jet crash story and went to South Glastonbury on the same day as the crash. A photographer also took pictures and an accompanying photo appears with the news article. It shows Lt. Dell with the South Glastonbury Police Chief George C. Hall. Irving M. Kravsow and Mary Coleman wrote *The Hartford Courant* news article that included information about Lt. Dells' bail out:

A Royal Air Force pilot, trapped in a powerless Sabre Jet, F-86, hammered his way out and parachuted to safety seconds before the plane crashed in South Glastonbury Tuesday…He pulled the button [lever] which was supposed to open the canopy over the cockpit and eject him from the plane. BAILS OUT AT 4,000 FEET.

The mechanism jammed, however, and Dell found himself trapped in the rapidly falling jet. He stood up and battered the canopy with his arms and helmet he said, until it opened. He was at 4,000 feet when he finally freed himself and jumped. His helmet landed on some telephone wires on Main Street in South Glastonbury. The pilot's seat missed Police Chief George C. Hall's house by a few inches and landed in his back yard. Dell made a perfect parachute landing in a field in the rear of Company 2 Firehouse in South Glastonbury.

The Bridgeport Telegram reported the crash on "WEDNESDAY MORNING, AUGUST 6, 1952." The Telegrams front-page headline reports:

JET PLANE PILOT CHUTES TO SAFETY AT GLASTONBURY
Royal Air Force Flier Hammers Way Out of Falling Craft
WAS TRAPPED IN SEAT

The Bridgeport Telegram picked up the crash story from the *Associated Press* on August 5, 1952, which was released by *The Hartford Courant*. It also reported the same information and reported on Lt. Dells bail out procedure but with a different sub article headline, "SMASHES WAY OUT."

The New Haven Evening Register also reported the crash on "WEDNESDAY, AUG. 6, 1952" on page two. Its headline story reports, "RAF JET FLIER ESCAPES DEATH IN STATE CRASH." This article was datelined August 6, 1952, and states in part, "East Glastonbury, Aug. 6 – (AP) – A Royal Air Force pilot parachuted to safety after pounding loose a jammed canopy in a conked out F-86 Sabre Jet here yesterday…Flying in a thick overcast, Dells aircraft failed at 10,000 feet. He yanked the lever to open the canopy over the cockpit. It was jammed. Furiously, the pilot battered the canopy with his arms and helmet. At 4,000 feet the canopy flipped open and he leaped out. He made a safe parachute landing in a field."

The nearby Hartford Courant sent their people to the site of the jet crash on the same afternoon the crash occurred and got their information shortly after. On the following day, The New Haven Evening Register reported their story from another *Associated Press* source with some updated information.

According to the original accounts of the incident, Lt. Dell freed himself from the cockpit when he stood up and battered the canopy loose with his helmet and arms. He then jumped out of the jet and parachuted to safety.

During the process of breaking out of the cockpit of the falling jet, he would have followed a procedure similar to the following steps I have outlined below:

1. Lt. Dell had to disconnect his oxygen tube.
2. Lt. Dell actually had to unharness himself from the seat's safety harness in order to stand up. Once he was free of the safety harness, he was able to stand up from the ejection seat.
3. He then took off his helmet and actually used it to batter the canopy with his forearms, which jarred it loose and caused it to open.
4. The pilot then jumped out of the jet. During his departure from the jet, he was not wearing his helmet because it was in his hands being used as a battering tool. Lt. Dell actually lost his helmet when he leaped from the plane and discarded it, then began his parachuting procedure. This included pulling his ripcord to open his parachute and then holding on to the parachute straps while descending.

This would explain why Lt. Dell said in his statement, "As I left the craft I lost my helmet." The original *Hartford Courant* also stated, "His helmet landed on some telephone wires on Main Street in South Glastonbury." Lt. Dell was not wearing his helmet.

Furthermore, at some point after Lt. Dell jumped out of the falling jet, the ejection seat did jettison and land in the town of South Glastonbury. The original *Hartford Courant* article stated, "The pilot's seat missed Police Chief George C. Hall's house by a few inches and landed in his back yard."

Lt. Dell also confirmed the ejection seat segment of the story in his statement in the Aircraft Accident Report, "I assumed the standard landing position and touched down in a small field immediately behind the South Glastonbury Fire Station. The ejection seat landed approximately 300 yards away and the aircraft approximately 2 miles away." I now ask the following questions.

1. Why is Lieutenant Dell's original story concerning his bail procedure different from what was recorded in the official Aircraft Accident Report? 2. Was Lt. Dell forced into changing his original story to a fabricated version? 3. What was the Air Force trying to hide concerning this jet crash? 4. Were there other events and circumstances involved in this crash changed as well? 5. How many segments of this story were changed and how much should we actually believe?

My next step was to visit the towns of Glastonbury and South Glastonbury to further my investigation into the incident. Two days after Christmas, I made the trip to upstate Connecticut once again with Don. We went into the town of Glastonbury and visited the Main Street library.

I made an inquiry at the reference desk about this 55-year-old jet crash story. I was greeted with four blank looks from the librarians behind the large desk. None of them were familiar with the story. One of the women brought me to a microfilm cabinet and showed me the holdings for their local paper, *The Glastonbury Citizen*. Shortly after I looked through the microfilm roll of this weekly paper, I found what I was looking for.

The entire front page of the August 8, 1952 issue was devoted to the story of the jet crash. The headline story reads, "RAF Pilot Visits Glastonbury" and another reads, "Pictures Record Firemen's Work." Along the top of the front-page reads, "First-on-the-Scene Photos by the Citizen." Underneath this headline are two large photos of the crash site taken immediately after the incident. One photo shows the wrecked jet in the woods with firefighters putting out a fire. Another photograph shows wreckage of the jet strewn about the woods.

The bottom of the front page also shows more photos of the devastated area of woods at the crash site. Don and I then drove into South Glastonbury and went into town in search of the local library in search of more information. We eventually found it but it was closed when we got there. We drove around the town, found the South Glastonbury Firehouse, and looked around the area. We left shortly after as darkness approached as we did not want to get lost up in this neck of the woods. Another trip was needed to familiarize myself with the area and find the crash site.

During the week, I reviewed all of the information in the *Glastonbury Citizen* article. There is no mention about Lt. Dells bail out procedure, but there are some interesting bits of information in the story. The article, "RAF Pilot Visits Glastonbury" gives the following information. I have listed the series of events in chronological order for continuity of the story.

1. "The British exchange pilot had run out of fuel while circling Hartford while waiting for clearance to land."
2. "Officer Dell came out of the clouds northeast of town to look for a landing field at 3:15 p.m. from his fogged in base, Westover Field, Mass.
3. "As he told townspeople later in the Glastonbury Drug store, he had come down out of the clouds and become certain he couldn't land before bailing out. He did not clear his plane until down to 2500 feet."
4. "Mrs. Harry Arnold of High Street saw a parachuted pilot drop gently into the area behind South Glastonbury's firehouse."
5. "He landed easily behind Company Two's clean brick firehouse and walked across Main Street to the drug where he phoned his base to let them know he was alright, if planeless."
6. In reference to the jet, "It was reliably reported as diving close to the ground just before it hit."
7. "Two men fishing in Great Pond saw the F-86 Sabre Jet crash Tuesday at 3:30 p.m. in the woods a quarter mile up the hill east of John Christian's farm buildings off South Main Street…It had fallen close to two miles southeast of where its pilot alighted."
8. "'Mommy, is it an atom bomb?' asked a youngster on nearby Hickory Lane…Two somewhat worried

mothers and their four children stood in the Glastonbury Drug Store, their children eating ice cream cones. They were in their homes on Hickory Lane at the time of the crash and explosion."

9. "Persons at the drug store reported he [Lieutenant Dell] was unshaken and casual as he chatted with them."

10. "At 4:00 p.m. a car driven by a man who identified himself as a reserve Captain at Westover picked up the Briton and started back to Massachusetts. Later the pilot was brought back to where his plane crashed and posed for pictures." Note: When the pilot was brought back to South Glastonbury, he talked to the Hartford Courant and posed for several photographs.

11. "The crash of the plane drew hundreds of spectators with cars. They were unable to get close to the crash site at first, because of whistling 50-caliber ammunition.

12. "By the time the fire trucks were in place to douse the burning wreckage, the State Police had taken over the holding back of the crowd."

13. "Captain Eric Kusche of East Glastonbury's Fire Company Three, directed efforts of firemen to put out small fires around the scene of the jet's crash."

14. All were breathing easier on learning the damped-down woods had not caught fire."

In the other article, "Pictures record Firemen's Work," the following information was given:

15. "At center of crash scene, four-foot-deep marks pit where body apparently exploded on impact."

16. "Plane broke into two main parts, tail and fuel mixer."

17. "Explosion showered small parts of blue and silver plane fuselage and fine earth over 150-yard radius in woods."

18. "Flames still blazed fiercely in small sections of plane body and wing."

19. "Exploding ammunition made area dangerous."

20. "Recent rain made area murky."

It is interesting to note that there is no mention about the pilots bail out procedure in this newspaper. Even though Lt. Dell talked to the local townspeople about the accident shortly after he landed in town and after his return, why is there no mention in the article about his hammering out and jumping from the jet episode? *The Glastonbury Citizen* article was the last article of all the newspapers to print this story because it was a weekly paper. The story was not published until three days later on August 8.

The Accident Board meeting was held the day before on August 7 at Otis AFB and the bail out story was already changed at that point! Did the Air Force tell *The Glastonbury Citizen* not to run this segment of the story?

The Hartford Courant stated, "The control tower at Bradley Field heard Dell and Air Force Captain Baca, pilot of the other Sabre jet talking about running low on fuel and looking for a place to land." *The New Haven Register* reported, "The control tower at Bradley Field in Windsor Locks reported hearing the pilots talking about finding a place to land their craft, because fuel was running low." Furthermore, *The Glastonbury Citizen* disclosed, "The British exchange pilot had run out of fuel while circling Hartford while waiting for clearance to land." I ask the following questions. 1. Why is there is no mention of any of this information in any of the follow up documents in the Aircraft Accident report including Bradley Field heard the pilots? 2. Did Lt. Dell "run out of fuel while circling while Hartford while waiting for clearance to land"? What actually happened on that afternoon may never be known, but there are more questions than answers.

Derived from the following quotes, I will raise another point that concerns the actual crash of the jet and its impact in the wooded area of South Glastonbury.

1. "At center of crash scene, four-foot-deep marks pit where body apparently exploded on impact."

2. The "explosion showered small parts of blue and silver plane fuselage and fine earth over 150-yard radius in the woods."

3. Four nearby witnesses, "were in their homes on Hickory Lane at the time of the crash and explosion."

4. "Captain Eric Kusche of East Glastonbury's Fire Company Three, directed efforts of firemen to put out small fires around the scene of the jet's crash."
5. "Flames still blazed fiercely in small sections of plane body and wing."
6. A photo description stated, "Steam rises from burning wreckage as firemen move past exploded tailpiece to put fires under control."
7. "The crash of the plane drew hundreds of spectators with cars. They were unable to get close to the crash site at first, because of whistling 50-caliber ammunition."
8. "By the time the fire trucks were in place to douse the burning wreckage, the State Police had taken over the holding back of the crowd."

This jet was said to be out of fuel. I ask how is it possible that it, exploded on impact, caught fire and blazed fiercely, set small fires in a wet terrain, ignited 50-caliber bullets, and had to be doused by water because it was burning in flames? The jet was supposedly out of gas, which was the reason that it was said to have gone down! It took several fire fighters to control and put out the fires near the crash, including the jet. Furthermore, there are on the scene photos from the Glastonbury newspaper to prove it, which brings up another important point. When I looked through the dozens of Aircraft Accident Reports on microfilm, I noticed that cases have on-the-scene photographs of the wrecked aircraft. Air Force officials would take several photos of the accident scene and the aircraft from numerous angles to document the crash. What I found odd about this case is that there are only seven photos in this case file. Four photos show the woods, including the impact area, the cut path made by the plane's approach and two photos of the woods with a debris field. Three other photos show parts of the plane: the engine, the seat, and a piece of wreckage with the aspirator. What is mysterious here is there is not one photograph showing the wreckage of the body of the jet, the burned jet.

The local newspaper said the, "plane broke into two parts, tail and fuel mixer," and showed two photos of the wreckage of the jet on page one. The paper also stated, "Steam rises from burning wreckage as firemen move past exploded tailpiece to put fires under control. Explosion showered small parts of blue and silver plane fuselage and earth over a 150-yard radius in woods." Why are there a no photos of the jets wrecked fuselage in any of the official Air Force photos? It is obvious that would be an indication that the jet exploded, was on fire and severely burned during the crash when it was supposedly out-of-fuel. Furthermore, there is not one single word in the official Aircraft Accident report, about the explosion or the fires that occurred at the scene of the crash. Consider the following questions.
1. What caused the jet to explode, catch fire and blaze fiercely, set nearby fires and ignite 50-caliber bullets throughout the area?
2. Was this jet really out of fuel when it crashed on that wooded farm in South Glastonbury?
3. Did this jet run out of fuel, causing it to crash or was there another reason?
4. Did the jet have in-flight electrical and or mechanical failures that caused it to go down?
5. Was this Sabre Jet forced down by another aircraft?

Throughout the end of the year, I reviewed all of the information that I had about the story. I bought several maps of the area including Connecticut and Massachusetts state maps and a detailed Hartford County map and pinpointed the locations involved in the incident. During the first week of January 2007, I made another trip to South Glastonbury, Connecticut and went with my sister in law Mary Jane. I brought the maps to find the location of the crash site and to get a better overview of the town area where the events took place. We also both brought along cameras to document the locations, I brought a video camera and Mary Jane brought a 35 mm camera. Glastonbury and South Glastonbury are located to the east of the winding Connecticut River. The towns of Wethersfield and Rocky Hill are located on the opposite side of the river across from Glastonbury and South Glastonbury. In Glastonbury, Route 17 runs directly south into South Glastonbury and parallel to the Connecticut River.

On August 5, 1952, when the pilot was lost, he proceeded south and had already bypassed Rentschler Field in East Hartford and Brainard Airport in Hartford. The August 6, 1952, Hartford Courant article stated, "Baca when his plane quit, glided into Rentschler but Dell, could not make it." When Dell ran out of fuel and being on the east side of the Connecticut River he was probably looking for Rentschler Field located about seven miles northeast of South Glastonbury.

Lt. Dell descended through the clouds over Glastonbury and flew along Route 17 on his flight path on the afternoon and continued south over South Glastonbury. When Lt. Dell dropped out of the clouds to the northeast of town, he proceeded south to look for a location to land his jet. Unable to find an airfield the pilot bailed out of his jet at 2500 feet and landed in a field behind the South Glastonbury Firehouse.

The South Glastonbury Firehouse NO. 2 is located in the center of town on the Route 17 also known as Main Street. The firehouse is located on the west side of the Main Street between High St. and Water St. It has changed from its 1952 brick building structure to a modern and expanded firehouse. Directly behind the firehouse is a parking lot that was once a field. This is the area where a witness on High St. saw the pilot descend. This is the area where Lt. Dell landed. Mary Jane and I took several camera shots of the area and we discovered that the Bakery shop across the street was the same building where the Glastonbury Drug Store was located. This is the spot where the pilot went after he made his landing made his phone call to Westover AFB and talked to the locals.

The Glastonbury Citizen had reported that Dell's fighter jet had crashed off of South Main Street and a quarter mile up the hill east of the John Christian farm buildings…It had fallen close to two miles southeast of where its pilot alighted." The Hartford Courant reported that witnesses reported that the jet, "skimmed over the Blackburn home on Kimberly Road, missed the roof by a few feet, and plowed into a patch of woods in back of the John Christian farm. The impact was followed by an explosion which sent parts flying for yards around the area." Another nearby witness reported, "The plane whizzed by him flying 'very low.' Suddenly, he said, it nose dived into the woods with an explosion and fire following almost instantly." *The Glastonbury Citizen* also reported a mother and her four children "were in their homes on Hickory Drive, near the crash scene at the time of the explosion" One child was the little boy who thought "an atom bomb" exploded nearby.

With all of my information at hand, Mary Jane and I got into the vehicle and left the center of town. We proceeded down South Main Street along Route 17 and continued to follow the same route that the abandoned jet flew after it was abandoned. In search of the crash-site, area while eating a doughnut from the bakery we went just over a mile down the road and made a left turn onto Kimberly Lane. We proceeded up the steep road that leveled off shortly after and continued west on this short road that had both old farmhouses and later model homes on it. The woods are sparse in the neighborhood where the old Christian Farm was back in 1952. We drove to the end of the road that intersects with Dayton Road. A good part of this area is still heavily wooded to the west and we took camera shots of this area. This was the vicinity where the abandoned F-86 Sabre crashed on that cloudy afternoon in August of 1952. We then took a right hand turn on Dayton and proceeded up a hill to Hickory Drive, where the family heard the explosion and left the area for fear of the fire that raged from the crash. Mary Jane and I turned around, drove back down Dayton to Kimberly lane, took more photos and enjoyed the scenery.

We discussed the crash incident and I commented that few people here probably do not know that an American fighter jet crashed in this neighborhood 55 years ago. If only the trees could talk, what a story they could tell. Jane and I then proceeded back into town and went to the South Glastonbury Library and we met two friendly women working there, a mother and her daughter. Neither had known about the 1952 crash and when I showed the mother the local article she told me that the names she recognized in the article were deceased. I was given permission to take some pictures on the wall of old photos and we talked a while. I left the town with a much better understanding of the area where the events of the jet crash incident occurred so long ago on that

August 5 afternoon. I continued to research for other unusual and unexplained incidents that involved Westover AFB in Chicopee Falls, Massachusetts, and found some interesting information.

On September 2, 1952, and only 27 days after the Westover AFB jet crashed in South Glastonbury, CT, another Westover AFB F-86 Sabre Jet crashed, killing the pilot. *The New York Times* reported on September 3, 1952, that an Air Force veteran of 100 combat missions in the Korean War died in the crash. First Lieut. John J. Burke, Jr. was killed when his F-86 jet fighter crashed near Westover AFB. It was reported that, "Air Force officials said the cause of the crash had not been determined. It happened, they said, five miles east of the field near the Ludlow reservoir." For his services in Korea, Burke received the Air Medal and the Korean service medal. Why was Westover AFB having such a difficult time keeping their fighter jets in the air during this period? Were these jets going down during UFO intercept attempts?

Ten days later on September 13, 1952, Westover AFB was in the headlines again. *The Springfield News* in Massachusetts carried the following story, "15 'Flying Saucer' Reports From N. E. Unexplained-Objects Spotted Form Holyoke, Long Meadow, Westover On List; Most of Sightings Identified." In part, this article states, "Washington, Sept. 12 – Reports of unidentified flying objects in the New England area continue to reach the Air Force, but all but 15 have been unexplained, officials said today."

The "15 unexplained reports from New England" were not among those that the Air Force considered "familiar things" such as; friendly aircraft, light aberrations, hoaxes, meteorological phenomena, other known natural occurrences or manmade objects. Among the 15 "unknowns" on the list was, "Westover Air Force Base, Chicopee Falls." The article further stated, "These [15 cases] are among the 400 'unexplained' sightings out of some 2000 reports from all over the country which the Air Force has attempted to investigate and analyze since it first took official notice of the phenomena five years ago."

The article ended with the following information, "The Air Force is continuing its investigation of unexplained sightings because it feels a responsibility to identify and analyze aerial phenomena that could possibly be a menace to the United States." Did Westover AFB fighter pilots, Captain Leo Baca, Lieutenant James Dell, and First Lieutenant John Burke, Jr., encounter UFOs that disabled them and forced them down?

The Westover AFB jet that force landed in Hartford, and the jet that crashed in South Glastonbury on August 5, 1952, was not the end of the unusual events that afternoon.

There was another sighting on that Tuesday afternoon, August 5, 1952. This report came from Granger Texas and appeared in *The Taylor Press* newspaper on August 7, 1952. The article reported, "A Taylorite, Gene Precuss, says he and two other fellows spotted what they called a 'flying saucer' over Granger Tuesday afternoon about 2:30 [p.m. CST/3:30 p.m. EST- 4:30 p.m. EDT].

It was said that the witness, "Precuss described the object as a silver ball with a dim black ring around it. It would move at a tremendous pace, then slow down and flop around and then speed up again." He also stated, "When the thing was moving fast it would taper off at the back, but when it slowed down you could tell it was in the form of a circle." Precuss added that, "the object was first spotted coming out of the east and that he and two companions followed it until it crossed the sky and disappeared into the sun." The witness stated, "I know one thing: it was no illusion, three of us saw it." The paper reported, "Precuss said the trio were in downtown Granger when they spotted the object. He said that it was the first time he had ever seen anything like it." The UFO sightings continued into the night and ended with a grand appearance over the nation's capitol.

On that night near Washington D.C., it was a hot and rainy night and most people were at home listening to their favorite radio program or watching television. At 9:46 p.m. EST/ 10:46 EDT, the UFOs returned once again. At Manassas, Maryland, a ground observer at his post spotted an "oval-shaped" object proceed south across the sky, according to a "Flyobrpt" [Flying Object Report], from the "29th Air Division at "Great Falls AFB, Montana." Shortly after, the UFOs returned to Washington and once again began to reconnoiter the Capital. The third summer flap of UFO sightings over Washington had begun. These sightings began 22 hours after the first UFO visit to Westover AFB, in Massachusetts, earlier that morning.

An *Associated Press* August 6th news wire reported the incident. *The New Haven Register* newspaper in Connecticut printed a front-page article, "Radar Screen Picks Up Fleet Of Flying Saucers In Capital."

The incident unfolded at Andrews AFB located in Camp Springs, MD. It was reported that, " A spokesman at Andrews Field said two unidentified objects showed on the fields radar at 10:20 p.m. moving slowly from Washington to Mount Vernon." At approximately the same time, a heavy rain started to come down over the Capitol area as they tracked the two blips; "An Air Force spokesman at the Pentagon noted that the radar sightings – tiny blips on a fluorescent screen – started just about the time a thunderstorm hit the Washington area with heavy rain." Andrews' AFB radars then picked up two more targets a few minutes later that were located to the east of their base field and moving at approximately 60 miles per hour. This article explains, "A few minutes later two more images appeared on the screen, four to six miles east of the field, which is about seven miles southeast of Washington. These objects appeared to move slowly, then stop, then fly away." The UFOs disappeared and the sightings over Washington D.C. had ceased, but only temporarily.

The next UFO appeared over the area of Camden, New Jersey at about 10:40 p.m. The New Jersey Newspaper, *The Camden Courier Post* reported sightings of this UFO the following day. Their August 6 headline stated, "8 Residents Report 'Saucers' On Nocturnal Sweep Through Sky." In part it states, "Eight Camden residents reported a 'bright, round orange object' in the western skies Tuesday night." At "10:45" Camden resident Mrs. Roger McGowan, "excitedly" called to her sister-in-law to tell her about a UFO. *The Courier-Post* article states, "There was a bright orange ball, like a fireball, over in the west," Mrs. McGowan said. "It didn't seem to move, and it was very high. After about Five minutes, it just faded away. It didn't blink like the light of a plane, and we didn't hear any noise. My two brother-in law [s], Chuck and Earl, saw it too."

It was repotted that three additional local residents also "saw a similar object in the west at the same time." One of the witnesses, "Mrs.Iezzi described it as low in the sky, and said it moved in the west to 'about a block away,' circled for a moment, and disappeared in the west." These were the last reports of a UFO sighting over the New Jersey area, but this was not the last sighting of the night.

Back in Washington D.C., around midnight, the radars at Andrews AFB picked up a UFO target. A big blip had appeared on their radarscopes. The blip indicated it was a UFO, and furthermore, it was over the nations Capitol. Shortly after, a scramble alert was issued and fighter jets from New Castle AFB took to the skies over Washington D.C. When the F-94 Starfires arrived over the area in question, the UFO had disappeared. . It was reported, "Two jets were sent up from New Castle Del., but pilots saw nothing unusual. The jets passed over the Washington area and then returned to their base in Delaware." The following day, an Andrews AFB spokesperson stated the following to the press, "No radar sightings were made while the planes were overhead." Throughout the night, as many as two to ten targets were picked up on radar. This article also stated, "The Washington Post said one official called it 'a veritable fleet.' It also quoted an experienced radar operator as saying, 'This is the most puzzling phenomenon we have ever observed. We have definitely not been seeing spots before our eyes.'"

An "AIR INTELLIGENCE INFORMATION REPORT" by "Captain Benjamin Berkon" dated "6 August 1952" and a "Spot Intelligence Report, by "Colonel Doyle Rees" of "Bolling AFB," states that the first target was picked up by Andrews AFB radar at 10:20 p.m. and its position on the scope indicated that it was only 2 - 1/2 miles from their field. At about 10:23 p.m. three more blips appeared on their radar screens and indicated they were about 4-1/2 miles from them, and then another appeared shortly after that. After 10:30 p.m., yet another blip appeared on the radar screens of Andrews AFB. These two documents contained in the Project Blue Book files do not state fighter jets scrambled that night, yet there is also a mention about a jet scramble in The New York Times on August 7, 1952. Why is there no official record of the scramble in Blue Book? Were the UFOs that flew over Washington that night, the same objects sighted earlier over; Westover AFB in Massachusetts...Baltimore, Maryland...Augusta, Georgia... and Granger, Texas? Where any of these UFOs involved in the F-86 Sabre Jet incident that led to the jet's crash in South Glastonbury, Connecticut?

AUGUST HEATS UP

On August 5, 1952, an F-94 Starfire fighter jet and a UFO were involved in yet another incident. This event occurred near Haneda Air Force Base, in Japan. Project Blue Book recorded this incident, as Case 1827 and evaluated it as an "Unknown." At 11:30 p.m. local time, Haneda AFB control tower operators watched a UFO as it passed over Tokyo Bay at about 1,500 feet. The object was described as being a dark round shape surrounded by a bright light with a curved outer edge with smaller lights around it.

While being tracked on radar, a scramble alert was issued at 11:55 p.m. and shortly after a Starfire jet from nearby Johnson AFB scrambled after the unknown object. The fighter jet, piloted by 1st Lt. W.R. Holder and radar observer 1st Lt. A.M. Jones chased the object, which accelerated away from the jet while being tracked on the Starfire's radar. During the next half-hour, the UFO disappeared and reappeared throughout the sky and would vanish when the jet closed on it. The Starfire crew searched over the Tokyo Bay airspace until 12:33 p.m. and were recalled back to Johnson AFB and landed shortly after. The sighting that lasted about one hour was never explained!

There was three-reported Project Blue Book "Unknown" cases on August 6, 1952. The Haneda AFB sighting over Japan was actually continued over to August 6 from the night of August 5, 1952 and was designated another case. These are the three-recorded cases.

1. Case 1841. Tokyo, Japan.
2. Case 1843. Belleville, Michigan.
3. Case 1845. Fort Austin, Michigan.

On August 7, 1952, a flying saucer was sighted over Silverton, Oregon, between 3:00 and 4:00 p.m., according to *The Capitol Journal* in Salem, Oregon, dated August 9, 1952. Two women of the GOC watchers reported seeing the UFO about three miles away from a Ground Observers Post. Later, two more women sky watchers "saw, the 'Saucer' a few minutes before 5 o' clock at approximately five Miles from the observation post." Information giving descriptions of the object stated, "All four women said that the color was a glistening aluminum color." One GOC observer said, "the saucer was at first triangular, and later appeared to be more of an inverted saucer." Another observer, "described it as flat on the bottom side and 'turtle back shape' on top."

The Silverton GOC watchers then contacted officials at Portland located north of them, at Portland International Airport. The airport provided a certain designated section for USAF units. Information states, "Their report was confirmed by army and air observers at Portland who said the object was being intercepted at that moment by jet pilot action." During this time, officials kept in contact with the Silverton GOC and questioned them about the unfolding incident. The article then stated what occurred next, "All four watchers agreed that it [flying saucer] was headed to the east, not too active a speed until it came in close to the intercepting plane when it darted 'fiercely' toward the interceptor plane." It was reported that, "All agreed that it circled the jet, much as one would swing a rope; that it darted at terrific speed; that it was close to the observation post."

Seemingly, the flying saucer did not want to be bothered when the plane was near it. The object quickly maneuvered toward the plane; a maneuver that could be interpreted as a threatening gesture to back off and keep away from it. It is a good thing that neither the jet pilot nor the flying saucer was trigger-happy during this encounter. How many other encounters between jets and UFOs had different endings that ended in duels of death?

On August 7, a UFO report came in from San Antonio Texas that was recorded as "Unknown" Case 1855 in Blue Book. The next "Unknown" case was on August 9, 1952. At 10:50 a.m., a UFO made another visit to reconnoiter Lake Charles AFB in Louisiana; the second sighting over that Air Force base in a week. This spectacular event was witnessed by Air Force Airman 3rd class J.P. Riley of the 806th Air Base group on that late morning. The witness reported that he saw a "Disc" out in the distance as it approached from the "north." The disc was on a direct course toward the base at a low altitude. Airman Riley said the object "flew very fast" and then passed over the base at an altitude of approximately "5,000 feet." Suddenly, the disc, stopped over the base, "hovered for 2 seconds," then "turned" and flew toward the west and disappeared from sight. Airman Riley stated the length of his incredible observation occurred over a time of about five to six minutes.

On Sunday August 10, 1952, alarming amounts of UFOs were sighted over Rockford, Illinois near Chicago. This prompted Air Force fighter jets of the 4706 Defense Wing at O'Hare International Airport to be scrambled once again. On August 11, 1952, *The Rockford Register –Republic* newspaper reported the following story, "SAUCERS' SIGHTED-Speedy Jets Are Alerted In Vain Hunt." In part, the article states, "Fifty-four flying saucers were sighted streaking over Rockford early Sunday evening by at least 14 persons. Two U.S. Air Force F-86 Sabre Jet interceptors based at O'Hare International Airport near Chicago came seeking the strange objects, but the pilots didn't see them. The report of the saucers here may be the most detailed of all and probably more of the objects were seen consecutively than ever before anywhere in the nation." Even though these powerful "detailed" statements appeared in the press, the incident was not recorded in the Blue Book unexplained files. The UFO sightings that night lasted from 5:20 p.m. until 7:30 p.m. CST... an amazing two hours and ten minutes! One must wonder why these objects were repeatedly sighted over this part of Illinois!

The New York Times also reported a mysterious jet accident that occurred on Sunday August 10 in an August 12 article titled, "JET CRASH VICTIM FOUND TO BE HERO…FALMOUTH, Mass., Aug. 11(UP)."

It was reported that a veteran fighter pilot was killed in an "unexplained crash of an F-94 all weather interceptor jet fighter." The pilot, Captain Hobart R. Gay Jr., was a 1949 West Point graduate and transferred to the Air Force. Captain Gay "completed 105 combat missions in Korea and earned the Distinguished Flying Cross and Air Medal with three oak clusters in thirteen months Far East duty." It was stated that, "An Air Force spokesman said shortly after the incident occurred, Captain Gay was believed to have been trapped in the cockpit of his plane when it crashed." The Air Force reported, "Fragments of the craft, including a wing tank, were found near the spot where it plunged into Vineyard Sound seconds after Captain Gay radioed he was landing. He was within minutes of the runway when a Coast Guard watchman said he saw the ship suddenly dive into the water." The Times reported, "An Air-Sea search for Captain Gay's body was resumed at dawn."

I will now ask the following questions:
1. Seconds after the pilot "radioed he was landing" he crashed. Why did he crash?
2. What problem arose that caused the jet to "suddenly dive into the water"?
3. The pilot was in radio communication seconds before the crash. Why was the Air Force unaware of the problem?
4. Why did the Air Force believe Captain Gay was trapped in the planes cockpit when it crashed?
5. What is the reason that Captain Gay did not bail out of his jet before he crashed into the water?
6. Why was this accident said to be "Unexplained" when the pilot was in radio communication with his base?
7. What were the circumstances that caused this Korean War veteran with 105 combat missions to crash?
8. Did this combat veteran fighter pilot actually die in combat against the same UFOs seen that day?
9. Was this accident dubbed an "unexplained crash" because it actually involved flying saucers?

The objects became bolder in their actions as the summer continued. The UFOs were making blatant appearances around the United States and seen over major cities, key installations, and Air Force Bases; in several cases, repeatedly over the same locations. The jet scrambles and pursuits after UFOs continued across the United States 24-hours-a-day. The armed forces protecting the skies over America were relentless in their pursuits of these objects in an attempt to "shoot them down."

On August 11, 1952, *TIME* magazine reported an incident that involved jets scrambled after several UFOs over New York. The following article appeared in the "SCIENCE" section of that issue, "In Chenango County, NY., citizens gathered in crowds to watch a 'whole flotilla of bright shiny balls moving rapidly in a northerly direction.' Jet fighters scrambled from Griffis Air Force Base in Rome, NY., but found nothing." Also appearing on this page in the same "SCIENCE" section was a mention about the July 26/27 Washington D.C. sightings. It reported, "Washington itself had just lived through a phantom invasion when unidentified blips on a Civil Aeronautics Authority brought jet fighters screaming over Delaware to hunt 'flying saucers.' (TIME, Aug. 4). The fighters had shot down no night-flying saucers, but two of them had found their targets. It appeared later that they had been drawing a head on each other." It is apparent that *TIME* knew the motive of the Air Force jets.

An "Air Intelligence Information Report" dated "12 August 1952," explained a UFO encounter reported by Second Lt. T. Boluch of the 148 FIS at Dover AFB. On August 10, the encounter unfolded when an F-94 B Starfire fighter jet was flying over New Jersey at an altitude of 20,000 feet at 0543Z [0043 EST/12:43 a.m.]. While cruising on a straight and level trajectory, the pilot and radar operator saw a glowing object. It was off to their left at a lower altitude than the jet and was sitting motionless in the sky.

The Starfire pilot redirected his aircraft and proceeded directly at the stationary light. The chase was on. The object quickly moved away from the pursuing jet that was bearing down on it. The object diminished in size and brilliance as it streaked away from the jet. Moments later, the object stopped over the vicinity of Cape May, according to the pilot. The pilot tried to contact the local Ground intercept station over the area but was unable to do so. At this point, the pilot discontinued his pursuit because the jet was running low on fuel. He turned and proceeded back to Delaware.

Shortly after, the tables were turned and the UFO began following the jet back towards the base! The pursued had now become the pursuer! The UFO continued to trail the jet that was continuously running low on fuel, and then closed on it. Without any warning, the UFO turned darted away and proceeded south. With out any further incident, the pilot and radar operator landed at Dover AFB a short time after. Luckily, for the pilot of the Starfire, this incident did not turn into a dogfight while the jet was low on fuel.

On the following day, another UFO incident occurred on the west coast that involved an F-94 Starfire fighter jet. In San Rafael, California on August 13, 1952, an official at Hamilton AFB received a telephone call from a concerned citizen in Oakland who just had a UFO sighting. At 9:10 p.m. the caller reported, "Two balls of fire" had made a ten-mile circle over the Oakland area and then proceeded in the direction of Hamilton AFB. The report was then forwarded to the base Airdrome officer, "Captain Broden." In turn, Broden immediately scrambled an F-94 fighter jet to search for the two objects. The Starfire searched the airspace between Oakland and Hamilton AFB with negative results. The intercept mission was called off shortly after. This "Flyobrpt" [flying object report] was sent from Hamilton AFB to ATIC officials on the following day, "14 Aug 52."

The UFOs continued their reconnaissance of Air Force bases around the United States. On August 13, 1952 at 7:11 p.m. EST., three UFOs were sighted over Tampa, Florida, near MacDill AFB... Two witnesses watched a UFO aerial display for 20 minutes and then contacted the base to report their sighting. On August 14, Captain W. J. Grant, an Intelligence officer at MacDill reported the following incident in an "Air Intelligence Information Report." He stated:

One object changed course abruptly to the west moving in excess of 600 mph. This same object then appeared to hover for about five minutes then moved at an excessive rate to the east, then resumed its course to the north and disappeared. The two other objects did not alter their course and disappeared.

It is interesting that Captain Grant referred to them as "Objects." There were 118 August cases of UFO reports documented between "Unknown" Cases 1771 on August 1 until "Unknown" case 1889 was recorded on August 13. Between August 1 and August 13, Project Blue Book recorded 12 of them "Unknown" cases.

On August 13, 1952, "Unknown" case 1889 involved a fighter jet encounter with a UFO over Tokyo, Japan. At 9:45 p.m., an "orange light" was sighted as it orbited at 8,000 feet above the Tokyo area. The speed of the UFO was an estimated "230 miles per hour." Shortly after, the object was reported to have "spiraled down" to an altitude of about "1,500 feet" and then stopped. The UFO stayed hovered in a stationary position over the Tokyo area for about "2-3 minutes." Marine Corps pilot, Major D. McGough was over Tokyo in his interceptor plane and attempted to intercept the UFO. According to the fighter pilot, when he approached the light, it "went out."

This intercept attempt was just another in the long list of military fighters going after UFOs during the summer of 1952. Air Force, Navy, and Marine Corps fighters across the world were on constant alert to intercept these UFOs and Project Blue Book continued to analyze the incoming barrage of reports.

On August 14, 1952, The UFOs came back to another one of their favorite cities, Lake Charles, Louisiana, home of Lake Charles AFB. At 10:30 p.m. that night, an object described as a "ball of light" and "yellow in color," rose, fell, and then swept over the Mathieson Chemical Corporation. This was the third UFO sighting over that city in less than two weeks. This sighting was reported to nearby Lake Charles AFB and documented in an "Air Intelligence Information Report" dated "16 August 52." Officials contacted ATIC once again.

An early morning UFO report from the Ground Observers Corp Post at Davis, California prompted an F-94 scramble from Hamilton AFB according to a base "Flyobrpt" dated "19 August 52." On August 15, GOC spotters at the Davis Post reported a UFO over their city at 4:20 a.m. They described the UFO as a "round object" that was rainbow-colored. The observers reported it "hovered" in the sky for about nine minutes, and then eight more UFOs joined it. Outside sources said, the GOC Post at Woodland also reported seeing the UFOs. At approximately 5:30 a.m., two more UFOs appeared in the sky over the Davis area. Shortly after, a filter station official notified Hamilton AFB and they scrambled an F-94 Starfire after the objects. The fighter pilot searched the skies at "10,000 feet" and then climbed to "20,000 feet" but claimed he did not see the objects. The Ground Observers stated otherwise. They claimed they saw the jet and UFOs in the sky simultaneously. Furthermore, the GOC spotters said the jet actually appeared to be at the same altitude of the UFOs at one point during the interception attempt! How many pilots were gagged about their UFO experiences?

Edward Ruppelt stated, "By the middle of August, Project Blue Book was back to normal Lieutenant Flue's Coca-Cola consumption had dropped from twenty a day in mid-July to his normal five." This was only a temporary situation though. There were 93 August cases of UFO reports documented between "Unknown" Cases 1920 on August 18, until Case 2013 on August 29, 1952. Project Blue Book recorded 16 of them as "Unknown" cases. There were more "Unknowns" recorded during the second half of August:

1. Case 1920. August 18, 1952. Fairfield, California.
2. Case 1928. August 19, 1952. Red Bluff, California.

An outstanding incident that did not appear in the "Unknown" case files occurred over the vicinity of Boron, California on August 19. This was the same day as the Red Bluff, California sighting. "Air Intelligence Information Report" dated "25 August 52" from the 750th AC & W, in "Boron, California," explained this UFO incident. On the night of August 19, 1952, a UFO was sighted high over the skies of Boron and above the "750th Aircraft and Control Warning" radar site.

As the incident unfolded, two fighter jets flew into the area to investigate the target while being guided by "Captain Borgrson" of the 750th AC & W. As the jets passed into the airspace looking for their bogey, pilot Lieutenant Otis was flying the lead jet. He informed Borgrson that, "He had a stranger at one o'clock." Moments later, the radar man asked, "What kind of aircraft is it?" The wingman replied that the stranger "appeared as a large craft." The 750th AC & W controller then instructed the pilots to close on the target and investigate the so-called "stranger."

Captain Borgrson stated, Lieutenant Otis, "reported that upon turning into the stranger [to change heading], it appeared to have no tail assembly and showed great acceleration in moving away from them in an easterly direction and moving into space." Borgrson stated that after landing, Lieutenant Otis told the controller at the 750th AC & W, and he "described the object as oval at the base and tapered to a heavy center section, he also reaffirmed that it did not have a tail section." Near perfect eyesight is required to be a fighter pilot. The object that fighter pilot Lt. Otis saw and described, definitely gave the appearance an unconventional aircraft!

On August 21, 1952, Sabre Jets of the 4706th Fighter Interceptor Wing based at O'Hare International Airport in Chicago were scrambled out on a UFO interception mission. On that night, a UFO was sighted over Elgin Illinois, located near Chicago, one of the UFOs favorite cities. This incident appeared in *The Chicago Herald-American* with the headline, "Saucer Outflies Jet Over Elgin."

A Ground Observer Corps supervisor at the Elgin Post, Mr. D.C. Scott, and an Operations officer of the Ground Observers Corps at the Chicago Filter Station, Captain Everett A. Turner were involved in the incident. In part, the article states the following; Mr. Scott said that the light first showed, "in the sky northeast of Elgin at 10:10 p.m." He also added, "It first appeared at about 2000 feet flying straight. At times it rose with a great burst of speed, and then appeared to hover."

The article reported, "Scott said the mysterious object was a 'yellowish white light five times brighter than a star and about the size of an orange [at distance seen]…Several times, he said, it appeared to rise to 5,000 feet within three minutes. Scott added, 'It's nothing like I have ever seen before. It looks like a light but casts no beam." Supervisor Scott then stated, "Turner told me to call when ever the thing settled down. After watching it for an hour and 23 minutes, we saw it begin to hover. Turner had alerted the O'Hare jets and they came at once. So far as I know, only one gave chase. At my direction, relayed by Turner, the pilot made four passes." The first pass the jet made was at 10,000 feet, the second at 5,000 feet, and the third pass was at 2,500 feet. Scott explained the fighter pilots fourth pass, "He repeated at 2,000 feet, this time turning off his running lights. Just as he got over the mark, the thing blinked out."

The article also reported, "the jet pilot was on 'a collision course' when the mysterious blinked out, Turner said. He went on: 'If it had been where it was last seen he [pilot] would have hit it. I don't know if it could maneuver that fast or what. That's something for the people at Wright Field to figure out."

After the fourth pass at the UFO, Supervisor Scott stated, "The pilot was forced to return to O'Hare because his fuel was running out." The pursuit was reported to have lasted until, "11:48 p.m." It was also reported, "The 'saucer' reappeared for a short time six minutes later, Scott said, apparently at about 25,000 feet in the southeast sky." He also added, "We have seen this thing five or six times the last two months, but never in the same place." This was not the last UFO scramble that the O'Hare fighter jets would be partaking against a "saucer."

Project Blue Book recorded three more "Unknown" cases over the United States on August 21, 22, and 23, 1952:
1. Case 1938. August 21, 1952. Neffesville, Pennsylvania.
2. Case 1944. August 22, 1952. Dallas, Texas.
3. Case 1956. August 23, 1952. Akron, Ohio.

Project Blue Book recorded three more "Unknown" cases that all occurred on August 24, 1952.
1. Case 1961. Hermanas, New Mexico.

2. Case 1964. Tucson, Arizona.

3. Case 1969. Levelland, Texas.

A most note worthy incident occurred on August 24, 1952, and involved a fighter plane and a UFO, Case 1961. An "Air Intelligence Information Report" written by the Commanding Officer of Turner AFB, Ga., and dated "29 August 1952" gave the details of this incident. Major John Albert, the CO, reported the name of the fighter pilot involved was, "Colonel Gerald W. Johnson." Colonel Johnson was piloting an "F-84G" Thunder Jet over New Mexico air space at an altitude of "35,000 feet" when he encountered two UFOs. The fighter pilot described them as "6' silver balls." The (AIIR) report states the pilot's sighting lasted for "10 minutes."

Shortly after the incident occurred, Albert Chop let Donald Keyhoe read a copy of the Intelligence report from ATIC. Keyhoe wrote about the incident in his 1953 book, *Flying Saucers from Outer Space*. He actually told the story about 20 years before the Blue Book "Unknown" cases were declassified and made public at the Air Force Archives located at Maxwell AFB.

In his 1953 book though, he gave the pilot a pseudonym name and called him, "Colonel Carl Sanderson," rather than his real name, "Colonel Gerald W. Johnson." Keyhoe stated that the pilot had, "been a skeptic." He also said this about the pilot, "In a coolly factual report he told Intelligence officers he was now convinced the discs were real." Donald Keyhoe reported the following excerpt of this fighter pilot's testimony:

I was flying an F-84 at 35,000 feet, en route to Turner Air Force Base, in Georgia. At 10:15, Mountain Standard Time [10:15 a.m. MST], I sighted two round silvery balls flying abreast over Hermanas, New Mexico. One made a right turn, in front of my F-84. Both disappeared at very high speed, and then reappeared over El Paso Texas, Texas. I saw one climb straight up, two or three thousand feet. Then the second one came in front of me and joined the other in close formation. In a few minutes, they both vanished. From their maneuvers and their terrific speed, I am certain their flight performance was greater than any aircraft known today.

The "Air Information Intelligence Report" gave the following remark in evaluating Case 1961, "The observed characteristics of these unidentified objects were such that would lead to no conclusion."

The UFOs continued their surveillance of Air Force Bases throughout the United States. An August 28, 1952, "Spot Intelligence Report" from Robins AFB near Macon, Georgia reported a UFO sighting. While on base, an employee sighted a "Spherical in shape" looking UFO at 8:30 p.m. and watched it for five minutes with his binoculars. In another episode that night, a UFO circled over the airfield of Barksdale AFB, near Shreveport, Louisiana. Multiple witnesses reported the object looked like a star as it made several repeated passes over the base, and then it would stop and hover. An "Air Intelligence Information Report" that was dated "2 September 1952," wrote, "Sometimes the speed was terrific and then again it just barely moved or stood still." One witness who observed the UFO thought it appeared to be, "inspecting Barksdale Field from different angles." This was a common thought amongst witnesses, especially military witnesses.

Project Blue Book recorded three more "Unknown" cases that all occurred on August 25, 1952.

1. Case 1972. Pittsburg, Kansas.

2. Case 1915. Delaware, Ohio.

3. Case 1979. Alamogordo, New Mexico. Holloman AFB.

Holloman AFB was the next location an "Unknown" UFO incident. Case 1979 reported that two Holloman base employees made an afternoon observation of a large UFO at 3:40 p.m. Two civilian supervisors, Mr. Frederick Lee and supervisor Mr.Aquilar sighted a "round silver object" that flew over Alamogordo and flew over an area of the base. The witnesses stated that they watched the UFO for nearly five minutes. During that time, it proceeded south over Alamogordo, then made a turn, and proceeded in the opposite direction on a northern heading. The UFO then made an amazing "360 degree turn" and ascended. The witnesses said the object "flew away vertically." Once again, like so many of the previous sightings, this UFO did not look like a conventional aircraft. The ball-shaped objects continued to be seen throughout the summer of 1952.

The UFO sightings continued to escalate toward the end of August and Project Blue Book recorded three more "Unknown" cases that occurred on August 26, 1952:

1. Case 1986. Lathrop Wells, Nevada.
2. Case 1987. Biloxi, Mississippi.
3. Case 1994. Mexico. (August 26, 27, and 30)

On the following day, August 27 at 12:05 a.m. EST, "a round, medium sized, amber colored object" was sighted over Richmond, Virginia on a western heading. The Air Force personnel who sighted this object at the Richmond filter station of the GOC said, "The object looked like a round light, was moving about 100 miles per hour, and disappeared near the horizon. The object remained in sight for approximately five (5) minutes." This information is stated in a Blue Book "Air Intelligence Information Report." It originated from the "771st AC & W Sq., Fort John Custis, VA."

About one hour later at 1:20 a.m., the object was sighted again. The report said, "It was reported the second time as being very large and resembling a bright white light moving up and down." At 1:29 a.m., the 771st AC & W Sq. contacted Dover AFB in Delaware. Dover officials then "scrambled two F-94 fighters –interceptor aircraft in an attempt to intercept the aircraft." At 2:06 a.m., "the pilot of one of the scrambled fighters reported a contact on a bright yellow light several miles south of Richmond. Contact was lost after three minutes." During this time, the GOC observers were relaying the coordinates of the UFO in relation to the fighters to the 771ST A C & W Sq. In turn, they relayed this information to the fighter jets in the air. The report then explains, "Each time, the pilot [Captain John A. Swezing] of the lead aircraft stated, that the planet Venus was at the position for the reported object." The Starfires searched the area for 15 minutes and "the search was discontinued." The two Starfires returned to Dover AFB without incident.

This incident was written off by Blue Book as the "Planet Venus." I ask why is there no further mention or evaluation about the original UFO sighting at 12:05 a.m.:

A. Observers said, "The object remained in sight for approximately five (5) minutes."
B. Observers said, the "object was sighted moving west over Richmond, Virginia."
C. Observers said, "The object ...was moving about 100 miles per hour and disappeared over the horizon."

Furthermore, there is no mention or evaluation concerning the objects' second appearance at 1:20 a.m.

D. It "was reported the second time as being very large and resembling a bright white moving up and down."

It is obvious that the Air Force in an attempt discard this incident, compiled the first two legitimate UFO sightings together with the planet Venus sighting, and then wrote the incident off as "astronomical"! Why did the Air Force not scramble fighter jets after the UFO when it was seen the first time? There are more questions here than answers. One point is obvious though; there was an intentional cover-up.

On August 28, another incident occurred that involved another Air Force base. Project Blue Book listed this incident as "Unknown" Case 2006. On that night, witnesses at Brookley AFB in Mobile, Alabama as well as witnesses in Chickasaw, Louisiana reported seeing UFOs. At Brookley AFB, the incident unfolded when control tower operators sighted UFOs over the vicinity of their base at 9:30 p.m. Also present was an Air Force OSI officer and numerous Air Force personnel...an official audience. Several civilians also witnessed the fascinating aerial display that the UFOs put on that night that lasted for "one hour and 15 minutes."

During that time, six UFOs with varying colors were seen. They were described as red, green, blue, and sparkling like a diamond. During the course of their visit, the objects flew "erratically up and down" and also "hovered." It was also noted that there was absolutely no military or civilian air traffic in the area at that time.

The final Project Blue Book "Unknown" case that occurred in August over the United States is listed as Case 2013. This aerial sighting is worth noting because it occurred over Colorado Springs, Colorado, home of

ENT AFB, Headquarters for the Air Defense Command. On the afternoon of August 29, 1952, a civilian Air Patrol pilot by the name of Mr. Magruder got the shock of his life when he sighted three UFOs that dwarfed his aircraft. Shortly after, the pilot contacted the Air Force and reported his sighting. It was later filed with Project Blue Book.

An account of Magruder's encounter is contained in an Air Force report. This report, "Flyobrpt" [Flying Object Report] is dated "30 August 30" and was sent from the Commanding General at "ADC - ENT AFB – COLO," to the "ATIC – WP AFB – OHIO." General Benjamin Chidlaw was the commander who sent this UFO report to Project Blue Book at the Air Technical Intelligence Center. This report is not complete but the teletype message gives all the pertinent details of the incident. I have included words in authors' brackets for continuity. The teletype message is as follows:

THREE ROUND OBJECTS, 50 FT IN DIAMETER BY 10 FT HIGH [were seen] FLYING IN TRAIL FORMATION. [The three] OBJECTS [were] ALUMINUM IN COLOR WITH REDDISH YELLOW EXHAUST. [There was] NO SOUND HEARD. [Their] SPEED EST [estimated at] 1500 MPH.

[The three] OBJECTS PASSED IN FRONT OF [the] MOON ON A SOUTH EASTERLY COURSE, THEN WENT STRAIGHT UP AND DISAPPEARED. 29/2335Z [29th of August/4:35 p.m. MST] FOR 4-5 SECONDS. VISUAL [type of sighting]. [Location:] COLORADO SPRINGS, COLO. [The three] OBJECTS WERE SIGHTED [in the] SOUTH AT [an altitude of] 5000 ft [and] TRAVELING SE [southeast].

The three UFOs seen by the pilot during that afternoon sighting were not explained. From the witnesses' description of the objects, they were obviously some type of metallic craft that emitted reddish yellow exhausts behind them. The objects seemed to be huge round discs that were thick and seemed to be controlled. This is apparent by the maneuvers they displayed while in flight. These objects were not conventional aircraft as is apparent by their size, shape and speed. What were these three objects and why were they here? They certainly did not come from the Soviet Union, so where did they come from? Was it just a coincidence that they were seen over Colorado Springs, Colorado, home of the ADC Headquarters? Furthermore, they were flying at a 5,000-foot altitude and would have been difficult to pick-up on radar at that height. Is that why Ent AFB did not scramble jets after the UFOs, when they were right in their own back yard?

On August 28, 1952, the same day as the Colorado UFO incident, a fighter jet exploded near Seattle, Washington over Puget Sound. The jet was based at Paine AFB, located in Everett, which is just northeast of Seattle. *The New York Times* reported this tragic jet fighter accident on August 30. It reported:

LONG ISLAND JET PILOT KILLED. EVERETT, Wash., August 29 (AP)—An airman who was killed in a jet plane explosion over Puget Sound yesterday [August 28] was identified as Capt. Paul M. Ellman, 27 years old, of South Farmingdale, L. I., N.Y. Paine Air Force Base said that he was the pilot. Lieut. Ike Barber of Louisville, Ky., the radar operator, parachuted to safety onto Camano Island.

I ask, what caused this fighter jet to explode in mid-air near the Seattle area? Did these men encounter a UFO similar to the objects seen over Colorado that day? Bremerton, Washington is located west of Seattle on the opposite side of Puget Bay. The coastal inlet waters of Bremerton lead through Rich Passage and flow into Puget Sound. This small waterside city reported a UFO on the same day that Captain Ellman's jet exploded over nearby Puget Sound.

The Bremerton Sun newspaper reported this UFO sighting on August 29, 1952. It also referred to a military plane that was sighted during the UFO incident. The article, "'Something' Seen over the City" gave the following information. The incident unfolded at 1:30 p.m. when, "at least three persons were known today to have sighted something in the 'flying saucer' category from Bremerton." One of the witnesses was C.A.

Williams a local movie operator. He reported to have, "seen the 'thing' in sight for over a five minute span." The witness was putting up a fence on his property, "when he saw the disc-like craft." Mr. Williams's sons, "Kenneth 18, and Conrad, 12," also saw the UFO.

Mr. Williams, a pilot with 24 years flying experience, "was watching the sky" when he saw, "a single-engined, low-wing plane pass over." He said that it "appeared to be a military-type trainer." The plane was flying at an altitude of approximately, "8,000 to 10,000 feet," on a northern heading.

The witness' attention was then drawn to a "Thing" flying to the "west." This UFO was on a "southwesterly course," as it proceeded across the sky. Williams said that he watched it for approximately, "a minute until the plane came back into sight." This sighting actually puts the plane and UFO in the same setting of the sky.

Did Air Force Captain Ellman die on August 28, 1952 while trying to intercept this UFO or another one over Puget Sound when his jet exploded in mid-air? Is it just another coincidence that a fighter jet was destroyed in the same area where a UFO sighting occurred?

On the following day, an incident occurred on the west coast that involved a fighter jet and a UFO. The 83rd FIS at Hamilton AFB in San Rafael, California was back in the picture scrambling after UFOs again. On August 2, 1952, they had scrambled F-86 Sabre jets after eight UFOs. Eleven days later on August 13, 1952, they scrambled an F-94 Starfire after three UFOs and on August 29, Hamilton AFB scrambled yet another F-94 Starfire after UFOs. A short Project Blue Book teletype from the Commanding General at Hamilton AFB described the August 29, UFO incident.

It was then sent to the ADC at Ent AFB, ATIC at Wright Patterson AFB, and USAF Intelligence at the Pentagon in Washington D.C. A "PROJECT 10073 RECORD CARD" was also filed with it. At 9:15 p.m., civilians in Selma, California sighted "four" UFOs over their city. They described them as "Lights" that were "moving up and down." Three of the lights were green, and one light was red. They reported their sighting to the "Pasadena GOC" who then passed the information on to the Air Force. Shortly after, an F-94 Starfire scrambled from Hamilton AFB after the objects. The jet was vectored into the target area, but the UFOs had vanished. The fighter pilot was unable to find any of the lights and after a short search of the sky, he returned to his base without incident. This report was very short and indistinct. It was evaluated in the 10073 Record card, "Conclusions…Insufficient Data for Evaluation." I wonder why the information in this report was so vague!

Edward Ruppelt wrote about the month of August and said, "Several reports had come in during early August that had been read with a good deal of interest in the military and other governmental agencies. By late August 1952 several groups in Washington were following the UFO situation very closely."

Even though the UFO sightings declined by the end of August and early September, the objects were still being seen over key government installations. This factor concerned military officials at the Pentagon and in Washington D.C. It seemed that the summer of 1952 would never end. The month of September would prove to be a very troublesome time for the United States Air Force as the sightings continued.

THE SPACE SHIPS RETURN

During September, the team at Project Blue Book received "124" reports and evaluated 25 as "Unknown" cases. There were eight cases that they listed which involved military sightings. Four of those unexplained cases directly involved Air Force base sightings. They are listed below:

1. Case 2025. September 2, 1952. Chicago, IL. O'Hare Int. Airport. (4706 Fighter Interceptor Wing)
2. Case 2045. September 6, 1952. Lake Charles AFB. Lake Charles, LA.
3. Case 2093. September 14, 1952. Olmsted AFB. Middletown, PA.
4. Case 2100. September 16, 1952. Warner-Robins AFB. (Near) Macon, GA.

On September 1, 1952, Blue book listed two "Unknown" cases, both over the United States:
1. Case 2022. Marietta, GA.
2. Case 2023. Yaak, Montana.

The Marietta, Georgia case involved multiple witnesses who had UFO sightings. They are as follows:

A.) At 10:30 p.m., an ex-artillery officer, Mr. Bowman and twenty-four other witnesses watched a UFO over the skies of Marietta for 15 minutes. The witnesses described it as multi-colored, white, red, and bluish-green object. The object was reported to have a spinning motion and gave of sparks.

B.) Also at 10:30, another witness had a UFO sighting over Marietta. He watched two UFOs with binoculars for 30 minutes. He continued to watch for 15 minutes longer than the other witnesses did. The witness said, the objects were large and looked like spinning tops in the sky. They were red, blue and green, and flew in a side-by-side formation and left sparkling trails. It is obvious that a second one after 15 minutes joined the first object.

C.) At 10:50, a World War II, Army-Air Force B-25 aircraft gunner, had a sighting over Marietta.

This veteran stated he saw two large discs that were white in color and trailed green vapor. He said that they flew in trail formation, one behind the other. The witness also said that they appeared to merge, then flew away very fast.

The Yaak, Montana case involved visual and radar sightings of multi-colored objects and a black object. The objects were reported by, the 760th Aircraft & Warning Squadron. Located in Coleville, Washington, Air Force personnel watched them over the course of one hour and tracked them on radar. Two Air Force witnesses made visual sightings and three men witnessed the radar tracking of them. These UFOs made erratic maneuvers throughout the sky and visual sightings indicated that the UFOs also left vapor trails. There were no military or civilian aircraft flying within 100 miles that would account for the UFO sightings or radar returns. The UFOs disappeared at dawn.

On the following day, September 2, 1952, only 23 days after veteran combat pilot Captain Hobart Gay died in his F-94 Starfire, another Korean War "hero" was killed in his fighter jet. On September 3, 1952, *The New York Times* reported this headline, "AIR FORCE HERO KILLED - Veteran of 100 Korea Missions Dies In Bay

State Crash." This article reported, "WESTOVER AIR FORCE BASE, Mass., Sept 2 AP. A veteran of 100 combat missions in Korea, First Lieut. John J. Burke, Jr...was killed today when his F-86 jet fighter crashed near here. Air Force officials said the cause of the crash had not been determined." First Lt. Burke was attached to the sixtieth Fighter Interceptor Squadron at Westover. In combat, in Korea, Burke shot down "two MIGs and a TU-2" and damaged "two" more." The fighter pilot had "received the Air Medal and the Korean service medal."

On September 2, the same day that First Lt. Burke was killed in his F-86 Sabre Jet, Project Blue Book recorded seven sightings across the United States. Blue Book evaluated four of these cases, "insufficient data" and two as "balloons." Fighter jets and pilots were dropping out of the sky as UFO sightings continued to pile up around the United States.

Case 2025 occurred on September 2 and was evaluated an "Unknown." It involved two Air Force F-86 Sabre Jets scrambled after unexplained objects over Illinois at 5:55 a.m. The UFOs were back over one of their favorite cities, Chicago, and this night, they came back in record numbers. This incident appeared in *The New York Times* and *The Hartford Courant* newspapers. The two Sabre Jets were part of the 4706th Fighter Interceptor Wing based at O'Hare International Airport. *The New York Times* headline reported, "Jets Fly 'Through' Target; 'Hot Air,' says Radar Man." It states, "Two Sabre Jet fighters…flew 'right through the sky' over Chicago where radar scopes on the ground were showing a reflection from some unexplained object."

The Hartford Courant headline reported, "Saucer Suspect' Rammed by Jet; Nothing There." The article stated, "An Air Force officer said today he flew his jet fighter plane – 'right through' a spot where radar had shown an unexplained object. He said he saw nothing but empty airs…Two Sabre Jets were summoned after night radar crews of the Civil Aeronautics Administration reported tracking a number of unexplained objects over the city," Captain William W. Maitland, one of the Sabre Jet pilots "and another pilot asked CAA radar men, 'Head us right for whatever you see. We'll ram it if necessary.' F-86 pilot Captain Maitland then stated, "We then passed right through the spot of reflection and didn't see or hit anything."

Luckily, these fighter pilots did not "hit anything" when they attempted to "ram" their anticipated target. The pilots' aggressive and offensive maneuvers indicate that the Air Force was not playing games with unidentified flying objects. How many other fighter pilots were not as lucky?

Project Blue Book recorded the incident as an "Unknown" case. The 10073 Record Card for this incident states, "Two F-86s based at O'Hare AFB, Chicago Illinois were diverted from Air Patrol…to investigate the objects." This 10073 document also stated the amount of objects that were sighted. It reported, "Number of objects - 30 Multiple." The report also commented that there was, "No inversion layer present." The staggering amount of UFOs seen that night was never explained. It is worth noting that the two jets were actually on an "Air Patrol" at the time they were diverted toward their targets. *The United States Air Force Dictionary* defines air patrol as follows, "A detail of airborne aircraft sent out for reconnaissance, combat, or guard purposes. See combat air patrol." It is obvious that these jets were in anticipation of an attack.

The sightings continued throughout the month of September. On September 3, 1952, a UFO was reported about six miles from Tucson, Arizona by a pilot-instructor for the Arizona based company, "Darr Aero Tech." An Air Information Intelligence Report, from Marana AFB, in Arizona was contained in Blue Book. It stated that two civilian pilots, the pilot-instructor and a friend sighted a dark elliptical object as it flew over Tucson and back again, before disappearing. On the following day, another dark object was sighted, but this object was "disc-shaped." Two Blue Book reports, "FLYOBRPT" from Hamilton AFB stated that two GOC posts, one in Sacramento, and one west of that city sighted the object. The first report stated the witness described the "disk" as having a "shimmering silver color." During the second sighting at Danville, the object was described as "silver" and circular in shape and about the "size of a fighter jet."

On September 6, 1952, Blue Book recorded two "Unknown" cases:
1. Case 2045. Lake Charles AFB. Lake Charles, LA.

2. Case 2048. Tuscon, AZ.

On September 6, a UFO sighting that did not receive a lot of attention occurred over Enfield, Connecticut. On September 7, 1952, *The Hartford Courant* carried a front-page article, "High-Speed 'Flying Saucer' Spotted By Osborn Guard." This incident was investigated by Ct "Civilian Defense Officials" and reported to the New Haven, Connecticut Filter Station, but does not appear in Project Blue Book. What is interesting about this incident is it occurred only 20 miles directly north of Glastonbury, where the F-86 Sabre jet crashed only one month before on August 5, 1952. The article reported that this UFO sighting involved "Fifteen witnesses; two prison guards and 13 prisoners of the "Osborn Prison Farm."

The incident unfolded at 10:10 a.m. Saturday morning, when two guards, Walter Borys and George McCracken, were in the farm enclosure of the prison with 13 prisoners. The group of men heard an unfamiliar noise in the sky, looked up, and to their surprise saw "an odd silvery object."

The Hartford Courant reported what guard Mr. Borys stated about the UFO, "He heard a strange noise in the northern part of the sky…the motor sound was unlike that of a jet or any airplane sound." Borys described the UFO as a "silvery oblong object." The prison guard also said, "The sound stopped and the object appeared to be drifting toward the earth in a zigzag course. As it descended, it assumed a fluffy appearance. Mr. Borys then stated, "After it had dropped a considerable distance, the object stopped. There was a loud report [sound] and with a puff of smoke it shot upwards at a right angle at an incredible rate of speed." The object went out of sight and disappeared.

Enfield Civilian Defense officials, "William J. Murphy and Russell Maylott visited the farm" and interviewed all the witnesses. Murphy stated, "All 15 stories were consistent and agreed except for minor details." *The Hartford Courant* reported, "He said that he had no explanation to offer about the incident."

I ask the following questions:
1. Why is this case not in the files of Project Blue Book?
2. Why was this 20-mile area of up state Connecticut having strange aerial incidents occurring in their skies in August and September 1952?

On the following day, September 7, 1952, Project Blue Book recorded two "Unknown" cases, 2049 and 2052. Both of them occurred over San Antonio, Texas. Several witnesses saw an orange object materialize and "explode" into view over the skies of San Antonio. On September 9, at 9:00 p.m., an Air Force intelligence officer had a sighting over the area of Rabat, French Morocco. An "Operational Immediate Message" from the "5th Air DIV Rabat" to Wright Patterson AFB, disclosed the following information according to witness E. J. Colisimo. It was reported the witness, "SIGHTED DISC-SHAPED SOUNDLESS AERIAL OBJECTS HEADING NORTHWEST [and] TURNING WEST TO SOUTHWEST. [The] FORMATION OF 6 WHITE LIGHTS [were] EVENLY SPACED. [They] APPEARED AS LIGHTS IN [a] FOG. [There was] NO BREAK IN [their] FORMATION DURING SIGHTING." Blue Book recorded this multiple UFO sighting, case 2062 and evaluated it an "Unknown."

On the following day, September 10, a saucer was seen in broad daylight near the airfield of one of their favorite bases, Andrews Air Force Base. The reconnoitering continued. A "civilian employees" wife sighted the object at 0230/2:30 p.m. that afternoon and reported her sighting to Andrews base officials shortly after.

An Andrews AFB "Air Intelligence Information Report" dated "10 September 52" and written by "Major Hammerlund" disclosed the witnesses' testimony. He stated the following:

The object was described as shiny, metallic [and] elliptical with no exhaust visible and emitting no sound. The sighting lasted two to three minutes during which [time] the object moved rapidly back and forth over a short arc. Finally, the object rose rapidly and disappeared.

It is interesting to note that there were no reports of this sighting from the Andrews tower operators who certainly would have been able to see this object…or did they!

On September 11, 1952, A *United Press* news story told of a UFO sighting that occurred over Miami Beach, Florida. Witness Abraham Friedman sighted an aerial object pass over the skies of Miami and with the assistance of a pair of binoculars; he got a good visual of the object. Friedman described the UFO as being shaped like a "salami." This type of unconventional aerial object was commonly seen throughout 1952 and was also described as, jet-shaped, and resembling the fuselage of an aircraft without wings. An official at the local Weather Bureau implied that the witness probably saw reflected light off a small cloud!

A "Washington, Sept. 12," News story carried by *The Greensboro Daily News* dated Saturday, September 13, 1952 reported, "AIR FORCE PROBES FLYING SAUCERS-Four State 'Disc' Reports Unexplained." This September 12 story references the recent "unexplained phenomena cited in North Carolina" and states, "So you wanna believe in flying saucers. Gather around, tuck in your credulity, and listen to what the Air Force has to say. To date, the airmen haven't been able explain about 400 of 2,000 reports that have come in on 'unusual aerial phenomenon.' Four of the reports are from the old north state…25 percent are reported by military personnel" This article also states, "Nonetheless, since these unexplained sightings persist, the Air Force will continue its investigations, giving the problem adequate but not frantic attention, spokesmen said." This quote made by the United States Air Force was an absolute understatement. On September 12, 1952, all hell broke lose over the skies of the United States when hundreds of Americans in eleven states reported seeing UFOs up and down the east coast.

The UFO flap of September 12, 1952, "Defense Day," began at approximately 1:30 am over Knox County, Ohio, near the small town of Bladensburg. This UFO incident appeared in the February 1953 issue of FATE magazine in an article titled, "Circling Object." It explains that two oil well drillers, William Darling and Donald Davis of Bladensburg, had an early morning sighting on September 12 while working the midnight shift. The next day, the two witnesses told their friend Jack Montgomery about the sighting. Montgomery said, "The incident was related to me by the two men the following morning." In turn, he then reported the incident to FATE magazine.

Mr. Montgomery explained, "They sighted an object about 2,000 feet from where they were working and about 150 feet from the ground. It was lit up very bright in the side [inside] and seemed to have windows only on one side. It circled near the ground for nearly half an hour making very little noise. Then all once it made a loud noise like steam blowing, and with a bright flash flew out of sight with the speed of a falling star." Shortly after this incident, another close range and low altitude UFO sighting occurred in Pennsylvania.

At 2:35 a.m. EST, the quiet star-filled sky over Middletown, Pennsylvania was shattered with a shocking noise that echoed through the night air. The noise which shook the area was the sound of heavy artillery being fired into the sky. A lone figure, a patrol guard on duty at Olmstead Air Force Base, gazed at a maneuvering craft as it flew across the nearby sky. This aerial craft was neither a plane nor a helicopter. It was an unconventional aircraft; an elliptical-shaped flying object. In 1952, Olmstead AFB housed an air materiel area set up by the Air Materiel Command of the United States Air Force. The patrol guard's sighting was reported to Project Blue Book at Wright-Patterson Air Force Base, the Air Force's investigative body for the acquisition and analysis of UFO data. The guard then received a Tentative Observers Questionnaire from the Air Technical Intelligence Center (ATIC) at Wright-Patterson and officially documented the incident.

The witness stated that he first noticed the object because he heard a noise that "sounded like heavy projectile artillery and saw a blue light in the sky." The object was oval-shaped. He added that the object "changed speed and direction as well as brightness." The guard made three sketches of the elliptical object and illustrated it as making unconventional maneuvers by drawing trail lines behind it. The guard said, "When the object disappeared the noise ceased," and added, "The object disappeared from sight behind some trees."

A question on the form asked, "In your opinion what do you think the object was and what might have caused it?" The witness answered, "Do not know."

What had the guard heard? Was the Air Force test firing their heavy projectile artillery guns at 2:35 a.m. EST? Was our military firing upon a UFO? Was it a coincidence that a UFO was seen in the area of an Air Force base at the same time heavy artillery fire was heard? On the day of September 12, an unusual heat wave blanketed the eastern United States with temperatures reaching around 90 degrees. Other than the intense heat that scorched the country that day, nothing else seemed out of the ordinary. That was about to change.

As the day slipped away into night, the summer sun set across the majestic skyline of Washington D.C. and the skies were clear. Around 8:00 p.m. EDT, the unseasonably hot air in Washington suddenly turned ice cold and President Harry Truman's worst fears had become a reality. The Air Defense Identification Zone (ADIZ), the United States airspace in which the control and recognition of aircraft was required, had been violated.

An unidentified craft soared west over the Atlantic Ocean through the coastal ADIZ and headed toward the mid-Atlantic coast. Because this aircraft had not given warning or properly identified itself according to protocol, it was considered a threat to the United States. Under the Air Force rules of engagement, the aircraft had shown just cause to be fired at. The Pentagon waited as the object headed further west on a direct course toward the Capitol. Shortly after, it passed over Washington D.C. and continued west. Who was this enemy, and where did this unidentified aircraft originate? Why was it flying over the Capitol and further more, why was it engulfed in flames?

Approximately two hundred and six miles west of Washington D.C., located in the rolling mountains of West Virginia, is the small town of Flatwoods. Set east of the Allegheny Mountain plateau, Flatwoods is the geographic center of the state. Located in Braxton County, Flatwoods was a thriving little town of farms and mills surrounded by forests of towering pine and oak trees. Friday night was just beginning, and the residents of Flatwoods settled in for another quiet evening.

About twenty-five minutes later, as dusk settled over Flatwoods, the shouts of boys were heard in the local schoolyard. The center yelled, "Hut-one, hut-two, hut-three, hut, hut, hike!" The boys dashed across the football field, scrambling into another play. An incomplete pass brought the boys back to the line of scrimmage, yelling at each other in opposition. Seconds later, someone shouted and pointed skyward. For a few moments, an eerie silence fell over the schoolyard. The game stopped as the bewildered boys focused their attention on a nearby mountaintop. Gazing toward the sky, they saw a flaming aerial object soar over the mountain and towards them. Seconds later, this object flew directly above their heads as it passed over the Flatwoods Elementary School playground. The low flying object then turned and proceeded over the nearby road and headed in the direction of a farm, barely clearing the treetops.

During my investigation, I contacted witness Freddie May, who still lived in the area. On my initial telephone call with Freddie, he refused to speak with me. After several follow-up calls, he remained reluctant to talk with me. I had fallen into the category of a pestering, fly-by-night reporter. Mr. May had been hounded by the press for years. He had seen reporters distort the truth of the incident, and he quit talking to them. He was tired of seeing misquotes and distortions released to the public. What this case needed was a thorough investigation, instead of reporters and writers who just wanted a quick, flashy story. As the years passed, these writers did more harm than good to the story. The incident had become just another fast, quirky story for the press.

After countless telephone calls, I finally convinced Freddie of my sincere interest in the case. The interview I had been patiently waiting for was quickly reversed. Freddie interviewed me. He wanted to know about the seriousness and depth of my investigation. After I finished explaining what I had uncovered in my research, he was amazed, even overwhelmed. After all those years, he had found the person he was waiting to talk to. Since our initial conversation, Freddie and I have spent countless hours discussing the incident in detail. Freddie verified the majority of the information I had discovered. I had also uncovered new facts about the case that I shared with Freddie. In this book, I am sharing the information from the combined efforts of Freddie May and myself.

Freddie agreed to be interviewed on the various locations where the incident occurred. For the first time ever, a witness to all the events of that evening was willing to tell the true story of the "Flatwoods Monster." Freddie's testimony began on site at the school playground, "The new school here sits on what used to be the old playground, where we were playing ball, and we were down about fifty yards or so from where the actual site used to be." Freddie then pointed to a mountain ridge in the northwest and said, "Somebody yelled, 'Look there,' and we all looked up and saw a fireball coming from over the mountain here. It came right over the top of our heads." He said it looked like a "round ball of fire," and looked "oval-shaped." The colors of the object were "red, yellow, and orange." Freddie said the fireball emitted a "small trail of fire," and "flames were trailing behind it." From his position on the playground, he "saw the object for three seconds" as it passed over the group.

One week after the incident, scientist/author Ivan T. Sanderson, a former British Naval Intelligence Officer, visited Flatwoods with his assistant Eddie Shoenenberger. They spent several days in Braxton County investigating. Sanderson was on assignment to cover the story for the North American Newspaper Alliance and for *True Magazine*. Sanderson stated, "One of the kids looked up and he said in so many words, 'What on earth is that?' And they all looked around the edge of a hill behind the village, the north of the village but lower than the peak of that hill—or the one [hill] opposite it, came a pear-shaped glowing red object, which was pulsing from cherry red to bright orange. It was traveling blunt-end first. It traveled quite slowly across the valley over their heads and managed to top the mountain on the other side." The boys who witnessed this event were, Neil Nunley (14 years old), Olin Shaver (14 years old), Ronald Jordan (14 years old), Edison May (13 years old), Teddie Neal (13 years old), Freddie May (11 years old), and Ronald Shaver (10 years old). Unknown ages, Don Eubank, John David Jordan and Lawrence Squires.

The sloping pasture of the Fisher Farm. The arrow indicates where the object landed on the back mountain top.

The Charleston Gazette reported the following information in an article "Did It Ride Meteor" dated September 14, 1952. "One boy told this story. ' We saw this fiery object go overhead and seem to come down in the hills. We started to look for it. It was just about dusk.'"

In their excitement, the boys began shouting as the fireball went flying over the playground. There were some mixed opinions. One boy shouted, "It's a flying saucer!" Another yelled as the object landed, "Watch out. It may be a flying saucer and a man from Mars will jump out and get you!" One of the other boys remarked, "I bet it didn't land up there at all." Another boy in the group, who saw the object as it descended upon the mountaintop, said about its trajectory, "[It] looked like a door falling flat wise."

Freddie May clarified the description of the object's landing. He gestured toward the southeast and said, "It came down and lit on the other side of the mountain right up there." He pointed to a mountaintop. "Just over the edge we could tell it came down up there." The object came down across from the playground on a mountaintop. The mountaintop is on the property of a farm, then owned by a Mr. Bailey Fisher. Some people also refer to this as a hill or a hilltop. For consistency, I will refer to it as a mountain or mountaintop.

Freddie and I went across the street and walked up to the farm. We hiked up a series of long paths and proceeded to the rear of the property. Upon reaching the foot of the mountain, I set my equipment down and took a break. The terrain of the mountain was not rough and rugged; rather it was a steep, grassy slope, which ascended to a level plateau on top. When we made it to the top, I was amazed to find a wide, open field. The area was nearly level, completely covered in grass and surrounded by trees. On the top, Freddie May said, "It's almost perfectly flat up here, a nice place for it to touch down. . . . As you can see, we're right on top of the mountain. It would have been a quick spot for an emergency landing."

Freddie described the plateau area where he saw the object land. "There used to be an old cistern that was torn down." (A cistern is a receptacle for holding water, especially rainwater.) Freddie pointed to some trees along the outlying perimeter of the field. He said, "It lit right over the top of the trees in this area." The object flew over the playground, about a mile away, passed over the trees, and then landed in the field on the mountaintop. Freddie continued by gesturing into the field where he was standing. He stated, "We could tell that it lit right here, and in this area is where we figured the thing [object] would be." He then reiterated the geography of the mountaintop, "A nice, flat spot, it makes a perfect landing place."

This portion of my interview with Freddie May concluded when I asked him his current opinion on what the object was. "I don't have any way, actually, of knowing what it was. My opinion is that it was a UFO from someplace else. We didn't have the technology in 1996, [to build] something that could come in as fast as I saw it come in, and slow down at the same time, and make a soft landing on earth, on the ground, and not explode or leave any evidence. I know what I saw and it's nothing that we built here on earth."

Ivan T. Sanderson made this statement, "This object, this large, glowing object, which appeared to be about the size of a house, seemed to pause when it topped the hill and then [began] to sink, instead of going down in a sort of trajectory. It stopped and sank slowly down the hill and they could see this light pulsing behind the crest of the hill." He added, "It had stopped and landed. I know that it landed because where it landed it had pushed a large circular depression into the ground. It was an overgrown field, knee and waist high and filled with lots of twigs and bushes." Sanderson explained, "All of that was completely flattened." He also stated, "The ground itself was flattened and there were considerable [sized] stones, not boulders, but stones the size of a man's head that had been pushed down. Also, at three points equidistant around [the area], there were three holes jammed into the ground at the edge of the circle which looked as if the object stood on a tripod, is what it looked like."

Freddie May conveyed what most of the boys thought the object was, "Well, we thought it was a meteorite, and we wanted to run up and see the meteorite burning and see if there were any rocks or anything we could save off of it, and stuff like that. That's what we were thinking when we went up."

The oldest witness to the fiery object was fourteen-year-old Neil Nunley. He suggested the object was probably a meteorite and that they should go find it. His teachers at school said that any meteorite fragments should be gathered up for the West Virginia State Geological Department.

During the course of my investigation, I met a Flatwoods resident named Jack Davis, a prominent businessman in the area. Davis explained that he witnessed the passing of the object as it flew over the area and landed. Mr. Davis agreed to be interviewed at his home. The following testimony is from that interview.

He stated, "I went over and visited my mother-in-law and father-in-law. I stayed there a little while that evening. Then I decided to leave as it was getting near dark. So - I was coming out and on the other side of the hill from the main road. When I topped the hill at the Stout Cemetery, why, I saw a lighted object coming through the sky. It crossed where the railroad cut is today and it was an oblong-shaped object, lit up. Well, my first thought when I caught the first glimpse of it was there was an aircraft coming down and it was in trouble. Then I recognized it wasn't and that it was bigger than an ordinary aircraft you'd see in this area at that time. It wasn't traveling at a great rate of speed in terms of that day and age. It came a little bit above the height of the trees at that time." Jack Davis then explained the color of this oblong object as it passed by. He stated, "It had a clearer, brighter illuminated light from the top and kind of an orange-red. Then as it came on down a little farther, the object was a little duller orange-red. The top of it had the reflection of a light that I would describe today as a mercury vapor light."

I asked Jack Davis if the object he saw pass over Flatwoods resembled a meteor. He replied, "It didn't resemble a meteor to me. To me, the object that I saw was a craft." Jack went on to describe the shape as "oblong" in nature. I then asked him, "Did it look like it was being controlled or did it look more like the flight of a meteor?" He said, "No, it looked like it was something controlled. Like I said, it wasn't traveling at a high rate of speed, and it basically seemed like it was slowing down when it was coming in, from where I was looking at it." I then commented, "It was decelerating then." Jack replied, "Yeah, decelerating." My next question was, "Did you hear any noise, Jack?" He answered, "I didn't hear any noise." I questioned, "And there was no sonic boom noted, no noise, no rumbling?" Jack answered, "I heard none."

I then asked, "The object that you saw over the trees, Jack, did it just clear the trees, or was it a thousand feet above the trees?" He replied, "No, it was just clearing the trees, just a little bit above the height of the trees there. I had the general feeling that whatever it was-had landed. Naturally, it was coming down, not very far over the treetops until it came in behind the trees that follow the ridge out, that ran parallel to the railroad at the time, with the school building down below that. I knew it was up there and I knew with the reflection, the light stopped there, and I could see the reflection of it through the trees. It was very obvious to see."

Jack lived in a house that actually bordered the farm where this incident happened. After the interview, Jack walked me to my car. I looked up toward the farm and walked up the road a few feet in that direction. I asked Jack, "Why didn't you go up there that night when you saw the thing land?"

Pointing up to the farm he said, "I wanted nothing to do with it. Frank, if you had seen it, you wouldn't have gone up there either." Then he joked, "Well, maybe you would have."

During a visit to Flatwoods, I spoke to the Mayor of Flatwoods, Margaret Clise, who lived in Flatwoods in 1952. A youngster at the time, she was outside in her yard and had seen the object pass nearby enroute to the Fisher Farm. Mrs. Clise told me, "The thing was oval-shaped and red. It was bright and glowing." She said, "It was big and it was flying at a very low altitude. It startled me when I saw it." She continued, It was so low, it was barely clearing the treetops." Mrs. Clise offered to take me to the yard where she sighted the object as it passed over the town. This section of Flatwoods is just west of the school playground at a higher elevation and overlooks the school area. While standing in the front yard near the house, Mrs. Clise pointed out a row of trees. She said, "The object passed over that area." According to my research, the flight path trajectory she pointed out to me was correct. The witness emphatically stated, "The treetops had all turned brown and were discolored," She informed me that, "You could only see this from certain elevations in town." Furthermore, Mrs. Clise said that the tops of the trees remained "brown" for about a year or more.

After the object landed, the boys raced up the street in hot pursuit of the flying object. They ran along the street for about a half-mile, then across the road and over the railroad tracks. They headed for a side street where the train depot sat. The road was the main access up to the Fisher farm. The road had a steep uphill, then immediately bent to the right behind the train depot. Located on this street were three homes. At the crest of the street was the home of the Mays. Joe Lemon, Freddie May's grandfather, owned the house. Mr. and Mrs. Lemon lived in the house with their two grandsons and the boys' mother, Kathleen May, age thirty-five.

As the boys approached the Lemon home, they raised quite a commotion, which drew the attention of the neighbors. Sanderson stated, "As they ran between the houses, several people had come out on their verandas and wanted to know what was going on. One of the younger kids said, "A flying saucer has landed."

As the chaotic group of boys scurried to the house, fatigued and out of breath, they started yelling in excitement. They piled through the front door of the house. Moments later the boys were met by Mrs. Kathleen May. During this commotion of mixed anxiety and excitement, some of the boys claimed the object was a meteorite, while others insisted it was a flying saucer. Ten-year-old Ronald Shaver blurted out to Kathleen May, "A flying saucer landed up on the back hill [Fisher farm mountaintop], and we wanna go look at it!" By then, dusk was turning into night and the boys were anxious to get to the mountaintop. Eighteen-year-old Eugene Lemon of Flatwoods was visiting at the house when the boys arrived.

Throughout my contacts with Mrs. May, I compiled large amounts of notes and taped her testimony with regard to the case. Mrs. May's account of the incident begins here: "I was sitting. I had just got home from work. I was working in Sutton at the beauty shop and still had my uniform on. I hadn't even taken it off or taken a shower. I bet I hadn't been home for ten minutes when the boys came running in the house. They had been in the lower end of town playing ball and said there was a flying saucer landing up there on the hill behind the house, and they were going up. My father had a flashlight on the coffee table in front of the couch. I reached down and got it. I said, 'You're not going by yourself. And I just took off with them.'"

This next segment of Freddie May's interview took place on the mountaintop of the farm. Freddie explained to me where he told his mother the object had landed, "It lit right in here some place. So that's where we told our mother that it lit, up on the old Fisher farm, up close to the old cistern. This is where we were coming, to this area right here."

At the house, Eugene Lemon heard the boys and decided to join the group going up to the farm. He also decided to take his dog along. I tried to clarify who was carrying the flashlight. (There were many conflicting reports about who carried the flashlight up to the farm that night.) Freddie May explained, "Gene had walked over to the house that night. When it got dark, you would need a flashlight to get around. You wouldn't walk around these parts of the woods without a flashlight at night. Gene and mother both had flashlights that night."

Mrs. May continued, "So, I grabbed the flashlight and took off with them, because it was getting pretty well dusk, and we started out and as soon as I stepped down into the road and was startin' up to the hill, I noticed this great big red flare, a purplish-looking flare."

One of Mrs. May's neighbors, Mrs. Neal (Teddie Neal's mother), heard the commotion as they headed toward the farm. She came outside to see what was going on and observed the light being emitted from the farm. The boys told her that something had landed on the mountaintop on the farm, and they were going to look at it. Mrs. May said, "Little Teddies mother, well…she seen the light when we were going up there, but she didn't want to go on up. She just stayed on home." Mrs. May adds, "I said; 'Now boys, we'll just go. We won't go clear up to it. We'll just go get the direction and the location of where it landed and then we'll just come back and call the law, and let them go up and investigate.'"

At this point, some of the original boys from the playground decided to go home instead. Five boys from the original group of witnesses proceeded up to the farm. They were Neil Nunley, Teddie Neal, Edison May, Freddie May, and Ronald Shaver. One more boy joined the group. He was six-year-old Tommy Hyer.

At about 7:40 p.m., the group departed in search of the mysterious object. They proceeded east of the May residence. The main access road dead-ended only a short distance away, at the boundary of the farm. The group followed a grass path uphill a short distance that leveled off into an open field. A few hundred yards away, toward the back of the property, was the small mountain where the boys saw the object land.

As they headed in that direction, darkness began to blanket them. Their apprehension steadily increased and their pace quickened. Their breathing became labored as the level path began to ascend.

To the right of the path, out in the distance, was a fence line made of wire and wooden posts. It ran nearly parallel to the grass path. Inside the fence, line was a wide-open, sloping pasture, set down in a valley. Mountains and hills overlooked the property, surrounding the entire area of farmland.

Lemon, May, and Nunley led the group and came upon their first obstacle about ten minutes into their quest. The obstacle was a five-foot high metal gate, which was wired shut to a large wooden post. The gate was the entrance to the main farm area, where livestock periodically grazed. The older boys unwired the gate and allowed the group to pass through. Then the gate was closed and rewired. They entered a thinly wooded area, leaving the grass path behind them.

The path continued, but the ground became hard-packed, rough, and rocky. The path cut sharply to the right. A wooded line of trees lay to their left, the fence line continued on their right, and beyond that was the sloping valley pasture. The group moved together, following a winding path that made four bends. Far off to their right, down the slope of the pasture, a large spherically shaped object rested in the valley. Some of the group became aware of the object's presence. It seemed to pulsate, dim, and brighten.

Some of the people in the group did not see the spherical object as it sat in the valley near a pear tree orchard. The people who did the object said it looked as big as a house off in the distance. One of the boys said it looked like a big ball of fire.

Frank at the metal gate

During Sanderson's investigation, he interviewed the boys who did see the object sitting in the valley. He said; "They pointed out to me, an outhouse, a sort of little barn and I said, 'How big was it?' And they said 'about that size.' We [Sanderson and assistants] measured that little two-story barn and it was about twenty-two feet high. They said this thing landed with the nose, the blunt end down . . . sort of standing out in the field [valley] sticking up."

On one occasion, during an interview with Freddie, he retraced the path made by the group that night. We kept our eyes focused on the beam of the lead person's light. As we continued retracing the footsteps of the witnesses toward the first gate, we noticed there was brush surrounding the valley and along the path to our right. I asked Freddie how high the brush had been and whether it would have prevented some witnesses from observing the object.

Freddie replied, "Back then, there was a lot of brush in the area, a lot of tall brush, more than there is now, which made it difficult to see [down into the valley]." Taking into consideration the location of the object as it sat down below eye level on an inner slope, I knew it would not have been readily visible, especially through tall brush.

Ivan T. Sanderson said about little Tommy Hyer in reference to the tall grass, "was at one of the houses and he tagged along behind, and to me, he is one of the most important witnesses in the whole case because of his extraordinary honesty. When we asked him certain things he said, 'But, mister, I couldn't see. I am too low down. There was grass in between me.'"

Another important point that Freddie brought up as he walked up the path that night was the direction some of the boys were focusing their attention. He stated, "We were looking up the path to where we saw the object land on the back of the farm on the mountaintop. I was looking ahead up the path to where I saw the object land. I was not looking to the right down into the valley. We [the boys in the schoolyard] thought it was a meteorite that landed back there. We were unaware that it had moved."

Another factor prohibited some of the witnesses from seeing the object. In 1952, there were several large trees in a pear orchard and the object had landed on the opposite side of those trees. Today, very few of those pear trees remain.

The Charleston Gazette article, "Did It Ride Meteor" reported the following statement made by one of the boys, "As we were going up the hill, we saw lights flashing on and off and got [whiff of] a horrible odor. It smelled like sulfur and really sort of made you sick."

Freddie stated, "The boys who saw the object...the older, taller boys, told me later that the thing they saw sitting down in the valley was pulsing. A couple of them said it would get a little brighter, then dim. They saw it to the right of the path in the grass on the inner slope."

About then, a warm fog-like mist began to engulf the area. The group detected a pungent, nauseating odor that permeated their noses and throats. They tried to ignore the odor and continued up the path.

Mrs. May described her account of the misty fog as the group approached the tree area. "Before we got up there, we could smell a kind of metallic odor, and it looked like it was getting foggy. I turned around, and looked toward the town to see if I could see the streetlights. And that metallic odor, oh, I can still smell it yet today. It was real misty." The fog obviously was not an ordinary early-evening fog that was settling through the mountains. That fog was isolated in one area, the area of the path.

Freddie May recalled the odor. "The smell was similar to the old TV tubes burning out in the old TV sets years ago. A tube would burn out and have that, what we'd call that metallic smell."

I asked Mrs. May about her reaction to the smell. She said, "I had a little irritated throat. [The odor] was very penetrating. It affected me a good bit, in the chest area [inhalation]." Mrs. May also said that some of the boys were severely affected by the smell. She recalled that Neil Nunley was almost overwhelmed by the smell. Mrs. May said this about Eugene Lemon, "He did have some irritation in his throat and nose, as well as I remember." On September 13, the day after the incident, *The Charleston Gazette* stated, "The atmosphere in the vicinity was reported as being 'close and hot, with the foul odor prevailing.'"

In Freddie May's interview with me on the path, he said, "Coming up the road, on down there at the beginning of the path, you could hear a whining noise which at the time (his 1952 interview), I think maybe I described it as a whining noise, but I had never heard anything like it before. Since then, with my employment, I have heard electrical compressors when they've been shut down, and they're what they call 'whining to a stop.' Same kinda noise…same kinda noise."

In the book, *Flying Saucers from Outer Space*, this same noise was reported by Donald Keyhoe in reference to another UFO incident, which occurred only ten days later on September 22, 1952 at Camp Drum in Canada. Keyhoe states, "For 30 minutes that night, the duty officer and several soldiers watched a round, red-orange object circle above the camp. At least three times, they heard what they later described as 'the whine of a generator or rotating discs.'"

It was now about 8:00 p.m. in Flatwoods, and Eugene Lemon was leading the group up the path with his flashlight. Suddenly, Lemon's dog froze, started to growl and its ears went straight up. The dog darted across the dirt path ahead of the group and out of sight in seconds. Lemon continued and followed the path to the inside of the tree line to his left. Beside him, to the right, was Neil Nunley. Kathleen May was following closely behind Eugene Lemon. To Kathleen's right was her oldest son, Edison. A few feet behind Kathleen May was Ronald Shaver, also following close to the tree line. Behind Ronnie Shaver were Freddie May, then Teddie Neal, and finally Tommy Hyer. Lemon, May and Nunley approached the fourth and final bend in the path when they heard the dog barking violently. Moments later, Lemon's dog raced by them, headed back down the path toward the house. Regardless, the group pushed on and only had only about a hundred yards to go until they reached the top of the mountain.

The location of the landed object was my main concern at that point. While in the schoolyard, the boys saw the object land on the Fisher farm's rear mountaintop. Little did the group now realize that the object had moved from the mountain and was sitting in the valley.

While on the mountaintop, Freddie explained the relocation of the object. He said, "Where we'd seen it come down there [he pointed down and off into the distance at the schoolyard], the angle it was coming in would have knocked trees over to get where it was (in the valley), and it didn't do that."

The boys' who did not know any better and thought the object was a meteorite were wrong. Pointing into the field of the gulley he stated, "It had to go down to there, or part of it moved down to there, whichever. This right here [mountaintop], if you're coming out of the sky, is the only place it could have lit," he said while pointing. Reiterating his stance Freddie said, "Right here." Until my interview that day, no reporter had ever learned that the object had moved from the mountain down to

Frank on the mountaintop, points into the valley of the farm where the object relocated as indicated by arrow.

the valley—that it had actually changed its location on the farm, landing twice. This object made an emergency landing and strategically placed itself on the plateau of this mountaintop. Shortly after, it retreated into the lower valley of the farm where it would be less conspicuous.

Chapter 12

SANCTUARY

The group ventured up the mountain and encountered another gate where the fence line to the right of the path ended. Beyond that area were tall grass, pear trees and irregular clumps of brush. I interviewed Freddie May on location. He stated, "Right down here was a wooden fence and that's where we [Freddie, Teddie, and Tommy] stopped. We came right up to that wooden fence. We didn't cross that wooden fence," he stated.

Arrow Indicates the Location of Tree

Frank at the remains of the wooden gate along the path

Some of the individuals in the group were focused on the path ahead, following the beam of Lemon's flashlight. Other group members had focused their attention on the object, as it sat off in the valley. Lemon was still walking along the inside of the path near the tree line. Kathleen May had now moved just ahead of him and was walking in the beam of his flashlight.

Mrs. May told me lightheartedly in the interview, "They let me lead the way. Just like an old buck, they sent the old doe out before them. We just kind of went around this little swag, [bend in the path] and it was kind of around that gate there." To their left, along the tree line, was a large white oak tree set back from the path about four feet. May said that she heard strange noises as they neared the tree. "We got up there and it was making a hissing noise, and it just sounded like it was frying bacon and flipping a silver dollar or something against a piece of canvas, stretched canvas." May and Lemon, the closest of the individuals to this tree, saw something near it. May said, "As I turned, I thought I could see it in eye view, eye level. I thought I saw something there." I asked Freddie about the misty fog as they walked along the path. He stated, "It was very hazy in the area along the path. It was also very misty along the tree area."

Lemon also saw something. He noted a pair of eyes thought to be those of an animal set high in a nearby tree. The eyes were glowing through the fog that had engulfed the area. Lemon redirected his flashlight beam toward the direction of the eyes. At the same moment, Kathleen May turned on her flashlight. Lemon made the following statement: "I saw a pair of eyes near a tree and threw my flashlight on them. I thought it was an opossum. Then there stood this — thing." Sanderson stated that, "The dog ran into the mist, barking at this object."

Shocked at the ghastly sight peering over them, the boys gasped and Mrs. May let out a blood curdling scream that was heard throughout the town. They were not the eyes of an animal perched on top of a 12-foot high tree branch; they were the eyes of a tremendous towering figure, which stood to the right of the tree.

That colossal figure is still commonly referred to as the "Flatwoods Monster," also known as the "Braxton County Monster." Mrs. May added, "I turned the flashlight on, and the thing [the figure] lit up from the inside." She then emphasized, "I turned on my flashlight and it lit up like a Christmas tree."

Lemon described it as, "A 10-foot monster with a blood-red face and a green body that seemed to glow."

Just after the beams of the witnesses' flashlights struck the monster, its dully-glowing eyes lit up brilliantly. The light from those eyes suddenly projected outward and cut through the fog, illuminating the area.

The stunned witnesses watched as the light beams shot forward and shone over their heads as the entire area glowed from the immense "monster."

During Sanderson's interviews with the witnesses, he was told about these beams of light. He stated that, "Coming out of what appeared to be glass on the front of the head of this creature were fixed beams. The thing was turning slowly around, waving from left to right and right to left as if it was searching the horizon with those beams. Somebody suggested that the thing ["monster"] was looking for its colleagues or looking to find out where it was."

Mrs. May told me that the monster lit up when she aimed the flashlight on it. I asked her, "So, it reacted to you." She replied unequivocally, "Yes." Sanderson also said, "Apparently, when the flashlight came on, the object [figure] turned so that those two little beams came over and concentrated on them."

Once the area was lit up, the monster was seen in its entirety for the first time. Some of the witnesses claimed the monster was green; others said it was dark. One of the boys said, "The monster was obviously black really, but as it was hot. It was getting red hot like a poker." Sanderson reported, "[It] was a sort of aluminum-gray color but reflecting the color of the bushes and such, which gave the idea of green."

Freddie said this about the encounter, "She [Kathleen] aimed the light on it, and it was standing in this neighborhood right here under this big tree, which was a big living tree at the time."

Over the years, I visited the tree dozens of times. That towering tree now stands only about nine feet tall, and is a decaying hollow shell. The remnants of the tree are steadily deteriorating, leaving little evidence of its former shape. It leans against a barbed wire fence. Freddie said, "From where you're filming right now, is where it was, the 'Braxton County Monster,' it was the main thing that we saw. It was standing right there."

I wanted to know if Mrs. May initially approached the monster or if it approached her. She said, "We came up on it. We got close enough to it so I could see exactly what it was, and we all saw the same thing. I was as close to it as the length of a car, a small car."

The monster had risen up, hovered above the ground near the vicinity of the tree, and barely cleared the tree limb just above its head. It moved away from the tree while propelling itself then glided down toward the dirt path. It then hovered over the path and passed directly in front of a horrified Kathleen May and Eugene Lemon. The immense figure hovered past a terrified Lemon who he fell to the ground and dropped his flashlight. It continued moving across the path in front of a shocked Neil Nunley.

Kathleen May told me what happened immediately after the monster moved toward her and Lemon. She said, "Gene fell over first, but he wasn't long in getting up. I don't know if he passed out, or his legs got rubbery, or what. Now anyways, he just fell to the ground." Lemon stated, "I screamed and fell over backwards."

Neil Nunley said that as the monster was coming toward them, it was actually moving in a downward direction as it crossed the path. Nunley said the figure was also "circling at the same time toward the globular object." Nunley described the movement of the monster as it passed in front of him. He said, "I couldn't move as it did. It just moved. It didn't walk. It moved evenly. It didn't jump."

Kathleen May clarified the monsters' movement: "It was just kind of floating. It was about a foot to a foot and a half off the ground, but it didn't have any kind of feet or anything that we could see."

As the monster glided over the dirt path in front of the three closest witnesses, it moved from their left to right, and passed in front of them. Initially, Kathleen May was the closest to the monster. She said, "I was as close to it as the length of a small car."

As the towering creature passed in front of her from behind a tree, hissing and making frying noises, it spewed an oily substance all over her clothing. Mrs. May explained to me, "I was close enough that it [the monster] squirted oil out all over my uniform." I then inquired if this oil burned her skin or work uniform. She answered, "No! I didn't even notice it on my uniform until after I got home."

I wanted to ascertain the actual height of the monster. Various publications over the years had said the height of the monster ranged from seven to fifteen feet tall. On location, Freddie May described the height of the monster to me, "This was the tree, what's left of the tree, right here. It had a limb that came over the road, like this limb right here. [He gestured toward another tree]. It was a little better than twelve feet up to that limb, and it was standing out and under that limb, so we figured it was about twelve feet tall, or in that neighborhood.

We estimated from where we saw him that it was approximately twelve feet tall, and I would have been oh, about five feet [tall] at the time. Now, I wasn't half the size of the height of it. It was [gestured with arms spread wide apart] big, you know, wide at the bottom, and the top was [indicated with his arms the width of the top of the monster as approximately three feet], it was, [he sighed] it was scary."

Kathleen May said, "They [investigators and townspeople] measured, and it was right under this limb of the tree, ten to twelve feet." One of the investigators who measured the height of the tree was Ivan Sanderson, "The first branch growing out of the oak tree, when measured from the [bottom] of the branch to the path on which they were standing, was 12 feet 6 inches."

The gigantic figure towered over the terrified witnesses just beneath the tree limb. It cast an eerie orange light over the area as it overlooked them. The beams of light cut through the mist, and the entire area glowed, making the so-called monster and everything around it visible. The group stared at the surreal image in utter disbelief. Their first instinct was to take flight, but their feet seemed welded to the ground. They were in a dream-like state for what seemed like an eternity.

The younger boys gazed wide-eyed and terrified as if trapped in a nightmare. Their legs finally started pumping madly as they careened back down the path into the darkness. I asked Kathleen May to describe the events directly following the encounter, "We just took off running!"

A shocked Gene Lemon gathered himself up off the ground and quickly caught up to the fleeing group. He said, "A boy standing near me jumped over me and took off down the hill with the rest of them behind him. I got up and took off too." Witness Neal Nunley, who was the boy who jumped over Lemon, said he saw the monster for a very short time. He said, "We just got a good look at it and left."

On location near the tree, I asked Freddie May what his reaction was when he first spotted the monster. He said, "To get out of here, we could have done the Olympics proud." Freddie and I then walked back down the path He turned and pointing up the path, said to me, "We had come up this direction and we took off in that direction [gesturing back down the path], the same direction which we came in."

Mrs. May expanded on her trip back down the path. She explained her encounter with the wooden fence across the path. "There was a wooden…ya' know how they lay the wooden pieces up across to make a little fence/gateway. That's what I jumped over and I don't even remember touching it. They [reporters] asked me if I ran, and I said I passed several of them [the boys] while I was running, and no one said a word all the way back to the house."

In what was supposed, to be only a search for a meteorite, Kathleen May said this about the younger boys, "They were just small tykes, you know, and naturally it would scare 'em, but they were of interest and they wanted to see what it was."

The terror-struck witnesses raced back down the path through the mist and darkness as adrenaline surged through their bodies. Mrs. May, Lemon, Nunley and Eddie May cleared the wooden fence and fled down the path. All the witnesses quickly approached a major obstacle, the five-foot-tall metal gate that they had wired shut. Instinctively, some of them went over the top of it. Others went around it, and the smaller boys went through it, uncertain whether the monster was following. They were finally out of the woods; they then entered the wide-open grass field where they gained momentum.

The ground was much easier to traverse as it flattened out. The only sounds were their pounding footsteps and their hearts thumping in their ears. Some of them passed the May house and continued running to their own homes. Kathleen May said, "Teddie Neal got so scared he ran home. He lived in Shaversville, I'd say about half a mile away. He ran all the way home, opened the door, and ran in, and his mother knew that something was wrong. She said it looked like he was scared to death. And he ran into his bedroom and turned his radio on, and he just would not talk to her for ever so long."

One by one, the others piled through the front door of Kathleen's home. Mrs. May explained, "After we all ran off the hill, the boys and I went in the house and we were all scared silly!"

The house had an air of chaos as they tried to regain their senses. Kathleen May instinctively tended to the traumatized boys. All of them had difficulty breathing. Some of the boys needed more attention because they were bruised and bleeding, while others were coughing and gagging. Their eyes were glassy and tearing. Their noses and throats were inflamed. Eugene Lemon, overcome by the gas, rushed straight to the bathroom and vomited profusely.

Freddie May recalled the scene, "When we got back to the house, we were all very scared. We were all pacing around the house, our adrenaline was pumping, and we couldn't stand still. As a matter of fact, it scared me so badly for weeks after the incident I didn't go out of the house after dark."

On September 19, 1952, *The Braxton Democrat* newspaper article "Flatwoods Folks See Monster" reported, "The Lemon boy was so overcome that ammonia and camphor were administered to him before he was fully restored."

Kathleen May said, "Gene vomited all night and I had to take my boys to the doctor the next morning. Their mouths and throats were as raw as a piece of meat. I got so scared it's a wonder I hadn't vomited my head off, but I hadn't eaten and that made the difference."

After tending to the boys, Kathleen May called the local sheriff's department. She placed the call at 8:15 p.m. or shortly thereafter. She said, "Cecil Rose [the jail keeper] answered the phone and he told me all the law enforcement had gone down to the river, investigating what they thought was a plane crash. But it was one of these things [the spacecraft] that landed, I'm sure. It was across the river though."

The area of the plane crash investigation was in Frametown, approximately twenty miles away, near the Elk River. Sheriff Carr could not respond to her call until he searched for survivors of an alleged small airplane crash. The West Virginia State Police had their Braxton County substation located in the Sutton Courthouse, and the office was just down the hall from the sheriff's office.

Jack Davis said this about the state trooper offices, "They had one or two troopers, at the most, assigned to Sutton. A lot of times, it was just one trooper at a time. Two troopers would handle the whole county."

The author stands near the remains of the tree where the "Flatwoods Monster" was sighted.

KNIGHT-FALL

Jail keeper Cecil Rose walked down to the State Troopers' office to request assistance after he received Mrs. Mays call. No one was available. State troopers Gumm and Tribet were out on calls. Soon trooper Corporal Ted Tribett called headquarters and spoke to Rose. Rose told him of Mrs. May's call and asked if he could respond. Tribett was detained but promised to send a representative in his place. Tribett contacted a photojournalist, A. Lee Stewart, Jr., who was working late in his office at *The Braxton Democrat*.

Stewart was an outstanding photojournalist for the paper and worked closely with the Sheriff's department and State Troopers' office. During that era in a small community, reporters and photographers often worked side by side with law enforcement officials. They would work closely with the authorities and assist them on accident and crime scene investigations. In Mr. Stewart's case, he would travel with the police to various scenes. He would help analyze the scene, report on it, and then photograph the scene for the police department. On the night in question, September 12, 1952, Mr. Stewart was empowered by the West Virginia State Police to represent the Braxton County Sheriff's Department, in the absence of Sheriff Robert Carr.

In the meantime, the news of the encounter with the monster spread like wildfire throughout the small community. Within ten minutes, the town had been alerted.

After witness Jack Davis saw the object land, he walked back into town to retrieve his car parked in front of the mill building. As he was driving on his way out of town, he saw a gathering of people at the local country store. He explained, "This building was operated as a pretty good sized country store. It was owned at that time by a gentleman by the name of Steorts. I pulled in there to kinda' see what the gathering of people was and I learned what they were describing. . . . [It had] later become the green monster."

One resident who lived nearby was eighteen-year-old Junior Edwards. Edwards was one of the first to hear about the story. About half an hour after the incident, he went up to the farm with his friend, nineteen-year-old Joey Martin. Uncertain as to where the actual encounter took place, they searched the area anyway. The boys did not see, hear, or smell anything unusual, and left the farm not knowing where the actual event took place.

Another neighbor, accompanied by some friends, drove his pickup truck to the May home and walked in on the hysterical group. He questioned them, trying to determine what had happened. Most of his queries were answered except for the exact location of the sighting. Since all the witnesses were still terrified, none of them would go with him. The neighbor drove up to the Fisher farm, through the first field to the metal gate. He opened the gate, and drove up the path. He continued up the path looking for the tree where the monster had been seen. He never found the correct tree and never reached the second field where the object had relocated. He considered his search unsuccessful.

During the course of my early investigation, I kept trying to locate a man who played a key role in the "Flatwoods Monster" incident, A. Lee Stewart, Jr. He was the first person of authority to arrive at the May residence after the sighting. There were many missing pieces to the incident, and only he knew the answers. After many frustrating attempts and countless inquiries to locals, I was still unable to find him. After six years of traveling to Braxton County, the only thing I had learned about him was that he had left the area in 1958 and might be living in Ohio or Indiana.

My Ohio and Indiana leads turned out to be dead ends. Luckily, I learned that the Sutton school had opened a new alumni archive. The collection consisted of past yearbooks, documents, and local memorabilia, overall a very impressive account of the school's history. Included in one of the class photographs was A. Lee Stewart, appearing among his graduating class. While I was photographing the picture of Stewart, the curator mentioned that Stewart had recently visited the town. Mr. Stewart's wife had passed away and been laid to rest in her native Braxton County. I went to the funeral home in Sutton and obtained Mr. Stewart's current address in North Carolina.

After an appropriate amount of time had elapsed, I telephoned Mr. Stewart. When Stewart left Braxton County in 1958, six years after the incident, he also left the story of the "Flatwoods Monster" behind. Stewart hadn't realized that the "Flatwoods Monster" incident was still popular. When I explained to him the amount of research I had compiled over the years, he was impressed. When I mentioned the horrendous inconsistencies of the case that had been recorded throughout the years, he was shocked. He did not like how he had been grossly misquoted and portrayed by previous reporters and writers.

Stewart said the story should be told once again, but this time to an investigative field reporter who would quote the facts correctly. I asked him if I could interview him and record him. He suggested we meet in person. With only a few days' notice, I set out on the thousand-mile trek to Stewart's home.

My excitement grew as I made the trip to North Carolina, as six years of questions raced through my mind. I arrived at his home at two o'clock in the morning. I was greeted courteously by Mr. Stewart, especially considering the time. We immediately sat down and talked about the incident. I showed Lee my compilation research book, which contained forty-four years of publications on the "Flatwoods Monster." We talked until four o'clock. Later that morning when I awoke, I walked into the living room and found Stewart intently reading my research book. I thought he had just begun reading the book, but to my surprise, he was just finishing. What had taken me seven years to accumulate, Stewart had read overnight. As I looked at Lee, he raised his head, shaking it in disgust at how the incident had been portrayed. After reading the previously available research, Lee spent the next four days in in-depth discussion with me, hoping to get the real story told.

The following is the account of the incident told by A. Lee Stewart, Jr., "In 1952, I was co-owner and publisher of *The Braxton Democrat*. I broke the story on what is known as the "Braxton County Monster." I have not discussed this subject since I left West Virginia in 1958. I would like to bring to light some of the things that have been said, and clarify some of the problems that have been written on this subject over the past forty years. An artist from Florida by the name of Frank Feschino contacted me some time ago concerning this. He has done extensive research concerning this particular thing, and has spent a lot of time in West Virginia. A lot of the material that he has picked up, which he has given to me, and we have gone over, is not true. A lot of tongue-in-cheek, a lot of disclaimer material that has no bearing whatsoever on what

A. Lee Stewart, Jr. during a taping segment of his interview

actually happened at that particular time [1952]." He continued, "The reason I am doing this [interview] is that I'd like to bring into focus some of the things that happened and what actually transpired on the night of the particular incident. It was not easy for the people who went through this incident, and it wasn't easy for the people who tried to report it."

Stewart's involvement with the story began about 9:00 p.m., "On September 12, 1952 I was contacted at my office at *The Braxton Democrat* by Corporal Ted Tribett of the West Virginia State Police. Tribett told me about the incident. He also said the sheriff was out on a call [the supposed Frametown airplane crash] and could not answer Mrs. May's call immediately. I proceeded out to the home of Kathleen May. As far as I know, and I'm saying as far as I know, it is the only involvement that the West Virginia State Police had with this particular reporting."

He stated, "On the road out to Flatwoods, I passed Steorts' store, and Bill Steorts was working at the store with his father, and I picked him up. He directed me to the house and, in fact, was there when I talked to the people. He also went up on top of the mountain with me that night. I was the first person [of authority] to get to the Mays. It was sheer turmoil. Three boys were very sick, sick to their stomachs, and all of them were wheezing and coughing. Mrs. May's eyes were as red as they could be and sort of weepy, and everybody talked at once, so I just sat and listened for a while. As soon as I realized that the whole thing took place on the mountain (on the Fisher farm) right behind the house, I started asking if I could get somebody there to direct me to the spot. Of course the answer was a very emphatic, NO."

After learning some of the details of the story, Stewart tried to find a willing volunteer to guide him to the exact area. Finally, he talked two of the witnesses into guiding him to the farm.

Stewart explained further, "After a little coaxing, I convinced the two older boys (Lemon and Nunley) to go up to the mountain with us. So we left, the boys, Bill Steorts, and I. We were armed. We had a twelve-gauge automatic shotgun and a couple handguns. Two or three other people who lived right around there came up and went with us; they were also armed. [Kathleen May's father, Joe Lemon was part of this group] On the way up, the boys were hesitating and wanting to go back [home], and we coaxed them on. As a matter of fact, I had my hand up around one of the boys' necks. And under his breath, he was actually crying like a whipped pup. We went on up to the tree where this thing was supposed to have happened."

With shotgun in hand and his backup revolver readily available, Stewart went into the area where the monster had been seen. "Upon arriving at the scene, we were always reminded by the boys about the odor that made them all sick. We got down close to the ground, and we could still pick up an odor. They [Lemon and Nunley] identified it as the same odor that made them sick."

The Charleston Gazette article, "Did It Ride Meteor," reported, "According to Stewart, there was a strong, sickening burnt metallic odor prevailing, but there was no sign of the monster."

They made a thorough sweep of the area near the tree where the monster had been seen. Stewart said, "We had two large flashlights-electric lanterns, so we quickly picked up the skid marks."

The skid marks that Stewart found were actually two paths running parallel to each other, each one about thirty feet long. The marks were located to the right of the tree and the path. The markings were on the grass, leading from the valley up to the area where the monster had been seen. Stewart said, "We just spotlighted around because not one of us was inclined to hunt for something we didn't know what it was in the dark. We decided we would go back to the Mays. We were on the mountain probably thirty to forty minutes."

Sheriff Carr went to the farm with a pair of dogs. Donald Keyhoe said, "When the sheriff arrived, a fog was settling over the hillside. Twice he tried to get his dogs to lead him to the spot where the monster was seen. Each time they ran away, howling, and he gave up until morning."

Freddie May said, "When the sheriff got to the house someone told him where we saw the monster. He went to the farm with two dogs, but they didn't get very far before heading back. He never even got up near the tree where we saw it. When Carr got back with his dogs, Joe Lemon [Kathleen's father] even offered to take him up there to show him where it happened."

Stewart said, "I went in and talked to the Mays, saying that maybe I could come up with a tape recorder the next day and interview the boys." Sheriff Carr, who was very skeptical of the whole incident, went back to headquarters in Sutton. Stewart stayed and continued talking to the witnesses. Gene Lemon, who had arrived back at the house with Stewart, was still feeling nauseous from the fumes he had inhaled and consequently stayed the night. Mrs. May explained, "Gene is the only one who vomited and my aunt sat up with him and put cold cloths on his head and took care of him until about 12:30 that night." Stewart explained what happened when he left the home, "I left the May residence between 10:30 and 11:00 and returned to Sutton. I took Bill Steorts home at that time. I came back to my office, and I called Buck Thayer in Gassaway to see if I could borrow his tape recorder, a big reel-to-reel he used in the theaters. So I called him and picked that tape recorder up about midnight for use the next day with the kids."

Stewart picked up the tape recorder about 12:30 a.m. and drove back to Sutton. Stewart wanted advice on breaking the story to the media. He said, "Then I called my attorney, Olin Berry, who I got out of bed, and asked him if I should contact the *Associated Press* or *The Charleston Gazette* or both. I went over to his house (about 1:00 a.m.), we ran over this thing, and he actually made the initial call to *The Charleston Gazette* himself. This was probably about two o'clock in the morning." Berry explained the legality of the situation, and that Stewart should be credited with the story. They concluded their conversation and Stewart left Berry's house about 2:45 a.m. Stewart's involvement in the incident ended shortly after. He stated, "I got home about 3 a.m. and slept the night."

I also found out that the United States Army National Guard had played a significant role in the "Flatwoods Monster" incident that night. The West Virginia National Guard was actually mobilized into Braxton County on the evening of September 12, 1952 under the direction of the United States Air Force. National Guard Army troops were also mobilized to the Frametown area to look for a crashed airplane. Frametown was the area that Sheriff Carr was investigating when Corporal Tribett of the WV State Police called State Police headquarters in Sutton. The time of this call was approximately 8:45 p.m. Earlier that evening, Sheriff Carr had responded to another call involving another alleged airplane crash. That call was received shortly after 7:30 p.m. from the small community of Sugar Creek.

Sugar Creek is located between Frametown and Gassaway. Frametown, Sugar Creek, and Gassaway all lay along the Elk River. After the Frametown and Sugar Creek investigations had discovered nothing, a small contingent of those troops was led to Flatwoods to investigate the Fisher Farm.

Stewart searched this area of the path near the tree where the encounter occurred.
A. Location of the nearest witnesses on the path.
B. Location of the monster near tree.

Chapter 14

AIR FORCE ENTERS

On April 19, 1953, *The New York Times* reported in an article titled, "SAUCERS-Air Training, published by the Air Training Command, says that more than one thousand reports of flying saucers were received at Wright Patterson Field, Ohio, in 1952. Twenty percent of these apparitions are of unknown origin. A team of four- two officers and two civilians – is evaluating all reports." This team was the understaffed intelligence group at Project Blue Book located at the Air Technical Intelligence Center. They made up only a small percentage of those in the United States Air Force who were trying to solve the UFO dilemma.

I discovered that the long arm of the United States Air Force had actually reached into Braxton County on the night of the Flatwoods encounter and contacted the West Virginia National Guard. Witness Kathleen May spoke to me about the military commander of the WVNG who was involved in the Flatwoods case. This Braxton County resident was actually contacted by the Air Force. His name was Dale Leavitt of Sutton, but the locals called him by his retired military rank, Colonel Dale Leavitt. Mrs. May told me that in 1952, Leavitt, then a captain, was the commander of the West Virginia National Guard and had visited the Fisher farm with some troops the day after the incident.

Colonel Dale Leavitt was the commander of the Special Forces Augmentation Section of the state headquarters of the West Virginia National Guard. Leavitt entered military service as an enlisted man in 1941. In 1943, he commanded a recruit training detachment at Fort Richardson in Alaska with the 4th Infantry Regiment. Leavitt then went to jump school in 1944 at Camp Kilmer, New Jersey.

Colonel Dale Leavitt

After qualifying, he was assigned to the 541st Parachute Regiment at Camp McCall, NC. He then saw service in New Guinea and Luzon, where he joined the 11th Airborne Division.

Colonel Leavitt then went to Japan and was among the first troops to land in Japan on August 28, 1945 a few days before the peace treaty was signed. Leavitt separated from active service in November 1945 and became a reservist. He transferred to the WVNG in 1948, as the commander of Company G, 150th Infantry, at Gassaway until 1955. He served as chief of staff for the West Virginia Guard from 1967 until 1968 and retired from active duty in 1973.

I asked Mrs. May if she thought that Leavitt would talk to me if I contacted him. She paused for a few moments and then replied, "Maybe you should let me call him first and tell him about you." Mrs. May didn't have to say anything else. I knew what she meant. Outsiders who came into these parts were not always readily welcomed, especially outsiders who were snooping around, talking about the monster. Fortunately, I had some relatives in Braxton County, which made me more acceptable to the locals. Mrs. May called Colonel Leavitt on my behalf, and Leavitt told her that he would talk to me.

The following day, I called Colonel Leavitt. I told him that I was surprised by the fact that there was very little known about the National Guard's involvement. Leavitt became very quiet and then asked me what I knew about the case. At that point, I gulped and had to decide quickly whether to divulge the amount of information I had. Knowing not to tip my entire hand, I was vague in my response. I did not know this retired Army colonel; I was leery of negative repercussions. As the conversation progressed, it was a touch-and-go situation, and I was uncertain whether I would get any information. Leavitt set the boundaries of the topic, and his demeanor was clear. However, toward the end of the conversation, Leavitt stated that he admired my persistence and agreed to talk again soon. Over the next few months, Leavitt told me a little bit more of the story via telephone.

I brought my mother with me on my next visit to Braxton County. I wasted no time in calling Leavitt. He said to meet him at his home in Sutton. When I called him the next morning for directions, he surprised me by saying, "Make sure you and your mom wear your sneakers or boots, because I want to take you both up to the Fisher farm to talk to you." We drove to Leavitt's house, picked him up and went to the Fisher Farm.

Leavitt explained to us that he went to the farm with several West Virginia National Guardsmen to investigate the site on the night of the incident. He said that his presence on the farm that night was strictly covert. The locals and the public were unaware that the National Guard was on the farm only hours after the incident occurred. Leavitt also explained that he had had troops down on the Elk River, looking for a crashed airplane in the nearby Sugar Creek and Frametown areas.

Leavitt told me that National Guard members throughout West Virginia were alerted and ordered to report to Braxton County for duty. He explained that he believed something highly unusual had occurred there. Shortly after our meeting, Colonel Leavitt mailed me a brief unsigned note. The note is as follows:

> Dear Frank, and your mother, I was glad to go back to the hill at Flatwoods, and to know that those people and I did what Washington wanted us to do. However, there are many sightings in various states in our world. Some people laugh and think people are crazy. It appears that there are beings on other planets that want to come and land on our planet. And they may have more knowledge of outer space from their planet than we do. I do think that sometime they will continue to come to our world and try to live on our world.

Upon receiving this short unexpected note, I was shocked. Even though Leavitt stated his opinion about extraterrestrial life, he left his note unsigned. This seemed unusual, but considering his rank in the military and his involvement with this case, I could understand his desire to remain cautious.

After several repeated telephone calls with Leavitt, I pleaded with him to tell his story in front of a video camera. I knew the truth about the government's involvement that night, and his testimony would lend more credibility to the incident. In a last-ditch effort to obtain this interview, I brought up the point that the people of Flatwoods deserved better treatment than all the ridicule they had received. Without Leavitt's testimony, the truth of the Flatwoods incident would be forever lost. Leavitt finally agreed to the interview and shortly after our conversation, I was headed to West Virginia once again.

Colonel Leavitt being interviewed by the author

The interview was conducted on the Fisher farm and videotaped. When we began the interview, he caught me completely off guard by discussing facts that he had never disclosed before. Due to the complexity of the case and the wealth of new information that Leavitt gave me throughout the interview, I have arranged the most important information in sequential order. For the purpose of accuracy, the following interview consists of quotes and a straight question-and-answer format as the interview progressed during the videotaping.

I began the interview with Leavitt as we stood on the dirt path near Kathleen May's home, which leads to the Fisher farm.

Frank: "Is this basically the same path you came up with your troops?"
Leavitt: "On the other side, down over the side a little bit. It was near the tree. It was close, not too far away from where we went."

When Colonel Leavitt and his troops arrived in Flatwoods to investigate, they didn't travel the main access road to the farm. The troops came through on a logging road on the back part of the property. They arrived at approximately 1:30 a.m.

Leavitt was called by the United States Air Force and was ordered to deploy National Guardsmen from around the state into Braxton County. The first target zone of investigation was the Sugar Creek and Frametown area along the Elk River where a downed aircraft had been reported. The second target zone of investigation was Flatwoods.

On the scene at the Flatwoods farm, Leavitt said, "When I got the word on it, I had to detour some of our people to come up here and look at it. What happened is they [USAF] wanted us to go, so I got the people together and brought it [the contingent of troops] up here, and then the airplane, that's the other part of it, and the car [UFO encounter with car]."

Realizing that Leavitt had arrived on the farm with a contingent of troops, I asked him how many troops he had with him.

Leavitt: "There were about thirty, when these guys came out [gesturing towards the Elk River direction], because they had to fan out and try to find that airplane. But there wasn't anything there."
An additional twenty to thirty troops joined the thirty initial troops that came with Leavitt to Flatwoods.
Leavitt: "I had a total of 180 something people but a whole bunch of them went down the river."
Frank: "Now how many stayed up in this area?"
Leavitt: "Oh, I'd say about 50 or 60."
Frank: "How long were you on this actual spot right here?"
Leavitt: "I'd say about 45 minutes."
Frank: "Now how long was everybody up here…a total time?"
Leavitt: "Well, we had about 50 people here, and I don't know how long. Well, they stayed the night."
Frank: [shocked reaction] "They did?"
Leavitt: "Yeah, to see if something else was going to happen."
Frank: "Now all this time your troops were out looking for a crashed airplane?"
Leavitt: "Well, yeah. Most of my people had to because it was a big area. We didn't find anything!"

During the 45 minutes that Leavitt investigated the scene of the monster incident, he had two specific missions to carry out. His first task was to form a cordon to prevent unauthorized entry into the area. Second, he had to gather specimen samples from the area in question.

Leavitt then explained the involvement of the USAF. "They called me on the phone and asked me to get them what they wanted, and I told them I would send it back to them. I did. And I came up here and got it. I dug some dirt, and all that sort of thing, leaves off the trees, and sent them in. That's all I did."
Frank: "Where did you have to send all this? Did you have to send it to Washington?"
Leavitt: [sternly] "The Air Force, that's what they wanted me to do."
Frank: "And they never told you any of the results?"
Leavitt: "No results. Never. They never do."
Frank: "Why do you think that? Do you think? . . ."
Leavitt: [interrupting] "You think something's wrong"!
Frank: "Do you think they were trying to cover something up?"
Leavitt: [Caught off guard by the question, he answered] "Maybe."
My next question involved the tree area where the witnesses claimed they saw the monster hovering. I
Frank: "What about the tree limbs or leaves? What did they look like? Were they wilted or burnt or singed at all?"
Leavitt: "No! It wasn't burned at all, the ones I got. I got them off the tree. But I got some of this oil, the little bits of this and that to see what it was, and I never did know what it was."
Frank: "Now this oily substance that was on the ground, did you have to take samples of that also?"
Leavitt: "I did, I did, and I took dirt, and leaves and some of the wood."
Frank: "Now, when these samples were sent out, they were sent to Washington directly. How did that process work?"
Leavitt: "Air Force People, that's who."
Frank: "Now, they contacted you?"
Leavitt: "Yeah."
Frank: "Through Washington?"
Leavitt: "Yeah and they wanted to know what it was."
Frank: "Were there any other reports from Washington?
Leavitt: "No! They never, they never gave me anything back."
Frank: "It was just this one time that they called you and you sent the samples?"
Leavitt: "Yeah."

Frank: "Yeah and that was the end of it?"
Leavitt: "That was the end of it for them."

The following conversation concerned the mysterious object that was seen sitting in the valley of the Fisher farm and was reported to have been the alleged vehicle of the monster. Leavitt was standing along the path pointing to the grass in the valley pasture when he said, "I saw all this stuff pushed over and everything [high grass] and it landed right here. Well, it landed gently because it didn't go down in the dirt or anything like that."

Frank: "So, it was a soft landing?"
Leavitt: "I don't know what they had underneath that place where they landed."
Frank: "What was it, just set down and pressed?"
Leavitt: "It just set down and got back up."
Frank: "How big was the section of grass that was pressed down?"
Leavitt: "Oh, it was probably about twenty feet."
Frank: "Was there much of a burnt area? Could you actually . . . ." [Leavitt interrupted]
Leavitt: "No! Nothing burned."
Frank: "So this object was definitely maneuvering. It didn't just crash down out of the sky? It was definitely able to maneuver?"
Leavitt: "No, they could go right or left I imagine."

An important point arises concerning the object that sat in the valley. Because this object was seen in flames just prior to its landing, I assumed it would still be very hot when it relocated in the valley. To my dismay, the Colonel told me there was nothing burned. This seemed odd to me. It did not seem feasible that the object's shell was able to cool down in such a short time after being on fire. Ivan Sanderson also had a discussion with some of the boys about the object as it sat in the valley. Sanderson had asked the boys if it was hot. The boys said that it had not been so.

Sanderson expounded on this. He stated, "One of the younger kids, and I don't remember which one now said, 'But mister, it wasn't hot!'" Sanderson said, "Everyone supposed [it would be hot], because of the tremendous light [and] that the thing [object] was hot and pulsing, but the boy said, 'No! No! No! It's not hot. It wasn't hot.'"

Sanderson added, "The boys also kept saying that it was black. I said that if it was pulsing cherry red to orange, how do [sic] you say it was black? And they said it was obviously a black object, which was giving out this light." It seems that the shell of the object that was just in flames only a short time before was able to cool down quickly after it landed.

Another important piece of evidence that was found in the field was the mysterious tracks, which were called skid marks. Colonel Leavitt investigated the tracks. He explained the correlation between the tracks and how they were made, "The tracks just stopped here and that's all there was to it, and it [the monster] got out just the same way." After the craft relocated into the gulley and landed, the monster exited and hovered away from it. It then proceeded across the field and headed toward the nearby woods. The monster went across the path and toward a large white oak tree for cover. It barely passed under a 12-foot high limb that extended from it. Leavitt explained that this limb extended out over the path and then arched downward across it.

He said this about the so called monster once it went under the branch, "It could move even though it went under this limb…it couldn't raise up very much or anything, but it must of backed off or turned around."

At this point, the figure was now facing the path and the direction it had just come from and then settled down. Leavitt explained the area of the tree where the monster was seen. "It just sat down. It just sat down under a limb. There was a limb here, and it scooted in underneath it. He went underneath something here [gestures upward] but it wasn't very high, maybe ten or twelve feet." Leavitt said that the proximity between the monster's head and the tree limb was close. He stated, "It was pretty close and that THING couldn't have got out very far. Cause it was a low limb that was down [gestures downward] through here."

When the three closest witnesses saw the so-called monster, it was next to the tree and looking down the path toward them. When the two closest witnesses shone their flashlights on the figure, it moved out directly away from the tree and under the highest point of the limb and hovered over the path and across them.

Earlier in this interview, Leavitt stated how he brought his troops to Flatwoods and then spoke about the airplane and "the car." On a break during the videotaping session, I asked Leavitt what he was referring to when he spoke about the car. He told me how a car encountered a craft on the night of this incident. This happened near the Elk River, at Duck Creek, which is about six miles west of Frametown. To my knowledge, this incident had never been documented.

Frank: "Now, could you explain about the craft that flew over the automobile and what happened with that? That's never been documented."

Leavitt: "No, it hasn't been documented, but other people have said what happened. They [the witnesses] said [a UFO craft] shut their car motor off and they couldn't get it started. Then when [the UFO] left, [the witnesses] went on up the road."

Frank: "And the engine just started up again?"

Leavitt: "Yeah, well they started it up."

Frank: "But while the craft was over the top of it, the engine went completely dead?"

Leavitt: "Yeah, that's what they said."

Frank: "Was that the same night this crash-landing happened here?"

Leavitt: "Yes, it was on the same night."

Frank: "Do you remember what part of town that was in?"

Leavitt: "Well, it was—do you know where Duck Creek is? It was back this way, it was."

The Duck Creek incident, the "Flatwoods Monster" incident and the massive search for a downed aircraft in the Sugar Creek/Frametown area were the three major items discussed by Leavitt. It is my opinion that there wasn't an airplane crash, but instead I believe it was a downed UFO, which departed the area shortly after it came down. Furthermore, I believe the Air Force knew what had actually transpired. Since they were also aware of the "Flatwoods Monster" incident, which occurred only a short distance away, I believe that it is conceivable that they made a connection between these two incidents. This is why the National Guard was called out in large numbers.

Leavitt expressed his opinion about the events of that night, stating to me, "Something was a cover-up! There was something down below too, but I don't really know what it was."

Frank: "When you were here in 1952, is this the only involvement you've had with this type of case?"

Leavitt: "Yes."

Frank: "That's the only one?"

Leavitt: "That's the only one. I've heard of some [others], but I've never gone to the place where it happened. This is the only one I know [has firsthand knowledge of] about."

In Donald Keyhoe's 1955 book, *The Flying Saucer Conspiracy*, he stated, "As I thought about these sightings, I wondered—and not for the first time—if I could be wrong in probing this mystery. And yet in 1952 Air Force Intelligence had fully cooperated with me. Since then more than one Air Force officer had urged me to tell the whole story. In spite of this, I felt a growing uneasiness. Could the silent group be right after all? Had they found something too frightening to tell the public?"

Up to this point in the story, the National Guardsmen who were involved in the search party area along the Elk River departed after a fruitless search. The contingent of troops remaining in Flatwoods "stayed the night" then departed before sunrise. These troops returned to central National Guard headquarters in Gassaway, where Leavitt released them to go home. The United States Air Force had covertly entered the picture and had Leavitt and his troops take control of the situation. However, much more had occurred that night over West Virginia and the Washington D.C. area that Leavitt and his troops were unaware.

The news of the visitor, which had terrorized Flatwoods, was received too late by *The Charleston Gazette* to make it to press on the following morning. However, the Gazette did publish an article on Saturday September 13, 1952, about an alleged meteor seen over West Virginia and Front Royal, Virginia.

The headline read, "Meteorite Spotted in Kanawha Area." The article stated in part:

A large meteorite presumably landed or exploded within a 50-mile radius of Charleston last night. . . . The object was sighted not only in the Charleston area, but in Wheeling and Parkersburg as well. . . . A pilot en route to Wheeling from the east reported sighting the object from the vicinity of Front Royal, VA over this general area

According to the article, it was believed that the object seen over Wheeling, Parkersburg, and Charleston was the same object seen over Front Royal, Virginia…it was not. Although the Gazette reported the object seen over the Charleston area as a meteorite, it printed this contradictory statement: "The object was also variously reported to have made hissing sounds and to have 'backed up and started over.'"

The Charleston Gazette also printed the following article on September 13, 1952, under the subtitle heading, "Who Heard [the] Crash?" that stated:

Geologists said that the appearance of the meteorite was not uncommon, although a crash in this area would mark the first time it had happened. Meteorite fragments should have been found somewhere in the area if the object came down near here.

No one reported any sort of explosion accompanying the disintegration or disappearance of the object. Presumably, a meteorite of this size would leave a depression in the earth near its disintegration point.

Meteorites are composed chiefly of nickel and iron and are fragments of other planets or meteors, which have been loosened by an explosion or by a collision. When they fall into the earth's atmosphere, they are traveling at a high rate of speed and are set afire by the extreme atmospheric friction. Normally, they disintegrate before striking the earth. Those that do hit, however, leave their mark. Large meteorites have fallen in the southwestern part of the U. S., and one which fell some years ago in Siberia wiped out an entire forest.

When one caller was told these facts, he replied, "That may be, but whatever it was it sure scared the hell out of me." *The Charleston Daily Mail* also reported on this story on September 13, 1952. Their headline read, "Fiery Objects Flash Across Sky in W. Va.—Many From Wheeling to Bluefield Puzzled Over Weird Spectacle." Unlike the Gazette article, which reported a single meteorite, *The Charleston Daily Mail* reported many objects. It begins, "Hundreds of West Virginians from Wheeling to Bluefield reported last night seeing strange meteor-like objects flashing through the sky."

The Charleston Daily Mail article also named locations where sightings occurred throughout West Virginia. Many of these sightings were not reported in *The Charleston Gazette*. It states, "Residents from Wheeling, McMechen, Fairmont, Parkersburg, Elkins, Morgantown, and Bluefield all reported seeing fiery objects in the sky about 7 p.m. About 40 persons in the Fairmont area said the object looked like a spotlight with a greenish tail and was traveling from 100 to 500 miles per hour. . . . Pilots of two or three commercial planes reported to the CAA in Wheeling they saw meteoric objects flash past their planes while aloft. One pilot said an object had nearly clipped the wing of his craft."

This article also reported a sighting over McMechen, WV, about thirty miles south of Wheeling. It stated, "Mrs. Mary Curitti of McMechen said she saw an object which appeared without noise, and was spitting blue and white fire from one end."

In reporting these sightings as multiple objects rather than one meteor, I find *The Charleston Daily Mail* was more accurate in its rendition of the story than the Gazette.

I next researched all the locations where sightings were reported throughout West Virginia. When I plotted these points on a map, they formed a pattern that could not have been the flight path of any one object. Two separate objects on two separate flight paths were sighted around 7:00 p.m. EST over West Virginia.

I plotted a definite flight path of the object that flew on a southwest trajectory into the Charleston area. I was also able to pinpoint its path within the city and then follow its departure route once it left Charleston and continued south. This object flew over the following West Virginia cities, towns and vicinities:

1. Morgantown, about 7:00 p.m. EST/8:00 p.m. EDT
2. Fairmont, about 7:00 p.m. EST/8:00 p.m. EDT
3. Wheeling, about 8:00 p.m. EDT
4. McMechen, about 8:00 p.m. EDT
5. Parkersburg, after 7:00 p.m. EST
6. Nitro, after 7:00 p.m. EST
7. Charleston/Spring Hill Cemetery area, after 7:00 p.m. EST
8. West of Charleston, after 7:00 p.m. EST
9. Charleston/South Hills area, after 7:00 p.m. EST
10. Charleston/MacCorkle Ave., after 7:00 p.m. EST
11. Ward, after 7:00 p.m. EST
12. Chelyan/Cabin Creek, after 7:00 p.m. EST
13. Bluefield, after 7:00 p.m. EST

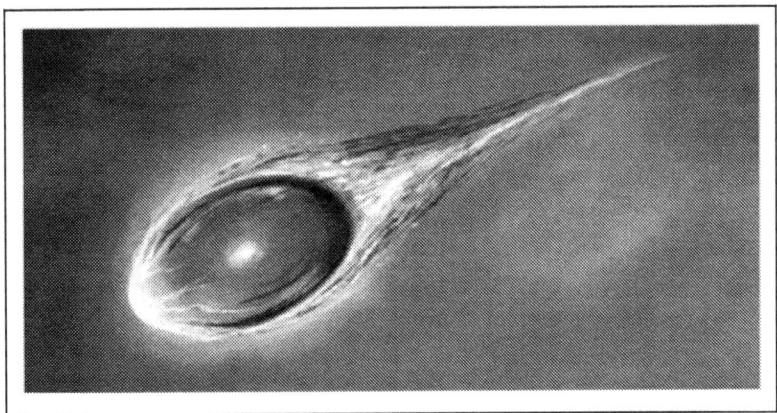

West Virginians actually saw one aerial pass over the above listed areas. The object that passed over Front Royal, Virginia was a completely different object on a western heading. A September 13, 1952, *Associated Press* news article from *The Daytona Beach Evening News* titled, "Saucer Talk In 4 States...Baltimore (AP)" states, "a pilot en route to Wheeling from the east reported sighting it in the vicinity of Front Royal, Va." There were actually two separate aerial objects on two separate trajectories, *not* a single meteor.

AIR FORCE INTELLIGENCE!

At about 7:00 a.m. on Saturday morning, A. Lee Stewart, Jr. walked onto the Fisher farm and was the first person to set eyes on the scene in daylight. As he looked across the scarred landscape of the property he scribbled notes on a pad, absorbing all the information he could, before curious onlookers besieged the area. Stewart stated, "I was back on the mountain at seven o'clock the next morning. I scanned the area of the tree as best I could, then stepped out into the tracks—the skid marks. There were several rocks that were turned over."

The two skid marks in the tall grass of the valley were each about thirty feet long. The grass was pushed down as if something had passed through it. Even though there was no ground contact made in these tracks, some outside force had turned over some rocks.

Stewart then explained his investigation. He said, "I walked up both of the skid marks and examined the area around [them]. That is when I realized I was getting the oil on my clothes. Upon examination, and of course I had gotten the same thing [on me] the night before—I actually thought of it the day [the previous night] that I ran into it, that it could be from the grasses. There is a grass in West Virginia called tar grass that leaves marks on your clothes, but the marks wash off. But these marks didn't come off. The oil that came from the scene adhered to your clothes, and was darker than anything you would normally get [from anything] such as tar grass."

Stewart analyzed one theory of how these track marks were made. He then said, "Somebody made the statement that the skid marks were probably made by a tractor. Well, these skid marks were probably ten or eleven feet apart and two feet to thirty inches wide." He sarcastically stated, "That takes a damn big tractor."

I also spoke to Lee about the landing area that was near the two track marks. He said, "Just a few feet away from the skid marks was a large pressed down area of grass. It was round and I'd say, about twenty feet across. It looked like something had set down there in a way that the tall grass was pushed down." This was the area where the craft landed after it relocated into the gulley of the farm.

I will now explain the true story of the so-called "Flatwoods Monster" and dispose of the folklore aspect of the story. This will also explain how the tracks were made in the gulley of the field and why the oil was found in them. The "Flatwoods Monster" was not an entity wearing a cloth garment.

The original drawing of the "Flatwoods Monster" was drawn back in 1952. A famous photograph shows Mrs. May holding this poster-sized drawing of it. One week after the incident occurred Mrs. May and Lemon appeared on a nation wide television show in New York called, *We the People*. Mrs. May and Gene Lemon sat down with an artist in the studio before the show aired and spoke of their encounter. The artist then drew a pencil illustration of the so-called monster from their descriptions. It was then shown to the national television at the opening of the show with scary orchestra music setting the scene, as the host narrated the beginning of the story.

In talking with Mrs. May and Fred May, I discovered that the artist's depiction of the 12-foot tall figure was actually incorrect. The artist turned the entity into a claw –waving monster that was outfitted with a garment similar to a hood and flowing cloth robe worn by a monk. It was depicted as wearing a tunic top, a pointed hood that covered its large red head, and wore a long pleated dress. After this picture was shown, the media then ran with the story and further distorted figure. What Mrs. May described as antennae protruding from the shoulder area of the upper torso was interpreted incorrectly. They were changed by the TV show artist to arms with claw-like hands. The overall description of the figure was misinterpreted. The press then had a field day, turning this entity into its own fictional creation. The incorrect physical portrayal of the monster is still seen today, and the entity is still represented as a Hollywood monster to the public.

In Mrs. May's interview, she said, "Now! It didn't have arms. The drawing showed arms [the drawing shown on the New York TV show], but it didn't [have them]." Mrs. May said, "It looked like, something like antennae sticking out from it, between the body and the head."

After several discussions and more in-depth interviews with the May family, I was able to make a composite image of the monster's true appearance. Freddie May assisted me in drawing an actual likeness of the monster. I did several thumbnail drawings based on his description and sketched my way into a rough draft.

Here in the eyewitnesses' own words, are their descriptions of the entity seen on September 12, 1952, in Flatwoods. Freddie May said, "For publicity, the monster got attention, and I think that's why the papers played it up with claws and things like that, as something alive. It was mechanical; it was not alive. Maybe inside the thing there could have been something that was alive, but what I saw was either a small spaceship or suit of some kind. Something it was wearing. It was mechanical."

Freddie told me while we were drawing the monster, "There was something in the upper torso area that I could see. From what I saw, they could have been antennae. I'm not sure what they were, but they were coming out from the body."

The ace of spades shape that was shown in the original 1952 drawing illustrated the shape of a cloth hood that surrounded the monster's head. As I sketched the monster, Freddie clarified the head apparatus, "Over the head was a big ace of spades covering, it was something that looked like a helmet, and I think it was. I would describe it as a helmet."

Mrs. May also explained the head apparatus to me, "It looked like — over the top of its head, was a great big black thing that looked like the ace of spades."

The Charleston Daily Mail was one of the first newspapers to report the monster. On September 14, they printed an article titled "Braxton Co. Residents Faint Become Ill After Run-In With 10-Foot Monster." This article contained information about the head apparatus. It stated, "Both Mrs. May and Lemon described the thing…They said it had a black shield affair in the shape of an ace of spades behind it." What was originally misinterpreted as a monk's hood surrounding the head was actually a large metallic helmet.

Set inside this helmet was the sphere-shaped head. Mrs. May explained, "The head and face were round. Now right around the neck it looked like the neck would rotate."

The original drawing showed a tunic-type flap of material hanging down over the chest of the monk-like garment. I thought the original portrayal of the chest area in the drawing was some type of armor plate covering. Mrs. May described the actual shape. She said, "It just came up, just like a human body." The depiction of the monk-like robe and tunic were a complete fabrication.

Freddie said that the upper torso was nearly cylindrical in shape. He explained to me that, "The overall body was metallic not cloth…the figure was made of metal." I asked Kathleen, "Did it look cloth-like or metallic?" She said, "No! It looked more metallic."

In Mrs. Mays' description of the lower torso, the original TV show artist and media writers interpreted her description literally. The sketch of the lower torso depicted the monster wearing a pleated dress. This was depicted as the lower robe section of the monk-like garment. Kathleen told me this about the lower torso. She stated, "It was shaped like drapes but it came out. It wasn't straight down like they had in that picture. It came out on the sides. It flared out." Based on her experience, drapes were the best example she had to describe the lower portion of the monster's body. The description of the monster in *The Charleston Daily Mail* September 14 article actually mentioned the pleated lower torso, but made one small mistake. The article stated that the monster "wore what looked like a pleated metallic shirt." The word "shirt" was mistakenly substituted for "skirt" thereby changing the description of the monster and its likeness. Freddie May clarified the pleated lower torso section of the monster.

Freddie described the lower torso as cone-shaped. He said, "What mother described as the pleats of hanging drapes, were actually tubes running vertically." We continued working on the drawing and as I sketched his descriptions onto paper, I drew tubes running from the waist area of the body toward the bottom. Freddie said, "The lower torso flared out." As I continued to draw, Freddie told me the tubes were equally spaced apart around the circumference of the body. He said that the thickness of the tubes could be compared to that of a "fireman's hose." Freddie also stated, "They were metal…actually metal pipes." Freddie then extended his arm out and said, "they were big…thicker than my arm." As the drawing began to develop, it appeared to me that the lower torso was taking on a shape, similar to a booster rocket.

I asked Freddie what he believed those tubes to be. He said, "I think those tubes were some sort of propulsion system. It was hovering about one foot off the ground." He then took my pencil and drew his own sketch of the tube pattern, circling the torso. He drew the end of the tubes as exhaust pipes. After I saw his drawings, I believed that those tubes were part of an exhaust system where the sulphurous mist/gas smell originated. Freddie agreed. During an interview with Mrs. May, I wanted to know if the "Flatwoods Monster" was throwing off any heat. Being so close to it, she may have noticed this detail. I asked," Did you feel any heat from it?" Mrs. May answered, "Yeah, you could feel-it was just like a warm mist." Hearing this, Mrs. May reinforced my theory that the mist she described as a "warm mist", was actually spewed out of the metal pipes of the monster itself.

The eyes of the monster were another area of discrepancy. The press portrayed them as eyeballs that emitted light, protruding and bulging. The eyeballs were described as having a wide variety of colors, but mainly red. Freddie said, "The monster, as the TV show and papers led us to believe, came out with the claws and the big red eyes and things like that." Freddie explained what the large eyes actually were. He stated, "The eyes were portholes. It's the way I described them, and the way most of us [the other witnesses] described them, as portholes. Say like a window in a house at night, with the light on, and you're looking in. That's what it looked like."

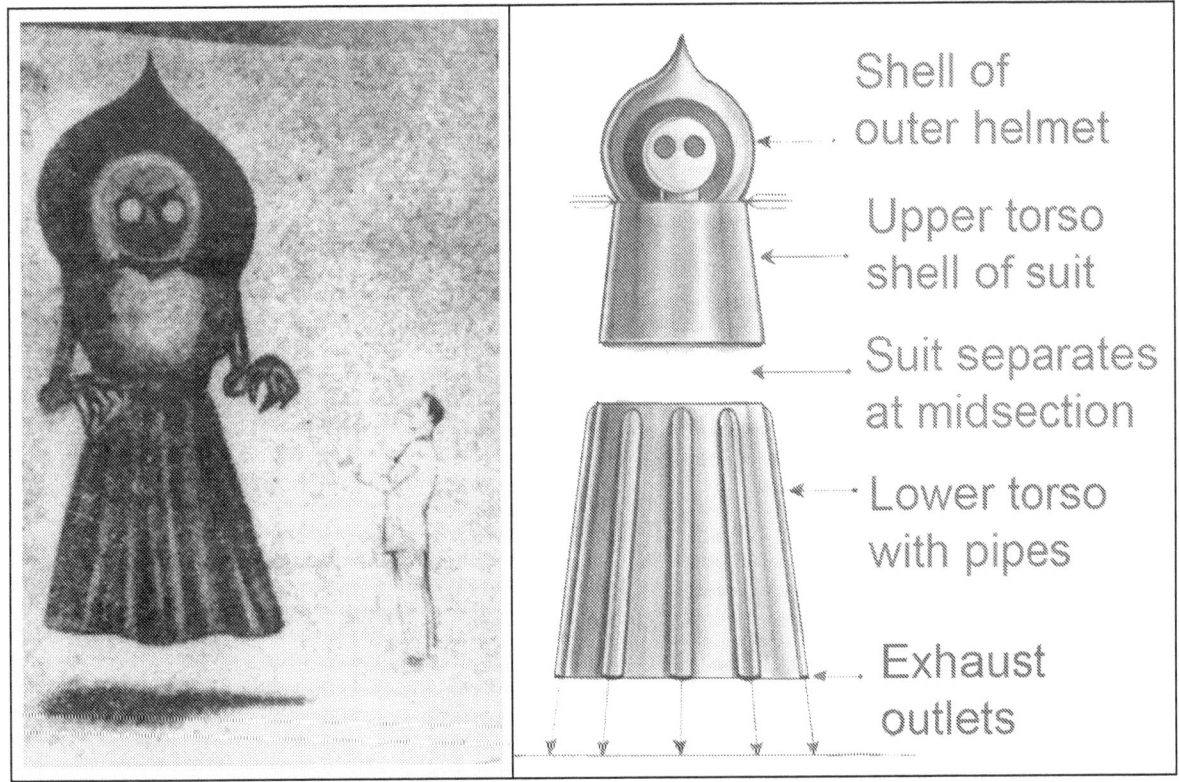

Mrs. May said, "It had great big eyes, portholes or whatever you want to call them, and basically lit up. It was a funny looking orange in the portholes. It looked like there'd be lights behind them."

I now had a working visual image to aid me in illustrating a rendition of the monster. I combined the descriptions from Freddie and Kathleen May and made an illustration of the "Flatwoods Monster." My illustration showed the monster as described by the actual witnesses. In making comparisons between the old and new renditions of the monster, I was able to establish several conclusions.

What the press portrayed as a monster wearing a monk-like garment was most likely a machine, some sort of spacesuit, or a large transport vehicle.

Surrounding the head area was a large ace-of-spades shaped covering. The early depiction of this covering was portrayed as a cloth hood with an opening in the front facial area. In reality, the hood was actually a metallic helmet with a circular opening that was covered by a transparent barrier. It resembled a pane of glass, similar to a window. An inner helmet was contained within the ace-of-spades shaped helmet. This inner helmet was sphere-shaped and red. It was thought to be the actual head and face of the monster.

The eyes were described as large and about one foot apart. The early depiction of the eyes portrayed them as large and protruding. Descriptions of eye color varied from red to green to orange. The eyes were thought to be eyeballs. Actually, they were porthole-type openings one foot apart. Behind the eye openings was a light source. (Note: When the monster reacted to a beam of flashlight cast upon it, the light source behind the eye openings increased. This forced the light through the openings into a beam like pattern.) The light source color changed from orange to green.

The original depiction of the neck indicated it was wrapped in a dark cloth. This was thought to be an extension of the cloth-like shirt, similar to a scarf.

According to witnesses, the neck was short, stout and cylindrical in form. The sphere-type inner helmet sat upon the neck that rested upon the top area of the upper torso. The upper torso from the shoulder area to the waist was depicted as wearing a monk-like robe. This area was shown to be in a human form. The monster, then, was illustrated as wearing a dark cloth like undergarment with a tunic type material across the chest. Actually, it had a metallic, cylindrical body, wide at the shoulders, which widened slightly down to the waist.

The biggest misconception about the appearance of the monster was that it had a pair of arms. My first-hand interviews revealed that antennae-like devices protruded out from the upper torso area, on the same horizontal plane as the shoulders.

Another misconception was that it was wearing a robe-like dress, which extended downward from the waist toward the ground. The contour of this dress was shown to have great folds running vertically from the waist to the bottom, like a pleated fabric.

The lower torso was said to be metallic and conical shaped, according to the witnesses. It flared out, resembling a booster rocket cone. The vertical folds were actually tubes that ran from the waist to the bottom of the cone, equally spaced. Freddie May said, "What really stood out was [sic] the big pipes on the bottom of the monster. They were metallic and silver in color and very bright."

After reviewing all the eyewitness descriptions of the color of the metallic outer shell, I concluded that the space suit was aluminum-gray and that the shell was hot and was becoming a darker color. As the metal turned "dark," it became "black," as "it was getting red hot like a poker." The dark oily-like substance that the structure was emitting covered portions of the metallic shell as well, adding to the dark appearance. When the flashlight beams hit the so-called monster, it reacted and lit up from the inside and projected beams of light from the eye area. At that point, the area became illuminated, "reflecting the color of the bushes and such, which gave the idea of green" against the metallic body shell of the figure. The visitor in question was definitely not a monster shrouded in a monk-like garment but rather a mechanical apparatus or probe if you like. Now…what lived within the probe is a whole other matter

Shortly after Mrs. May returned from New York after appearing on *We The People*, she claimed she was notified in a letter by the United States government that the monster was actually an experimental craft. This explains her government craft story. *The Charleston Gazette* printed the following story, "What Happened to the Monster?" The sub-headline read, "Braxton County Woman Feels Glowing Object Was Jet Ship Discovery in 1952 Stirred up Nation-Wide Martian Debate." The article stated, "Flatwoods, Oct. 6 - The woman who set off a four-year debate when she saw a mysterious object near her home here said today she was convinced she didn't stumble on a craft from Mars. Mrs. Kathleen May said the 'Braxton County Monster' was nothing more than some new type governmental-owned jet or rocket plane." Shortly after Mrs. May returned from New York after appearing on *We The People*, she claimed she was notified in a letter by the United States government that the monster was actually an experimental craft. This explains her government craft story.

When I interviewed Colonel Leavitt, he also knew that the so-called monster was some kind of a machine.

He stated the following to me in our interview:

Leavitt: "Well, there was something here that could fly backwards or anywhere it wanted to go, just anywhere, as long as it didn't tear up its equipment. But it was right here."

Colonel Leavitt's comment about equipment damage was in reference to oil that he found that night. This oil was emitted by the figure, the same oil that spewed on Mrs. May's clothing during the encounter. Leavitt actually found an oil puddle near the tree where the monster was seen. This puddle was obvious to see at night with flashlights. Leavitt explained, "It just sat down. It just sat down under a limb. There was a limb here, and it scooted in underneath it." I asked Leavitt if the oil that he found near the tree was splattered all over the place.

Leavitt: "No, not all over the place. Where it sat, it had some oil coming out. Whatever-it was."

Frank: [lightheartedly] "I guess spaceships have oil leaks too."
Leavitt: "Maybe so."
I then asked Colonel Dale Leavitt his opinion about the craft, called the "Flatwoods Monster."
Frank: "Do you seem to think it was an experimental craft, or do you think it came from someplace else?"
Leavitt: "No. I think it came from someplace else, personally."
Frank: "What was the general thought of the local people around here?"
Leavitt: "They thought it was silly, crazy."
Frank: "Did they ridicule, make a big joke of it?"
Leavitt: "Yeah, they made a joke out of it. They made all kinds of different pictures [he laughs]. I saw some of 'em."

In analyzing A. Lee Stewart's findings of the strange oil-like substance in the grass and Leavitt's findings near the tree, I reached a conclusion. Based on witness testimonies and news reports, I theorize the marks were actually two separate paths made by the monster as it hovered and glided across the field. The force of the propulsion system parted the grass and over turned small rocks as it hovered over the area. The oil-like substance was emitted from the monster after it had departed its craft, through, and over the grass. This created the path en route to the tree.

Once near the tree, the monster continued to emit or leak the oil. Upon reaching the tree, it sat down and leaked more oil. This was the oil puddle that Leavitt and hi troops found and collected. Shortly thereafter, the witnesses encountered the monster. In my interview with Kathleen May, she said, "I was as close to it as the length of a car. I was close enough that it squirted oil out all over my uniform."

After the witnesses saw the monster, it hovered back toward the landing area, leaving a second track that ran parallel to the first one. The monster continued to leak oil on its return trip back to the craft.

Stewart found something else while walking through the large tracks. He said, "It was at that time that I found a piece of metal. It looked like somebody had taken a soldering iron and just dripped solder. The piece of metal was shiny and silver, very easy to see in the daylight. I don't think we would have ever found it at night, even if we looked. It was about this big [making a circular shape with thumb and forefinger], rugged on the edges like any dripped metal would be."

After examining the scene for about an hour and a half, Stewart went back to his car and got the large reel-to-reel tape recorder to record the witnesses. He went to the May residence and spoke to Mrs. May, the Lemons and Kathleen's two boys. The other boys and their families congregated at the house throughout the day and the Mays were swarmed by curious visitors from the town. Stewart eventually interviewed four of the witnesses that morning, and the remaining three in the afternoon.

Stewart said, "One point that you've got to remember on this, is that you're dealing with an age range of from six to eighteen years of age. These kids were not modern street punks; they were country kids. They had not been exposed to TV or monster movies [or the sophistication] that kids [have been] in this day and time. You've got to remember, this was 1952 in central West Virginia."

Stewart explained his procedure in interviewing the witnesses, "I interviewed each one of these people separately and privately and asked each the same questions. Approximately thirty questions on anything and everything I had heard the night before, and ones [questions] I had been able to come up with since that time. After I finished with each one of these kids, I'd change the questions. I would take a couple or three of the questions and change them around so I could expect another answer. They'd always come back to the same things they had said before. Then I would jumble the thing up in such a way that, I said, 'Well, you said so and so,' but they always, [he paused] always went back to the same answers."

Stewart said this about the witnesses he interviewed, "They were sincere, truthful, [and] to be quite honest with you, I believe they believed everything they said. It is surprising to be able to sit down, go through that many questions to kids of that age, and still get the same answers, regardless of what you did to the question."

Ivan Sanderson talked about the witnesses that he and his colleagues interviewed throughout Braxton County and stated, "None of those people were telling lies. They never deviated from their story, one single iota. They never deviated in their overall story and I think that's a very powerful factor."

As the day progressed, hundreds of people overran Flatwoods. Droves of local residents and outsiders congregated near Kathleen May's home. Flatwoods had now become a target of investigation by both amateur and professional information seekers. Before long, local West Virginia newspaper reporters arrived on the scene. Some of the people who visited the area were from the local sheriff's department and the West Virginia State Police. In addition, there were local political figures Glen Cochran, the mayor of Flatwoods, and J. Holt Byrne, the mayor of Sutton. Byrne was also the owner, publisher and editor of the Braxton Central, the rival of *The Braxton Democrat*. Olin Berry, the prominent attorney who broke the story to the Gazette, was also present. Arriving that afternoon was the small group of National Guardsmen led by Colonel Dale Leavitt.

Drawings made by five of the boys that witnessed the monster

I also talked to several people who actually visited the Fisher farm after the incident. They told me that the farm was overrun with people in the days following September 12. Several of them saw the "pressed down" area in the lower field and the "two path marks" near it. At least twenty people that I spoke to, told me about an odor that was described as a "sulphur smell" scattered all across the farmland. According to one man's account, he visited the farm over a week later and the "sulphur smell" remained in the area.

A *Charleston Gazette* article written by James Haught on October 31, 1954, titled "Martian or Mirage" stated, "The day after the sighting [September 13, 1952] visitors reported finding 'large marks', oil spots, scraps of metal and pieces of black plastic-like substance on the ground." A photograph of Leavitt appears in the story showing him in his civilian work uniform holding a pencil with his thumb pointing to the tip of the pencil. The caption stated, "Metallic fragment the size of the tip of a pencil was found at the spot where the 'monster' was seen by National Guard Capt. Dale Leavitt. Also, found were 'skid-marks, oil spots and pieces of black, plastic-like material."

I found this article 10 years after my videotaped interview with Colonel Leavitt. It seems as though Leavitt actually found at least one scrap metal fragment on the site where the monster had been. At the time of my interview with Leavitt, I was unaware that Leavitt and some visitors had actually found "scraps of metal" fragments and "pieces of black, plastic-like material" on the farm. I retrieved my video tape of Leavitt from storage and reviewed it again.

Leavitt did mention something to me that I did not understand at the time of the interview when I asked him about the samples he collected. When we were standing in the field on the farm, Leavitt was explaining and gesturing his hands across the field and talking about the grass and dirt samples that he had collected.

He then stated, "I got some of this, - all of this, little bits of that [pauses] to see what it was, and I never did know what it was." I was not aware that there was a black-plastic like substance and metal pieces found on the farm at the time of Leavitt's interview. It was not until I spoke to Stewart in 1996, about three years after

Leavitt's interview, that I realized fragments were found on the farm. James Haught's 1954 article was very useful when he informed that, "The day after the sighting visitors reported finding 'large marks', oil spots "scraps of metal and pieces of black plastic-like substance on the ground."

Colonel Leavitt also went to the farm with some of his troops on that following day to control the overwhelming number of visitors. He told me, "There were so many people that came up here and ran all over the place, they might have gotten killed or something." Freddie May said, "When Leavitt and his troops arrived, there was a lot of people at our house and on the farm. It was chaotic. The access road to the farm was cordoned by the Guard so no one else could get in." Mrs. May stated, "The amount of people that came up here later the next day was unbelievable. The National guard roped of the area at the access road." I ask; how many visitors found and picked up pieces of the metal and black plastic-like material on the farm that day?

When Sheriff Carr arrived on that Saturday, he spoke with some of the witnesses and local newspaper reporters. Carr spoke with J. Holt Byrne. He told Byrne that he and Deputy Long had previously investigated another crash-landing of what was thought to be a small cub airplane at Sugar Creek. Woodrow Eagle, a resident of Duck Creek, made a call, saying he had witnessed a flaming object crash into a hillside while traveling in his car. Byrne reported the following statement to *The Charleston Daily Mail* dated September 15, 1952, "Woodrow Eagle of Duck Creek, along the Braxton County line, was traveling toward Flatwoods as the aerial phenomenon made its appearance. He reported to Braxton County Sheriff Robert Carr that a small airplane had crashed against the mountainside. A later search [by the sheriff] failed to disclose any remnants of the wreckage."

During my interview with Mrs. May, she said that about one month after the incident she read a government letter explaining the events that took place on September 12. She told me that the government had an explanation for the objects seen in Braxton County. She was informed that they were actually experimental crafts being tested in the area. The one craft that had trouble was the one that landed in Flatwoods.

She said, "They notified us that there were four crafts in Braxton County that night. One of them lit here [Flatwoods], one down the river [Sugar Creek crash- Frametown crash, same craft], and one up in Holly [a town just south of Flatwoods]. And I don't know what happened to the other one [James Knoll crash, Frametown]."

Donald Keyhoe also investigated the Flatwoods case between 1952 and 1953 on a governmental level. He associated with various people connected with the federal government, including Albert Chop, who was the USAF press officer and public liaison for Project Blue Book.

Interestingly, I discovered that the federal government denied being involved with this case. Officially, they made no public investigation. I have combined my research findings with Keyhoe's early governmental findings. Together, they show a correlation between the United States government and the "Flatwoods Monster" incident. In 1952, Keyhoe refers to this case as the "Sutton Monster Incident." The town of Sutton neighbors Flatwoods to the southwest and is the county seat of Braxton County.

When Keyhoe first heard about the case, he said, "I found myself faced with another puzzle, the case of the Sutton Monster. Of all the eerie saucer stories, this was the weirdest. When the story first appeared, I put it down to hysteria. As a joke, I phoned Chop."

Keyhoe asked Chop, "How many intelligence officers are you rushing down to Sutton?" Chop answered sourly, "You too? We're not even bothering to investigate. Several astronomers said a meteor went over there. Those people must have dreamed up the rest."

Keyhoe, during the course of his investigation, said, "Later from a source outside the Pentagon, I heard that intelligence had followed this up by sending two men in civilian clothes who posed as magazine writers while interviewing witnesses. Even if this was not true, and the Air Force denied it, their check through the state police showed more interest than they had admitted."

I found out from Kathleen May that intelligence actually did send men to Flatwoods the day after the incident. She said, "Two men came and knocked on my door and they told me they were editors from Clarksburg. Well, they said they were reporters from Clarksburg at first and they would like to go up and see the place where it landed. Freddie went up with me, Eddie was too sick to go, and we went up there."

Mrs. May, Freddie, and the two supposed reporters left the house and went to the Fisher farm. This was the first visit to the farm for both Mrs. May and Freddie since the incident had occurred. Upon reaching the farm, they went to the field in the valley. Mrs. May said, "And one said he was going to cross over the fence and go down toward Shaversville. That's the way the thing came in that night and landed."

While Kathleen, Freddie and the two supposed reporters were standing in the valley near the track marks and second landing area, they conversed about the events that had taken place. Kathleen said, "We were just talking about the thing and they saw the skid marks. These skid marks went right down a little slant. One stayed there with Freddie and me, and one went across [the fence] and went down. Well, he was gone about thirty minutes and came back."

Mrs. May explained what happened when the supposed reporter came back from the tree area covered in oil. She said, "He came back and said to the other guy, *'Now what do you think Ed's gonna think of this when we send these in for analysis?'* **That's just the way he said it** [Gesturing with her arms down at her sides and held out away from her body]. And he was covered. They had beautiful, nice suits on with hats to match, and he was striped. He looked like a zebra, with oil. Everything he touched left oil marks on his suit and hat."

Questioning her further, I asked, "So when this guy came back he held his arms out and he was covered with oil?" She replied, "Yeah, he was just covered, on his arms, his legs, his hat and everything. He had oil all over him." Shortly after these events, the two supposed reporters left the scene.

One of the legitimate reporters on location that day was a representative from *The Charleston Gazette*. He worked with A. Lee Stewart, Jr., and the following article appeared in the Sunday morning September 14, 1952 edition. (Special to the Gazette). "Did It Ride Meteor?" The article began, "The 'meteorite' which flashed through eastern skies Friday night may have had a passenger, according to reports from nearby Flatwoods."

The newspaper had made a correlation between the alleged meteorite Friday night and the "Flatwoods Monster." The alleged meteor was seen over numerous parts of the state between Morgantown, Fairmont, and Wheeling. It was also seen over the city of Bluefield along the southern border of West Virginia.

It was also, "Considered to be one of the most brilliant meteors to streak across the sky in recent years."

The Charleston Daily Mail reported on September 14, "Braxton Co. Residents Faint, Become Ill After Run-In With Weird 10-Foot Monster." This article gave the monster an inaccurate description, "Seven Braxton County residents Saturday reported seeing a 10-foot Frankenstein-like monster in the hills above Flatwoods."

Not only was the monster's description reported inaccurately in the article, but also the following remark was included. It discredited the story even more, "However, state police laughed the reports off as hysteria. They said the so-called monster had grown from seven to seventeen feet in 24 hours."

Donald Keyhoe said this about the West Virginia State Police involvement: "I discovered that the Air Force had not ignored the Sutton report. To avoid public attention, intelligence had worked through the West Virginia State Police, securing all the details."

I spoke to Jack Davis about the involvement of the state police in the Flatwoods case. He stated, "I was in Sutton and a patrolman, by the name of Gumm talked to me a little bit. He expressed to me that any remarks or anything that people might ask about it [the monster], not to give them any information and not to discuss it." Davis then told me about other state troopers that spoke with him in Flatwoods, concerning the monster. "They told me just not to discuss it with anyone. They said, 'that [it] was to be discussed with no one and not to tell a bunch of tales about something I'd seen that I didn't know anything about,' That if you couldn't tell them what it was, then you didn't tell them some phenomenon [sic] tale."

Davis also told me about seeing the state police in Flatwoods. He told me, "I would notice that very, very often they'd just come along and stop at the local stores in the areas of Flatwoods—basically, just in my opinion, to disperse the loafers or whatever you would want to call them."

I believe that the debunking phase of the government's plan had begun at this point through the West Virginia state police.

On Sunday, September 14, the two supposed reporters who spoke with Kathleen May returned and took her back up to the Fisher farm. She said, "And then the next day they came back and they begged apologies. They said they were from Washington, D.C. They said they were from Washington and they had flown in and rented a car and came up here."

I asked, "Why do you think they didn't tell you the truth the first time?"

She replied, "They were afraid that if they wanted information and we knew they were investigators we wouldn't tell them anything."

Mrs. May and the two men conversed about the incident. Pressed further, Mrs. May again mentioned that during her encounter she was squirted with oil. One investigator was adamant about getting a sample.

She said, "They did go down to the house and scrape some oil out of my uniform. . . . So I guess he just wanted it for analysis or something, to see what kind of oil it was."

I asked, "Do you remember the oil in particular? Did you get it all over yourself when the monster sprayed it on you?" She replied, "No. It just hit the front of my uniform." I asked, "What did you do with your uniform? Did you keep it or did you throw it out?" She answered, "I kept it for a while and then I think I threw it away. I'd never have gotten that (oil) out of it anyway."

These statements by Kathleen May demonstrated the government's involvement and interest in the case. It also corroborated Keyhoe's source who had heard that intelligence had sent two men in civilian clothes posing as magazine reporters while interviewing witnesses.

A striking part of this interview was the name that Mrs. May clearly remembered after her first encounter with the intelligence officers on the farm. She remembered the officer who was covered in oil specifically using the name Ed. He stated, "Now what do you think Ed's gonna think of this when we send these in for analysis?" The Chief of Project Blue Book at that time was none other than Captain Edward J. Ruppelt and the two men who visited Flatwoods were undoubtedly officers from Project Blue Book. Ruppelt had three officers who were available for field investigations, Lieutenant Kerry Rothstein, Lieutenant Robert M. Olsson and Lieutenant Andrew Flues. Which two men met with Mrs. May and which officer needed a new hat and suit?

The level of participation by the federal government in the case far exceeded the interest they were willing to admit. The two intelligence officers returned on Sunday and revealed their identities in a desperate attempt to get further information and obtain the oil sample from Mrs. May's uniform.

Lt. Rothstein & Lt. Olsson

DOUBLE JEOPARDY

At this point, I knew there were actually two objects that flew over West Virginia about 7:00 p.m. EST that night. It had become clear to me, that not all the reported sightings across the state could be blamed on one single meteor. My next step was to trace the flight paths of these two objects back to their origins.

I searched through newspaper archives for information. My first goal was to locate articles related to alleged meteor reports for that evening. Once I located those articles, I was overwhelmed by the fact that there had been multiple sightings of supposed meteors throughout the east coast. The newspapers had inadvertently combined all the sightings of this supposed single meteor, not realizing there had been more than one.

Donald Keyhoe said the following about the "Flatwoods Monster" incident, "I found myself faced with another puzzle, the case of the Sutton Monster." Investigator Gray Barker also referred to the "Flatwoods Monster" case as a puzzle, He stated, "I can only begin to cope with the mass of data and the correspondence, the pieces of the jigsaw puzzle containing the answer to the entire mystery—if it could only be put together!"

The overwhelming number of UFO sightings that occurred that night throughout the east coast was indeed similar to pieces of a jigsaw scattered about in a shotgun pattern. It took me over a decade to search out and collect a list of locations where these so-called meteor sightings occurred. I used newspapers from around the country, including daily and small weekly regional publications. I also used actual Project Blue Book documentation to obtain information about these UFO sightings and spoke with actual eyewitnesses who saw the objects.

To put this gigantic jigsaw puzzle together I used several maps and plotted all the areas where the UFOs were sighted that night. My master map consisted of several aeronautical maps that I pieced together that made one huge map of the eastern United States. I used this master map throughout the course of my investigation and as I discovered new sightings, I would plot the points on the map. I also used several regional maps to plot UFO sightings that occurred over local areas and then made several maps of my own. I then combined all of the information that I had accumulated, including times and started connecting the plotted points on my maps. In other words, I connected the dots and started forming flight path trajectories across the country. This is how I was able to reconstruct the events as they unfolded on the night of September 12, 1952.

I discovered an article that provided the first half of the flight path for the object that was seen from the Wheeling area. It appeared in *The New Haven Evening Register,* September 13 AP news article, "Fiery Object Streaks across Skies of 4 States—A Meteor? Could Be." The article in part reported, "The streak of fire first was reported over Baltimore shortly after dusk about 8:00 p.m. EDT. In quick succession came reports to the west from Frederick, Hagerstown, and Cumberland, MD, and Charleston, Wheeling and Parkersburg, W. Va."

The first object seen that night over this vicinity was the object passing over Baltimore that proceeded into northern West Virginia. I will now refer to this as the Baltimore/WV Object.

This object was **first** reported flying over Baltimore, MD shortly before 8:00 p.m. EDT/7:00 p.m. EST. The object was described as "a fiery object that streaked through the night sky with a great greenish-white light." On September 13, *The Baltimore Sun* featured an in-depth article about the object, "Scores of Baltimoreans See Meteor-Like Objects In Skies." The article reported:

What was it? It definitely was not an airplane streaking across North Baltimore, its engine on fire. And it was not a comet. It could have been a meteor. In fact, it probably was. But you cannot convince scores of Baltimoreans who witnessed its spectacular dash over the city that it was not a flying saucer. Not since Baltimore, with the rest of the world, first began to read about flying saucers several years ago has anything approaching so close to what local residents considered the 'real thing' made its appearance here. The first excited call came in a few minutes after 8 p.m. And they kept up for more than an hour. Mrs. Felix Blair, for example, said she and her husband were sitting on their back porch in the 1300 block of West North Avenue, when: "Suddenly this thing came swooping down from the eastern skies. It looked like it was right above the housetops. It was a ball of bright greenish fire with a long tail." Then there was the army veteran who was driving along Cold Spring Lane, near Loch Raven Boulevard. He would not give his name ("people might kid me"), but to him, it was a flying saucer. "I thought it was a flare at first," he recounted. "That is, I thought it was a flare until the darn thing swooped down, and then up again. It seemed to follow the contours of the road."

The **second** sighting occurred shortly after. The object passed over Catonsville, located on the outskirts of Baltimore. *The Baltimore Sun* reported this sighting in a September 13 article titled, "Scores of Baltimoreans See Meteor-Like Object In Skies." A subtitle states, "Seen In Catonsville" and gives the following information, "Numerous Catonsville residents saw it too. Most of them thought it would hit the ground in that area. It didn't though." After passing over the Catonsville region, the blazing object continued on its westerly flight path. It veered slightly to the north and passed near Frederick, MD., where it was reported for a **third** time. This same article stated, "A few minutes later, four farmers near Frederick described a ball shooting across the horizon."

This object, engulfed in flames and searing through the sky, continued on its northwest trajectory before passing over Hagerstown, MD., where it was reported for the **fourth** time. *The Baltimore Sun* also reported this sighting by stating, "And it was next heard of in Hagerstown, where at least a dozen persons called police or the local newspaper." The **fifth** sighting was made over Cumberland, MD, where it was still heading in a northwesterly direction. Police and newspaper switchboards were flooded with reports in Cumberland. As the object continued on its path, it was seen for the **sixth** time over Garrett County, Maryland.

A Baltimore Sun September 12 (AP) headline read, "A Meteor Seen Whizzing across Maryland Skies." This article stated, "It first was sighted over Baltimore and traced westward across the state over Frederic [sic], Hagerstown and Cumberland, 140 miles away. It was last seen by a state trooper atop Negro Mountain in westernmost Garrett County, headed into northern West Virginia."

After passing over Garrett County, along the Maryland-Pennsylvania border, the object continued on its northwest flight path and was sighted a **seventh** time in Preston County, West Virginia. The time of this sighting was about 7:00 p.m. EST. (Preston County observed Eastern Standard Time.) Soon thereafter, the object was spotted for the **eighth** time in Morgantown, WV. *The Dominion News* printed an article on Saturday, September 13, 1952. The headline states, "Large Meteorite Reported Sighted in This Section." The article reported:

Several Morgantown and Preston County families called *The Dominion News* last night to report the appearance of a "large glowing ball" streaking through the heavens. One resident who phoned was certain it was a "flying saucer." Another was more cautious, reporting only that what he saw appeared to be "a large ball of fire. It appears, however, that the object traveling through space was not one of those mysterious and elusive "saucers." Instead, it apparently was a large meteorite, and it appeared possible that it landed and exploded in the Charleston area.

The **ninth** sighting of this supposed meteor was by residents of Fairmont, WV. Fairmont is located about 15 miles southwest of Morgantown. The time of this sighting was about 7:00 p.m. EST/8:00 p.m. EDT. *The Charleston Daily Mail* reported this sighting in its Saturday evening, September 13, 1952 edition, "About 40 persons in the Fairmont area said the object looked like a spotlight with a greenish tail and was traveling from 100 to 500 miles per hour." *The Wheeling Intelligencer* reported the object on the front page on September 13, 1952. It reported:

Mystery Lights Zip Through Skies Here Stirring Mild Furor—Flashing Light Believed Caused By 'Low' Meteors—Night Sky Watchers Swamp Phone Circuits In Reporting Event. A series of brilliant flames flashed across the sky over the Ohio River last night and jittery valleyites feared they were in for another siege of "flying saucers." Hundreds of calls flooded area law enforcement offices, local airports, and The Wheeling Intelligencer last night describing a brilliant flaming object blazing across the sky at a low altitude.

After I reviewed this article, I realized that there were actually two objects sighted near Wheeling that night. Wheeling observed Eastern Daylight Saving Time. The first UFO, whose flight path I have plotted proceeding northwest, was sighted around 8:00 p.m. EDT. The second UFO was sighted shortly after 9:00 p.m. EDT, in the Wheeling area. The first UFO had passed across the lower region of the West Virginia panhandle and proceeded into Ohio. The rest of the article stated:

The CAA office at Stifel Field, Wheeling Ohio County airport, received a call late last night from a Martins Ferry man who claimed to have seen what looked like a light plane on fire crash to the ground between the transmitters of radio stations WHLL and WKWK atop Glenwood Heights. State Police from the Triadelphia barracks were searching the countryside late last night but the unofficial report was that the flying objects were thought to be meteors flashing through space. W. A. Garrison of West Liberty called the Intelligencer to report seeing an object resembling a Roman candle flash over his home at 8:06 p.m. [EDT] toward the southeast, approximately the same direction as the object seen by the Martins Ferry man. The CAA office at Stifel Field said that offices in Pittsburgh, Morgantown, Zanesville, OH, and several other points were swamped with calls from persons who thought they saw burning planes crashing to the ground.

Pilots of two or three commercial airliners, however, reported seeing meteoric objects flash past their planes while aloft. The mysterious brilliant flames were even sighted over the nation's capital last night and jittery Washingtonians flooded newspaper offices with calls giving all sorts of stories to describe the phenomenon. Descriptions of the "flames" varied widely, but all the witnesses agreed the blazing objects moved horizontally across the heavens and came "awfully low."

At the U.S. Naval Observatory, a spokesman said the reports "sound like a typical meteor." The National Airport Observatory said flatly the objects were not "flying saucers." There was no trace of any unidentified object on radar screens, observers said.

Mrs. Mary Curitti and her parents, Mr. And Mrs. James Butler, of McMechen were on their lawn last evening when they witnessed the strange fire-spitting display in the sky. Mrs. Curitti said it appeared without any noise and was spitting blue and white fire from one end, "It disappeared over the Riley hill at McMechen." The Brookside station of the Ohio highway patrol received a number of calls from eastern Ohio concerning the strange visitor in the sky, spotting it in the vicinity of Piedmont and Tappan Lakes. Mr. and Mrs. H.F. Penney of Shawnee Hills witnessed the light. Mr. Penney described it as a luminous ball that was moving downward diagonally and apparently parallel to Route 88. Mrs. Penney stated that there was no noise and she was confident it was not a plane. Apparently, it should have come down in the vicinity of Oglebay Park. The Cambridge station of the Ohio highway patrol reported calls from Columbus and Akron, where persons reported seeing the meteor. Many thought it was a plane that was about to crash.

I found more information about aerial activity in this area that night. The Columbus Citizen reported this incident on September 13, 1952. The article gave pertinent facts concerning the flight path of an object seen around 8:00 p.m. EDT. The article also tells of two additional UFO sightings, which occurred after 8:00 p.m. EDT as well. These occurred at 8:06 p.m. and 8:30 p.m. EDT. The article headline read, "Fireballs Shower City Area: Meteor Fall Blamed as Cause of Scare." The article stated:

Reports of "balls of fire" and "flaming planes" deluged newspaper offices and police stations in four states Friday night. Civil Aeronautics Administration officials said today witnesses probably saw a meteor shower. Reports were made at Columbus, Mt. Vernon, Zanesville and Chillicothe, in addition to a number from eastern Ohio points, Pennsylvania, Virginia, West Virginia and Washington, D.C.

Mt. Vernon state patrolmen said they received a report at 7:05 p.m. [EST] from G. S. Gollopy of Danville, reporting a "plane on fire going down." He said the crash seemed to be near Millwood, 12 miles east of Mt. Vernon. Patrolmen said no crash could be found, however.

In Zanesville, CAA officials at the Municipal Airport said an Army pilot at 10,000 feet reported what looked like a burning plane. Other calls to newspapers there described "flying saucers" and "flaming planes." Other people said they saw a streak of light in the southeast.

In Chillicothe, patrolmen said a Frankfort man reported a "burning plane falling" north of town about 8:30 p.m. No plane could be found they said.

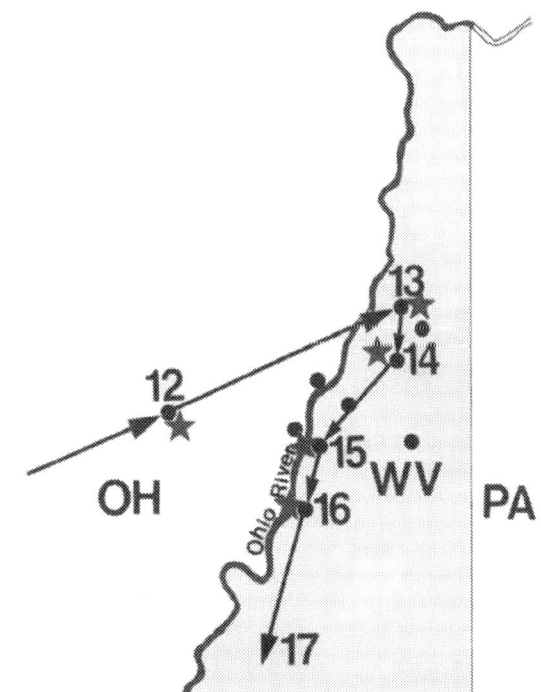

The flight path of the #2 Balt./WV object after it redirected east from the Zanesville-Columbus, Ohio area

12. St. Clairsville, OH
13. Wheeling-OH County Airport, WV
14. Oglebay Park, WV. Landed
15. Wheeling, WV
16. McMechen, WV
17. Proceeded South West to Parkersburg, WV

Columbus patrolmen said they received no local calls on the reports but did receive a number from other posts. CAA officials at Port Columbus concurred with Zanesville CAA officials in describing the phenomenon as probably a meteor shower.

In Washington, residents of the nation's capital feared they were in for another siege of "flying saucers." Residents in Harrisonburg, VA reported a "cigar-shaped object trailing blue-green flames" streaking across the sky. Police in the "bombarded" states reported they were searching the countryside for some clue to the strange phenomenon. However, police officials said they believed the objects sighted were meteors.

A spokesman at the U.S. Naval Observatory said the reports "sound like a typical meteor display." Descriptions of the weird spectacle varied widely but all witnesses agreed the blazing objects moved horizontally and zoomed "awfully low. . . ."

Next, the Baltimore/WV object made an astonishing maneuver for a meteor. After proceeding from Baltimore on its northwest path, it changed directions. This object made a 45-degree turn near Selma, OH turning northeast, passing over Columbus. The object continued on a northeast trajectory passing over Zanesville, OH, fifty-five miles from Columbus. These two episodes are plotted as the **tenth** and **eleventh** sightings respectively, and occurred shortly after 8 p.m. EDT. This alleged meteor then went approximately 60 miles northeast of Zanesville and passed over St. Clairsville, OH at approximately 8:02 p.m. EDT. This was the **twelfth** sighting of the object. *The Wheeling News Register* reported this sighting on September 13, 1952, with the heading, "Residents of Ohio Valley Excited as Heavenly Meteor Hurls Off Bright Fragments." In part, the article read,

A gleaming meteor sped silently over the Ohio Valley at 8:02 last night throwing saucer-conscience residents of four states into excited speculation…Many Ohio Valley football fans saw the object as they trooped into stadiums up and down the river. The massed bands of St. Clairsville and Powhatan had just finished playing the national anthem, when the meteor flashed over the west horizon, sped toward the east, broke into several pieces and vanished in a sparkling shower at the south end of the field.

The **thirteenth** sighting occurred approximately 20 miles northeast of St. Clairsville, over the vicinity of the Wheeling-Ohio County Airport in West Virginia. *The Wheeling Intelligencer* article above reported, "Pilots of two or three commercial airliners reported seeing meteoric objects flash past their planes while aloft . . . one pilot said the object nearly clipped the wing of his aircraft. Tower control men at the Wheeling CAA reported a bright ball of fire flashing through the sky and disappearing to the south or southeast. According to the spotters, the thing appeared simply to disintegrate in their general area."

The next sighting occurred four miles away. This object reappeared and was now in the area of Oglebay Park. This marks the **fourteenth** sighting of the object along its path. The sighting was described as a "luminous ball," which made "no noise," was not traveling at a high rate of speed, and was about to land. The object at this point was descending but not engulfed in flames, it had cooled.

This UFO was looking for an isolated area to land after being sighted by several pilots. The following report came from Triadelphia, located about five miles southeast of the Oglebay Park area. The Intelligencer stated, "State police from the Tridelphia barracks were searching the countryside late last night, but the unofficial report was that flying objects were thought to be meteors flashing through space." According to this information, West Virginia state police tried to locate the downed object. Were the police looking for meteorites, downed aircraft, or aliens?

After the craft took off again, it headed in a southerly direction along the Ohio River toward Wheeling. Many residents in Wheeling sighted this UFO. *The Wheeling News Register* reported, "Hundreds of calls flooded area law enforcement offices, describing a brilliant flaming object blazing across the sky at a low altitude." The sightings over Wheeling account for the **fifteenth** location where the UFO was seen.

The object was still blazing southbound after passing Wheeling, trying to ascend to a higher altitude. Shortly thereafter, the UFO was sighted for the **sixteenth** time over McMechen, approximately five miles south of Wheeling, also along the Ohio River. When the craft followed the river to McMechen, it was sighted and reported by local residents to *The Wheeling Intelligencer*. This damaged object was having problems, as it was seen spitting fire over McMechen. The object "appeared without any noise," which meant it was not a conventional airplane, jet, or helicopter. *The Charleston Gazette* September 13, 1952, edition reported this information:

The object was sighted not only in the Charleston area, but in Wheeling and Parkersburg as well. Tower control men at Civil Aeronautics Commission stations in the latter cities reported a bright ball of fire flashing through the sky around dusk and disappearing to the south or southeast. According to the spotters, the thing appeared simply to disintegrate in their general area. . . . Appearing at the same time in those cities, the meteor was at a very high altitude.

Parkersburg observed Eastern Standard Time. Wheeling observed Eastern Daylight Saving Time. After the object passed over Wheeling, it passed in to the Eastern Standard Time zone.

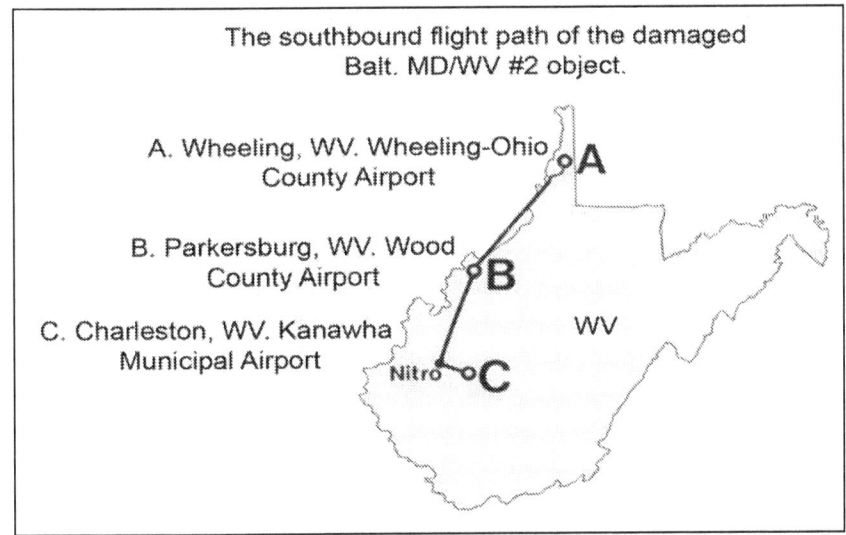

The Parkersburg report made this the **seventeenth** sighting of the craft. Even though "the thing" appeared to simply disintegrate in their general area, as the sky watchers gazed on, it reappeared once again.

Next, the **eighteenth** sighting of the object was made southwest of Parkersburg over the town of Nitro.

Witnesses there stated the object was seen about 7:00 p.m. EST. The flight path showed that this object was actually seen after 7:00 p.m.

The Charleston Gazette received this Nitro report, "Sergeant Major L.C. McDougal of the Salvation Army, his wife and sister-in-law, Mrs. Homer Murray, also reported sighting the object." He said, "It was about 7 p.m., and we were driving through Nitro. I saw the thing and told the rest of the passengers in the car to look. My sister-in-law said she saw something dropping from the thing. It [the flying object] was a greenish color, shaped like a top. Two Nitro high school boys were also with us. It seemed to disappear about the edge of the entrance to the rubber plant." Like the two previous sightings, the object again seemed to disappear or disintegrate.

After passing over Nitro, the object made a maneuver very unlike a meteor. It changed its flight path and followed the Kanawha River southeast toward Charleston. *The Charleston Gazette* reported in a September 13 article "Meteorite Spotted In Kanawha Area" that, "The Gazette switchboard was deluged with calls from anxious Charlestonians who saw the object."

The next series of sightings took place in the Charleston area. Charleston observed Eastern Standard Time like the rest of the state, except Wheeling and the northern panhandle. The sightings of the object in Charleston and the following areas that occurred after 7:00 p.m. Eastern Standard Time, translate to 8:00 p.m. in the Eastern Daylight Saving Time zone areas.

I plotted the **nineteenth** sighting as it neared the Kanawha River in Charleston. *The Charleston Gazette* reported in the same September 13 article, "One woman was standing in the Spring Hill Cemetery at the time the meteorite appeared [to her]. The witness said, 'One of the small planes had just landed, and my daughter and I were still looking at the sky. Suddenly this enormous thing appeared and veered in the general direction of Shadowlawn or Meadowbrook.'"

When the object proceeded southeast towards Charleston from Nitro, it followed the Kanawha River. What the witness had been watching initially was a small seaplane that had landed in the Kanawha River at the Capitol City and Marine Service of Charleston. This was a community access area for seaplanes that used a 6,300-foot section of the river as a runway. When the witness watched the seaplane land, she was looking northward in the direction of Nitro. After the plane landed, she saw an "enormous light" appear. She also said, "It looked like a big star and was brighter than anything I have ever seen before. It made a sort of a putt-putt noise. One corner seemed to fall off, and I saw sparks for a moment. Then it just seemed to disappear." This craft was definitely damaged as indicated by this witness's description.

The object appeared as an enormous light that veered. Meteors do not veer during flight. It was also noted to have "made a putt-putt noise," also uncharacteristic of a meteor. This kind of noise indicates an engine noise, possibly stalling or having problems. The only sound a meteor would make is a sonic boom. If this witness were close enough to the object to hear a putt-putt noise, she clearly would have been close enough to hear a sonic boom. *The Charleston Gazette* also received the following information from local eyewitness accounts.

1. "The object was variously reported to have made hissing sounds and to have 'backed-up and started over.'" This startling eyewitness account, defies the laws of physics and logic by describing a meteor going in reverse.

2. Another eyewitness, Andrew Burkhardt, gave the following description of the "thing." He stated it, "had sparkles all around it. It was white. I was standing out in our front yard and it went to the right, behind a neighbor's house and just went away."

It evident that the object was not a meteor, but instead, was an unidentified flying object. It was damaged, giving off sparks with pieces falling off it. Even after the object disappeared, it actually reappeared once again. This time it was seen west of Charleston. This was the **twentieth** location where a sighting occurred. A Mrs. Alice Williams witnessed a glowing object, which was seen to be flying low and moving slowly.

Williams was a member of the Speleological Society and a very credible witness. She said it, "disintegrated in a rain of ashes" at a height of "no more than a few hundred feet," above her. The strange disappearances the object made seemed to form a pattern. These locations are listed in sequential order from the St. Clairsville, OH area sighting to the West Virginia sightings:

1. St. Clairsville, Ohio - "broke into several different pieces and vanished in a sparkling shower."
2. Wheeling and Parkersburg - "The thing appeared to simply disintegrate."
3. Nitro - "It seemed to disappear."
4. Charleston/Spring Hill Cemetery - "It just seemed to disappear."
5. West of Charleston - "Disintegrated."

It seems that the object was actually dematerializing and then reappearing at different locations. It was sighted for the **twenty-first** time by Mrs. F. W. Emory of Forest Hills, who made the following report to *The Charleston Gazette*, "[She] reported seeing the object appear to land in or near South Hills." Furthermore, she told the Gazette, "It was very close, and at first I thought it was an airplane in trouble. Then it appeared to be a very bright light, and it looked as though some little pieces fell from it. It seemed to fall right in South Hills."

This is the third time a witness reported seeing something falling from the object and the second time the craft appeared to land. It was sighted once again, for the **twenty-second** time, east of South Hills, Charleston. According to *The Charleston Gazette* in the September 13 article, "Another woman reported seeing the same thing near Morris Harvey College." The witness stated:

I was driving east on MacCorkle Avenue when I saw it. It appeared to be falling in a very slight arc to the south, in the hills back of Watt Powell Park. It looked like a giant skyrocket and there was a very bright light. The light seemed to go out just before the thing hit, and it looked like a very, very faint puff of smoke rose where it landed.

The object seemed to be in trouble, which would explain the reason it landed a third time. As I analyzed the flight path of the craft over the Charleston area, it appeared to have flown purposefully over the outskirts of the city, disappearing and reappearing as it proceeded southward. In doing this, the craft was able to locate one isolated area after another, desperately hoping to land because it was damaged. Examples as follows.
1. Nitro, **eighteenth sighting** - "saw something dropping from the thing."
2. Charleston/Spring Hill Cemetery, **nineteenth sighting** - "one corner seemed to fall off and I saw sparks for a moment. It made a sort of a putt-putt noise."
3. West of Charleston, **twentieth sighting** – "a rain of ashes."
4. Charleston/South Hills, **twenty-first sighting** - "At first I thought it was an airplane in trouble. It looked as though some little pieces fell from it."
5. Charleston/MacCorkle Avenue, **twenty-second sighting** - "It looked like a very, very faint puff of smoke rose where it landed."

The Charleston Gazette reported in the September 13 article, "Meteorite Spotted In Kanawha Area" that "A large meteorite presumably landed or exploded within a numerical 50 mile radius of Charleston last night, according to reliable reports received by the Gazette."

The NASA FIRST EDITION book, *Dictionary of Technical for Aerospace Use* defines a meteorite as, "Any meteoroid which has reached the surface of the earth without being completely vaporized." The same Gazette article also stated, "Geologists said the appearance of the meteorite was not uncommon, although a crash in this area [Kanawha Co.] would mark the first time it happened. Meteorite fragments should be found somewhere in the area if the object came down here." These same geologists also made the following statement to *The Charleston Gazette*, "Presumably a meteorite of this size would leave a depression in the earth near its disintegration point." Contrary to normal documentation procedures applied to astronomical discoveries, this object that landed in Kanawha County was neither documented nor recorded in any official scientific reports. This so-called "large meteorite" was actually the damaged Baltimore/West Virginia object.

After making its third emergency landing in Charleston, the object took off again. It once again crossed over the Kanawha River and headed southeast, following the river.

The next sighting was over the town of Ward, WV, approximately 7 miles southeast of Charleston. This was the **twenty-third** sighting of the craft.

On September 14, *The Charleston Daily Mail* reported, "2-In-One Meteor Seen Over Ward." The article stated the following information:

James Blount of Ward, an employee of the state Liquor Control Commission, said he viewed the object and that it appeared to be two balls of fire, one over the other, with a connecting tail. He said the bottom ball was about 14 inches in diameter, the connecting tail about 3 feet long, and the top ball about 4 inches in diameter (Relative size of objects seen at a distance). Blount said the color of the object was orange.

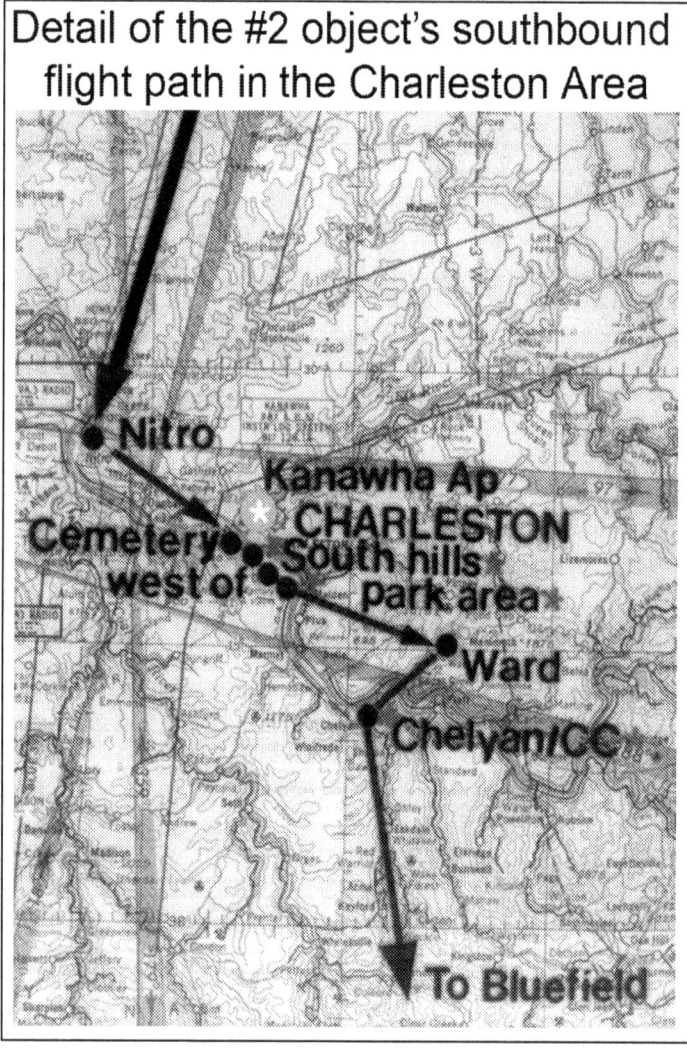

Detail of the #2 object's southbound flight path in the Charleston Area

The witness to this sighting referred to the object as two balls of fire, never referring to it as a meteor, as the headline stated. When the craft passed over Ward, it was heading southeast. Then it changed direction and headed southwest, where it was seen thirty-five miles away by a witness from the town of Chelyan. This was the **twenty-fourth** sighting of the craft. The *Charleston Gazette* reported in the September 13 article, "A man in Chelyan said it seemed to land at the point of a hill near Cabin Creek."

The witness described the object as "about twenty or thirty feet across. . . It looked like it dropped either in Mill Hollow or the hollow to the right." However, the key statement that the witness made was, "I don't think it was a meteor because it looked like it stopped right in mid-air just before it came down." This marks the fourth landing of the craft.

Bluefield was the last location where the object was reported along its flight path in West Virginia. This final sighting was made approximately 65 miles southeast of Cabin Creek near the state's southern border. This was the **twenty-fifth** location where the object was sighted on its southern heading. The in-depth flight path I have re-created shows that this object was not a meteor Every indication is that it was, instead, an intelligently controlled craft.

Furthermore, the craft was maneuvered across the state, making multiple landings. Moreover, this object was not the craft that landed in Flatwoods, the same object previously seen enroute to that town by the pilot over the area of Front Royal, VA. He said it was "tremendously large and seemed to disappear in a bunch of sparks."

The plotted 25 locations for the object that was first seen over Baltimore before 8:00 p.m. EDT indicate that it flew on a northwest path along the northern border of West Virginia. It then passed over Ohio, turned and then redirected northeast over the northern West Virginia panhandle. Again, it turned, then redirected and proceeded on a southern flight path over the state.

On September 13, *The New Haven Evening Register* headline read, "Fiery Object Streaks Across Skies Of Four States—A Meteor? Could Be." It stated, "Washington viewers flooded the weather bureau,

Naval Observatory, and even the Pentagon there with calls. . . . No blips showed on Washington area radar screens to record the object's passing." The article continued and reported, "Operations personnel at Andrews Air Force Base near Washington put a similar label on it. And Naval Observatory officials said reports they received made it sound to them 'like a typical meteor.'"

The meteor seen over the Washington area and the meteor seen over Baltimore were reported by the press to be the same object. The confusion of what was thought to be a single meteor over Washington and Maryland by the press appeared in an article in *The Massachusetts Springfield News* on September 13. The headline read, "Flaming Object Seen at Capital." It was reported:

A flaming object believed to have been a falling meteor tonight flashed across the skies startling hundreds of Washington area residents. The object was seen over the capital and near Maryland and Virginia. The Weather Bureau, Naval Observatory and newspaper offices were jammed with a flood of calls from persons wanting to know what the mysterious looking object was. National Airport observation tower crewmen said there was no trace of an unidentified object on their radar screens. A U.S. Naval Observatory spokesman said, "It sounds like a typical meteor" which probably burned itself up before it hit the ground.

To establish a second flight path I needed more information about this supposed meteor sighting over Washington. The Saturday, September 13, 1952, edition of *The New York Times* reported the following article, "Flame Over Washington—Brilliant Streak Across the Sky—Probably a Meteor." It reported:

A brilliant flame, apparently a meteor, flashed across the sky near the nation's capital tonight prompting jittery Washingtonians to believe they were in for another flying saucer scare. Newspaper offices were flooded by calls from witnesses of this phenomenon who sought an explanation. Descriptions of the flame varied widely, but they agreed the blazing object moved horizontally across the heavens and came "awfully low." The National Airport's observation tower said the object was not a "flying saucer. There was no trace of any unidentified object on radar screens. At the United States Naval Observatory, a spokesman said the reports "sound like a typical meteor." The Air Force said it knew absolutely nothing about the object.

At this point, I would like to stress two points from this article:
1. The "Flame over Washington" was said to be "apparently a meteor;" which was,
2. "Prompting jittery Washingtonians to believe they were in for another flying saucer scare."

This comment refers to the numerous UFO sightings that had taken place over the skies of Washington during July and August at the height of the UFO flap during the summer of 1952.

Since this object "moved horizontally across the heavens" and "came awfully low," and was traveling near to the ground, is it possible that it could have been seen in Baltimore, thirty miles away, at the same time?

The following three segments of this article show official statements made by prominent organizations in the DC area. The truth of these statements is questionable. Based on my research they show a discrepancy.

1. "The National Airport's observation tower said the object was not a 'flying saucer.' There was no trace of any unidentified object on radar screens." The observation tower declared the flame as an "object," which would make it a solid target. If this object was not a UFO, it was an IFO (Identified Flying Object). If this object was identified, why was it not reported as such? Furthermore, the reason that there was no radar trace of this "object" over Washington is because it had actually flown under the radar when it passed over the city.

2. At the United States Naval Observatory, a spokesman said the reports "sound like a typical meteor." This statement has little relevance, being made by a non-witness, and only based on other reports.

3. The Air Force said that it knew absolutely nothing about the object. They did not want to admit that, again, Washington had UFOs over its skies in great numbers, as it had in July, and August.

Furthermore, they were not going to tell the public that they had called Colonel Leavitt in West Virginia, and activated the National Guard in Braxton County. In addition, they would not report, as they did to Leavitt, that they wanted to know what the object was.

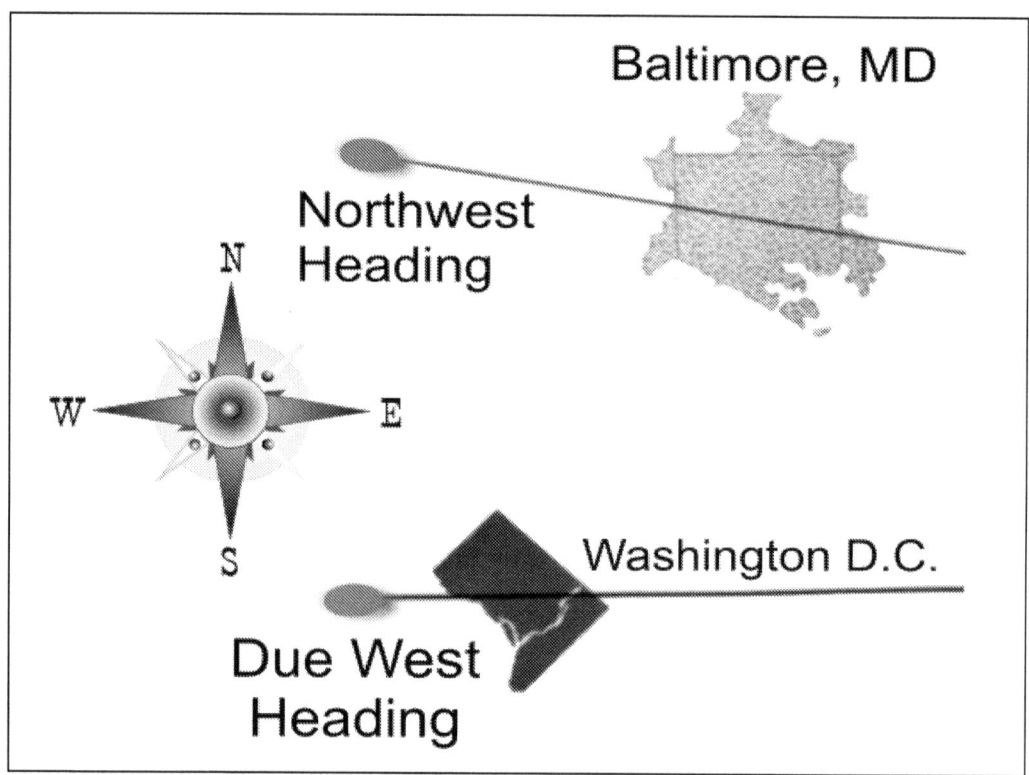

The UFO cover-up in 1952 continued. Again, a curtain of silence had been dropped in front of the American public. A disinformation directive, developed by the government, was being implemented.

I plotted the easternmost area where an alleged meteor had been seen over Washington. Then I plotted the town of Flatwoods, which lies approximately two hundred miles due west of Washington. I connected these points with a solid line, representing a flight path. This line ran almost parallel to the 39-degree latitude meridian line. I examined this plotted flight path line and found the answer I was seeking.

Sixty miles west of Washington, DC, along the flight path line I had drawn is Front Royal, VA. This is the area where a pilot reported an object thought to be a meteor. Continuing along this straight line to the west, 85 miles away, is the town of Elkins, WV. *The Charleston Daily Mail* article on September 13 referred to "Fiery Objects Flash across Sky in W.Va." and reported, "Residents of Wheeling, McMechen, Fairmont, Parkersburg, Elkins, Morgantown, and Bluefield all reported seeing fiery objects in the sky about 7 p.m." The town of Elkins did not fit into the flight path of the Baltimore/WV Object, which I plotted from Baltimore to Bluefield. Elkins did fall in line with the Washington-Front Royal object's flight path. Fifty miles west of Elkins is the Braxton County borderline.

I reached a definite conclusion based on the geographic locations of all these sightings. There were actually two individual objects and two very distinct flight paths. The other flight path indicates that this craft had passed over Washington, D.C. and proceeded west. It then traveled 60 miles, veered slightly to the southwest, and passed over the vicinity of Front Royal, Virginia. Continuing westward, it was next sighted 85 miles away over Elkins, West Virginia. It continued to fly another 50 miles farther west and reached Braxton County. This westward flight path went directly over the town of Burnsville, which is located about ten miles northwest of Flatwoods.

Several Flatwoods residents told me that there was a man who had witnessed the flight of this craft before it reached Flatwoods. The witness lived in the town of Burnsville at the time of the sighting. Eventually, I found out the witness' name was Wally Hefner and located his current residence in Flatwoods. I asked him if he witnessed the passing of the object over Burnsville before it reached Flatwoods. He told me, yes that he did see it. Mr. Hefner agreed to do an interview, which I taped. Mr. Hefner stated, "I was sitting in front of the taxi stand. It came from my right heading left toward Flatwoods. It was so much lower. That is what caught my attention, and it wasn't an airplane or a weather balloon, but it was traveling fast, and I'd say it looked like a ball. It wasn't on fire, but it was reddish-orange and went very fast but I knew as low as it was, just clearing the treetops, that it was going to land someplace close, someplace very close in our county. And of course, I'd heard the next day about it landing in Flatwoods, and I knew that I had seen it."

When I analyzed the westward flight path of this craft after it had passed over Elkins, I was astonished. This alleged meteor, which was traveling from east to west, had made an amazing aerial maneuver. It had made a 90-degree turn toward the south and proceeded over Burnsville en route to Flatwoods.

While en route to Flatwoods, the object had traveled due south. It passed to the west of the small community of Heaters and then proceeded about five miles farther to Flatwoods. This object I will now refer to as the Washington/Flatwoods Object.

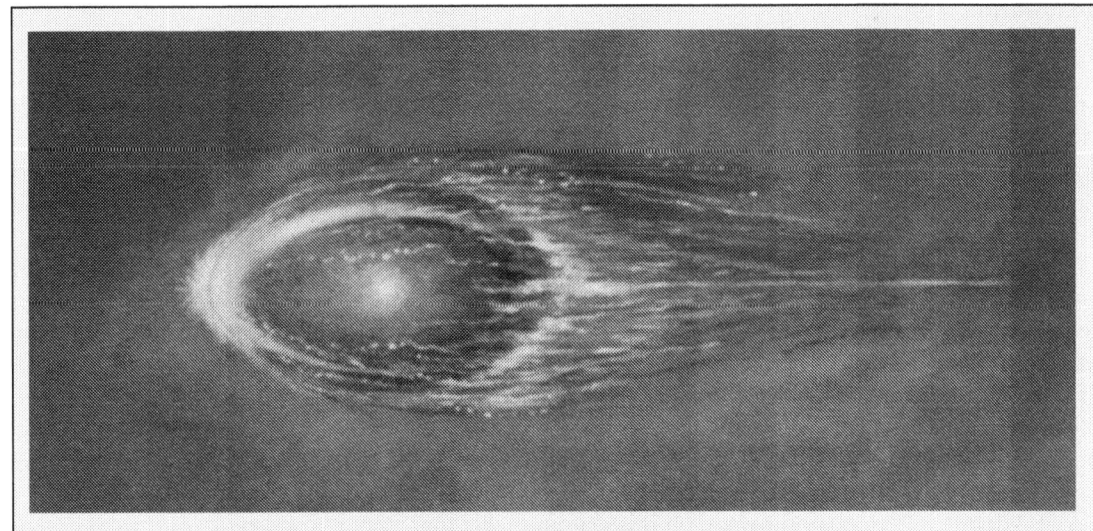

The Washington/Flatwoods Object

Chapter 17

TRIPLE THREAT

My plotted flight paths indicate that there were two objects seen flying on westward paths over the mid-Atlantic United States. These two objects were both seen at approximately 7:00 p.m. EST/ 8:00 p.m. EDT. They were the Baltimore/WV and the Washington/Flatwoods objects.

After establishing the flight paths of what was supposedly one meteor, I referred back to the Baltimore, September 13, AP article. "Fiery Object Streaks Across Skies Of Four States—A Meteor? Could Be." It stated the following:

> A ball of fire seen in the sky over Kingsport, TN, about the same time, set off a fruitless search for a wrecked plane. There were no reports of missing aircraft, but Tennessee highway patrolmen, the Kingsport lifesaving crew and several ambulances combed an area of almost 15 square miles after an aerial object was reported to have struck the ground after streaking across the sky.
>
> A spokesman at Tri-Cities Airport near Kingsport said the object had been identified as a meteor.

When the newspaper reported the Baltimore sighting at "about 8 p.m. EDT" and that the Kingsport, TN ball of fire was seen "about the same time" they were correct. Because Kingsport observed Eastern Standard Time instead of Eastern Daylight Saving Time, the Kingsport area sighting that occurred at 7:00 p.m. EST, was actually occurring "about the same time," as the object sighted over Baltimore at 8:00 p.m. EDT.

The Kingsport Times-News sent me a detailed article about an object seen in their area. After I read this article, I discovered that the object was actually seen at 6:50 p.m. EST. The actual time the Baltimore, Washington, and Tennessee objects were sighted was about 8:00 p.m. EDT. *The Kingsport Times-News* published the following article, dated Saturday, September 13: "Sky Object Seen Here—Search Ends for Wrecked Aircraft." The opening paragraph is about an object that landed about two miles to the northeast of Kingsport, "A flying object described variously as 'like a full moon with a tail on it', 'a streak of silver' and as 'big as a car with a flaming exhaust,' reportedly fell to the ground somewhere in the Bloomingdale area about 7:00 p.m. Friday."

The path revealed that this was a completely different object from the two seen over the mid-Atlantic about 8:00 p.m. EDT and was an isolated incident.

The landing of the Tennessee object brought the total number of objects that flew into the United States at about 7:00 p.m. EST to three. The following documentation is the plotted flight path of the Virginia/TN object arranged in sequential order.

1. It was first reported by "airport communication sections from Roanoke to Pulaski, VA."

2. "Tri-Cities Airport tower operators in Johnson City sighted it," as it crossed into Tennessee.

3. "A communications office operator said the tower sighted the object at 6:50 p.m. [EST] in the sky northeast of the airport in the direction of Kingsport. The source said operators described it as a 'bluish-green brilliant light with an orange tail.'"

4. "Tri-Cities Airport tower identified [it] as a meteor, a brilliant ball of fire that flashed across the sky in the vicinity of Kingsport Friday night. Several had reported it was a plane in distress."

As this object passed over the Tennessee border, it fell to the ground in the small town of Arcadia, four miles northeast of Kingsport.

5. "First to call the newspaper was Mrs. Nettie R. Taylor of Kingsport. Mrs. Taylor said she and her husband, W. G. Taylor, saw the object from their front porch. She described it as a 'flaming streak of silver.'"

6. Another witness to the passing of the object gave this report, "Guy Lewis who lives in McCrary Manor on Bloomingdale Road, apparently saw the same object, which he said looked to him like a meteor."

7. Another witness to this object was H. L. Williams, a fifteen-year-old boy, who said he was driving some cows in from a field when the object went over. He said, "It was shining bright and big as a car, and when it went down over the hill back of Joe Newland's tobacco patch, it sprouted a tail."

The *Kingsport Times-News* article of September 13 stated what happened shortly after the object was seen going down in Arcadia:

> Since most of the early reports came from Arcadia, about five miles out the Bloomingdale Road, Tennessee Highway Patrolmen and county officers, led by persons who saw the object, formed search parties to comb the area.
>
> An ambulance and the Kingsport Life Saving and First Aid Crew sped to the area and stood by after patrolmen reported sighting what they believed to be distress flares from the ground near where the object was supposed to have fallen.

The *Kingsport Times-News* follow-up article of September 14, stated, "Many who called in felt certain it was a plane in distress." Even though the object was classified by a communications office operator as a meteor, the Tennessee Highway Patrolmen and county officers thought otherwise. Although the search continued for three hours on the possibility that a private craft might have gone down, no wreckage was found.

The description of the object as it was seen going down stated, "it was shining bright and big as a car." This weakens the supposition it was a meteor. If it were a meteor as big as a car that fell to earth, there would have been substantial material evidence to that effect including a very large conspicuous crater. I visited Arcadia on one occassion and searched the area in question. I went to the locations mentioned in the newspaper and photograhed the area as well. I never saw a large meteorite impact pit, nor had any of the locals that I spoke to. Over the many years that had passed, no one had ever reported such a crater's existence.

Another point to consider was that when the object went down over the hill it was said to have, "sprouted a tail." Why was there no sign of a tail during the alleged meteor's flight? When I considered the descriptions of the object's appearance and behavior from the sightings, along with the complete lack of physical evidence of a meteor or downed aircraft, it became evident that the object was not an airplane or a meteor.

Whatever landed in Arcadia shortly before 7:00 p.m. EST on that night was capable of taking off after it landed. The object must have taken off almost immediately after it landed, because the search parties who arrived on the scene shortly afterward found no evidence of it.

Another issue regarding this sighting remains. An ambulance and the Kingsport Life Saving and First Aid Crew were called to the area by patrolmen. These patrolmen reported sighting what they believed to be "distress flares from the ground, where the object was supposed to have fallen." Consider these questions.

1) Officials at Tri-Cities Airport said all their aircraft were safely accounted for. What craft or person launched the flares seen by the patrolmen?

2) If a downed aircraft from somewhere else launched flares because it needed assistance, why was no wreckage or physical evidence found?

3) The Tri-Cities Airport tower identified the object as a meteor. Since meteors do not launch rescue flares, what actually landed or happened in Arcadia? Were the flames something other than flares?

The next sighting was made about 7:00 p.m. EST over the town of Rogersville, about forty miles southwest of Arcadia. Sam F. Miller of Rogersville reported seeing a ball of fire resembling a meteor about 7 p.m. [EST] headed east. Miller said, "It looked like a full moon with a tail on it." After the object reached Rogersville, heading southwest, it then made a 45-degree turn and headed east, where it was seen by the witness.

The *Kingsport Times-News* reported in the September 13 article that highway patrol officers in Rogersville said, "Numerous calls were coming in all evening reporting meteors and shooting stars." Unlike a meteor, this object had already landed once and then taken off. Once airborne again it was described as resembling a full moon with a tail on it, looking like a ball of fire, and resembling a meteor. This object was actually a damaged craft that was having difficulty flying.

The next report was made over the area of Sullivan Gardens, at about 7:15 p.m. EST. *The Kingsport Times-News* stated, "Later reports throughout the evening placed the fallen object 'just over the ridge' in Wadlow Gap, Moccasin Gap, and Sullivan Gardens." The object passed over Rogersville headed east, then changed direction and headed back toward Arcadia, where it had originally landed. This was the Sullivan Gardens area:

Reports were still coming in late last night from residents of the Moccasin Gap and Wadlow Gap sections saying they had seen the object but had not reported it earlier for fear of "being laughed at." Edgar Bowlin and his wife said they were visiting at the home of Mr. and Mrs. Tom Lane. They were talking together on the front porch when they saw an object "almost big as a full moon and with a fluorescent glow" streak past. Bowlin said the "thing seemed to burst as it went down over some trees on top of a mountain and left only a short glowing trail."

This object was referred to as a "thing" by these witnesses. Witnesses who saw the Baltimore/WV object also referred to the object as a "thing." This object in Tennessee seemed to burst and disappear, just like the object in the Charleston area did several times.

The final sighting of this object was over Tennessee, twenty-five miles to the southeast, near Elizabethton. Highway patrol officers reported receiving numerous telephone calls all evening from local residents "reporting meteors and shooting stars."

At this point, I have demonstrated the flight paths of three separate objects seen over the United States on the evening of September 12, 1952 over the eastern seaboard around 8:00 p.m. EDT. They are listed below:

A.) The northernmost object, the Baltimore/WV craft, flew over Baltimore, proceeded northwest into Ohio, redirected and passed over northern West Virginia, then turned southwest over the state and exited south over the Bluefield area.

B.) Just southwest of Baltimore, the object that flew over Washington, DC, the Washington/Flatwoods craft, proceeded west over Virginia, then flew over West Virginia and turned south toward Braxton County and then landed in Flatwoods.

C.) The southernmost object, the Virginia/TN craft, traveled southwest over Virginia, then passed over Roanoke and Pulaski, Virginia before reaching Tennessee and then landed in Arcadia, Tennessee.

At this point, I needed assistance to figure out the rest of the timeline. A man that I had met at a military show who is a historian of military strategy helped me. I took out my master map, hung it on the wall and showed it to him. He studied it intently then took a yardstick and pencil and then extended the flight path of each object back to the east coast. Soon, I realized that the trajectories of two of these objects first passed over New Jersey, and one passed over Delaware. He continued to extend the lines of the three flight paths east and out across the Atlantic Ocean. Now the flight paths showed an amazing conclusion; all three-flight paths converged and intersected ninety miles off the eastern seaboard and directly east Washington D.C.

"So what does this mean?" I asked. He told me, "You're thinking one-dimensional with this piece of paper hanging on the wall." We took the huge map off the wall, laid it down on the floor and stood over it. He then said, "We just put this map into a three-dimensional setting." He reached in his pocket and took out three coins as I stood and watched. "This is the atmosphere above the map," he stated, and "these coins are the three objects." From waist level, he dropped the three coins one at a time over the intersection point on the map and they all landed on top of each other. He turned and looked at me and said, "This intersection point over the Atlantic Ocean indicates the area where the three objects made their descents into the atmosphere." Now it made sense to me. He continued, "These three ships were dropped from a main craft that was hovering above the atmosphere." This three-dimensional demonstration illustrated how the three objects dropped down one at a time, hence the area where all three-flight paths converged. He then said, "Now look at the area where these three coins are sitting," and pointed to a perimeter line on the map that said ADIZ.

He picked up my USAF dictionary and flipped to a page. "Here, read this!" he said, "ADIZ. The airspace above a specified geographical area in which the control and ready recognition of aircraft is required." I read further, "The *coastal* ADIZ, an ADIZ established over an oceanic area adjacent to the international boundary lines of the U.S. or its territories or its possessions." This intersection point ninety miles off the coast indicates that the three objects were within an Air Defense Identification Zone, the Atlantic ADIZ. Any aircraft within this air zone must properly identify itself. If it didn't, the aircraft would be considered possibly hostile, and a threat to the United States. I looked at him and he said, "Radar picked them up. This is where the jets got them as they dropped." He then said, "Boy, they must have been surprised by our rockets!" Looking back at the map, he explained a partial scenario from the plotted points, flight paths, locations and times of the sightings. We continued to work together and I showed him more research as I found it. The timeline of events tightened up over the years and the pieces of the puzzle finally fell into place. This sequence of events begins here.

By following the flight paths of the three damaged objects from the intersection point in the Atlantic ADIZ back west, indicates they actually spread out in a fan-like pattern. The UFOs passed over the Atlantic Ocean and across the United States on western trajectories. I will reiterate the following July 28 *United Press* news story that appeared in the press only weeks before the September 12, 1952 UFO flap. "Air Force Alerts Jets to Chase 'Flying Saucers' Anywhere In U.S." ... "WASHINGTON, July 28 (UP)-The Air Defense Command alerted jet interceptor pilots Monday to take off instantly in pursuit of any flying saucers sighted in the country...interceptor planes are ready to go aloft at any time." Further information states, "The Air Defense Command's mission is air defense of the United States and it is virtually interested in anything unidentified that flies in the air a spokesman said."

Each of the three objects sighted on September 12, 1952 shared several characteristics. They displayed the characteristics of being damaged as they flew over the United States along their flight paths. These objects were described as being on fire, exploding, had pieces falling from them and moreover seen flying at low-level altitudes across the country and making forced landings then taking off again.

Jets Told to Shoot Down Flying Discs

I will now reiterate another July 28 news story that appeared in *The Fall River Herald–New* of Massachusetts. It reads, "Jets Told to Shoot Down Flying Discs – Air Force Puzzled But No Longer Skeptical." It reported, "Jet pilots are operating under 24-hour nationwide 'alert' to chase the mysterious objects and to 'shoot them down' if they ignore orders to land."

This appeared in the press only weeks before the September 12, 1952 UFO flap occurred along the eastern United States when damaged UFOs were falling out of the sky and landing throughout the country. Based on the locations where these damaged objects were sighted and the times they were seen on September 12, the three objects actually flew over land one after another. They are listed below:

1.) The *Virginia/TN* object actually flew in first and later landed near Kingsport, TN in Arcadia, just after 6:55 p.m. EST/7:55 p.m. EDT. Its flight path indicates it passed over the U.S. over Delaware.

2.) The second object was the *Baltimore/WV object*. This craft was seen over Baltimore just before 7:00 p.m. EST/8:00 p.m. EDT. Its flight path indicates that it passed over New Jersey along the coastline of the United States.

3.) The third object was the *Washington/Flatwoods* object called the "Flame over Washington."

The *United Press*, which carried this article, did not state the time that it was seen. Since the Washington craft and the Baltimore craft were thought to be the same, the third object passed over Washington about the same time, actually shortly after. Of the three objects that passed over the Eastern Seaboard, the third object had the shortest flight path before landing and had a later landing time, about 7:25 p.m. EST. The Washington/Flatwoods object passed over the United States coastline over New Jersey, and then passed over Delaware. The "Flame over Washington," was the severely damaged craft that landed in Flatwoods.

Several coastal Air Force bases were close to the three UFOs and had superior fighter jets available to scramble. The flight path of the Baltimore/WV object as it passed over Delaware, en route to Baltimore, actually passed over the area of Dover AFB. Dover AFB is strategically located to dispatch jets over the Atlantic into the ADIZ and would have been among the first to scramble. In 1952, Dover AFB was the home of the 336th Fighter Interceptor Squadron. This Air Defense Wing Squadron possessed superior F-86 and F-94 jet interceptors that were equipped with new electronically fired rockets.

About thirty-five miles to the northwest of Dover AFB is another Delaware base known as New Castle AFB. At New Castle, the Air Force had F-94A, F-94B and F-94C Starfires in their inventory, always ready to scramble. Another nearby base located about fifty-five miles to the northeast of New Castle AFB is McGuire AFB, in Wrightstown, NJ. McGuire is the closest AFB to the Atlantic Ocean in this part of the country. This base was home of the 52nd Fighter All-Weather Wing, and was assigned to the Eastern Air Defense Force of the Air Defense Command. They possessed both Sabre Jets and Starfires, several of which were equipped with 2.75- inch rockets. These Air Force Bases were three of the nearest installations to the objects with the best fighter jets available to scramble after them. There were also several others as well as Navy and Marine Corps Air Stations.

In 1953, Donald E. Keyhoe made this statement in *Flying Saucers from Outer Space*, "The public ought to know its serious business, chasing a flying saucer. Right now, they read some newspaper story where the pilot says the object made a tight turn and came near his ship. Even people who don't brush it off as a joke won't feel any need to worry—and I think it's time they did begin to worry."

Notice the similarities of the eyewitness descriptions that indicate the three objects were damaged.

A. VISUAL APPEARANCES
1. *Virginia/TN Object*
   Arcadia, TN - "Flaming streak of silver" and "flaming exhaust"
   Rogersville, TN - "ball of fire"
   Moccasin Gap, TN - "plane on fire"

2. *Baltimore/WV Object*
   Baltimore, MD - "streak of fire"
   Preston County and Morgantown areas - "a large ball of fire"
   Morgantown, WV - "burning planes"
   Zanesville, OH - "burning planes"
   Ohio River, OH/WV border - "brilliant flames"
   Pittsburgh, PA - "burning planes"
   Wheeling, WV area - "brilliant flaming object"
   McMechen, WV - "spitting blue and white fire"
   Wheeling and Parkersburg, WV - "bright ball of fire"
   West of Charleston, WV - "fiery object"
   Ward, WV - "two balls of fire"

3. *Washington/Flatwoods Object*
   Washington, DC - "a brilliant flame" and "blazing object"
   Flatwoods - "ball of fire," "small trail of fire" and "flames were trailing behind it"

B. DESCRIPTIONS OF OBJECTS
In flight low level altitudes
1. *Virginia/TN Object*
   Moccasin-Wadlow Gap area, TN – "went down over some trees on top of a mountain" (low altitude)

2. *Baltimore/WV Object*
   Wheeling area, WV - "across the sky at a low altitude"
   West of Charleston, WV - "low flying"

3. *Washington/Flatwoods Object*
   Washington, DC - "came awfully low"
   Burnsville, WV - "low as it was, just clearing the treetops"
   Flatwoods, WV - "just about cleared hilltop" and "just clearing the trees, just a little bit above the height of the trees."

Type of light from objects (overall brilliance)
1. *Virginia/TN Object*
   Arcadia, TN area – [object passing over Virginia across Tennessee border] "brilliant light"
   Arcadia - "it was shining bright"
   Moccasin Gap - "a fluorescent glow"

2. *Baltimore/WV Object*
   Ohio River, OH/WV border - "brilliant flames"
   Preston County and Morgantown areas - "glowing ball"
   Oglebay Park, WV - "luminous ball"
   Wheeling area, WV - "brilliant flaming object"
   Wheeling and Parkersburg - "bright ball of fire"
   Charleston, WV - "enormous light" and "brighter than anything I've seen before"

West of Charleston, WV - "glowing object"
Charleston area - "had sparkles all around it"
Second Charleston sighting - "there was a very bright light"
Forest Hills, WV - "then it appeared to be a very bright light"

3. *Washington/Flatwoods Object*
Washington - "a brilliant flame"
Flatwoods - "luminescent glow, white similar to a mercury vapor light" and "illuminated from the top"

C. DISAPPEARANCES WHILE IN FLIGHT
1. *Virginia/TN Object*
Moccasin Gap, TN - "thing seemed to burst" and "left only a short glowing trail"

2. *Baltimore/WV Object*
Wheeling and Parkersburg - "the thing appeared to simply disintegrate in their general area"
Nitro - "it seemed to disappear"
Charleston - "saw sparks for a moment, then it seemed to disappear"
West of Charleston - "witnessed the disintegration"

3. *Washington/Flatwoods Object*
Front Royal, VA - "disappeared in a bunch of sparks"

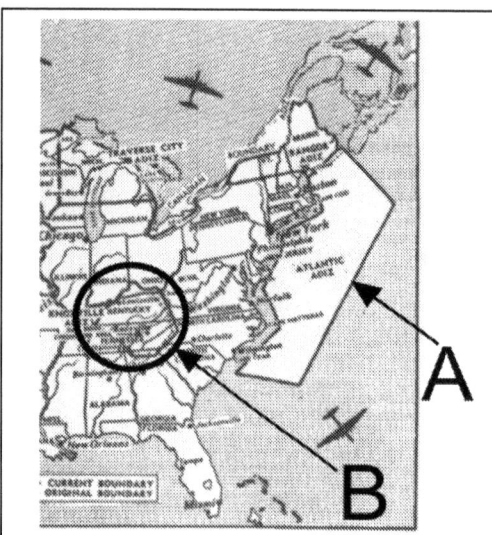

Air Defense Identification Zones

A. Atlantic ADIZ
B. Oak Ridge National Laboratory ADIZ

D. LANDINGS
1. *Virginia/TN Object*
Arcadia - "when it went down over the hill"
Sullivan Gardens, Wadlow Gap, and Moccasin Gap areas - "later reports throughout the evening placed the fallen object 'just over the ridge' in Wadlow Gap, Moccasin Gap, and Sullivan Gardens."
Moccasin Gap - "thing seemed to burst as it went down over some trees on top of a mountain and left only a short glowing trail."

2. *Baltimore/WV object*
Morgantown, WV - "crashing to the ground."
Zanesville, OH - "crashing to the ground"
Oglebay Park, WV - "moving downward diagonally" and "apparently it should have come down in the vicinity of Oglebay Park."
Charleston, WV - "the light seemed to go out just before the thing hit and it looked like a very faint puff of smoke rose where it landed."

Cabin Creek, WV - "it looked like it stopped right in mid-air just before it came down" and seemed to land at the point of a hill near Cabin Creek."

3. *Washington/Flatwoods Object*

    Flatwoods - "We don't have the technology yet today [in 1996], that something could come in as fast as I saw, it come in, slow down at the same time, and make a soft landing on earth, on the ground, and not explode or leave any evidence."

    Flatwoods - "Well, it landed gently and undoubtedly because it didn't go down in the dirt or anything like that. I don't know what they had under that place when it landed."

    Flatwoods - "It was slowing down as it was coming in, decelerating."

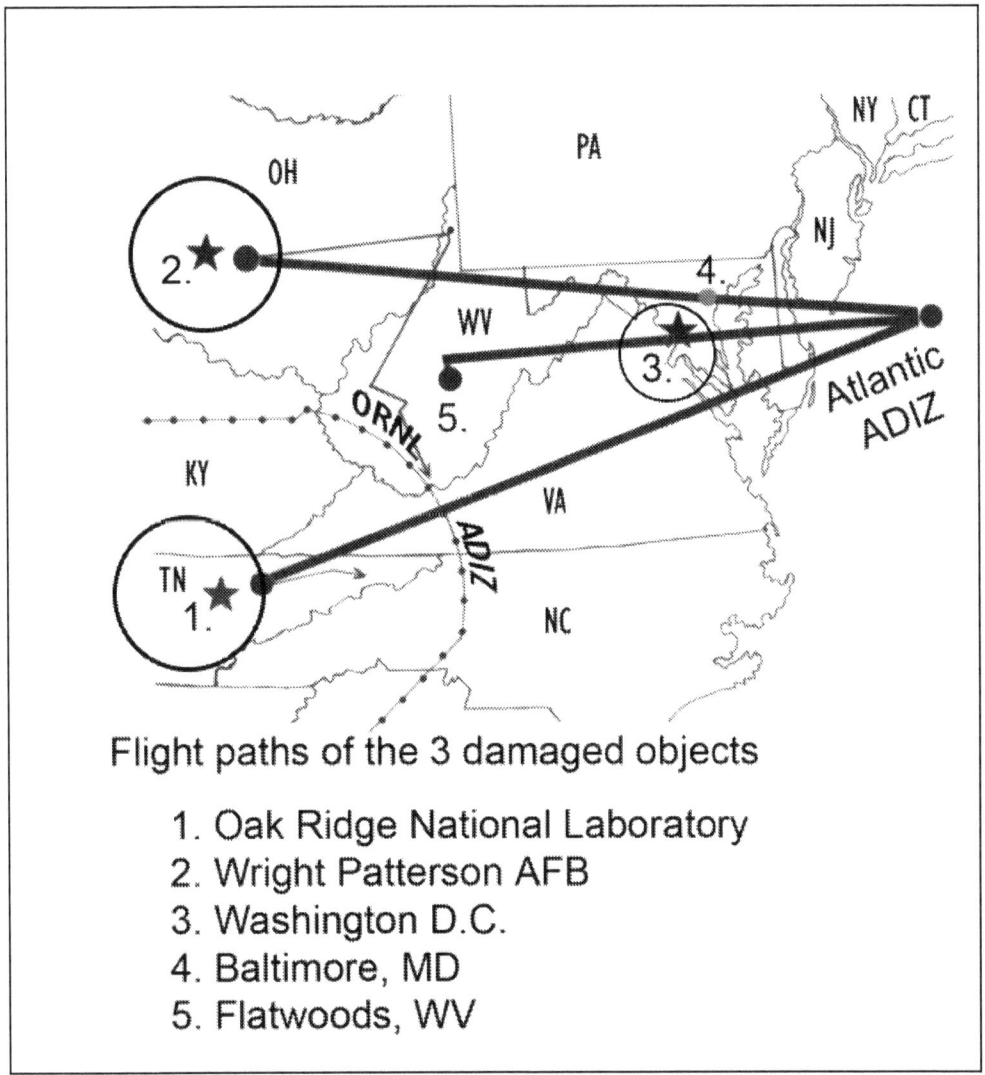

Flight paths of the 3 damaged objects

1. Oak Ridge National Laboratory
2. Wright Patterson AFB
3. Washington D.C.
4. Baltimore, MD
5. Flatwoods, WV

These three spacecraft were shot out of the sky over the Atlantic Ocean ADIZ by American fighter jets. The similarities of the three damaged objects were uncanny.

SHOT DOWN

In Major Donald Keyhoe's book, *Flying Saucers From Outer Space*, Albert Chop expressed the USAF opinion of the incident: "Several astronomers said a meteor went over. Those people must have dreamed up the rest." This statement prompted me to find the records.

After I reviewed the file segment for the Project Blue Book September 1952 cases on microfilm I was shocked. This section contained about 200 pages of documents for September 12 and 13. I discovered that the majority of the September 12 documents all pertained to what the government called a single 'meteor' sighting over the mid-Atlantic. Specifically, the U.S. Air Force called it the "Washington area meteor." Included in the government's single meteor explanation were the Virginia/TN object, the Baltimore/WV object, and the Washington/Flatwoods object. Upon further examination of these reports, I discovered that additional sightings were also reported that night up and down the eastern seaboard of the U.S. These sightings were made from locales throughout Maryland, Virginia, West Virginia and North Carolina. These sightings were being described as a single meteor by the U.S. government, but were actually made at different times, locations and directional headings throughout each of these states.

It was while examining Project Blue Book for clues about the "Flame Over Washington" object that I discovered the Air Force had kept a close record of the entire incident. The following quotes are from September 12 radio broadcasts aired in Washington, DC that evening. These pages were transcribed from Project Blue Book T1206, tape 15, 2000-2167:

1. The flying saucer fad nearly made a comeback in the nation's capital tonight.
Many residents in the area saw a brilliant flaming object flash across the sky . . .
and thought it might be a saucer. But a spokesman at the naval observatory says the reports
"sound like a typical meteor."
And the National Airport Observation Towner [sic] said flatly the object was not a
saucer. Newspaper offices were flooded with calls from persons who wanted to find out more
about what they had seen. Descriptions of the object varied . . .
but eyewitnesses generally agreed that the blazing matter moved horizontally across the sky and
came "awfully low."

2. A brilliant flame—apparently a meteor—flashed across the sky near the nation's capital tonight. Newspaper offices were flooded with calls by persons wondering about flying saucers. Most witnesses agreed that a blazing object had moved horizontally and came "awfully low." The National Airport Observation Tower said the object definitely was not a flying saucer.

3. Here is the station's 10 o'clock headline. "A Flaming Object Whizzed Through the Sky Over Washington Tonight. It's Believed to Have Been a Meteor. Listen at –o'clock for the next complete news report.

4. Objects believed to be meteors have soared through the skies in three states and the nation's capital. The display caused many residents in Virginia, Pennsylvania, and Ohio to think they were seeing flying saucers. Several commercial pilots said they saw balls of fire flash by their airliners. The show in the skies resulted in many calls to police, civil aeronautics offices, and news offices.

This following report contained in Project Blue Book was released to the *Associated Press* from Baltimore, MD:

A fiery object that streaked through the night sky with a "great greenish-white light" stirred "flying saucer" talk among residents of four states from Maryland to Tennessee last night. Weather bureau observers here saw the object but made no official report of it. The streak of fire first was reported over Baltimore shortly after dusk. About 9 p.m. in quick succession came reports to the west from Frederick, Hagerstown, and Cumberland, MD, and Charleston, Wheeling and Parkersburg, W. VA. Washington viewers flooded the Weather Bureaus, Naval Observatory and even the Pentagon. No blips showed on Washington area radar screens to record the object passing.

This Baltimore September 13 AP article is actually an edited version of the article, "Fiery Object Streaks Across Skies Of Four States—A Meteor? Could Be." The final ten paragraphs containing explicit details of the supposed meteor have been deleted. Whether this was done intentionally, I do not know. I do know that much of the information contained in the original article was deleted in Project Blue Book. Upon closer examination of the Air Force's edited version of this article, I discovered an inconsistency from the original. The original article stated the time of the object's passing "over Baltimore shortly after dusk about 8 p.m. EDT." The edited version contained in Project Blue Book stated, "Over Baltimore after about 9 p.m."

I wondered why this change was made. Researcher Ivan T. Sanderson stated that he discovered "a local Baltimore account later picked up by the wire services but not extensively used. It related to the passage of a 'fireball' over that city at 7 p.m. [7:00 p.m. EST, 8:00 p.m. EDT] on Friday, September 12."

Sanderson also stated that he and his assistant met two witnesses while driving into Baltimore from West Virginia "who had seen a slow-moving reddish object pass over from east to west." He also wrote that this object "was later described and 'explained' by a Mr. P.M. Reese of the Maryland Academy of Sciences staff as a 'fireball meteor.'" According to Sanderson, Mr. Reese "further stated that it 'was burned out.'" However, a similar, if not the same object, was seen over both Frederick and Hagerstown [Maryland]. The object that passed over Baltimore, MD at 7:00 p.m. EST did not burn out over that vicinity. The object proceeded on a western course and then flew over both Frederick and Hagerstown.

There were actually two different times reported for the object passing "over Baltimore shortly after dusk." This would explain the confusion in stating the times set by the press. According to my research, the 7 p.m. EST time was the most accurate.

The sighting of the alleged meteor became a primary topic in many of the country's newspapers for days. On Monday, September 15, three days after the incident, the *United Press* (UP) released a story. Picked up by *The New York Daily News*, the headline read, "The Thing, 10 Feet Tall, Terrifies Party of 7."

This article described the monster as, "an evil-smelling fire breathing monster, 10 feet tall, with a bright green body and a blood-red face." Clearly, the misinterpretation of the monster had already begun.

On Monday, September 15, an article by the *United Press* in *The Washington Daily News* headline read, "The Monster of Braxton County - Around a Bend They Saw a Pair of Bulging Eyes."

The lead paragraph read as follows, "Sutton, W. Va., Sept. 15- A short time after a meteorite—or something—blazed across this town last Friday and seemed to land nearby, an evil-smelling, green bodied monster 12 feet tall with bulging eyes and clawy [sic] hands sent seven young citizens running for their lives."

Another article dated Monday and carried by *The Binghamton Press* (New York) ran this headline: "Flashes of Life—Green Monster with Blood-Red Face Scares Wits Out of Seven Hill Folk."

On Monday, September 15, the *United Press* released another article carried by *The Fairmont Times* of West Virginia. The headline reads, "Police Say Braxton Monster Product of 'Mass Hysteria.'"

Now the story of the monster was being given a negative slant, "Police figured the smelly boogie man was a product of mass hysteria." This article also stated, "Police laughed. They said the monster had grown from seven to 17 feet in 24 hours."

Another negative article on the monster was printed by *The Charleston Daily Mail* on Monday, September 15, 1952. The headline stated, "Braxton Folks Divided Over Visitor—'Monster' May Have Been Due To Dead Tree, Meteor, Beacon." It reads in part, "A coincidental combination of light from a revolving airplane warning beacon and the fiery trail of a blazing meteor reflected against the trunk of a dead tree standing alone atop a steep ridge at nearby Flatwoods may have been the 'glowing monster' who made a strange visit Friday night to Braxton County. . . But the combination of the 'orange to green glow' of the heavenly body that roared through space to the south—casting off fragments as it sped along—and the stark white from the beacon is the best explanation yet offered about the formation whose height ranged upward from seven to 17 feet tall."

Even though Charleston several newspaper articles were inaccurate in their description of the monster, *The Charleston Gazette* reported it quite accurately. On Monday, September 15, 1952 the headline read, "Braxton Monster Left Skid Tracks Where He Landed."

This article subtitled, "Special to The Gazette," was written with the assistance of A. Lee Stewart, Jr. The article gives a rather accurate account of the incident. It nicknamed the monster for the first time as, "The Phantom of Flatwoods," and one of the few articles that came close to the truth. In part it stated, the so-called Phantom of Flatwoods, **"Wore a suit of green armor; looked like a mechanical man; was 10 feet tall, four feet wide; had a blood-red face; sported a black, spade-like cowl that extended a foot or more above its head. It had claw-like 'toy' hands too and orange eyes the size of half dollars, according to Mrs. Kathleen May."**

The Witnesses

Back Row: Fred May - 11, Kathleen May - 32
Gene Lemon - 18, Neil Nunley - 14
Front Row: Eddie May - 13, Theodore Neal - 13
Ronnie Shaver - 10
Missing from photo is witness Tommy Hyer - 6
Photo taken by A. Lee Stewart, Jr, on the Fisher Farm, September 20, 1952
Photo Courtesy of A. Lee Stewart, Jr.

This accurate description of the so-called "Flatwoods Monster," actually appeared in this article five days before the inaccurate rendition of it appeared on the *We The People* TV show. This article also marked the first time that a photograph of most (seven of eight) of the witnesses was published.

The *Wheeling Intelligencer* also reported this incident in a straightforward manner with the front-page headline, "Boogie-Man Has B.O.—Monster From Space Roaming W. Va. Hills?—Police Discount Half-Man, Half-Dragon Figure Seen in Hills as 'Saucer' Hysteria." It states in part:

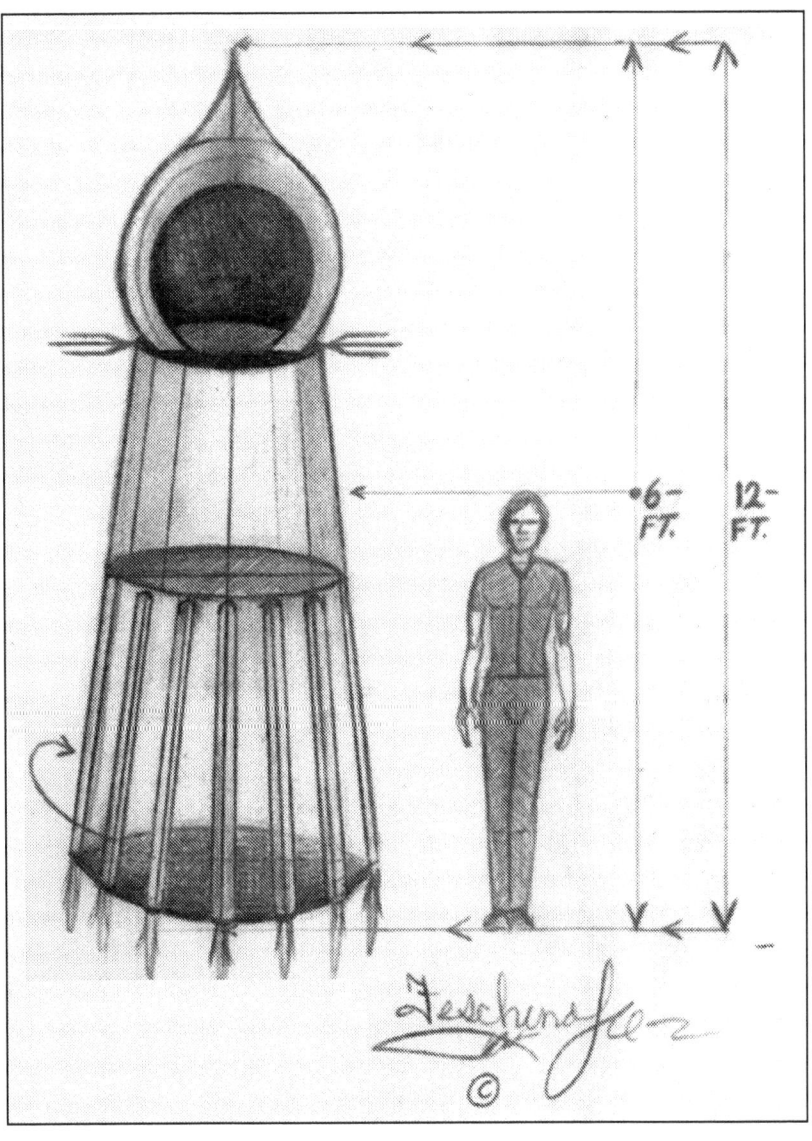

The thing… had not been reported seen since Friday night but residents of the area said a foul odor still clung to the hilltop yesterday. All of this started when Mrs. Kathleen May . . . found a "fire breathing monster, 10 feet tall with a bright green body and a blood-red face," that waddled toward them with "a bouncing, floating" motion and sent them scurrying down the hillside.

Police laughed. They said the so-called monster had grown from seven to 17 feet in 24 hours. The "flying saucer," officers speculated, might have been a meteor crashing to earth. But Mrs. May stood her ground. She said she went back to the hilltop today and found "skid marks," one and a half car lengths long…She said Lemon was leading the party when he saw something move in a tree. Lemon said at first he thought it was a "possum or a coon" but that when he shone a flashlight on it he saw the 10-foot monster with the flushed face and green body "that seemed to glow."

She said the monster exuded an overpowering odor 'like metal,' that so sickened them they vomited for hours afterward. "It looked worse than Frankenstein," said Mrs. May. "It couldn't have been human. . . ."

Lee Stewart . . . said Mrs. May and her boys "must have seen something." Stewart said he and several men, armed with shotguns, returned with Lemon a half-hour to an hour later and reported a sickening odor was still present "I don't know what to think," he said today. "I hate to say I believe it but I hate to say I don't believe it. Those people were scared—bad scared, and I sure smelled something. The odor was still there. It was sort of warm and sickening. And there were two places about six to eight feet in diameter where the brush was trampled down.

After reviewing the above article, I believe the information concerning the actual events to be highly accurate. The headline describing a "half-man and half-dragon" entity is not accurate. I am unaware of the source of this quote, but this description was taken literally by many readers, as well as the police.

The "Flatwoods Monster" was described from the waist up as being in the general shape of a human figure. The half described as a dragon had to have been the lower torso section, where the propulsion system exhaust was emitted.

I believe the writer of the following piece was closer to the truth than was realized. The headline in *The Wheeling Intelligencer* for September 15 read, "Monster From Space Roaming W. Va. Hills?" Omit the question mark and that is exactly what happened.

On September 15, *The Wheeling Intelligencer* headline story read, "Metallic Odor Indicates Meteor — Officers Shake Heads Over W. Va. Ogre Tale." It reported, "Authorities said they believed the 'flying saucer' which Mrs. May's sons saw, was a meteorite. The incident occurred during a meteor shower over a 3-state area." Many other states reported sightings that night. The entire list included Illinois, Maryland, North Carolina, Ohio, Pennsylvania, Tennessee, Virginia, Washington DC., California, Delaware, and West Virginia. However, if Mrs. May's sons saw a meteor go down, then where did it land? As previously stated, a "Meteorite is any meteor which has reached the surface of the earth without being completely vaporized."

At the time of this incident, there were no traces of meteorites found in neither Braxton County nor anywhere else in the United States. These discrepancies evident in the above statements set the stage for the controversy and put in motion a cover-up that is still the official explanation of the entire series of events.

The *Wheeling Intelligencer* also printed an article regarding the "Flatwoods Monster" on September 16. The article carried no headline, "Mayor J. Holt Byrne thinks he has the answer to the 'monster' mystery that has this little central West Virginia town all a-twitter. Byrne, who besides being mayor is also publisher of one of the town's weekly newspapers and Republican nominee for West Virginia secretary of state, said today he believed what seven persons saw on a remote hillside near here was "vapor." …Byrne said it probably was vapor and that it was possible the vapor was left by a meteor which was reported to have flashed over the state Friday night. The "foul odor" which witnesses said engulfed the area where they saw the 'monster' could be attributed to the vapor and some strong-smelling weeds growing on the hillside, Byrne said.

Was Mayor Byrne suggesting that seven local people could not tell the difference between "some strong-smelling weeds," which area residents would have recognized, and something alien, wholly unknown to them? According to the mayor, these "weeds" were the source of the overpowering stench—an easy, though highly unlikely explanation.

Could the mayor's bid for state office have influenced his attitude? Was he seeking to please the authorities, possibly grasping at straws for explanations?

Even though most newspapers had given a negative or dubious slant to the story, the popularity of the "Flatwoods Monster" was far reaching. It had captured the public's imagination. A ballad was written about it by radio announcer Donald Lamb and sung by radio singer Cindy Coy, the title of which is The Phantom of Flatwoods. As the story spread across the country, Flatwoods became the center of attention. Even though the Air Force and others tried to stifle the story, saying the Flatwoods witnesses had dreamed it up, the story didn't die. Radio commentators repeated and repeated it all over the country.

The Braxton Democrat was a weekly publication that circulated on Fridays. Since A. Lee Stewart, Jr., broke the story, his newspaper office had become the makeshift headquarters for media inquiries about the monster. On September 16, A. Lee Stewart, Jr., Kathleen May, and Eugene Lemon received and accepted an invitation to appear on *We the People*, a popular television show aired nationwide from New York. This show was to be aired live from an NBC studio in New York on Friday evening, September 19.

Opinions throughout the country were as divergent as those expressed in Braxton County. Many people in the area doubted that the event had occurred. Long-time Flatwoods resident Jack Davis said, "You find the culture of people in this area to be very skeptical unless you can really prove something to them. People don't [believe something] if they only hear talk of it."

UFO witness Wally Hefner stated, "People heard that they [May, Lemon and Stewart] were going to New York to be on TV and they [local residents] thought that was kind of ridiculous, that they'd be better off staying in Flatwoods than to be on TV in New York City talking about a monster in West Virginia." Mr. Hefner continued, "Over the years West Virginia has had [paused], you know, we haven't had the best publicity."

Kathleen May, regarding some of the local residents, said, "They razzed me. They said we were drunk and we'd seen a deer that got caught in somebody's mesh, you know. Some said we were making moonshine." Even though there were many wild and absurd explanations as to what the monster actually was, some people were taking this event seriously. On Wednesday, September 17, only one day before the three Braxton County residents were to leave for New York, Mr. Stewart was paid a surprise visit. Three people came to see him inquiring about the piece of strange metal and the odd oily substance he found in the track marks. Stewart explained in his interview, "I brought that [piece of metal] back to the plant and it sat on my desk there for several days. My father suggested that I remove it, because everybody wanted it [locals], everybody that saw it.

Well, I had taken that piece of metal and taken a torch that I had available there; a soldering torch and I couldn't melt it. I took it to a shop there in town [Sutton], and they took that particular piece of metal and put it in a prong devise and then they turned it around and put two torches, gasoline blowtorches, on it to try to melt it. We couldn't melt it. Now as everybody knows that's ever melted solder and dripped it, it comes out relatively thin.

What happened to that metal is I had three people come to my house on Wednesday. I took them out to the site; I invited them into my house that evening. They were a man and wife and a friend of theirs who worked in Virginia. They had taken a few days off and they were driving up through the mountains to see the site, and they asked me about the piece of metal. They asked me about the stains on the clothes so we [Stewart and his wife] showed them the pair of pants that was there with the stain on them. They took a piece of paper out that they had with them, and with a hot iron transferred the stains from the pants to the piece of paper.

The following day was newspaper day. It was the day in the weekly newspaper business when you gave it your all from seven in the morning 'til the paper was out. Then it went out to the post office [for Friday afternoon delivery]. About ten o'clock in the morning they dropped by the office and wanted to know if they could get a little clipping off that [metal]. At that point they admitted to us [Lee and his father] that they worked for the Treasury Department, but were in no way connected with the federal government as far as this trip was concerned. They also wanted to take scrapings from the legs of the pants that I had worn. We quickly jumped into the car and ran to my house.

I set the little vial out with the metal in it. I went down to the basement and got out a pair of tin snips, and I cut that little piece of metal into three pieces. I gave them a piece no bigger than the end of my finger [showing his pinky finger from joint to fingertip]. My wife went into the bedroom to get the pants that the lady took and scraped. She [Mrs. Stewart] took them back. I put the little piece of metal into an envelope, and they took it with them. We jumped back in the car and they delivered me back to the shop. When I went home for lunch, I picked up the vial that had the metal in it, and the balance of the metal was gone.

I had their names, their addresses. They were to call me back with an analysis of the little piece of metal, and an analysis of the scrapings. I waited a month, six weeks. I heard nothing. I called the telephone numbers, wrote the addresses, and at that time I realized I had been taken. To this day I've never heard from them."

The metal vanished only a few hours prior to his flight to New York, where he was to appear live on a nationally televised talk show with two of the seven eyewitnesses. The strangers' appearance had to be more than coincidence. First, they transferred the evidence of oil traces from the cloth pants to a piece of paper with a hot iron. The next day, on their way back to wherever they had come from, they removed more oil by scraping it from the material of the pant legs. The only other evidence Stewart possessed was the metal fragments. They, like the oil smears, were now gone.

Kathleen May had also been investigated by two intelligence officers from Washington who initially claimed to be reporters. They, too, took scrapings of the strange oily substance from her clothing. Now she, like Stewart, had no physical evidence to present on national television. Later that Thursday afternoon A. Lee Stewart, Jr., Mrs. May, and Eugene Lemon flew to New York. The guests were given accommodations at the Belmont Plaza Hotel for their stay in the city.

On Friday, September 19, the two local Braxton County weekly papers went on the stands with their first articles concerning the monster incident. The first headline read, "Mysterious Monster Pays Visit to Braxton County." J. Hoyt Byrne wrote that the residents of Flatwoods did indeed see something. He gave three possibilities for the sighting: 1. That it had been a man from another planet. 2. Vapor from a falling meteorite, which took the shape of a man. 3. An omen of disaster

Byrne referred to a "meteor" that was seen on September 12 over "Pennsylvania, Maryland, and West Virginia." He also stated that the meteor passed over Flatwoods at 7:15 p.m..

The other local newspaper that carried the story was *The Braxton Democrat*. Its headline read, "Flatwoods Folks See Monster." This article gave an account of the incident without interjecting personal or editorial opinion. It stated, "The story as it appeared in the daily paper has caused much comment and many questions. Calls have come into this office from New York, Washington, Los Angeles, and many other places. . . . Several news syndicates and magazines have shown an interest in further information, with the objective of using the story. Mrs. May has also been flooded with phone calls and letters."

Among the many people arriving in Flatwoods to investigate the incident were Ivan T. Sanderson and Gray Barker. Sanderson, a naturalist and researcher, visited Flatwoods on Friday, September 19 to research the story for an upcoming article for *True Magazine*. Later that day, Barker, local Clarksburg businessman and former English department head, came into the area. Barker investigated the incident for Fate magazine. Both of these men were unaware that the three key figures with whom they most needed to speak were in New York for a television appearance.

Later that Friday afternoon, Mr. Stewart, Mrs. May, and Mr. Lemon were driven to NBC studios to prepare for the live airing of *We the People*. The three met with talk show host Dan Seymour and his staff, and reviewed the story with them. During the course of their initial interview, an artist stood by and drew his interpretation of the monster. This poster-sized drawing of the creature was to be shown on air during the broadcast.

I asked Mrs. May about the sketch artist and the drawing. She told me, "They just told me they'd like to draw a sketch of it, and Gene and I together had told them what we'd seen, and they drew the sketch."

I continued, "Why did he draw arms on it then, because you told me it had antennae?" She responded, "I told him that [about the antennae] too, but that's what he drew on it. To make it look more like a monster, I guess."

The drawing that evolved is an inaccurate rendition of the monster. It portrayed the monster as having menacing claw-like hands, wearing a monk-like robe and a cloth cowl, which looked like a dress. This illustration can still be found in publications today. The network was probably trying to emphasize to its viewers the threatening appearance of the monster with arms and claws. Its inaccurate depiction of the monster eroded the story's credibility by showing a dress-wearing, claw-waving caricature of the creature.

Master of Ceremonies Dan Seymour began the show by setting the stage of the incident for viewers while the orchestra performed soothing background music. He said, "Imagine a scene in the autumn dusk, in a lonely secluded spot which you reach right after viewing a fiery meteor in

the sky. This was easy to imagine." Suddenly the drawing of the monster was flashed on the screen and the music from the orchestra then turned eerie, intensifying. "This," he said, "was not so easy."

While showing me a 1952 picture of Mrs. May holding the original monster drawing from the TV show, Stewart said, "The picture in question that always seems to be in a lot of the articles that I've seen is the one right here. The artist at *We the People* drew that in New York on the actual day we were there. In fact, it was the focal point of the entire show. They started interviewing Mrs. May, and then went to Lemon, which was all a question-and-answer situation. They gave me the opportunity of summarizing the thing in general and then again finished with this particular picture. That was basically the entire program."

An interesting fact about the airing of this program was that the Huntington channel that telecasts into the Sutton area did not carry the show. The residents of Flatwoods saw only a garbled transmission from other, more distant markets. Messages and letters from West Virginia residents in areas who had received better reception of the show reported the story to the Braxton County residents.

Mrs. May described the scene that greeted them at the airport upon their arrival home from New York: "When we got off the plane down here in Charleston, Lord, there were photographers and everything else. They had taken pictures of me, and they were all waiting for us."

A. Lee Stewart, Jr. began handling the public relations, becoming the primary spokesperson for interviews with the media. Among numerous reporters who visited the May home after their return from New York was one from *The Charleston Gazette*. A. Lee Stewart, Jr. and a Gazette photographer took numerous photos of May in her home, while she held the monster drawing she had brought back from New York. These famous photographs have been published repeatedly.

Among the others in Flatwoods that day was Colonel Dale Leavitt, commander of the West Virginia National Guard. Leavitt was accompanied by local guardsmen and was soon once again on the farm.

Kathleen explained an incident that happened the afternoon of her return to Flatwoods. She spoke with Dale Leavitt regarding the monster saying, "I hadn't been home too long until this truck came up and it had all the troops and everything on it, and Dale came in. He asked me if he could borrow the picture and he took it out and showed it to all the boys. After a while he came back in and said, 'Well, I want you to take a look at this' and he just turned it [the picture] sideways and said, 'This is a complete missile.'"

I asked Mrs. May what that meant and she responded with, "It means it was some kind of missile craft, you know." She also told me that she had been very proud of the National Guard unit in their county. "They did all they could and they tried their best to find out—and now—but the government, I just don't know. I'm still puzzled as to what the government—[the few] answers, the government gave us. And I guess I always will be."

Investigator Major Donald E. Keyhoe made this statement, "Then Mrs. May and the Lemon boy appeared on *We the People* and retold their frightening experience. It was obvious they believed the monster was real, and a dozen papers and magazines sent writers to Sutton for new angles on the story."

Mrs. May told me how far the news of this incident had reached: "We got telegrams, even from Japan, Steve McNeil, he's over at Sutton, he was in Japan at the time and he sent us a telegram. They'd heard it over there in Japan."

Shortly thereafter Keyhoe contacted Air Force public liaison, Albert Chop, as stated in *Flying Saucers From Outer Space*, "This could get out of hand," Keyhoe told Chop. "Why doesn't the Air Force squelch it?" Keyhoe asked. "We've already said the object was a meteor," Chop retorted. "A lot of people don't believe it. And the way this has built up, it's bad," replied Keyhoe. "It'll die out," Chop insisted.

Keyhoe responded, "But people will remember it later if something breaks. Why doesn't intelligence go down there and kill it? They sent Ed Ruppelt to Florida [Desvergers incident, August 19, 1952], and that thing didn't have half the potential danger."

Chop's reply, "We didn't know the answer to that one [Florida]. This time we do. All those people saw was a meteor. They imagined the rest. We can't send intelligence officers out on every crazy report. Project Blue Book hasn't the people or the funds."

CASE #2078-WAS ASTRONOMICAL

I have mentioned various actions taken by the government to cover up the incident. These are summarized as follows:

1.) False information given to the *United Press* news releases. The "Flame Over Washington" article dated 12 September 1952 UP stated, "The Air Force said it knew absolutely nothing about the object." On the contrary, Colonel Dale Leavitt stated, "They called me on the phone and asked me to get them what they wanted and I came up here and got it. The Air Force, that's what they wanted me to do."

When Major Donald Keyhoe spoke to Albert Chop about the incident, Chop made the excuse of having insufficient funds and limited personnel. He said he could not send intelligence officers "out on every crazy report." Keyhoe apparently didn't believe this because he said, "Major Fournet [Major Dewey Fournet, Jr., Pentagon liaison for Project Blue Book] and other investigators were available in Washington; a plane from Bolling Field could get them there in one hour."

2.) Through my own interviews with witnesses who had personal dealings with these individuals, I found it obvious that government intelligence agents had come to Flatwoods. Kathleen May said, "These two guys came out from, well; they said they were reporters from Clarksburg, at first, but they were investigators or some men from Washington, D.C."

In addition, A. Lee Stewart, Jr. said, "They admitted to us that they worked for the Treasury Department, but in no way were they connected to the federal government as far as this trip was concerned. I had their names, their addresses. I called the telephone numbers, wrote to the addresses, [and never received a response]. At that time, I realized I had been taken. To this day, I've never heard from them."

3.) Government officials acquired landing-site samples from witnesses involved in the case. Kathleen May said, "They scraped oil out of my uniform. They just scraped the oil out of it, that's all they did."

A. Lee Stewart, Jr., speaking about oil on his clothing, said, "They took a piece of paper out that they had with them, and with a hot iron, transferred the stains from the pants to the piece of paper. I put the little piece of metal into an envelope. When I went back home for lunch, I picked the vial up that had the rest of the metal in it, and the balance of the metal was gone."

Major Donald E Keyhoe, in reference to the investigation, said, "If the Air Force had sent investigators publicly in hope of killing the story, it might have backfired. Papers and magazines would picture the intelligence officers as making a serious investigation. It might seem like proof to some people that the Air Force was soberly impressed by the report, or at least the "giants from space" were considered a strong possibility."

I was put in touch with eyewitness Neil Nunley. When Gray Barker interviewed Nunley back in 1952, Barker wrote extensively about him. Nunley seemed surprised that he was mentioned in so many articles and books by Barker. Like so many of the witnesses, he had no idea that this incident had been written about so extensively. I then gave Nunley some copies of Barker's articles and writings in which Nunley was featured.

Shortly after Neil read them, he told me, "You can pretty much take that story to the bank as far as I'm concerned. The only thing that wasn't mentioned was the fact that some people claiming to be with the federal government were shutting everybody up and telling them not to talk to any reporters. My parents both told me at the time that that would be for the best and to this day, I haven't said a lot about the whole ordeal. So you can quote any, or part, of that article, [Saucerian article] and it would be fine with me."

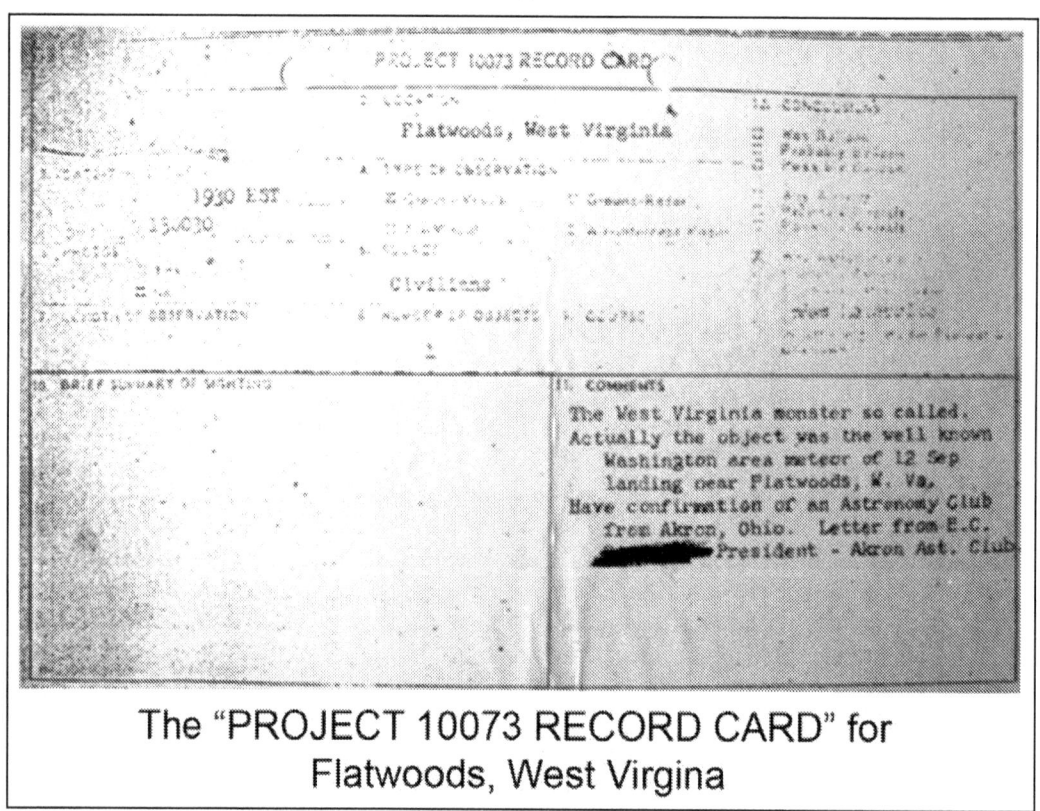

The "PROJECT 10073 RECORD CARD" for Flatwoods, West Virgina

As I searched Project Blue Book for the official document stating the USAF explanation of the "Flatwoods Monster," I kept thinking about the comment Albert Chop had made to Donald Keyhoe: "Several astronomers said a meteor went over there. Those people must have dreamed up the rest."

The "Flatwoods Monster" incident was given the designated case number #2078. The definitive answer I sought I found in a "Project 10073 Record Card ATIC Form 329 (REV 26 sep 52)." [Note: The typed-in information on the document appears in bold print.] This document stated:

1. Date. **12 Sep 52**
2. Location. **Flatwoods, West Virginia**
3. Time. **1930 EST** [7:30 p.m. EST/8:30 p.m. EDT]
4. Type of observation. **Ground Visual**

5. Photos. **No**
6. Source. **Civilians**
7. Length of observation. [Blank]
8. Number of objects. **1**
9. Course. [Blank]
10. Brief summary of sighting. [Blank]
11. Comments: **The West Virginia monster so called. Actually the object was the well-known Washington area meteor of 12 Sep landing near Flatwoods, W. Va. Have confirmation of an Astronomy Club from Akron, Ohio. Letter from E. C.** [blacked out] **President-Akron Astr. Club.**
12. Conclusion: [**X**] Was astronomical.

It is interesting to note that three of the most important sections of this document were incomplete and left blank: #7, length of observation; #9, course; and #10, brief summary of sighting. #11 reports that the object was a meteor. The proper term is actually "meteorite." Again, if a meteorite had landed as claimed by the USAF, why was no trace of it found?

Project Blue Book concluded that this object "Was astronomical." I researched the Blue Book files for September 12 again and found a copy of the letter from the president of the Akron Astronomy Club sent to Project Blue Book that confirmed the sighting of this object. The following is a verbatim copy of the letter. After this letter was received by Project Blue Book at, ATIC, handwritten notes were added. [Note: the handwritten notes appear italicized and the typed-in information on the document appears in bold print.]

EXAMPLE Typical Meteorite (Fireball)
12 Sep Fireball - September 12, 1952-Flatwoods, W.Va.

Direction: **From about 30 ° north of east to 30 ° south of west**
Angle of Flight: **About 30 ° from the horizontal**
Duration: **5-6 seconds**
Size: **about twice the diameter of the moon at zenith, but believe the object looked larger than it actually was because it was so near the horizon**
Time: **Approximately 7:00 p.m. EST**
Color: **Brilliant greenish white**
Shape: **Egg-shaped with smaller radius in front; bluish green at rear**
Distance: **Assuming that it passed over Cumberland, MD in the flight to Flatwoods, West Virginia it passed within 160 miles of Akron.**
Arc: **Was observed while passing through an arc of approximately 45 °**
Length of visible flight: **Based on a distance of 160 miles from Akron and an arc of 45 °, the flight was observed for approximately 135 miles.**
Altitude: **When first observed the object was about 65 miles above the ground.**
Velocity: **25 miles per second**
Actually Velocity: **27 miles per second**

Fireball (also see Dr. LaPaz + Dr. Olivares report) 7-3719-17

Observed by a number of people between Cumberland, MD to a point 160 miles from Akron, Ohio (All computations tally with speed description trajectory and other characteristics of a meteorite.)

The information contained in this report was used for the Air Force's final evaluation for the Project 10073 Record Card. There is no explanation for the conflicting data between this letter/report and the final Project Blue Book Project 10073 Record Card.

The Akron report stated the time the supposed meteor was seen was "approximately 7:00 p.m." The final Project 10073 Record Card stated the time of the sighting in Flatwoods was 7:30 p.m.

The Astronomy Club stated, "Assuming that it passed over Cumberland, MD in the flight to Flatwoods, it passed within 160 miles of Akron." Since an object did pass over Cumberland, the Astronomy Club assumed "that it passed over Cumberland in the flight to Flatwoods." The distance from Cumberland to Flatwoods is approximately 110 miles. According to the Akron Astronomy Club report, they assumed a meteor passed over Cumberland at approximately 7:00 p.m. en route to Flatwoods. According to the Project Blue Book report card, the object landed near Flatwoods at 7:30 p.m.-110 hundred miles away from Cumberland, Md. This shows a time lapse of about thirty minutes. If this object's actual velocity were "27 miles per second," as the Astronomy Club stated, it would have reached Flatwoods in about four seconds, not thirty minutes.

The next inaccuracy of the assumed flight path is the direction this object flew en route to Flatwoods. The direction of its flight was given as "from about 30 ° north of east to 30 ° south of west," which according to the Astronomy Club was the assumed flight path from Cumberland, MD to Flatwoods. This object was called the "Washington area meteor" by Project Blue Book. It is the same meteor that "flashed across the sky near the nation's capital." If this alleged meteor flew over Washington, DC headed west, it would have been impossible for it to pass over Cumberland and then change direction and head south to Flatwoods. The Akron Astronomy Club's assumption of the meteor's direction and flight path was dead wrong. The object the Astronomy Club sighted within 160 miles of Akron was actually the Baltimore/WV object heading towards Wheeling. What Project Blue Book called "the well-known Washington area meteor" and the newspapers called the "Flame Over Washington" actually flew over Washington, DC on a straight due west flight path before landing in Flatwoods.

Once again, these two objects—the Washington/Flatwoods object and the Baltimore/WV object—were mistakenly thought to be the same.

Another important item in the Akron Astronomy Club letter is their assumption about the object "in the flight to Flatwoods, WV." They sighted the meteor 160 miles away, flying at 27 miles per second. The duration was said to be 5-6 seconds. If the Astronomy Club wrote this report based on the information from their sighting, how did they know the object was in flight to Flatwoods? This letter was perhaps written later, probably in collaboration with Project Blue Book.

The Akron Astronomy Club report had a handwritten message on it, written by someone from Project Blue Book. This message state, "Fireball (also see Dr.'s LaPaz and Olivares report) 7-3719-17."

Dr. Lincoln LaPaz, head scientist of the University of New Mexico's Institute of Meteorites, was known worldwide as an authority on meteorites. In the late 1940s, LaPaz worked closely with intelligence officers in New Mexico trying to solve the green fireball mystery. LaPaz was called upon numerous times by the U.S. government to assist in various sighting cases. In the Flatwoods case, where the monster was explained as a meteor, the confirmation document from the Akron Astronomy Club stated in a handwritten note that LaPaz and Olivares made a supplemental report about this supposed meteor.

I was unable to find this report in the files of Project Blue Book for the September 1952 cases. Handwritten on this document are statements referring to a fireball meteor. Handwritten statements were obviously added after the letter was supposedly received by the Air Force. These statements seem to indicate that there was a supplemental report written by Dr. LaPaz and Dr. Olivares. This would account for the statement made by the Air Force's public liaison, Albert Chop, to Donald Keyhoe: "Several astronomers said a meteor went over there."

There are some interesting questions to bring up about Dr. LaPaz's and Dr. Olivares' message that was written on the Akron Astronomy Club report.

1. Did Project Blue Book officials contact LaPaz and Olivares because they felt unsure about the report from the Akron Astronomy Club?

2. Was the USAF trying to reinforce their cover-up by using Dr. LaPaz and Dr. Olivares' opinions?

3. The letter showed a handwritten reference note that read "fireball (also see Dr. LaPaz's and Dr. Olivares' report)." This note told of the existence of an important document. If Dr. LaPaz and Dr. Olivares wrote a report, stating the object in question was a fireball, why did officials at Project Blue Book use the confirmation of an amateur astronomy club report in their final Project 10073 Record Card?

4. Is it possible that the Akron Astronomy Club report was actually a complete forgery, made up by ATIC officials?

After I determined the flight paths of the three objects, I analyzed the Project Blue Book reports that explained all of the sightings as a single fireball meteor. I needed further assistance to help sort out the facts concerning the Air Force's single meteor explanation. I contacted an astronomer who is a meteor expert as well, Harold (Hal) Povenmire from Florida. Povenmire wrote a book titled Fireballs, Meteors, and Meteorites and was an active participant in the field of astronomy. Povenmire worked with world-renowned astronomer J. Allen Hynek, a key figure in UFO studies who served as a consultant to Project Blue Book.

Harold Povenmire responded to my interview by talking about his association with J. Allen Hynek. He said, "I first met Dr. Hynek when I was a high school student and he was a professor of astronomy at Ohio State University. I worked with Dr. Hynek with satellite tracking cameras out in Pasadena, CA. I also worked on board a ship with him off the coast of Africa during the solar eclipse of 1973. Later on, around 1975, I helped set up some of the lectures and demonstrations on his UFO studies. So my actual association went on with him for more than twenty years. During that time, I saw him change his attitude quite a bit toward the flying saucer-UFO phenomenon."

In the early days, Hynek did not take any of these stories seriously; [saying] that most of them could be accounted for by identified flying objects, such as aircraft, balloons, balled lightning, and things like that.

However, Povenmire also said this about Dr. Hynek, "He often said, 'I hear incredible stories from basically credible people!'" I asked Mr. Povenmire, "What constitutes a meteoritic fireball?" He answered,

"A fireball is a small Apollo asteroid, or a meteorite that is orbiting the sun along with the earth, and it happens that their paths or their orbits cross, and this small object enters the earth's atmosphere. As it does, it is retarded by the atmosphere and begins to oblate or burn, and can become incredibly bright. Much brighter than the full moon. It can be bigger than the full moon. If it is heavy enough and moving slow enough, it can descend into the lower atmosphere. If it gets below eighteen to twelve miles above the surface, it can produce a sonic boom."

I asked Mr. Povenmire, "Would the average person notice this boom?"

He answered, "Yes, if it's close, it can be extremely intense. I felt one sonic boom from a fireball that was actually a jolting experience. On one other occasion, I could hear the reflected rumble. In both cases, the rumble sounded like distant thunder and was approximately forty seconds in length."

In reference to the Flatwoods case, there is no mention in either the Akron Astronomy Club report or the Project Blue Book report of a sonic boom. Even though this alleged meteor was traveling at an extremely low altitude, none of the witnesses who sighted this object mentioned a sonic boom. This object had traveled well under the 12-to-18 mile range and would have created a very audible sonic boom.

I then asked Mr. Povenmire, "After the object had dropped and landed, a very bright light had flared up and appeared from the area where it had landed or crashed. Is this typical for a meteor or any [celestial] body?"

Povenmire answered, "Absolutely not. Whatever you're describing there, [it] is not a meteoritic fireball or a meteorite impact. I can say that with certainty."

I also asked Povenmire if oil deposits would have any relativity to a fireball.

He responded, "To my knowledge, there would be absolutely no connection of any sort of an oily deposit and a meteorite impact. The two are completely incompatible with each other."

The most uncharacteristic flight path of what was called a meteor was the Baltimore/WV object. I handed Mr. Povenmire a map showing the flight path of this alleged fireball meteor.

I asked him, "Is this a typical path?"

He answered, "Now, I can tell you with absolute certainty that a meteoroid or a fireball could not possibly entertain such a course. Its ability to change course would only be caused by deceleration by the atmosphere, or an explosion, and at most it could only change one or two degrees in its path."

Mr. Povenmire expounded further about fireballs, "If it descends further and is slowed enough, then it may produce meteorites which are portions of the object that actually land on earth. Very few meteoritic fireballs produce meteorites."

Mr. Povenmire explained two kinds of meteorite craters that would have been relative to the alleged fireball meteors seen landing that night.

He said, "The first one is what we call an impact pit. That's where a small meteorite falls from the atmosphere and all the cosmic velocity—that's the velocity that it had in space—has been damped out by the retardation effect of the atmosphere, and so it's dropping just by Newton alone—by the force of gravity—and when it hits the ground, it's like a brick that's tossed off of a building, and it will form a small impact pit.

A second crater would be a much larger one, called a simple crater. This is where a meteorite of some size still retains a bit of cosmic velocity and plows out a good size pit, maybe a thirty-or-forty-foot-wide crater and throws the dirt out and will always leave a raised rim.

There was not one impact pit reported in West Virginia or Tennessee where these objects landed on September 12, 1952. To this day, there has been no impact pits reported in these areas. What the officials at Project Blue Book concluded as "the well known Washington area meteor of 12 Sept landing near Flatwoods, W.Va." was actually three separate UFOs. I have given those objects designated numbers in the order that they appeared. The #1 object, the #2 object, and the #3 object. After each object passed over the eastern seaboard, they continued on western headings and fanned out across the country. These sightings occurred between 6:50 p.m. and 7:25 p.m. EST (7:50 p.m. and 8:25 p.m. EDT). The following is a chronological list of locations where the three objects passed over and near after they flew over the Mid-Atlantic coastal region of the United States:

I. **VIRGINIA/TENNESSEE # 1 OBJECT**
1. Roanoke, VA
2. Pulaski, VA
3. Johnson City, TN - Tri-cities Airport sighting
4. Arcadia, TN –landed
5. Kingsport, TN
6. Rogersville, TN
7. Moccasin Gap, TN –*went down*
8. Wadlow Gap, TN
9. Elizabethton, TN

II. **BALTIMORE/WEST VIRGINIA # 2 OBJECT**
10. Baltimore, MD
11. Catonsville, MD
12. Frederick, MD
13. Hagerstown, MD

14. Cumberland, MD
15. Garret County, MD
16. Preston County
17. Morgantown, WV
18. Fairmont, WV
19. Columbus, OH
20. Zanesville, OH
21. Saint Clairsville, OH
22. Wheeling- Ohio County Airport, WV — near mid-air collision between object and aircraft
23. Oglebay Park Resort, WV — *landed*
24. Wheeling, WV
25. McMechen, WV
26. Parkersburg, WV
27. Nitro, WV
28. Charleston (Spring Hill Cemetery), WV
29. West of Charleston, WV
30. Charleston (South Hills), WV –*landed*
31. Charleston (Park Area), WV –*landed*
32. Ward, WV
33. Chelyan/Cabin Creek, WV –*landed*
34. Bluefield, WV

III. **WASHINGTON D.C./FLATWOODS # 3 OBJECT**

35. Washington, DC
36. Front Royal, VA
37. Elkins, WV
38. Burnsville, WV
39. Heaters, WV
40. Flatwoods, WV –*landed* at approximately 7:25 p.m. EST

These sightings took place over a period of approximately thirty-five minutes. The Akron Astronomy Club report stated that the duration of the alleged single fireball meteor was 5–6 seconds. It would be impossible for all these sightings to have occurred within a period of 5–6 seconds over all of the areas above. Povenmire explained about the time durations of fireball meteors and meteors, "Anytime that you have a meteor that lasts for more than seven seconds, its path would be considered very long. Nine seconds is a near record for a typical fireball, and anything longer than that would be considered extraordinary."

The Akron Astronomy Club report said it was a "typical meteorite," a "fireball." On the contrary, it would not have been possible for a fireball meteor to change directions several times and be seen flying over forty locations. The characteristics, geographic locations, and flight patterns of what were sighted that night are completely inconsistent with humankind's knowledge of meteors, and instead point to unknown crafts. Could all of the different sightings been a meteor shower? I asked Mr. Povenmire, "In which months do we not see any significant meteor showers?"

Povenmire answered, "The months that would be considered not to have meteor showers would be February and March. Then we go into June without any significant showers, and then September. Really every other month has some sort of known annual shower."

In 1952, Harvard University established the Harvard Meteor Project. The project was in existence from 1952-54 and photographed 2,529 meteors and their flight paths. During that time, renowned UFO debunker, Donald H. Menzel, was the director of the Harvard College Observatory. Interestingly enough, there were no photographs taken by this project on the day of September 12, 1952.

The December 1952 issue of *Sky and Telescope* magazine had an article titled "Astronomical Highlights of 1952." The article gave a list of the top ten astronomical highlights for 1952, as of October when their meeting was held. Amazingly, the overwhelming amount of alleged meteors that the military insisted occurred on the night of September 12 did not make the list.

To reiterate a point, the definition of a "meteorite" is as follows, "Any meteoroid which has reached the surface of the earth without being completely vaporized." An astronomer that I know in Charleston, West Virginia, assisted me with my research concerning the alleged meteorites of West Virginia on September 12, 1952. I asked him if he could find documented information about the history of West Virginia meteorites. He told me that he would get in touch with other astronomers in the state and ask them to look through their private astronomy book collections. Several weeks went by and he called me back. Several of his astronomer friends went through their books and copied everything they could find about the history of meteorites in West Virginia. Some of the books they got information from are actually very rare and have been out of print for several years.

Shortly after, I received a package in the mail with a wealth of information I was seeking. I discovered there are only three documented cases of known meteorites in the state of West Virginia. It was no surprise that none of these meteorites fell in West Virginia on September 12, 1952. One of the valuable sources of the material that I received is information from, "THE SMITHSONIAN INSTITUTE CATALOG." It states the following three meteorites of West Virginia:

1. GREENBRIER COUNTY, West Virginia. Coarse octahedrite. Found 1880. Original weight: 5 kg.
 Description: A mass of 5 kg. was found near the top of Alleghany Mountains, 3 miles N of White Sulpher Springs.
2. JENNY'S CREEK, Wayne County, West Virginia. Coarse octahedrite. Found 1883. Original weight:
11,987.6 g. Description: Three masses of about 10.4 kg. , 1134 g. and 453.6 g. were found in 1883-1886 but only about 907 g. have been preserved.
3. LANDES, Grant County, West Virginia. Iron. Silicate bearing octahedrite. Found about 1930,
recognized as a meteorite in 1968. Total weight: 69.8 kg. (1) Specimen. Description: Plowed up in a hillside cornfield one mile east of the Landes Post Office about 35 to 40 years before it was brought to the attention of G. I. Huss.

To reiterate my point, Project Blue Book recorded the following in a, "Project 10073 Record Card ATIC Form 329 (REV 26 sep 52)" and stated, "11. Comments: The West Virginia monster so called. **Actually the object was the well-known Washington area meteor of 12 Sep landing near Flatwoods, W. Va.** Have confirmation of an Astronomy Club from Akron, Ohio. Letter from E. C. [blacked out] President-Akron Astr. Club. The following handwritten notes appeared on the Akron Astronomy Club letter that was sent to Project Blue Book, "**EXAMPLE Typical Meteorite (Fireball) 12 Sep Fireball - September 12, 1952-Flatwoods, W.Va.**" Further information stated, "(All computations tally with speed description trajectory and other **characteristics of a meteorite**.)"

Major Keyhoe explained the major reason that the incident was covered up. He stated, "When the time came to admit that the saucers were real, the slightest official hint of possible menace would be quickly remembered. From that angle, the Sutton story was dangerous, with its picture of a fearsome creature intelligent enough to build and control spaceships. It was far better to brand the whole thing as a hallucination, which Intelligence evidently believed was the answer." Donald Keyhoe's statement makes absolute sense and the time is nearing...

Chapter 20

KEYHOE SPEAKS OUT

It is safe to say that the Air Force's official viewpoint of the incident was one of contrived disinterest. The Air Force repeatedly claimed that the so-called West Virginia Monster was a meteor that landed near Flatwoods.

In 1952, shortly after the event occurred, Major Keyhoe contacted the Air Force for its viewpoint about this case. He again spoke to Albert Chop, requesting an update. Chop told him, "We're simply not bothering with monster stories. We've got enough trouble with confirmed sightings." Chop's statements were misleading if not untrue. If the Air Force was "not bothering with monster stories," why did USAF representatives contact Colonel Dale Leavitt, A. Lee Stewart, Jr., and Kathleen May, among others? If the object was a meteor, why was the National Guard activated in Braxton County? What was the Air Force representative referring to in, "We've got enough trouble with confirmed sightings?"

As I searched through Project Blue Book, I found documentation that at the least the Air Force was reading and saving the monster stories. I found an article Blue Book had obtained about the monster. The headlines read, "The Thing, 10 Feet Tall, Terrifies Party of 7." This article had handwritten notes across the top of it stating the source as *New York Daily News* September 14, 1952. Along the bottom of this page was written "in Sutton, West Virginia." Along the side of the document appeared the same code number that was handwritten on the Akron Astronomy Club report, "7-3719-17."

Another article contained among the Blue Book September 12 documents was from *Infinity* magazine. The article was an interview with Ivan T. Sanderson. This article also had the same handwritten code number on it: "7-3719-17."

Another article among these documents was a synopsis of the "Flatwoods Monster," written by Gray Baker. This article was a retyped facsimile and gave a detailed account of this incident.

Also within the files was another document, this one taken from a page of the book, The World of Flying Saucers, by Donald H. Menzel and Lyle G. Boyd. It was a synopsis of the works of Gray Barker and Donald Keyhoe. Handwritten notes stated "12 Sept 1952" and "Sutton, West Va." The original copyright of the book was 1963. It was apparent the Air Force was still interested in UFO stories for at least eleven years after the Flatwoods incident occurred. The monitoring of these stories seemed odd considering the Air Force's supposed disinterest in the incident. The following statement was made by Albert Chop, four months after the incident:

A. "First, the glowing object seen by Mrs. May and the boys was actually a meteor; it merely appeared to be landing when it disappeared over the hill."

B. "Second, the group did see two glowing eyes, probably those of a large owl perched on a limb. Underbrush below may have given the impression of a giant figure, and in their excitement they may have imagined the rest."

C. "Third, the boys' illness was a physical effect brought on by their fright."

D. "Fourth, the flattened grass and supposed tracks were caused by the first villagers when they came to investigate."

It seems that the Air Force spent a lot of time and effort trying to explain away the details of the incident! Following are points concerning the Air Force explanation given to Keyhoe, by Albert Chop (in quotations), followed by my rebuttals:

1. "First, **the glowing object seen by Mrs. May** and the boys was actually **a meteor**." Actually, Mrs. May was not at the Flatwoods Elementary School playground playing football with the boys when the object went overhead. Mrs. May was at home when the boys on the playground saw the object pass overhead. Besides the documentation of this "meteor" in Project Blue Book, I did not find any other official record of it in any astronomical history or record books. There are no West Virginia meteorites recorded for September 12, 1952.

2. "It merely **appeared to be landing** when it disappeared over the hill." Albert Chop's quote contradicts the Project Blue Book "Project 10073 Record Card" comment; **"the meteor of 12 Sep. landing near Flatwoods, W. Va."** If it disappeared, how did they become aware of its landing near Flatwoods?

This illustration compares the size relationship between the 12-foot tall "Flatwoods Monster" and a 6-foot tall barn owl. Note the 6-foot tall human figure for size comparison

3. "The group did see two glowing eyes, **probably** those of a large owl perched on a limb." The use of the word "probably" showed the Air Force was speculating. The witnesses tell a different story.

4. "Underbrush below **may have given** the impression of a giant figure." The Air Force again used speculative terminology to dismiss the sighting; may have given. Again, the witnesses tell a different story.

5. "In their excitement they **imagined the rest.**" It is highly unlikely that every witness "imagined" the same description, especially when the boys were separated and interviewed privately by professional writers and drew similar pictures of what they saw.

6. "The boys' illness was a physical effect brought on by their **fright**." The USAF could only guess it was caused by fear. Eighteen-year-old witness Eugene Lemon vomited for hours after the encounter due to the gaseous odor that emanated from the monster. Several other witnesses also became ill with the same symptoms from this gas.

7. "The flattened grass and supposed tracks were caused by the first villagers when they came to investigate." This was another excuse given by the USAF. The local residents did not flatten the grass into specific markings with a well-defined pattern.

In Keyhoe's book, *Aliens From Space*, Edward Ruppelt told Keyhoe, **"We're ordered to hide sightings when possible, but if a strong report does get out we have to publish a fast explanation—make up something to kill the report in a hurry. We must also ridicule the witness, especially if we can't figure a plausible answer."** The Flatwoods case was definitely a strong report that got out to the public and received a fast explanation in an attempt to kill the incident. As far as a plausible answer, the team at Project Blue Book could not figure out an answer, there explanations were speculative. Furthermore, Edward Ruppelt did not mention one word about the Flatwoods incident in his book, even though this incident was one of the biggest news stories of 1952.

There were several sightings of unexplained objects in Braxton County on the evening of September 12. If the supposed single meteor sighted over Washington, DC did indeed land in Flatwoods, then that does not explain the multiple sightings in Braxton County that night, or the lack of a meteor pit.

During my interview with Kathleen May, she made the following statement about the government letter she had received, "They notified us there were four of them [objects] in Braxton County that night." Colonel Dale Leavitt, in my interview with him, also told me about different objects seen that night throughout the area: The Flatwoods object, the Sugar Creek-Frametown crash (one object), and the Duck Creek UFO encounter, which involved a car.

In 1954, writer Harold T. Wilkins researched the case and made this articulate statement, "The local police, however, admit that on that day of the incident a fleet of pear-shaped objects—dull red, white and gleaming—had been seen flying in formation over the region. They hovered in mid-air, ascended almost vertically, descended, then flew level, and three strange objects had crashed in the dense woods."

Investigator Gray Barker said, "Within a 20-mile radius of Flatwoods, numerous persons saw what they variously described as shooting stars, flying saucers and meteorites. Evidently, these objects were different from the one seen in Flatwoods."

It is evident that Braxton County was the target of a "UFO flap" that night. This UFO flap would account for the confusion of the original investigators in formulating accurate flight paths of these various objects over Flatwoods.

Investigator Ivan T. Sanderson documented many of the objects seen that night. He stated, "As a result of plotting the incidents on a map," he said, "we are of the opinion that a flight of intelligently controlled objects flew over West Virginia on the evening of September 12 and further that one of them landed or crashed, a second and third crashed, and a fourth blew up in the air." Even though Sanderson's individual investigations were thorough, I believe his overall theory to be incorrect. Even though Sanderson was unable to formulate the flight paths of these individual objects, he did reach the following conclusion about them, "The one that reached Flatwoods landed rather than crashed and its "pilot" or "occupant" managed to get out before it disintegrated." This object did not disintegrate; it took off from the farm after it landed.

Gray Barker made this statement, "I can only begin to cope with the mass of data and the correspondence, the pieces of the jigsaw puzzle containing the answer to the entire mystery—if it could only be put together!"

The four landing sites that Mrs. May described to me were amazingly accurate except for one point. What the government told Mrs. May were four individual experimental crafts were actually two crafts that were damaged and landing repeatedly throughout the Braxton County area.

The first craft made two landings in Braxton County, one in Sugar Creek near the Elk River, and then in Frametown. The second craft, the "Flatwoods Monster" craft, made three landings in Braxton County. It first landed in Flatwoods on the Fisher farm, then in Holly, and then later crash-landed on James Knoll in Frametown.

Gray Barker, interviewing A. M. Jordan, described the first object seen over Flatwoods. Barker stated, "This strange event had taken place simultaneously with sightings of aerial objects over several states." The a.m. Jordan sighting in Flatwoods occurred simultaneously to some of the earlier sightings, at approximately 6:50 p.m. EST.

Barker stated in his interview with Jordan, "He saw the object, which later landed on the hill, and was able to describe it in a cold matter of fact." Barker assumed this was the object that later landed on the mountaintop of the Fisher farm about 7:25 p.m. EST. He believed this was the "Flatwoods Monster" ship.

Jordan's description of the object was not the round-oval shaped craft seen over the schoolyard that landed on the Fisher farm. Barker, based on his interview with Jordan, said this about the object, "Evidently it came from over the horizon from the southeast as he was sitting on the porch. He [Jordan] did not look up until it had come into his view overhead and flashed in a southwesterly direction toward the hilltop opposite him. It was an elongated object. The top of it was a light shade of red. From the rear shot balls of fire."

Barker explained what Jordan believed this object to be, "He thought it was a jet plane at the time, though he saw no wings. He did not see the nose of the object clearly. It proceeded across the sky, then halted suddenly, seemed to fall rapidly toward the hilltop." This was not the same object seen passing over the schoolyard. The description given by Jordan—and his drawing—had little or no resemblance to the descriptions of the "Flatwoods Monster" ship.

Gray Barker spoke to the children who witnessed an object pass over the schoolyard. Barker said, "The children were unanimous in disagreeing with Mr. Jordan about the shape." I believe these were two entirely different ships.

Additional witnesses saw this object pass over Braxton County on September 12, 1952. Mr. Morrison, his father, mother and a sibling saw this UFO from their backyard when they lived in "Ben's Run," near Newville. This area is approximately four miles southeast of Flatwoods. They saw this elongated object fly near them shortly before it passed over Flatwoods. I spoke to Mr. Morrison and he told me what occurred on that early evening, which he witnessed at the age of eleven.

He stated, "My dad had seen it first. He was out in the wood yard getting stove wood and had an armload of stove wood and hollered and said 'By God' and said everybody look. When we all ran and started to look, he said 'Look up there' and pointed right at it. It was in a low gap and it was clear at the time and we all seen it go through." Mr. Morrison told me what he saw, "I seen a big huge thing that looked like a bottle gas tank."

He also stated, "It was red in color. I remember very well what I'd seen. I'd say it was probably forty-feet long…my estimation about it. The object was probably a quarter a mile away…from where I was lookin' at it. It was very low. It was skippin' the tops of the trees." He also stated that the area of the tree line "was on a mountainside…I was lookin' up at it." This witness gave a further description of the UFO, "There was no indication that I could see of anything being on the outer shell of it…at all." I asked him if he saw wings or appendages and he answered, "There wasn't no wings on it…at all. When he [father] hollered, we had seen the whole thing. We even seen both ends of it and it came through that low gap. It was rounded on both ends and it was floatin' straight through." When I asked Morrison how fast the elongated object appeared to be moving, he answered, "It was goin' very slow when we seen it. It was goin towards a little community right below where I lived at Ben's Run, Har. It [object] went ahead and vanished behind…there was another hill there, and it vanished behind it."

After speaking to a witness and resident of Har who also saw the object, Morrison stated, "They seen the same thing down there and it came toward Har then veered toward the right…came over the store. Everybody down there seen the same thing that we seen up here. They all said it was red in color and huge. They said it left and the last they seen of it, it was headed right smack dead for Flatwoods when it disappeared."

It is evident that this jet-shaped object was actually the same one that was later seen over the Fisher Farm. Upon reaching, the farm in Flatwoods this jet-shaped object dropped a homing device onto the hilltop. This occurred when the ship appeared to halt suddenly, then fell rapidly toward the earth. The device would guide the damaged ship that was approaching the Washington area on a western heading. The damaged ship was the Washington/Flatwoods #3 object, also known as the "Flame Over Washington."

The following sequence shows the order of the objects as they appeared:

1. **The Virginia/TN #1 object** first passed over the coastline and then landed in Arcadia, TN at approximately 6:57 p.m. EST.

2. **The Baltimore/WV #2 object** passed over the mid-Atlantic coast then passed over Baltimore before 7:00 p.m. EST/8:00 p.m. EDT, heading over West Virginia and north of Braxton County.

3. **The jet-shaped UFO** was then seen by A.M. Jordan over the Bailey Fisher farm at about 6:50 p.m. EST.

4. **The Washington/Flatwoods #3 object**. The "Flame Over Washington" was the object that contained the "Flatwoods Monster." It eventually landed on the Fisher mountaintop about 7:25 p.m. EST.

Actually more than two objects passed over Flatwoods that night besides the jet-shaped UFO and the "Flatwoods Monster" ship. Gray Barker said the locals reported several other objects passing over the area of Braxton County. Harold T. Wilkins said the local police admitted, "on that day of the incident a fleet of pear-shaped objects—dull red, white and gleaming—had been seen flying in formation over the region. They hovered in mid-air, ascended almost vertically, descended, and then flew level." Ivan T. Sanderson stated, "We are of the opinion that a flight of intelligently controlled objects flew over West Virginia on the evening of September 12." Why were there other UFOs flying over Braxton County that night? Moreover, why were objects seen over the town of Flatwoods? Furthermore, where did they come from? The answers to these questions were contained in Project Blue Book. Several other alleged "meteor" sightings had also been reported earlier that evening on September 12.

These sightings did not come from the mid-Atlantic area however; they were reported south of West Virginia over North Carolina and were thoroughly documented in Project Blue Book. The first of these alleged "meteor" sightings actually occurred shortly before 7:00 p.m. EST. At this point, we know no there is no official documentation of any meteor for September 12, 1952 other than Project Blue Book's records.

It is no surprise, the USAF tried to explain the series of sightings over North Carolina as a single "meteor." The Directorate of Intelligence Agency stated in a document entitled "Air Intelligence Report" that a flying object was reported in the Lumberton, NC area September 12 at 7:00 p.m. EST/8:00 p.m. EDT. Four witnesses at four different locations confirmed its appearance. This report covered sightings from Lake Waccamaw to Fayetteville, North Carolina. The object was traveling from southeast to northwest and described as a ball shape with a trail three times the length of the body. The speed was so fast that most witnesses got only a hurried glimpse. According to Fayetteville and Raleigh, NC newspapers, a meteor was observed at approximately the same time and place, and had the same flight path.

After examining all the official Air Force reports and eyewitness accounts contained in the Tentative Observers Questionnaires I began to notice major discrepancies about this alleged "meteor." The first discrepancy; the numerous locations that this alleged single "meteor" passed over during the duration of its flight. Next, the witnesses' descriptions of details were varied. The descriptions included different sizes, shapes, and colors. Next, this alleged "meteor" displayed various types of trajectories over different locations, unlike a meteor. When I dissected these reports and analyzed the descriptions reported by the witnesses, I discovered there were actually five different objects sighted, not a single "meteor."

Project Bluebook received the following information from a witness to this alleged single meteor. This information was contained in a Tentative Observer Questionnaire. For clarity and continuity, I have named this object, the "#1 Object." The witness stated:

At about 7 o'clock on September 12, in front of [service station name blacked out] in Lumberton, NC . . . I saw a large seeming ball of fire, traveling from east to west . . . it seemed to be a bright glowing mass with a contrasting colored tail at least three times the diameter of the ball. . . . I saw it for approximately two or three seconds traveling on a downward plane. When it got below apparent tree height, it seemed to level off, but never came into view again… It seemed to be traveling at least 600 mph and perhaps more…The mass or object appeared round and flat with the flat side down … I have seen many falling stars and meteors but this was larger, closer and different from any I have seen before…The object appeared to be about a mile and a half away and 12 to 15 feet in diameter. . . My seeing this object was not a hallucination as I saw it long enough to call [name blacked out] attention to it and he saw it also.

Another description of a North Carolina sighting stood apart from the #1 Object called a "ball of fire." This object I have designated Object #2. The following information was contained in another Tentative Observer Questionnaire. The witness stated, "On Friday afternoon, Sept. 12, 1952 at dusk, my attention was called to an unusual object in the sky. This object was round in shape and white in color, with a trailing streamer of darker color. It was traveling to the northwest at a very high rate of speed. Another witness driving on Highway 301, three miles north from Lumberton, NC, reported sighting the object directly in front of him crossing his windshield from right to left. In both cases [military witness and Highway 301 witness] the object was moving from the southeast to the northwest."

According to this intelligence report, another witness "was fishing five miles east of Elizabethton, NC. He reported the object to be between 15-20 degrees [percent] of the tail of the object." The witness who sighted the object here reported he saw it "immediately after dark." It is interesting to note that the sighting of the #1 Object and the #2 Object were both made during dusk. This witness saw neither the #1 nor #2 Objects. The object he sighted was seen at dark.

It seemed apparent that the Air Intelligence Information Report combined all of the sightings reported in the area, and explained them as one single meteor. At that point, the object sighted, "immediately after dark" did not fall into the time frame of the two earlier reports made during daylight. This lone object passed over the area after dark, about one hour after the other two objects did. Even though the descriptions, the flight directions, and the times as observed by different witnesses varied, the USAF still claimed those incidents were a single meteor sighting. The intelligence report gave yet another account of this supposed single meteor sighted over North Carolina. It stated, "Another person in the vicinity of Lake Waccamaw, a distance of 45 miles from Lumberton, reported sighting this same object."

To this point, we have learned about two different objects with two very distinct descriptions, both seen over Lumberton:
1. A large ball of fire compared to an object that was white in color.
2. A round and flat object with a flat side down compared to an object that was round in shape.

An Air Force C-46 plane northwest of Lumberton also sighted the #1 Object over Greensboro NC, approximately 110 miles away. A Project 10073 Record Card document stated the object was a "meteor" shaped like a "ball of fire." It also stated that it was traveling at a "high speed" in a "steady dive." It said the object was the "12 Sep meteor sighting throughout east coast area."

Also contained in the Project Blue Book files was the original two-page report that told a completely different story. The original document was filed under an official "CIRVIS" [sur-vees] report.

According to the *JANAP, Joint-Army-Navy-Air Force* publication 146(D), it defines and states, "Canadian - United States/Communications Instructions For Reporting Vital Intelligence Sightings."

In "Chapter I - JANAP 146 (D) - General Description and Purpose of Communications Instructions For Reporting Vital Intelligence Sightings" the scope of CIRVIS is explained as follows:

102. SCOPE - A. This publication is limited to the reporting of information of vital importance to the security of the United States of America and Canada and their forces which in the opinion of the

observer, requires very urgent defensive and/or investigative action by the U.S. and/or Canadian armed forces.

USAF personnel, who witnessed the object from a C-46 aircraft of the "514th troop carrier wing, Medium-132", filed the "CIRVIS" report. The most relevant information contained in this report is arranged in a chronological order and is as follows:

A. "Unidentified aerial object directly over Greensboro, North Carolina (3605 N dash 07948 W)."
B. "Observing aircraft flying over Greensboro, North Carolina at 7,000 feet."
C. "Pilot of observing craft —Colonel"
D. "object appeared at 11 o'clock high approximately 200-500 feet above observing aircraft as a brilliant streak of fire"
E. "Observed one unidentified flying object traveling on heading of approximately 330 degrees"
F. "Course of object a steady dive at extremely high speed, from altitude of approximately 7200 or 7500 feet to a point somewhere near below altitude of and in front of observing aircraft"
G. "After object had passed observing aircraft it appeared as a round ball of fire which then erupted into sparks and disappeared."
H. "Object in view approximately five seconds."
I. "Sighting verified by 2 CR/MS [crew members]"
J. "Also observing phenomena were persons in control tower at Greensboro Highpoint Airport."

C-46 Aircraft and the #1 North Carolina object

The Project 10073 Record Card for Flatwoods, WV stated, "Actually the object was the well known Washington area meteor of 12 Sep. landing near Flatwoods" This North Carolina Blue Book case reported the "Unidentified aerial object directly over Greensboro, North Carolina," at 2400 hours GMT.

North Carolina observed Eastern Standard Time. 2400 hours Greenwich Mean Time translates to 7:00 p.m. EST, or 8:00 p.m. EDT. The Akron Astronomy Club letter sent to Project Blue Book stated the time as approximately 7:00 p.m. EST [8:00 p.m. EDT].

The alleged "Washington area meteor" flew "awfully low" over the Capitol around 7:00 p.m. EST/8:00 p.m. EDT. It was on a western heading when it passed over Washington D.C. and was said to have an official duration time of five to six seconds. This alleged "meteor" could not have flown "directly over Greensboro, North Carolina," it was not possible. These two objects flew directly over two different cities, located in two different states and were proceeding on completely different flight paths. An interesting point to note in this CIRVIS report is that a crew of Air Force pilots filed it. ATIC ignored the pilots' judgment and opinion and declared this object a meteor. When a Major, a Colonel, and a Captain in the Air Force filed a report naming something as a threat to national security, it was arrogant and deceitful for the ATIC to dismiss it as a meteor.

On September 16, 1952, *The Greensboro Daily News* featured a lengthy article about sightings that occurred over the area of Reidsville, NC. The town of Reidsville is about 120 miles northwest of Greensboro. The object that was sighted there was actually the #2 Object sighted along its northwest flight path. The object was first sighted over Lumberton en route to Reidsville. The following headline and opening paragraph detail this sighting, "Many Report Thing in Sky at Reidsville. Reidsville, Sept. 16—A strange light which streaked through the heavens Friday night in Reidsville has been described by W. E. Lambeth, postal clerk, who saw the object about 6:55 p.m. [EST] through a skylight in the post office building, as "like a traveling flashlight."

The witness gave no description of the #2 North Carolina Object being on fire. This article also said, "A group of boys sighted two objects in Reidsville about 6:50 p.m. While watching an object in the sky they initially thought to be a star, another object passed over them trailing fire." The #1 and #2 Objects passed over Lumberton and followed parallel flight paths over Reidsville.

The Greensboro Record also ran an article on September 16 about the Reidsville sightings, titled, "Aerial Whazzit Seen Here Friday." It refers to the sightings as "strange objects" using the plural tense. A paper in the nearby town of Leaksville ran an article headlined, "'Flying Saucer' Reported Seen By Mrs. Blackwell." This low flying object was described as trailing a red streak that looked just like fire. This description is similar to the ones of the #1 Object sited over Reidsville and Lumberton.

There was yet another sighting of a different object over North Carolina. This object was sighted over two different areas to the northwest of Lumberton near the North Carolina-Virginia border. This object was sighted 30 miles west of Greensboro after it had been sighted over Winston-Salem approximately 115 miles away.

The object was then sighted over Mount Airy at the North Carolina border approximately 40 miles away from Winston-Salem. This object I have designated Object #3. It was described as a "shooting star" over both of these locations.

In *The Mount Airy News* dated September 19, a headline read, "Flat Rock Man Calls News to Report Flying Saucer–Local Residents See Ball Of Fire in the Sky." This article combined the reports of various sightings as being a single object. It reads, "A streak of fire that appeared and suddenly disappeared again was seen by a group of people last night at about 7 o'clock." The article gave information about the sighting of the object that was seen over Winston-Salem. It stated, "At Winston-Salem many puzzled witnesses called the airport for information. Men on duty at the tower saw the spectacle and said it was a larger-than-usual shooting star that remained in sight at least two or three seconds." The #3 Object was then sighted along its northern flight path approximately 40 miles away over the Mount Airy area. The Mount Airy witness, Bernice Harris, described the object as follows, "I thought it was either a shooting star or a falling star with a tail on it." The single meteor explanation became even more unlikely when still another description of it was given.

The next report indicated a UFO was seen over North Carolina within the same period as the first three objects, and was seen over Flat Rock, North Carolina along the South Carolina border. This is the #4 North Carolina Object. Information concerning this sighting was in the same article, "Flat Rock Man Calls News to Report Flying Saucer." The article stated, "One of the observers, James Newman, of Flat Rock, called the News to report the object as a flying saucer. Mr. Newman was the only person to call the spectacle a 'flying saucer,' but plenty of other people did see it." This saucer description stood apart from the previous objects.

I have designated the next object the #5 North Carolina Object. The sighting of this object is the one that took place immediately after dark. It was first sighted over Lake Waccamaw. It then headed northwest over Elizabethtown, then northwest over Fayetteville. The Air Intelligence Information Report stated:

The newspaper Fayetteville Observer, reported on 13 September [name blacked out] of Fayetteville had seen a huge ball with a tail heading northwest after 1900 Eastern Time 12 September 1952. He reported the color as a greenish blue; the newspaper reported the object as a meteor. Several newspapers in Raleigh, North Carolina, it is reported, carried articles about the sighting of this meteor.

According to the description in this intelligence report, the color of the object was a "greenish blue." It was not described as a "ball of fire" or "white in color." This object was seen immediately after dark, which also puts it after the period that the first four objects were sighted.

This #5 Object was described as a "huge ball with a tail and heading northwest," which was the same directional heading of the previous four objects. The end of this intelligence report raised a major discrepancy concerning the Fayetteville sighting of the #5 Object and its flight path.

This information appeared in the section "Comments of the preparing officer." He stated, "I have interviewed the three witnesses in the above report. All reports, in my opinion are reliable." The final line in this report stated: "The witness at the point east of Elizabethtown reported the object to have a flat trajectory; whereas the other two said it was definitely curved." The two referenced sightings, that had 'definitely curved' trajectories were the Lake Waccamaw and Fayetteville sightings. This was the first area where the #5 Object was sighted on its flight path. When the object passed over Lake Waccamaw, it had a trajectory that was "definitely curved."

Located 20 miles northwest of Lake Waccamaw is Elizabethtown. After the object passed Lake Waccamaw, it continued over Elizabethtown where it was then noted to have a "flat trajectory." This would mean that when the object was first sighted over Lake Waccamaw while its trajectory was curved, its flight path was arching downward because it was actually descending. As the object neared Elizabethtown and proceeded over that area, it then leveled off, causing it to have a "flat trajectory." The object then continued in a northwest direction and proceeded another 30 miles where it was sighted again over Fayetteville. It was stated in a Fayetteville newspaper that the trajectory of the object over the area was curved. At that point, while the object was over Fayetteville still heading northwest, its trajectory changed to a curved trajectory once again. This area is where the object began to descend even closer toward the earth.

During my interview with meteor expert Harold Povenmire, he made the following statement concerning a horizontal meteor's path and trajectory. He stated, "Now if it's going to have a horizontal path, that means that it's entering the earth's atmosphere almost tangent to the earth's surface and it's going to continue on until it either leaves the earth's surface, or it oblates down to essentially nothing."

Povenmire then said, "Nearly horizontal meteors are not terribly rare, but they're not going to change course." If this object had been a meteor, it would not have been able to change its course three times during its flight path. When this alleged meteor was observed to have a flat horizontal trajectory over Elizabethtown, it should have left the earth's atmosphere or disintegrated into nothing. This object did neither.

After dark, the #5 Object descended over Lake Waccamaw, it flew on a northwest flight course over Elizabethtown, and then Fayetteville. Shortly after, the object passed near Pope AFB at Fort Bragg, located just north of Fayetteville. I find it more than coincidence that another one of these objects was near another major Air Force base. The object proceeded farther northwest and was sighted again as it flew over Raleigh, NC, located to the northeast of Fayetteville. The Air Intelligence Report confirmed this sighting, "Four different witnesses at four different locations confirmed its location." According to the Fayetteville and Raleigh newspapers, "a meteor was observed at approximately the same time, day, place and the direction of the flight…." This supposed meteor was observed passing to the west of Raleigh then later ascended out of North Carolina.

The Project Bluebook Intelligence report concerning the so-called meteor incident ends by stating, "It is the personal opinion of the reporting officer that the flying object sighted by witnesses in and around Lumberton and the meteor report made by the Fayetteville paper are the same."

It is evident that there were actually five different UFOs sighted over North Carolina, and not a lone "meteor." The following is a list of the five North Carolina UFOs and the designated numbers that I have assigned to them:

A.) **# 1 North Carolina Object**. The "ball of fire" sighted over Lumberton at approximately 7:00 p.m. EST.
B.) **#2 North Carolina Object**. "The white in color" object sighted at dusk over Lumberton at Approximately 7:00 p.m. EST.
C.) **#3 North Carolina Object**. The "larger-than-usual shooting star" sighted over Winston-Salem at approximately 7:00 p.m. EST.
D.) **#4 North Carolina Object**. The object reported as a "flying saucer."
E.) **#5 North Carolina Object**. The "greenish blue "object seen "immediately after dark."

The following are descriptions of the five objects that were sighted over North Carolina:

A.) #1 North Carolina Object. It did not manifest the characteristics of a meteor in flight; namely, it changed its course from a downward trajectory to a level trajectory. Its characteristics indicated it was being controlled and maneuvered. The Lumberton witness who sighted this "ball of fire" called it "the mass or object," but not a meteor.
B.) #2 North Carolina Object. The primary Lumberton witness who saw the object, which was "white", Called it "an unusual object," but did not call it a meteor. None of the other eyewitnesses called it a meteor either.
C.) #3 North Carolina Object. Winston-Salem tower men said it was "a larger-than-usual shooting star."
D.) #4 North Carolina Object. Observer James Newman described the object as a "flying saucer."
E.) #5 North Carolina Object. When referring to it, the Fayetteville witness had seen "a huge ball." This object changed its flight three different times.

The witnesses involved in four of these sightings did not refer to the objects as meteors. The tower men though said the object that they saw was a "shooting star" but also stated it was, "larger than usual." Next, I plotted all of these objects on my master map, including their origin points, locations and the times they were sighted. The origin points actually indicate the areas where the five objects descended upon North Carolina. Next, I connected the plotted locations of their origin points to the other points where they were sighted and formed flight path lines that headed north. It was evident that these five North Carolina objects were not "meteors." They actually had a specific task when they descended upon North Carolina. These were on a search and rescue mission, their target area – Flatwoods, West Virginia.

The first three objects descended over North Carolina at approximately 6:50 p.m. EST and proceeded on northwest trajectories toward Flatwoods, West Virginia. The fourth and fifth objects hovered high over North Carolina, guarding the area from any potential air strikes against the three northwest bound rescue objects.

The #4 Object described as a "flying saucer" descended over Flat Rock North Carolina near the South Carolina border. This area lies within the perimeter of the Oak Ridge Laboratory restricted no-fly zone. Furthermore, Donaldson AFB in Greenville, South Carolina is located just south of the Flat Rock area where this UFO descended. The #4 Object passed over Flat Rock, proceeded on a northeast flight and flanked the three rescue ships to the west to assure them of unobstructed flight to Flatwoods. Even though this UFO descended into the ORNL ADIZ just north of Donaldson AFB, it was not intercepted!

The #5 Object hovered out of sight when the other objects descended and positioned itself to the east of them. It guarded the area as a backup role in this rescue mission and then descended southeast of the Lumberton area about one hour later. Upon it's descent it headed northwest as far as the Raleigh area along its flight path then ascended. This flight path was actually a flight corridor that the damaged objects would use upon their departures to exit the United States. The #5 object was patrolling the flight path corridor awaiting the damaged objects to reach the area. This exit corridor was predetermined when the four objects descended.

This search and rescue operation was definitely a programmed plan from beginning to end. I have now designated the five objects as the "North Carolina Rescue Objects." The following is a list that shows the vicinities where each of the five North Carolina Rescue objects descended then passed over the state.

#1 North Carolina Rescue Object
1) Lumberton, NC - *Descended*
2) Greensboro, NC
3) Reidsville, NC
4) Draper, NC

#2 North Carolina Rescue Object
1) Lumberton, NC - *Descended*
2) Reidsville, NC

#3 North Carolina Rescue Object
1) Winston-Salem, NC - *Descended*
2) Mt. Airy, NC

#4 North Carolina Rescue Object
1) Flat Rock, NC - *Descended*

#5 North Carolina Rescue Object
1) Lake Waccamaw, NC - *Descended*
2) Elizabethtown, NC
3) Fayetteville, NC
4) Pope AFB, Ft. Bragg, NC [in line of flight path]
5) Raleigh area, NC

Up to this point in the storyline, three-damaged mid-Atlantic UFOs had all met resistance from U.S. fighter planes that were scrambled to intercept them over the Atlantic Ocean ADIZ. They suffered damages in an aerial battle and were forced down. During this time, four objects were observed to be damaged, on fire and flying erratically; the three Mid-Atlantic objects and the #1 North Carolina Rescue Object. The three damaged mid-Atlantic objects all had one common denominator though; they were all forced to make landings. The #1 North Carolina Object was not forced down over North Carolina, which does not fit into this pattern of a damaged ship. However, it did go down shortly after. After it reached West Virginia, it crashed in Braxton County just outside of Flatwoods. The characteristics of the #1 North Carolina Object actually does fit the profile of a damaged ship, which would also indicate it met fighter jet resistance. I continued my search and looked for mysterious incidents that involved fighter jets, and found what I was looking for.

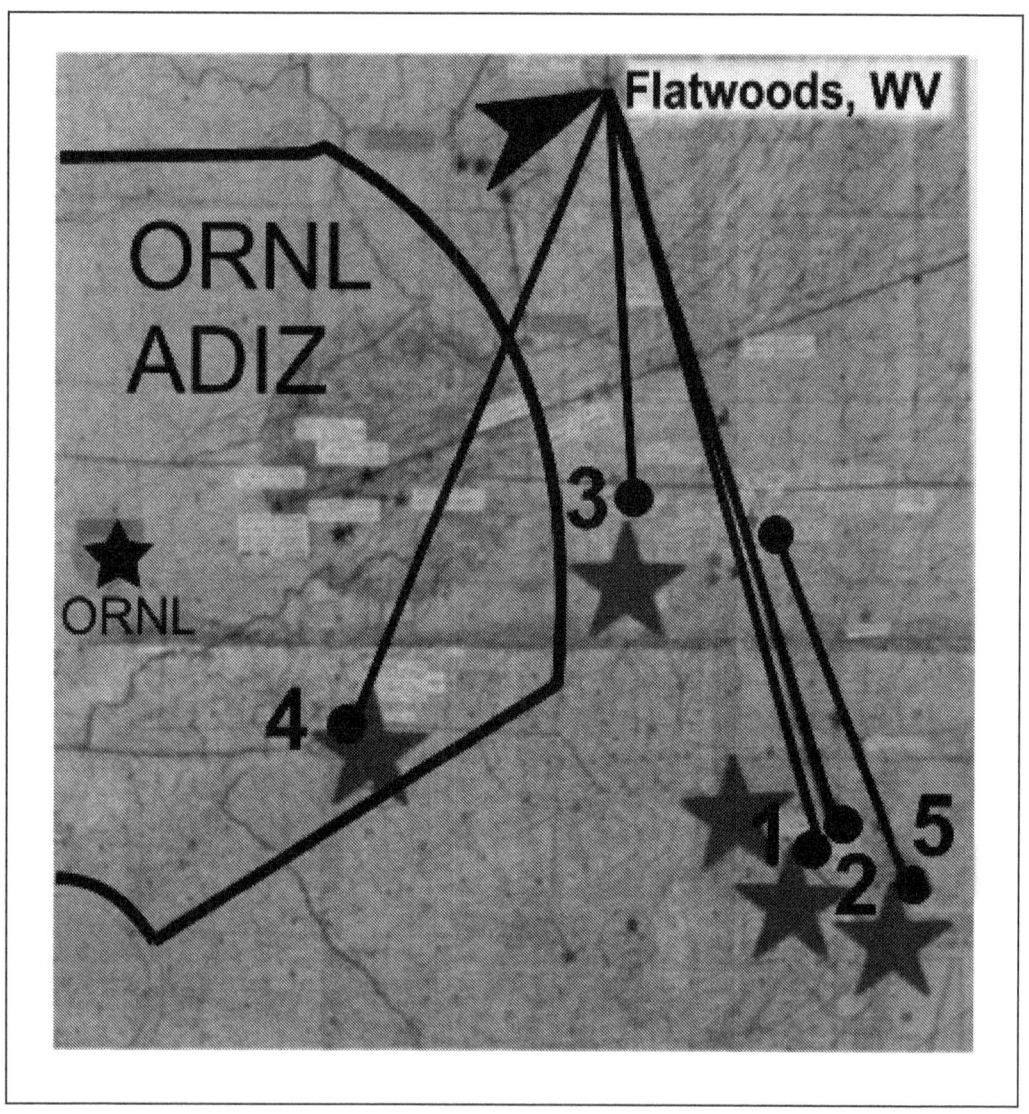

Map detail showing the vicinities where each of the five rescue objects descended over North Carolina. The #1, #2, #3 and #4 objects proceeded North while the #5 object patrolled the flight corridor exit.

THE AIR FORCE FIGHTERS

While researching, I found several newspaper articles that discussed an unusual fighter jet incident that occurred on September 12, 1952. This article led me on a long search. The article appeared in *The Daytona Beach Morning Journal* dated Tuesday, September 16, 1952 with the heading, "Lost Pilot Was From Sanford, AF Reports." It reads:

The Air Force yesterday identified a jet pilot and radar operator missing since Friday in a flight from Tyndall Air Force Base here to MacDill Field, Tampa. The pilot was 2nd Lt. John A. Jones, Jr., 544 Palmetto Ave., Sanford, attached to the Air Defense Command. The radar operator was 2nd Lt. John S. DelCurto, of Pine, Ore., a trainee at Tyndall.

A large-scale air-sea search has been underway for the two since their F94 all-weather night fighter and interceptor radioed it was having trouble at 5:52 p.m. Friday [5:52 p.m. EST/4:52 p.m. CST]. The search continued yesterday after shifting 200 miles west of Tampa in the Gulf of Mexico.

This incident took place only about an hour before the first mid-Atlantic UFO went down in Tennessee. The following points are important:

1. The lost jet was an F-94 all-weather night fighter and interceptor, one of the Air Force's elite jets.
2. This fighter jet was carrying state-of-the-art radar and tracking technology.
3. The U.S. Air Force reported this jet "missing" in a flight from Tyndall AFB in Panama City en route to MacDill Field in Tampa. It should have been a routine flight over the Gulf of Mexico, especially for a jet capable of traveling at speeds of 600 miles per hour.
4. This jet disappeared off the Florida coast surrounded by Air Force Bases with sophisticated military radar systems as well as radar stations.

I found the mysterious disappearance of this F-94 fighter jet disconcerting. The article raised questions that made me want to dig more deeply for answers, in part because this incident had occurred on September 12, in the midst of 18 ½ hours of UFO sightings.

I began to research the missing airmen story in earnest. I was instructed to contact the Air Force Historical Research Agency at Maxwell AFB in Alabama. I sent a letter to this agency requesting further details. I asked if the airmen had been found and asked for any additional data pertaining to the story. Shortly thereafter, I received a letter from the AFHRA with this response: "Thank you for your letter requesting information about the lost pilots. Regrettably, our holdings do not contain the historical data you've requested. Sincerely, David R. Mills, Captain, USAF, Chief, Inquiries Branch."

It seemed unbelievable that the Air Force had no documentation on this subject. They had released the information to the *Associated Press* in 1952; where had it gone?

How could an incident of such magnitude, involving two missing airmen and a fighter jet, go undocumented by the Air Force, especially in light of the huge air and sea search that took place following their disappearance? I did not believe it.

The next lead took me to The Air Force Safety Agency at Kirtland AFB Albuquerque, New Mexico, as suggested by Maxwell AFB. I spoke to a representative there about the two lost airmen. I gave him the information I had, including the names of the pilot and radar operator, their addresses, the date of the incident and the location, including the area of search. I was even able to give him the reported time of the pilot's last transmission.

He asked, "How did you find out about this incident, and where did you get your information?" I told him I had found an article in the *Daytona Beach Morning Journal*, dated September 16, 1952. I was puzzled at the officer's question about how I had found out about the incident. His response led me to believe that he was familiar with the story, and surprised by the amount of information I had. As our conversation progressed, the officer asked me, "Why are you fooling around with a story like this from so long ago?"

I found his questions disconcerting enough to make me uncomfortable disclosing that my research was related to a UFO incident. I told him that I had stumbled across the article. I said the fact that I lived in the area where it had occurred had made me curious as to whether the airmen had ever been found. He told me that in the early 1950s there were numerous planes for which there had been no accounting and that it would take a very long time to search through the many documents in their archives to find out about this incident.

I asked him, "Even with all the information I just gave just you about this incident? I even have the time reported that the last transmission was made by the pilot. How much more do you need?"

At this point, the officer became agitated. His courteous demeanor changed, and I could tell that our conversation was coming to an end. He said, "Doing research like this could become very expensive." Then he requested my name, address and a telephone number at which I could be reached. He said if he found any information, he would contact me.

I told him that I had not realized what a big job the search would be and that at that point I was no longer interested. He suggested that I contact the Maxwell AFB AFHRA. I realized I would have to take a different course of action to obtain the information I needed.

Since the National Archives had referred me to Maxwell, where this wild goose chase had begun, I figured I had reached a dead end. I tried contacting Maxwell AFB again in hopes that they had overlooked something in the search of their records. Again, I sent a letter of inquiry, this time directed at the missing airmen in reference to the history of Tyndall AFB. Tyndall was the base that these pilots were assigned at the time of their disappearance. I thought that perhaps by directing my angle of inquiry toward the history of Tyndall AFB, they might have a record of their missing personnel.

My response from them was not what I had expected. Their letter read, "Thank you for your letter. We checked the history of Tyndall AFB FL for the time period mentioned in your letter, but did not locate any information on the incident you mentioned. You may wish to contact the Air Force Safety Agency at Kirkland AFB . . . Sincerely, Archie DiFante, Archives Branch." Once again, my request was given the runaround. I either began to think that the Air Force had lost the records concerning the incident or were reluctant to disclose the relevant information.

My next step was to contact the Florida Office of Vital Statistics. As Jones had last resided in Florida, the state records should have had a death certificate for him. The letter I received stated, "Florida vital records have been carefully searched, but no record has been found that exactly matches the information on your application. The attached record which is a partial match may be the correct record."

I examined the Certificate of Death and found the partial match to be, "John Anthony Jones," not John A. Jones, Jr. This death certificate was for a man who was born in 1888 with a death date of 1953, one year after Jones and DelCurto were lost. This Mr. Jones died at age 64, far older than any jet fighter crewman. It seemed I had again reached a dead end.

Because the Air Force had no records of these men or their disappearance, I thought that perhaps the names cited in the newspaper were wrong. I had no choice but to return to the source where I had originally discovered the story, the newspapers. I searched several library collections and contacted several other libraries in Florida and Oregon. I found new articles, and after reviewing them, I began to develop new leads. I found that the missing radar operator had had his name spelled at least three different ways. The variations were John S. Del Curton, John S. Del Curto and John S. Curto. I contacted different libraries and looked through directories and Web sites to find any one of the variations of this airman's name. My big break came when I received a telephone call from a librarian in Oregon.

This librarian not only gave me the correct spelling of the name, but she had also found one of the relatives of a John S. DelCurto. She had gone far beyond what I would have expected. She had made many telephone calls on her own time to help me.

Shortly after her call, I talked to John's brother via telephone. He was able to give me insight into his brother's life and death. He verified John's disappearance as the navigator of the F-94 jet. He told me of John's love for the Air Force, and the tragic impact his disappearance had on his family. He explained to me that he had received a telegram from the Air Force informing him of John's disappearance, and that the Air Force was attempting to locate the jet and the missing airmen. The family had received several updates via telegram about the search, but there was no new information. He said, "There was never any wreckage found whatsoever, and the boys' bodies were never recovered." About six weeks after the jets, disappearance the Air Force contacted them again. John's official date of death was October 22, 1952.

One year after the incident, a military memorial was held in Pine, Oregon and a headstone was erected in memory of 2nd Lt. John S. DelCurto. I experienced a deep sadness for this family who had never had any closure on this terrible tragedy.

Next I tried to find information about the pilot of the missing jet, John Jones. The Seminole County Public Library in Florida helped in this quest. Although the Florida Bureau of Vital Statistics had no record of John A. Jones, Jr., another resourceful librarian tracked down the information. A librarian had found a microfilm copy of *The Sanford Herald*. On Monday September 15, 1952, *The Sanford Herald* ran a front-page story with the headline, "Lt. John A. Jones is Reported Missing." This article was written from information given by the brother of Lt. Jones. After reading this article, I started searching through local Sanford business facilities. Eventually I spoke with someone at a historical museum there. This small museum had records going back to the 1950s. There was no record of John A. Jones, Jr., but there was information on a surviving brother. I found a telephone listing for him and immediately called him.

I asked this man if he had a brother, John Jr., who had served in the Air Force and who had disappeared while piloting a jet fighter. I told him I was researching the entire incident involving his missing brother and the radar operator. I explained that I had found numerous inconsistencies in the available information and an odd aura of mystery surrounding the whole incident. He agreed and said that even to this day the incident was unsolved. After nearly half a century (when we spoke), he still could not believe no wreckage of the jet had been found. He told me that the Air Force had contacted him by telegram informing him of John's disappearance. The USAF also contacted him by telephone and sent several more telegrams.

To my surprise, he told me that he still had the original Air Force telegrams and a letter that had been sent to him. These did not state the type of aircraft that John was piloting when he disappeared. He told me that in one telephone conversation the Air Force had said that the jet John was flying was a "current, state-of-the-art jet interceptor." I told him that the newspaper accounts of the incident reported it as an F-94 all-weather night fighter and interceptor. He did remember, he said, being told by the Air Force that the jet was one of the most recent models in use. In the Official GOC Magazine, *The Aircraft Flash* Vol. 1, No. 1, October 1952, Brig. General Kenneth P. Berquist made the following statement in an article titled "ADC Deputy for Operations Explains Air Defense System." He stated, "On July 14, 1952, the GOC [Ground Observer Corps] system along our eastern and western seaboards and along the Canadian Boundary went into continuous 24-hour-per-day operation. Some of the finest and fastest jet fighters in the Armed Forces have been allocated to ADC for the interception mission. They are the F-94 and the F-89, both all-weather fighter interceptors." John's brother asked me if I wanted copies of the telegram and letter sent to him to use in my research and shortly after, he mailed them to me along with an original photo of John.

The brother also put me in touch with a man who was a Civil Air Patrolman at the time of John's disappearance. This man said that he had gone to MacDill AFB to assist in the search for Jones and DelCurto, but was told by officials at MacDill that his services were not needed. They had everything under control.

The following information is the official documentation that the USAF sent to the brother of 2nd Lt. John A. Jones, Jr. These were the telegrams and letters sent to the family of John A. Jones, Jr., pilot of the lost jet. They are presented here in chronological order with the first, a *Western Union* telegram, dated "1952 SEP 15 P.M. 348." It states:

> Western Union (40)
> AB65
> A-TP A 662 Long Govt PD—MacDill AFB FLO 15 327P=
> ASHBY Glen Jones=
> Palmetto Ave Sanford FLO= DAAD-A 53042.
>
> It is with deep regret that I officially inform you that your brother, John A. Jones, Jr. has been reported as missing. He was on a local routine training flight from Tyndall AFB on 12 Sept 1952 when the weather deteriorated. All aircraft were recalled and instructed to proceed to Moody AFB, Georgia which was the alternative landing field. Your brother was unable to contact Moody by radio and notified Tyndall AFB that he was not positive of his position. The Tyndall control tower was directing him to MacDill, AFB Flo the nearest base when he informed them that his engine had failed. Immediately thereafter Tyndall AFB lost radio contact with your brother. No further information is available at this time, however, please be assured that everything is being done to locate the aircraft.
>
> Additional information as it becomes available will immediately be forwarded to you—General Benjamin W. Shidlaw (sic) Commanding General Air Defense Command ENT AFB Colorado Springs Colorado=

The next document is a *Western Union* telegram dated "1952 SEP 16 P.M. 851." It is an updated telegram sent out the next day.

> 1952 SEP 16   51
> AB8I

TPA895 Govt NL PD=MacDill AFB FLO 16
Ashby G Jones=
2544 Palmetto Ave Sanford FLO=
Reference is made to my message of 15 Sept 1952 informing you that your brother is missing. Being located in Florida you are probably in contact with the rescue operations now being conducted. Results of the search now in fourth day are negative. Search this far has covered area of forty-six thousand miles=
General Benjamin W. Chidlaw, Commanding General, Air Defense Comm=.

The next document is a letter, which is hand typed, including the heading:

Headquarters 3625TH Flying Training Wing (Advanced Interceptor)
Tyndall Air Force Base, Florida

17 September 1952
Mr. A.G. Jones
2544 Palmetto Avenue
Sanford, Florida

Dear Sir:

In addition to our telephone conversations, perhaps this letter will bring a little more light as to just what happened last Friday afternoon. John and his Radar Operator, Lt. DelCurto, were on a routine weather training mission. When the weather started to become near our minimums, all of the aircraft were called to come back to the field. Supervisory personnel in the Control Tower advised John and three other aircraft to go to Moody Air Force Base about 15 minutes north of Tyndall; however he was unable to contact the Moody tower or the Moody Approach Control. He indicated that he was not sure of his position at 4:20; however, the Tyndall radio directional finding gave him a steer to Tyndall Air Force Base. MacDill Air Force Base directional finding was able to pick up John's voice and gave him a directional steer also. Shortly afterward, he said he had a flame-out at 15,000 feet.

Immediately, Air Sea Rescue was alerted for a search. Since last Friday, almost 125 sorties, which at one time included 52 airplanes, have been searching. Over 46,000 square miles have been searched with aircraft and surface vessels. All available leads are being thoroughly investigated. I wish that I could give you some positive hope and information; however, at this time all I can say is that the Air Force is doing everything possible to find John and his Radar Observer. Search is continuing. I am sure that you have received some information from newspapers that is not, in all cases, factual information; however, any leads that we get are thoroughly investigated. For example, today an area is being thoroughly searched by helicopter in an attempt to run down a lead that some fishermen possibly heard shouting. Please be assured that the Air Force will continue to search in the hopes of finding John and his Radar Observer. My deepest sympathies are with you at this time. In the event we develop any additional leads, I will call you direct [sic].
Very sincerely yours,
B. T. KLEINE
Colonel,
USAF - Commanding

The next telegram update was dated "1952 SEP 20 P.M. 258." It states:

> Western Union
> AB56 KA251 1952 SEP 20 P.M. 258
> K.CGA 139 Govt D.IPD=ENT AFB Colorado Springs Colo 20 1235P
> Ashby G. Jones. Report Delivery=
> 2544 Palmetto Ave Sanford FLO=
> Reference is made to my message of 16 September 1952.
> Results of the search now in eighth day are negative=
> General Benjamin Chidlaw CG HQ ADC ENT AFB Colo=

The last document is another telegram. It is dated "1952 OCT 23 P.M. 750." It is the death notification of John A. Jones, Jr.

> AB90 KB321   1952 OCT23 P.M. 750
> K.CGA349 Govt PD=HQ ADC ENT AFB Colo Springs Colo 23 523P
> Ashby G. Jones=
> Report delivery 2544 Palmetto Ave Sanford Flo=
>
> ADAAD-4 56 345. It is with deep regret that I officially inform you that on 22 October 1952, the Chief Of Staff, Headquarters United States Air Force notified this command that your brother John A. Jones Jr. was declared dead. The body was not recovered, however after the extensive search conducted by the Air Force it was determined that conclusive evidence existed to warrant this action. Please accept my sincere sympathy in your bereavement.
> General Benjamin W Chidlaw Commanding General Air
> Defense Command ENT Air Force Base Colorado Springs Col=

2D LT. John A. Jones, Jr.

THE AIR FORCE SPEAKS

The UFO activity near Florida and along the Gulf coast was plentiful in August and September of 1952. Edward Ruppelt made this statement in his book, "September started out with a rush and for a while it looked as if UFO sightings were on the upswing again. *For some reason we began to get reports from all over the southern United States.* Every morning [for] about a week or two, we'd have a half dozen or so new reports."

The United States Air Defense Command was on a constant full alert, ready to scramble jets at any unidentified aircraft deemed a national threat. One incident involving a USAF base that had a direct encounter with a UFO occurred during the summer of 1952 at MacDill AFB. This UFO report was on file with the National Investigations Committee on Aerial Phenomena. According to their archives, MacDill AFB picked up a "UFO target" on its radar and tracked it. This Unidentified Flying Object was flying at an altitude of "40,000 ft" at a speed of "400 knots (460 mph)."

This aircraft was a B-29 plane, which was manned by a USAF colonel pilot and a co-pilot. When these airmen "investigated [the] radar target, [they] saw [a] maneuverable egg-shaped object!" This UFO was also described as being an "elliptical UFO."

Even though the exact date of the MacDill event is unknown, there were many correlations between that incident and the events of September 12, 1952. They follow.

1. Both events occurred during the summer of 1952.
2. The UFO in this incident was described as an egg-shaped object.
3. The UFO visual sighting report of the object in this event stated it was maneuvering.
4. This event involved MacDill AFB in Tampa, Florida.

The following newspaper articles about the two missing airmen are listed here in chronological order of their publication dates. They span a period from September 13 through September 17, 1952.

On Saturday, September 13, 1952, the first two articles appeared in two different newspapers talking about September 12 stories. Both were Tampa-based newspapers. The article that appeared in *The Tampa Tribune* was datelined September 12. It reported the missing flyers incident within the headline story of another incident, "Pilot Bails Out, Lands Safely After MacDill Hears Distress Call." It reads in part:

The pilot of a jet observation plane ran into technical trouble during a training flight today and bailed out after heading the plane in the direction of the Gulf of Mexico. The pilot was reported to have landed safely between Tyndall Air Force Base here and Apalachicola… Earlier MacDill Air Force Base at Tampa reported a jet has been unheard from since it radioed it was out of fuel at 5:42 p.m. [5:42 p.m. EST/4:42 p.m. CST]

MacDill and the Coast Guard base at St. Petersburg sent out planes along the course being followed by the fighter. The pilot was unable to give his exact position, and MacDill said the fighter could have been anywhere up to 70 miles northwest of Tampa at the last radio report. MacDill's Public Information Office reported late tonight that crash boats and two search planes had discontinued the search but would resume looking for the missing plane at daybreak pending conformation of the report that the pilot had parachuted to safety.

This article gave the source about Jones and DelCurto's disappearance as well as the time it was reported to the press, "MacDill's Public Information Office reported late tonight"—"late tonight," meaning late Friday night, September 12. The press received the information contained in this article late Friday night from MacDill AFB officials and also reported the "pilot of a jet observation plane," had bailed out "today." This article also stated that "earlier" on September 12, MacDill had reported a missing jet fighter—the plane piloted by Jones and navigated by DelCurto. The information given claimed that Jones and DelCurto and their jet fighter actually disappeared before the pilot of the jet observation plane bailed out and headed his plane out over the open waters of the Gulf of Mexico on September 12.

The Tampa Daily Times also ran a story about Jones and DelCurto as well as the pilot who bailed out. The headline read, "Last Heard From Late Yesterday—MacDill Searches for Pilot Down In Flight Over Gulf." This article also talks about the "jet observation plane." It states, "MacDill Air Force officials were unable to confirm an earlier report that a jet observation plane pilot headed his plane toward the Gulf and bailed out after he ran into trouble on a training flight *Thursday*." The article states:

Thirty-two planes fanned out over a wide area of the Gulf from Panama City to Bradenton in search of an Air Force jet plane last heard from at 5:42 p.m. yesterday. MacDill Air Force Base Public Information Officer Paul E. Mitchell said the plane was identified as a Lockheed F-94 all-weather night fighter and interceptor flying from Tyndall Air Force Base, Panama City to MacDill. Lt. Col. Charles J. Rosenblatt, base operations officer, said the last coherent radio contact with the plane disclosed the pilot had engine trouble at 15,000 feet over the Gulf. The last radio sound indicated the disabled craft was down to 8,000 feet, Captain Mitchell said. The time was 5:42 p.m.

Captain Mitchell said the plane was apparently lost, and Air Force officials speculated that its radio compass had failed. First inkling that the craft was in trouble came when the pilot called Tyndall Air Force Base. He was directed to land at Moody Air Force Base at Valdosta, GA, but for some reason, failed to comply with the orders, Captain Mitchell said.

The next contact was made with MacDill radio tower, which gave the plane three fixes, the MacDill information officer said. It was by means of these fixes that the plane's approximate location was determined. The assumption is that the pilot bailed out over the Gulf. The two Air Force Bases, MacDill and Tyndall, and the Coast Guard are participating in the search today. Combing the Gulf are 36 Air Force planes, six Coast Guard planes, and six crash boats from MacDill.

MacDill Air Force officials were unable to confirm an earlier report that a jet observation plane pilot headed his plane toward the Gulf and bailed out after he ran into trouble on a training flight Thursday.

The information in this article was received later than the information that appeared in *The Tampa Tribune*. The Tribune had picked up the story from the Panama City, September 12-(UP) wire and used their story. *The Tampa Daily Times* printed their article from information they received later in the day, hence the headline, "Last Heard from Late Yesterday." It stated, *"MacDill Air Force officials were unable to confirm an earlier report that a jet observation plane pilot headed his plane toward the Gulf and bailed out after he ran into trouble on a training flight Thursday."* USAF officials from MacDill were unable to confirm the "Thursday" report that had come from Panama City because the "training flight" accident actually occurred on Friday September 12, not Thursday September 11. This was the reason MacDill officials were unable to confirm the report of a plane lost "on a training flight Thursday." *The Tampa Daily Times* made a mistake.

Both jets in these incidents departed Tyndall AFB in Panama City on September 12, 1952. In each case, they were reported as having radioed Tyndall and both were reported as having mechanical difficulty. The jets in both stories were lost. In one the pilot bailed out, in the other Jones and DelCurto were not reported to have exited their plane.

The following day, Sunday, *The Tampa Tribune* published a follow-up story about the two missing airmen. "Planes Hunt For Missing Jet Fighter." It reads in part:

The missing plane was identified as a Lockheed F-94 all-weather night fighter and interceptor bound from Tyndall Air Force Base, Panama City, to MacDill, according to MacDill Public Information Officer Captain Paul E. Mitchell. Thirty-two planes from Tyndall and MacDill, with six Coast Guard planes and six MacDill crash boats took part in yesterday's search for the two crewmen who were presumed to have bailed out when the plane had engine trouble 15,000 feet over the Gulf while en route from Tyndall to MacDill.

Lt. Col. Charles Rosenblatt, MacDill Base operations officer, said, "The last thing we heard was the pilot had a flameout (power failure) at 15,000 feet on course between Tyndall and MacDill. There was complete radio fadeout at 5:43 [EST/4:43 p.m. CST] at about 8,000 feet. Standard procedure is for the crew to bail out."

First notice that the craft was in trouble came when the pilot radioed Tyndall Air Force Base. He was instructed to land at Moody AFB, Valdosta, GA, but for some reason failed to comply with the orders. Captain Mitchell said the plane was apparently lost, and Air Force officials speculated that its radio compass had failed. The next contact was with MacDill radio tower, which gave the plane three radio fixes. Captain Mitchell said, "The plane took off on a routine training mission from Tyndall Field at 3:08 p.m. [EST/2:08 p.m. CST].Friday and last radio was two hours and 35 minutes later when MacDill received the last message at 5:43 p.m. [EST/4:43 p.m. CST]."

I next found an article in *The Panama City News Herald* that appeared on Sunday, September 14, 1952. The large bold print read, "Fliers Hunt Tyndall Pair." The only real difference between this report and the other articles was the time given when the pilot was last heard from, 4:52 p.m. Central Time. The other three Tampa articles gave the period as 5:42 p.m. EST to 5:43 p.m. EST.

This article also mentioned a pilot reported to have bailed out. It stated, "An *Associated Press* story from MacDill said public information officers there had been unable to confirm reports that the pilot had parachuted to the ground between Tyndall and Apalachicola, but Tyndall officials said the reports 'are not correct.'"

The reason they were not correct was that they were two entirely different stories. In this article, two tragic jet incidents had been combined into one story in this article. The newspapers were having a difficult time keeping track of the two September 12, 1952 jet accident incidents. The report of the jet observation pilot who bailed out was never followed up, but the missing jet story continued to receive further press coverage. The names of the two flyers that were presumed missing had not yet been released by the Air Force.

The September 14 article titled, "Fliers Hunt Tyndall Pair" said:

A vast air and sea search continued last night for two Tyndall airmen missing on a routine training flight between the Panama City base and MacDill Air Force Base, Tampa. Public information officers said the plane, an F-94 all-weather jet fighter was last heard from at 4:52 p.m. Friday when the pilot radioed MacDill that he was having engine trouble.

MacDill operations told him to attempt a landing at Valdosta, Ga. and gave him a "fix." Capt. Paul Mitchell, MacDill's public information officer, said the craft had messaged earlier that it had engine trouble 15,000 feet over the Gulf.

Failure of a radio compass was believed to be the cause of the pilot's non-compliance with the order directing him to land in Valdosta. Directions to the Tampa base were also given the pilot, but the out-of-fuel message was received about six minutes later. The plane's position at the time of the last message was unknown, except that it was northwest of Tampa and probably within 70 miles of here. Names of the pilot and radar man, the only two occupants of the plane, were not immediately available.

An *Associated Press* story from MacDill said public information officers there had been unable to confirm reports that the pilot had parachuted to the ground between Tyndall and Apalachicola, but Tyndall officials said the reports "are not correct."

The bulletin report article followed the main article on Monday September 15, 1952. The name of one of the missing men was released. It stated, "TAMPA (AP)" ...His name was 2nd Lt. John S. DelCurto of Pine, Oregon. DelCurto was the radar operator of the missing Tyndall jet."

The Pine, Oregon local newspaper that carried the story was *The Baker Democrat-Herald*. The headline read, "Pine Airman Lost in Flight." The article informed of DelCurto's disappearance and stated the following about Second Lt. Jones, "The pilot was attached to the Air Defense Command and his name is being withheld pending notification of next of kin. Their F-94 all-weather night fighter and interceptor has been unreported since 2:52 p.m. (PST) Friday when the pilot radioed he was having engine trouble."

[This article also stated the missing time/pilot transmission as 5:52 Eastern (5:43 p.m. EST gave which conflicted with the time of the disappearance originally stated by the USAF.]

At the time of publication of the Pine, Oregon article on September 15, 1952, the pilot's name was withheld "pending notification of next of kin." At the same time, a late article appeared in *The Sanford Herald*, a Florida paper, bearing the headline, "Lt. John A. Jones Is Reported Missing." The name of the missing pilot was then known, not through wire service reports but rather through Jones' brother, his next of kin. The article from *The Sanford Herald* was more personal than the other articles. It contained quotes from the "missing" notification telegram sent by ENT AFB in Colorado Springs, CO, to the missing pilot's brother on Monday.

In 1952, according to city directories, John's brother, Ashby, was listed at the address to which the "missing" notification was sent. Ashby was the next of kin and upon his receiving the telegram from the Air Force, he contacted *The Sanford Herald*. The following missing notice was reported to *The Sanford Herald*, "Lt. John Jones Is Reported Missing. Lieutenant John A. (Buddy) Jones, Jr., 22, Sanford, has been reported by the Air Defense Command as missing after he took off from Tyndall Air Force Base, Panama City, last Friday." This information actually reached the press shortly after the incident occurred on Friday night September 12. Since it was released to the press on that night when the two airmen disappeared, why was 2nd Lt. Jones' brother, who was his next of kin, not notified until Monday, September 15 about his brother's death?

Why did the Air Force wait until nearly three days had passed to notify John's brother when the MacDill Public Information Office told the press about the incident on Friday night, September 12?

I was able to put together a time line of the events that happened that night. The only discrepancy I found was the last transmission time. I used the original time of disappearance of 5:43 p.m. EST as released to the Tampa papers by the Air Force. I do not know why the time of the disappearance was changed afterwards to 5:52 p.m. EST. It remained at 5:52 p.m. in all the AP articles appearing afterward until the story was dropped.

According to the telegram received by Ashby Jones, 2544 Palmetto Avenue, Lt. Jones was on a "local, routine training flight" when the "weather deteriorated." The telegram, bearing the name of General Benjamin W. Chidlaw as the sender, further stated that all aircraft were recalled and instructed to proceed to Moody AFB Georgia, the alternate landing field. It reads, "Your brother was unable to contact Moody by radio," the telegram said, "and notified Tyndall AFB that he was not positive of his position." The Tyndall control tower was directing him to MacDill AFB, which was the nearest base, when Lt. Jones informed the tower his engine had failed. Immediately, radio contact was lost.

I raise the following points concerning Air Force statements contained in the telegram and article:

1. None of the other articles stated that the "weather deteriorated" while the jet was en route to Tyndall.

2. None of the other articles stated that all aircraft were recalled and instructed to proceed to Moody AFB. The scenario projected by the USAF on the missing jet was that it was on a solo mission. There was never any indication given by them that Jones was flying with three other planes.

3. None of the other newspapers stated, "Your brother was unable to contact Moody by radio."

4. None of the other newspapers stated that Jones "notified Tyndall he was not positive of his position."

On Tuesday, September 16, 1952, three newspapers carried updated stories concerning the missing Tyndall airman. The names of both missing men were then finally announced but only in two of the newspapers. Oddly enough, the newspaper that did not list both of the men's names in the article was *The Panama City News Herald*, the point of origin of the event. That newspaper listed only John S. DelCurto.

The two papers that named both the pilot and radar observer were *The Tampa Daily Times* and *The Daytona Beach Morning Journal*. Both of these papers carried articles that were AP press releases from Panama City. The Daytona Beach article, "Lost Pilot was from Sanford, AF Reports" stated, "The Air Force yesterday announced a jet pilot and radar operator missing since Friday…."

The Tampa Daily Times article read, "Missing Airmen's Names Announced . . . Panama City, Sept. 16 (AP)." Why didn't *The Panama City News Herald* print John A. Jones' name in its September 16 article if it was released on September 15?

Both the Tampa and Daytona papers listed the time of the men's disappearance as 5:52 p.m. EST. This inconsistency from the original report made by Air Force officials of 5:43 p.m. EST was still being published incorrectly on September 16.

Were the times of the disappearance of Jones and DelCurto intentionally changed by the U.S. Air Force (by approximately ten minutes)? If so, then why? If the time change was a simple error, why was it not corrected in subsequent correspondence? If the mistake was made by news reporters, why was it not caught by the Air Force or at least by an editor who had access to Air Force information?

The following article appeared in the *Panama City News Herald* on September 16, 1952:

Planes Press Search for Jet Fighter.

Air Force planes today widened their Search for an F-94 jet fighter from Tyndall, missing over the Gulf of Mexico with its crew of two since Friday. Planes from Tyndall, Eglin and MacDill, plus five SB-29s of flight C, Fifth Air Rescue, Maxwell Field, shifted their hunt west of Tampa and included a land area southeast of St. Petersburg. By nightfall, the search will have covered 46,000 square miles. The SB-29s bear 33-foot rescue boats with inboard motors that can be dropped by parachute.

The final article I found regarding this incident was published in *The Tampa Tribune,* five days after the disappearance. The second paragraph of the article, "CAP To Continue Plane Search," states, "CAP planes flew six sorties yesterday [Tuesday], and one Monday in the Crystal Bay-Chassahowitzka Bay area after fishermen reported hearing calls for help in the vicinity Monday." These calls probably were not from the missing airmen because the article continued, "No trace of the missing plane or its crewmen had been found since it disappeared Friday afternoon." Was this a false alarm, or was someone calling for help in that bay area on September 15? If not the missing airmen, who was it?

I extracted Air Force information from the articles, along with the telegrams and letter sent by the Air Force to the Jones family and created a timeline. I arranged the following timeline of events according to several quotes. They appear in chronological order below:

1.) "MacDill Air Force Base Public Information Officer Paul E. Mitchell said the missing plane was identified as a Lockheed F-94 all-weather night fighter and interceptor flying from Tyndall Air Force Base to MacDill."

2.) "The Air Force reported Monday that a jet pilot and a radar operator were missing in a flight from Tyndall Air Force Base here to MacDill Field, Tampa."

3.) "The plane took off on a routine training mission from Tyndall Field at 2:08 p.m. [CST/3:08 p.m. EST] Friday."

4.) "He was on a local routine training flight from Tyndall AFB on 12 Sept. 1952 when the weather deteriorated."

5.) "Colonel B. T. Kleine, USAF commander of headquarters for the 3625th Flying Training Wing stated, 'John and his radar observer, Lt. DelCurto, were on a routine weather training mission. When the weather started to become near our minimums, all of the aircraft were called to come back to the field, John and three other aircraft. . . .'"

6.) "MacDill and the Coast Guard base at St. Petersburg sent out planes along the course being followed by the fighter."

7.) "A vast air and sea search continued last night for two Tyndall airmen missing on a routine training flight between the Panama City base and MacDill [sic] Air Force Base, Tampa."

The press was not notified by the USAF that this was a "routine weather training flight," nor was there any mention at all that they were diverted to Tyndall or Moody due to deteriorating weather. In fact, there was no mention of deteriorating weather to the press from any of the Air Force public information officers.

This key factor was left out when the Air Force briefed the news media. *The Tampa Tribune* weather report for September 12 was for "moderate variable winds with scattered evening showers." The September 12, 1952 Tampa Daily Times, published a weather map showing the symbol for rain over Tampa. It was no secret rain was coming in the direction of Tampa on that day. Air Force weather officials were quite aware of the status of the weather. The weather map also revealed a large arrow marked rain located over the Gulf of Mexico, with a point of origin just south of Tampa. The arrow was shown as a continuous sweep from the southeastern U.S. across the Gulf heading northwest past Panama City and continuing across the entire Gulf. This indicated the rain pattern was moving from Tampa right into the flight path of the jets. The weather forecast was for rain for the entire southeast United States.

The Panama City News-Herald [the Tyndall area] reported the weather as, "partly cloudy to cloudy today, tonight and Saturday with scattered thunderstorms." This indicated that the rain pattern from South Florida was moving in the direction of the Florida Panhandle and sweeping northwest, passing over the Gulf of Mexico.

Had the press found out that an F-94 all-weather jet interceptor on a "routine weather training flight" was recalled because of poor weather conditions, they would likely have raised too many controversial questions. This jet was designed (and named) for just such conditions. The F-94A and F-94B Starfires were the Air Force's first operational jet interceptors capable of operating in weather conditions described as, "adverse."

One must wonder if the deteriorating weather was really a factor in recalling the jets. In addition, why was there no mention to the press that Jones was flying with three other jets? The only mention of the additional aircraft involved was sent to Lt. Jones' family.

The Air Force reported that all aircraft were ordered to return to Tyndall field. The supervisory personnel in the Tyndall Control Tower advised John and the three other airmen to proceed to Moody Air Force Base. There was no explanation given for the change of flight orders.

The reports said, "All aircraft were recalled and instructed to proceed to Moody, AFB, Georgia, which was the alternative landing field." This was a mere puddle jump for these fighter jets.

General Chidlaw said in a telegram, "Your brother [Lt. Jones] was unable to contact Moody by radio and notified Tyndall AFB that he was not positive of his position." The September 17 letter from the commanding colonel of the 3625th FTW said, "However he [Jones] was unable to contact Moody tower or the Moody Approach Control." It is puzzling that two airfields that handled the most highly sophisticated aircraft the U.S. possessed were unable to keep track of their planes. It was also interesting that no mention was made of the other three aircraft that were apparently accompanying Jones.

At this point, Jones had radioed and notified Tyndall AFB that he was not positive of his position and was unable to contact Moody AFB. Captain Paul F. Mitchell said, "He was instructed to land at Moody AFB, but for some reason failed to comply with the orders." Mitchell further said, "The plane was apparently lost, and Air Force officials speculated that its radio compass had failed."

Even if Jones could not contact Moody AFB, they were still in radio contact with Tyndall AFB. Why were Tyndall officials unaware of the problems onboard?

MacDill attempted to aid the two flyers. In 1952, MacDill was operating a very high frequency directional finding system. This radio directional finding station was nicknamed "Homer." Contact was established between the F-94 and Homer. Mac Dill's public information officer related the following information: "The next contact was made with MacDill radio tower, which gave the plane three fixes." It was by this means that the plane's approximate location was determined. One of the three established fixes was a landing fix. "MacDill operations told him to attempt a landing at Valdosta, Ga. and gave him a fix."

Once again, Jones did not land the Starfire at Moody. This was the second time that the pilot did not land when he was instructed to.

Why was the crew of the F-94 jet unable to make contact with Moody? This raises the following questions:

    1. What distances were the planes from one another when Jones became lost? Why was pilot Jones isolated from them and why did no one realize he had become lost?

    2. Why didn't Jones contact the three other jets and notify them that he was unable to contact Moody? What was the radar operator, John Del Curto doing during this time?

    3. All of these aircraft should have been in communication with one another and should have been able to overhear each other's transmissions. Why were they not in communication with each other? This dangerous situation could have lead to disastrous mid-air collisions!

4. Why did the other three aircraft, which were flying on this "routine weather-training mission", proceed to Moody field and abandon Jones and DelCurto?

5. Why were all four jets redirected to Moody after being called back to Tyndall? Was the weather too treacherous for these all-weather fighter interceptor jets?

6. I ask, was it pilot error, mechanical failure or something undisclosed that caused Jones to become lost?

7. Why did Jones not make a landing attempt in the Moody area?

8. Why did Jones refuse to attempt a landing at Moody the second time, after receiving further instruction from MacDill, which included three radio, fixes on his location? If Jones were unable to contact Moody to land, this would indicate he was near Moody AFB and planning to land. The pilot then "notified Tyndall AFB that he was not positive of his position. " Since Jones was unable to contact Moody AFB to land," why didn't Tyndall AFB just direct him back to their base field, 140 miles from that area?

According to General Chidlaw, "The Tyndall tower was directing him to MacDill AFB, which was the nearest base."

In Colonel Kleine's Sept 17 letter he stated, "However he was unable to contact Moody tower or Moody Approach Control." He also wrote, "He indicated he was not sure of his position at 4:20. The Tyndall radio directional finding gave him a steer to Tyndall AFB…Shortly afterward, he said he had a flameout at 15,000 feet."

This supposed flameout occurred at 5:42 p.m. EST. Kleine in his letter indicated that the pilot "was not sure of his position at 4:20 [4:20 p.m. CST/5:20 p.m. EST]." The letter tells us the following:

1. Jones was given a steer by Tyndall tower to their base field.

2. The pilot was then given a steer by MacDill AFB, but Kleine neglected to state that the steer also given to Jones by MacDill AFB was not to Tyndall AFB. From the time Jones indicated he was not sure of his position at 4:20 p.m. until "he said he had a flameout at 15,000 ft." at 5:42 was a span of 22 minutes, all of which leads to the following questions.

a) If all the involved bases were in radio contact to the point of being able to monitor Jones' transmissions, give him positional fixes, and landing orders, how could he be lost?

b) What was Jones doing during the times when he repeatedly failed to land at Moody?

c) Jones was lost near Moody AFB and not positive of his position, while being tracked by both Tyndall and MacDill radar systems and receiving steers. Why did he go anywhere near Tampa?

d) How could both MacDill and Tyndall be unaware of the problem with the jet's radio compass as each had had radio communication with Jones? Why no mention of the onboard radar operator's involvement?

e) Why was Jones not directed to another nearby AFB over land when he was lost at 4:20 p.m.?

f) At this point Kleine stated, "The Tyndall radio directional finding gave him a steer to Tyndall AFB. Then MacDill AFB picked up John's voice and gave him a steer also." While Tyndall AFB was steering Jones toward their base in Panama City, MacDill AFB stepped in and redirected the pilot toward their base in Tampa. General Chidlaw stated Tyndall Control Tower was directing him to MacDill AFB. Why did Chidlaw fail to say that Tyndall AFB was steering the pilot toward their base? During this time, Jones was being steered by both Air Force bases.

g) Why did Tyndall and MacDill controllers both steer Jones away from Moody AFB toward Tyndall, then attempt to bring the jet all the way across the Gulf of Mexico towards the Tampa area 245 miles away?

h) Why would Tyndall and MacDill take the risk of bringing a jet across water when it was running low on fuel? If the jet did run out of fuel, which supposedly caused the flameout, why was Jones not aware of his fuel consumption to that point, when the fuel gauge was directly in front of him?

Lt. Col. Charles Rosenblatt [MacDill] said the last coherent radio contact with the plane disclosed the pilot had a flameout at 15,000 feet while on course between Tyndall and MacDill and the crewmen were presumed to have bailed out when the engine trouble occurred.

MacDill, at Tampa, reported that the plane had been unheard from since it radioed that it was out of fuel at 5:42 p.m. EST. At 15,000 feet, Jones' jet supposedly had engine failure because, "it was out of fuel." This caused a flameout, the extinguishing of the flame of the jet while in flight. 5:42 p.m. was the "last coherent radio contact with the plane," according to Rosenblatt.

One minute later at 5:43 p.m., "The last radio sound indicated the disabled craft was down to 8,000 feet," according to Captain Mitchell. Lt. Colonel Rosenblatt added, "There was complete radio fadeout at 5:43 at about 8,000 feet."

i) The jet was now in a dive, dropping 7,000 feet between 5:42 and 5:43 p.m., MacDill said the planes position was unknown at the time of the last message and the fighter could have been anywhere up to seventy miles northwest of Tampa. What did the Air Force mean when they stated the "last coherent transmission" from the jet was at 5:42 p.m.? At 5:43 p.m., "the last radio sound" from the jet indicated it was down to 8,000 feet. Was this transmission incoherent? What actually occurred at 8,000 feet when the radio faded out?

j) Did the jet run out of fuel, or was this a cover story? *Since the jet was running low on fuel, why was it over Gulf waters?* Had the jet used extra fuel during the time Jones was lost? Or had Jones put his plane into afterburner (which requires more fuel)? Why would Jones engage afterburners if he was low on fuel? The engagement of afterburners indicates Jones was attempting to intercept or outrun another aircraft.

k) During this entire time Jones' plane would have been visible on radar as well as in radio contact with three bases. Search planes would have been sent out to search along his route if his course was known. It seems unlikely that the radar systems at all three military bases as well as radar stations along the coast were unable to keep track of the jet. These radar systems were not only used to track U.S. aircraft but to detect any potential threatening aircraft entering U.S. airspace. Another puzzling question is; why did Jones and DelCurto not bail out, which is standard procedure for the crew of a doomed aircraft?

The Jones-DelCurto incident was not the only odd occurrence in northern Florida that night. The article "Odd Balloon Is Found In Tree" was published on September 16, 1952, in *The Daytona Beach Morning Journal* and appeared next to the story of the missing airmen:

Members of the Tallahassee Civil Air Patrol yesterday reported recovering a strange paper balloon from the top of a tall pine tree where they saw it land Saturday. CAP men engaged in a search for a missing plane spotted the object drifting along about 25 miles an hour near the Tallahassee airport. CAP Col. Wally Schanz, State Aviation Director, reported the location of the tree in which it landed. The next morning, a CAP cadet shinnied up the tree and pulled it down.

It was a hot air balloon apparently made of rice paper over a wire frame. The paper was in panels of white, green and blue. Attached to it were streamers of white, green and red paper. It contained no writing or markings. In the inside, there was a wire bracket for a heating element. The interior was badly smoked but there was no indication of what type of fuel was used to provide hot air to raise the balloon. It is being turned over to military authorities.

The CAP is a semi-military volunteer organization supervised and administered by the Air Force and trained to assist in emergencies. The balloon was first sighted on September 13 when it landed in a tree. Its location was reported and it was retrieved the following day. The strange balloon was discovered the day after two Air Force jets disappeared. Had the CAP men been searching for Lt. Jones' missing fighter jet or the lost observation jet when they found the balloon? Did something unreported occur in the Tallahassee area on September 12 that linked the balloon to the missing jets? This story raised more questions than it answered.

Another story called "Mystery Object Frightened His Cattle" was reported in *The Daytona Beach Morning Journal*. This article appeared on the same page as the "Odd Balloon" story in Tallahassee:

Floyd Brown, a milker at the Everglades Experiment Station, said yesterday "a large red lighted object" scared some cattle he was trying to milk early Sunday. Brown told civil defense authorities he went out to milk the cows about 4:30 a.m. and saw "a large red lighted object over the barn in the trees, about 100 feet above the ground.

The lighted object settled down to within about 40 feet of the ground with a whistling sound and the cattle bolted, he declared. Then the object moved off. Brown said he rounded up the cattle and was just driving them into the barn. When the object appeared, again the cattle bolted. The milker was alone at the time.

Belle Glade is on the south side of Lake Okeechobee. This object was "100 feet above the ground in the trees," which precluded it having been a conventional aircraft. Brown also said it settled to within 40 feet off the ground, which I interpreted to mean hovering downward from 100 feet. No mention was made of engine noise or any sounds associated with conventional aircraft. This object appeared again after having moved off the first time. This is not behavior exhibited by a meteor, but instead is consistent with controlled maneuvers made by a craft with intelligent guidance.

The search for the Starfire continued on Monday, shifting to the Gulf of Mexico. The last piece of information I found occurred on Wednesday. This was two days after fishermen had reported hearing shouts while fishing, and six consecutive days of search for Jones. I found no further newspaper reports on the search. However, General Benjamin Chidlaw told Jones' family the search had continued for eight days.

I believe that the story told by the USAF concerning the disappearance of Jones and DelCurto to be a partially fabricated one. The military's story had too many inconsistencies, time gaps, and vague explanations. Whatever happened to these two men, their families and the public were given misinformation. The communications from the Air Force to the next of kin and news services were not all outright lies. Instead, they were fragments of truth, fragments that did not mesh to form a logical timeline or a coherent set of facts. The military's story had too many holes in it.

It is worth noting that when I was corresponding with several Florida newspaper archivists who were sending me articles, several of them called me and had raised points of inconsistencies contained in the news releases! I believe that news of the Starfire's disappearance spread so quickly that the Air Force did not have time to prepare a sufficiently believable cover-up story.

Chapter 23

FORGOTTEN

To this day, the two flyers and their F-94B Starfire jet have never been found. Second Lt. John A. Jones Jr. and Second Lt. John S. DelCurto simply vanished off the face of the earth without a trace. For more than 50 years, they were forgotten about by most and their families never had closure. I will never forget the moment that I found Second Lt. Jones memorial head stone marker at the cemetery located in Ocala, Florida in the summer of 1999. I found it after researching this story for about seven years.

At first, I was excited because I found it, and then I became sad. As I looked down at the head stone that was over grown with grass and weeds, I knelt down and cleaned them away from the stone marker. I brushed away the sediment from the face of the stone and a chill ran through me when I saw the date of Jones' death carved in stone. The date of his death was the day that he vanished on "September 12, 1952." Not the day he was officially declared dead by the Air Force on "22 October 1952."

As I stared at the memorial, John Jones Jr. became more than just a name that I had read about in a few newspaper articles and reports. I felt very sad as I put a small American flag into the ground next to his long forgotten and neglected memorial. I then thought, "John, if only I could talk to you, I would have a lot of questions to ask!" I needed some answers to the many questions about this incident.

When Stanton T. Friedman obtained the unclassified July cases of major "Aircraft Accidents of 1952," he also obtained the microfilm reel for the September 12, 1952 cases. The Jones and DelCurto case was verified and contained on it according to the microfilm representative that Friedman talked with. Stanton Friedman received the reel with the September 12, 1952 dates and then sent it to me. I scanned the reel and the incident involving Second Lt. John A. Jones Jr. and Second Lt. John S. DelCurto was indeed on the microfilm. I reviewed it and transferred it to paper. Furthermore, this incident was only one case out of eleven known cases that were documented on September 12. The Jones and DelCurto case was recorded by the USAF as case number "52-9-12-4." It was the fourth major accident documented of the eleven recorded for that day.

When I looked through the eleven case files, the first thing that I noticed was that two major aircraft accident cases were removed. The two files missing were case numbers three and five. These were the cases just before and after the Jones and DelCurto incident case. There is no reference at all to these two missing cases, they are simply absent from the microfilm. There is not one page of documentation for either one of these cases... they are gone! The only way I knew that both cases were missing is they are listed in sequential order and the case numbers jumped. These two cases were actually pulled and put into another higher classification than the others that were already considered "restricted."

Why were both cases "52-9-12-3" and "52-9-12-5" removed from the major Aircraft Accidents for September 12, 1952? What was contained in each of the cases that the USAF does not want the public to see? How many aircraft were involved in each of these major accident reports and what kind of major accidents were they? *Moreover, were there any more September 12, 1952 cases removed after the last known case, the eleventh case that was recorded as the "52-9-12-11" accident case? We would never know because there would be no way to track and identify any cases after the last listed case. An ingenious way to remove documents from the record without leaving a trace of evidence, there would be no sequential case numbers to compare after the eleventh accident case!*

When Stanton Friedman visited the National Archives in 2005 to research the declassified Air Force accident reports he focused on 1952. Friedman requested, received and looked through the 1952 aircraft accident documents. The Air Force recorded aircraft accidents for each month that included statistical documentation, which contained fighter aircraft accident information. Friedman went in search of the September 1952 statistics documents and discovered they were all removed. *Once again, official 1952 Air Force aircraft accident documents for the month of September were missing. How many fighter jet accidents and disappearances really occurred on September 12, 1952?*

Another major jet accident that occurred on September 12, 1952 that involved Tyndall AFB, was not documented in the "Aircraft Accidents For 1952" files. *The Tampa Tribune* documented this incident on September 13, 1952. The information appeared in the article, "Pilot Bails Out, Lands Safely After MacDill Hears Distress Call." It states that, "The pilot of a jet observation plane ran into technical trouble during a training flight today [September 12], and bailed out after heading the plane in the direction of The Gulf of Mexico." The pilot of the jet was said to have, "...radioed in to his base at Tyndall that he was setting the controls so the jet would come down far out in the Gulf."

Why is this accident not documented by the Air Force? Was the incident one of the two cases that were missing from the eleven known September 12 documented cases? Regardless, this major accident is not documented.

The Tampa Tribune article that disclosed this incident also stated the following information about the pilot in this incident: "His name wasn't learned immediately." I have never found the follow-up story about this pilot at all. This major accident was forgotten about long ago.

The Jones and DelCurto incident was not forgotten about. Even though this incident never made headlines across the country, the Florida press heavily documented it. It does not surprise me that this case was finally declassified after more than a half century. If this case involving the two lost airmen and their jet had not been declassified and made available to the public, it would have raised more suspicion…especially since the U.S. government became aware of my Jones and DelCurto research after I submitted my first book manuscript to the Library of Congress for a copyright back in 1999. It was just a matter of time until my first book came out, so why not make the records public…disproving any further conspiracies.

I read and reviewed the case # "52-9-12-4" involving the mystery of the lost jet and its crew. It was more than 65 pages long. Sixty-five pages of some of the most convoluted information I have ever read. The information set forth in the Jones and DelCurto incident was comparable to the Air Force's meteor and

"Flatwoods Monster" explanation for that same night. Whoever concocted the explanations given about the "Flatwoods Monster" Incident, probably wrote the script for the Jones and DelCurto story.

Of course, the documents in the case did not refer to flying saucers or UFOs. That would have made it too obvious and easy to link the lost jet together with the UFO events that night. I had never expected that there would be any reference to UFOs or saucers in the Jones and DelCurto documents. After I reviewed this case many of my questions were finally answered, but several more questions arose. The intentions of the Air Force in this particular incident were blatant and it is obvious by the information that appears in this accident report…COVER UP. This incident was covered up and I will say that it was covered up very poorly.

These two flyers were allegedly on a "routine weather training mission" according to Colonel BT. Kleine of Tyndall AFB. Air Defense Commander Benjamin Chidlaw stated that what occurred next: "When the weather deteriorated all aircraft were recalled and instructed to proceed to Moody AFB."

I read and reviewed the 65 pages of declassified documents and found that several documents in the case file were not there. There were several chosen extracts from other documents included but not the entire reports. Included in the 65 page report were Air Force forms, a preliminary report, the AF Aircraft Accident report, statements and aircraft information, to name a few. Also included were the very important transcripts for two "Board proceedings" conducted by "The Aircraft Accident Investigating Board." The first meeting occurred on "29 September 1952" and the second on "3 October 1952." Both board proceedings were held at Tyndall AFB in Panama City, Florida.

The Directorate of Flight Safety Research located at Norton Air Force Base in San Bernardino, California, received information on aircraft accidents as they occurred. Their officials decided whether if their personnel would conduct the investigation or those of a local base. Author Alfred Goldberg explains this in, "A History of the United States Air Force: 1907-1957." He states, "Directorate personnel actually investigated only a small percentage of the USAF major accidents, selected because they involved new aircraft, indicated new accident trends, or presented unusual technical difficulties."

I extracted information from these documents where information was given. I then formed a detailed timeline of the incident. I compared information from several different documents and reports and pieced them together. I also compared and cross-referenced the information contained in these 65 pages with the telegrams and letters sent to the pilot's brother shortly after the incident occurred. In addition, I utilized the Florida newspapers that followed the Jones and DelCurto incident. The earliest of these articles were quite valuable as they contained the first information about the incident from the September 12, 1952 USAF press conference in Tampa.

By utilizing, the information contained in all of these sources I was able to put together a complete time line of events according to what the USAF said happened. The incident involving the disappearance of Jones & DelCurto still does not add up according to the USAF version. The declassified documents are more convoluted than the press information and the information contained in the Air Force telegrams and letter.

I will point out the many inconsistencies in the Air Force's story. The USAF officially stated, "The primary cause of this accident was the pilot failed to keep himself oriented at all times while on instruments." The convoluted time line of events tells a different story, which indicate Jones and DelCurto were not on a "routine weather training mission" on September 12, 1952.

Some of the most pertinent information I found useful in this case, was extracted from the two board proceedings held at Tyndall AFB. The opening of the first board proceeding stated, "1. The Aircraft Accident Investigating Board convened at 0830 hours, 29 September 1952 in the Wing Conference Room at Tyndall Air Force Base, Florida for the purpose of investigating a major aircraft accident involving F-94B, NO. 50-819A piloted by 2nd Lt. John A. Jones, Jr. To date the aircraft and crew are still missing."

The six men from the board present were, "Major Peter E. Pompetti, the acting board president, 3 members; Major Roderick E. McCaskill, Major Wesley I. McKee and Major Joseph E. Wisby. Medical member, Captain Leo Jivoff and the recorder Captain John L. Armour." The purpose of the board was said to be "strictly fact-finding."

During this Investigation, the board questioned three key Tyndall persons involved in this incident. They were Captain Oran E. Need, weather officer; Capt. Phillip P. Harrison, flight instructor of "B" flight and 1st Lt. Robert A. Dunn, Tyndall AFB approach control officer. After these individuals were questioned, the board decided it needed "additional evidence." It would be "necessary in order to reach a comprehensive conclusion in this case."

On "3 October 1952", The Aircraft Accident Investigating Board reconvened. During this meeting, the Directional Finding Controller/ Approach Controller who was on duty in Tyndall AFB tower were also questioned. His name S/Sgt. Ernest S. Bolen. Each man was called before the board for questioning. They were administered the oath then testified before the board. Major Pompetti used the same basic opening to each man before the questioning commenced. He stated, "The purpose of this board is strictly fact-finding. It is not punitive in any sense of the word. We are here to read the testimony in file and to listen to other testimony, which might not be covered in the statements; to delve into the circumstances surrounding this accident and try to reach a conclusion, which might prevent accidents of this nature from occurring again. Do you understand?"

It is interesting to note that the only individual who was not asked, "Do you understand" was the flight instructor, Captain Harrison. On several occasions throughout the two board proceedings, Major Pompetti and his men had trouble getting straight answers from the Tyndall AFB men. Numerous times, when the board members asked them direct questions, they only received very vague answers. The Tyndall AFB men involved in the Jones and DelCurto incident were blatantly evasive with several of their answers, when board members asked direct questions.

It is obvious that the persons at Tyndall AFB, as well as several others involved in this incident from other bases and locations, were silenced. After I analyzed and dissected the transcripts of these two board meetings, I found several inconsistencies in the story. It was obvious that the Aircraft Accident Investigating Board was frustrated with many of the answers it received. Furthermore, because the first board meeting was so convoluted, another board meeting had to be rescheduled to reach a conclusion. I believe that the Aircraft Accident Investigating Board was in the dark concerning the Jones and DelCurto incident. They were the outsiders. By separating, comparing and cross-referencing all of the information I had concerning the incident, the inconsistencies built up. The blatant lies and outlandish cover-ups began to surface as well.

Tyndall AFB was the headquarters of the advanced Interceptor, 3626 Fly Tng-Gp. (AI) Tyndall AFB, FL. Jones had his wings and DelCurto was in training at the time they disappeared.

The jet that the two flyers were flying was said to be a Lockheed F-94B Starfire, "No. 50-819A", the second Starfire jet in the series. The F-94A and F-94B Starfires were the USAF's first operational jet interceptors capable of flying in adverse weather conditions. The F-94B preceded the F-94C and 356 were ordered by the USAF and put into operation. This jet was a two-man fighter that carried a rear-seat radar operator. The F-94B had a maximum speed of nearly 600 MPH. It was equipped with a Hughes E-1 Fire control system and AN/APG-33 radar system. The F-94B was armed with four .50 caliber cannons each allocated with 300 rounds of ammo.

To this day, the two flyers and their F-94B Starfire jet have never been found. Second Lt. John A. Jones Jr. and 2nd Lt. John S. DelCurto simply vanished off the face of the earth without a trace 55 years ago. They have been forgotten about by most and their disappearance has never been officially explained. The Air Force does not know where these two airmen are…or do they! Occasionally I will visit 2nd Lt. Jones memorial head stone marker at the cemetery located in Ocala, Florida. Some of us remember…and some want us to forget!

Chapter 24

THE TRUTH?

The United States Air Force Dictionary gives the following information, "Tyndall Air Force Base. An AF base at Panama City, Florida, named for Lieutenant Frank B. Tyndall, a WW I fighter pilot, killed in 1930." As I was researching this case and writing this book, I often wondered; what questions would Lt. Tyndall have asked if he were present at those two "Aircraft Accident Investigating Board" meetings? How would this fighter pilot have handled the situations as they unfolded? Would Lt. Tyndall have believed the testimonies that were being told to the board? Now, ask yourself the same questions as you read the following declassified information.

Second LT. Jones disappeared in a LOCKHEED F-94B STARFIRE similar to the jet pictured here

POINT 1: THE ADDITIONAL JETS INVOLVED

The first point to raise in this incident; there was no mention to the press at the original press conference, that Lt. Jones was flying with "three other jets." It was presumed that he was flying alone. The only mention of the additional aircraft involved was sent to the Jones family. The recently declassified documents now state, that Jones and DelCurto were said to be part of the "B" flight with five other jets. All six jets were said to be F-94B Starfire all-weather interceptors, on a "local weather proficiency flight." The first segment of this incident involves the actual take-off time of the six Starfires from Tyndall AFB. They were said to have departed Tyndall AFB between 1:47 p.m. and 2:26 p.m. CST. Lt. Jones and DelCurto were documented as the fourth jet to depart the base at "1408C," 2:08 p.m. CST in jet # 0819.

POINT 2: AIRCRAFT OF "B" FLIGHT WERE NOT RECALLED BECAUSE OF DETERIORATING WEATHER

On September 13, 1952, Tyndall sent a teletype of their "Preliminary Report of a Major Accident" to several USAF bases. The Directorate of Flight Safety Research at Norton AFB received one of the reports. Contained in the declassified documents was a letter from the Office of the Inspector General at Norton AFB, California to Tyndall AFB. In this letter, the Executive Director of Flight Safety Research, Lt. Col. Warlick, asked seven questions in reference to the Jones/DelCurto Incident. It stated, "req fol info" [request following information]. The letter was dated "16 September 1952." Two questions of interest are as follows:

Question #5, "Description [of] weather deterioration from takeoff time until recalled to Tyndall?"
Question #6, "What was forecast weather and why were aircraft not recalled sooner?"

On the following day, "17 Sept 1952" Tyndall AFB sent a teletype to Norton AFB with answers. Question #5 was answered, "Aircraft were not recalled, were holding and letting down on IFR [Instrument Flight Rules] clearances under control of Tyndall Approach Control." Question #6 was also answered. It stated, "1500 BN 8000 overcast 2 miles rain; all aircraft were on IFR clearances and under control of Tyndall Approach Control."

I will now show the four previous statements made by the USAF between September 13 and September 17, 1952:

1. *Sept 13, 1952. 8:54.*
Preliminary Report Of A major Accident AFHQ Form O-309..."When weather started to deteriorate, all aircraft were recalled"

2. *Sept 13, 1952. 9:04.*
Teletype of Preliminary Report Of A Major Accident..."When weather started to deteriorate all aircraft were recalled."

3. Sept 15, 1952. 3:27 p.m.
MacDill Western Union Telegram. General Benjamin W. Childlaw - Commanding General ADC - Ent AFB, Co. MacDill..."When the weather deteriorated. All aircraft were recalled and instructed to land at Moody."

4. *Sept 17, 1952.*
Letter from "B. T. Kleine Colonel, USAF Commanding. HQ 3625th FTW - Tyndall AFB (Advanced Interceptor)..."When the weather started to become near our minimum, all of the aircraft were called to come back to the field."

It is obvious that Norton AFB officials were obviously puzzled by the explanations that Tyndall AFB officials presented and wanted some answers. Why did Tyndall AFB officials release four prior false statements? What were the officials at Tyndall AFB trying to conceal? How many other false statements were made by Tyndall AFB officials?

POINT 3: INFORMATION REVEALS TYNDALL AFB LOSES POWER AS JETS PREPARE TO LAND

The truth has been revealed that the six jets were not recalled because of deteriorating weather. What was said to have occurred next, as the first of six jets prepared to land at Tyndall AFB, is questionable. Tyndall AFB Flight Instructor Capt. Harrison stated the following information on Sept. 29 to the Aircraft Accident

Investigating Board members, "About an hour after the first one got off they were all at altitudes on top and working assigned quadrants of range; it came for approach times and one of them was already making his approach. About that time, Tyndall range went off the air. Immediately several called in and said their radio compass was out and all they could hear was static. I advised them the range was off the air."

Captain Harrison gave the following information in his statement dated, "23 September 1952." In this document he states, "No difficulties arose until Tyndall Range went off the air. At that time about three ships called for steers; one was Lt. Jones in aircraft #819."

The Report of AF Aircraft Accident reported the following information in "Section O. Description of Accident." It stated, "Tyndall radio range went off the air at 1440 C and was off until 1445 C. During this time, Lt. Jones called for a D/F steer back to the station."

The following information appeared in the Tyndall AFB teletype, "Preliminary Report of a Major Accident" dated Sept. 13. It stated, "When jet acft started letting down procedures Tyndall Range went off the air. It was off the air from 1440 to 1445 CST." [2:40-2:45 CST]

Norton AFB official Lt. Col. Warlick asked the following in his "16 September 1952" letter to Tyndall AFB officials, "Reason Tyndall range went off air." On "17 September 1952," the following day Tyndall answered, "AACS power maint. Personnel were making a power change-over CH in order to test the emerg power. The emerg power did not take over and the radio range went off the air until the tower operators called in and ADV the power maint personnel to reset the commercial power."

The "Airway and Air Communications service" at Tyndall AFB actually claimed to have tested their emergency power while the six jets of "B Flight" were preparing to land. They claim that the emergency power failed to go on and their "radio range went off the air" for five minutes. The power maintenance personnel were supposedly contacted by the Tyndall tower operators and advised to reset the commercial power.

This scenario as presented by Tyndall AFB is absurd. Power Maintenance personnel do not pull the plug on an air force base and make a "changeover" so they can "test the emergency power," whenever they feel like it. This would be a very dangerous practice. A test of this nature would have been scheduled with the entire base. A surprise power outage could have had catastrophic results especially when a group of six F-94 Starfire jets was preparing to land. This explanation does not seem plausible.

During this time in 1952, the US government was anticipating a Soviet nuclear assault by long-range bombers. Tensions ran high and air force bases were on a 24-hour alert to scramble fighter jets towards any airborne intruders. Was it common practice during the Cold War, for base commanders to allow their Power Maintenance personnel to perform unscheduled power change-over tests? Did Tyndall AFB actually allow such risky and dangerous actions to take place? Tensions were high enough at these bases without the addition of any other surprises, like cutting your power unannounced.

How many other equipment malfunctions actually occurred on that day besides the "radio range" power loss? Was the power loss at Tyndall AFB really caused by an unscheduled power changeover test?

Captain Harrison explained the following information when he was questioned by Major Pompetti and board members, "Q. How long was the [Tyndall AFB] range off the air — Do you know? A. It was off the air long enough for them to finish one pilot up from penetration and bring another one all the way down. Why did the board ask Harrison, "Do you know?" Harrison was the flight instructor and should have known. It seems the board was becoming more suspicious evident by their sarcasm?

Pompetti also asked, "Q. How many ships at one time were they working? A. About three." Capt. Harrison also told the board, "The man [pilot] who was making a letdown was brought in using D/F. The next man was brought in all the way with D/F."

The pilots of these jets actually made visual landings with the aid of Tyndall AFB directional finder to guide them in. The pilots used VFR/Visual Flight Rules procedures. The visibility in the Tyndall AFB area was good at that time, so the aid of instruments or IFR/Instrument Flight Rules was not necessary.

Approach Controller 1st Lt. Dunn actually stated in his signed "Certificate" that the first two jets "cancelled their instrument flight rules" plans.

At this point in the incident, the first two F-94 jets of B-Flight were brought down and landed at Tyndall AFB, they were "AF-1332" and "AF-0867." Four jets remained in the air, including Jones and DelCurto in jet "AF-0819." Captain Harrison said the following in his statement, "By this time the weather was getting a little bad (light rain) so I decided to send the top four ships in the stack to their alternate [Moody AFB]."

An actual photograph of F-94B STARFIRE 0867 that was part of the "B-Flight" on September 12, 1952

Captain Oran E. need, The Tyndall AFB Weather officer on duty that day was questioned by Major Pompetti and the board. He stated the following information about the four jets that did not land at Tyndall.

Captain Need stated, "After 1500 C [3:00 p.m. CST] there was not much doubt in my mind — but what they would have to [do is] make IFR letdown at the home terminal, Tyndall or cancel and go to their alternate." Captain Need then made this statement contradicting Capt. Harrison's decision to land the four jets at Tyndall using IFR, "In my opinion, I could not see why the pilots could not clear IFR [Instrument Flight Rules]."

Why didn't the jets land at Tyndall AFB using their Instrument Flight Rules? Why did Captain Harrison redirect the four jets away from Tyndall AFB because of "light rain"? Even the Tyndall AFB weather officer could not understand "why the pilots could not clear IFR." Was there another reason that flight instructor Captain Harrison redirected the four jets toward Moody AFB in Valdosta, GA?

POINT 4: CONVOLUTED STATEMENTS FROM TYNDALL TOWER — THE COVER-UP BEGINS TO UNRAVEL

At this point in the incident, I cross-referenced information between flight instructor Capt. Harrison, Tower Approach Control Officer, 1st Lt. Dunn and Approach Controller S/Sgt. Bolen. Harrison stated the following, "At this time #819 was not over the station so I told the Tower Officer [1st Lt. Dunn], who was working with him on D/F to direct him [Jones] to his alternate when he got back over the base, which he did. Capt. Harrison explained this segment further to Major Pompetti and the board members, "#819 [Jones] was not back over the station at that time. About five minutes later they [approach controllers] got him over the station." Harrison also told them, "When Lt. Jones got back over the station, he was at 29,000 ft and acknowledged he was proceeding to his alternate [Moody AFB]."

Tyndall AFB Approach Controller, S/Sgt. Bolen told a different story to Major Pompetti and the board members. The board asked the following question which was answered by Bolen, "Q. Do you feel sure in your mind that the aircraft [0819] was ever actually over the station before he [Jones] departed Moody — that he actually departed from Tyndall to Moody? A. I can't say."

Capt. Harrison continued his version of the incident and told the board the following, "I asked Lt. Dunn to tell #819 [Jones] to pick up a heading of 075° to Tallahassee and when over Tallahassee, to contact Moody D/F on 'D' channel and call for a homer."

Tyndall Approach Control Officer Dunn stated the following to the board concerning this section of the incident, "Q. Did you relay instructions to #819 [Jones] to depart to his alternate [Moody AFB]? A. yes sir. Q. In these instructions, was he instructed to report to Moody D/F over Tallahassee? A. Not that I remember."

It is obvious that flight instructor Captain Harrison was not on the same page as his men. Why was Captain Harrison telling a different version of the incident from what the two approach control operators told?

Were these statements involving this segment of the incident a fabrication? Was the entire scenario involving this incident a complete fabrication?

POINT 5: CONFLICTING INFORMATION CONCERNING JONES REDIRECTION DEPARTURE TIME TO MOODY AFB

There are two different times in the 65-page report for Lt. Jones redirection departure time to Moody. This was the point in time when he was sent to his alternate base, while flying over the Tyndall area. The "Report of AF Aircraft Accident" states Jones' time of redirection at 3:35 p.m. It states, "It is assumed that 0819 departed Tyndall AFB at 1535 with 289 gallons of fuel on board."

A signed "CERTIFICATE" by 1st Lt. Dunn, Approach Control officer states, "Pilot asked for a VHF/DF steer to the [Tyndall] field and was brought back over the field at 29,000 [ft] and instructed to go to his alternate at approximately 1525 [3:25 p.m.]."

Why did the Air Force have to assume the information they used in this segment of the incident? Why is there a ten minute differential between these two documents for the same event? Was the time 3:25 or 3:35; a big difference when in a jet? Was this just another hapless mistake on the part of the Tyndall Tower controllers when logging their times, or just a sloppy mistake in record keeping? Was the USAF intentionally trying to confuse the times and facts contained in the incident? Whatever the excuse may be, it is obvious that the USAF could not keep track of their story—or their jet!

Harrison explained what allegedly occurred next, "In the meantime we contacted Moody. They were alerted and had already worked one aircraft sent over there. Others were on their way; there were three already gone. Lt. Jones was the last one. Now Jones and DelCurto were allegedly en route to Moody AFB in Valdosta, GA. That was the last we heard of him for a while until we heard him calling Moody Approach Control on 'B' channel. He [Jones] was coming in clear at that time."

1st Lt. Dunn explained what happened next while in front of the board during his questioning, "Q. Did the person who was monitoring D/F in Tyndall Tower [or working D/F], did they hear 0819 calling Moody D/F for a steer over Tallahassee? A. I heard him calling Moody on 'B' channel."

The board then made an inquiry about the time and asked, "Q. When you first heard him ask Moody for a steer do you know what time it was? A. Somewhere around 1600 [4:00 p.m. CST] — I can't be sure." Why was Lt. Dunn unsure of the time?

Lt. Jones should have reached Moody AFB in about fifteen minutes from Tyndall AFB. After an approximate twenty-five to thirty-five minute time lapse, the pilot was finally heard over the airwaves. At approximately 4:00 p.m. CST, Jones and DelCurto were still en route to Moody and had not landed yet. Where were the airmen during this time they were overdue and what were they doing? Why had they not landed yet?

Lt. Dunn was questioned further by the board. The following transpired:

Q. At any time during this incident did you or anyone else instruct #819 to switch to 'D' channel?
A. No-not to my knowledge.
Q. Was there some reason for not switching to 'D' channel?
A. No – I don't know of any reason for not switching to 'D' channel. [Note: There was contact with jet)
Q. The reason I asked the question is because it is obvious from the statements in file that at approximately 1600 [4:00 p.m. CST] this thing was reaching emergency stages, yet we evidently did not go to emergency frequencies. My question is why?
A. There I think it is the pilot's responsibility to go to D channel if he considers himself emergency."

When Jones and DelCurto were overdue, and not heard from between twenty-five and thirty-five minutes later, were they actually on another mission? Is this why there was a delay in their arrival time at Moody? Furthermore, was the reason that Lt. Jones did not go to an emergency frequency, that he did not consider himself in an emergency? Was Jones really lost at 4:00 p.m.?

POINT 6: THE TRUTH ABOUT THE RADIO COMPASS

Jones and DelCurto proceeded towards Moody AFB to attempt a landing. At this point in the incident, the pilot was in radio contact with Tyndall AFB tower.

Another Air Force base that was monitoring the situation intervened. MacDill AFB in Tampa stepped into the picture and attempted to assist the pilot. MacDill's RDF named Homer, a high frequency radio directional finder had tracked Lt. Jones and DelCurto. *The Panama City News Herald* stated the following information on September 14, 1952, "MacDill operations told him [Lt. Jones] to attempt a landing at Valdosta, GA. and gave him a fix…failure of a radio compass was believed to be the cause of the pilots' non-compliance with the order directing him to land in Valdosta."

MacDill AFB Public Information Officer Captain Mitchell stated the following at the Sept. 12, 1952 press conference in Tampa, "First inkling that the craft was in trouble came when the pilot called Tyndall Air Force Base. He was directed to land at Valdosta, GA [by MacDill] but for some reason, failed to comply with orders."

The MacDill Public Information Officer also said, "The plane was apparently lost and Air Force officials speculated that its radio compass failed." They said this may have been the reason Lt. Jones "failed to comply with orders" to land.

At this point in the incident, at approximately 4:00 p.m. CST, the USAF "speculated" that the radio compass had malfunctioned. During this time, the Tyndall AFB tower operator was in contact with the pilot of the supposedly lost jet. Captain Harrison then stated, "We were reading him very weakly."

The first radio compass information released by the USAF at the September 12 press conference actually was not speculative. Captain Harrison revealed the truth about the condition of the Starfire's radio compass on September 29 to Major Pompetti and the board. Harrison was asked the following question, "Q. Did he [Lt. Jones] mention any malfunction of the radio compass after the [Tyndall AFB] range went back on the air? A. No sir." replied Harrison.

At this point in the incident the Air Force stated, "The plane was apparently lost." Could the weather over Moody AFB in Valdosta, GA, have been a contributing factor to Jones being "apparently lost"? Captain Need, the Tyndall AFB Weather Officer on duty during the incident, stated the following information to Major Pompetti and the board:

"Q. Did the forecast at Moody change any from what you forecast it to be during the period from the time the aircraft were flying?

A. It never changed to IFR. It did get very light rain, visibility remained 10 mi., VFR weather, ceilings remained the same. I believe that appears on the clearance."

The weather over Moody AFB was not bad at all, only "very light rain." There was a ten-mile visibility the pilots that preceded Jones to Moody AFB "never" had their orders "changed to IFR." Because there was a ten-mile visibility, the pilots were able to bring in their jets and land visually without instruments. These pilots used "Visual Flight Rules" because the weather was not a deterrent factor.

When Lt. Jones "called Tyndall AFB" and was "directed to land at Valdosta, GA," what was the reason he "failed to comply with orders to land"?

The "Medical Report of AF Aircraft Accident" document explained what occurred next, "He [Jones] called Tyndall Approach Control and was given a VHF/DF steer to return to TAFB [Tyndall AFB]."

POINT 7: TALLAHASSEE AIRPORT STEPS INTO THE PICTURE

Captain Harrison explained this segment, "Tyndall started giving him [Lt. Jones] steers since #819 couldn't read Tyndall, instructions were being relayed to Tallahassee tower." Harrison told Major Pompetti that "By working through Tallahassee Tower, which was able to read him, [Lt. Jones could not hear Tyndall AFB, but could hear Tallahassee Airport tower], we [Tyndall tower controllers] relayed headings and steers for him and Tallahassee relayed back information which Lt. Jones had to give."

Tallahassee Airport intervened and allegedly became the go-between communicators for Lt. Jones and Tyndall AFB tower controllers. Why were two USAF bases with the most advanced state-of-the-art equipment unable to communicate with their jet, yet a small airport in Tallahassee was able to have full communications with Lt. Jones?

What occurred approximately fifteen minutes later at 4:15 p.m. CST was never released to the public or the brothers of the two flyers in 1952.

POINT 8: 2ND LT. JONES DECLARES AN EMERGENCY

At 4:15 p.m. CST, pilot 2nd Lt. Jones declared an emergency to Tyndall AFB tower controllers.

This information was found in the 65 page case file in an "Extract from Air Rescue Service Report." This report was sent to "Maxwell AFB, dtd 24 Sept. 52 (to headquarters, Fifth Air Rescue Service), from Tyndall AFB, Panama City FL." It states, "At approximately 1615 C [4:15 p.m. CST]. 12 September, 819 [Lt. Jones] called Tyndall Tower and declared an emergency…"

Five days later after Tyndall AFB wrote this letter addressed to Maxwell AFB, Capt. Harrison answered the following question, addressed to him during the first board proceeding, "Q. Did the pilot at any time declare an emergency? A. No sir."

What was flight instructor Captain Harrison trying to hide from the board? The cover-up continues to unravel. Why did Lt. Jones declare an emergency at 4:15 p.m.? Why is there no record of what occurred at 4:15 p.m. that prompted Jones to declare an emergency? What occurred at 4:20 p.m. CST and afterward is the most convoluted segment of this incident?

B. T. Kleine, Colonel USAF commanding, Tyndall AFB stated the following in a letter to Lt. Jones brother, "He indicated that he was not sure of his position at 4:20, however, the Tyndall radio directional finding gave him a steer to Tyndall Air Force base."

The following information was contained in the "Report of AF Aircraft Accident" document, "At 1620 [4:20 p.m.] Tyndall Tower heard 0819 [Jones] calling Moody on channel 'B' and took a fix on him."

The report goes on to state, "The inbound steering to Tyndall AFB was 318-degrees." The following information concerning this segment of the incident transpired at the board meeting between Major Pompetti and S/Sgt. Bolen, "Q. [Pompetti] When you heard 819 calling Moody, after that you were able to hear transmissions, were they loud and clear or work?

A. [Bolen] They were very weak to start with. When he received our first steer of 318-degrees, from that point on - his volume would increase until it was four by four."

[NOTE: A four by four course refers to a radio range that beams on-course signals in four different directions.]

S/Sgt. Bolen also told the board that, "Tallahassee advised they were reading 819 loud and clear. Tyndall Tower relayed 318-degree steer through Tallahassee Tower. The aircraft acknowledged steer through Tallahassee."

There is not one word of information in the 65 page case report of Lt. Jones location at 4:20 p.m. when Tyndall "took a fix on him." At that time, Tyndall actually knew where the jet's location was. Why is there no information in the AF records about Lt. Jones location at 4:20 p.m.? Was the pilot really lost at that time or were the two airmen of jet 0819 on yet another mission? Why were Tyndall AFB officials being evasive?

POINT 9: FUEL CONSUMPTION OF JET #0819

At 4:20 p.m. CST, the USAF stated that Lt. Jones F-94 Starfire had "94 gals. of fuel left." The "Report of AF Aircraft Accident" document stated the amount of fuel that the jet had when Lt. Jones supposedly was redirected to Moody AFB at 3:35 p.m. It states, "It is assumed that 0819 [Jones] departed Tyndall AFB at 1535[3:35 p.m. CST] with 289 gallons of fuel aboard." By using these Air Force quotes, the following information can be formulated.

Tyndall AFB supposedly redirected Lt. Jones towards Moody AFB after he departed the Tyndall AFB area at 3:35 p.m. CST. At 4:20 p.m. CST, Lt. Jones was supposedly lost and redirected back towards Tyndall AFB. Tallahassee tower relayed information back and forth between Tyndall tower and the jet.

During that 45-minute time span between 3:35 p.m. and 4:20 p.m. CST, Lt. Jones jet used 195 gallons of fuel. Captain Harrison gave the following information in his statement dated "23 September 1952." He said, "The alternate I named was Moody AFB, Georgia. A distance of 139 nautical miles [160 statute miles] and would take 190 gallons of fuel from [Tyndall AFB] deck to reach if it were necessary."

Colonel B. T. Kleine stated the following information in his "17 September 1952" letter to Lt. Jones' brother, "all of the aircraft were called to come back to the [Tyndall AFB] field. Supervisory personnel in the Central Tower advised John and three other aircraft to go to Moody Air Force Base about 15 minutes north of Tyndall."

By combining Capt. Harrison's information together with Colonel Kleine's information, an F-94B would consume 190 gallons of fuel over a distance of 160 statute miles in about 15 minutes, from Tyndall AFB to Moody AFB.

The September 17 Tyndall teletype stated, "1620 CST [4:20 p.m. CST] pilot called in with 94 gals." The "Report of AF Aircraft Accident" document stated, "0819 had 94 gals. of fuel left. This information was relayed by Tallahassee Tower because 0819 could not read Tyndall Tower."

Lt. Jones jet consumed almost the same amount of fuel — 195 gallons, yet he was in the air for 45 minutes between 3:35 p.m. and 4:20 p.m. CST.

How was Lt. Jones Starfire able to stay in the air for 45 minutes on approximately 15 minutes worth of fuel? Why did the USAF have to assume that #0819 had "289 gallons of fuel onboard" at 3:35 p.m.?

At 4:20 p.m. CST, Lt. Jones was in an emergency situation over land and just northwest of Tyndall on a 318- degree bearing.

According to Tyndall Tower controller S/Sgt. Bolen, Jones had acknowledged the 318-degree steer from Tallahassee Tower from Tyndall Tower. S/Sgt. Bolen stated the following, "At this time tower contacted Jacksonville control and advised of the situation. Also called Florida State Police to patrol the area between Tyndall and Apalachicola vicinity." S/Sgt. Bolen also stated, "Jacksonville had alerted rescue facilities."

POINT 10: LT. JONES DECLARES ANOTHER EMERGENCY

One minute later at 4:21 p.m. CST, Tyndall AFB relayed a message to Tallahassee Airport who in turn contacted Lt. Jones. The "Report of AF Aircraft Accident" document stated the following, "At 1621C [4:21 p.m.] a second bearing of 320-degrees was given by Tyndall AFB."

The Tyndall AFB "Direction Finding Log" also disclosed more information of what occurred at 4:21 p.m. CST. At that time, the log recorded that Lt. Jones had declared another emergency. The D/F log states, "A/C IDENT-0819. COURSE - 320. TIME - 1621. REMARKS - EB EMER. [Emergency]."

This was the second emergency declared by Jones in six minutes. The first was at 4:15 p.m. CST. At approximately 4:21 p.m., Tyndall tower controllers were steering the jet on a 320-degree course toward their base when the emergency was declared. Lt. Jones was actually on a southeast trajectory near Tyndall AFB when the USAF said he declared the emergency situation. What occurred between 4:21 p.m. and the supposed last contact with the jet at 4:42 p.m. is an absolute travesty. Lt. Jones and Lt. DelCurto never landed at Tyndall AFB, overshot the base, and continued proceeding southeast. The two flyers passed over the area between Tyndall AFB and just west of Apalachicola. This is the stretch of coastline where S/Sgt. Bolen referenced when the Tyndall Tower allegedly "called Florida State Police to patrol area between Tyndall and the Apalachacola vicinity." Jones and DelCurto never attempted to crash-land their jet along this stretch of land either. They continued proceeding southeast, passed over the coastline, and proceeded out over the Gulf of Mexico.

Why did Jones and DelCurto not land at Tyndall AFB? Tyndall Tower supposedly contacted the Florida State Police. The police were informed to patrol between Tyndall and the Apalachacola vicinity for the jet if it went down along that stretch of coastline.

Tyndall Tower controllers therefore must have instructed Lt. Jones to make an emergency landing between those two points. Why did Jones not crash land along the coastline on land between Tyndall AFB and Apalachacola? Did Jones actually declare an emergency at 4:21 p.m. because he was preparing for a crash landing? Why did Jones continue proceeding southeast over the Gulf waters with only about 90 gallons of fuel left?

POINT 11: THE WEATHER

Jones and DelCurto were on a northwest to southeast trajectory, proceeding across the Gulf of Mexico, when their bearing was changed back to 318-degrees by Tyndall. The "Statement of Weather Officer," by Oran E. Need, Captain USAF gave the following information. On 26 September 1952 Captain Need stated, "This is our stability chart valid for today, 12 September 1952, which shows very unstable air over the entire local area, state of Florida and most of Georgia and South Carolina, with the flow being from SE to NW. We expect thunderstorm activity over that entire area and shower activity. At 1230C, 12 September, Suntan, which controls the radar operations at this base [Tyndall], is painting solid thunderstorms from 35 miles SE of the station due East for 120 miles throughout the entire SE quadrant approximately 120 miles." Captain Need also stated, "The greater percent of the weather is well to the south and southwest of your alternate, which is Moody, and will not affect your alternate since the flow is to the NW."

Jones and DelCurto were actually flying through and into the direction of the oncoming weather. Why didn't Tyndall AFB controllers turn Lt. Jones around and redirect him back towards their base? Why did Tyndall let the jet proceed across the Gulf waters when the jet was low on fuel? Lt. Jones continued to proceed southeast across the Gulf waters when another Air Force base intervened into the situation, MacDill AFB in Tampa.

The very evasive Captain Harrison answered the following question when asked by Major Pompetti and the board, "Q. At what time did MacDill start working him [Jones]? A. I would say it must have been around 1625 [4:25 p.m. CST] because we were giving him, [Lt. Jones] steers through Tallahassee on 'B' channel. All of a sudden he switched to 'C' channel – someone else was working him."

1st Lt. Dunn also made this statement in his signed certificate, "Aircraft switched from 'B' channel to 'C' and started working MacDill."

Captain Harrison was also evasive and vague when he made his official "statement" on "23 September 1952" concerning this incident. He also forgot that he answered "No Sir" to the board when he was asked, "Did the pilot at any time declare an emergency?"

His statement concerning this segment of the incident when MacDill took over is as follows. Harrison stated, "Tyndall started giving him 'steers' since #819 couldn't read Tyndall, instructions were being relayed by Tallahassee Tower. At this time, the tower alerted Jacksonville control of the emergency. About this time, McDill (sic) AFB started working #819 and the Tyndall tower was unable to read any further transmissions from #819. What happened after this time was relayed to Tyndall Tower from McDill (sic) AFB." [End Statement]

Signed Phillip P. Harrison - Captain, USAF.

Besides First Lt. Dunn's questionable answer, concerning the time that MacDill took over and began to steer Jones, there is no official documentation recording the time.

Another document contained within the 65-page case file states the following information, "Extract from Air Rescue Service Report, Maxwell AFB, dated 24 September 1952." It states:

A) "819 was given steer of 318-degrees to Tyndall, no time." [No time entered on the log for steer given]

B) "At approximately the same time, MacDill AFB also gave him a steer of 120-degrees to MacDill, no time logged for the steer."

C) "At 1635C [4:35 p.m.], MacDill gave 819 a confirmed class 'A' steer 104-degrees to MacDill; at 1637C [4:37 p.m.], a second bearing of 112-degrees was given."

The information contained in these extracts is very odd. The B. Information extract gives no time for the first MacDill steer of 120-degrees. The information contained in the C. extract does not even recognize the first steer of 120-degrees.

THE FOLLOWING MAP SHOWS AN OUTLINE OF THE LOST AIRMEN'S FLIGHT PATH

THE LOCATIONS OF THE FOUR AIR FORCE BASES AND AIRPORT INVOLVED IN THE INCIDENT ARE LISTED BELOW:

A. MOODY AFB. - VALDOSTA, GEORGIA

B. TALLAHASSEE AIRPORT, FLORIDA

C. TYNDALL AFB. - PANAMA CITY, FLORIDA

D. MACDILL AFB. - TAMPA, FLORIDA

E. EGLIN AFB. - VALPARAISO, FLORIDA

A map displaying the steers that MacDill gave is identified as "mission 5-C-9-12 SEP 52 — (SUSP)" is as follows, [NOTE; MacDill is spelled incorrectly]:
1. "steer of 120 degrees given by McDill – 1" [no time logged]
2. "steer of 112 degrees given by McDill – 2" [4:37 p.m. CST]
3. "steer of 109 degrees given by McDill – 3" [4:41 p.m. CST]
4. "steer of 104 degrees given by McDill – 4" [4:35 p.m. CST]

"bearing of 318 degrees given by Tyndall"

NOTE: The 318-degree bearing given by Tyndall AFB was the southeast trajectory that Jones followed out over the Gulf of Mexico.

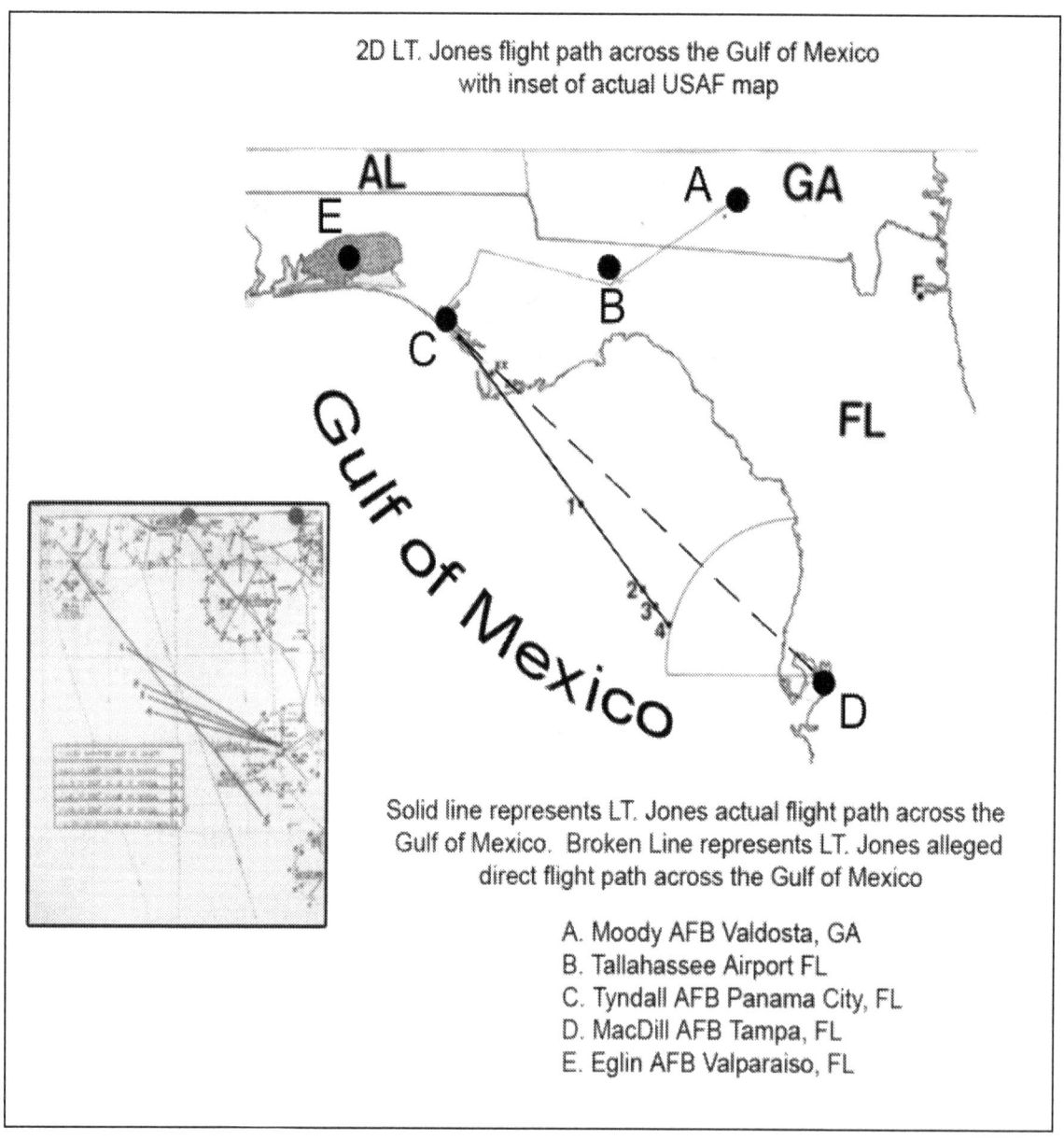

2D LT. Jones flight path across the Gulf of Mexico with inset of actual USAF map

Solid line represents LT. Jones actual flight path across the Gulf of Mexico. Broken Line represents LT. Jones alleged direct flight path across the Gulf of Mexico

A. Moody AFB Valdosta, GA
B. Tallahassee Airport FL
C. Tyndall AFB Panama City, FL
D. MacDill AFB Tampa, FL
E. Eglin AFB Valparaiso, FL

On the map, the 318-degree bearing is represented by the solid line between C. Tyndall AFB and number the #4 point, the 104-degree steer given by MacDill AFB.
This map also shows all the locations for the four steers, 1, 2, 3 and 4 along the solid line, the 318-degree bearing line. This solid line shows the plotted first steer, 1. "steer of 120 -degrees given by MacDill" to Lt. Jones. The location of the first steer; 1. Steer of 120-degrees that was given by

MacDill AFB is 100 statute miles southeast of Tyndall AFB. This point is actually less than half the distance between C. Tyndall AFB and D. MacDill AFB.
The broken flight path line on the map illustrates a direct flight path from C. Tyndall AFB, in Panama City to D. MacDill AFB in Tampa. The distance along this flight path is approximately 245 miles.

Captain Harrison told Major Pompetti this segment of the incident concerning MacDill's takeover from Tyndall AFB, "By working through Tallahassee Tower, which was able to read him, we relayed headings and steers for him [Lt. Jones] and Tallahassee relayed back information which Lt. Jones had to give. MacDill then started working since he seemed to be closer to them."

Air Defense Commander, General Chidlaw stated the following in his Western Union telegram to Lt. Jones brother on Sept. 15, 1952, "The Tyndall Tower was directing him to MacDill AFB FLO, which was the nearest base."

Tyndall AFB Colonel B. T. Kleine stated the following in his letter, "The Tyndall radio directional finding gave him a steer to Tyndall AFB. MacDill Air Force Base directional finding [Homer] was able to pick up John's voice and gave him a steer also." Captain Harrison stated, "MacDill started working him [Jones] since he seemed to be closer to them?"

MacDill tower controllers gave Jones his first steer when he was only 100 miles southeast of Tyndall. In contrast, the jet was 145 statute miles northwest of MacDill in Tampa. Why didn't they redirect the flyers back to Tyndall field, which was closer?

Captain Harrison said in his statement, "The alternate I named was Moody AFB, Georgia, a distance of 139 Naut. miles [160 statute miles] and would take 190 gallons of fuel from the [Tyndall] deck to reach…" Once again, by using Harrison's numbers in this statement to approximate fuel consumption and distance, how could Lt. Jones Starfire have reached MacDill AFB in Tampa from Tyndall AFB, approximately 245 statute miles away, on about 94 gallons of fuel? Lt. Jones jet would not have even come close to reaching the half waypoint across the Gulf of Mexico to MacDill in Tampa.

Furthermore, the jet was said to have disappeared approximately 70 miles northwest of MacDill AFB, an area approximately 175 miles away from Tyndall.

On September 13, *The Tampa Tribune* article reported, "MacDill said the fighter could have been anywhere up to 70 miles northwest of Tampa at the last radio report." MacDill Public Information officers stated, "The plane's position at the time of the last message was unknown, except that it was northwest of Tampa and probably within 70 miles of here [Tampa]." Lt. Jones jet obviously had more than 94 gallons of fuel left at 4:20 p.m., shortly before he crossed out over the Gulf waters near Apalachacola on his 318-degree bearing. The "Direction Finding Log" shows the "course" for "0819" at "1631" or 4:31 p.m. CST was still "318."

According to the Air Force map that illustrates the four-plotted steers that MacDill gave the jet, the point nearest to MacDill is the number "4" steer.

This plotted location of the jet indicates that it was approximately 70 miles northwest of MacDill. This indicates the farthest point that the jet reached along its southeast flight path toward Tampa on its 318-degree bearing given by Tyndall AFB. On the map, I illustrate an arc that represents the 70-mile point from MacDill AFB, in Tampa. Why is the time at this point documented by the Air Force as 4:35 p.m. CST? The jet allegedly flamed-out at 4:42 p.m. CST. Furthermore, the previous steer, the number "3" steer, is documented at 4:41 p.m. CST. This plotted location indicates the jet at a point approximately 80 miles northwest of MacDill at a later time, six minutes later. The number "2" steer, just before the number "3" steer, documents a time of 4:37 p.m. CST at a distance of 90 miles away from MacDill in Tampa.

The plotted points indicate the following information:

A.) Plot 4. When Jones was nearest to MacDill AFB along his southeast trajectory, approximately 70 miles from Tampa, he turned back northeast at 4:35 p.m. CST. (104-degree steer)
B.) Plot 2. Lt. Jones proceeded approximately 20 miles northwest of MacDill to an area about 90 miles away from Tampa at 4:37 p.m. CST. (112-degree steer)
C.) Plot 3. Jones then redirected southeast once again and proceeded 10 miles. Four minutes later, at 4:41 p.m. CST the pilot was approximately 80 miles from MacDill in Tampa. (109-degree steer)

Why was Lt. Jones going back and forth when he should have been continuing towards Tampa to land at MacDill AFB? Why did he redirect away from Tampa at 4:35 p.m., when this was the nearest he came to the base and the coastline? Jones' 318-degree bearing was never aligned with the direct path to MacDill in the first place. Even those outside Military and Aviation institutions are obviously aware that the shortest distance between two points is a straight line. This logic however was not employed this fateful day.

The following information comes from the transcript between Approach Controller S/Sgt. Bolen and the board, "Q. Did you ever hear 819 transmit to MacDill on any channel? A. I did not. Q. Did anyone else in the [Tyndall] tower? A. Not to my knowledge. Q. At this time you were on B channel. A. D/F was still on B channel. The aircraft then flamed out as I was advised by Tallahassee tower. I believe Lt. Dunn received that transmission on C. Q. From the aircraft? A. Yes — from the aircraft. MacDill then gave the aircraft a steer of 109-degree to a point of nearest land. Q. Where did you get that information? A. That was given [to] me by Tallahassee Tower. That was all the contact with the aircraft. We had several advisories at the time from their operations–Captain Gillette and Captain Harrison – as to emergency procedure to be given [to] the aircraft. I relayed information to Tallahassee and MacDill to attempt contact or transmission in the blind 819."

POINT 12: LT JONES AND THE EMERGENCY FREQUENCY CHANNEL – "D" CHANNEL

The Aircraft Accident Investigating Board asked First Lt. Dunn the following question that concerned the emergency "D" channel. "Q. At any time during this incident, did you or anyone else instruct #819 to switch to 'D' channel? A. No – Not to my knowledge," answered Dunn.

S/Sgt. Bolen gave a contradicting statement concerning the "D" channel situation. Major Pompetti and the board asked the following questions of S/Sgt. Bolen concerning the "D" channel, "Q. There was no advice to him [Lt. Jones] to switch to D channel? A. He had only switched to D channel once and there was no contact at all. Q. Who told him to go to D channel? A. I'm not sure who told him as we were unable to contact the aircraft. Q. Did you hear this yourself or did someone tell you about it later? A. No. It was over plan 62 [plan 62, a term used in Military Air Transport Service to Designate a Specific Communication System for transmitting messages regarding the movement of aircraft]. There was no conversation addressed to me. I heard people talking among themselves —Tallahassee Tower and others. I am not sure who they were. Q. They mentioned for him to go to D channel and he never heard them? A. Right. B. Channel was the best working frequency at Tyndall that day."

Approach Control officer 1st Lt. Dunn, and approach controller S/Sgt. Bolen were in the same control room at Tyndall tower during this time. Yet both men gave different information about Lt. Jones being advised to switch to the emergency "D" channel. Why were the two controllers unaware what was going on with their own jet? Why were these two men so unaware in what was going on in their own control room? Who were the other people involved in this incident that Bolen was unable to identify? Why didn't S/Sgt. Bolen make an inquiry to the "others" and find out who they were?

Were the unknown people involved in the incident who were said to have advised Jones to switch to "D" channel fabricated by S/Sgt. Bolen? At this point in the incident, was Lt. Jones really in an emergency situation or was he involved in another situation? Why didn't Jones declare an emergency situation during this time in the incident when he was flying back and forth over the Gulf of Mexico?

POINT 13: JET #0819- THREE FLAME-OUT TIMES

    Captain Harrison explained the flame-out segment of the incident to the board. He stated, "When he got low on fuel, I gave instructions to turn him 90-degrees towards land and when he reached 5,000 ft, bail out. That was the last we heard."

    There were actually three recorded times that Lt. Jones jet was said to have flamed-out. These times were all contained in the 65-page case file report. The entire list of documentation is as follows:

1.) 4:42 p.m.. Extract from Flight Service Center – Daily Operational Log, Maxwell AFB dated 12 September 1952. **"At 1642 pilot stated he had just flamed out and was preparing to bail out."**

2.) 4:34 p.m.. Airways and Air Communications Service — 1922 AACS Squadron, Tyndall AFB, FL. Date. 12 September 1952 **"1634 A/C [aircraft] flamed out."**

3.) 4:34 p.m. Tyndall AFB Telegram — Preliminary Report of a Major Accident – Aircraft Missing. Sep 13 – 9:04. **"Pilot said he had flamed out at 1634."**

4.) The official "Report of AF Aircraft Accident," actually gave two different times that the jet flamed out within their same report. 1. 4:34 p.m.. "Section – General Information. Missing Aircraft Report…5. Hour and Time Zone: **1634 CST**…Duration of Flight since last takeoff: 2 + 26." [2 hours + 26 minutes=2:08 CST until 4:34 p.m. CST]. The second time in this report; "Section O. Description of Accident…MacDill D/F heard him say at 1642C that he flamed out and was at 15,000 ft., still in weather and preparing to bail out. **"4:42 p.m. CST."**

5.) 4:34 p.m. CST. Medical Report of AF Aircraft Accident. "Time of Accident. 1634 CST…**At 1634 he reported a flameout**…Length of use: 2:30 Hrs." [2 hours +30 minutes]

6.) 4:42 p.m. Extract from Ltr. to Flight Service Hq., Washington D.C., from Flight Service Center, Maxwell AFB, dtd 16 September 52. "At **1742E**, the pilot stated that he had a flameout and was preparing to jump."

7.) 4:34 p.m. Tyndall AFB Telegram – Ref 11 - #9/47z. 17 September 1952. "1620 CST P/T called in with 94 gals, **flamed out at 1634 CST."**

8.) 4:37 p.m.. AACS, Tyndall AFB – "CERTIFICATE" by 1st Lt. Robert A. Dunn, Approach Controller. 18 Sep. 52. "Overheard pilot to say **he 'flamed-out' at 1637."**

9.) 4:42 p.m. Extract from Air Rescue Service Report, Maxwell AFB, dtd 24 Sept 1952. **"At 1642C, 819 reported out of fuel** at 15,000 ft IFR."

10.) 4:42 p.m.. Letter. HQ 3625 FTW – Tyndall AFB. Joseph E. Wisby – Major USAF Flying Safety Officer. "The accident occurred on 12 September 1952 at approximately **1642 hours** Central Standard Time."

    Why were there three different times stated for the jet's flameout? The alleged flameout was caused because of the jet being out of fuel, which could only occur once. Why was the USAF unable to keep track of its own story? How much of this story was a fabrication and when did the jet actually flameout? Why did Major Pompetti and the board fail to address the matter concerning the three different times during their two meetings?

    The following information was released at the Sept. 12 press conference in Tampa shortly after the jet vanished, "The last radio sound indicated the disabled craft was down to 8,000 ft," Captain Mitchell said. The time was 5:42 p.m. [EST/4:42 p.m. CST]. Captain Mitchell also stated, "The plane was apparently lost, and Air Force officials speculated that its radio compass had failed."

Captain Harrison was asked the following question by the board, "Q. After he called 'Flame-out,' did you get another call from him? A. No – the only information we got was from MacDill. I believe they were the last to hear from him at 8,000 ft."

It is very interesting to note, that at the end of flight instructor Captain Harrison's questioning he was asked. "Q. Would you care to voice your opinion as to what brought about this accident?" "A. No Sir." Harrison answered.

Why didn't Harrison care to voice his opinion as to what brought about the accident? He was the flight instructor in charge of the "B flight" that day and should have known every move being made. He should have known what brought about the accident and been able to voice an opinion…unless he was covering up what actually occurred.

Was Captain Harrison being evasive when he wrote his "Statement," concerning the times involved in the Jones and DelCurto incident? These are some of his quotes.

1. "At that time."
2. "at that time"
3. "by this time"
4. "At this time"
5. "At this time"
6. "About this time"
7. "after this time"

At any time, did Captain Harrison know what was going on during this incident?

The following quotes were taken from Harrison's answers, during the "September 29 board meeting."

1. "About that time"
2. "at that time"
3. "About this time"
4. "at that time"
5. "At one time"
6. "I cannot remember exactly…"
7. "I think he based it…"
8. "At one time we found him [Jones] where he was…"
9. "I don't know…"
10. "I don't remember"

Was flight instructor Captain Harrison hiding the truth from Major Pompetti and the board during his questioning? Harrison was not the only one who gave the runaround to Pompetti and the board members during the first board meeting. The following answers were given by 1st Lt. Dunn.

1. "Not that I remember."
2. "There must have been…"
3. "I can't be sure"
4. "I would say it must have been around…"
5. "No–not to my knowledge."

When the Investigating Board re-convened on October 3, 1952, they interviewed Approach Controller, S/Sgt. Bolen. The following quotes were taken from Bolen's answers when the board questioned him during this second fact finding meeting.

1. "sometime later…"
2. "At this time"
3. "No sir – I do not remember."
4. "I am not sure…"

5. "I could not say."
6. "Not to my knowledge."
7. "I am not certain."
8. "I am unable to say."

These three men, Harrison, Dunn and Bolen, were all in the Tyndall Tower during the Jones and DelCurto incident. Do their quotes reflect sincere honest answers, or were these men hiding something that involved a cover-up? Why were these men being evasive?

Did the Air Force fabricate the Jones and DelCurto incident as a cover story and coerce the Tyndall Tower men into using it to hide the truth? Would the Air Force go to the extent of fixing all of their official reports to cover-up another story? Would this explain all the inconsistencies in their documentation of this incident?

Why did the Air Force have such a difficult time in keeping track of their story concerning the missing aviators? Did the Air Force silence everyone involved in this incident? Why were there only three men from Tyndall AFB questioned by the Aircraft Accident Investigating Board, when so many people were involved? More people being questioned meant more inconsistencies.

Would the Air Force also go to the extent of doctoring up Lt. Jones military records and actually downgrading the missing pilot?

The "Medical Report of an Individual - Involved in AF Aircraft Accident" talked about Jones in the "Personal Factors (pilot or crew member only)" section of their report. John Jones graduated from "Advanced Single - Engine Pilot Training Course" on May 10, 1952 at Vance AFB, OH. He went to Moody AFB for "jet transition training" then reassigned to Tyndall AFB for "All-Weather Jet Interceptor Training." This document states, "At the time of the accident total time was 290:30 hrs." The "Report of AF Aircraft Accident" document states the "Total Pilot Hours" at "292:55," a time difference of two hours and twenty-five minutes.

The "Medical Report of an Individual" states, "He had approximately 2:45 hours of weather time," while the "Report of AF Aircraft Accident" states, "Total 1st pilot Instrument Weather Hours — 5:10." This is a time difference of three hours and five minutes. The "Medical Report of an Individual" states that Jones had "56 hours" of flying time in "jet-type aircraft." The "Report of AF Aircraft Accident" states, "Type and model 1st pilot experience in similar aircraft: T-33A – 52:00 and F–80B – 4:55" hours. This is a total of 56:55 hours, a time difference of 55 minutes from the other report.

The "Medical Report of an Individual" states that Jones had "70 hours of hood time." The "Report of AF Aircraft Accident" document states Jones hood times, including weather and hood times as, "21:35, 26:45, 25:00" for a total of 73:20 hours; a time difference of 3 hours and 20 minutes from the other report. Why these inconsistencies in Jones' flight record? Which documented times are correct? Moreover, are any of these documented times correct or were they all tampered with?

The "Report of AF Aircraft Accident" document states in the "General Information" section; "HOUR AND TIME ZONE" of the accident was "1634 CST" or 4:34 p.m. CST. In another section of the document, "Description of Accident" it states, "MacDill D/F heard him say at 1642C [4:42 CST] that he had a flame-out and was at 15,000 feet, still in weather and preparing to bail out." These two times in the same document show a time difference of 8 minutes for the same accident.

The "Report of AF Aircraft Accident" document states the length of the flight as follows, "Duration of Flight since last takeoff: 2 + 26 [2 hrs = 26 minutes]."

The "Medical Report of AF Accident Report" states, "Length of use: 2:30 Hrs [2 hours/30 minutes]," a time difference of four minutes.

Medical examiner, Captain Leo Jivoff, wrote the following in Lt. Jones "Medical Report of an Individual" that was dated "8 Oct 52." Jivoff states, "Early in the accident flight he [Jones] was faced with an emergency situation requiring the use of the pitot heat button. He did not know where it was and was told by another student via radio."

First off, was Captain Jivoff possibly trying to type the words "pilot heat button"?

Secondly, Lt. Jones was allegedly unable to find this "pilot heat button" when he was faced with an emergency situation, early in the accident flight. Lt. Jones did not declare his first emergency until "1615C" or 4:15 CST," when he called Tyndall Tower and declared an emergency…two hours and eight minutes into his flight." His flight only lasted another 18-26 minutes longer, depending on which AF document is used as reference. Jones was near the end of his flight when he declared his first emergency situation, not "Early in the accident flight."

Furthermore, why is there no record of this "emergency situation" that supposedly occurred during the early part of Jones' flight? Why was this point never raised at the investigating board proceedings? Thirdly, what type of emergency situation arose that required the use of the "pitot heat button"? The only other emergency situation occurred five minutes after the first emergency. It was documented at 4:21 p.m. CST.

Point #4 involves the "student" who allegedly told Jones "via radio" where the "pitot heat button" was during the alleged emergency. Who was this "student" and why is there no record of the "student" in any Air Force documents and no record of a name?

Was this entire statement by Jivoff a complete fabrication to degrade Second Lt. Jones to make him appear incompetent?

The "Medical Report of An Individual -Involved in AF Aircraft Accident" was written by Jivoff and dated "8 Oct 52." This document was actually dated five days after the final Aircraft Accident Investigating Board proceeding ended.

Also contained in this report within the "Personal Factors" section of this document is information about Lt. Jones background and progress.

The Air Force made the following statement about Lt. Jones, "He was a quiet, retiring individual who always kept himself in the background and did not mix with other pilots…He never visited the officers' club and preferred going to movies alone. No one knew him well." The Air Force also stated, "The impression of his [Jones] fellow students was that he was always visibly tense and apprehensive of flying and that he lacked self confidence."

The Air Force documented the unsubstantiated impressions of fellow students who portrayed Jones in a negative manner even though "no one knew him well." Why was the Air Force documenting degrading accounts from unnamed sources about Lt. Jones? Furthermore, if Jones was "apprehensive of flying," then why was he in the USAF flying planes and jets?

The Air Force also gave the following unsubstantiated account of Lt. Jones. One fellow student who knew him for 15 months and had been through pilot training with him said, "I wouldn't fly with him. He was uncoordinated, tense, responded poorly in emergencies and could not make decisions. He was even tense in B-25 aircraft and would grip his hands so tightly on controls that his knuckles would be white." Once again, the USAF made allegations about Lt. Jones incompetence as a pilot by using unnamed sources…students.

Why did the USAF intentionally go out of their way to degrade Lt. Jones and repeatedly make accusations about his flying? Why did the USAF permit Lt. Jones to fly aircraft if he was so incompetent?

This same document also gives accounts of Lt. Jones flying progress during the previous days leading up to his last flight. It includes information about his other flight missions including "interceptor missions in B-25" aircraft and his F-94 transition flights. The Air Force continually showed Lt Jones' weak points in this document and actually stated, "This officer verbalized less than the average student but had expressed dislike for jet fighter aircraft."

The Air Force even stated the following assertion, "On the day before the accident he verbalized his doubts in his abilities to fly the [F-94B] aircraft." This statement seems absolutely absurd. Who were the persons that Lt. Jones allegedly verbalized to, when he made these statements?

The Air Force gave a summary of Lt. Jones progress during these days prior to his disappearance.

It states, "The following is an instructors' summary of pilots' progress, 'This student had difficulty on landings with the F-94. He tried to force the aircraft on the runway [8 September 1952], which resulted in a hard landing, porpoising and ran off the runway damaging the tire on the aircraft. He was given a check ride in the T-33 [trainer jet] and it was unsatisfactory due to his poor judgment and his inability to think ahead of the aircraft. He was given another check ride, the following day, which was satisfactory, and it was recommended that he be given more transition in the F-94. He was transitioned again and completed eight very satisfactory traffic patterns and landings.'"

On September 11, the day before Jones and DelCurto vanished the following was said to have occurred, "On 11 September 1952 subject officer was given a check ride in a T-33 because of unsatisfactory performance on the previous day. At this time he completed 8 transition landings satisfactory."

The Air Force also stated what was said to have happened on September 12, 1952. This report states, "On the day of the accident, during B-25 interceptor mission pilot [Lt. Jones] again was noted to be slow in executing commands and demonstrated other weaknesses (i.e. 'range weak, could not hold altitude, let heading drift, airspeed control weak')."

According to the "Report of AF Aircraft Accident" document, the "primary Duty Assignment" of Lt. Jones was a "Stu Plt (Grad)," student pilot graduate. His "Organizational Assignment" was Hq ADC, Ent AFB, Colorado."

Second Lt. John DelCurto's "Organizational Assignment" was "ARTC, CTAF, 3626 Fly Tng Gp (AI) Tyndall AFB Fla. This translates as follows, Air Training Command, Crew Training Air Force, 3626 Flying Training Group (Advanced Interceptor) Tyndall Air Force Base Florida.

Why is there not one word in the 65-page report case file about DelCurto's participation during the incident? Jones and DelCurto were both members of the "3626 Flying Training Wing-Advanced Interceptor," yet there is no mention of DelCurto's involvement in any of the Air Force documents. The "Medical Report of an Individual - Involved in AF Aircraft Accident" concluded the following, "It appears that this officer's [Lt. Jones] relative incompetence, apprehension and inability to handle emergency situations were the prime factors in this accident."

Medical Officer Leo Jivoff, Capt. USAF, stated the following in the "Medical Officer's Recommendations" section of Jones,' "Medical Report of AF Aircraft Accident." He stated, "Recommend that student pilots be screened prior to an assignment to high performance jet aircraft performing All Weather Interceptor Mission in attempt to remove 'minimum satisfactory' students and those apprehensive of this type aircraft and mission." What kind of mission was Jones actually involved in.

Was 2nd Lt. John A. Jones Jr. actually a "minimum satisfactory" pilot as stated by the USAF? Were the prime factors in the Jones and DelCurto accident caused by Jones "relative incompetence," apprehension and inability to handle emergencies? Right up to the day that Jones and DelCurto vanished, the USAF claimed that Jones had several unsatisfactory flight performances.

The Air Force made several unsubstantiated degrading statements about him and portrayed him in a very negative way. The Air Force made it appear as though Lt. Jones was struggling right up to the day he stepped into the cockpit with DelCurto. Jones was also said to have "verbalized his doubts in his abilities to fly the [F-94B] aircraft on September 11, 1952 on the day before the accident."

The Air Force made the following assertions in this case report.

1. "This officer [2nd Lt. Jones] verbalized less than the average student but had expressed dislike for jet fighter aircraft."

2. "The following is an instructors' summary of pilots' progress, 'This student had difficulty on landings with the F-94. He tried to force the aircraft on the runway [8 September 1952], which resulted in a hard landing, porpoising and ran off the runway damaging the tire on the aircraft.

3. "On the day before the accident he verbalized his doubts in his abilities to fly the [F-94B] aircraft."

4. "On 11 September 1952 subject officer was given a check ride in a T-33 because of unsatisfactory performance on the previous day. At this time he completed 8 transition landings satisfactory."

5. "On the day of the accident, during B-25 interceptor mission pilot [Lt. Jones] again was noted to be slow in executing commands and demonstrated other weaknesses (i.e. 'range weak, could not hold altitude, let heading drift, airspeed control weak')."

I now ask the following questions about this incident.

1. If Jones was a "minimum satisfactory" pilot who doubted his own abilities to fly the F-94 jet and was having problems, then why was he put into the cockpit with a student radar operator with less experience?

2. Why was trainee 2nd Lt. DelCurto in the cockpit with 2nd Lt. Jones instead of a skilled flight instructor who's job it is to transitions student pilots, especially student pilots who are said to be having difficulties?

3. Why is there no mention in the 65-page Aircraft Accident report case file about 2nd Lt. John DelCurto's participation in this disastrous incident?

At the end of the transcript for the Oct 3, 1952 Aircraft Accident Investigating Board proceeding, the board stated, "After a discussion of all evidence in file and all testimony, the following conclusions were reached by the board." These conclusions also appeared in the "Report of AF Aircraft Accident" document as well, "FINDINGS: The primary cause of this accident was that the pilot failed to keep himself oriented at all times while on instruments." It states:

CONTRIBUTING CAUSE FACTORS:
1. Pilot failed to exercise proper emergency facilities available to him.
2. Tyndall Tower failing to properly advise the pilot to declare an emergency and go to the emergency channel "D" channel)."

Was Lt. Jones incompetent or were the Air Force controllers on the ground incompetent? Did the USAF actually use Second Lt. John A. Jones Jr. as the scapegoat? The Aircraft Accident Investigating Board ended their investigation with their recommendations.

They stated:

RECOMMENDATIONS:
1. That this accident be brought to the attention of all pilots, informing them that in case they were confused on orientation and their status of fuel was such as to place them in emergency condition, they should not hesitate to go to 'D' channel and declare an emergency.

2. The emphasis be placed on using the radio compass in the loop position to overcome the effects of thunderstorm activity and/or static.

3. That the Tower personnel be reminded that in case of an emergency or suspected emergency that the pilot be advised to utilize his emergency procedures, specifically switching to 'D' channel and also advising him of further navigational aids that may be utilized by him."

The "AUTHENTICATION" section was signed by the members of the board at the end of the report, but there was a discrepancy. In this section, there is a rebuttal area segment, where conclusions can be refuted. The following segments were marked off in boxes.

"1. X. Personnel Responsible for this Accident have been offered opportunity of Rebuttal." The word "tower" was typed above the word "personnel" in this area. "X. Rebuttal Statement attached"

"2. Personnel Responsible Not Available Because of: X. Death. X. Other (Explain) [typed-in] Missing - Presumed dead." Dead men tell no tales.

The "REBUTTAL STATEMENT" was dated "6 October 1952" and signed by A. J. Vickers - Captain, USAF - Tower Officer-In-Charge. It states:

Reference item 2 under Contributing Cause Factors on AF Form 14, at the time was ascertained that an emergency existed [and] the aircraft was not within range of the Tyndall Towers Transmitter. Furthermore, declaration of emergency rests entirely with the pilot, and his usage of radio frequencies is to be determined by existing conditions. If his emergency can be satisfactory handled on a frequency other than "D" channel, his channel of first contact is normally used.

AT the time Tyndall Tower heard #819 calling Moody Approach Control, contact was attempted with the aircraft with no success. After this time further contact was made through relay of Tallahassee Tower and in such condition, it is felt that all traffic be held to a minimum to lessen error in relay."

It is obvious that Capt. Harrison, 1st Lt. Dunn and S/Sgt. Bolen all spoke the same evasive language as Captain Vickers, the Tower officer-in-charge. In Vickers short rebuttal statement, he does not give any times to use as reference points that would indicate Lt. Jones location. He only states:

1. "At the time"
2. "At the time"
3. "After this time."

All four-tower men were fluent in this evasive time tactic-speak. Why did all of them intentionally avoid stating the locations and times of the jet during this incident?

Did the Air Force contrive the timeline of events in this incident to make it appear as though Jones was lost? Jones did declare two emergencies that were documented by the Air Force. The first emergency occurred at 4:15 p.m. CST. The second emergency occurred at 4:21 p.m. CST. The Air Force never disclosed the jets' locations during those times either. If the Air Force had pinpointed the jets' locations along with the times, it was over those specific areas that would have shown their timeline as incorrect. Is this why Captain Harrison made a statement like, "at one time we found him where he was…"

On "5 January 1953," Vickers' rebuttal was granted by command of the chief of staff via a letter to the "Commanding General, ATC - Scott AFB, Illinois."

This letter opens by stating, "Reference is made to the major aircraft accident involving F-94B, serial # 50-819A, which occurred on 12 September 1952. Wreckage of the aircraft has not located to date."

In part it states, "This office does not concur with the finding of Tyndall Tower failing to properly advise the pilot to declare an emergency and go to the emergency (D channel), as a contributing excuse factor to this accident. This factor has been deleted as a contributing cause to this accident," signed – Thomas C. Marbin – Major General US Air Force – Acting Deputy Inspector General. Had the Norton AFB officials finally been told the cover story? When this contributing factor was deleted from the official record, there was only one contributing cause factor remaining, "1. Pilots failure to exercise emergency facilities available to him."

Tyndall Tower was cleared of being incompetent and the full blame was put on Second Lt. John A. Jones Jr. Blame it on the dead man. In closing this chapter, I would like to mention two documents that have reference code tabs attached to them. These documents are labeled "RE-1 1342." Both documents are signed with the initials "ASA" and do not bear any other identifying name on them. What are interesting in both of these documents are the handwritten notes that appear on them signed by "ASA." The first document is a "BASIC CODE SHEET" and states, "CHECKED BY: 3 November ASA." In the "CAUSE FACTOR" section of this document, a handwritten note appears, "Failed to declare emergency." This note references the contributing factor that caused the accident involving Jones & DelCurto.

The other document containing a handwritten note by "ASA" appears on "Accident Information Checklist." It states, "For accident no. 52-9-12-4." Checked off on the first list is "FIGHTER." Three headings state, "DATE-CHECKED BY DATE" and handwritten under them is "11/26-ASA-1 DEC."

The second checklist is titled "SUBJECT." The section here that was checked off states, "Supplemental Accident Information." Just below this section at the bottom of the page is the area designated "REMARKS." The following handwritten note appears in that area, "Upon receipt of Command Correspondence determine whether or not re-evaluation of accdt [accident] is appropriate — Make final decision. ASA."

What is the name of the bearer with the initials ASA and what is the person's responsibility? Why did ASA make the remark about questioning the evaluation of the Jones & DelCurto accident? Did these two airmen die in vain? Finally, I ask, why are there several missing documents in this Aircraft Accident Report and why were they deleted from the case file?

WITHOUT A TRACE

On Wednesday, September 24, 1952, CIA Director of Scientific Intelligence, H. Marshall Chadwell, sent a memorandum to the Director of Central Intelligence, G. Walter Bedell Smith. This memorandum was in reference to recurring UFO sightings and incidents across the United States. The four-page memo was declassified in April 1977. It is quoted in part below:

1. "Recently an inquiry was conducted by the Office of Scientific Intelligence to determine whether there are national security implications in the problem of unidentified flying objects, i.e. flying saucers."
2. "The public concern with the phenomena indicates that a fair portion of our population is mentally conditioned to the acceptance of the incredible. In this fact lies the potential for the touching-off of mass hysteria and panic."
3. "In order to minimize risk of panic, a national policy should be established as to what should be told to the public regarding the phenomena."
4. "A worldwide reporting system has been instituted and major Air force bases have been ordered to make interceptions of unidentified flying objects."

Considering this memo was dated only five days after the airing of the "Flatwoods Monster" segment on the, *We The People*, TV show; there probably was a definite connection in reference to these points.

The account the Air Force had given concerning the Jones and DelCurto case of September 12, 1952 was illogical. With my extensive research and the help of several persons, including military personnel, I reconstructed a detailed storyline of the Jones and DelCurto incident according to the Air Force. The story made absolutely no sense at all and did not add up. This case was filled with lies, discrepancies, convoluted timelines, and incorrect storylines that left large gaps in Air Force's version of the incident.

Then, I used all of the information I had at hand and by utilizing my master map, recreated another scenario of events for this "cold case." The routine weather-training mission that Jones and DelCurto were said to have been on is an implausible story. It seems unlikely that their disappearance was due to a flameout, weather conditions, or to being lost. I have concluded that the flyers deaths occurred as the result of a conflict with several UFOs when they attempted to "shoot them down." This incident triggered a nationwide crisis that night and evolved into a series of events that ended up in Flatwoods, WV. It was also the beginning of what became a modern-day War of the Worlds. The Jones and DelCurto incident was the first of a sequence of events that evening that caused the three mid-Atlantic UFOs to be fired upon by U.S. military forces.

In his 1973 book, *Aliens From Space*, Donald Keyhoe made the following statement in reference to UFOs vulnerability to fighter jet armaments in the 1950s. He stated:

In the late 1950s, as a number of futile U.S. chases mounted, some pilots were convinced that the UFOs were immune to gunfire and rockets. Several Intelligence analysts believed the aliens might be using some negative force linked with gravity control to repel or deflect bullets and missiles. But the top control group disagreed. In a special evaluation of U.S. and foreign reports they found evidence that UFOs were not invulnerable. Some had been temporarily crippled, apparently from power or control failures, and a few others had been completely destroyed by strange explosions. In one or two cases, it appeared that missiles or rocket fire could have been the cause.

The events on September 12, 1952 that involved damaged UFOs, which fell from the sky was one such probable case that showed UFOs were vulnerable to fighter jet firepower. Based on my research, the following scenario is a feasible explanation for the events that occurred on September 12, 1952. The incident unfolded off the coast of Florida over the waters of the Gulf of Mexico.

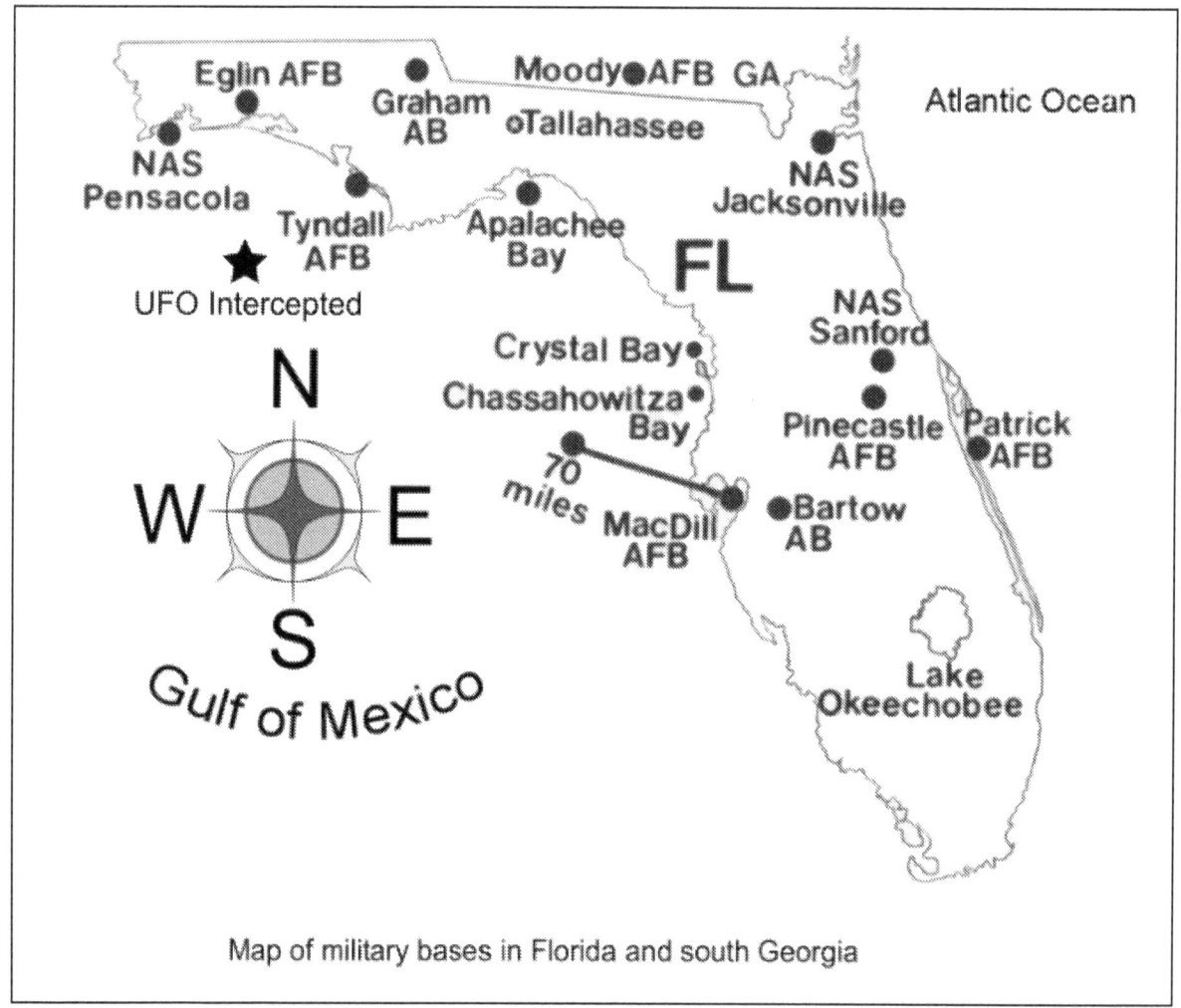

Map of military bases in Florida and south Georgia

The events on September 12, 1952 unfolded shortly before 2:08 p.m. CST. Several southeast Air Force bases tracked sixteen UFOs on their radar screens flying several miles above the Gulf of Mexico waters, south/southwest of Tyndall AFB.

The sixteen UFOs were separated into four groups, with each group consisting of four objects. All the UFOs were surveying the Florida panhandle coast, while moving high above the Gulf waters. These Air Force base radars formed a radar net that surrounded the Gulf of Mexico area. Radar net is defined as, "a network of radar installations set up to detect aircraft entering a defined airspace." Furthermore, these USAF base radar installations formed a "warning net," defined as "any system of communications set up to give warning of aggressive enemy movements, esp. enemy aircraft."

In addition to these nearby Air Force bases, the Jacksonville Naval Air Station, on the east coast of Florida, was also tracking the groups of unidentified objects. These UFOs were within and over the restricted boundaries of the Air Defense Identification Zone. Any aircraft that intends to enter the United States through one of these zones, in this case it was a coastal ADIZ, is required to file a flight plan. This flight plan would have been filed with the Military Flight service or the Civil Aeronautics Administration. If pilots did not file a flight plan or did not follow their flight plans in these ADIZ areas, fighter jets would have intercepted them. Several radio contacts were attempted by the Air Force to establish contact and verify the identification of these unidentified aircraft. There was no response.

Within minutes, all southeast Air Force bases and Naval Air Stations were on alert. The USAF Air Defense Command headquarters at ENT AFB in Colorado Springs was simultaneously informed. The ADC "yellow warning light" flashed on. Simultaneously, the large "warning bell" sounded, thereby alerting ADC officials unknown aircraft were being detected at that time.

The locations where these UFOs were situated above the Gulf of Mexico, near Tyndall AFB justified a full air defense readiness, declaration by the ADC. At that point, Ent Air Force Base contacted the White House, alerting President Harry Truman. Truman contacted Robert A. Lovett, Secretary of Defense, and the National Security Council. Simultaneously, the Pentagon and the Joint Chiefs of Staff were alerted. All defense forces throughout the entire eastern United States were now on "red alert."

Three Florida Air Force bases began to deploy combat air patrols over and near their bases. Two were from the panhandle, Tyndall AFB in Panama City and Eglin AFB in Valparaiso and the third was the west coast's MacDill AFB in Tampa. During this "red alert" situation, time was of the utmost essence. Fighter pilots and radar operators dashed to awaiting fighter jets to race aloft after unknown targets. Tyndall AFB scrambled six F-94B Starfires into the air between 1:47 p.m. CST and 2:26 p.m. CST. It was during this red alert that pilot 2nd Lt. John A. Jones, Jr. was paired into a waiting F-94B Starfire with radar operator trainee 2nd Lt. John S. DelCurto. The commanders at Tyndall AFB, headquarters of the Advanced Interceptor "3626 Fly Training Group," used the best fighter aviators they had available at that time. With no time available, to access or assign duty to who would be most qualified for the mission, fighter jets were scrambled into the air.

The time elapsed when Jones jet departed at 2:08 p.m. CST until he was supposedly lost at 4:20 p.m. CST was two hours and twelve minutes. From this time until Jones' F-94 jet supposedly has, a flameout en route to MacDill AFB at 4:42 p.m. CST was another 22 minutes. One minute later at 4:43 p.m. CST, the last radio noise was heard from the jet and the jet disappeared. The total time of Lt. Jones and Lt. DelCurto's flight was two hours and thirty-five minutes. Following the storyline, the four groups of UFOs continued moving at very high altitude above the Gulf of Mexico.

The movements of the UFOs were being monitored by Air Force radar on the ground as well as Ground Control Intercept Stations along the Gulf coast. The UFOs continued to ascend but stayed just above the ceiling range of the climbing jets that were being guided toward them. Shortly afterwards, the four groups of UFOs spread out into different directions toward the coast. The six jets now patrolling the skies and searching for these UFOs were in constant radio contact with ground radar controllers, who kept the jets informed. Suddenly, one group of UFOs began to descend as they moved closer to the Florida panhandle. The fourth object from that group ceased its descent and circled above the three companion ships.

The remaining three groups of UFOs stayed just above 50,000 feet, above the reach of the jets and began to hover in place. The three objects that had descended to a lower altitude had reached a "warning point." This is defined, as "any point which when reached gives warning that a critical moment or action is to follow." The warning given upon reaching the designated warning point of a restricted area is called a "warning order." This is defined as "a preliminary notice that another order or action is to follow, designed to allow time for making plans and preparations." Meanwhile, Tyndall AFB had sent up another Combat Air Patrol of four jets over their base.

Tyndall AFB as well as the pilots of the four nearby interceptors issued a warning order to the three descending UFOs. The warnings went unacknowledged. At that point, another major concern arose. The airspace this group of UFOs was nearing was close to Eglin AFB. This Air Force installation operates the Air Proving Ground Command (APGC). The mission of the Air Proving Ground, Eglin AFB, is the operational suitability testing of all Air Force aircraft and equipment. This includes the development of tactics and techniques for the tactical employment of this equipment. This installation conducted many top-secret aircraft tests and experiments from many of its base area test sites. The installation was heavily restricted to air traffic and required many special air traffic rules upon any craft entering its air spaces. Besides the concern that the UFOs could be extraterrestrial, there was the possibility that they were advanced Soviet aircraft, planning an aerial assault against U.S. bases.

Shortly afterward, while still descending, the three UFOs passed into the service ceiling height area where the jets were capable of flying. Immediately, three nearby patrolling Tyndall jets moved in and issued another warning to the objects that continued to descend. Once again, there was no response. I will now reiterate the words, "'shoot them down' if they refuse to land." While the other three Tyndall jets were tracking and flying near the other groups of UFOs, Tyndall officials ordered the other three jets to intercept the three descending objects. They had been considered possible enemy aircraft and probably hostile. Just before 2:40 p.m. CST, GCI guided the jets toward the three unidentified aircraft. Final warnings were issued by the pilots with no response. The fighter jets then approached their descending targets to "shoot them down."

The UFOs were sighted in the distance as the pilots closed in on their targets. The objects were identified as not being Russian aircraft and were recognized as unconventional and unknown crafts. They were oval and spherically shaped and approximately 20-25 feet in size with a smooth, metallic skin. The objects were not sleek saucer-shaped objects; they were very large and cumbersome, similar in comparing a Greyhound bus to a Ferrari sports car.

The three F-94s moved towards their targets. Seconds later, the jets had the UFOs locked on their radar systems, closed and then fired upon them. The UFOs scattered as the F-94B jets unleashed a barrage of cannon fire that blanketed the sky. Simultaneously a strange vibration filled the air and sky lit up. Seconds later, one of the objects took a direct hit, exploded, and then caught on fire. Sparks erupted and showered the sky and the object began to fly erratically. Simultaneously, the three jets pulled out of the fray but something was wrong. The two nearest jets had been hit by an unknown wavering shock. The pilots immediately contacted Tyndall AFB's tower through a static transmission. The messages however, were not positive. F-94 jets #1332 and #0867, the two nearest the UFOs, had developed electrical difficulties with some of their onboard systems. The jets were acting erratic and had intermittent problems with their instruments and radar systems.

The jet pilots told Tyndall tower about the strange powers that the objects possessed and informed them these UFOs did not possess the agility of a saucer- shaped craft. Tyndall tower controllers immediately ordered the two damaged and struggling jets back to base as the combat air patrol pilots listened in on the airwaves.

These UFOs possessed a propulsion system that produced an anti-gravity field. This field was generated by an onboard power source unlike any known system. The field, an electromagnetic-type field actually surrounded the UFOs. This field had adverse affects on any electrical systems at close range, but moreover, the power systems of these objects also acted as weapons systems.

The UFO that was intercepted had its anti-gravity field damaged by the jets firepower, causing it to lose power, fly erratically and drop in altitude. This object was in desperate need of electrical power and needed a source to regenerate itself. The damaged object being escorted by another UFO, quickly descended as the third object ascended back into the sky. With no time to waste, the destination of the damaged object was Tyndall

AFB. Meanwhile, all three jets were also en route to Tyndall as the two damaged jets struggled through their descent. Tyndall tower men watched their radarscopes as the two UFOs descended and approached the base on northeast headings. They were unsure if the base was being targeted for an attack. The tower advised their jets to remain above the objects in their stack formation. Minutes later, the damaged UFO and its escort approached Tyndall AFB and started their final descent. Stunned officials sounded the warning siren as pandemonium broke lose. Vehicles filled with heavily armed guards scrambled across the field and followed the two objects as they passed across the base.

The damaged UFO then hovered over a giant generator as it struggled to stay airborne. A strange device was lowered and it absorbed energy into its electrical power system. The other UFO hovered over the base between the approaching guards and the damaged UFO to safeguard the area. The power drainage caused Tyndall's radio range to go offline. Power maintenance personnel tried switching over to emergency power, which was also already incapacitated. As personnel scrambled to overcome the problem, the tower operators contacted the power maintenance crew and told them to try resetting the commercial power.

Near the UFOs, a strange electrical vibration intensified throughout the area. This stalled the approaching vehicles and shocked the guards who backed off. Officials were aware of the damaging electrical powers the objects possessed but were unaware if they possessed any deadly armaments. If these objects did have deadly weapons and chose to use them, Tyndall AFB could become the scene of a raging battlefield. At this point, there was another major concern; would the other objects hovering above and along the Florida coastline descend upon the base? To complicate matters, three aircraft were descending to land at Tyndall Field and two were damaged. The guards were ordered to stand down and not to fire at the objects until further notice.

This segment of the incident involving the power loss was stated in the "Preliminary Report Of A Major Accident," dated 13 September 1952: "When jet aircraft started letting down procedures Tyndall Range went off the air. It was off from 1440 to 1445 CST." [2:40 p.m. to 2:45 p.m. CST]. The official "Report Of AF Aircraft Accident" stated, "Tyndall Radio Range went off the air at 1440C and was officially off until 1445C." During this time, Lt. Jones called for a D/F steer back to station. "In an official statement by Captain Phillip P. Harrison, Flight Instructor of the 3625 Interceptor Training Squadron dated September 23, 1952, he said, "No difficulties arose until Tyndall Range went off the air. At that time about three ships called for steers, one was Lt. Jones in aircraft #819 (F-94B, AF-50-0819)."

The explanation of the power loss was detailed in the Air Force document dated 12 September 1952. Ref 11 #9/47z explained, "AACS (Airway and Air Communication Service, Tyndall AFB) power maintenance personnel were making a power change-over check in order to test the emergency power. The emergency power did not take over and the radio range went off-the-air until the tower operators called in and advised the power maintenance personnel to reset the commercial power." This explanation seems both unlikely and dangerous, that a power change-over to test emergency power would occur during a flight operation with three jets "letting down procedures."

As Jones and the two damaged craft were letting down their jets heading for Tyndall AFB, they proceeded to radio the tower. As previously stated, on September 29, 1952, the first board proceeding was held at Tyndall AFB in the Wing Conference Room. Six members of The Aircraft Accident Investigating Board were present including acting president, Major Peter E. Pompetti. Major Pompetti spoke to Capt. Harrison at length. Capt. Harrison explained, "It came for approach times and one of them (Jet #1332) was already making his approach. About that time (2:40 p.m. CST), Tyndall range went off-the-air. Immediately several [pilots] called in and said, their radio compass was out and all they could hear was static. I advised them that the range was off-the-air." This was the time, when the power was being drained by the UFO hovering over the base, between 2:40 and 2:45 p.m. CST.

During this time when the Tyndall Radio Range went off the air, the three jets were guided in by Tyndall tower using radio "D/F," Radio Direction-Finding; the act or process of determining the direction from which a transmitted signal originates, hence, a method for establishing the bearing or position of an aircraft. The three jets were being guided by this method because Tyndall's Range being off-air enabled them to utilize their IFR, or Instrument Flight Rules. IFR is the collection of rules in AF directives, which govern flight procedures under "instrument conditions." The jets on-board radio compasses would not function during off-air times. Capt. Harrison also stated, "Several of them [pilots] called for directional steers…Lt. Jones called for a steer and there were a couple more. The man who was making a letdown was brought in using DF." This was aircraft #1332.

Just after 2:45 p.m. CST, the damaged UFO began to ascend a short distance away from the base. The escort craft began to follow. The power for the radio range was switched to commercial. About 2:47 p.m. CST, the two UFOs ascended to a higher altitude, but the damaged craft was still unstable as it struggled to climb and attempted to leave the atmosphere. At 3:00 p.m. CST, Tyndall radar continued to track the UFOs slow ascent. Meanwhile, Tyndall officials were in touch with officials at The Pentagon keeping them informed of this unfolding situation in Florida. The Air Force wanted the damaged UFO before it could retreat. Tyndall contacted the three jets on combat air-patrol with orders to intercept it. They also contacted Lt. Jones and redirected him towards the other three fighters. At this time, all three jets were positioned above the two UFOs, the damaged one and its escort. The three combat air-patrol jets descended as Jones was vectored toward them.

Minutes later, Jones joined formation as Ground Control Intercept began to guide the fighters toward the UFOs. The pilots were informed that the UFOs could wreak havoc on their electrical systems at close range with some kind of unknown weapons system. They were warned to keep their distances. Separating into pairs, two jets targeted the damaged UFO while the other two targeted the escort craft. As GCI vectored the jets toward the UFOs, onboard radar observers picked up the targets on their scopes.

The four jets closed in diving toward the UFOs. Jones and his wing mate closed in on the damaged object. The two pairs of jets both flew toward their designated targets. The escort object changed its course onto a head-on collision course and proceeded toward two of the jets. The jets and the escort object headed at each other and not planning to play chicken, the jets fired at the UFO then broke away. The object avoided this strike, dove below the jets, and sharply banked and set a course for the other two jets. The escort UFO dove towards them as they closed-in on the damaged and struggling object. However, the approaching UFO did not reach the area in time and the damaged object was hit by the cannon fire from the two attacking F-94s. Meanwhile, the two jets that had engaged with the escort UFO only moments earlier were experiencing electrical problems. At this time, Tyndall ordered all four jets back to base. Colonel B. T. Kleine stated the cover story in his letter, "When the weather started to become near our minimums, all aircraft were called to come back to the field."

Meanwhile, the now severely damaged object turned away from the coastline and headed southwest in the opposite direction of its pursuers. The escort UFO then followed the damaged ship; its condition was deteriorating and it was having trouble staying airborne.

As the objects were making their escape, F-94, #1331 was approaching Tyndall to land. The Direction Finding Log dated 12/9/52 stated that while "1332 was on a course of 314 degrees at 1447/2:47 p.m. CST." Remarks were stated that an "BE EMERG" was declared during the jet's approach. This emergency was declared because the UFOs were still in vicinity of the base.

The first jet approaching Tyndall field did not land until nine minutes later…after declaring its emergency. An Airways and Air Communications Service document dated September 18, 1952 and titled "Certificate" states, "AF1332, F-94…cleared for approach at 1445 (2:45 p.m.). Cancelled instrument flight rules flight plan at 1456 (2:56 p.m.)." To avoid a confrontation, the approaching jet was diverted away from Tyndall for nine minutes, which is how long it took the UFOs to be out-of-range.

Capt. Harrison continued his statement by speaking of the next jet to land…F-94, AF-0867. He stated, "The next man was brought in all the way with D/F." The Direction Finding Log dated 12/9/52 stated that this jet was "cleared for approach at 1540 (3:04 p.m. CST). Cancelled IFR flight plan at 1512 (3:12 p.m. CST)."

Meanwhile another UFO re-entered the picture. This was one of the three objects involved in the original confrontation when the damaged UFO was initially hit. After that exchange, it ascended to a higher altitude hovering unnoticed above Tyndall, observing the fray. No longer on the sidelines, the third UFO began its descent back toward the panhandle coastline. Tyndall AFB had just scrambled four fighter jets toward the damaged UFO and the escort object accompanying it. The intent of this third object was to keep the scrambled jets away from the two retreating UFOs by heading them off. GCI was guiding the four jets. As the jets met this new threat, they knew that the UFO seemed vulnerable to their firepower but possessed an advanced weapon system. The onboard radar observers on the F-94s carefully guided their pilots toward the incoming ship despite the risks.

A little wiser and more prepared for round two, these F-94s planned to fire at their targets at a distance a little farther away. They intended to riddle the sky with .50 caliber rounds, then immediately pull out of range to avoid the UFO's strange shock wave force. Unfortunately, the pilots also found out the full effects of the armaments they were now up against when they fired upon them. The energy from this shock wave could fry their jet's electrical system and incapacitate them if they received a direct hit. An indirect hit could damage the aircraft or temporarily disable it and stun them. Another form of defense the UFOs utilized was a devastating high-intensity energy beam. Upon direct contact, the beam engulfed the target and completely disintegrated it. These weapons though, had a major drawback; they would drain the power of their craft if used repeatedly over a short time. This would lessen the strength and range of their weapons and slow down the craft.

The striking jets closed on the third UFO and blasted a round of cannon fire at it. The object banked, narrowly escaped being hit and struck one of the jets trying to bypass it with a shock wave. It was a direct hit. The jet was incapacitated and fell out of the sky as the remaining three jets scattered after the pilots saw what had just occurred. Shortly thereafter, the jets attempted another interception. As they fired their cannons, the third UFO retaliated and destroyed another jet. Seconds later, cannon fire was shot again at the object by the remaining two F-94 jets. They missed it. Meanwhile, the damaged UFO and the craft escorting it headed southwest out over the Gulf waters and decelerated. Traveling out over the Gulf waters could be fatal for the damaged and struggling craft should it go down. As the damaged craft struggled to stay airborne, it ceased its ascent over the Gulf of Mexico to assess its damage and stopped heading further southwest.

At that point, Air Force officials tracking the UFO's movements believed they might have been regrouping for a retaliatory attack. Eglin AFB directed their four CAP fighter jets toward them. Meanwhile, the first four jets, including Jones' jet were in contact with Tyndall tower. The two damaged F-94 jets informed Tyndall that they were still struggling with their electrical systems, which were intermittently malfunctioning. Tyndall AFB controllers guided all four jets toward their base to attempt landings. Jones and his wing mate were stacked above the two damaged jets and they all continued toward Tyndall field.

Meanwhile, Tyndall tower was simultaneously in contact with the two remaining jets in battle with the third object that was descending toward the base. Tyndall redirected Jones and his wing mate back toward the descending UFO to assist the two remaining jets in overcoming it. Just as Jones and his wing mate arrived into the air battle area, the two jets had been overcome. They attempted to intercept the third object as Jones wing mate fired his remaining ammunition but missed his target in a desperate attempt to overtake it. The UFO bypassed the two jets and continued descending as the two jets were ordered to return to Tyndall immediately. At this point, a major concern had arisen. The UFO was still descending and heading for Tyndall in addition to the last two jets that had sustained electrical problems.

During the Aircraft Accident Investigating Board proceedings, flight instructor, Capt. Phillip P. Harrison stated, "Lt. Jones called for a steer and there were a couple more. The man who was making a letdown was brought in using D/F [pilot of AF-1332]. The next man was brought in all the way with DF [pilot of AF-0867]. At about this time the weather was getting bad with light rain. I had been instructed if there were any rain showers to send them to their alternate. So at this time I told Lt. Dunn on Approach Control, to send the top four ships in the stack to [Moody AFB] the alternate."

Lt. Jones and the other three jets were never actually recalled back to Tyndall AFB because of bad weather. The first two jets ahead of Jones and the other three jets had already landed ahead of them, before the "light rain" started. Colonel Kleine, USAF commanding, from Tyndall AFB stated in a letter to Lt. Jones brother, dated 17 September 1952, "When the weather started to become near our minimums, all aircraft were called to come back to the field." This statement contradicts Capt. Harrison's statement of September 29, 1952. Colonel Kleine then states: "Supervisory personnel in the control tower advised John and three other aircraft to go to Moody Air Force Base about fifteen minutes north of Tyndall." Colonel Kleine neglected to say that there were actually six jets and two of them had already landed at Tyndall Field before Lt. Jones and the three others.

Colonel Kleine made it appear as though the bad weather was the factor that caused Tyndall AFB personnel to call the jets to come back to the field. The weather was not a factor. At this point, two jets were struggling with their electrical systems, another jet was out of ammunition and Lt. Jones was the last behind the group and low on ammunition, as they proceeded to their home base.

Meanwhile, the damaged UFO hovered erratically, had trouble staying airborne, and continued to lose altitude. The decision to make an emergency landing along the Florida coastline was inevitable. The damaged object and the escort object accompanying it stopped, turned and redirected. They proceeded on a northeast trajectory over the Gulf of Mexico toward the coastline behind the descending third UFO. Meanwhile, four combat air patrol jets from Moody AFB had been vectored southwest toward the area of the three descending UFOs. Simultaneously, the Eglin jets also headed southeast towards them. At that point, the three UFOs were surrounded by Air Force bases with jets closing in on them from different directions. Another confrontation with Air Force jets could prove fatal for the damaged UFO if it were hit again.

Shortly after, all three of the UFOs, including the damaged one, grouped together and descended. They proceeded northeast toward the Florida Panhandle so the damaged one could make an emergency landing. As the Four Eglin jets headed toward the three objects from the northwest and four Moody jets approached from the northeast, the entire situation changed. The remaining groups of thirteen upper-level UFOs hovering high in the atmosphere began to descend and take control of the situation.

The descending objects separated and spread out in a shotgun pattern, moving into strategic positions toward other military installations. As they fanned out in different directions, they formed an aerial blockade around their damaged craft. The UFOs maneuvered and cut off several access points of the military jets. Some UFOs moved into strategic Air Force operating areas and actually neutralized several airfields from scrambling any further jets. Their main objective was to protect the damaged craft from being destroyed or captured by the Air Force. The main objective of the Air Force was to destroy these objects before they invaded the United States. Within moments of their descent, these UFOs jammed communications of the USAF bases and naval air stations. The UFOs neutralized or made temporarily useless the following military installations. They are arranged in a clockwise order starting from an area just south of the Apalachee Bay.

1. Tyndall AFB, Panama City, FL. Flight paths neutralized and jets intercepted, airfields neutralized.
2. Eglin AFB, Valparaiso, FL. Flight paths neutralized and jets intercepted, airfields neutralized
3. Pensacola Naval Air Station, FL. Flight paths neutralized and jets intercepted, airfields neutralized.
4. Brookley AFB, Mobile, AL. Flight paths neutralized
5. Craig AFB, Selma, AL. Flight paths neutralized
6. Gunter AFB, Montgomery, AL. Flight paths neutralized
7. Maxwell AFB, Montgomery, AL. Flight paths neutralized
8. Lawson AFB, Columbus, GA. Flight paths neutralized.
9. Graham AB, (5 miles north of Marianna), FL. Flight paths neutralized

10. Bainbridge AB, Bainbridge, FL. Flight paths neutralized
11. Dobbins AFB, Marietta, GA. Flight paths neutralized
12. Turner AFB, Albany, GA. Flight paths neutralized
13. Robins AFB, Macon, GA. Flight paths neutralized
14. Spence AB, Spence, GA. Flight paths neutralized
15. Moody AFB, Valdosta, GA. Flight paths neutralized and jets intercepted
16. Hunter AFB, Savannah, GA. Flight paths neutralized
17. NAS. Jacksonville, Jacksonville, FL. Flight paths neutralized
18. NAS. Sanford, Sanford, FL. Flight paths neutralized
19. Pinecastle AFB, Orlando, FL. Flight paths neutralized
20. Patrick AFB, Cocoa, FL. Flight paths neutralized
21. MacDill AFB, Tampa, FL. Flight paths neutralized and jets intercepted

The first Air Force bases descended upon and neutralized were Tyndall AFB and the main runways of Eglin. During this time, one of the descending UFOs actually encountered a jet observation plane near the coast. Tyndall had dispatched this jet toward the Gulf of Mexico to survey the area and look for survivors. The UFO did not fire at the jet but got close enough to cause its electrical system to malfunction.

This is when the "jet observation plane ran into technical trouble." The pilot saw the object coming toward him, and considering the problems it had caused with the jet's electrical system, "bailed out after heading the plane in the direction of the Gulf of Mexico." Shortly thereafter, the pilot landed near Tyndall AFB and the UFO continued towards Tyndall AFB and circled over their airfields. Another UFO that had descended near the coast dropped in over Eglin and circled over the main runways. These strategic maneuvers prevented jets from scrambling into the air after the damaged UFO.

Meanwhile, every military radar installation in the southeast was tracking the thirteen descending UFOs. They also tracked the first three UFOs, including the damaged object, which was quickly losing altitude and heading toward Florida. It was feared the objects might attack, crash-land into a populated area, or make a kamikaze maneuver into a nearby Air Force base.

In the meantime, the third UFO left the damaged craft and the other escort object and headed toward the four incoming Eglin jets to head them off at the pass. The intentions of this object were not to destroy the jets but only to stop them from advancing. Because the Eglin fighter pilots were not aware of the UFO's strategy, the first jets fired upon it and missed. Seconds later, the UFO retaliated and destroyed them. The remaining jets were hit by an indirect shock wave and were damaged. They were ordered back to Eglin, told to land at one of the smaller fields, and guided in. The third UFO then continued to descend over the Gulf of Mexico and followed the jets back toward Eglin AFB. Shortly after the jets landed, the UFO descended over another area of that large base and circled other airfields. At that point, Eglin AFB actually had two UFOs hovering over their airfields to thwart off any more jets that may have been scrambled.

Meanwhile, across the Gulf, MacDill AFB had vectored four CAP jets northwest toward Tyndall through a rainstorm. The four MacDill jets were detected by four UFOs from above. The four UFOs descended through the clouds and rain. Two of these UFOs moved to the west of Crystal Bay and the Chassahowitzka Bay coastline over Gulf waters. They were positioned to form a horizontal blockade where they could make lateral movements across the Gulf of Mexico. Simultaneously, the two other UFOs headed towards the west coast of Florida. The intentions of the two objects over the Gulf waters were to prevent the MacDill jets from going any further northwest. The Air Force interpreted this as an offensive strategy. These UFOs were above U.S. restricted airspace and deemed enemy invaders. While tracking the UFOs, one pair of jets moved toward one UFO, while the other pair of jets headed towards the second UFO. The UFOs continued to descend, moving into the jets' flight paths. The jets continued on their intercept bearings to overtake and bypass the

UFOs. The first jets opened fire on the UFO in front of them; they missed. The UFO retaliated with fire, destroying the two jets. Seconds later, the second pair of jets closed in on their target and fired, narrowly missing it. This UFO attempted to shock wave the jets but missed a direct hit. The two jets were partially hit though and flying so erratically they did not pose a threat anymore. The two pilots struggled to control their jets. They retreated to MacDill AFB where one jet crash-landed and the other landed safely.

Meanwhile, the Air Force and Navy scrambled more fighters from MacDill AFB in Tampa, Pinecastle AFB in Orlando, Sanford NAS in Sanford, and jets from Patrick AFB in Cocoa. Radar stations discovered that two of the UFOs were moving toward populated areas. One UFO circled high above Ocala in the clouds, while the other hovered in the Inverness area, forming a north-south aerial blockade against the jets. The military could not afford aerial battles over populated areas. They did not know if the UFOs would strike civilians. Another concern was how many more UFOs there were in a position to descend upon Florida. The northwest bound jets from the central and west coast of Florida was recalled, as well as the jets moving over the Gulf from MacDill. At that point, the situation along the west coast had turned into a standoff.

Air Defense Headquarters in Colorado and Air Force Headquarters officials at the Pentagon were flooded with calls from southeast officials. Government military officials became aware of the devastating power of these UFOs. Pandemonium was raging, and it was far from being over. Military installations were being neutralized throughout the southeast as well as all the flight paths leading into the Gulf of Mexico. Within moments, nearly the entire southeast United States would be neutralized, rendering military installations helpless.

Meanwhile the four F-94B jets that were approaching Tyndall for landings could not land because the descended UFO had neutralized the base. This UFO had cut off their airfields and was circling over and above the area. Fighter jets were unable to get off the ground and the four incoming F-94 jets were unable to land as well. Jones was approaching Tyndall with his wing mate who was out of ammunition as the other two damaged jets flying below them struggled with their electrical problems. Tyndall personnel including Capt. Harrison analyzed the situation along the coastline southwest of their base. The two damaged jets and the jet depleted of its arms were then redirected to their alternate landing base…Moody AFB in Valdosta, Georgia.

Jones and DelCurto were also contacted with new orders. They were instructed to assist the four Moody jets in the interception of the damaged UFO and the remaining escort UFO. Jones and DelCurto then redirected their jet. As the four Moody fighters headed toward the damaged object and its escort, they were tracked coming in. The escort object descended, redirected toward the four jets and attempted to intercept them as they neared. The first pair of jets closed and fired upon the escort object, which deftly outmaneuvered their barrage of gunfire. The object quickly retaliated against the jets, and disintegrated them. The other two Moody jets immediately broke off their attack. They banked away, reorganized and then prepared to intercept the escort UFO from another approach.

In the meantime, the damaged craft approached the Florida panhandle on a northeast trajectory across the Gulf in flames. It decided against Tyndall AFB as a power source and looked for another source along the panhandle coast. It descended, dropped off radar and then passed over the St. Joseph Peninsula. The flaming object proceeded toward the coastline as Tyndall towermen watched it descend out in the distance and disappear from sight. The damaged UFO flew over the coast near Port St. Joe and began to decelerate to prepare for its landing near some power lines. The craft struggled to hover atop the trees, made its final descent inland between Mexico Beach and Port St. Joe, southeast of Tyndall AFB and finally landed.

During that time, the Air Force was unaware of the object's exact location but knew it was near the coast and just southeast of the base. It became apparent, because of the damaged craft's trajectory, that it had been forced to make an emergency landing. The primary objective of the Air Force was to now locate the downed craft until it could be reached by ground forces and be retrieved. Officials ordered contingents of men to gather arms and explosives and prepare to advance to the area in vehicles in an attempt to retrieve the object. Their first obstacle was to get off base without being noticed by the UFO circling over Tyndall.

The "strange paper balloon" that was found drifting along near the Tallahassee airport by the Tallahassee Civil Air Patrol "where they saw it land in a tall pine tree" now enters the scenario. This "hot air balloon" was "apparently" not positively "made of rice paper over a wire frame." Inside of the so-called balloon was a "wire bracket for a heating element." The interior of the balloon was "badly smoked." Furthermore, "there was no indication what type of fuel had been used to provide hot air to raise the balloon." This odd balloon was "being turned over to military authorities" because the balloon was directly related to the craft that landed. When the UFO had been damaged, the electrical field around it was broken, which was directly related to its propulsion system.

When the object was forced to land, it landed near the power transmission lines, which were located along the coastline of the Florida panhandle. This object had to regenerate by drawing electricity from a power source. The "odd balloon" was the conductor used by the craft to draw electricity to itself. When the damaged UFO landed near the power transmission lines, it launched the electrical conductor balloon into the air. When the balloon neared the power transmission lines, the electrical flow of energy was transferred within and through the balloon conductor back to the object. The UFO could recharge itself. Meanwhile, Lt. Jones' wing mate and the two damaged F-94s were directed away from Tyndall to Moody AFB in Georgia.

At this point during the incident Captain Harrison explained, "In the meantime, we had contacted Moody. They were alerted and had already worked one aircraft sent over there." This aircraft was F-94, #0842. Harrison then stated, "Others were on their way." The other jets that were on their way were #0851 and #0849.

The AACS at Tyndall AFB stated the following in a certificate dated 18 September 1952, "AF 0842 F-94 …landed 1535C (3:35), AF 0851 F-94 …pilot advised to go to his alternate at approximately 1520C (3:20), AF 0849 F-94, [Tyndall AFB] was unable to contact aircraft. Jacksonville control advised aircraft was working Moody D/F station." This document does not show landing times for the last two jets sent to Moody. Furthermore, Tyndall AFB was unable to contact the last jet; Jacksonville control line had actually informed Tyndall tower that Moody AFB was guiding the jet back to their base. Captain Harrison then stated, "There were already three gone. Lt. Jones was the last one…and acknowledged he was proceeding to his alternate."

In turn, the four jets were redirected and vectored toward their alternate field, Moody AFB. The official AF Accident report stated, "It is assumed that 0819 [Lt. Jones] departed Tyndall AFB at 1535 (3:35 p.m. CST) with 289 gallons of fuel." In an official statement given by Capt. Harrison, he said, "#819 said his fuel was 289 gallons and that his altitude was 29,000 ft. I gave him a course of 075-degrees to fly to Tallahassee, FL and told him to contact Moody AFB D/F on 'D' Delta when he got over TAL. The tower took care of his clearance. He [Lt. Jones] acknowledged these instructions and it was assumed that he was proceeding to his alternate."

The official AF Accident report also stated, "The instructor in the tower, Capt. Harrison advised Tyndall Approach Control to send 0819 [Lt. Jones] to his alternate, Moody AFB, when he got back over the station. Capt. Harrison advised 0819 to depart for Tallahassee radio on a heading of 075-degrees and to contact Moody D/F when over Tallahassee, on D channel for a steer." At the AAI board meeting, Major Pompetti asked Capt. Harrison if one of the Ground Approach Controllers had acknowledged Lt. Jones calling Tyndall upon reaching Tallahassee. Pompetti asked Harrison, "Does he [Ground Approach Controller] remember if #819 [Lt. Jones] reported or called over Tallahassee as he was instructed?" Harrison answered, "I don't remember whether he [Ground Approach Controller] said he [Lt. Jones] was over Tallahassee or not."

Approach control operator, 1st Lt. Robert A. Dunn told a different story when he was questioned by Major Pompetti at the AAI board meeting. Major Pompetti asked Lt. Dunn the following, "Q. Did you relay the instructions to #819 [Lt. Jones] to depart to his [Moody] alternate. A. Yes, Sir. Q. In these instructions, was he instructed to report to Moody D/F over Tallahassee? A. Not that I remember," answered Lt. Dunn.

It is evident by the statements that this incident was a convoluted mess and officials seemed to have selective memory. Why was everyone unaware of Lt. Jones location? I believe these men actually knew where the pilot was. Jones was in communication with Tyndall AFB and was being tracked on radar. How could they not know where Lt. Jones was? Why were Captain Harrison and Lt. Dunn unable to remember what occurred?

In the meantime, the two remaining Moody fighters regrouped and attempted to intercept the escort object again. A fierce battle ensued as the UFO warded off yet another intercept by the jets. By keeping their distances, the jets survived this confrontation as well and then passed out over the Gulf waters, ascended, and regrouped for another attack.

Meanwhile, Tyndall tower officials contacted Jones and gave him new orders. He was told not to head into the air battle of the escort object and the two remaining Moody jets. Moody AFB had just scrambled four more fully armed fighter jets toward the air battle area to attempt an intercept against the escort UFO. At this point, Second Lt. Jones was reordered to the Port St. Joe area where the damaged object was seen going down and told to find it. Tyndall radar operators steered Jones and DelCurto to the coastline. As the jet descended and approached the area, the pilot looked for the downed UFO with orders to immediately radio its location so ground forces could find it. Jones was also ordered to attempt an air strike to assure the object stayed down.

Jones and DelCurto kept descending; they saw the damaged object on the ground. The pilot took notice of the odd balloon that was connected to the power lines. They radioed back to Tyndall AFB, reporting the object and its location. Tyndall responded by telling the pilots to take out the balloon and and/or the power lines and try to separate the balloon from the craft. During the time the damaged craft was grounded, it was continuously absorbing electricity through its conductor to regenerate itself.

The jet approached and fired at the downed object and the odd balloon. Simultaneously, the UFO fired back. A barrage of gunfire soared through the air in the vicinity of the object and ground throughout the area. As .50 caliber bullets hit the power lines, they were instantly set ablaze, damaging the balloon. After completing their successful air strike mission, pilot Jones and DelCurto departed the area and radioed Tyndall AFB.

Meanwhile, the ground contingents were alerted of the downed object's location. Hurriedly, they split-up and headed southeast toward the target area on separate paths. As the ground forces left the base, the UFO hovering over Tyndall tracked one of the groups of men. It moved in the direction of the contingent, descended toward their vehicles and fired in their vicinity in an attempt to stop them from advancing. The object circled back and forth between Tyndall's airfields and the advancing contingents in an attempt to neutralize them, which proved to be a difficult task. The contingents continued to advance southeast on different courses while the patrolling UFO relocated and circled the airfields to intercept any jets that may have been scrambled.

In the meantime, Tyndall AFB control tower personnel ordered Jones to proceed to Moody AFB. At this point. Lt. Jones was advised by Tyndall AFB tower personnel to go to Moody AFB, the alternative landing field because their armaments were nearly depleted. They advised that Jones should not enter the battle against the UFO because Moody AFB had already vectored two fully armed jets toward this area. Meanwhile, the escort UFO had overcome the two relentless Moody jets engaged in battle against it.

The next objective for this UFO was to neutralize nearby Moody AFB, but two more fighter jets had already been scrambled. The escort UFO headed northwest toward Moody AFB and the pair of incoming Moody jets. A confrontation was inevitable. Second Lt. Jones had informed the incoming Moody jets of the exact location of the downed object. Within minutes, the Moody jets were about to strike at the escort object headed toward them in an effort to bypass it and continue after the downed object.

The two Moody jets were vectored by CGI towards the UFO. Moments later, the radar operators had the object on their scopes and directed their pilots toward their target. The pilots took control and shortly after approached the UFO and closed on it. The jets fired at the UFO with rapid gunfire from the fixed gun armaments and gunfire blanketed the sky. The UFO evaded the onslaught by pulling up and away and then banked away and passed over the nearest striking jet and disintegrated it. The remaining jet pulled away and climbed to an even higher altitude to escape the UFO. Likewise, the UFO maneuvered and climbed in the opposite direction away from the jet. Once again, the remaining jet received orders to attempt an intercept on the UFO, which had positioned itself between the downed object and the jet.

Meanwhile Lt. Jones and Lt. DelCurto were vectored towards Moody AFB, bypassing the air battle area after their air strike against the downed object. During this time between 3:35 p.m. and 4:00 p.m. CST, they were allegedly flying by Tallahassee en route to Moody AFB. There was an elapsed time of approximately twenty-five minutes. During this time, Captain Harrison made this statement to Major Pompetti, "That was the last we heard of him for a while until we heard him calling Moody Approach on 'B' channel. He was coming in clear at that time."

Approach control officer, Lt. Dunn told Major Pompetti what occurred next, when he was questioned:

Q. When you first heard him [Lt. Jones] ask Moody for a steer, do you know what time it was?
A. Somewhere around 1600 [4:00 p.m. CST] I can't be sure.
Q. Did you at any time ask him to switch to the 'D' Channel?
A. No. I did not.
Q. At any time during this incident, did you or anyone else instruct #819 to switch to "D" channel?
A. No — not to my knowledge.
Q. Was there some reason for not switching to "D" channel?
A. No, I don't know of any reason for not switching to "D" channel. (NOTE: There was contact with jet.)
Q. The reason I asked the question is because it is obvious from the statements in file that at approximately 1600 [4:00 p.m. CST] this thing was reaching emergency stages, yet we evidently did not go to emergency frequencies. My question is why?
A. There I think it is the pilot's responsibility to go to "D" channel if he considers himself in emergency.

At this stage of the incident, Lt. Jones did not declare an emergency because he simply was not in an emergency situation at this juncture. Furthermore, the electromagnetic field of the UFO hovering over Tyndall AFB was the cause of the airwave communication problems. Meanwhile, Jones and DelCurto were en route to Moody AFB to land when Jones contacted Tyndall Tower. He was overheard by MacDill AFB in Tampa who was monitoring the situation. At that point, MacDill tower controllers intervened.

What occurred during the time that MacDill made their takeover was documented in *The Panama City News Herald* on September 14, 1952 in an article titled, "Flyers Hunt Tyndall Pair." It states, "McDill operations told him [Lt. Jones] to attempt a landing at Valdosta, GA and gave him a fix…Failure of a radio compass was believed to be the cause of the pilot's non-compliance with the order directing him to land in Valdosta [Moody AFB]."

USAF explained what allegedly happened at this point in the incident. MacDill AFB public information officer Captain Mitchell stated the following at the Sept. 12, 1952 press conference in Tampa, "First inkling that the craft was in trouble came when the pilot called Tyndall Air Force Base. He was directed to land at Valdosta, GA [Moody AFB] but for some reason, failed to comply with orders to land."

I believe that this portion is a fabrication. Jones had not notified Tyndall by radio that he was unsure of his position. Since he was in radio contact with Tyndall tower, why didn't he also explain why he could not contact Moody AFB? Why did the Air Force have to speculate that Lt. Jones radio compass failed? Furthermore, why did Jones fail to comply with orders to land at Moody?

Major Pompetti questioned Captain Harrison about Lt. Jones' onboard radio compass. The question as to whether the radio compass was functioning was answered. Furthermore, the question as to whether there was contact between Tyndall AFB and Lt. Jones at this point was also answered:

Q. Did Lt. Jones ever mention any difficulty with the radio compass, other than the [Tyndall] range going off the air, after the range went back on?
A. At one time, when we found him where he was I instructed the tower operator to have him [Lt. Jones] check the slave compass against the magnetic compass and we never did get a satisfactory reply. We were reading him very weakly and could not make out exactly what he said.
Q. Did he mention any malfunction of the radio compass after the [Tyndall] range went back on air?
A. No sir.

Lt. Jones approached Moody AFB to land his jet, but there was trouble on the ground. Two of the three jets that Tyndall tower redirected to Moody ahead of Jones had just crashed. The two damaged jets that were struggling with their electrical systems had approached Moody erratically and upon touching down, crashed, caught fire, and tied up the airfields. At that point, it was not possible for Lt. Jones to land. Jones and DelCurto were given orders to go into a holding pattern and await further instructions. At this time, while the aviators were circling near the base in their holding pattern, they were said to be lost and unable to contact Moody tower. While Jones kept the jet in a holding pattern and awaited his landing orders from Moody tower, there was a change in events.

The "medical report of AF Aircraft Accident" document explains this section of the incident as well. It states, "He [Jones] called Tyndall Approach Control and was given a VHF/DF steer to return to TAFB [Tyndall AFB]." At this point in the incident, Jones and DelCurto were supposedly being steered back toward Tyndall AFB in Panama City. The airmen had been listening via radio to the transmissions of the lone Moody airmen who were about to go into a one on one battle against the escort UFO. The Moody jet ascended and was about to attempt another intercept against the UFO. The jet went into a dive, approached the object and locked on to it. As gunfire careened through the sky, the object veered away fired and missed as the two veered away from each other at blinding speed. The jet continued to dive, maneuvered past the UFO and headed toward the downed object. The UFO then turned and reversed positions and headed toward the jet.

When Jones and DelCurto were said to be returning to Tyndall AFB, they were actually en route to assist the lone Moody AFB jet that was about to go one on one against the UFO. They kept in constant radio contact with Tyndall AFB tower controllers, who were directing the two flyers toward the air battle of the UFO and the remaining Moody AFB jet. Colonel B. T. Kleine's September 17, 1952 letter should have stated that the Tyndall radio directional finding had given Jones a steer in the direction of the air battle to assist the lone Moody jet, which was at odds against intercepting the UFO. The time was approximately 4:00 p.m. CST. While Jones and DelCurto were en route toward the air battle area, the UFO was attempting a diversionary maneuver to divert the jet away from the downed object sitting near the power lines.

Jones proceeded southwest as the UFO continued toward the Moody jet, the Moody pilot informed Jones that he believed the object was closing in on him to strike. This pilot decided to counter maneuver and go after the UFO. The pilot completed a wingover and dove directly toward the object. As the Moody jet approached the UFO, it struck first and fired.

The object maneuvered away from the diving jet, and fired back. With blinding speed, the jet veered away unharmed. It headed toward the UFO again. The fighter pilot fired and once again missed the target. Simultaneously, the UFO fired, hitting and disintegrating the jet. Jones and DelCurto continued southwest having heard what had just occurred. The UFO turned toward Moody AFB, wanting to neutralize that base before any more jets could be scrambled. Moody AFB runways were ablaze from the jet fuel of the two crashed fighter jets. Ground crews were still trying to clear the twisted metal wreckage so they could safely scramble more jets as a fiery carnage raged across their fields.

Jones and DelCurto were redirected on a northwest heading around and away from the UFO. Its intention was to descend upon Moody AFB to prevent any more jets from being scrambled. The Air Force's intention however, was to have Jones avoid a deadly confrontation, then redirect him back toward the Panama City area and go after the downed object again. Jones continued on his northwest heading as the UFO continued in the other direction on a northeast heading toward Moody AFB.

At approximately 4:15, Lt. Jones declared an emergency because this time he actually was lost and requested directions toward Panama City. During the Aircraft Accident Investigating board proceedings on 29 September 1952, Major Pompetti asked Capt. Harrison the following, "Q. Did the pilot at any time declare an emergency? A. No sir." This answer was an outright lie. The following information appeared in the Extract From Air Rescue Service Report, Maxwell AFB dated September 24, 1952. [To Headquarters, Fifth Air Rescue Service] from Tyndall AFB and contradicts Harrison's answer. It stated, "At approximately 1615C [4:15 CST] 12 September 1952, 819 [Lt. Jones] called Tyndall Tower and declared an emergency, lost, and five minutes fuel left."

When Jones declared his emergency, he was temporarily lost. He became lost when Tyndall controllers redirected him away from the UFO, not because he had five minutes of fuel left as the Air Force stated. Lt. Jones actually needed directions back towards the Panama City area. The jet did not allegedly flameout until 4:42 p.m. CST, which is a time lapse of twenty-seven minutes later, not five minutes. The emergency information contained in the preceding extract sent to Maxwell AFB by Tyndall only contained a partial truth!

At approximately 4:15 p.m. CST, the situation took a turn for the worst at Moody AFB in Valdosta, GA. As fighter jets hit the runways to takeoff, the UFO descended upon the base and began to circle the airfield. The object fired towards the ground near the jets. Supervisory personnel ordered their tower controllers to keep their jets grounded. At this point, if the jets attempted to takeoff, it would have been like shooting ducks in a barrel. The jet pilots on the ground preparing to scramble were contacted and told not to takeoff.

To complicate the situation, the electromagnetic fields of the objects that hovered over the two bases had disrupted the Air Forces airwave communications. Simultaneously, Tyndall redirected Jones back south through Tallahassee tower controllers and towards Panama City.

At this point, Tyndall AFB tower controllers directed the jet over the Florida panhandle through Tallahassee Airport. This F-94 Starfire was being tracked on radar throughout the state. The USAF and the two aviators realized the situation had now taken a turn for the worse and was hopeless. The flyers' options had run out. Jones and DelCurto, aware of their dire situation, were actually trapped between both bases and unable to land at either one. Moreover, military ground forces were unable to reach the damaged object and the Air Force was concerned it would escape before they reached it.

Documents from the case reported information about Lt. Jones fuel capacity at 4:20 p.m. CST. A September 17 teletype from Tyndall to Norton AFB stated, "1620 CST pilot called in with 94 gals." The "Report of AF Aircraft Accident" also stated, "0819 had 94 gals of fuel left." This information was relayed to Tallahassee Tower because 0819 could not read Tyndall Tower. Approach Controller S/Sgt. Ernest S. Bolen explained the following to Major Pompetti, "Tallahassee advised they were reading 0819 loud and clear. Tyndall Tower relayed 318-degree steer through Tallahassee Tower. The aircraft acknowledged steer from Tallahassee." The Tyndall "Direction Finding Log" recorded the time of their 318-degree steer at, "TIME-1620 (4:20 p.m.)."

S/Sgt. Bolen continues, "At this time, Tower contacted Jacksonville control and advised of the situation. Also called Florida State Police to patrol area between Tyndall and Apalachicola vicinity. MacDill then got in contact with the aircraft on another channel and Jacksonville control had alerted rescue facilities."

The situation that Tyndall AFB had alerted the Jacksonville control about was an emergency. At 4:21 p.m. CST, Tyndall AFB relayed a message to Tallahassee Airport who in turn contacted Lt. Jones.

The "Report of AF Aircraft Accident" document stated the following, "At 1621 C [4:21 p.m.] a second bearing of 320-degrees was given by Tyndall AFB." The Tyndall AFB "Direction Finding Log" also disclosed more information of what occurred at 4:21 p.m. CST. At that time, Lt. Jones had declared another emergency.

The "D/F log" states, "A/C IDENT - 0819. COURSE - 320. TIME-1621. REMARKS - EB EMER. [Emergency]."

This was the second emergency declared by Jones in six minutes. The first was at 4:15 p.m. CST. What supposedly occurred next was the most convoluted segment of this entire incident. Although Lt. Jones had declared a second emergency at 4:21 p.m., the USAF never disclosed the location of the supposedly lost jet at 4:20 or 4:21 p.m. The coordinates were never given and the information concerning this segment of the incident is vague in details. This was obviously never disclosed because it would have raised too many questions concerning the validity of this incident. Jones and DelCurto were actually northwest of Tyndall AFB, and proceeding on a southeast trajectory towards it.

The jet was supposedly being steered back to Tyndall AFB with just over 90 gallons of fuel remaining, back into the area where they were redirected away from because of supposedly bad weather. During this emergency, Tyndall officials were said to have alerted the Florida State Police to patrol the Tyndall-Apalachicola area according to tower controller S/Sgt. Bolen. Jacksonville control was supposedly alerted of the emergency as well. In turn, they were said to have alerted rescue facilities. This emergency was not a premeditated crash landing area for Jones' jet though. This was the Air Force's cover story. This was the area where the damaged object was down along the coast. Military officials actually contacted the State Police because they did not want civilians in the area if there was an opportunity to retrieve the object. The rescue facilities were contacted in case a situation did rise between the Starfire and the downed object and the airmen needed emergency attention. At this point, all the bases were being covered to hide the outcome of this event.

Between 4:21 p.m. and 4:25 p.m., Tyndall was steering Lt. Jones back toward Panama City and ordered him to survey the area just southeast of the base. Jones was told to find the downed object, fire upon it and make sure it stayed grounded. Ground forces were advancing slowly to the area. It would be a while longer before the area could be reached. Jones flew southeast passing directly over Tyndall on course with this objective. Moments later the jet passed over the St. Joe area, the landing site of the downed UFO.

The jet descended and several small smoldering fires could be seen, damped out by the falling rain. Billowing smoke could be seen near the power lines, rising from a black and burnt area on the ground near a utility pole. As Jones made a closer pass, both he and DelCurto noticed that the downed craft was gone. They passed over the area searching for it, to see if it had relocated nearby. Jones followed the power lines and the object was spotted a few miles away. Once again, the object had its balloon apparatus aloft at a power line and continued to replenish its electrical power.

As the jet, headed toward the downed craft, Jones informed Tyndall AFB of the craft's exact location and told them he was going to attempt an air strike. Seconds later, the downed craft lifted off, disconnecting from the balloon's umbilical cord that was connected to the power line. Moments later the balloon separated from the power line and drifted away into the sky. Rather than risk another air strike that could permanently disable it, the craft began to flee and fired at the maneuvering jet but missed.

Jones quickly banked the Starfire, put the jet in a dive and chased the fleeing UFO toward the Florida coastline. As the UFO picked up speed, it continued to ascend, with Jones in hot pursuit. If not for Jones and DelCurto, the damaged UFO would have been able to charge itself to full capacity. Instead, the weakened UFO was unwillingly forced to deal with a jet that was desperately trying to take it down. Jones closed the gap on the UFO as it neared the coastline west of Apalachicola on a southeast trajectory. Shortly after the damaged object passed over the Gulf waters with Jones and DelCurto following right behind it.

At 4:25 p.m., MacDill intervened once again and began steering Jones and DelCurto. The following segment concerns this point in time of the incident. Tyndall Approach Control Officer, 1st Lt. Dunn was asked by Major Pompetti, "Q. At what time did MacDill start working him? A. I would say it must have been around 1625 [4:25 p.m. CST] because we were giving him steers through Tallahassee on 'B' channel. All of a sudden, he switched to 'C' channel—someone else was working him."

First Lt. Dunn also made this statement in his signed certificate, "Aircraft switched from 'B' channel to 'C' and started working MacDill." When Capt. Harrison was questioned by Major Pompetti and the board concerning this segment of the incident, the following conversation transpired:

Q. When did MacDill D/F take over?
A. We [Tyndall] did not have any way of telling exactly when they took over. We got information from Tallahassee and they just notified us MacDill was working him [Jones] and we discontinued giving steers.
Q. Can you tell us how long this aircraft was following Tyndall's D/F from the time they regained contact with him?
A. I would say about five minutes or longer. When we first made contact with him again through Tallahassee Radio, I made inquiry about fuel and he had 94 gallons."

Tyndall AFB colonel B. T. Kleine stated the following in his letter, "The Tyndall radio directional finding gave him a steer to Tyndall AFB. MacDill Air Force Base directional finding [Homer] was able to pick up Jones' voice and gave him a steer also." Air Defense Commander, General Chidlaw stated the following in his Western Union telegram to Lt. Jones' brother, on 15 September 1952, "The Tyndall tower was directing him to MacDill AFB FLO, which was the nearest base." Capt. Harrison told Major Pompetti this segment of the incident concerning MacDill's takeover from Tyndall. He said, "By working through Tallahassee Tower, which was able to read him, we relayed headings and steers for him [Jones] and Tallahassee relayed back information which Lt. Jones had to give. MacDill then started working him since he seemed to be closer to them."

What did Capt. Harrison mean in his statement that MacDill was working with Lt. Jones "since he seemed closer to them"? Lt. Jones had just passed over the Florida panhandle coast on a 318-degree bearing, just southeast of Tyndall AFB. The direct flight path to MacDill in Tampa on the West Coast peninsula; however, was about ten degrees east of where Jones was actually being steered. Then when MacDill AFB gave Jones his first steer, the jet was 145 statute miles away from their base in Tampa, yet only 100 miles from Tyndall in Panama City. At this point, Jones would have had less than 90 gallons of fuel left…only enough to get him part way to MacDill AFB across the Gulf of Mexico. This apparently would have been a one-way trip! Jones and DelCurto never had any intentions of going to MacDill AFB when they passed over the Florida coastline.

Furthermore, Jones had more fuel than what the USAF stated; this was the Air Force's cover story. Jones was not lost and low on fuel…he was actually in hot pursuit of a fleeing UFO. The damaged UFO started to overheat as it sped away from the jet and was forced to slow down. It was burning up and could not risk flying any faster. If the damaged object did not decelerate as it traveled further south over the Gulf, it would deteriorate even further and be unable to get back to the coast. Meanwhile, the Starfire was in afterburner and consuming a large amount of fuel. Jones kept a watchful eye on his fuel gauge to avoid the same problem of being unable to reach land. Jones began to close the distance between them, as both aircrafts proceeded farther out over the Gulf.

The overheated object flew erratically to compensate for its loss of speed, trying to outmaneuver the jet. This strategy caused the damaged craft to lose control slightly. Jones pursued the object and guided his Starfire toward his erratic moving target with the assistance of DelCurto. Jones followed the object, momentarily got a lock-on it and then fired. However, the UFO had decelerated, pulled abruptly out of the fray, reversed direction and avoided the gunfire. The damaged object quickly ascended into some clouds and disappeared. After their failed intercept over the Gulf, the nearest base at this point was actually MacDill AFB. As Colonel B. T. Kleine explained, "MacDill Air Force Base directional was able to pick up John's voice and give him a steer also."

As Jones and DelCurto proceeded further southeast, MacDill radar officials alerted the flyers that the UFO had now started pursuing them. The aircraft's ammunition was nearly depleted as MacDill officials continued to steer the jet southeast. Controllers advised Jones and DelCurto to redirect their flight course and proceed towards Tampa and put their wheels down. The UFO continued to trail the Starfire, intending to follow it back to MacDill from a distance and from a higher altitude. It slowly descended, keeping the jet below and in front of it, trying to prod it to a lower altitude until it reached the coast and landed.

Meanwhile at MacDill, the combat air patrol jets continued to circle their base in anticipation of an aerial attack. However, the CAP fighter jets were not vectored toward the incoming UFO. MacDill officials believed doing so would result in deadly results for Jones and DelCurto. There were still two UFOs hovering north of Tampa along the coastline that could maneuver and attack at any moment. Any fighter jets maneuvered toward the direction of the damaged UFO might prompt attack by the two additional UFOs on the Starfire. An attack at this point could have proved disastrous for all of the jets. The situation had developed into a dangerous standoff. Frantic MacDill radar controllers advised the flyers to immediately direct toward the coastline and to continue descending. The pilot and navigator were still aware that the UFO was still following behind them, forcing them to fly at a lower altitude. Jones and DelCurto believed they were being maneuvered for an intercept attempt.

At 4:35 p.m. CST/5:35 EST, Jones and DelCurto were in afterburner, trying to outrun the UFO approximately 80 miles northwest of MacDill AFB. They were in radio contact with MacDill radar controllers who were tracking both the jet and UFO. Again, the flyers were ordered toward Tampa and told to attempt a landing at MacDill. The UFO continued to trail the Starfire while descending in altitude.

Jones was fully aware of the descending UFO's position and simultaneously descended. Both aircraft continued southeast toward the coast, cutting in and out of clouds and rain. Jones continued to drop in altitude, but had no intention of leveling off and proceeding to MacDill AFB. He contacted MacDill tower and made controllers aware that he intended to go after the object. A reverse maneuver would put the Starfire onto a northwest heading towards the object. Ground Control Intercept could guide the fighter jet onto an intercept course at the damaged UFO, since the jet had enough ammunition left to attempt one more good strike.

Jones then put the Starfire into a steep climb and ascended back up into the heavens. As the jet soared through sky, he quickly redirected it and completed a renversement. The jet was now on a northwest heading and the UFOs intent to trail the jet had failed. MacDill GCI guided Jones and DelCurto onto a direct intercept course toward the oncoming UFO. The Starfire soared through the air as DelCurto guided the jet toward the object. The autopilot was coupled with the jet's radar. As the two aircraft neared one another at blinding speed, the Starfire obtained a lock-on onto its target. The UFO accelerated, went into a dive and then changed direction as cannon fire blanketed the sky and partially hit the diving object, which burst into flames.

The damaged object did not go down and struggled to pull out of its dive as the Starfire continued heading northwest, completely out of ammunition. The damaged object slowly pulled out of its dive but was having trouble-attaining altitude as it continued southeast being tracked on radar. MacDill then radioed the flyers and told them that the object was still airborne. At 4:37 p.m. CST/5:37 p.m. EST, Lt. Jones contacted MacDill and alerted them that even though he was out of firepower, there was one remaining offensive maneuver to attempt.

"Ramming" as defined by the USAF, "In air combat, an act or instance of deliberately flying or crashing into an enemy aircraft, engaged in only as a tactic of last resort." Jones and DelCurto had decided against proceeding to MacDill to land and opted to go after the UFO. Their plans; to set the jet on to a collision course at the object and to eject from the jet before impact. The pilot began his renversement to go back south and maneuvered the Starfire into a wingover. Colonel Kleine should have made the following statement in his September 17 letter, "Shortly afterward, Jones said that he and DelCurto had decided to engage with the UFO and ram it." General Chidlaw should have stated the following in his September 15 telegram, "He informed MacDill AFB that they were going to attempt to ram the UFO."

General Chidlaw's September 17 telegram should have explained, "Immediately thereafter John completed a renversement and proceeded on a southeast heading after the damaged UFO to ram it." MacDill AFB began to direct the two flyers onto a course to approach the damaged object in a lead-pursuit intercept attack. Meanwhile the fleeing UFO had burst into flames as it continued southeast over the Gulf waters. Its power supply had diminished and the object needed to locate power lines where it could land and replenish its energy. At this point, the damaged object opted to go near the populated west coast area and did it want to risk going anywhere near MacDill AFB who still had their jets on combat air patrol. It redirected and proceeded on a northwest course toward the Florida Panhandle with the intention of landing in an isolated area to recharge.

At this point, both aircraft had reversed their flight headings and were now proceeding toward each other. MacDill alerted Jones that the UFO had just reversed its course away from the West Coast area and was now headed northeast in their direction. The UFO proceeded back north in the direction of the oncoming and diving F-94 Starfire, while struggling to keep its altitude steady. It flew erratic in an attempt to turn away from the jet and shake it. It then accelerated in an attempt to go below the diving jet so to continue past it heading north in the opposite direction away from it.

At 4:41 p.m. CST/5:41 p.m. EST, MacDill gave Jones a steer towards the northbound UFO flying below them. At 4:42 p.m. CST/5:42 p.m. EST, MacDill guided the jet on an intercept course and Jones brought the jet down to an altitude of 15,000 feet. The jet continued to proceed toward the object in a dive, as the UFO tried to pass below it in the opposite direction. At this point, the jet supposedly had a flameout. Colonel B. T. Kleine stated, "Shortly afterward, he [Jones] said he had a flameout at 15,000 feet."

The Tampa Daily Times reported the following on September 13, "Lt. Col. Rosenblatt base operations officer [MacDill AFB], said the last coherent radio contact with the plane disclosed the pilot had engine trouble at 15,000 feet over the Gulf." It also gave the following information about the Starfire, "an Air Force jet plane last heard from at 5:42 p.m." *The Tampa Tribune* reported the following information about the flameout, quoting the same time as *The Tampa Daily Times*, "Earlier MacDill Air Force Base at Tampa reported a jet fighter has been unheard from since it radioed it was out of fuel at 5:42 p.m. [EST]." *The Tampa Tribune* also reported the following, "The pilot was unable to give his exact position, and MacDill said the fighter could have been anywhere up to 70 [nautical] miles northwest of Tampa at the last radio report."

According to the USAF version, the Starfire had a flameout. I compiled the following list of events in sequential order, as given by the USAF. I used the 4:42 CST flameout time. [The official report gave 3-times].

1. The Starfire radioed that it was out of fuel at 4:42 p.m. CST.
2. The pilot had engine trouble at 15,000 feet over the Gulf.
3. The Starfire had a flameout.
4. The flameout occurred at an altitude of 15,000 feet over the Gulf of Mexico.
5. The pilot was in radio contact with MacDill AFB when he notified them of the jet's flameout.
6. Jones was unable to give MacDill AFB tower his exact position.
7. The last coherent radio contact from the pilot occurred at 4:42 p.m. CST.
8. The last coherent radio contact from the pilot disclosed the jet was at 15,000 feet.
9. The jet had not been heard from since it radioed that it was out of fuel.
10. MacDill AFB said the Starfire could have been anywhere up to 70 miles northwest of Tampa at the last radio report.

According to the USAF version, when Jones reported the jet's flameout at 15,000 feet, the Starfire then descended 7,000 feet. At 4:43 p.m. CST, the last radio sound heard from the jet indicated it was down to 8,000 feet. The UFO accelerated and began to flame up into an inferno. It swerved and tried to avoid the jet, which was now descending and heading in its direction. Jones and DelCurto proceeded at the object with the assistance of MacDill GCI and achieved a radar lock-on moments later. The pilot put the engine into afterburner, flashed through sky, and headed directly at the UFO. The object veered away from the descending jet and tried to avoid a mid-air collision but was too slow to out-maneuver it.

The Starfire continued to approach the object to ram it and showed no sign of turning away. The swerving UFO began to accelerate while redirecting its heading northeast. This maneuver proved ineffective. The descending Starfire closed on the UFO in afterburner and still locked-on to ram it. As the Starfire closed on the object and the flyers were about to eject, the object hit the jet with a tremendous shock causing its electrical system to go haywire and malfunction, blowing the circuit breakers. The jet was fried and the stunned airmen were knocked unconsciousness as the jet dove at the damaged UFO. At that point, there was complete radio fadeout and contact was lost. The F-94 B Starfire cut through the air like a javelin as it approached the damaged object. Sadly, the "ramming" technique chosen by the two flyers had unwillingly turned into a kamikaze mission.

Seconds later, at 4:43 p.m. CST, the UFO fired on the approaching jet and disintegrated it. Air Force personnel on the ground were unaware if the crew had bailed out of the jet. Radar operators tracking this incident only knew that the jet had disappeared from their radar screens. This segment of the incident agrees with the original statement made to the press, by MacDill AFB Public Information Officer Captain Paul Mitchell. On September 13, *The Tampa Daily Times* reported that Mitchell stated, "The last radio sound indicated the disabled craft was down to 8,000 feet. The time was 5:43 [4:43 p.m. CST]." MacDill base operations officer, Lt. Col. Charles A. Rosenblatt, stated the following: "There was complete radio fadeout at 5:43 [EST/4:43 CST] at about 8,000 ft. Standard procedure is for the crew to bail out."

The damaged UFO continued toward the Florida panhandle coastline and transmitted a call to the other UFOs hovering throughout the southeast. It notified them that its power was nearly drained and it desperately needed to land and regenerate. Meanwhile, the MacDill AFB combat patrol jets patrolling the base were ordered to stay over the vicinity of Tampa and not to pursue the object over the Gulf of Mexico. Very slowly, the damaged UFO proceeded across the Gulf and received instructions to land near the Apalachee Bay area, south of Tallahassee, where it could recharge its nearly depleted system.

The damaged object continued to burn-up as it descended en route to its destination to make a landing. Furious Washington officials were being informed of the unfolding events throughout the southeast, including the recent Jones and DelCurto incident. Air Force bases along the Florida coast alerted them that radar was still tracking the damaged UFO. During this time, Air Force officials from Tyndall AFB informed Washington that it was inevitable the damaged UFO was going to land again to recharge. The government had another opportunity to attempt to capture the damaged craft once it landed but how long would it be on the ground was another question.

Government officials were fully aware that Air Force and Naval Air Stations along the Gulf of Mexico were still neutralized as well as military flight paths leading to the Gulf waters. Brookley AFB and Pensacola NAS already had their flight paths into the Gulf of Mexico neutralized by a UFO hovering off the coast and were out of the picture. Jet attacks through corridors over populated areas to reach the damaged object were ruled out. Upon landing, this object had to be kept on the ground until it could be retrieved.

Air Force officials jointly devised a plan to utilize fighter planes from their Alabama bases. They would head southwest toward the Florida panhandle coastline and then proceed out over the Gulf of Mexico west of Pensacola NAS. The planes would then redirect east and head toward the area where the object was descending toward the Apalachee Bay coastline. If they reached the area, they would attempt an air strike. The planes from Alabama were deployed shortly after and headed toward the Gulf waters along the southern Alabama coastline. However, as they neared the coast to flank around Brookley AFB there was a sudden change in events.

While en route, their movements were being tracked. As they neared the coast to proceed across the Gulf, an object that hovered over the Gulf near Brookley AFB and two objects that patrolled the coastline near

Pensacola NAS and Eglin AFB descended and moved into strategic positions. The UFO out over the Gulf waters south of Brookley AFB turned inland toward the Alabama coastline and moved northwest as the two other objects shifted west as backup. The first object continued northwest, passed over Mobile Bay and did a flyby over Brookley AFB. It then descended on the city of Mobile, and began to circle the area. Moments later, for fear of negative repercussions on Mobile, the entire attack plan was aborted, as the heavily armed UFO continued to patrol over that densely populated city. The planes then headed back to Alabama.

Meanwhile, at about 5:45 p.m. EST/6:45 p.m. EDT, the damaged UFO continued descending as it proceeded northwest and neared the Apalachee Bay coastal area. The object continued to descend over the Gulf toward the panhandle coast as Tyndall officials tracked it until it dropped below radar to the southeast of their base. Tyndall radar operators and officials realized the object needed power and knew its objective. Simultaneously, Tallahassee Airport officials also tracked the object and actually had a visual on it as it neared the coast just southeast of them only a short distance away. Moments later, the object passed over land, decelerated and headed for the powerlines along the coast and prepared to land.

Tallahassee Airport officials knew the approximate area where the object was going to land near the coast and notified Tyndall officials of the location. In desperate need of electricity, the damaged UFO headed toward the power lines and transformers along the panhandle coastline. Tyndall officials immediately contacted the contingents of heavily armed ground forces who were in the Port St. Joe area. The ground forces were ordered to redirect toward the Apalachee coast area in an attempt to reach the relocated object. Moments later, they headed east. The cat and mouse game continued in the densely wooded Florida swampland...

Wrapping up the events up to this point, the UFOs that descended on the southeastern United States on September 12 had all, actually, originated from one main large craft. This enormous craft was a carrier, or mothership, capable of holding and transporting many smaller crafts. It was positioned over the southeastern Unites States, high above the outer atmosphere of the earth, known as the exosphere. The mothership hovered in space and had dispatched the sixteen smaller crafts toward Earth. These crafts made atmospheric entries and observed the Florida panhandle coastline; they were on an aerial reconnaissance mission to examine military installations throughout the southeast. When three of these crafts descended toward the Gulf, fighter jets intercepted them. One of the UFOs was hit and damaged, and it sustained a major power loss. It was unable to ascend out of the earth's atmosphere and reach the mothership. When the Air Force attempted to intercept the damaged object again, the remaining UFOs descended to protect it and the situation escalated. Jets were lost, several were damaged, and many were recalled back to their bases. Moreover, military installations and flight paths were neutralized.

During this entire event, the United States military was the aggressor. The UFOs used their armaments only in retaliation after being fired at. During these air battles, the United States military became well aware of the objects superior armaments. Even though the UFOs had superior propulsion systems, their armaments drained them and slowed them down. Therefore, the more power used, the less powerful their arms.

The UFOs had another disadvantage, they were also large, cumbersome and when their power drained, they became less agile. The UFOs still overcame the jets even when they were outnumbered by a ratio of 4 to 1 because of their devastating powers, yet they were vulnerable to the armaments of Air Force fighter jets. During these air battles, the American jets were the slugger going up against the boxer. Above all, the jets were at another major disadvantage, while they were trying to outmaneuver the UFOs, the entire area was being monitored by the mothership hovering high above the Gulf of Mexico. This craft was directing the objects below it and keeping them informed of the fighter jets' maneuvers during these air battles.

"SHOOT THEM DOWN"

The damaged UFO continued to descend and landed near the power lines along the Apalachee Bay coastline at approximately 5:55 p.m. EST/6:55 EDT. In the meantime, the mothership that was positioned over the Gulf off the Florida coast, had headed northeast over the United States. The downed and damaged object then launched another balloon-type apparatus toward the power lines at the transformer and began to charge itself as ground forces headed toward it. Meanwhile, the mothership proceeded northwest above the atmosphere and passed high over Virginia. It then flew over Delaware, continued south of New Jersey, and passed out over the Atlantic Ocean. The mothership continued northwest over the Atlantic, stopped and located about 90 miles off the coast of New Jersey. It positioned itself near the 39-degree latitude/73-degree longitude mark, an area approximately 200 miles east of Washington D.C. The time was approximately 6:00 p.m. EST/ 7:00 p.m. EDT.

The position of this craft across from the nation's Capitol was not a coincidence. This was the area where the three flight paths of the damaged mid-Atlantic UFOs converged. These three flight paths all converged near the 39-degree latitude/73-degree longitude point. This was the area where the three mid-Atlantic objects were actually dropped from their mothership. The three objects made their atmospheric descents into this area shortly after 7:00 p.m. EDT.

This descent into the atmosphere east of Washington and into the radar net of the Atlantic ADIZ was an assertive act to make their presence known to Washington officials. The intention of the three UFOs was not to attack Washington; they could have already done that by descending on the city. Their objective was to warn Washington officials to keep away from their damaged craft in Florida and leave it alone. The "pilots" of the UFOs knew the damaged craft sitting in Florida needed time to regenerate before it could lift off again.

Meanwhile, radarscopes along the mid-Atlantic and northeast coastline had picked up the three descended UFOs, and the Pentagon was immediately notified. Washington officials had not interpreted the appearance of the objects as a warning. They interpreted their appearance as a threatening maneuver to attack Washington. President Harry Truman pulled- out all the stops and the entire situation took a turn for the worse.

Secretary of Defense Robert Lovett advised President Truman that an all-out air assault against these objects was inevitable, that the UFOs should not compromise the United States any further. An enraged Truman agreed. I cannot help but echo the words stated by President Truman in 1949, *"It is much better to go down fighting for what is right than to compromise your principles."* President Truman then ordered the nearest east coast Air Force bases and Naval Air Stations to scramble their rocket-bearing and cannon-armed jets to intercept the UFOs. At approximately 7:05 p.m. EDT, U.S. fighter jets were en route to intercept the objects ninety miles off the coast, with orders to *"shoot them down."*

The nearest Air Force bases that scrambled fighter jets toward these objects are as follows:

1. McGuire AFB, Wrightson, NJ - 90 miles away
2. Dover AFB, Dover, DE - 120 miles away
3. Mitchel AFB, NY – 125 miles away
4. New Castle AFB, Wilmington DE – 135 miles away
5. Stewart AFB, Newburgh, NY – 175 miles away
6. Andrews AFB, Camp Springs, MD – 193 miles away
7. Westover AFB, Chicopee Falls, MA – 205 miles away
8. Langley AFB, Hampton, VA – 220 miles away
9. Otis AFB, Falmouth, MA – 235 miles away

The following four Naval Air Stations scrambled fighters:

1. NAS New York, NY - 120 miles away
2. NAS Willow Grove, PA - 140 miles away
3. NAS Patuxent River, MD – 180 miles away
4. NAS Norfolk, VA – 220 miles away

Additional jets were put into action over the United States. These jets began combat air patrols around Washington to protect the President and all government officials. They were dispatched from the following military installations:

1. Bolling AFB, Washington, DC
2. Andrews AFB, Camp Springs, Maryland
3. Quantico Marine Corps Air Station, Quantico, Virginia
4. NAS Patuxent River, MD

The United States Navy had the duty to patrol the Potomac River area, which included the District of Columbia. On duty in this area were the Potomac River Naval Command and the Severn River Naval Command. The best fighter jets the Air Force, Navy, and the Marine Corps possessed at that time are as follows:

AIR FORCE
1. Thunder Jets a) F-84E b) F-84G
2. Sabre Jets a) F-86D b) F-86E c) F-86F
3. Starfires a) F-94B b) F-94C

NAVY
1. Banshees a) F2H-2
2. Cutlasses a) F7U-1 b) F7U-3
3. Sky Knights a) F3D
4. Panthers a) F9F-2 b) F9F-3 c) F9F-4
d) F9F-5

Republic F-84E Thunder Jet

MARINE CORPS

1. Panthers a) F9F-2   b) F9F-3

The jets I have listed here were the superior fighter jets during that time of the various models of aircraft possessed by the military. Three of these fighter jets were armed with powerful twenty-four 2.75-inch rockets nicknamed the "Mighty Mouse." This air-to-air rocket was four feet long and weighed 18 pounds and carried a seven-pound explosive warhead. These rockets had a greater range than aircraft machine guns, which made them more deadly. They served as an optional weapon on the F7U-3 Cutlass were standard-issue on the F-86D Sabre Jet and came equipped on the Air Force's newest aerial defense innovation, the F-94C Starfire.

The other jets that I listed were also armed with powerful weapons. The Air Force jets carried multiple .50 caliber cannons and the Navy and Marine jets carried 20 mm machine guns that could deliver thousands of rounds of fire. The F-84E fighter jet armed with six .50 caliber cannons was also capable of carrying wing loads of thirty-two 5-inch HVARs (High Velocity Aircraft Rockets). In combination, all of these military fighter jets had the capability to deliver devastating firepower against airborne enemies.

Chance Vought F7U-3 Cutlasses

Shortly after, East Coast Air Force bases and Naval Air Stations vectored their fighter jets after the UFOs being tracked on radar. The pilots knew that these objects were vulnerable to the cannon firepower of their jets and were aware of their opponent's weapons. The fighter pilots received strict orders to keep a safe distance from them and to be extremely cautious. Unlike the aerial battles over the Gulf, the circumstances of this situation would be different. Several of these fighter jets were armed with rockets including the new 2.75-inch rockets. "Mighty Mouse" was about to go into battle.

On September 13, 1952, *The Boston Globe* reported this unusual incident that involved jets on September 12, 1952. This incident took place over Rhode Island, forty miles from the coastline:

Unidentified Jets 'Buzz' R.I. Town

Residents of the Tarklin section were thrown into near panic today when two unidentified jet planes "buzzed" the area. According to complaints they roared 30 feet above the ground at one time. Raymond F. Cahill, town Civil Defense director, said he would report the incident to Army and Air Force authorities at the New Haven [CT] filter center.

Mrs. Cyril Bruineel of Tarklin Road reported it was only a "miracle" that her house wasn't hit by one or both of the jets. She said the planes flashed by at lightning speed almost at rooftop level, barely missing telephone wires. The woman said she threw herself flat on the ground during the "buzzing" and that terrified farm animals kept up a noisy chatter for 45 minutes. Another Tarklin woman, Mrs. James A. Starck, of Barnes road described the experience as "harrowing." She said it appeared as though the planes would crash into houses or trees at "almost any second."

This article informs us of a highly unusual episode that occurred over Rhode Island that involved two jets. In 1952, the only American jets flying over the United States were fighter jets. The article states the aircraft were "two unidentified jet planes." The nearest Air Force base to the Tarklin area was Westover Air Force Base, in Chicopee Falls, Massachusetts. This base is located about 55 miles northwest of Tarklin and home of the 4707th Defense wing, 60th Fighter Interceptor Squadron. These two jets were probably Sabre Jets from Westover AFB. These jets would not be flying at such a low altitude under normal circumstances as to endanger the lives of innocent civilians. Their very low altitude would indicate they were flying well under radar to go undetected or "In the weeds." Nevertheless, why were the two jets fighters flying at such a dangerously low altitude and where were they going "at lightning speed"? The unusual circumstances of this event lead me to believe that they were scrambled on an intercept mission…into the Atlantic ADIZ.

Ground Control Intercept stations along the coast guided the jets towards the objects and minutes later, the first jets from McGuire AFB reached the UFOs. Within seconds, these fighters unleashed an aerial assault. The UFOs retaliated with return fire and destroyed the nearest striking jet. As jets and UFOs scattered, the remaining jets prepared for another attack. Several more fighters arrived from Dover AFB and NAS New York and entered the air battle. A full-scale air battle was underway and the sky was covered with dozens of 2.75 rockets and thousands of rounds of gunfire.

The UFOs started firing against the striking jets. Some were destroyed while others had their onboard electrical systems temporarily jammed causing malfunctions. Fighter planes then arrived from Mitchel AFB and fired at the UFOs, unleashing a barrage of cannon fire. The UFOs shocked nearby planes and fighter pilots struggled with their aircraft's electrical systems. Some were recalled and returned to nearby bases. Seconds later, a wave of jets from New Castle AFB arrived. The New Castle jets were also heavily armed with rockets and salvoed their FFARs while the UFOs attempted to strike at the swarming jets. The UFOs were becoming weaker and slower as their weapons drained their power sources. During this episode, one of the UFOs had been separated from the other two crafts, becoming a primary target. While jets continued their relentless fire on the other two UFOs, fighter jets from NAS Willow Grove arrived into the battle and fired at the objects.

Dozens of fighter jets swarmed throughout the air battle, launching Mighty Mouse rockets, HVARs and firing countless rounds of cannon fire. The singled out UFO became a target and was overwhelmed with relentless firepower. It managed to temporarily paralyze a closing jet, but more and more kept attacking and attacking. The relentless fighter jets fired at the UFO from every angle and direction then quickly pulled out and away. The long-range rockets were a surprise to the intruders and the repeated firing of their weapons at the striking jets was starting to take its toll. Their weapons were getting weaker as their electrical systems were being depleted. They were also starting to slow down. The rocket-bearing jets had an advantage in this particular air battle while the cannon-bearers followed up during several attacks.

Fighter jets continued to barrage the lone UFO with rocket and cannon fire and the sky looked like a hailstorm. This onslaught was a success. At approximately 7:20 p.m. EDT, the object was hit by several rockets followed by a barrage of cannon fire. The electrically charged gravity field surrounding the object exploded like a fireworks display as sparks flew in every direction and covered the sky. The damaged UFO instantly lost altitude, went into a rapid dive and then burst into flames as it careened through the atmosphere.

The two remaining UFOs withdrew from the air battle. They attempted to return to the safety of the carrier ship hovering high above the atmosphere. Their attempt was futile as fighter jets had surrounded the entire area and cut off their access points to the mothership. The fighter jets continued to fire mercilessly on the two remaining UFOs as a pair of Navy fighters arrived into the air battle area.

Meanwhile, the worst-case scenario involving the damaged object occurred. It had descended and headed toward the United States coastline. A fighter jet attempted to intercept it, fired on it, but this attempt was not successful. The pursuing jet fired on the object again, hit it, and then banked away. The blazing object did not go down but drastically lost altitude and continued toward the eastern seaboard of the United States.

Minutes later, the UFO passed over the Delaware coastline. The NAS Patuxent River and Stewart AFB jets had reached the air battle area and had begun to fire on the two other UFOs. The remaining jets, which had run out of ammunition, headed back to nearby Air Force bases, but additional fighters from the east coast were being scrambled into service. The entire air battle area was once again swarming with maneuvering fighter jets firing on the two crafts. The UFOs attempted to shock some of the nearest striking jets but the jets kept their distances. The objects also fired at them but only managed to take one more down as the jets kept redirecting, closing, firing and quickly breaking away.

At approximately 7:35 p.m. EDT, the two UFOs attempted to ascend and reach the carrier ship high above them. Before they could reach their destination, however, they were attacked by yet another wave of fighter jets from Andrews AFB. One of the objects managed to outmaneuver the onslaught of firepower, but the other object was caught by a barrage of rockets, hit and exploded.

This damaged UFO became the second victim of the fighter jets. Sparks fell like rain as it began to head toward land at about 7:36 p.m. EDT. It had sustained more damage than the first damaged UFO. This craft suffered damage to its gravity field as well as to its structural shell and proceeded toward land at tremendous speed in a dive. A pair of Navy jets chased it, fired on it with cannon fire and the object was hit again. The damaged object exploded again, burst into flames and continued to dive as it headed northwest toward the east coast engulfed in flames. Meanwhile, the third object was involved in a lone raging confrontation with fighter jets over the Atlantic. This object desperately sought to ascend to the mothership when jets from Westover AFB arrived into the air battle area.

While these events unfolded over the mid-Atlantic, another series of events had simultaneously developed over the southeastern United States at 7:36 p.m. EDT. In Florida, ground forces continued east after the damaged object that was still recharging. Several vehicles of men neared the object with explosives and firearms but were noticed. Even though the damaged object was not fully charged and up to par because it was heavily damaged, the object had enough power to fly and possibly attempt to exit the atmosphere. The object rapidly lifted off and finally left Florida soil. The remaining UFOs neutralizing the southeast military installations made their exit as well and ascended out of Florida with it. The military retrieval had failed.

Meanwhile, off the mid- Atlantic coast over the Atlantic Ocean, yet another UFO had descended from the carrier ship as fighter jets from Langley AFB and NAS Norfolk reached the battle and began to fire. This jet-shaped UFO made its atmospheric descent into the air battle to assist the third object, but arrived too late.

At 7:40 p.m., Otis AFB jets arrived into battle from above and joined the Westover jets that were now swarming the third object while keeping a safe distance from it. These fighters then launched an all-out devastating bombardment of rockets and cannon fire that blanketed the sky and hit the UFO, which failed to retaliate. The crafts gravity field exploded around it while rockets caused severe structural damage to the body. Sparks covered the sky, fire engulfed the UFO and it immediately dropped in altitude then went into a dive. It changed its heading and then proceeded due west toward the east coast. The blazing UFO continued to descend, leveled off and then was attacked by a merciless onslaught of firepower from another pair of pursuing jets. Sparks and pieces exploded from the object as it wobbled and continued to descend but failed to go down. The severely damaged UFO headed on a western heading…directly toward Washington D.C.

The second damaged object, which had been hit about five minutes before, had already crossed into Delaware. The first damaged UFO was continuing on its southwest heading over Virginia, nearing Roanoke. It was approximately 7:40 p.m. EDT and all three mid-Atlantic objects had been damaged. They were the:

1. The Virginia/TN #1 Object
2. The Baltimore/WV #2 Object
3. The Washington/Flatwoods #3 Object

Meanwhile, the jet-shaped UFO was still in air combat with fighter jets. While the fighter jets were trying to intercept this UFO, the three damaged objects headed farther west. All of the UFOs that had departed Florida were heading toward Washington, DC, making the capitol their target. This red-alert crisis had gone out of control and was escalating toward total disaster. Aviators had perished, numerous jets had fallen, and an enemy with frightening potential had made a base 90 miles off the coast of the United States above the atmosphere. Moreover, there were also three damaged UFOs inevitably going down in the United States.

In the following ten minutes, between 7:40 and 7:50 p.m. EDT, United States government officials had to make the biggest military decision in history. When the three mid-Atlantic UFOs were damaged over the Atlantic and forced down, they all took different flight paths. The Virginia/TN #1 Object proceeded southwest. It had sustained a minimal amount of structural damage. However, it was unable to travel at maximum speed because its gravity field was damaged. The Baltimore/WV #2 Object went northwest, having sustained significant structural damage.

The Washington/Flatwoods WV #3 Object flew due west towards the coast. It had suffered the most severe structural damage to its body and had the slowest rate of speed. The three damaged UFOs were spreading out in a fan-like pattern. Their objective was to reach and threaten key government locations including military installations. Each UFO had a different geographical target.

A.) *The Virginia/TN #1 Object* headed southwest toward Oak Ridge National Laboratory.
B.) *The Baltimore/WV #2 Object* had targeted Wright Patterson AFB in Dayton, Ohio.
C.) *The Washington/Flatwoods #3 Object* headed due west to Washington D.C. This craft's target was the Capitol.

These three damaged UFOs chose these targets to get the attention of Washington officials and to intimidate them into withdrawing their jets from the Atlantic air battle. [Note: See map on page 167]. Before the three UFOs were damaged, the main concern of the UFOs was to get their damaged craft out of Florida. When southeast military forces were relentless in trying to capture it, the mothership situated off the Florida coast decided to position itself east of Washington over the Atlantic as a warning to officials to back off from their downed craft in Florida. This warning did not work. Washington officials deemed this action as a maneuver to attack the capital and the military aggressively attacked the three UFOs that descended from the mothership.

The first damaged UFO undoubtedly intended to neutralize the Top-Secret, Oak Ridge National Laboratory [ORNL]. Oak Ridge is the home of the atomic bomb and was "ground zero" for nuclear research and in 1952, simulated hydrogen or 'fusion' bomb tests were being tested at Oak Ridge.

Targeting ORNL would surely be an extreme action that would clearly indicate a message to Washington officials to back off the downed craft in Florida. ORNL was no secret to the UFOs. Edward Ruppelt made the following statement in his book, "UFOs were seen more frequently around vital areas to the defense of the United States. The Los Alamos-Albuquerque area, Oak Ridge, and the White Sands Proving Ground rated high. Strategic Air Command bases and industrial areas ranked next." During this time, both the FBI and USAF wanted to downplay all UFO sightings because they were directly responsible for the security of these installations, and the seemingly at-will breaches were becoming an embarrassment to J. Edgar Hoover.

The second damaged UFO proceeded toward Dayton, Ohio, with the intention of neutralizing Wright Patterson AFB. Washington officials had not yet realized the intentions of these two damaged crafts proceeding inland.

In Florida, the grounded craft struggled to ascend and shortly thereafter, discovered it was still unable to climb out of the atmosphere. Simultaneously, the rest of the southeast UFOs ascended with it. They exceeded an altitude above the reach of any fighter jets that may have went after them and then headed north. The damaged ship, being escorted by four other objects led the way flying at high altitudes in the upper atmosphere. The intentions of all the objects were to drop in over the capital and several surrounding areas. This strategic maneuver actually involved a main plan and an optional plan. Depending how the government handled the unfolding events would determine how and when these plans would be implemented.

The main plan, descend over the capitol and other populated areas in a blatant aerial display. This maneuver by the UFOs would certainly make their presences well known and would easily enable military radar stations to track them and their movements. If this threatening maneuver worked, it could possibly pressure military officials into withdrawing jets from the mid-Atlantic air battle and their combat patrol jets from over and near Washington. Then, the situation would be over.

The optional plan: if the jets were not withdrawn from the Atlantic air battle and the combat air patrol areas over the coast, then several of the UFOs would descend where needed between the coast and Washington D.C. to clear a path for the incoming westbound damaged craft. This plan would result in an air battle along the coast or over Washington with combat patrol jets. If complications developed and the damaged ship went down in the area in a confrontation, one of several ships would be there to extract it.

The Washington/Flatwoods #3 Object targeting Washington was being tracked on radar as it descended towards the east coast. It also wanted to pressure officials to withdraw jets from the Atlantic air battle. This damaged UFO was contacted and made aware that several more ships from the south were en route to Washington and nearby areas. If Washington did not withdraw any of the coastal combat patrol jets when the UFO passed over land, the UFOs would attempt to force the jets out of the way to let their damaged craft by.

Meanwhile, several fighter jets had focused their attention on intercepting the last mid-Atlantic UFO, the jet-shaped object. Fighter jets swarmed around the UFO and continued to mercilessly fire upon it. The UFO was trapped and unable to reach the mothership hovering above as waves of incoming jets kept going after it.

The third damaged object continued to descend toward Washington on a direct flight path and showed no sign of turning away. This was the point when Washington officials had ten minutes to decide the fate of the United States and possibly the world.

In the meantime, the mothership was high over the Atlantic, and dropped yet another object from its hull. This UFO was another jet-shaped UFO object, the #2 Jet-Shaped UFO. The #2 Jet-Shaped Object did not drop into the air battle area though, it descended near the coast of the United States. This object was traveling at tremendous speed at a high altitude toward West Virginia. Its mission was to locate an isolated area where the damaged "Flatwoods Monster" craft could make an emergency landing. Should the damaged ship reach this area, it could make repairs, and then depart the area after dark. It could then relocate to an area near the power lines where it could regenerate itself and leave. The emergency landing area to be chosen for this incoming ship had to be located to the west of Washington, but along its direct western flight path. The area had to be situated far away from any Air Force bases. The area had to be situated at a high altitude where the damaged ship would have clear access to land, especially if it was flying erratically. The location had to be a very high hilltop with a clearing. The damaged ship was contacted and informed that the beacon drop plan was underway.

The #2 jet-shaped UFO quickly continued toward central West Virginia. Washington radar stations and Ground Observer Corps stations continued tracking it and officials were unsure of its intentions. This maneuver around Washington might have been a flank attack against the capital. This maneuver might have been a plan to bypass Washington and proceed toward Oak Ridge, Tennessee or Dayton, Ohio. In any event, the UFO complicated the problem for Washington officials. They had to decide how to handle the situation of the third incoming damaged craft. Meanwhile, the #2 Jet-Shaped Object flew south of Washington, passing over southern Maryland and northern Virginia en route to West Virginia. Several people sighted the #2 Jet-Shaped Object as it passed over Virginia.

The Baltimore Sun, September 13 (UP) article, subtitled "Like A Flaming Jet," stated, "Persons throughout Virginia saw what they variously described as a 'big star,' a 'flying saucer' and something 'like a flaming jet plane.' They said it ranged in color from pale yellow to greenish and reddish and was noiseless. It moved from east to west." As this so-called flaming jet plane continued west, it was sighted over Harrisburg, VA, twenty miles from the West Virginia border. *The Ohio Columbus Citizen* reported on September 13 in an article titled "Fireballs Shower City Area…Residents in Harrisburg, VA reported a 'cigar-shaped' object trailing blue-green flame [which] streaked across the sky."

The southwest-bound object was still heading toward Oak Ridge and was nearing Roanoke, VA. The northwest-bound object en route to Dayton had just passed over the Delaware coast. The third damaged mid-Atlantic object was over the Atlantic Ocean, heading toward Washington D.C. In the meantime, the entire southeast group of UFOs was high above Georgia, quickly moving up the coast toward Washington. The Ground Observer Corps and radar stations were tracking the Virginia/TN #1 Object. As reports of the UFO's location were being forwarded to Washington and the ADC, military officials were quickly plotting its flight path. Shortly after 7:40 p.m. EDT, Washington officials realized this UFO's projected flight course was Oak Ridge, Tennessee. It was only 240 miles away from its designated target.

Meanwhile, the Baltimore/WV #2 Object, engulfed in flames, decelerated and descended over Baltimore at approximately 7:46 p.m. It buzzed the city at a very low altitude. The UFO then accelerated to a higher altitude, blazed past Baltimore, and headed northwest. During this time, Washington officials still had not withdrawn its fighter jets from the air battle area over the Atlantic. Unbeknownst to these same officials, the group of sixteen UFOs from Florida was still headed northeast toward them above the atmosphere...undetected.

The #2 Jet-Shaped UFO, at about 6:55 p.m. EST chose the Fisher farm in Flatwoods for the emergency landing location. The jet-shaped UFO, according to witness A.M. Jordan, "proceeded across the sky, then halted suddenly [and] seemed to fall rapidly toward the hilltop." This was the point when the UFO dropped a homing device onto the Fisher farm hilltop for the damaged object to follow. The jet-shaped UFO then quickly departed the area.

This particular drop area in Flatwoods, West Virginia was by no means a randomly chosen site for the emergency landing. The state of West Virginia has no Air Force bases located within its borders. Several of the nearest ones are located in other surrounding states that encompass West Virginia.

As the damaged object proceeded on its due west trajectory after passing over Washington D.C., it actually "threaded the needle" of Air Force bases around it. The object continued to descend along its flight path. During this time, it was actually flying under radar. This maneuver made the object virtually impossible to track by radar as it headed west to Flatwoods while avoiding any potential jet interception attempt.

Furthermore, Flatwoods being the geographical center of the state, was an ideal location to make an emergency landing. There were no nearby bases to impose an immediate threat against the damaged object once it landed ... mainly the threat of a capture by force. In addition, it would be nearly impossible for the Air Force to find the grounded object from the air in this mountainous region, especially at night. The following Air Force bases encompassed Flatwoods, WV. They are listed in a clockwise order starting from the north. I have also listed the approximate distances from each Air Force base to the town of Flatwoods:

1. Greater Pittsburgh Airport, PA. Base for the 71st Fighter Interceptor Squadron. [F-86 Sabre Jets] -125 miles north of Flatwoods
2. Olmsted AFB., PA- 240 miles northeast of Flatwoods
3. Andrews AFB., MD- 200 miles east of Flatwoods
4. Bolling AFB., Washington D.C.-195 miles east of Flatwoods
5. Langley AFB., VA-. 250 miles southeast of Flatwoods
6. Pope AFB., NC- 255 miles south/southeast of Flatwoods
7. Shaw AFB., SC- 320 miles south of Flatwoods
8. Donaldson AFB., SC-280 miles southwest of Flatwoods
9. Godman AFB., KY- 280 miles west/southwest of Flatwoods
10. Clinton County AFB., OH- 170 miles northwest of Flatwoods
11. Wright Patterson AFB., OH- 205 miles northwest of Flatwoods

The mothership contacted the damaged westbound object headed toward Washington and notified it that an emergency landing area had been found, and the homing device had been dropped. The damaged ship notified the main craft that its propulsion system was damaged and drastically deteriorating. It did not know if it would be able to regenerate itself if it reached the designated landing area safely, it might be stranded.

Meanwhile, the first five UFOs that departed Florida were also in contact with the mothership. One of these ships was the damaged object that was downed in Florida and unable to ascend out of the atmosphere. It was flying at a high altitude and being escorted by the other four ships, but was losing altitude quickly. The damaged Florida object was experiencing problems again and beginning to overheat. It began to flame-up from friction brought on by its extreme velocity. The five were ordered to immediately change their flight paths away from the Washington D.C. area and make their way to West Virginia.

The downed Florida object had become such a major concern that the mothership felt it safer to redirect it towards the relatively unpopulated woods of Braxton County with its escort ships. This damaged craft was in no condition to travel to Washington D.C. and assist with the plans to descend over the capitol. If a battle ensued this object would not be able to fight. They already had a severely damaged object headed west toward Washington D.C. and two more within the United States. At this point another plan was implemented, a rendezvous and rescue mission. I designated the five northbound objects the North Carolina Rescue Objects.

The objective of the rescue mission was to rendezvous with the incoming westbound damaged object in Flatwoods when it landed and keep these two inbound damaged objects in the same area. Upon reaching the rendezvous area, the Fisher Farm, the two damaged objects could land, cool down, and possibly make repairs, then leave. If they were beyond repair, they would leave their crafts behind on the farm or a nearby area. They would then be picked up by the escort ships, and ascend out of Braxton County. The westbound damaged object, the Washington/Flatwoods #3 Object was notified of the plan in progress. The damaged Florida object continued to lose altitude as the five objects continued northbound over North Carolina at approximately 6:50 p.m. EST. Shortly after, the damaged object descended over Lumberton. The second object also descended into the Lumberton area and the third object descended into the Winston-Salem area. Two additional objects were part of the rescue mission. They were the #4 North Carolina and the #5 North Carolina Rescue Objects.

The #4 North Carolina Rescue Object descended over the area of Flatrock, North Carolina, located along the North/South Carolina border. This area is approximately 25 miles northeast of Greenville, South Carolina. Greenville and was home of the Donaldson AFB 18th Air Force. This base is situated along the Oak Ridge National Laboratory, ADIZ perimeter. The #5 North Carolina Rescue Object hovered high over North Carolina and patrolled over the area south of Pope AFB, Fort Bragg.

Both objects hovered over North Carolina to thwart off any possible offensive maneuvers against the three northwest bound objects and guarded their flight path corridors. The remaining eleven southeast objects continued north toward the Washington area above the atmosphere and completely undetected.

The three rescue objects that had descended in North Carolina then picked up the signal of the homing device on the farm in Flatwoods. Upon their descents, several witnesses throughout North Carolina began to report sightings as the three UFOs passed over the state and continued toward their destination in Flatwoods. The #4 North Carolina Rescue Object that hovered over Flat Rock, left the area, headed north and followed the three objects toward West Virginia.

Meanwhile, Ground Observers throughout the mid-Atlantic were calling in the sighting of the Baltimore/WV #2 Object. Washington area radars were simultaneously tracking it, for it was still ablaze as it-neared Cumberland, MD. At that point, military intelligence had projected the object's flight path and calculated that it was en route to Wright Patterson AFB. Every military official involved was aware of the possible consequence.

President Truman was then alerted by several military sources. He was informed that the third damaged UFO they had been tracking just passed the east coastline. It was descending and still on a trajectory toward

Washington. If the worst-case scenario occurred, the craft would crash in the city, putting thousands at risk. Truman was then notified that nearby radars were tracking several UFOs headed toward the Washington area at a high altitude. The UFOs had blatantly descended and made their presences well known. Shortly after, they arrived over Washington and other nearby states, maneuvered into position, and descended further. These UFOs stopped, hovered and then waited above the ceiling ranges of the combat patrol jets. Washington officials were wondering whether Washington and or nearby areas were going to be attacked from the sky above. Key targets would be the Capitol and surrounding military bases.

President Truman and the National Security Council, including Secretary of Defense Robert Lovett, discussed the options with the Department of Defense. A quick decision had to be reached regarding the withdrawal of the fighter jets from the air battle over the Atlantic. President Truman, as Commander in Chief of the Armed Forces, gave the order to withdraw the jets from over the Atlantic Ocean air battle area.

Shortly after, the jets withdrew, but there were still several combat air patrols of jets on alert patrolling the area between the capital and the coastline. The front line jets guarding the coastline from the Washington area against an enemy attack were still on combat air patrol. Suddenly, the UFOs that were hovering over the different areas began to descend slowly. Truman was once again alerted by nearby radar stations. The President being concerned with a possible assault by the descending UFOs instructed the frontline combat air patrol jets to withdraw from the coastal regions. The incoming damaged UFO was not to be intercepted.

The combat air patrols over and near the immediate area of Washington were not ordered to withdraw. They were ordered to intercept the incoming UFO only upon receiving direct orders. Truman would have to decide whether to give these orders as the situation unfolded. If Truman gave the order to intercept the UFO coming toward Washington, what course of action would the two UFOs heading toward Oak Ridge and Wright Patterson take? If President Truman ordered the incoming damaged UFO taken down, it would inevitably crash near Washington. To attack this incoming UFO would probably mean catastrophic outcome, considering that several UFOs were hovering over Washington and might descend and strike against the jets, nearby bases and the city.

By approximately 7:51 p.m. EDT, the jets off the mid-Atlantic coast were disengaged from battle against the jet-shaped UFO and heading back toward their bases. The large carrier ship contacted all three damaged westbound UFOs and ordered them to abort and cease their progression toward their targets. The first jet-shaped UFO had departed the air battle area and proceeded back toward the mothership. Moments later, the mothership proceeded due west toward the coastline and headed toward Washington D.C.

The Air Force had sent combat air patrols into the perimeter of the Oak Ridge Air Defense area from three separate bases, forming a triangulation net pattern surrounding Oak Ridge. The three Air Force Bases were Dobbins AFB in Marietta, GA, Godman AFB in Louisville, KY, and Donaldson AFB in Greenville, SC. The patrolling jets within this highly restricted area were ordered not to make any aggressive maneuvers. They were instructed only to attempt an intercept upon receiving direct orders from their base superior commanders. Wright-Patterson AFB had also put up jets around their perimeter in anticipation of an attack as well.

Meanwhile, the Virginia/TN #1 Object had been called off from the Oak Ridge National Laboratory. It began to decelerate to find a location to land. It had already traveled approximately seventy miles into the Oak Ridge Air Defense area. At about 6:55 p.m. EST, this UFO landed just across the Tennessee border in Arcadia, about 110 miles northeast of Oak Ridge without any incident.

The Baltimore/WV #2 Object that had targeted Wright Patterson AFB in Dayton was over Morgantown, WV, when it was called off. It began to decelerate and sought an area where it could land.

The third mid-Atlantic damaged object was the "Flatwoods Monster" ship. It was engulfed in flames and approached Washington on a due west course. The nearby Washington area fighter jets on combat air patrol around the Capitol and other areas had not yet been ordered to withdraw. This strategy was deemed as an offensive maneuver against the damaged UFO. Still hovering above the atmosphere, the mothership craft continued west, headed toward Washington, and reordered the other two westbound objects toward their original designated targets again.

Seconds later, the Virginia/TN #1 Object, which had just landed in Arcadia, took off and once again proceeded toward Oak Ridge. Simultaneously, the Baltimore/WV #2 Object, which was searching for an area to land near Morgantown, continued toward Ohio. When this object started toward Dayton once again, the residents of Fairmont sighted it. *The Charleston Daily Mail* reported; "About 40 persons in the Fairmont area said the object looked like a spotlight with a greenish tail and was traveling from 100 to 500 miles per hour."

Military radar installations had again begun to track the Virginia/TN #1 Object. Washington officials were immediately alerted that it was moving toward Oak Ridge again. Nearby military installations also alerted them that the UFOs being tracked on radar over Washington were now descending upon them. President Truman had to decide if he should let the damaged flaming UFO get closer to Washington D.C.

If Truman let the incoming UFO through to Washington, what would it do upon arrival? Would it bypass Washington and go farther west, or would the damaged object execute the worst-case scenario? If President Truman let the UFO through, would it land in the city in front of thousands of witnesses, or would it attack Washington and destroy it? On the other hand, if Truman struck at the object as it approached DC and the craft went down in the city, it could kill many civilians and the Capitol could be attacked from above as well. If that happened, the President of the United States would have to tell the American public that the government had known that extraterrestrial aircraft were visiting earth. Moreover, if Truman did choose to strike at the incoming object, what would happen if the other two objects continued on to Oak Ridge and Dayton?

Equally important were the series of events that unfolded above them. The UFOs that were hovering over Washington, Virginia and Maryland continued descending as the mothership neared the Washington area. If the nearby combat air patrol jets were not withdrawn, the Washington, DC area could be the scene of a raging full-scale air battle.

Truman and his military advisors held the fate of the nation in their hands. With only minutes remaining to make a decision, Truman decided to call off the fighter jets on Combat Air Patrol. Then all he could do was hold his breath, wait and pray as the object headed toward Washington D.C. Shortly after, at about 8:00 p.m. EDT, the damaged "Flatwoods Monster" ship passed over the northern part of Washington. *The New York Times* called this object the, "Flame over Washington." This UFO actually buzzed Washington as it passed over the heads of "jittery Washingtonians." When *The New York Times* reported the incident, the reporter wrote, "The blazing object moved horizontally across the heavens and came 'awfully low.'" This is the UFO that I designated, the Washington/Flatwoods #3 Object.

The mothership passed high over the Washington area overseeing the situation and then contacted the Virginia/TN #1 and the Baltimore/WV #2 Objects. They were immediately called off from their targets because the "Flatwoods Monster" ship had passed over Washington without incident. The Virginia/TN #1 Object redirected its southwest heading after traveling another 35 miles toward Oak Ridge. It headed east over Rogersville, Tennessee. One witness was "Sam Miller of Rogersville [who] reported a ball of fire resembling a meteor passed over there about 7 p.m. heading east. Miller said it 'looked like a full moon with a tail on it.'"

The Baltimore/WV #2 Object was called away from Dayton also. It was engulfed in flames and burning up, traveling at near maximum speed. This damaged craft slowed and searched for a spot to land. It could not land immediately as it was over a heavily populated area near Columbus, OH. The craft redirected northeast and flew directly over Columbus, heading for the northern West Virginia panhandle. Shortly thereafter, it passed over Zanesville. *The Columbus Citizen* reported CAA officials at Port Columbus concurred with Zanesville CAA officials in describing the phenomenon as "probably a meteor shower."

The Columbus Citizen also reported, "In Zanesville, CAA officials at the [Zanesville] Municipal Airport said an army pilot at 10,000 feet reported what looked like a burning plane." What the pilot actually saw was the damaged UFO engulfed in flames. A distress call was made to the mothership and the damaged UFO was instructed to land in an isolated area near an easily recognized landmark and wait for assistance. As the damaged object headed toward the West Virginia panhandle, it followed the signal of the Wheeling-Ohio County Airport in Wheeling, WV. Upon reaching their airspace, "One pilot said the object nearly clipped the wing of his aircraft." After this near mid-air collision, the UFO redirected on a southern heading and searched for an area to land. Shortly after, it landed a few miles away in the area of Oglebay Park. Meanwhile, the Washington/Flatwoods #3 Object was following the homing signal to Flatwoods as the three North Carolina rescue ships were traveling more than twice as fast toward that small town being followed by their back up, the #4 object.

At this point, the "Flatwoods Monster" craft was west of Washington D.C. and passing over Virginia. It was reported, "A pilot en route to Wheeling from the east reported sighting the object from the vicinity of Front Royal, VA." This pilot had actually sighted the Washington/Flatwoods #3 object. He noted that it was "tremendously large" and "seemed to disappear in a bunch of sparks." It was flying erratically at a low altitude and was having trouble staying airborne. This object was literally burning up and the farther it traveled, the more damaged it became. It had to slow down so it did not crash before reaching its rendezvous point in Flatwoods.

In the meantime, military officials had ordered combat air patrols into the air around all major military installations throughout the country. These fighter patrol jets were ordered not to make any offensive maneuvers toward the UFOs. Radar operators had sighted the three rescue ships over North Carolina proceeding northwest. Military officials realized that all this UFO activity was a rescue mission in progress. Washington officials decided that the safest and most logical way to proceed with such an incredible situation was to leave it alone.

At about 7:00 p.m. EST, the three North Carolina Rescue Objects were sighted passing above the Appalachian Mountains in Virginia, with the #4-rescue ship trailing them. It was reported, "Persons in southwest Virginia saw at least three flashing objects that were described as meteors."

After these three objects passed over Virginia on northwest trajectories, they crossed over the southern West Virginia border and passed over Monroe County and then Summers County. Shortly after, they flew over Greenbrier County and continued onward towards Flatwoods to rendezvous with the incoming damaged craft. While over Greenbrier County the #4 object received word to go directly to the Wheeling area where the Baltimore/West Virginia #2 object had gone down. The #4 North Carolina Rescue Object was needed in the Wheeling area to participate in another search and rescue mission. This "flying saucer" immediately ascended to a higher altitude, departed the area on the double and headed toward the northern panhandle area. The three North Carolina Rescue Objects continued north and passed over Nicholas County then crossed over the border into Webster County. The next county they would fly over would be Braxton County

When the three objects passed over into Webster County on their northern flight path, they were seen. I spoke to the witnesses about this sighting. I received a letter from a man who lived in Gauley Mills, West Virginia back in 1952, and now resides in Florida. This witness, Mr. Frank Woods, contacted me after hearing me on a talk radio program. He wrote, "I was listening to George Noory's program and heard Linda Moulton Howe talking about Frank Feschino." He stated, "I thought you might like an eyewitness account of the 'UFOs' of 1952." Mr. Woods wrote me the following letter, "I was a teenager in the eighth grade, living in Gauley Mills, Webster County, West Virginia on the night of the "Flatwoods Monster" incident." Gauley Mills is a small town located approximately 25 miles southeast of Flatwoods. "I, with two or three other playmates saw three bright lighted objects streak across the sky in a northerly direction. It was about 7:00 p.m., shortly after supper." Several adult witnesses also saw these three objects as well. Mr. Woods stated what they thought about the lights, "Adults who saw the 'UFOs' (not called that at the time) said they were meteors." He then gave the following information:

They were close together in a triangular formation. We were too young to determine the altitude of the objects. Airliners did not fly across that part of the state, so it was uncommon to see anything larger than a piper cub. We dismissed the sighting until the next couple of days; *The Charleston Gazette* had run front-page pictures of the "Flatwoods Monster." I was not exactly sure where Flatwoods was located, except it was near Burnsville and Sutton and I knew where these towns were.

Shortly after receiving this information, I phoned Mr. Woods. He had no idea how the three objects he saw that night fit into the timeline of events that took me years to figure out. I asked him if we could meet and talk further about what he had seen. He agreed to meet me and we arranged a meeting in Orlando. A couple of weeks later, Mr. Woods met me and he talked further about his sighting. As we talked, I drew sketches and took notes about the incident. I was very adamant about knowing the direction that these three objects were headed. Mr. Woods explained to me "a boy growing up in the woods of West Virginia had to know his directions." He said it was "second nature."

By using "mountain ranges" and "rivers" as landmarks in the vicinity, as well as the location of the sun, one would be accustomed to directions. Mr. Woods was very distinct and detailed in his descriptions. He told me these three objects were "very bright" and "not small like stars." He stated, "They were not airplanes, or jets — there were no contrails." He added, "They were large." He told me, "They were heading North/Northwest at a high altitude," and "flying in a triangular formation when they passed over Gauley Mills, WV." I drew three sketches, and witness Frank Woods signed and dated the information I had written accompanying the drawings. The location of this incident, Gauley Mills, was then plotted on my master map.

At that time, none of the three rescue ships knew the location of the damaged ship, nor did the mothership since the damaged ship had descended to such a low altitude and was having difficulty transmitting.

At about 7:05 p.m. EST, the lead ship, the damaged ship, reached Flatwoods and was desperate to land. The other two objects arrived shortly after and then began their search for the "Flatwoods Monster" ship. Meanwhile, as the "Flatwoods Monster" ship headed west, navigating had become treacherous. About 80 percent of West Virginia lies in a plateau region of towering mountain ridges and narrow valleys. East of this plateau is rolling countryside. The mountains of West Virginia had now become the enemy as it struggled to stay in the air and began losing the signal of the homing beacon device.

As the damaged #1 North Carolina Rescue Object worked its way toward the homing device it descended below tree level and flew over the Fisher farm. It passed over the mountaintop on the rear of the property to rendezvous and land with the other damaged craft, the Washington D.C./Flatwoods #3 object. There was a major problem though...the "Flatwoods Monster" had not arrived yet. Within moments, all the rescue ships were engaged in a sweeping search and conducted in a thorough grid pattern and looking for the damaged craft in the likely event, it had crashed nearby.

These three objects had entered Braxton County from the south. The damaged ship flew over the Fisher Farm; another had flown to the north of Flatwoods and passed over the town of Heaters and the third object flew south of Flatwoods over the nearby Sutton Airport and began its search there. Each of these objects eventually made U-turns and then swept back to the south. The incoming damaged westbound ship, unable to contact its comrades, was still on its way to the rendezvous point on the farm and was over the Monongahela National Forest area.

The overheating ship struggled, decreasing its speed and had difficulty following the signal as it passed over the mountainous terrain. It veered off its direct course to Flatwoods and headed toward northern Braxton County. At about 7:15 p.m. EST, the "Flatwoods Monster" ship passed over Elkins, WV, engulfed in flames and continued west. Several residents in Elkins reported seeing this fiery object pass over them.

Meanwhile, the three rescue ships desperately continued their search. I was able to distinguish among the flight paths of the three North Carolina rescue ships by using all the information I had compiled:

1. The #1 North Carolina Rescue Object was damaged and on fire when it passed over the Bailey Fisher mountaintop to near the cistern to land.
2. The #2 North Carolina Rescue Object went five miles north of Flatwoods and passed over the town of Heaters.
3. The #3 North Carolina Rescue Object flew just three miles south of Flatwoods and passed over the Sutton Airport.

Investigator Gray Barker reported this information in his September 1953, Vol. 1, No. 1 issue of the Saucerian. Barker interviewed Mr. Hoard, who had seen an object pass over the Fisher farm and stated:

Mr. Hoard said he'd be glad to tell me everything he saw. At approximately 7 p.m. [actually 7:15 p.m. EST], he had gone out in his front yard to feed his chickens. His attention had been drawn to a fiery object coming over the horizon, though in a slightly different direction than the others reported. It had not landed but had gone across the sky. It went over the Bailey Fisher cistern and it was about here (he pointed to a location in line with his house) that a piece of fire broke off it. As it neared the horizon, toward the Sutton Airport, it exploded and went out.

This incident puzzled Barker because he thought this object was the "Flatwoods Monster" ship. This object reported by Mr. Hoard was actually the damaged #1 North Carolina Rescue Ship. It flew over the farm searching for the downed ship as to rendezvous with it and then land. Barker also stated, "And if Hoard were in his yard at the time, why did he not see the amazing occurrences on the nearby hilltop, easily within his view?" There was a reason that Mr. Hoard did not see "the amazing occurrences" that involved the monster encounter on the nearby hilltop; it was not the "Flatwoods Monster" ship.

Meanwhile, the #2 North Carolina Rescue Object was five miles north of Flatwoods over Heaters searching for the downed object. During one interview with Mrs. May, she said, "Jerry Marples from Heaters called the sheriff's office and said there was a flying saucer coming down behind the hill in Flatwoods."

Investigator Ivan T. Sanderson also reported the UFO sighting over Heaters. He said, "A bright globular object was seen passing fairly slowly through the sky at low altitude and at the same time as the others, slightly to the east of the settlement known as Heaters. This was allegedly seen by several people along a line to the southeast and to a point about due east of Sutton." It was leaving the vicinity after making its sweep of the area.

Sanderson also reported a "similar object was said to have passed over Sutton airport at the same time." This was the #3 North Carolina Rescue Object called the "shooting star," sighted over Winston-Salem and Mount Airy. These three North Carolina rescue ships did not locate the "Flatwoods Monster" ship and the designated rendezvous area on top of the Bailey Fisher farm was completely missed. The condition of the #1 North Carolina Rescue Object was also worsening and although there was still enough daylight to continue circling and sweeping the area, it would have drawn further attention to them, which they did not need. The three objects were ordered to leave the area and the damaged UFO needed to find another area to land.

Meanwhile, the damaged "Flatwoods Monster" ship continued west. The craft struggled to stay airborne, had difficulty following the homing beacon, and actually overshot Flatwoods to the north. It finally reached northern Braxton County, slowed down and then made a 45-degree turn and headed south, following the signal of the homing device on the farm. It then passed south over the town of Burnsville, located approximately ten miles north of Flatwoods. It flew over that town just above tree level and continued south following the road below it while moving through the valley of the surrounding mountains. The UFO then passed over Heaters, six miles south of Burnsville, continued to follow the road on its southern heading and neared Flatwoods, now only four miles away. Upon reaching Flatwoods, the object veered slightly off course as it continued to struggle and then burst into flames as it barely cleared a mountaintop in front of it.

Moments later, while proceeding south, it passed over the Flatwoods Elementary School playground where a group of boys was playing football. It then turned east, passed over the main road, continued to follow the signal and barely cleared the treetops as it passed over the Fisher Farm where the homing device was located on the back of the property. The damaged craft followed the signal to the back of the farm and landed on the grass in the wide-open field on the mountaintop at approximately 7:24 p.m. EST/8:24 p.m. EDT. The object sat aglow on the mountaintop, severely overheated and in dire need of assistance, awaiting the three rescue ships.

As the minutes passed, things became very grim. The occupant of the damaged craft had missed the rendezvous with the rescue ships by a matter of minutes and had missed its opportunity to make an escape. The ship was not in flames, but its interior was extremely hot. The propulsion system inside the craft was severely damaged. It was still glowing from the friction damage it had sustained from burning off plasma while traveling through the atmosphere.

The outer shell was severely damaged from the missile and gunfire it had received. The pilot of the ship needed to move the ship off the mountaintop to a less conspicuous location. It lifted off and moved into the pasture of a nearby valley. At approximately 7:30, the craft landed in a grassy field near the bottom of the sloping valley. Extreme heat caused by the damaged and leaking propulsion system radiated throughout the craft's cabin. The generator was barely producing power and the communication system was barely functioning.

Minutes later, communication was established with the mothership. A faint signal revealed that the pilot had reached the beacon on the mountaintop. The occupant was notified that the first rescue mission had been aborted, but another rescue mission would be underway shortly after dark. The alien was told to stay near the ship and beacon, so it could be found.

The occupant departed its ship to the cooler atmosphere outside the craft. When this tremendous creature emerged from its ship, it was wearing a metallic space suit. This space suit, which resembled a small shuttlecraft, was capable of hovering and was maneuverable. It was also damaged. The creature hovered toward the ground in its battle-damaged suit and descended over the grass. Its main objective was to head for cover where it could not be seen. The "Flatwoods Monster," then traveled across the open field and up the slope of the valley and maneuvered toward some nearby woods for cover.

It spewed oil from its damaged metallic suit leaving behind a scarred trail in the grass caused by the force of its propulsion system. Upon reaching the crest of the valley, the "Flatwoods Monster" hovered to a level grassy area. It traveled a short distance through some tall grass and brush and then hovered across a narrow dirt path bordering the woods blowing rocks and dirt aside. The creature then hovered up next to a large oak tree at the outskirts of the woods along the dirt path. Once there, it settled to the ground and concealed itself. The creature went undetected and waited to be picked up by the second rescue party.

Meanwhile, the damaged #1 North Carolina Rescue Object had difficulty flying. It did not leave the area with the other two North Carolina rescue ships that had already ascended out of Braxton County. The craft continued to struggle and was having trouble staying airborne; its propulsion system was in dire need of electrical power. The craft needed to find a power source at some location where it could land and regenerate. Before it found a source though, it crashed. I found documentation that pertained to a damaged object seen in Braxton County during that time. This object was undoubtedly the damaged rescue ship that was forced to make a temporary stay in Braxton County.

After Mr. Hoard saw the fiery object, circling over the back mountaintop of Fisher farm, it left the area and flew toward the nearby Sutton airport then a piece of fire fell from it. Mrs. May had told me that another one of the objects went down in Braxton County that night landed in Holly. Holly was an isolated, wooded area about five miles southeast of the airport. This site would account for the object after it was seen heading toward the airport. After the ship landed in Holly, it cooled off then departed the area. Again, it was reported in Braxton County when it crash-landed in the community of Sugar Creek located along on the Elk River.

On September 15, *The Charleston Daily Mail* reported the story, "Braxton Folks Divided Over Visitor." It stated, "Woodrow Eakle [sic] of Duck along the Braxton-Clay line was traveling toward Flatwoods as the aerial phenomenon made its appearance. He reported to Braxton County Sheriff Robert Carr a small airplane had crashed against a mountainside. A later search failed to disclose any remnants of the wreckage." Investigator Ivan T. Sanderson spoke with several witnesses. Sanderson said of the object after interviewing Woodrow Eagle, "He saw a flaming object, which he thought from his army experience to be a small Piper Cub plane, shoot over a saddle to his left, cross the main road, the river, and the rail line beyond, and crash into the wooded side of a steep hill immediately to the south."

Another witness "who lived on a farm above the road, had that night seen the flaming object come around the low hill opposite him, horizontally and below its crest, making a neat turn and then go into the valley where Mr. Eagle said he saw it crash. He described it as a 'flaming bucket with a tail.'" A man who lived in Sugar Creek said this to Sanderson, "He and others had been puzzled by the smoke that hung about the face of the hill in question on the evening of September 12, and remarked that there had been 'a strong smell of woods burning.'"

Woodrow Eagle reported the crash in Sugar Creek to the Braxton County Sheriff's Department. This was the first call that Sheriff Carr and Deputy Long responded to involving a supposed plane crash. When they arrived in Sugar Creek, they did a visual scan of the area and found no signs of an airplane wreck. The damaged craft that had crashed there had already taken off again.

The craft had actually crashed into a hillside along the Elk River, then lifted up, and landed on a mountaintop, where it could not readily be seen from the valley area below. It cooled down and rested shortly before it was able to take off again. Ivan Sanderson and four other men investigated the landing site at Sugar Creek. The "Flatwoods Monster" ship landed on the Bailey Fisher farm about the same time that the #1 North Carolina Rescue Object crashed in Sugar Creek. Shortly thereafter, yet another plane crash was reported about eight miles southwest of Sugar Creek along Elk River in Frametown. This plane crash incident was actually the crash landing of the damaged #1 North Carolina Rescue Object, after it departed Sugar Creek.

Gray Barker reported this incident in Vol. 1, No. 1, of the Saucerian. He said, "A Piper Cub plane, an excited hitchhiker was reporting, had crashed into a hillside near Frametown and was burning. He had seen it from a car from which he had received a 'lift,' then driven to the first available phone to report this incident. Sheriff Carr and a deputy [Burnell Long] rushed the seventeen miles to the scene but could find no trace of the burning plane." I retraced this same route by automobile as stated by Barker and traveled the same seventeen-mile distance along Route 4. The trip from police headquarters to the scene of the crash placed me about two miles west of the Frametown line. This was the area where the hitchhiker witnessed the alleged airplane crash. I noted a mountain in the nearby area that I believe to be the hillside referred to by this witness. It was across the Elk River from Route 4 where I was parked; this area was clearly inaccessible without a boat.

When the sheriff went to the site, he did not find a downed airplane because the object had already taken off again. While the sheriff was searching for the downed aircraft at about 8:15 p.m. EST, Cecil Rose, the Braxton County sheriff's office jailer, received the call from Mrs. May, who reported the monster incident in Flatwoods.

The next report of a UFO occurred about nine miles southwest of Frametown in the Duck Creek area along the Elk River. This was the next area where the #1 North Carolina Rescue Object was sighted. It is interesting to note that after the damaged object left the Holly area it followed the Elk River. It is evident that this damaged object flew above the river as it navigated between the mountains for safety reasons as it proceeded out of the area looking for a power source. The UFO sighting that occurred over Duck Creek was from an automobile along Route 4. Mrs. May explained what happened: "I heard a man and wife were driving through Duck [Creek] when they saw the thing. She was scared to death and in the hospital for about two days."

I then asked Mrs. May, "Why did the lady have to go to the hospital?"
She answered, "She thought it was a plane on fire, at first."
I then asked her, "What was it that scared her so badly?"
She answered, "It was one of those things flying around Braxton County that night."
I discussed with Colonel Leavitt the Duck Creek incident involving an automobile.

Frank: "Now, could you explain about the craft that flew over the automobile and what happened with that? Now that's never been documented?"

Leavitt: "No, it's never been documented, but it has been said from other people what happened. They [witnesses] just said the [UFO] shut its engine off and they couldn't it get started again. Then when it [UFO] left, they went on up the road."

Frank: "And the engine just started up again?"

Leavitt: "Yeah. Well, they started it up."

Frank: "But while the craft was over the top of it, the engine went completely?"

Leavitt: "Yeah, that's what they said."

Frank: "Was that the same night the [Fisher farm] crash happened here?"

Leavitt: "Yes. It was on the same night."

Frank: "Do you remember what part of town that was in?"

Leavitt: "Well, it was [pauses]; do you know where Duck Creek is? It was back this way."

According to my research, this was the last time the damaged #1 North Carolina Rescue Object was seen in Braxton County. This object was the same UFO shot down earlier near Florida and once again had difficulty flying. Furthermore, this same UFO engaged in the final aerial combat with 2nd Lt. John Jones and 2nd Lt. John DelCurto.

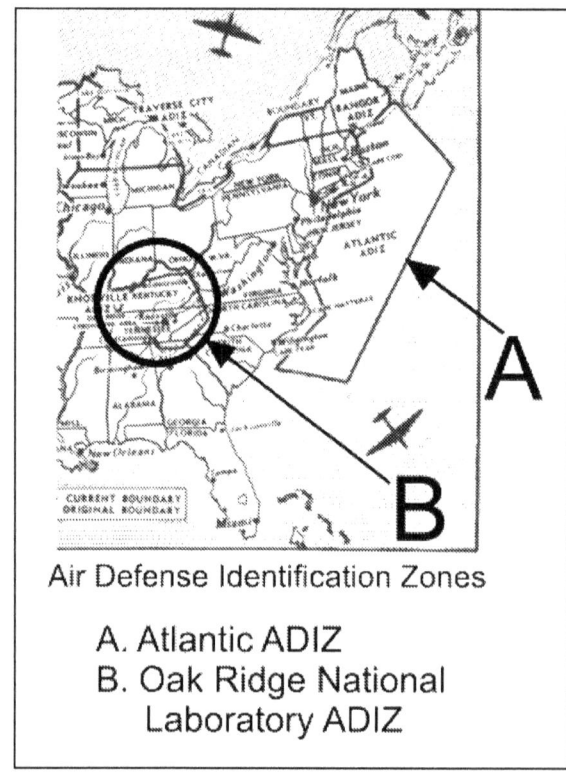

Air Defense Identification Zones

A. Atlantic ADIZ
B. Oak Ridge National Laboratory ADIZ

Chapter 27

DESCENDING GUARDIANS

Project Blue Book led the public to believe that the single "Washington area meteor of 12 Sep." was the cause of all the sightings over the Washington area.

I probed more deeply into the Project Blue Book files, hoping to find further information that would explain the discrepancies between these sightings. What I found were more documents that reported several additional UFO sightings made that evening. These documents included several Project 10073 Record Cards, numerous ATIC compilation reports and Tentative Observers Questionnaires. These reports all referred to several objects seen around 8:00 p.m. EDT. These sightings occurred on September 12, over the areas of Washington, Virginia, Maryland, and Pennsylvania.

ATIC explained away the numerous sightings that night within a Project 10073 Record Card and stated, "One of numerous Wash. DC area reports of 12 Sept. meteor."

Next, I combed through all the Project Blue Book reports and documents and put them into a comprehensible order. The most difficult task I had was separating the multiple sightings; the number of sightings reported does not directly correspond with the actual number of objects. I categorized the numerous sightings of the objects by their times, locations and descriptions.

I arranged all the information, picked out the most relevant facts, and constructed a chart comparing these objects. I was able to establish the number of objects seen over the Washington, Virginia, Maryland, and Pennsylvania areas around 8:00 p.m. I arranged the objects in order by the times of their appearance. I gave each object a designated number because so many of them were sighted around 8:00 p.m. EDT.

Based on my research of the sightings; there were two waves of UFOs that passed over the eastern United States that evening. The first wave of UFOs passed over the mid-Atlantic coastline shortly before 8:00 p.m. EDT. They were the first three damaged objects.

The second wave of UFOs were positioned over their designated areas and prepared to descend and assist the incoming damaged object as it proceeded west toward Washington D.C.

A witness from Washington, DC who saw this supposed single meteor recorded the following segment in Project Blue Book. It demonstrates the confusion that arose regarding the single meteor story when it appeared in newspapers.

"From newspaper accounts of other observers in the Washington area there was a very wide variation in the size, color and direction the object was traveling which, assuming they saw the same object as we did indicates the observation[s] of many people are unreliable in many respects."

Chart of the 13 UFOs that descended over Washington D.C., Virginia, Maryland, and Pennsylvania.

Object #	TIME ↓EDT	Location Direction	color	shape	Description
#1-UFO	8:00pm EDT	WDC.-SW.	yel.-white	○—	Ball
#2-UFO ↓	8:00pm ↓	WDC-West ↓	Green ↓	↓	slightly-oblong ↓
#2ᴮ-UFO	8:00pm	McLean. VA.	Green-Wh.	◯	oval w/ pink
SECOND SIGHTING of #2 object - WDC. west to McLean VA.					
#3-UFO	8:00pm	WDC-SW to west	Greenish-blue w/red trailer	⬭	Balloon-shaped tonight size of dirigible
#4-UFO	8:00pm	WDC "zoomed to the west"	white to red w/green tail	NO REAL SHAPE "ZOOMED"	exploding plane soundless rocket
#5-UFO	8:00pm	Arlington VA. West-NW.	Green Ball Type	●	Ball— little flattened
#6-UFO	8:00pm	WDC - south-SW	bluish-yellow yel-tail-fringe	◯	flaming ball
#7-UFO ↓	8:01pm ↓	WDC - Georgetown	light-Green flame color	▬	plane on fire + size & shape of fuselage of plane
#7ᴮ-UFO	8:02pm	WDC - Georgetown	white to red Green at tail "GLIDING"	▬	plane on fire
SECOND SIGHTING of #7 object over Georgetown is #7ᴮ					
SECOND SIGHTING was "GLIDING" towards the northwesterly direction"					
#8-UFO	8:03pm	WDC	silvery-white red-orange tail	○—	spherical shape- white ball
#9-UFO	8:03pm	Fairfax, VA. Lt commander USN-Aviator	Greenish-wh. white rim	⬭	slightly oblong
#10-UFO	8:04pm	District Heights Maryland	Bright Blue Green-white in center, tail-blue-grn	⬭—	size of an automobile This thing was being flown
#11-UFO	8:05	Beltsville Maryland	light blue lt blue tail	◯—	large round thing
#12-UFO	8:10pm	Alexandria Virginia	yellowish-white	⬯	round front- tapered to a point
#13 UFO	9:07pm	Middletown pennsylvania	Bright white Light	○	auto headlight at distance

This is exactly how the government's disinformation plans work. Give out false information or a lack of information to the public through the media to cause mass confusion, which discredits witnesses. Large portions of information contained in these Project Blue Book files were from "Tentative Observers Questionnaires." These forms were sent out by the Air Force to witnesses upon request. Each questionnaire was a standard format that contained thirty different questions pertaining to a UFO sighting. The questionnaires were completed by the witness and then sent back to the Air Force for review and evaluation.

The following information concerns the sightings of thirteen different UFOs that descended over the United States. Between 8:00 p.m. and 8:10 p.m. EDT 12 different UFOs dispersed, over four states and were sighted as they descended. The last UFO, the # 13 Object of this group, situated itself over Olmsted AFB in Middletown, PA at a very high altitude and hovered while standing guard over the situation. This UFO was sighted one hour later when it descended at 9:07 p.m. EDT.

Object #1. Source: Tentative Observers Questionnaire. The #1 Object was seen by a man and wife at 8:00 p.m. EDT as they were driving their car along Western Avenue in Washington D.C. The man filled out the questionnaire. His wife called his attention to the object "thinking it was fireworks." They were looking "southwest" in the sky and "the object appeared solid." The witness said, "It gave off a yellowish-white light" and there was "no sound audible."

The question was asked, "Was this the first time that you have seen an object like this? Yes, although many meteors have been observed but none as intense as this one or that appeared to travel as slowly." This witness also stated it looked "like an auto headlight but somewhat more yellowish." The couple was looking to the "southwest" when the object disappeared from their sight. When this witness initially contacted PROJECT BLUE BOOK and reported his sighting, ATIC documented the following, he stated, the "Object was shaped like a ball with light radiating from it...tail was almost as bright as object itself." This object actually passed over Washington D.C. from the "northeast" and continued "on a southwest trajectory before it disappeared."

Baltimore, MD is located to the northeast of Washington DC where another description of this object was previously made. A previously mentioned September 13 Baltimore Sun article gives the following information, "Not since Baltimore, with the rest of the world, first began to read about flying saucers several years ago, has anything approached so close to what locals considered the 'real thing' made its appearance here. The first excited call came in a few minutes after 8 P.M. [EDT] And they kept up for more than an hour...to Herman Rosenthal, when he first saw it swinging 'treetop height' near his home in 2700 block of Spring Hill Avenue, it looked, at first like a 'plane on fire.' He soon realized that it was no plane however. 'But it was that big.' he said." He described it as a large, sun-colored ball with a tail.

Object #2. Source: Witness Compilation Report & Tentative Observers Questionnaire. The #2 Object was seen at 8:00 p.m. EDT by a witness from 21st Street NW, Washington D.C. While calling his girlfriend, he "saw a bright green light through the window" from his eighth-floor apartment. He "first noticed a plane circling for a landing." After the "plane disappeared from view" the witness said he, "saw a green light where the plane was and it dove toward the ground. It sort of leveled off and disappeared." The witness described this UFO as a "solid object" that was "slightly oblong" in shape. He stated the object emitted a "bright-green light." The said the object was traveling "toward the west." The length of time the object was seen was "8 seconds," a near record for a meteor sighting. Moreover, unlike a meteor, this object appeared to level off after making a dive toward the ground. The witness also noted the object had "no tail."

Another description of this object was made to the west in McLean, VA by a fifty-year-old male who worked for the Army. This sighting occurred while he was traveling in his car with his wife. This witness stated:

The object looked like an oval Roman candle descending at the speed of a passenger plane until it suddenly disappeared, leaving for a second the black or gray outline of an arrow or rocket, which could have been either an object or smoke. It was a greenish white light as I first saw it. My wife who was with me agrees with the above but adds that she would include pink in her description of the object.

The witness also stated, "The object was no more than 2,000 feet above the ground." A question asked, "How far was it from you?" The witness answered, "Near enough for us to debate stopping the car for fear of what might happen when it landed." The witness also answered the following question in the questionnaire, "In your opinion, what do you think the object was and what might have caused it?" The answer, "I don't know."

This object was close enough to the witness that he actually saw what it was, and was scared it was going to land near them. There was no sonic boom noted, even though he stated it was only about 2,000 feet above the ground. This object also suddenly disappeared or dematerialized, like so many of the objects seen earlier. It seems unlikely that a witness who worked for the Army would be afraid of a meteor.

Object #3. Source: Tentative Observers Questionnaire. The #3 Object was seen from the corner of Massachusetts Avenue and 39th St. NW, Washington, DC, at 8:00 EDT. This witness saw the object disappear from the "southwest to west" direction as he was driving a car through a residential neighborhood. He said it was "greenish-blue with a red trailer," and noted that there was, "no sound." The witness said the UFO was about "as big as a dirigible" and stated that he had "no idea" what it was. The Air Force witness compilation report initially stated it looked "onion shaped" with a streamer tapering gradually. The color was, "bright light green with a yellow-red tail." The object appeared to be "heading northwest." The observer also stated it, "seemed to be traveling remarkably slow."

Once again, this object did not demonstrate the characteristics of a meteor. The most striking description besides the size of this object was that "it seemed to be traveling remarkably slow." If this "dirigible" sized object was a meteor that had actually disintegrated that close to Washington, every person in the city would have heard it and felt its percussive landing. The witness answered the following question in the questionnaire, "In your opinion what do you think the object was and what might have caused it?" The witness stated emphatically, "I haven't the faintest idea."

Object #4. Source: Tentative Observers Questionnaire. The #4 Object was seen by a couple at 8:00 p.m. EDT while with their two children. The sighting was made from the banks of the Potomac River, near the Lincoln Memorial. The fifty-three-year-old wife is the one who filled out this questionnaire. This witness stated, "Our family was watching the sky-sunset and airplanes going toward the airport." The witness was looking to the south when she "first saw the object," and saw the object "disappear to the west." It "looked transparent" and the witness said its changed size, color and brightness. The following descriptions were given, "SOUND- none… "COLOR- Blazing white, with red, then green tail." The size of the object was described as "about the same as a small airplane."

The observer said the striking points about this object were "its sudden appearance in the sky as though from nowhere." The witness was shocked by "the suddenness of its disappearance over the hills, but as though it had burned out in the sky before it could have possibly landed. Just appeared, zoomed toward the opposite horizon moving very fast like a comet's flash or a rocket, but soundless, and then just couldn't be seen. I personally thought it might be a non-lethal guided missile."

The most interesting part of this statement concerning the object's appearance was "its sudden appearance as from nowhere." Again, these objects seemed to be materializing and dematerializing. The witness answered the following question in the questionnaire, "In your opinion what do you think the object was and what might have caused it?" This witness stated, "Can't imagine what it was."

Object #5. Source: Witness Compilation Report. The #5 Object was seen at 8:00 p.m. EDT from Arlington, VA. While driving in a convertible with top down, the witness "saw a luminous green ball type object. A little flattened with a short orange-yellow tail." The Object was sighted "toward the west." The observer stated it "looked similar to a Roman candle if seen at close range. Could not judge distance or speed. No sound." The witness stated the object was seen for "5 seconds" and it was "on a west-northwest heading until it disappeared behind a hill."

Object #6. Source: Witness Compilation Report. The #6 Object was sighted at 8:00 p.m. EDT from the vicinity of the National Guard Armory in Washington D.C. The report stated, "One flaming ball, bluish in color, yellow in fringe." The witness said it was, "falling toward earth." The UFO had a "tail" that was described as" yellow" in color. From the witnesses' location the object "looked smaller than a baseball" at a distance. The observer's point of observation was near the National Guard Armory, "facing south-southwest." The witness said the object was "heading in the direction of the National Airport."

It is clear that even though these six sightings were made at 8:00 p.m. EDT, they were definitely not the same object. There are far too many discrepancies regarding the shapes, colors, directions of flight and movements made by these witnesses for all of the 8:00 p.m. sightings to have been one object.

Object #7. Source: Witness Compilation Report. The #7 Object was seen from Georgetown at 8:01 p.m. EDT. The Object was described as "about size and shape of fuselage of plane. Light green in color and glowing incandescently." The witness stated, "It looked at first like a plane on fire." He said the, "color varied from green to flame color toward tail, almost giving it a teardrop shape." There was no mention of the object's disappearance. The observer said his sighting lasted for "about five seconds."

Another "Georgetown" witness described this same object. He said it was "no more than 500 feet in the air." Its color was described as, "White turning to red and green at the tail." The witness said, "It made no noise." This witness also described the object's movement as it descended along its flight path over Georgetown. He stated that the "object" was "gliding towards the ground." The "Washington area meteor" according to Blue Book stated its speed as "27 miles per second" in a very non-gliding fashion.

This object was also noted to have "disappeared in the sky with a flash," which indicates it may have actually dematerialized.

The #7 Object and the #4 Object were very similar in their descriptions, as both were elongated UFOs and both thought to be planes on fire. Both of these UFOs descended from the sky approximately one minute apart and proceeded in different directions.

The descriptions of these two objects are nearly identical to the description of the jet-shaped UFO previously seen over Flatwoods by A.M. Jordan, the same UFO that dropped the homing beacon on the hilltop.

Object #8. Source: Project Blue Book Teletype & Record Card. The #8 Object was sighted at 8:03 p.m. EDT over Washington D.C. The report is as follows:

FM HQ USAF WASHDC [From-Headquarters-U.S. Air Force-Washington, DC]
[TO JEDEN/Commanding General Air Defense Command-Ent Air Force Base, Colorado]
[JEDWP/Chief, Air Technical Intelligence Center - Wright-Patterson Air Force Base, Ohio]
JEPLB/CG TAC LANGLEY AFB VA
[JEPLB/Commanding General - Tactical Air Command-Langley Air Force Base, Virginia]
 Presently on duty as security officer, JCS reports following flying object sighting: "Spherical effect appearing as a ball spinning clockwise. Reddish orange tail protruding from brilliant silvery-white ball with brilliance of phosphorous. Tail about half-length of diameter of object. Observed at 122003 [8:03 p.m.] for two seconds falling with trajectory like Roman candle. Object observed at angle of 40 degrees altitude moving in north-northwest direction. Size about two-thirds that of moon on bright night when moon is at 75 degree angle. Looked as if it might be about 3 miles away and would fall on outskirts of D.C. Brightness seemed more-white than sun. Further observation prevented by mass of buildings and woods. Observed from position in front of 2641 Conn Ave, N.W. Facing 2606 Conn. Ave. N.W. Source has plotted map-showing angles of observation in his possession.

The following information comes from the 10073 Record Card of that report. It states, "One of numerous Washington, DC area reports of 12 Sept. meteor." Furthermore, the conclusion stated, "Was astronomical-meteor." It is hard to believe that Project Blue Book logically concluded this object was the "12 Sept. Meteor."

This is even more unbelievable considering that the Pentagon [HQ USAF WASHDC] contacted Ent AFB, Wright-Patterson AFB and Langley AFB. In 1952, Ent AFB was the headquarters for the Air Defense

Command (ADC). It seems inconceivable that the Pentagon would have contacted all these Air Force bases with regard to a meteor.

Object #9. Source: Tentative Observers Questionnaire & Project 10073 Record Card. The #9 Object was sighted at 8:03 p.m. EDT over Fairfax, VA. Enclosure 3 is questionnaire completed by LCDR [Lieutenant Commander—blacked out] USN [United States Navy], following his telephonic report of a sighting to this office. He stated, "I was sitting at the dinner table facing the window when the object flashed by the window." He said the object looked "solid" and the object gave off "a greenish-white light." The observer stated the color was, "white rim about a greenish-white core" and there was "no sound." The actual size of the object as he saw it was the size of a "basketball." The witness was looking "southwest" in the sky when the object disappeared. He described the object as, "slightly-oblong" and said it was, "moving in a horizontal path over ground." He reported that the object had, "no tail or sparks." He also noted it displayed a "solid incandescent outline."

The questionnaire asked, "In your opinion what do you think the object was and what might have caused it? I don't know. The newspaper said it was a meteor, but it had no tail and was not falling and was larger than any meteor that I ever saw." This witness, like many of the other witnesses, questioned the Air Force's meteor explanation.

The Project 10073 Record Card read as follows, "Local newspaper reported object as meteor. Duration of sighting was only 3 seconds and observer was in poor position."

Once again, Project Blue Book had two informative points to comment on about this sighting. The card also stated that this witness was "source-Naval Aviator (Lt. Cmdr.)." It seems that even though this witness was a Navy aviator, Project Blue Book did not consider him a credible witness.

Object #10. Source: Tentative Observers Questionnaire. The #10 Object was sighted by a man from District Heights, MD, at 8:03 p.m. EDT. This sighting was made "in the residential section of the city." The witness was "on [his] porch facing SSW," when he noticed the object.

In response to the questionnaire, he stated these answers to the following questions:

How did the object look? Solid.
Give off smoke? Yes.
Did the object give off light? Yes.
What color was the light? Bright blue-green.
Sound? None audible.
Color? Very white in center to blue green on edge.
Which of the following objects is about the same size as the object you saw? Automobile.
How did the object disappear from view? Gradually.
What direction were you looking when the object disappeared? West.
How long was object seen? 11 or 12 seconds.
Clouds? Clear sky (very).

The witness said that the object, "disappeared below horizon in west," and stated the, "entire object was a constant very bright glow traveling at steady rate." A question asked, "In your opinion what do you think the object was and what might have caused it?" the witness answered, "This is your job. I have seen many meteors. This was not one—much too large. It was not an image or reflection. The object's trajectory was constant in a swooping arch following the curvature of the earth and eventually going behind the horizon. It didn't fall toward the earth." The testimony this witness gave at the end of the report was even more convincing. He stated:

For a person with limited knowledge about things of this nature, I can give an opinion that may be of too little value. I do not know what it was I saw and will insist on what it was not. I have seen meteors, and the newspapers will have a hard time telling me I was looking at a meteor on 9/12. Maybe it sounds good to persons who didn't see the object. This thing was being flown. Picture for yourself a jet plane going over and into the horizon. Now set it on fire to a bright glow and have it travel 3 times as fast, covering the same trajectory in 1/3 the time. Does it look like a meteor? In summarization, this may sound as though I am inferring some fraud in the reports given to the public. Perhaps responsible parties believe they are true and the best information available, but did they see the thing on 9/12?

This report was obviously written by a man who was very adamant of what he saw and was not afraid to tell the U.S. Air Force his opinion. The lone fireball meteor theory became weaker the more questionnaires and reports I read.

Object #11. Source: Witness Compilation Report. The #11 Object was sighted over Beltsville, MD, at 8:05 p.m. EDT. The witness report said the object looked like "a large round thing resembling a child's ball." It was said to, "like a moon with a tail." The witness said it was traveling about "the speed of a plane." When he first observed the object, it was "very high but heading toward the ground" in the direction of the plant at Industry Station, in Beltsville, MD. Note that this object was descending on a trajectory "heading toward the ground." Did this alleged meteor change its course to avoid impacting the earth? The report said, "The source was unable to give a direction of flight but said it was "toward the west. Second observer at same time and place was Mr. [blacked out], an employee at Bolling AFB." This object was seen northwest of Washington D.C. at 8:05 p.m., five minutes later than the first six objects seen over Washington D.C.

Object #12. Source: Witness Compilation Report. The #12 Object was sighted from Alexandria, VA, at 8:10 p.m. EDT. The witness "saw a yellowish-white, very bright light about one-half the size of a full moon." The witness said the object "had a vaguely rounded front with a tail about twice the diameter and tapering to a point. The object made no sound. Observer was at home facing southwest and saw object through open window in house. Traveled west in a straight line." The object was seen "for 3 seconds."

Object #13. This object hovered over Middletown, PA for approximately one hour before it descended. Source: Air Intelligence Information Sheet; Project 10073 Record Card and Action Synopsis Sheet. The #13 Object was seen at 9:07 p.m. EDT from Middletown, PA, over Olmstead AFB by a civilian observer. The following information was from the Air Intelligence Information Report:

[Name blacked out] an employee of this base reported seeing an unidentified flying object while at work at 0107z [8:07 p.m. EST/9:07 p.m. EDT] on 12 Sept 1952. Mr. [blacked out] described the object as a bright white light that looked like an automobile headlight at a considerable distance. The light moved in a straight line from the southwest to the northwest and disappeared behind a tree. Its speed was described as "slower than an airplane." The light was visible for "three or four" minutes, but Mr. [blacked out] reported that during this time it dimmed "considerably" for a period of approximately five seconds after which it regained its former brilliance. No exhaust or sound was noted. There were no local aircraft in the air at the time. Weather was clear with twelve miles visibility, winds calm.

Mr. [blacked out]'s estimate of the length of observation discounted astronomical phenomena such as meteors. Although no sound was heard and he maintained that the object did not resemble an aircraft, the object's speed and level flight strongly suggested the possibility of an aircraft. The bright light sighted over Olmstead AFB at 9:07 p.m. EDT bore a striking similarity to an earlier sighting. Olmstead AFB was also the location where an earlier sighting of a UFO took place at 3:35 a.m. on September 12, 1952. In both Olmstead

AFB cases, the reports stated an object changed brightness while being observed. Was it just another coincidence that this was the second UFO seen flying near Olmstead AFB that day?

It is interesting to note, "There were no local aircraft in the air at the time." Yet, at the end of this report they said, "The object's speed and level flight strongly suggest the possibility of an aircraft." In the Project 10073 Record Card, the U.S. Air Force stated its conclusion as "possibly aircraft." It is also interesting to note that in the Air Intelligence Information sheet report, the Air Force stated, "This office can offer no definite explanation of the sighting." This sighting was put into a synopsis report by Olmstead AFB, stamped "ACTION," and then sent to several other Air Force bases. It was deemed important enough to be immediately sent to the Director of Intelligence Headquarters, USAF; the ATIC, Wright - Patterson AFB; the Commanding General, Air Materiel Command Wright-Patterson AFB; and the Commanding General, ENT AFB, Colorado Springs, CO.

Between 8:00 p.m. EDT and 8:10 p.m. EDT, I discovered there were at least twelve known objects that flew over Washington, Virginia, and Maryland. The majority of these objects were sighted heading in westerly directions. However, the #13 Object hovered high above Olmsted AFB keeping a watchful eye over the area until 9:07 p.m. EDT. After this hour-long surveillance was completed, the object descended upon the base and departed shortly thereafter. Olmsted seemed to draw the #13 Object like a moth to a flame. It makes me wonder what indeed was at Olmsted AFB to attract the UFOs.

Based on my years of research data, the following scenario fits the chronological order of events that occurred at 8:00 p.m. EDT that night. These UFOs were eleven of the sixteen UFOs that neutralized the southeastern military installations. The "Flatwoods Monster" ship that was engaged in an aerial battle over the Atlantic Ocean was damaged and headed west toward the coastline enroute to Washington D.C. At that point, the group of sixteen objects that departed Florida was passing over North Carolina. Three of these sixteen UFOs went on to Flatwoods, West Virginia to rendezvous with the "Flatwoods Monster" ship; they were the North Carolina Rescue Objects.

The fourth and fifth rescue objects hovered over North Carolina near the vicinities of Pope AFB and Donaldson AFB, to guard against any potential military aggression towards the three other North Carolina objects. The #4 North Carolina Rescue Object then descended over Flat Rock, just north of Donaldson AFB then proceeded north and followed the three rescue ships over Virginia and into West Virginia. The #5 North Carolina Rescue Object descended to a lower altitude just after dark. At that point, it was sighted. It patrolled the skies over North Carolina and stayed behind, securing an escape route.

The remaining eleven UFOs headed towards the Washington area, arrived shortly after and moved into their strategic positions. The two jet-shaped objects dispatched from the mothership then moved into position with the other eleven UFOs. They waited and then began to descend, stopped and watched over the area. When the combat patrol jets showed no sign of withdrawal, they continued to descend to lower altitudes. If the military had not withdrawn their patrolling combat patrol jets, all thirteen UFOs would have descended in an attempt to clear the area in order to let the damaged ship through. If there had been a confrontation along the damaged ship's flight path as it neared Washington and it went down, these thirteen UFOs would have been there to extract it. As the damaged ship neared Washington, President Truman withdrew the combat air patrol jets, the corridor was opened, and the damaged UFO passed over Washington D.C. without incident. Twelve of the thirteen ships descended upon Washington, Virginia and Maryland as the mothership watched the situation unfold as it hovered high above Washington. The UFO situated over Pennsylvania hovered high over Olmsted AFB and then descended about an hour later.

The objects that had dropped in over Washington D.C. and nearby areas were tracked on radar by Washington National Airport, Andrews AFB, and Bolling AFB. After the twelve UFOs descended, they proceeded west at low altitudes. This was a deliberate and direct maneuver to follow the damaged craft and to show their power. Hundreds of unsuspecting and shocked residents, who were later told that they had seen only meteors, sighted these objects. The UFO extraction mission commenced when the "Flatwoods Monster" got a safe distance from Washington en route to West Virginia. The last of these 12 ships were seen at 8:10 p.m. EDT.

During that ten-minute time, there were other UFO sightings reported over eastern Ohio and the northern panhandle of West Virginia. At 8:05 p.m. EDT, two different objects were seen in two different locations in eastern Ohio. One object, which resembled "an enormous skyrocket," was sighted in the area of Freeport and Tappan Lakes. Another object that resembled "the shape of a frying pan" was sighted from Lafferty, OH, also at 8:05 p.m. The Freeport and Tappan Lakes areas are approximately 35 miles northwest of Wheeling, WV. Lafferty, OH is located approximately 18 miles almost due west of Wheeling.

The Columbus Citizen reported another incident that occurred approximately 50 miles west of Freeport. "Mt. Vernon State Patrolmen said they received a report at 7:05 p.m.[EST/8:05 p.m. EDT] from G. S. Gallopy of Danville [OH], reporting a 'plane on fire going down.' He said the crash seemed to be near Millwood, 12 miles east of Mt. Vernon. Patrolmen said no crash could be found, however." This article also stated, "Police in the 'bombarded' states reported they were searching the countryside for some clue to the strange phenomenon. However police officials said they believed the objects sighted were meteors."

The residents of Akron, OH also sighted an object in their vicinity. The Cambridge highway patrol reported, "Many thought it was a plane about to crash. . . ." Persons in Akron also reported, "Seeing a meteor!"

CAA offices in Pittsburgh "were swamped with calls from persons who thought they saw burning airplanes crashing to the ground." These sightings were reported to the Greater Pittsburgh Airport, located in Coraopolis, to the east of Wheeling. Pittsburgh observed Daylight Saving Time, as did the northern West Virginia Panhandle (Wheeling).

Two September 13 Pittsburgh UP articles had the following headlines, The first reported, "Four States 'Bombarded' by Meteor-Like Objects" and the second reported, "'Balls of Fire' in Pittsburgh'- Jittery Citizens Report Planes in Flames over Wide Area."

At 8:06, another sighting occurred in West Liberty, WV, ten miles northwest of Wheeling. This UFO was described as "an object resembling a Roman candle."

The information concerning these two nearby 8:05 sightings of UFOs in eastern Ohio was contained in *The Times-Leader*. The headline on September 13, 1952 read, "Authorities Probe Flashes in Area Skies: Strange Lights Observed over Four States."

The information concerning the 8:06 sighting over West Liberty was in *The Wheeling Intelligencer*. The headlines on September 13, "Mystery Lights Zip Through Skies Here Stirring Mild Furor—Flashing Light Believed Caused By 'Low' Meteors."

These articles both reported that objects thought to be airplanes, blazing objects, meteors, and brilliant flames appeared in the skies over eastern Ohio and the northern WV panhandle before 8:10 p.m. The search and rescue mission to Braxton County was not called off until 8:10 p.m. EDT.

The objects sighted before 8:10 p.m. EDT were seen over different areas not even close to Braxton County. These objects were not searching eastern Ohio and northern West Virginia for the "Flatwoods Monster." They were over this area for an altogether different reason. These ships were looking for another stranded occupant from one of their other crafts. This occupant was from the damaged Baltimore/WV #2 Object that landed in the Oglebay Park area. When this craft was damaged over the Atlantic Ocean, one of the occupants was injured. When it proceeded toward Dayton, OH, the condition of the ship deteriorated. The object overheated so severely that the living conditions inside the damaged ship became nearly unbearable.

When the craft was called away from its route toward Wright-Patterson, it slowed and changed to a northeasterly path. It passed over Columbus and Zanesville en route to West Virginia. It radioed a distress call. Passing into West Virginia, it followed the beacon signal being transmitted from the Wheeling-Ohio County Airport. The UFO nearly hit a passenger plane as it approached the airport area before landing in Oglebay Park.

At 8:05 and 8:06 p.m. EDT, the first rescue ships began to descend into eastern Ohio, but there were major problems. The rescue ships did not know whether the damaged ship had reached its destination. Moreover, they also did not have the exact location of the destination. *The Times Leader* reported the 8:05 sightings with the headline, "Authorities Probe Flashes in Area Skies—Strange Lights Observed Over Four States." It stated:

Civil Aeronautics Authority officers were still trying to find an explanation today for a flurry of bright flashes seen in the skies of eastern Ohio and three other states by hundreds of people the previous night shortly after 8 p.m. Switchboards of law enforcement officers, newspapers and airports were swamped with calls last night with reports of the meteor-like flashes that appeared over Washington, Pittsburgh, and Virginia, as well as above the Ohio valley.

The U.S. Naval Observatory at Washington said the reports 'sounded like a typical meteor,' but the most persistent report in eastern Ohio was that a plane had crashed in the Freeport-Piedmont Lake area. O. C. Frantz, Martins Ferry postmaster, said he and two other post office employees, Roy Lucas and Dave Smith, were fishing in Piedmont Lake when a flaming object appeared in the sky at 8:05. The men first thought it was a 'flying saucer' but said it looked like an enormous skyrocket. It was big enough to be a plane they said, and they thought later it might have been a bomber or large passenger plane.

The Patrol investigated the report, but could find no evidence of a plane crash. Other reports of the flashing objects all confirmed the time at 8:05 last night. Three cheerleaders from Lafferty High School told the Times-Leader that what they saw a flying saucer appearing at the same time [8:05]. The girls, Nancy Azallion, Madelyn Calovini and Seania Bayat, said they were practicing cheers at the high school when an object 'the shape of a frying pan,' appeared. It was very white and bright and had sparks shooting from the tail, the girls said. They saw it come from east to west and disappear over a hill in the west —in 30 seconds. Carol Santini, a former Lafferty cheerleader, incidentally was in town and supported a similar object.

This "flying saucer" described as "the shape of a frying pan" over Lafferty, Ohio was previously seen over Flatrock, NC. This UFO was the #4 North Carolina rescue ship that descended as back up over North Carolina. The object then followed the three North Carolina rescue UFOs over Virginia, into West Virginia and then ascended and headed toward the northern West Virginia panhandle area. It then proceeded into Lafferty, Ohio, about 18 miles due west of Wheeling and was sighted there at 8:05 p.m. The search had begun.

The Wheeling Intelligencer reported, "The Brookside station of the Ohio highway patrol last evening received a number of calls from eastern Ohio points concerning the strange visitor in the sky. One of these reported it was seen in the vicinity of Piedmont and Tappan Lakes."

The object sighted at 8:05 p.m. that "looked like an enormous skyrocket" was actually one of the ships descending into eastern Ohio, as part of the search and rescue mission. I then reviewed the reports of all the other objects seen that night and compared them. It seems this object was the same ship sighted over several other locations across the country at different times. This UFO was sighted over the following four locations.

1. Harrisonburg, VA. It was said, "Residents in Harrisonburg, VA, reported a 'cigar-shaped object trailing blue-green flame' [that] streaked across the sky." This object had just previously left the air battle area over the Atlantic Ocean.

2. Flatwoods, WV. When this object reached Flatwoods, Mr. A.M. Jordan saw it. After interviewing Jordan, Gray Barker said, "Evidently it came from over the horizon from the southeast as he was sitting on the porch. It proceeded across the sky, then halted suddenly, seemed to fall rapidly toward the hilltop [of Fisher farm]." This object dropped the homing beacon. After this object left Flatwoods, it rendezvoused with the mothership high above Washington D.C. Shortly after it then departed.

3. Georgetown, Washington, D.C. This object was then sighted over Georgetown at 8:01 p.m. EDT. It was actually the #7 Rescue Ship. It was sighted over Georgetown again at 8:02 p.m. EDT. The witness stated the,

"Object looked like a plane on fire at first, and then like some sort of flare gliding toward the ground in the general direction of the Lee Memorial." During this sighting this UFO actually "seemed to flash and disappear" in the sky. The witness reported it to Project Blue Book. Again, the ship was capable of de-materializing and disappearing. It then proceeded to the Ohio and West Virginia areas to search for the other stranded occupant.

4. Freeport, OH—(Piedmont Lake area) at 8:05 p.m. EDT. After this object "disappeared" at 8:02 p.m. over Georgetown, it then reappeared over eastern Ohio. At 8:05 p.m., "a flaming object appeared in the sky." What these witnesses actually saw was the #7 Rescue Object descending into the area.

The description of this #7 Rescue Ship seen across the country that night was also similar to the description given of the #4 Rescue Ship. Both of these UFOs were described as being elongated and shaped like a rocket or a wingless aircraft. The #7 Object was reported to be a much larger craft than the #4 Object. These elongated wingless objects were also well documented by the USAF. Some of these elongated wingless objects appeared in *Flying Saucers: An Analysis of the Air Force Project Blue Book Special Report No. 14*. Some of the elongated wingless UFOs that appeared in this report were categorized in the report as "Cigar Shape – Cases IV and V." The first listed was "Case IV (Serial 4599.00)"; "two cigar-shaped objects" that "both had an exhaust at one end" were sighted on July 19, 1952.

The second listed was "Case V (Serial 0565.00 to 0565.00)" multiple sightings made from "DC-3" aircraft by pilot, copilot and a passenger. These sightings occurred on "JULY 24, 1948." Drawings also accompanied these two case reports. These objects were almost identical to the descriptions of the elongated wingless objects, which were sighted on September 12, 1952. I own a copy of the drawing made by Mr. A.M. Jordan, who saw the wingless jet-shaped UFO over Flatwoods. His drawing and description of the UFO he saw is nearly identical to the UFO sighted by the DC-3 pilot on July 24, 1948.

The other object sighted at 8:05, was over Lafferty, Ohio. This object was a flying saucer described as "the shape of a frying pan." I would classify this UFO as a disc-shaped object with a tail. This UFO's description was almost identical to another well-documented UFO sighting in *Flying Saucers: An Analysis of the Air Force Project Blue Book Special Report No. 14*.

The UFO's sighted at 8:05 p.m. in eastern Ohio were the first rescue objects that had descended into those areas. The objects were sighted to the west of the Ohio River. The area where the stranded occupant was dropped off was to the east of the Ohio River near Oglebay Park Resort.

The Times Leader also reported this sighting, W. A. Garrison of West Liberty reported seeing an object that looked like "a Roman candle flash over his home and at 8:06 it headed southwest." *The Wheeling Intelligencer* also reported the same incident. The object seen by the Martins Ferry, OH man occurred later that evening in Glenwood Heights, WV, about 7 miles southwest of West Liberty. [This object will appear chronologically in the story at the time it was sighted.] The mid-Atlantic rescue ships were sighted between 8:00 p.m. and 8:10 p.m. before their initial extraction mission was called off at 8:10. I re-examined the mid-Atlantic sightings that occurred before the 8:06 West Liberty, WV sighting, which was said to resemble a "Roman candle." The following mid-Atlantic rescue objects were reported to have had similar characteristics. Following are the objects said to resemble a Roman candle: A.) #1 Object, Washington, DC - 8:00 p.m.-"thinking it was fireworks." B.) #2 Object, McLean, VA - 8:00 p.m.-"The object looked like an oval Roman candle." C.) #5 Object, Arlington, VA - 8:00 p.m.-"Looked similar to a Roman candle."

Then I re-examined the directions that these three objects were said to be heading. Only one of these objects was noted to be heading in a direction toward West Virginia's northern panhandle. The Virginia witness to the #5 North Carolina Rescue Ship said it was moving north-northwest.

That flight course would actually be heading away from Braxton County. The #4 North Carolina Rescue Object was the craft that proceeded north-northwest to West Liberty. This is the area where the damaged Baltimore/WV #2 Object had landed earlier and dropped off the injured occupant from the craft. The #4 North

Carolina Rescue Object was the first rescue ship to search for the stranded being in West Virginia. The other two UFOs were searching in eastern Ohio.

A later sighting in Chillicothe, OH appeared to be a plane on fire, falling from the sky. The *Columbus Citizen* reported, "Fireballs Shower City Area: Meteor Fall Blamed Cause Of Scare." The article stated, "In Chillicothe, patrolmen said a Frankfort [OH] man reported a burning plane falling north of town about 8:30 p.m. [EST]. No plane could be found they said." This article also named two locations where "what appeared to be a plane crash" occurred, Mt. Vernon and Chillicothe, Ohio.

The Chillicothe sighting was one of the rescue ships. This UFO landed only 30 miles northwest of Clinton County AFB in Wilmington. This UFO had landed 30 miles away from Clinton County AFB as a warning to the military officials to stay out of the Wheeling area. That was why it positioned itself between this base and Wheeling.

Two of the rescue objects were the elongated wingless jet-type #4 and #7 objects that emitted flames from their crafts through their propulsion systems. Those aircraft looked similar to a plane on fire when they descended. Some of the other objects produced tails of various colors while passing through the earth's atmosphere. These tails were produced by the "plasma phenomenon." This is caused by extreme heat surrounding the energy field of a craft while passing through the earth's atmosphere at tremendous speed.

For nearly two hours, the objects made desperate attempts to locate the stranded being. *The Wheeling Intelligencer* reported that their "editorial room was also swamped with calls between eight and ten o'clock from residents on both sides of the river." The Intelligencer also stated the following information in its September 13 article concerning a late night sighting, "The CAA office at Stifel Field, Wheeling-Ohio County airport received a call late last night from a Martins Ferry man who claimed to have seen what looked like a light plane afire crash to the ground between the transmitters of radio stations WHLL and WKWK atop Glenwood Heights." Glenwood Heights is located approximately 15 miles southwest of the Oglebay Park area where the injured alien was left off from the damaged Baltimore/WV #2 craft.

This maneuver was a final effort by one of the rescue objects to find the stranded being. This object landed at Glenwood Heights at a high point where it could be easily sighted. In all probability, this object was one of the elongated wingless ships. Obviously, the craft that landed on the hill between two radio towers was capable of taking off again. Since no plane or wreckage was found, the flaming aircraft must have been an unconventional-type aircraft.

The Times-Leader also reported the following in its September 13 article, "All witnesses agreed that the blazing objects, planes, meteors, rockets or whatever zoomed horizontally and awfully low." This supposed meteor shower finally ended when the search and rescue mission was abandoned at around 10 p.m. EDT/9 p.m. EST.

At about 8:05 p.m. EST, the "Flatwoods Monster" boarded its craft after being sighted. While preparing to depart the Fisher farm, it contacted the mothership over the Capitol. The damaged craft needed to relocate to a nearby area before it was threatened by the locals. The damaged ship was not capable of regenerating. Because its power was nearly depleted, it could not go far. This would probably be its last transmission. Shortly after taking off, the "Flatwoods Monster" gained enough altitude to rise above the hills and mountains. It picked up momentum and rose out of the valley. There was only one witness, who saw the "Flatwoods Monster" craft depart the Fisher farm that night. Mrs. May talked to me about this witness, "This editor from Webster Springs was over there [at the sheriff's department] when I called. And he got in the car and he went down Monkey Row [local nickname for Salt Lick Road] and he saw the thing up there, the light, and he went upon [sic] the field trestle (a railroad bridge located in back of the Fisher farm) and stood up there and watched it. And he said it went down a little grade like this (gesturing downward motion) and he said it went around and around and took off and went to the airport. It turned and then went right back down the river."

Just southwest of the Sutton airport is the small town of Little Birch. *The Charleston Gazette* reported the following incident on September 14, "Residents of Little Birch reported seeing a fiery object flash overhead shortly after the monster was reported. It was conceded that the monster may have climbed in its 'ship' and taken off again shortly after his untimely visit." According to all my research, this analogy was quite accurate.

It changed direction and headed northwest to Frametown. This incident was documented in the *Braxton County Democrat*, September 18, 1952. The article by J. C. Dean told about a fiery object that had landed in Frametown on a mountaintop. One week after the above incident occurred, investigator Sanderson went to the home of Mr. Dean in Frametown. Sanderson said that Mr. Dean "had reported on the previous day that still another aerial object had crashed or landed on a nearby farm. Mr. Dean received us most courteously and informed us that a craft had landed on an overgrown and isolated field atop a hill known as James Knoll or Knob but that, although seen by the two young James boys, it had not been investigated because it had been regarded as a fireball." By no means, was it coincidental that it crash-landed on James Knob atop a field. James Knob is located in a very mountainous and isolated region in Braxton County. It is a wide-open field on top, a good location for a damaged ship to land where it could not be reached very easy. James Knob was a perfect and accessible location for an emergency landing. This was the last known location where the damaged ship was seen that night.

"B" INDICATES WRIGHT PATTERSON AFB. IN DAYTON, OHIO

The Baltimore/West Virginia #2 Object flew northwest to "**A**". It then redirected northeast toward the northern West Virginia panhandle to the Wheeling-Ohio County Airport, "**C**". It then redirected and proceeded southwest and dropped off the injured being in Oglebay Park, "**D**". For 2-hours, UFOs descended throughout the WV panhandle area and eastern Ohio in search of it. White Stars represent what were called, blazing objects, planes, meteors, crashing planes and rockets.

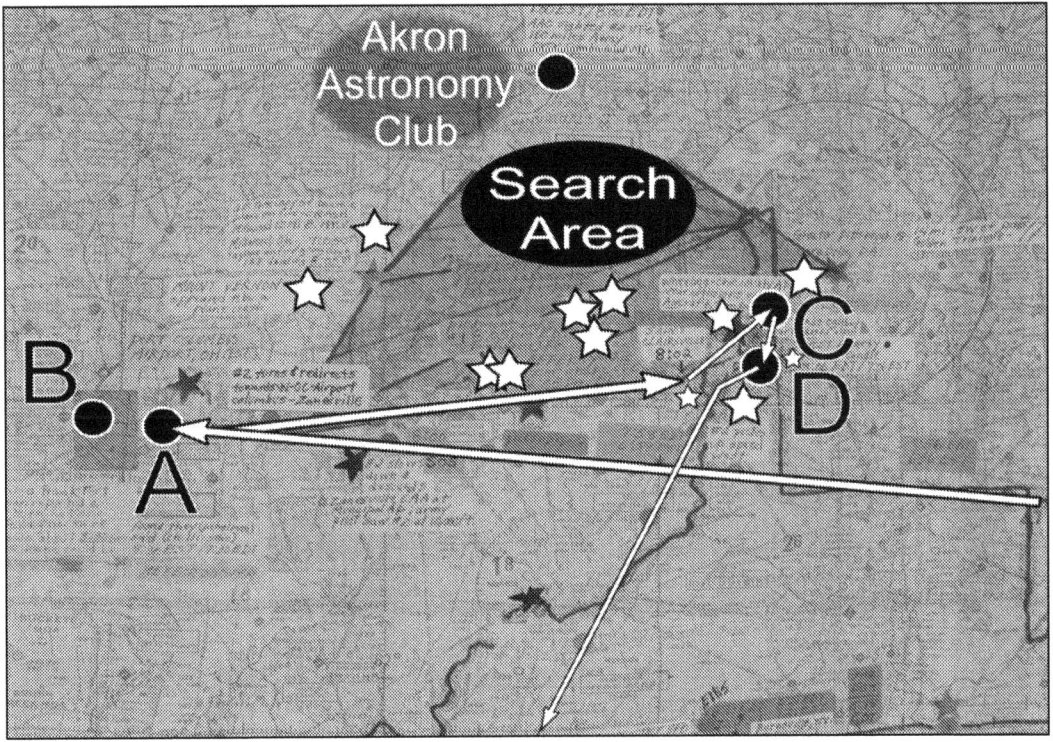

EXIT

I was able to trace the flight paths of the following ships; 1.) The three damaged mid-Atlantic objects. 2.) The jet-shaped UFO. 3.) The five southeastern North Carolina Rescue Objects. The following list indicates the locations where these nine UFOs were last seen:

1) **The three mid-Atlantic UFOs**;
   The damaged Virginia/TN #1 Object was last seen airborne and traveling east over Elizabethton, TN.
   The damaged Baltimore/WV #2 Object was last seen over Bluefield, WV.
   The damaged Washington/Flatwoods WV #3 Object was last seen crashing into James Knob in Frametown, WV.
2) **The one jet-shaped UFO**;
   This object was last sighted over Flatwoods.
3) **The five southeast North Carolina Rescue UFOs**;
   The damaged #1 North Carolina Rescue Object was last seen airborne over an automobile in Duck Creek, WV before it departed the area.
   The #2 North Carolina Rescue Object was last seen airborne over Heaters, WV. It also ascended into the upper atmosphere.
   The #3 North Carolina Rescue Object was last seen airborne over the Sutton airport. This ship also ascended into the upper atmosphere.
   The #4 North Carolina Rescue ship, a backup ship, was reported over Flat Rock, NC. It was then sighted over Virginia with the other three NC rescue ships heading north and was later seen over Lafferty, OH.
   The #5 North Carolina Rescue Object was a backup ship, last seen over Raleigh, North Carolina

Of the nine UFOs listed, four were damaged—the three mid-Atlantic objects and the #1 North Carolina Rescue Object, the UFO intercepted by fighter jets over the Gulf waters earlier.

I closely examined the characteristics that these four ships displayed. The ships were all described as having been on fire at one point or another during their flight paths and crash-landed. While in flight, these ships were seen emitting sparks, had pieces fall off of them, exploding, and hurling off fragments, to name a few.

After the ships initially landed, they were seen airborne several times afterward, except for one ship. The only ship I could not find an extended flight path for was the "Flatwoods Monster" ship. It remained on James Knob in Frametown and that is where its flight path ended. The other three damaged ships were seen airborne heading out of each of the states that they landed in, two departing West Virginia and one departing Tennessee. Upon examining the Project Blue Book case files, I found additional reports of objects sighted after 7:00 p.m. EST. These reports all relate to two separate incidents reporting three separate objects. They were sighted at 7:45 p.m. EST/8:45 p.m. EDT, and 8:03 p.m. EST/9:03 p.m. EDT.

The 7:45 p.m. incident involved the sighting of two UFOs flying together. The second incident involved the sighting of a single object. All were seen near Greensboro, NC, along the flight path where three of the North Carolina rescue ships traveled en route to Flatwoods.

In examining the eighteen-minute time span between these two incidents, it is clear that these objects were actually the three damaged ships making their departures. Greensboro was a designated departure point along the escape route. This was also the same route used by the rescue ships earlier.

The first sighting at 7:45 involved two of the damaged objects that were unable to make atmospheric ascents. These two objects were the Virginia/TN #1 Object and the #1 North Carolina Rescue Object. The two objects flew one in front of the other. One object described as a "huge light," was in front of and attached to a "fiery ball" that was flying as if it were in tow. This incident was recorded in a Project Blue Book Tentative Observers Questionnaire by the Greensboro eyewitness.

Another incident also involved two objects flying together in unison over Ward, WV, and occurred shortly before the Greensboro incident. *The Charleston Daily Mail* article, "2-in-One Meteor Seen Over Ward," reported that the witness said two objects, "appeared to be two balls of fire, one over the other, with a connecting tail." These alleged meteors were actually the damaged Baltimore/WV #2 Object and the #1 North Carolina Rescue Object. The Baltimore/WV #2 Object had lost power and had trouble staying airborne. It had already landed on the outskirts of Charleston twice trying to get to safety and then landed in Cabin Creek.

At some point between the Charleston and Ward, West Virginia, it actually made a rendezvous with the #1 North Carolina Rescue object. The damaged #1 North Carolina object had just departed Braxton County after regenerating its power supply, and then headed southwest towards Charleston. When these two craft made their rendezvous, they connected in midair so the #1 North Carolina Rescue Object could transfer energy to the failing Baltimore/WV #2 Object. This process is similar to the in flight fueling method. During this process however, the damaged Baltimore/WV #2 Object began to overheat and caught on fire, igniting the #1 North Carolina Rescue Object. The Baltimore/WV #2 Object was forced to land once again. It landed in the area of Cabin Creek, West Virginia, just southeast of Ward. The #1 North Carolina Object, now low on power, continued on a solo flight and struggled towards Greensboro, NC.

During that time, the last damaged ship that was unaccounted for, the Virginia/TN #1 Object, reentered the scene. It was last seen headed east over Elizabethton, TN, approximately 120 miles northwest of Greensboro. As the fleeing #1 North Carolina Rescue Object got close to Greensboro, the Virginia/TN #1 Object tracked it from the west. As they reached Greensboro, the Virginia/TN #1 Object intercepted the rescue craft, the #1 North Carolina Rescue Object. The two crafts linked and energy was successfully transferred. Minutes later, both of these craft moved over Greensboro at a low altitude heading southeast. The Virginia/TN #1 Object was described as a huge light, headed in front of the fiery ball object, which was the #1 North Carolina Rescue Object.

Eighteen minutes later, at 8:03 p.m. EST, Project Blue Book reported another incident near Greensboro, North Carolina. According to my research, this was the last damaged ship, the Baltimore/WV #2 Object that had just landed in Cabin Creek, West Virginia to cool down. It was last seen heading south across the southern West Virginia border over the town of Bluefield. The following is a record of the incident in Project Blue Book, called a Flying Object Report. It states, "One oblong fiery object, whitish glow trailing red sparks was observed from B-25 aircraft, 20 miles south-southwest of Greensboro, North Carolina by Captain [blacked out]. Special Investigations Unit Bolling AFB, Washington. Object observed for approximately 15 seconds, object disappeared going north very fast. Altitude of B7-25 [B-25] was 2000 feet, air speed 215 MPH. Time of sighting 12/2003 [12 September/8:03 p.m. EST]."

During this time, the #4 North Carolina Rescue Object that descended over North Carolina earlier, stayed behind to secure the area. Its purpose was to protect the damaged outgoing ships against any potential jet intercepts. It patrolled the skies over North Carolina after dark along a southeast to northeast corridor. This North Carolina escape route was also the same corridor used by the rescue ships upon entering the air space.

After the damaged Baltimore/WV #2 Object passed over Greensboro, NC on its southeast flight path, it redirected its flight path when the B-25 aircraft came into the area. This object then proceeded on a northern heading to avoid a confrontation with this military plane, then redirected its flight path again and proceeded towards the east coastline of North Carolina then headed southeast. When the Baltimore/WV #2 Object was seen earlier by the Akron Astronomy Club, it was described as "egg-shaped with a smaller radius in front." Later, when the object was sighted over Charleston, WV, a witness said he "saw sparks for a moment." Afterward, when it was seen over the skies of Greensboro, it was reported as "trailing red sparks."

After the three damaged ships were seen passing over the Greensboro, North Carolina area, they headed southeast until they reached the coastline and passed out over the Atlantic Ocean.

Meanwhile, the large mothership over the Washington area was relocating. Moving high above the atmosphere, it headed southeast toward the North Carolina coast for a rendezvous. Upon reaching the North Carolina coastal area, it situated itself a few miles off the coastline over the Atlantic Ocean. It descended low into the atmosphere and met the three damaged ships that were circling and waiting. The large carrier craft picked the three damaged ships up, ascended and then headed back north. The rendezvous was successful.

The North Carolina Exit Corridor

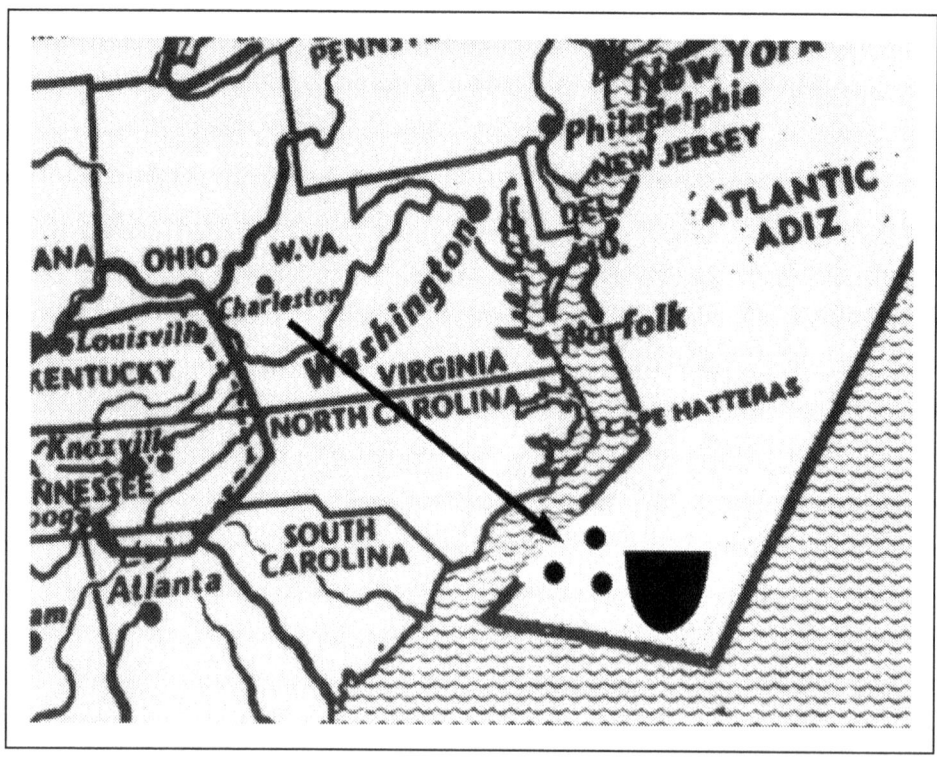

CEASED

The next sighting of a UFO occurred over Allen, MD. It was seen about one-half hour after the search and rescue mission for the injured being in Wheeling had been called off.

Project Blue Book heavily documented this case, and recorded the sighting as "Unknown" case #2077. The witnesses, Mr. And Mrs. Kolb made their sighting report at 9:30 p.m. EST to the Baltimore, MD Ground Observer Corps Filter Station. They also reported the sighting to the 647th AC & W ["'Aircraft Control and Warning'...as in *AC & W facility, installation, system, unit."*] in Manassas, VA. A Teletype report from the 647th AC & W was sent to two Air Force bases and the Pentagon. This document stated, "Object was round with streamers, flashing greenish-white light, with a red rim. Moving at about 2,000 feet and under observation about 35 minutes. Visibility was 10 miles. No aircraft were detected with radar; however, low-level emissions were sighted." Shortly after the 647th AC & W made this report, it was Teletyped to the ATIC at Wright-Patterson AFB. Upon receipt, it was hand-stamped "ACTION."

Shortly afterward, a follow-up report was completed. This report was an "Air Intelligence Information Report." This two-page report was also copied and sent to ATIC Project Blue Book for evaluation. The document read:

SUMMARY: a report received at 0245z [9:45 p.m. EST] 12 September 1952 from the Baltimore Ground Observer Corps Filter center stating that an unconventional flying object had been sighted at 0230z [9:30 p.m. EST]. Object was round with streamers, flashing green, white light with red rim, moving mid-Atlantic at approximately 2,000 feet. Object was observed through field glasses for a period of thirty-five minutes during which time the red rim around the object grew fainter and object faded altogether. A check of the area of reported sighting was made by this station using all electronic equipment available and no targets were detected.

After ATIC reviewed this report, a handwritten note was added in the margin, disregarding the possibility the object was a low-level mission being conducted: wind 90 degrees [arrows indicating direction] = could not be a weather balloon. No split [arrow indicating direction].

After Project Blue Book officials analyzed this report, they gave their final evaluation on the sighting of the object. This was recorded in a Project 10073 Record Card.

Comments: Does not coincide with regular releases in area.
Conclusion: Unknown.

The 647th AC & W Squadron Air Intelligence Information Report stated a check was made on all electronic equipment available, and no targets were detected. Why was this object not detected? After receiving this report at 9:45 p.m. EST and checking for an object on radar, they were unable to find it even though the object appeared in the sky for another twenty minutes.

The Baltimore GOC Filter Station must have thought the sighting of the UFO was important enough to contact an Aircraft Control and Warning squadron.

The UFO was surrounded by USAF bases and Naval Air stations at all points except over the Atlantic Ocean. The UFO positioned itself in the middle of the following military installations:

1.) NAS Patuxent River, 35 miles west of UFO
2.) Dover AFB, Delaware, 65 miles NE of UFO
3.) Andrews AFB, Maryland, 75 miles NW of UFO
4.) Bolling AFB, Wash, DC, 80 miles NW of UFO
5.) NAS Quantico, VA, 85 miles NW of UFO
6.) Langley AFB, VA, 90 miles SW of UFO
7.) NAS Norfolk, VA, 100 miles SW of UFO
8.) NAS Oceana, VA, 105 miles SW of UFO.

After the Baltimore GOC station reported this strange UFO, the military could not detect the object. The object was hovering so low that radar could not pick it up. The 647th AC & W squadron did not scramble fighters, but they contacted the Pentagon, Wright-Patterson AFB, and ENT AFB.

Why did the USAF leave this object alone? The military officials knew what the UFO was and probably knew its motive. The UFO did not position itself in the middle of these military bases to go undetected. It wanted to be seen, hovering at an altitude of 2,000 feet for thirty-five minutes. The craft was round, with white light and a red rim. It was flashing green and blinking. It had streamers flowing from its body. The object was acting as a beacon to guide the Flatwoods ship toward the coastline.

Approximately 108 miles northeast of Allen, MD, another UFO was sighted in Claymont, DE hovering at 2,000 feet. *The Wilmington Journal* printed an AP article from Baltimore dated September 13, 1952, titled, "Fiery Object in Sky Stirs 'Saucer Reports' in 4 States." It stated, "Several persons living in the vicinity of Claymont called State Police and the weatherman at New Castle Airport last night inquiring about 'the spinning tops in the sky.'"

The Wilmington Morning News printed another story about these sightings. The headline read, "Flashing Meteors Scare Residents In Three-State-Area." It stated, "They had seen what they described as a spinning top in the skies north of Wilmington. (The object resembled a spinning top in shape, which remained in one position and did not travel through the skies.) Paul Ridgeway said it appeared to be about 2,000 feet in the sky . . . and slightly smaller than a dirigible."

This top-shaped object and the round object over Allen, MD both acted as beacons. If the damaged Flatwoods ship had departed West Virginia, it would have had the option to move toward either one of these beacons. A projected flight path from Braxton County to either of these beacons would have taken the object around Washington D.C.

The top-shaped craft was the large mothership that had descended over the Claymont area. This huge craft descended to 2,000 feet and waited to pick up the damaged "Flatwoods Monster" ship if it came that way.

Taking into account, the bold actions of these two crafts so near to Washington, it was wonder military interceptions were not ordered against them but Government officials were well aware of their presence. Just prior, installations across the country were tracking and reporting the three damaged objects. They were sighted across the country by countless civilians. Washington officials definitely knew something was going on. These two low hovering UFOs were actually awaiting the damaged "Flatwoods Monster" craft. The officials did not know if the rescue missions would be successful.

About three hours after the object was seen over Allen, a Teletype was sent from U.S. Air Force headquarters to the Pentagon, Ent AFB, Wright Patterson AFB, and Langley AFB.

The following statement was made, "One Navy pilot over Patuxent River, MD, and one Air Force pilot over Greensborough [sic] NC reported seeing shooting stars at about the same time of the sightings."

According to the Teletype, the U.S. Navy pilot reported this sighting to the Pentagon. Why did a Navy pilot report shooting stars to the Pentagon? It seems that the Teletype was forwarded to three Air Force bases because the Pentagon was aware these alleged "shooting stars" were actually UFOs. This Navy report was the first hint of a cover-up, foreshadowing the "single meteor theory" that would be given.

It is hard to believe that the U.S. Air Force could explain away all the sightings that night with their single meteor theory. Washington's explanation was accepted by the public in 1952, but looking at the evidence today, we see that the single meteor explanation fails to explain much of anything. Furthermore, not one word about any of these sightings appeared in Edward Ruppelt's book!

The final UFO sighting that occurred that night was in Braxton County, in Flatwoods, over the Bailey Fisher farm. Investigator Gray Barker discovered the story and reported it in the Saucerian Vol. 1 No. 1. Barker reported, "I often puzzle over one account I drove fifty miles to obtain. It was said that Bailey Frame of Birch River, had been on the scene, and had witnessed a rocket ship take off from the hill. I found him in a tavern at Birch River, where he hastily denied most of the report, but did say he had seen a strange object in the sky after the 'monster' incident."

Barker added, "It was a large orange ball, he said, flattened on top, from which jets or streams of fire shot out and down around the sides. It circled around in the sky, and was seen from a small valley at Flatwoods, near the hilltop, where Bailey Frame had driven half an hour after hearing about the matter. After circling for fifteen minutes, it suddenly left at great speed toward the Sutton airport."

Barker said, "This, I thought, was most important. For it filled an important gap—the exit of the 'monster.'" Barker explained the following episode involving Bailey Frame. "He said he'd be glad to meet me at a restaurant that evening, drive to Flatwoods with me, and take me to the exact spot where he had seen the thing. He did not show up. I was not greatly impressed by the report anyway."

I believe Barker was not impressed because the sighting of this object and its description did not fit the profile of the "Flatwoods Monster" ship. Barker had hoped this was "the exit of the 'monster'" ship.

The "Flatwoods Monster" ship was described to me as elliptically shaped, not round. Witnesses Jack Davis and Freddie May both described the incoming damaged ship to me in a rather detailed manner. Their descriptions of the object did not sound like Mr. Frame's description.

The object seen circling the mountaintop of the Fisher farm was actually a later sighting of a rescue ship, making a last-ditch effort to find the monster. This would explain why the object circled the hilltop of the Fisher farm for fifteen minutes. From Mr. Frame's description of the object's circling flight pattern in the sky, it appears that the object was intently searching the area.

I re-examined the shapes and descriptions of the 8:00 p.m. rescue ships seen over the mid-Atlantic and found a striking resemblance to one of the objects. The #5 UFO, which was witnessed flying over Arlington, VA, was a nearly identical match to Mr. Frame's UFO sighting in Flatwoods.

Frame described the shape of the object he saw as a "large orange ball…flattened on top." The Arlington, VA witness described the object as "a luminous green ball-type object, a little flattened with a short orange tail." The reason for the color differences is that the object seen by Frame was hovering and emitting jet streams of fire, reflecting against the body giving it an orange appearance.

In both sightings, the witnesses described the object as being round and having a flat side. These two objects were the only two described as ball-shaped with a flat side.

Furthermore, the Arlington area sighting at 8:00 p.m. EDT and the West Liberty, WV sighting were both said to resemble a Roman candle while in flight. I believe that this particular object was seen over three separate locations throughout the night.

Gray Barker said that Bailey Frame had "driven half an hour after hearing about the matter." He did not give the time that Frame heard about the incident. According to my research, Frame's sighting occurred after A. Lee Stewart, Jr. and the sheriff left Mrs. May's house in Flatwoods between 10:30 and 11:00 p.m. EST.

The object had headed toward Flatwoods, called by the homing beacon. It followed the beacon signal to the Fisher farm and circled over its several acres. Nevertheless, the "Flatwoods Monster" was stranded in Frametown atop James Knoll, unable to transmit any messages from its overheated ship.

After the rescue object circled the Fisher farm for fifteen minutes, it departed. Trying to locate the damaged ship at night in the mountains of West Virginia without any communications had been virtually impossible. All search and rescue attempts had ceased.

In the meantime, the UFO over Maryland and the Mothership over Delaware ascended, then rendezvoused and departed the atmosphere. The large carrier craft headed northwest and then hovered back over Washington D.C., just above the atmosphere.

All the rescue objects that were searching for their two stranded comrades over eastern Ohio and throughout West Virginia rendezvoused with the mothership and waited...

This illustration depicts the UFO that was sighted by the GOC for 35 minutes over Allen, MD

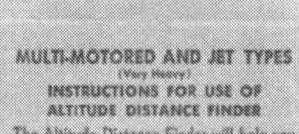

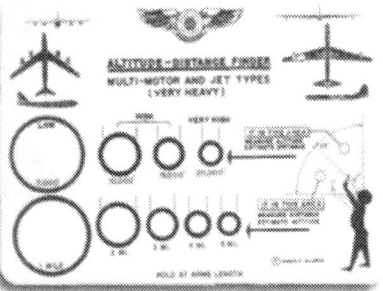

GOC Altitude Distance Finder

THE REPTILIANS

It was Saturday morning on September 13, 1952. While newspapers around the country had released articles about the strange phenomenon of the previous night, nobody was fully aware of the aftermath.

The "Flatwoods Monster," the occupant of the craft described as the "Flame over Washington," was stranded in Frametown, atop James Knoll. Moreover, the occupant of the damaged Baltimore/WV ship was still awaiting rescue near Oglebay Park. The pilot of this craft did not make its presence known until Monday night, September 15.

When this occupant was sighted in Wheeling on Monday night, it was also called a "monster." It had been stranded in the area since Friday night, when it had been dropped from its craft because it had sustained injuries. The area where the creature was sighted was the Vineyard Hill Housing Development, approximately five miles from Oglebay Park.

On Tuesday, September 16, 1952, the following article appeared on the front page of *The Wheeling Intelligencer*, "Powered by Suggestion? 'Monster' From Outer Space Arrives Here Via 'Saucer.'" It reads:

"Bashful Billy," the monster from outer space and southern West Virginia, arrived in Wheeling by flying saucer yesterday and promptly set tongues wagging and telephones burning. Even the Wheeling police prepared to call out all space cadets. Telephones of The Wheeling Intelligencer and city police kept humming last night as anxious residents attempted to confirm rumors, but in true Hollywood style, the monster apparently vanished without pausing to light a single cigarette with his fiery breath.

One call to the Intelligencer office asked if it was true that the horrible burned body of a woman was found at Vineyard Hill and that, a city policeman was burned mysteriously about the arm. Since no members of the department are equipped with Buck Rogers rocket guns, Lieutenant Murphy declined to assign men to the area. "The only green-eyed monster I ever heard of was a jealous woman," Detective Howard Miller said.

Callers also reported that an unpleasant odor was produced by the monster, who evidently hasn't heard of chlorophyll since he's newly arrived on this planet, and police admitted there was something smelly about the way the rumor was started from no apparent source. Lieutenant Murphy said undoubtedly the rumors were caused by over-active imagination following yesterday's Intelligencers story of an outer-world monster, reportedly spotted in the woods near Sutton, W. Va.

Wheeling monster must have been a "Bashful Billy," however, as none of the people who called the Intelligencer or police had actually seen the fugitive from fairyland, but were merely passing on reports from people who had talked to people who had talked to people who had heard about the Vineyard Hill Frankenstein.

Meanwhile three disbelievers of the flying saucers story had a change of mind last night when they reported seeing a 'ball of fire' soar through the heavens to the west, just outside of Independence, Pa. Ernest Mitchell, of 1038 Capline Street, William Downey, who lives at the Wheeling Country Club, and Katherine Meyers, of

Barnesville, Ohio, were returning to Wheeling from Aspenwall last night after visiting Downey's brother when they sighted the object.

"We were watching an airplane from the Independence Airfield when the ball of fire zoomed over the horizon." Mitchell said, "And then it was gone in no time at all." Mitchell's statement was verified by Miss Meyers, who said the object was seen between 7:30 and 7:45 o'clock [EDT] headed due west. "I've been watching every night since I first heard of flying saucers and I've never seen one, until tonight that is," Downley said. All three described it as a plain ball of fire, quite small, and said it wasn't trailing sparks.

They estimated that it appeared for one to two minutes. Due to the length of time the object was sighted, this was not a typical fireball meteor, nor any kind of meteor.

This witty and sarcastic newspaper article was actually filled with a lot of valuable information, much of it very close to the truth. It was reported, "One caller to the Intelligencer office asked if it were true that the horribly burned body of a woman was found at Vineyard Hill and that a policeman was burned mysteriously about the arm."

Further reports about this Wheeling city police officer were made to the police department. Their response was, "Police Lt. John P. Murphy reported similar calls pertaining to an injured policeman, and in one incident was asked to send a patrolman to Vineyard Hill for guard duty. Lieutenant Murphy declined to send a man to the area."

It was also noted, "Callers reported an unpleasant odor was produced by the monster."

When the Wheeling Police Department received such a large number of calls, why would Lieutenant Murphy allegedly refuse to send a police officer to the Vineyard Hill area? Even if the calls were only rumors and Lt. Murphy placed no credibility in the story, it is the police department's duty to protect and serve its citizens. I am surprised Wheeling Police Department officials stayed at their office answering phone calls instead of going out to Vineyard Hill to talk to their concerned citizens.

I find it odd that Detective Millard saw fit to mock one of the callers with the comment, "the only green-eyed monster I ever heard of was a jealous woman." Had the Wheeling Police Department actually already responded to the call, and knew quite well what was happening at Vineyard Hill?

Was it a rumor or a fact that an officer had "been burned mysteriously about the arm"? If this was a fact, had the officer been dispatched to Vineyard Hill to respond to the calls about a green-eyed monster?

Was the body of a "horribly burned woman" found at Vineyard Hill, or was this the cover story for what was actually found? If a body had been found, was some attempt made to ascertain the identity of the victim? Under these circumstances, why didn't they try to establish whether the victim in question was involved in an accident or a homicide? Why is there no follow-up story or death record about this alleged dead woman?

Did an officer respond to the call and have to handle a burnt human body? On the other hand, had he been exposed to the body of a burnt extraterrestrial that caused his injury?

Cover stories aside, I believe there were sightings of an extraterrestrial being in that area. It was actually discovered dead. That would explain why the Wheeling police gave no public statement about already having responded to the calls by sending an officer to the area. The officer in question would have responded to the reported calls of the monster sighting.

This is another scenario of that incident, unlike the newspaper reported. After reaching Vineyard Hills, the officer actually found the burnt extraterrestrial body of an occupant from the damaged Baltimore/WV #2 ship.

The alien sustained severe injuries while onboard its craft during a direct confrontation with USAF jets on Friday night. When the living conditions inside the craft became intolerable, the craft landed. The cooler atmosphere outside the ship was the creature's only chance of survival.

Shortly after the being was dropped off, several rescue ships searched in vain for approximately two hours to recover the injured, stranded pilot.

The rescue ships that repeatedly descended to the earth looking for their comrade were labeled a meteor shower. There is no official documentation for this meteor shower.

For three days, this injured being waited alone in the West Virginia woods near Wheeling to be picked up and then died. Shortly after, the extraterrestrial was found dead by persons from Vineyard Hills.

It was reported, "Callers also reported that an unpleasant odor was produced by the monster." That "unpleasant odor" was the smell of the exhaust that was emitted from the metallic spacesuit of the being. This stench was also present on the Fisher Farm in Flatwoods and sickened the witnesses. It also lingered for some time.

After the body was discovered, a call was then made to the Wheeling Police Department. An officer was escorted to the area by the witnesses. The officer approached the horribly burned body. The officer was himself burned when he were exposed to the body and metallic suit, apparently sustaining injuries to one or both of his arms because of the contact. This burn was more than likely a type of radiation burn that was later described as "mysterious."

The author's rendition of "Bashful Billy"

Shortly thereafter, the West Virginia State Police were notified of the incident as well as officials in Washington. The area where the body was discovered was cordoned off; the body was removed from the scene.

During that time, in Vineyard Hills, rumors started circulating about the "horribly burned body of a woman" having been found. This was the cover story. It was told to the Wheeling residents that had seen or heard of the "monster."

Another point to bring up regarding the "green-eyed monster" comment made by Detective Millard is he obviously heard this description from someone who contacted the police department. This information is mentioned nowhere other than in the newspaper article attributed to Millard. It is, therefore, interesting that the Intelligencer article that Murphy cited [September 15 "Monster from Space Roaming West Virginia Hills"] did not refer to a green-eyed being. How did Detective Millard learn about this detail?

On Wednesday, September 17, *The Wheeling Intelligencer* printed another article mentioning a monster. This article refers to two Ohio sightings on Tuesday night, September 16. The following is a complete quotation of the entire article, "Bashful Billy Plagues Patrol" It stated:

Reports of a roving monster which have been coming in from various sections shifted to Ohio last night, much to the discomfiture of the State Highway Patrol at Bridgeport. At about 9:30, a boy telephoned to headquarters and said: 'Yes, I saw the thing. It was from 10 to 15 feet tall and had a green body and a red head. It was spitting flames from its mouth.'

Another call came from a man in Bellaire who said his grandchildren were 'almost scared to death' by something they had seen but their descriptions were vague. The names of the callers are not known.

Were these roving so-called monsters actually a search and rescue group trying to locate their injured comrade? What really happened to the being nicknamed "Bashful Billy" will never be known. However it seems, that the being "Bashful Billy" never made it off this planet alive. I believe the crash incident and retrieval operation was handled in a manner similar to the Roswell, NM area crash of July 1947.

The fate of the "Flatwoods Monster" stranded in Braxton County awaiting rescue atop James Knoll in Frametown was quite different. The outcome of that incident resulted in a successful rescue on September 13, the day after its ship went down. On the evening of the 13th, a family driving through Frametown, West Virginia in Braxton County also had a terrifying encounter with a so-called "monster." The family was so distraught that that they did not speak about the incident publicly for three years.

In 1955, the president of the Flying Saucer Research Institute, Paul Lieb, wrote a story entitled "The West Virginia Monster." This story was a narrative told to Mr. Lieb by a witness, George Snitowsky. It was published in Male magazine in July 1955. I was amazed by the article's content. The evidence is overwhelming that there was a direct connection between this incident and the "Flatwoods Monster" incident.

In December 1993, I sent Mr. Snitowsky some of my research material about Braxton County and expressed my interest in his story. Shortly afterward, I received a signed receipt for the material. I then contacted George Snitowsky by telephone. George acknowledged that he was the witness interviewed by Paul Lieb and that indeed the story was true. As we talked, I took notes about the incident including a description of the being that he saw that night.

After our conversation, I asked George if he would work with me and possibly do a taped interview. He told me that he had gone with this story once, and preferred not to deal with the repercussions again. I respected his request and did not push him further. Most of what Snitowsky told me appeared in the 1955 article by Paul Lieb. The following information is from that article as told to Mr. Lieb by George Snitowsky.

George Snitowsky, his wife, Edith, and their eighteen-month-old son had traveled from Queens, New York, to visit a relative in Cincinnati, Ohio. After a three-week vacation, they left Ohio and began their drive back to New York. The Snitowsky couple had not been in a hurry, so they visited small towns and enjoyed the scenery along the secondary roads. Dusk approached as George drove into Braxton County. It was about 8:00 p.m. EST on September 13, 1952.

What was supposed to be a peaceful sightseeing trip through the mountains literally turned into a night of absolute terror. The Snitowsky's automobile inexplicably stopped and they were stranded along the roadside.

George said, "According to the map, we were in Braxton County, WV somewhere around Frametown and Sutton." Several attempts to start the engine failed. It seemed the car battery was dead which was odd. Snitowsky stated, "It was a relatively new battery and there had been no indication that it was running down."

As George continued trying to start the car, the fresh mountain air became filled with a sickening odor, something "like a mixture of ether and burnt sulfur." Immediately George jumped from the car and raised the hood, thinking the engine was burning. He found no problem with the engine.

As the odor worsened, the baby began to cry uncontrollably as he lay in a small crib in the back seat. George got back into the car and closed all the windows, as the odor grew stronger.

By that time, it was getting dark and George did not want to leave his wife and baby alone in the car while he sought help. The nearest town was Frametown, about twelve miles away. George thought it best to wait until another car came and could assist them.

Suddenly, the car was bathed in "a dazzling flash of light with a wavering, unsteady beam." The light was emanating from a wooded area bordering the road. The diffused light was described as "a soft, violet hue, blinding to the eyes." George opened the window to get a better look. It had become difficult to see because the area had now become engulfed in a cloudy haze.

When he opened the car window, this dusty, cloudy haze filled the car, causing everyone to gag. A nauseating stench made them sick to their stomachs. The poor baby was crying uncontrollably. George said at that point, "I didn't know what the hell was going on."

George got out of the car to investigate the light in the distance. He walked toward the light, and after only a few steps, he was overcome by the odor and vomited heavily.

As he tried to regain his balance, he gazed down into the woods at the light source. Off to the side of the road, the ground sloped down into a valley and George was able to look between some trees. What he saw was only the beginning of the nightmare into which they had stumbled. About "200 or 300 feet away behind a few trees", there was an object that George described as "some kind of luminescent spheroid." He stood gazing at the object in disbelief, trying to comprehend what he was seeing.

As George neared the object, trying to get a closer look, he became sicker from the stench permeating the air. Upon closer examination he said, "It was like a frosted street lamp a couple hundred times enlarged."

This large spheroid was not sitting on the ground, but "it seemed to float on one end, moving slightly back and forth."

Walking closer to the spheroid, George became more nauseated from the odor that still filled the air. He walked about half the distance to the floating object when he became hot. George then felt a strange "tingling sensation" coursing through his body.

Despite these adverse conditions, his curiosity overcame him and he moved closer to the spectacle. After taking only a few more steps, George felt a sensation he described as feeling like "thousands of needle-like vibrations," and "like a low-grade electric shock." He jerked away and stumbled back toward his car. During his walk to the car, George fell repeatedly, his legs numb and rubbery from the electric shocks he had received. He drew closer to his car and staggered against a tree, attempting to regain his balance and catch his breath.

As he tried to pull himself together to continue onward, a blood-curdling scream pierced the air. It was Edith. George, in fear for his wife and child, instinctively overcame his physical distress and dashed back to the car.

He shouted to her, "Edith - for God's sake - what's the matter?" Edith was paralyzed with fear. George stated, "Her lips moved and her eyes were wide open and staring at something behind me." George turned to look, seeking the source of her terror, and the image he saw buckled his knees.

George gave this statement regarding what he saw that night, "The figure was standing immobile, on the fringe of the road, about 30 feet off to my right."

It was silhouetted in the light emanating from the large spheroid. George described the figure as, "a good eight or nine foot tall, and in the general shape of a man." He further described it as having "a head and shoulders and a bloated body."

Frightened, George "fumbled" with the car door handle, then climbed in and "slammed the door." Their baby was crying hysterically from the commotion. He stated, "'Try to quiet him! Muffle his mouth - !' I said to my wife. She was whimpering in sheer terror."

He grabbed for the glove box where he kept a knife, and pulled his wife and baby down to the relative safety of the car floor. He huddled over them, shielding them from what was standing only a short distance from their car.

According to George, while they were "on the floor for several minutes," they were unaware that the huge alien figure had moved closer to their car. George raised his head to assess the situation and was shocked to see the monster standing directly in front of the car. He stated, "My chest was hammering like a sledge. I poked my head up and got a close-up of whatever it was–out there."

The hysterical couple, anticipating their next move, stayed on the floor of the car. George, still peering over the dashboard saw the giant creature near the car. He stated, "Reaching across the windshield from above, a long, spindly arm was forked into two soft ends. It seemed to be examining the surface of the car." George added, "If I ever prayed in my life, I was praying then."

He then explained, "Seconds later, without making any hostile moves toward us, the creature started back to the woods." He said, "It wasn't walking and I couldn't make out anything that might be called legs." Furthermore, "the lower torso was a single solid mass that seemed to glide across the uneven road surface" as it made its way back into the woods.

The sickening stench was still in the air as George watched the creature hover away, He stated, "The figure vanished among the trees." Shortly thereafter, with the mysterious giant gone, George assisted his wife and child up from the car floor. He stated, "My wife became hysterical and I put the baby in the car crib and tried to calm her." He suddenly "caught sight of the ascending iridescent globe over the trees" as it moved up into the sky. The object he had seen hovering over the forest floor only moments before was now airborne.

George gave the following description of the object he saw departing: "It rose slowly and made intermittent stops, hanging in mid-air for a split second before continuing upward. And then, at about 3,000 feet I guess, it swung back and forth like a pendulum gathering momentum. Suddenly it swooped up in an elliptical arc and with a dazzling trail of light, shot completely out of sight."

George, still badly shaken, instinctively attempted to start the car again. This time the engine started without any problem. He then drove until reaching a 24-hour truck stop/diner, which I believe was in the Sutton area. The Snitowskys went into the diner to unwind after their ordeal. They decided not to tell anyone about what they had just experienced, not then, anyway.

After a short stay at the diner, they left, stopping at a hotel for the night. The following morning, as they were preparing to leave, George noticed something odd on the hood of his car. The hood showed a discoloration, which was dark in appearance where the creature had touched their car the night before. It looked as though the metal on the hood of the car "had been singed. The outline was fork shaped.

The following are comparisons between the "Flatwoods Monster" and George Snitowsky's account of the Frametown creature:

- Both George Snitowsky and Eugene Lemon vomited from a nauseating smell that was present in the area where a so-called monster had been seen.
- Both Snitowsky and the Flatwoods witnesses described an alien figure that was huge, very tall and had no legs.
- In both cases, witnesses described a cloudy, foggy mist in the area of their encounter.
- In both cases, a burning smell and sulpher odor were noticed nearby.
- Both cases took place in Braxton County, about seventeen miles apart.
- Both cases took place one day apart.
- In both cases, the figure was described as gliding, hovering, or floating above the ground as it moved.

The "Flatwoods Monster" was described as about "twelve feet tall" by all of the witnesses. The Frametown Monster was described as being "a good eight or nine feet tall, in the general shape of a man, with a head and shoulders and a bloated body." In comparison, by adding a three- foot high helmet onto the shoulder area of a nine-foot tall figure contained in a metal space suit would make the overall spacesuit apparatus, twelve feet tall.

Based on the sizes and the heights of the figures seen in both incidents, it is feasible that an eight-or-nine-foot figure in the general shape of a man could easily have fit inside a twelve-foot metal space suit. By comparing the descriptions of both figures from the eyewitness testimonies in both incidents, I have concluded that the Frametown Monster was actually the same creature seen in Flatwoods the night before. I will explain.

After the alien landed in Flatwoods on September 12, it was seen wearing a space-suit apparatus when it was outside its ship. The space suit, which also functioned as a vehicle, was capable of hovering and traveling over and above the ground. It carried the alien via a propulsion system, which was contained in the lower half of the suit.

When the alien was seen the following night in Frametown, it had removed the upper half of its spacesuit apparatus. In reference to the lower portion of the figure Snitowsky said, "The lower torso was a single solid mass that seemed to glide across the uneven road surface." The lower torso was actually the lower half of the metal space suit, which contained the propulsion system.

Snitowsky could not see any legs on the figure because the alien was standing inside the lower torso section. The lower half of the space-suit apparatus carried the alien above and across the road.

What George Snitowsky saw when he described the upper torso of the huge figure was the exposed body of the alien. What these witnesses smelled was the exhaust emitted from the propulsion system. As the alien hovered and passed near the areas where it had been observed, it polluted the air around it.

On September 12, the alien was wearing its entire space suit when it landed in Flatwoods after having been shot down. After it was seen, it departed Flatwoods and made another emergency landing in Frametown, on James Knob, and was stranded overnight. It had abandoned its damaged ship. The monster left the area where its ship went down in the event the military located the crash site and attempted to take further hostile actions.

While roaming the area of Frametown, and hovering in its vehicular suit, it was inadvertently seen by the Snitowsky family who were simply in the wrong place at the wrong time. The Snitowskys actually witnessed the rescue of the stranded "Flatwoods Monster."

An associate who worked with Major Donald Keyhoe on the book, *Flying Saucers from Outer Space*, spoke about the "Flatwoods Monster." He wished to remain anonymous in his interview with Keyhoe for the book. This man whom Keyhoe called James Riordan was a captain in the U.S. Air Force. He also had connections with the Air Technical Intelligence Center, the headquarters for Project Blue Book. This officer was an F-86 Sabre jet pilot who fought in the Korean War.

The following conversation took place between Keyhoe and this captain concerning the "Flatwoods Monster": Keyhoe: "I started to ask him about the Sutton Monster story. What was the ATIC's conclusion?"

Captain: "They swear they didn't analyze it, but I'm positive they did check into it."

Keyhoe: "I told him what I knew about the case."

Captain: "(shaking head dubiously) It sounds as if there was something to it. Not a monster—I still can't see that—but it might have been a robot of some kind, the way they [witnesses] described it."

Ivan T. Sanderson spoke with the boys who witnessed the "monster" and had them draw it. He concluded that the "Flatwoods Monster" was a large suit that contained a being. Sanderson stated, "They all did sketches and we put together a composite of it. It looks exactly like one of the most modern Navy diving suits, which is solid [outer shell], the person is inside." Sanderson also likened the being inside to a "pilot" or "occupant." This spacesuit or the equivalent of our deep-sea-diving bells was regulated to counteract gravity by adjustment to the density of air at ground level. Sanderson believed the "pilot" of the UFO that landed in Flatwoods was "obviously contained in some kind of suit."

It is obvious from the testimony of the witnesses that what was called a monster was instead a living being inside a space suit. The space suit was metallic, served as a protective outer covering, and served as a small vehicular craft, by which the creature could move around. The metallic suit or craft and its living entity had emerged from a large ovoid craft, which it had originally controlled and landed.

The metallic space suit was actually a mechanical probe. Its function was life-supportive, maintaining a controlled environment and protecting the entity within from hostile atmospheric conditions or beings. This creature's metallic suit seemed to be damaged. This had most likely occurred during the aerial confrontation with the military over the Atlantic.

Colonel Dale Leavitt: "Well, there was something here that could fly backwards or wherever they wanted to go, just anywhere, I think, as long as they don't tear up their equipment."

Mrs. May: "It was making a hissing noise and sounded like it was frying bacon." (Possibly very hot and burning up.)

"I was as close to it as the length of a car, a small car. I was close enough that it squirted oil all over my uniform. . . . You could feel it was like a warm mist. It must have come from the creature."

Lee Stewart Jr.: "I walked up and down the skid marks area and that's when I realized I was getting oil on my clothes. The oil was darker than tar grass and adhered to your clothes. There were rocks turned over in the skid mark area, and that's when I found the piece of metal . . . it was a dripping, like a piece of dripped solder, it was rugged on the edges . . . it was shiny like silver."

It seems evident that this metal space suit or vehicle was damaged. Once the alien left Flatwoods and landed in Frametown, it discarded the upper portion of its suit. This alien realized either it was able to tolerate the Earth's environment or it had no choice because the upper torso of the suit was useless.

Apparently, a large spherical object landed in Frametown to rescue the alien. This gigantic being then disappeared into the woods and the sphere-shaped craft took off moments later.

An interesting point to rise involving the Frametown and Flatwoods incidents is the comparison of lights noted at each of the sights. Purple and violet covered lights were described in each of these cases where the objects were located. Mrs. May stated the following information concerning a flaring light she saw on the Fisher Farm, "As soon as I stepped down into the road and was startin' up the hill, I noticed this great, big red flare, a purplish-looking flare." This was the vicinity where the "Flatwoods Monster" craft landed.

George Snitowsky also gave a similar description of light where he saw the object hovering above the ground in Frametown. He described the color of light as "A soft violet hue, blinding to the eyes." Snitowsky also stated it was "a dazzling flash of light with a wavering unsteady beam." Both witnesses had "seen the light," and it was intense.

Prior to the 8:00 p.m. EST rescue of the stranded being in Frametown, another series of UFO events had occurred. Project Blue Book stated that UFOs were sighted between 6:40 p.m. and 7:07 p.m. EST in Pennsylvania, Virginia, and Maryland.

I established that there were four objects sighted over those areas. After plotting their locations, the times they were seen, and their directional headings, I concluded that those four objects were a reconnaissance team.

On the night of the 12th, there had been no communications to or from the downed "Flatwoods Monster" craft. The specific location of the damaged craft was unknown. A last minute effort to locate the craft by circling over the Fisher farm for fifteen minutes proved futile.

The transmitter device of the overheated craft was nonfunctional when it landed in Frametown on September 12. On September 13, the circumstances were different.

The scenario involving this reconnaissance mission unfolded at about 6:30 p.m. EST on September 13. The main carrier craft located above Washington, DC received a faint transmission signal from the downed object in West Virginia. A ship was dispatched from the carrier so it could obtain a better fix on the signal. The ship descended into the atmosphere over Allentown.

Project Blue Book lists this UFO case as an unidentified case, #2085. The location was Allentown, PA. The witness was W. A. Hobler of New York. Hobler was an inactive Air Force Reserve captain at the time. Hobler submitted a letter to the commanding General at Mitchel AFB in New York regarding his encounter.

The following information is the verbatim letter from Mr. Hobler:

Dear Sir:

If I had not seen the enclosed clipping, I probably would not make the following report. However, since other people in the vicinity where I saw an unusual phenomenon, saw the same thing, I thought perhaps I should describe my experience.

On 13 September 1952 at about 1940 [about 6:40 p.m. EST], I was flying alone at ten thousand feet from Allentown, PA, to the Caldwell-Wright Omni Station in a Beechcraft Bonanza. Visibility at that altitude was about twelve miles. There were no clouds of any kind although there was some haze . . . from the ground to more than 12,000 feet.

I was approximately 15 to 20 miles NE of Allentown when suddenly a bright object, which appeared to be shaped like a fat football and three feet in diameter, flaming orange-red in color, appeared at a distance of 150 to 200 yards ahead of me at eleven o'clock high.

It was descending at about a 30-degree angle. . . . My first impression was that it was a "falling star" and that I was on a collision course with it. I immediately pulled up into a steep climb to avoid hitting it; but the object, instead of continuing on its downward course, very suddenly pulled up into about a 65-degree climb and went directly over my windshield. I quickly made a 180 to the right but could no longer see the ball of fire. If the object was at the distance and was of the size that it appeared to me to be, I would estimate it was traveling at better than 700 miles an hour. If what I saw was actually a physical object, the rapidity with which it altered its course was astonishing.

Since I was able to see it for not more than two seconds, I hesitated to report what I saw. After the object went by, I resumed my course and for the next 20 minutes tried to be sure that what I had seen was not a light reflection on the windshield. I regret now that I did not make this report immediately.

Even though the description of this oval object is similar to the other descriptions of similar objects seen on 12 September, the Air Force identified the object as unknown.

After the UFO had been sighted, it quickly descended below the five-thousand-foot radar range. With the reconnaissance mission now in jeopardy, the craft looked for an isolated landing area.

The craft went southwest and landed in York County after traveling more than 100 miles. York County borders Dauphin County, separated by the Susquehanna River. Olmsted AFB, located in Middletown, is located in Dauphin County, near the Susquehanna. The UFO came down in a wooded area near Conewago Lake and awaited orders from the main craft. The object sat until approximately 7:00 p.m. EST. It received orders to abort the mission and depart the area traveling north at a very low altitude. The UFO then passed over Middletown, Pennsylvania. Shortly after, it was sighted over Olmsted AFB by base employees. This was the third sighting of an object over the vicinity of Olmsted AFB in two days.

1. The first sighting occurred September 12 at 3:35 a.m. EDT. A guard stated that while on patrol he became aware of the object after hearing what "sounded like heavy projectile artillery and saw a blue light in the sky."

2. The second sighting occurred a few hours later at 8:07 p.m. EST/9:07 p.m. EDT. This object was the #12 Rescue Ship. An employee "sighted a strange object while at work" and "described the object as a bright white light. . . . The light was visible for 3 or 4 minutes. . . . Its speed was described as slower than an airplane."

3. The third sighting occurred on September 13 at 7:04 p.m. EST. Project Blue Book explained and recorded this sighting as a meteor.

I was able to establish that this sighting was a UFO based on several Project Blue Book documents. The first document was the original Teletype report from Olmstead AFB, designated "RE AFL 200-5" [reference Air Force Letter 200-5]. This report was typed at 10:09 p.m. EST to four different Air Force facilities. Along the top of this document were two hand-stamped messages. In large letters were the words "Operational Immediate" and underneath was the word "Action."

The following is the "FLYOBRPT" [Flying Object Report]:

On 13 Sept 1952 at 0004Z observers from Dauphin and adjacent counties sighted object in sky. Number of base employees sighted same object and reported it to be a meteor traveling from Southeast to Northwest. Apparent size was approximately 25 inches in diameter [size of object at distance] out near ground. Last sighted at 40-10N, 76-40W appearing to go below hills to west of field across Susquehanna River. Light was bluish-white turning to yellow. Fast rate of speed. No sound. Slight tail said by observers to be merely due to great rate of speed. Weather at time of sighting clear with 7 miles visibility. Surface winds calm 2000 feet 280 degrees at 7 knot. (95 4000 ft 320 degrees at 6 knots). No air traffic at time. All observers making reports were on ground, observers appear to be reliable at least two are base guards.

Upon examining this Teletype, I had numerous questions about it.

1. This object was reported to be a meteor by the Olmstead base employees who sighted it. Yet the meteor made no sound. If the object was indeed a meteor, why did Olmstead AFB send a Teletype describing the incident to the Pentagon, ATIC, Wright Patterson AFB, Air Material Command, Wright Patterson AFB and the commanding General of Ent AFB?

2. Why would a meteor sighting receive a hand stamp by ATIC designating the report "Operational Immediate" warranting "Action"?

I believe the reason that Olmsted AFB relayed the original sighting report was that the flying object had passed in the near vicinity of their Air Material Area, which housed air defense equipment and supplies. Following procedure by filing this report was appropriate. It does not seem like a valid response if personnel had spotted a passing meteor.

Three days later, Olmsted Intelligence Officers followed up their initial teletype report with an additional report. This report was an "AIR INTELLIGENCE INFORMATION REPORT." Two copies of this report were sent to Wright Patterson...one to ATIC and the other forwarded to Strategic Intelligence in Washington D.C. Was it logical to send a report about a "meteor" to Strategic Intelligence, a government agency responsible for collecting and evaluating information about the enemy or potential enemies for national security reasons?

This "AIR INTELLIGENCE INFORMATION REPORT" Titled: Country–United States SUBJECT–(UNCLASSIFIED) Unidentified Flying Objects

Reporting (Short Title: FLYOBRPT) contained vital information regarding this sighting.

It is interesting to note that the "EVALUATION" segment of this report was left blank. The reason this follow-up report was filed is stated in the following summary statement:

"SUMMARY-Reference teletype 13/0259Z [September 13/10:59 p.m. EDT], this headquarters, according to base observers this object was unquestionably a meteor. This report is submitted only to nullify teletyped referenced above."

The last document recording this case in Project Blue Book was the Project 100073 Report Card. It states the following information, "COMMENTS - Possible meteor. CONCLUSIONS - Possibly astronomical. Meteor [handwritten]."

Even though Olmsted AFB nullified its original teletype report about the sighting of a meteor, Project Blue Book concluded that the object was possibly a meteor anyway. Why did Project Blue Book ignore the nullification of this teletype by Olmsted?

At approximately 7:00 p.m. EST, the reconnaissance ship lifted off and passed near Olmsted AFB. It then made its atmospheric ascent out of Pennsylvania toward the carrier ship.

At approximately 7:00 p.m. EST another reconnaissance plan was implemented that involved three objects. The first ship made its atmospheric descent over Richmond, VA. It was sighted at 7:02 p.m. EST. One minute later the second ship made its atmospheric descent over Colonial Heights, VA. Two minutes later the third ship descended over Patuxent, MD at 7:05 p.m. EST. The three rescue ships immediately began to search for the transmission signal from the downed West Virginia craft.

Project Blue Book recorded these sightings in three different documents by the 771st AC&W installations, located in Fort John Eustis, VA. The Virginia sightings were all reported to this installation, but the Maryland sighting was reported to the 26th Air Division Defense (Roslyn, NY) and then relayed to the 771st AC&W. The AC&W is defined in the United States Air dictionary as follows, "Aircraft control and warning. A service or activity in which aircraft (including guided missiles) are detected and tracked in flight and reported, followed by evaluation and plotting of the information obtained, which information is then used in a warning network and in the control of fighter aircraft, anti-aircraft artillery, and other combative forces."

The 771st AC&W initially recorded these incidents, documented them, and relayed the information via Teletype to five different Air Force installations across the United States. When received by Project Blue Book, it was hand-stamped "ACTION."

The most interesting point I found when analyzing these three documents was that even though the 771st informed all these Air Force installations about the sightings, the ATIC later evaluated the incident as a single meteor. The following information was contained in the original Teletype document sent to ATIC before a final evaluation was made by Project Blue Book:

One blue ball of fire with a long tail was sighted heading west over Lovingston, VA at 0007z [7:07 p.m. EST]. The observer stated that a four-engine aircraft was in the area at the same time and the pilot could possibly have seen the object. Two airmen of the Richmond Filter Center of the GOC (Ground Observation Corps) reported seeing an object of the same description approximately five minutes earlier [7:02 p.m. EST]. The object danced for a few seconds then took off toward the West. At 0115 [8:15 p.m. EST] the Richmond Filter Station called this station again with the report that the same object had been sighted over Colonial Heights, VA., at 0003z [7:03 p.m. EST].

After translating this report into non-technical language, I realized there were actually four sightings of three separate objects. I concluded the three Virginia sightings were actually two objects seen over three different areas. The last object was sighted near Patuxent, MD, Charles County, near Washington D.C.
The sightings and times of these objects are as follows:
1. First sighting: approximately 7:02 p.m. EST over Richmond, VA. Observed for a few seconds.
2. Second sighting: 7:03 p.m. EST over Colonial Heights, VA.
3. Third sighting: pilot of cavalier aircraft sighted meteor at 7:05 p.m. EST near Patuxent, MD.
4. Fourth sighting: 7:07 p.m. EST over Lovingston, VA.
The Colonial Heights object was reported to be the same object that was seen over Richmond, which would be impossible. The Richmond object left on a westerly course at 7:02 p.m. EST. Colonial Heights lies almost twenty-five miles south of Richmond.
The third sighting was made four minutes later over Lovingston, VA at 7:07 p.m. Lovingston is to the northwest of Richmond and Colonial Heights. Lovingston is also near the West Virginia border, southeast of Braxton County. The document gave a more detailed accounting of the Lovingston, VA sighting. It stated, "One blue ball of fire with a long tail was sighted heading west over Lovingston, Virginia at 0007z [7:07 p.m. EST]. The observer stated that a four-engine aircraft was in the area at the same time and [the pilot] possibly could have seen the 'object.'"
The Richmond and Lovingston sightings had the same description; the Richmond sighting was seen five minutes earlier because it was the same object, traveling westward.
I believe the first Virginia object was seen twice, five minutes apart and traveling from east to west, and that it was the first reconnaissance ship in the area. The object sighted over Maryland was another ship. The two Virginia objects and the Maryland object were part of the second reconnaissance mission.
My conclusions regarding these rescue ships were reinforced after reviewing the ATIC's Project Blue Book "Project 100073 Worksheet" and the "Project 100073 Report Card." The documents related to the Virginia and Maryland sightings contained many errors.
The Project 10073 Worksheet was the follow-up report made by Project Blue Book to the original report made by the 771st A C & W. Section 2 of the worksheet shows an error. One of the questions in the section was standard, but the response was inaccurate:
Q. What astronomical activity was noted? A.: Yes.
The answer to this question was handwritten and stated, "yes;" not an answer to the question.
The section that was highly questionable was the evaluation portion. There were three evaluation questions asked in this section. The answers for each section are as follows, taken from multiple choices given on the form.

Evaluation of source: The answer checked off is "poor" concerning the multiple witnesses.

Details of Report: The answer is recorded as "fair."

Final Evaluation: The answer checked off is "was astronomical."

The Lovingston, VA object was explained as a meteor that was seen near Patuxent, MD. This evaluation was based on the information from the "26th Air Division Defense" in Roslyn, NY.

The following are inconsistencies and oddities contained in the Project 10073 Worksheet. They declared all of the Virginia sightings and the lone Maryland sighting all to have been a single meteor.

1. Why did the U.S. Air Force try to establish that an object that had passed over Lovingston, VA was a meteor sighted over the Washington area, over 125 miles away?

2. Why did the comment section of the document state that several people in the Washington area had seen the meteor? The original document stated that a single "pilot of cavalier aircraft sighted meteor…."

3. The Intelligence at ATIC at Wright-Patterson AFB receiving the original report from the 771st AC&W knew that "two airmen of the Richmond Filter Center of the GOC reported seeing an object of the same description approximately five minutes earlier."

4. A single meteor could not have been seen over Richmond, VA at 7:02 p.m., then fly south over Colonial Heights at 7:03 p.m., then fly northeast to Patuxent, MD at 7:03 p.m., and then turn back to the southwest and once again fly over Lovingston at 7:07 p.m.

5. Another inconsistency in the Air Force's meteor explanation is "the object danced for a few seconds then took off." It seems unlikely that two men in the U.S. Air Force would mistake a dancing UFO for a meteor.

6. Another weak point in the Air Force's evaluation was their evaluation of the source. This was stated to be "multiple" and "poor." This seems odd since the first Virginia sighting was made by trained aviators. The Air Force's low estimation of a sighting by trained personnel seems like an effort to facilitate the cover-up.

The final document pertaining to this case is the evaluation report, Project Blue Book's "Project 10073 Record Card." The ATIC recorded inconsistencies follow:

"Type of observation - Ground visual, air visual."

The ground visual sightings were made in Virginia. The air visual sighting was made in Maryland. ATIC labeled all the sightings over Virginia and Maryland as one single meteor.

"Source – multiple."

Once again, the Air Force tried to label these reports as one lone meteor, seen by multiple witnesses from two states.

"Length of observation - a few seconds."

This is a very general answer. Multiple witnesses sighted the object over three Virginia locations and one witness saw it over Maryland. How did the ATIC arrive at its conclusion, "a few seconds" when the alleged meteor was seen over a five-minute time span?

"Number of objects – One."

"Course – West."

The ATIC's flight path analysis was equally illogical One meteor could not have passed over all the locations, across multiple states if it only headed in a westerly direction.

A Brief summary of sighting - states the Lovingston, VA object was, "a ball of fire" that "appeared to dance for a few seconds." Real meteors do not dance. It is a physical impossibility for a meteor to "dance" during its trajectory for a few seconds and then take off.

Another inconsistency in the 10073 Record Card was the attribution of the prior description to the Lovingston object. The description of an object that appeared to "dance for a few seconds" was made over Richmond, not Lovingston, as the record card stated. The Lovingston sighting occurred at 7:07 p.m. EST, five minutes later. It gave the directional heading as west, and there was no mention of the object dancing over Lovingston.

"Comments - Several sources saw an object with a tail streak across the sky, seen for a few seconds only. Aircraft in the area reported a meteor at approximately the same time."

The several sources who saw an object with a tail streaking across the sky were the Virginia witnesses. The aircraft in the area that reported a meteor at approximately the same time was actually in Maryland.

"Conclusion - Was astronomical." [Answer checked off in block; next to this standard response, the word "meteor" was typed in.]

My conclusions differ drastically from those of Project Blue Book. I believe the four objects seen throughout the Mid-Atlantic were actually reconnaissance ships. Each of these four rescue ships descended to obtain a better fix on the Flatwoods ships' signal.

When the first object had a near collision over Pennsylvania, the reconnaissance mission was temporarily aborted. Soon thereafter, three more ships descended south of Washington, DC to find their comrade.

The first Virginia object was seen over the Richmond area at 7:02 p.m. EST and the second Virginia craft was seen over Colonial Heights a minute later. The Richmond sighting "danced for a few seconds then took off toward the West." This blue ball of fire with a long tail was next seen over Lovingston, VA five minutes later at 7:07 p.m.

I believe this first Virginia craft obtained a solid lock on the signal at 7:02 p.m. EST. The other two ships descended shortly afterward and continued as part of the mission.

After the ship past over Lovingston, it followed the signal to West Virginia. The ship passed high over Frametown and pinpointed the location of the downed craft on James Knoll. The fix had been obtained.

The coordinates of the downed craft were then transmitted back to the main carrier craft. At that point, though, it was not dark enough to descend into the area without being noticed. The object ascended out of the atmosphere, along with the other two objects over Virginia and Maryland. All three ships moved back to the carrier ship.

The ship chosen to go back to West Virginia and retrieve the stranded being was the original Pennsylvania reconnaissance craft. This was the football-shaped object involved in the near collision near Allentown. It headed to Braxton County high above the atmosphere. It descended and followed the signal into the densely wooded Frametown area looking for the craft and stranded pilot.

However, the signal was not being transmitted from the damaged craft. The signal was being transmitted from the woods below James Knoll approximately two miles away. The alien had removed the transmitter from the ship after connecting it to another smaller portable source. The stranded being left the immediate vicinity of its ship for fear of being captured by the military and sought cover along the perimeter of the nearby woods. The transmitter was placed in the woods and the alien roamed the outskirts of the woods, staying within close proximity of the device.

The rescue ship circled over James Knoll at a low altitude making a visual inspection of the terrain. It descended and followed the transmission signal. An intense spotlight emitted from the craft aided in the search. Shortly thereafter, the rescue ship was sighted by the stranded pilot, and the alien moved out of the woods into a clearing, where it could easily be spotted. This clearing was a paved road.

The alien was sighted by the rescue ship. The ship landed a short distance away in the woods to wait for the stranded pilot to reach it. This is when George Snitowsky drove his car into the area. The alien quickly left the road and went back to the edge of the woods.

Minutes later, the alien emerged back on the road. As it headed toward the waiting rescue ship, it encountered Snitowsky. After the alien reached the ship, Snitowsky saw the spherically shaped UFO shoot "completely out of sight." The rescue had finally been completed. The alien beings had rescued their comrade.

I have established that the "Flatwoods Monster" was actually a mechanical probe of metallic construction. It also acted as an armored space suit, which contained an alien being that used it as a mode of transportation.

On Sept. 13, the Snitowskys saw the upper portion of the alien being during their encounter. The upper half of the metallic suit including the torso shell, inner helmet and outer protective ace of spades helmet were removed. This revealed the head, bloated body, arms and hands of the being that was standing inside of the lower half of the probe. The lower half of this probe was a flared shell that consisted of a mechanical propulsion system. This enabled the probe to hover, enabling the occupant standing inside of it to traverse above and across the ground.

When the being landed in Flatwoods and left its craft, it was wearing, the full armored metal space suit. On the following evening, only the lower half of the space suit was utilized to transport the being.

The lower shell of the suit apparatus was very large. Witness Fred May told me, "The lower part of it flared out and was over four foot wide at the bottom." He also stated that, "there were pipes that went around it, and they were as thick and round as a fireman's hose."

These pipes were part of the propulsion system and emitted a gaseous odor similar to sulfur, when it propelled the apparatus. When the being removed the upper protective armor section of the suit in Frametown, why did it still use the lower half?

This portion of the suit apparatus was very large and cumbersome. Even though it was being used as a transportation device, it would not be easy to maneuver a machine over throughout the densely wooded area of Frametown, especially a four-foot wide machine between trees, shrubs and rough terrain of the West Virginia Forest. The alien's mobility would be severely limited. Why had the alien not discarded the lower transport section and simply walked. This would have allowed it to move easier and faster throughout this wooded area than a hovering probe would have. Furthermore, that segment of the suit emitted an obnoxious sulfur-like odor that drew its attention to the occupant, thereby making it conspicuous. Did the alien need the transport device because was slow and not agile? Was the alien even capable of walking, and better still, did it have legs? Who were these aliens and what race of beings were they. Did these aliens leave any physical evidence behind that was found and not covered up, that gave information about them?

There were several landings made throughout West Virginia and Tennessee that night. Numerous landings occurred in Braxton County, including Flatwoods, Sugar Creek and Frametown. In Sugar Creek, biological evidence was found in the area where a landing occurred. It was found by investigator Ivan T. Sanderson and a group of his men.

Sanderson gave details about the specimens he found at Sugar Creek on two occasions. This information was contained in his "Uninvited Visitors" book and his 1968 interview with Long John Nebell. The following information given by Ivan T. Sanderson is from those two sources, "We made the best attempt possible to investigate the hill at Sugar Creek, but the terrain was difficult. There were five of us, Eddie Shoenberger, Gray Barker, Raymond Walter and one other gentleman from MonSanto and myself. The first cliff rose about 800 feet almost perpendicularly. There was a mile-long saddle above and two 500-foot hills beyond. We searched this mountainside on our hands and knees clawing our way up, because it was so steep. We found nothing until we got to the top. There was a little swamp up there with small trees behind the big forest, of tall trees.

In there I found a huge –like a skid mark, which had knocked these bushes down. Sanderson also stated an observation made by Shoenberger, who looked up at the trees from the direction that the object had come in, before it landed. He states, "Before it had apparently crashed in the swamp, he said 'look at that,' and there was a whole treetop knocked off and several other branches, all recently shattered. As though there was a hole in the top of the trees."

Sanderson explains what he found in the vicinity of where the object crash-landed, "There was a depression in that [area] and also two of these tremendous hoof-life things pushed into the ground and beyond it, a whole mass of little pieces, little coils of white plastic-like material, scattered all over the ground." Sanderson states, "The depression itself was about 15 foot across, we measured it – 15 or 16 foot but you couldn't, of course, tell where it ran out. It was a disc-shaped [round] depression."

At this point, I will analyze Mr. Sanderson's findings at Sugar Creek. The UFO that landed at Sugar Creek was the damaged #1 North Carolina Rescue Ship. When the object landed, it did not hover and descend vertically to make a soft landing when it touched down. It descended on a downward trajectory, knocked off an entire treetop, and shattered several other nearby branches. The damaged object continued on this trajectory until hitting the ground. It made a belly-landing and crashed, leaving a skid mark path and knocking down bushes as it plowed through the earth. When the elliptical-shaped object came to a halt, it left a depression in the terrain about 15 foot across that was disc-shaped in nature. The other depressions found near the landing site were the two "tremendous hoof-like things pushed into the ground." These large hoof-shaped impressions seem to indicate the shape of the lower torso section of the metallic suit made by the occupant upon touching down after hovering out of the downed ship. It seems the alien occupant departed the object in its spacesuit probe and when it settled to the ground, its tremendous weight caused the lower torso to be "pushed into the ground." Thus leaving a partial impression described as, "hoof-like things." Were there two aliens?

Sanderson expounded on the evidence he found concerning the "white plastic-like material", he found. He states, "On the comparatively open saddle above the cliff, we found three shallow holes. Beyond each of these, there were wedge-shaped spatters of a strange white substance in small, curled cylinders. This at first looked to us like dried up snake or turtle egg shell, but we collected some and had it subjected to x-ray and general chemical analysis. Sanderson explained what occurred, "We did have this funny white stuff analyzed. My friends took it down to MonSanto and they couldn't be much better there." Sanderson, actually references the "Monsanto Chemical Company." Plastics and synthetic fabrics had become a primary segment of Monsanto's business by the 40s and during that era. An ideal place for Sanderson to have his "white plastic-like material" specimens analyzed.

Sanderson states what the lab discovered, "They had numerous spectrograph analysis machines and they were unable to find out what it was. It seemed to be of a plastic nature, but – to be of an organic structure. The only thing that they could think it was, that it looked more like the dried up skin of a snake more than anything else." Mr. Sanderson explained the structural characteristics of this material as well as an analysis of it, "It proved to have three layers, the outer smooth, the inner rough, the central, columnar in structure, as far as it could be ascertained. It contained aragonite, and the whole was porous, which would seem to agree with the description of a reptile shell." Sanderson went into further detail about material and said, "However, one of the lab assistants down there managed to soften it up. They had been trying to soften it up in everything. He said, 'Why don't you try water' and they did. One of these little rolls of stuff, which were only about the size of my little finger, when outstretched, measured nine and one half inches." Sanderson then asked, "I would like to know, what snake's egg found in the United States, or anywhere else [pauses] from which you could get a strip nine and one half inches long?"

Ivan T. Sanderson made the following statement and ended his 1968 interview with Long John Nebell by saying, "The parting shot, was a humorous one made by John DuBarry when I told him all about this. He said, 'UT-oh, perhaps they were space people, but perhaps they're reptiles and were looking for somewhere to lay an egg."

In 1968, this statement may have seemed to be humorous. Did Sanderson and his associates have the evidence right in their hands, that would have show what kind of race of alien beings landed on September 12, 1952. Were these gigantic beings actually of a reptilian race with snake-like bodies and without legs or feet?

Were the lower segments of these armor suits flared-out to accommodate coiled alien bodies? Is that why these aliens needed mechanical probes to transport their bloated, slow moving and clumsy hulking bodies?

The December 1952 issue of *Sky and Telescope* magazine had an article titled "Astronomical Highlights of 1952." The article gave a list of the top ten astronomical highlights for 1952, as of October when their meeting was held. Amazingly, the overwhelming amount of alleged meteors that the military insisted occurred on September 12 and 13 did not make the list. On those two nights—there were no meteors.

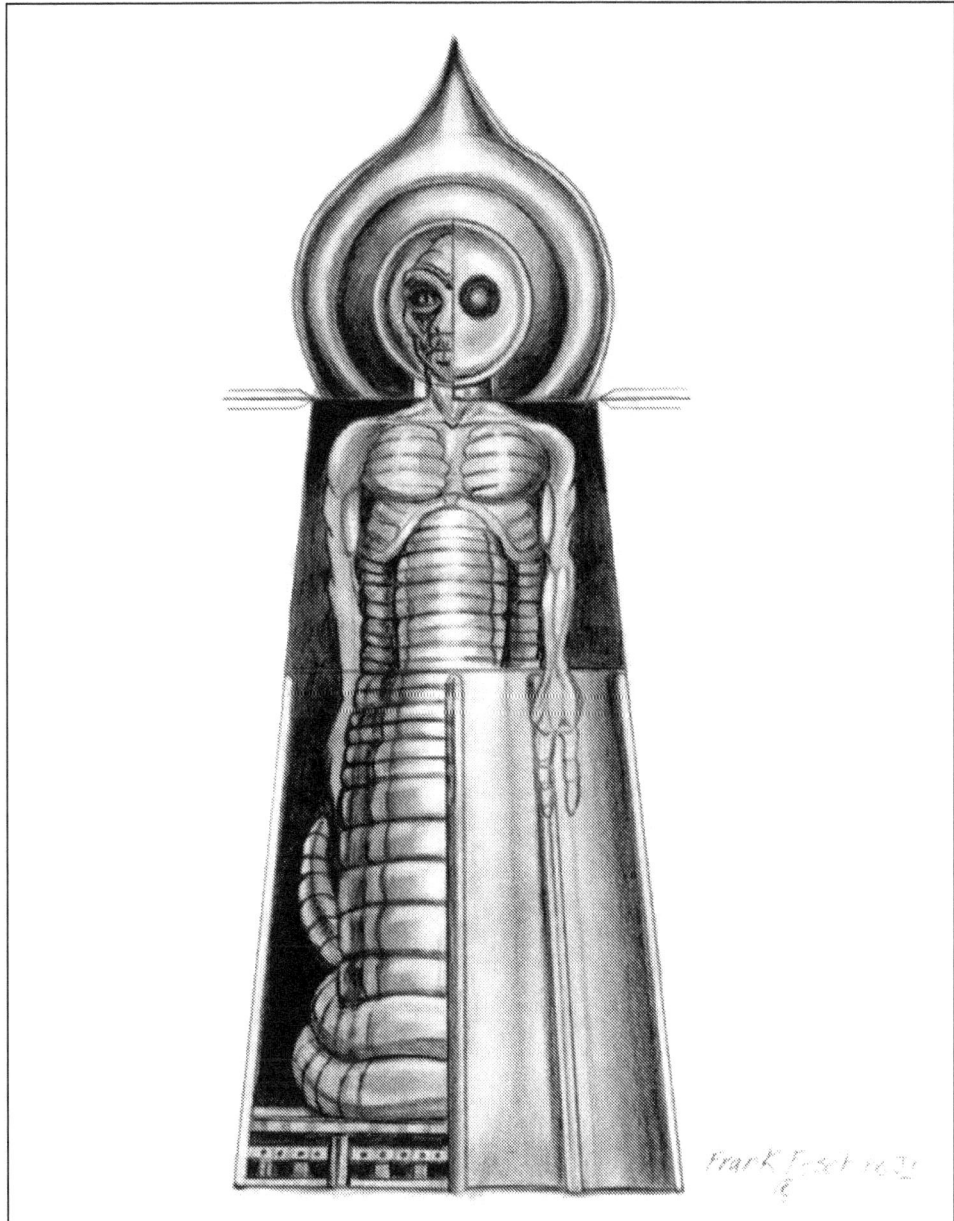
The author's depiction of the reptilian inside of its spacesuit

THE SUMMER ENDS

The total amount of "Unknown" cases that Project Blue Book recorded for the month of September was 25 cases of the 124 they received. These unexplained cases were listed for a time span between September 1 and September 29, 1952. The summer of 1952 ended on Sunday September 21, 1952. Project Blue Book evaluated and recorded eight "Unknown" cases after September 13, 1952. They were the last remaining "Unknown" cases for that summer. These cases were recorded between September 14 and September 17, 1952. Five of those cases were recorded on September 14 alone, two on September 16, and one on September 17, 1952, which closed out the "Unknown" cases for the summer of 1952. They are listed below:

September 14, 1952
1. Case 2086 - Santa Barbara, California
2. Case 2087 – Operation Mainbrace
3. Case 2089 – White Lake, South Dakota
4. Case 2092 – El Paso, Texas
5. Case 2093 – Middletown, Pennsylvania - Olmsted AFB

September 16, 1952
6. Case 2099 – Portland, Maine
7. Case 2100 – Macon, Georgia area-Warner-Robins AFB

September 17, 1952
8. Case 2105 - Tucson, Arizona

The UFO flap of September 14, 1952, spanned across the United States and as far away as the North Atlantic, during a military exercise. The first "Unknown" case from Santa Barbara, California, involved an Air Force C- 54 Sky master cargo pilot. The incident started at 8: 40 p.m. when the pilot Mr. Tarbutton, saw a UFO that he described as a "Blue-white light." He said that he watched the UFO for about "30 seconds." The observer said during that time the object's trajectory was, "straight and level." Tarbutten said the sighting ended when the object ascended, "went up" and disappeared from sight.

The second case, Case 2087, involved UFO sightings that occurred during "Operation Mainbrace," a North Atlantic Treaty Organization naval exercise. This naval exercise program was the largest held by the combined NATO fleet up to that time. Units of eight NATO governments and New Zealand participated in the maneuvers in Norwegian waters and the North Sea. It commenced on September 13, 1952, lasted for twelve days and involved 80,000 men, including 200 ships and 1,000 planes.

During night maneuvers, just north of Bornholm Island in the Baltic Sea, Danish Lieutenant Commander Schmidt Jensen, of the Danish "Destroyer Willimoes" had a UFO sighting. At 10:30 p.m., the commander and several crewmembers sighted a formation of three "bluish-green" objects. They were flying in a "triangular" formation across the sky at an altitude of about "3,000 feet." It was estimated that the objects were flying at about "1,500 Kilometers" per hour. During the sighting, the witnesses reported that the UFOs changed their flight course. They maneuvered from a "bearing of 320 degrees" to a bearing of "240 Degrees" during a time span of "approximately 7 seconds," before they vanished. The UFOs were also said to have emitted a "white light exhaust." Another incident occurred between Ireland and Iceland that involved a single UFO sighting. Several military witnesses aboard numerous naval vessels from different countries sighted a "blue-green" object described as "triangular-shaped." The UFO was traveling to the southwest and disappeared out in the distance.

The third September 14, "Unknown" case involved a Ground Observer Corps observer in White Lake, South Dakota. The witness reported a UFO sighting over that area that lasted between, "30 to 40 minutes." Case 2089 explained that witness, L. W. Barnes watched a large "cigar-shaped" object through a pair of binoculars while at the local GOC post. The object was described as "red" in color and showed "puffs" trailing behind it during its flight. The witness said that the object flew to the west, redirected toward the south, and then disappeared from sight. The "cigar-shaped" object reported by the GOC witness in this case was one of most common besides the saucer shape during the summer of 1952. This type of UFO was also reported throughout the night of September 12 over Washington D.C., Virginia, and West Virginia.

Case 2093 was the last "Unknown" Project Blue Book case recorded for September 14, 1952. Once again, it involved a UFO sighting over an Air Force base in the northeast United States. Furthermore, this base was a primary focus of UFO reconnaissance during the previous days, Olmsted Air Force Base, located in Middletown Pennsylvania.

A "FLYOBRPT" was sent from the Commanding officer of Olmsted AFB to ATIC at Wright Patterson AFB on that night described the incident. On that evening, a pair of civilian base guards was doing a security check in the parking area of the west gate. The men noticed a large aircraft sitting motionless in the sky that they described as a "blue watermelon." The guards stated that the object made a "humming sound" during the time that they saw it. Shortly after, the UFO that they described as "glowing a brilliant blue," started to ascend up into the sky. The object then moved horizontally and disappeared behind some trees in the area and the guards lost sight of it. The length of the sighting lasted for approximately, "three minutes." This description of the UFO described in this sighting was very similar to the sightings that occurred only days before over that same base.

On the following day, Monday September 15, 1952, the UFOs were back in the skies over the United States. This time they appeared over the state of Kansas on three separate occasions. The September 17, 1952 edition of *The Topeka Capital* newspaper reported the following first and second incidents. The first Kansas UFO sighting of that day occurred at 2:15 p.m. and involved five witnesses who saw six UFOs northeast of Topeka. In part, this article states:

Flying Objects 'Invade' State; 6 Seen From Highland Park.

A wave of "flying saucer" reports apparently has passed over Kansas. Five residents of Highland Park reported Tuesday that they saw metallic objects in the sky. Two Wichita airmen at the Wichita Air Force Base said a "saucer" flew parallel to their car a few minutes near Douglas Kan.

"I'm not trying to be sensational and I'm not superstitious but there were six metallic objects up there in the sky northeast of Topeka," said O. W. Bobo Jr., of 1720 Hudson. He said he, his wife, his wife's mother, his mother, and a neighbor, Mrs. Harold Hibbs of 1701 Hudson watched the objects for about 20 minutes at 2:15 p.m. Monday... The Highland witnesses also reported that the objects, "twinkled like stars as they reflected the sun, and apparently hovered in the air before taking off."

The September 16, 1952 edition of *The Wichita Evening Eagle* gave a detailed report about the second sighting that day which involved the two Wichita AFB flyers that saw a UFO from their car. Their encounter occurred six hours later at 8:15 p.m. The opening of the article states:

'Egg-shaped' Flying Saucer Sighted Near Douglass, Kan.

An egg-shaped "flying saucer" emitting orange-colored flames along with a shower of sparks was reported in the vicinity of Douglass, Kan., Monday night…

I have arranged the events of the incident contained in this article into a chronological order for continuity of the story:

A. "The airmen are Staff Sergt. Carlyle McLendon, 39, a motion picture projectionist with the visual aids section at the base, and Staff Sergt. William Muse, 26, a classification and assignment clerk in the flying training program."

B. "They were returning home from a hunting trip in their car when they saw the object in front of their car about 200 feet off the ground and a little to the left they said."

C. "They had sighted the strange object for two minutes at about 8:15 p.m. Monday at a point five miles south of Douglass."

D. "The 'saucer' appeared to them as being 30 to 40 feet in length and about 20 feet wide and both agreed that they felt no heat and heard no noise from the strange object."

E. "Sergeant McLendon said the orange-colored flame shot from what appeared to be portholes. However, Sergeant Muse believed the fire came from a dome-shaped object. They said also that flames shot from the rear of the oval."

F. "The sergeants said another car ahead of them slowed down to watch the object but when the two cars stopped [including them] it veered sharply to the right and 'disappeared in a streak of flame.'"

G. "A few moments later, when they told of seeing the strange object while in a roadside café near Douglas, the operator of the establishment agreed that he had sighted a 'streak of light' passing over Douglass at about the same time."

The description of this oval-shaped object bears an uncanny resemblance to the UFOs sighted during the previous days throughout the eastern coast of the United States. The September 16, 1952 edition of *The Wichita Evening Eagle* also reported the third and final UFO sighting that occurred that Monday over that section of Kansas.

Their other article stated, "Fiery Object Seen by Man At Clearwater." It reads in part, "James Eugene Haak, 34, of Clearwater, said at 9:15 Tuesday that he saw a mysterious fiery flying object at 9:15 p.m. Monday." This Clearwater sighting occurred one hour after the two flyers made their sighting near Douglass. Two witnesses are known to have seen the UFO that night. They were Haak and another girl walking back from a free show in the Clearwater Park. He reported his sighting to The Eagle newspaper the next morning.

This article states, "He saw the object seconds before a girl named Mary Blumenshine, whose age is estimated at 13 years shouted, 'Hey! Look there!' and pointed at the flaming object." The paper reported that "Haak said the object, all red, orange, blue and white and apparently afire, came from the northwest and appeared to have landed somewhere between Wichita and Clearwater" Eugene Haak told the paper, "If it landed, it landed five, six, or seven miles northeast of here." This may have been the same object sighted by the Wichita flyers earlier that night at 8:15 p.m.

The next Project Blue Book "Unknown" Case 2099 occurred over the region of Portland, Maine on September 16, 1952. This incident involved the crew of a United States Navy P2V Patrol plane. This aircraft was a long-range maritime patrol aircraft built by Lockheed. It was armed with machine guns located in a dorsal turret, had provisions for under wing rockets, and up to 8,000 lbs. of bombs, depth charges and torpedoes. This aircraft was characterized by its large radar radome located beneath the forward fuselage. During this incident, the plane's crew saw a "group of five lights," that were unexplained. The large radar system of the aircraft simultaneously tracked the objects, which was characterized as a "thin blip" on their screen. The entire episode lasted approximately, "20 minutes."

The second "Unknown" case on September 16, 1952 occurred over another Air Force base. This incident was recorded as Case 2100. Air Force officials reported that two UFOs flew "abreast" over Warner-Robins Air Force Base located near Macon, Georgia at "7:30 P.M." The witnesses, three Air Force officers and two civilians, described the pair of flying objects as "round objects" that were "glowing white." The two UFOs passed over the base at an altitude of "5,000 feet" at approximately 100 m.p.h.

It was reported on two separate occasions that the two objects "emitted a small bluish flame from the underside. The emissions were 30 seconds to a minute." The length of the UFO sighting was said to have lasted for "15 minutes." Similar descriptions of these type objects were reported only four days before on September 12, 1952. This was the final "Unknown" UFO sighting to have occurred over an Air Force Base in the United States during the summer of 1952.

The final Project Blue Book "Unknown" case recorded for the summer of 1952 occurred on September 17. It is recorded as Case 2105. This UFO incident occurred over Tucson, Arizona, and involved multiple objects. The witnesses, a husband and wife, Mr. and Mrs. Theodore Hollingsworth had their sighting during the late morning, at "11:40 A.M." During their "two minute" sighting, the couple reported that "two groups of objects" passed through the sky above them. Each group consisted of "three large objects" that were described as "flat and shiny." The witnesses stated the objects flew in "tight formations" as they passed overhead. The first group flew "slow" and the second group of objects flew at a "faster" speed. They could not explain their sighting. This was the last UFO sighting during the summer of 1952 that Project Blue Book evaluated and recorded as an "Unknown" case. The UFO sightings continued until the last day of summer and culminated into a mass sighting just west of Washington D.C.

These UFO sightings occurred over Virginia on Sunday September 21, 1952. This frenzy of sightings ended the summer of saucer incidents over the United States. They occurred over the town of Centerville located southwest of Washington, directly north of Manassas, Virginia. A Centerville, VA September 22 INS report, and three Washington area newspapers carried this news story. *The Washington Daily News* reported the story on September 22, 1952. *The Washington Times* and *The Washington Post* carried stories on the following day. I extracted the most pertinent information from each newspaper and arranged the story into a sequential order for continuity.

In Centerville, at approximately 12:30 a.m., the Hazelwood family noticed a horrible odor and thought something was burning outside the vicinity of their house. Mr. and Mrs. Hazelwood and their two daughters, Marie and 18-year-old Dorothy, went out into their yard in search of the source.

The family looked up into the sky and noticed "four objects" casting off light over the vicinity of their property. Marie explained, "Whatever it was" lit up the yard, "just like the early morning sun." She also said the "odor" was still permeating throughout the air, and "it made my mother ill for a while." Mrs. Hazelwood described the UFOs moving above her. She said they were, "Orange, red and blue and about the size of an automobile headlight." She said that these "things" were moving and "bouncing in the cloudy sky above her home." According to the INS report, "at 12:50 a.m.," Mrs. Hazelwood telephoned the "Fairfax County Police" station and notified them about the UFOs. Shortly after, the police received several calls for "Help" from the locals. *The Washington Times* reported, several officers then went outside and looked over out over Centerville. They saw a "bright, white light" in the sky. The light resembled a "headlight", was said to have a "small tail" trailing behind it, and flew at an altitude of "4,000 feet."

The Washington Post reported that two Fairfax Police Officers, Officer John Wahl and Officer Julian Burke immediately went to Centerville to investigate, "Burke said one of the objects were the size of 12 quart buckets and appeared to be 2,000 feet high. He saw four." He also said, "One would pop out here and then a few seconds later another would pop out there. His partner Officer Wahl stated, "One of the objects hovered in the sky for a few moments, then rose rapidly into the sky trailing a blue flame." *The Washington Daily News* reported that another police officer went to Centerville and saw the UFOs. Private Dunn stated, "I saw three or four of them at one time, but they weren't in any formation" He also added, "The lights looked like a white ball of fire coming through the clouds. They would get real bright and light up the sky and then sort of go up and fade away." Dunn said, "They were solid objects." Throughout this entire time, Mrs. Hazelwood said she "saw six or seven" UFOs over the area.

The Washington Daily News also reported that a UFO then flew over the "Fairfax County Police Station," at approximately, "1:30 a.m." This area is located just northeast of Centerville and west of Washington. Officer Marvin Eherell who saw the object from outside of the station stated the UFO, "looked like a big auto headlight." He said, "It lighted up the sky," over that area. Officer Eherell added, "It made a circle, got real bright and then climbed back up again. It just kept that up. It would come down, get real bright, swing a circle, fade out, and climb back up again." After watching this aerial display, Officer Eherell went back into the station and called, "The Defense Department," in Washington D.C. Eherell said that authorities told him that the sightings would be "investigated."

The Sept. 22 International News Service report on the incident said the following statement was made by the Air Force at "9:00 am," that Monday morning, "Right now, we have no idea what they were. They might have been weather balloons or something." *The Washington Daily News* reported that the Civil Aeronautics Commission was also contacted that night about the sightings. It was reported, "CAA said its radar control tower at [Washington] National Airport noticed nothing on their radar screens. They said, however, they received a call from Fairfax police and a man who identified himself as an Air Force Captain saying they saw the lights." It was also reported, "All the stories the CAA heard agree in almost every detail, they said." The long hot summer of 1952 was officially over on September 21, 1952.

During the previous three months, Government officials in Washington D.C., the United States military, and Project Blue Book's staff at ATIC all had their hands full with UFO sightings. The American public, including the Ground Observer Corps had their fair share of sightings that summer and were tired of the saucers. It was a trying period in United States history. Between the UFOs, the threat of a Soviet nuclear assault and the Korean War, the United States held together. During the summer of 1952, between June 1 and September 17, 1952, Project Blue Book recorded 111 "Unknown" cases.

The year 1952, was a record year for UFO reports sent to Project Blue, 1,501 reports. The staff at Blue Book recorded 303 of them as "Unknown" cases; these numbers were never equaled again. During the months of June, July, August, and September, Project Blue book received 1,134 UFO reports. The following is a monthly breakdown of the reports received by Project Blue book for 1952:

Month 1. January - 15
Month 2. February -17
Month 3. March - 23
Month 4. April - 82
Month 5. May - 79
Month 6. June - 148
Month 7. July - 536
Month 8. August - 326
Month 9. September - 124
Month 10. October - 61
Month 11. November - 50
Month 12. December – 42

On April 19, 1953, *The New York Times* released the percentage of 1952 "unknown," UFO cases as recorded by Project Blue Book in a small article, which reads:

SAUCERS

Air Training, published by the Air Force Training Command, says that more than one thousand reports [1,501] of flying saucers were received at Wright-Patterson Field, Ohio, in 1952. Twenty per cent of these apparitions are of unknown origin. A team of four Officers and two civilians – is evaluating all saucer reports.

It is interesting that *The New York Times* still referred to the objects as, "flying saucers," rather than UFOs or "Aerial phenomena," as the Air Force preferred.

In the doorway of the building at Wright Patterson AFB where the Project Blue Book office is located are Ruppelt, Rothstein, and Olsson.

AUTUMN EXPLANATIONS

A complex and controversial aspect of the "Flatwoods Monster" case involved a government letter received by Kathleen May. She said the letter explained that the objects seen throughout Braxton County that night were experimental military aircraft. The controversy surrounding this letter involved Kathleen May and A. Lee Stewart, Jr. Since 1952, they have vehemently disagreed with each other about the content of the letter. Mrs. May maintained that the letter was governmental in origin, while A. Lee Stewart, Jr. maintained that it was merely a press release for an upcoming issue of *Colliers* magazine.

This controversy was first reported and documented by Gray Barker in September 1953. He reported in *The Saucerian*, Vol. 1, No. 1, that Mrs. May's "father told me (Barker) that Mrs. May had received a letter from the government, which explained what the whole thing actually had meant, and advised that a report was to be *released* to the public that week, after which she could talk freely about it. Her father said that since the release date had passed he could tell me that the 'monster' was a government rocket ship, propelled by an ammonia-like [sic] fuel, and which could travel at terrific speeds."

Barker also said, "I could hardly wait to look up Editor Stewart who, I was told, could give me details on the government report. Stewart laughed as he pulled out an 8" x 10" photo, attached to a publicity release from *Collier's* magazine. The issue of October 18 was to contain the story about a moon rocket, and the photo was the cover art. It was to be released that week, he explained. He had shown the picture to the May family, because there was some resemblance between the rocket ship and their descriptions of the 'monster.'"

Since that time, there have been many opinions expressed about the contents of this letter and the integrity of the involved parties. Some researchers believed A. Lee Stewart, Jr. actually showed Mrs. May a magazine press release and that Mrs. May simply misinterpreted the source of the material as being governmental.

Some researchers have tried to explain the dispute by alluding to increased age and a failing memory on the part of Mrs. May. Those opinions are unfair and inaccurate. Since 1952, Mrs. May has never wavered in her assertion that the letter was from the government. Some researchers have even suggested that Stewart intentionally misled Mrs. May into believing this letter was from the government. Mrs. May always maintained the same story. Not once did she ever waver on a single point.

The following story was related to me during an interview with Mrs. May, "It was a week or ten days after we got back from New York. Stewart called and wanted to know if I could get the boys gathered up and have them at my house at seven o'clock that evening.

He said he had received a letter from the government and he couldn't open it until seven o'clock. That is when *Collier's* magazine went to the newsstand, seven o'clock that night. He opened the letter and they had a 5" x 7" picture in there of the machine that they were building to send to the moon. And they said that the Navy Department had put the machine up, you know, the one that had come over that evening and that I had given the best description of it even to those that had built it, helped to build it."

Frank: "Now the letter was actually from the Navy, or from Washington?"
Kathleen: "From Washington, the government, uh-huh. They said the Navy Department was putting it up, building the machine."
Frank: "Now this photograph, that came with the letter, it was an actual picture of the craft?"
Kathleen: "Yes, uh-huh."
Frank: "And it looked similar to it?"
Kathleen: "Yes, uh-huh, the one that I—the one that we saw . . . and they said there'd be two men in it or more."
Frank: "Inside the actual craft?"
Kathleen: "And they told us how they would be strapped down, you know, and all this, that and the other and how they would get around and operate in the machine."
Frank: "And this was the Navy who supposedly built this?"
Kathleen: "Yeah, the Navy, and they also said, in the letter, that there were four ships around in the vicinity that night."
Frank: "They said there were four of them that night?"
Kathleen: "Uh-huh, and one of them landed in Flatwoods." Mrs. May added, "It also said the one that landed in Flatwoods was having oil trouble."
Mrs. May's mother also attended when the letter was presented to the gathered witnesses. She made the following statement to Terry Marchal of *The Sunday Gazette-Mail State Magazine*, in 1966, "The letter said it was a test plane with two men in it and then took off again." This next portion of Mrs. May's testimony clarifies her assertions that the information she received was from the government.
Kathleen: "The National Guard and A. Lee Stewart wrote the government and told them they wanted a report. They wanted to know just exactly, what it was. And they were concerned over the children with the gas, you know, and they said they wanted to know if it was one of our own."
This would explain her claims regarding the letter she had received informing her about the experimental ships.

It is a fact that Leavitt did ship off samples from the landing site to Washington upon their request. When I asked Colonel Leavitt if any reports or explanations ever came from Washington, he replied, "No! They never gave me anything back."

Stewart informed me that when the Treasury Department acquired his metal sample they informed him "in no way were they connected to the federal government as far as this trip was concerned." Stewart claimed they also took the balance of his metal fragment without his knowledge or permission. It was clear that the Treasury Department people who visited Stewart and obtained his metal samples were actually government investigators.

Mrs. May said that the government letter reported the results of the site samples. "They [government] said it was our own native oil and metal." A press release would not have contained information on the results of the oil and metal samples found at the landing site.

Mrs. May did possess knowledge of four experimental ships seen throughout Braxton County that night. She also stated that these experimental craft had a two-man crew, and one craft had landed in Flatwoods.

The October 18, 1952 issue of *Collier's* magazine was only a one-part segment in a series of space articles. Collier's editor, Gordon Manning, created a symposium from a team of space experts; they created the series. The articles dealt with all aspects of theoretical space exploration, and they were published by Collier's in 1952, 1953, and 1954. In 1952 there were only two titles released from the series. The first article, "Man Will Conquer Space Soon," was published on March 22, 1952. The following article, "Man on the Moon," appeared in two consecutive issues published on October 18 and 25, 1952.

Stewart claimed *Collier's* magazine sent him a press release for the October 18, 1952 issue that had a photo attached to it of a moon ship. He in turn showed it to Mrs. May and the witnesses. What puzzled me about Mrs.

May's letter was why the United States government would send a letter to Stewart rather than to Colonel Leavitt.

Stewart during an interview spoke about the letter and the Collier's October 18, 1952 issue

Frank: "Why do you think that Colonel Leavitt didn't receive any letters, and they sent it to a news reporter? What baffles me is that the newspapers are usually the last people the government wants to deal with, given their propensity for blowing a story out of proportion. Colonel Leavitt, who ran the investigation, told me he didn't get any information at all."

Kathleen: "No, I don't know either."

Frank: "Doesn't that sound. . . ."

[Interrupted]

Kathleen: "A. Lee had that letter that he brought down and didn't open it until he came out to our home."

Frank: "But the government sent it to him, right?"

Kathleen: "Uh-huh."

Frank: "What do you think about the whole story yourself?"

Kathleen: "Well, I didn't know and I still don't know. The government just tells you what they want you to believe."

In closing, I asked Mrs. May about the whereabouts of the letter. I asked her if she had it or if Stewart had it. She said, "He never would release the letter, and I don't know what he's done with it."

During my interview with Stewart, he explained his version of the controversial letter. Before I started taping, I asked him if he still had the letter. He told me it might be in storage in his attic. I explained that it would be great evidence for my story. It would clarify that Mrs. May might have actually been wrong in interpreting that the letter had come from the government.

Stewart told me he had kept several boxes of documents from *The Braxton Democrat* over the years. He said that some of this was the original correspondence concerning the "Flatwoods Monster." He said his late wife had taken care of the old Braxton Democrat records, packing them away, and that he did not know where she had put them. He told me we didn't need the letter anyway, that he was going to tell me what had happened. When I stressed the importance of the letter as the only hard evidence to prove who was right, he grew upset with me. I decided not to push the issue and started taping his testimony.

To aid in his recollection of events, I gave Stewart my copy of the October 18 *Collier's*. I also gave him a copy of the infamous photograph of Mrs. May holding the monster drawing, the one drawn by the *We the People* artist.

This is Stewart's version of the events, "*Collier's* contacted me after seeing the television show, remarking about the similarity to what they were getting ready to use in their magazine, to the subject they saw on television. So here are the two side-by-side, which there is some similarity, maybe you need a broad view of mind to see it, but there is some similarity, much more similarity in 1952 than in 1996. The only reason that I received this piece of material was the fact that they had seen this on television. It had nothing to do with the federal government, or anything to do with this, except the fact of the similarity, which they saw. We didn't. We hadn't seen this yet."

After hearing his statement, I was no closer to understanding the controversy than when I had started. Both Mrs. May and Stewart were still telling me the same stories they told Gray Barker in 1952.

As Stewart and I discussed the story, we spoke of the odor of oil at the landing site on Fisher farm. He said, "We got close down to the ground, and we could still pick up an odor."

I told Stewart that I knew he entered the Air Force following graduation from high school. After completing his service, he returned to West Virginia to run the newspaper with his father. Stewart had recently returned from Air Force duty at the time of the monster incident. Because of Stewart's military training, he knew to check close to the ground for the gas odor because he had learned that gases settle.

I asked Stewart to expound upon his military experience while being filmed. I explained that his background would reinforce his competence when he investigated the landing site.

Much to my shock, Stewart adamantly told me, "There's no need for anybody to know about my Air Force background." I pushed the issue but he refused to discuss his Air Force experience with me at all.

The following day was my last with A. Lee Stewart, Jr. I asked Stewart what he really thought had taken place that night. He told me that something unusual did land on the Fisher farm. He then asked what I thought had really happened. I told him I believed that the monster was actually an alien in a space suit who had landed in a damaged space ship.

He answered, "You're probably right." Stewart said that after the incident he had returned to the landing site on numerous occasions. Over the years, he had attempted to piece together the strange encounter on the farm. He would sit out at the farm, sketchpad in hand, attempting to retrace the steps of the event and the flight paths of the objects.

I went out to my car to retrieve one of my paintings, the full color illustration that depicted the farm at the moment of the encounter. I showed it to Stewart and he said, "You know, it didn't land there. It landed on the mountaintop and moved into the valley." I was stunned that he knew this.

Stewart then took my sketchpad and started to draw the Fisher farm. We drew a compilation sketch together and compared notes while we reviewed the incident. Amazingly, our facts about the encounter on the farm coincided. I had underestimated Stewart's knowledge of the story.

I said to Lee, "So you believe it was an alien in a space ship, too."

"Yes, it was," he replied. Lee then looked back at my painting and said, "There were more trees in the valley, to the left of where the ship landed the second time. They were pear trees." He told me I should correct the picture if I wanted it to be accurate.

Shortly thereafter, I began to pack up my equipment for the long trip home. As I thanked Lee for helping me in my research and having me in his home for four days, he made one more comment. I was walking out the door when Lee said, "My dad said, 'I think the aliens knew to land in West Virginia because no one would ever believe us here.'"

After spending four days with A. Lee Stewart, Jr., I came away with a much clearer understanding of the "Flatwoods Monster" case, and a much deeper understanding of A. Lee Stewart, Jr. Because of my opportunity to speak with Stewart at length, over a period of four days, the letter incident that had confused me had taken on a new dimension. I began to see this story from a different angle—an angle I dreaded even thinking about.

I tried unsuccessfully to contact Stewart numerous times to see if he had found any documents, supposedly packed away in storage in his home. I continued to call sporadically for over a year, but was unable to reach him.

During that time, Freddie May made an arrangement for me to interview his mother once more. I wanted to review some final details for the book before finishing it. During our meeting in November 1998, Mrs. May informed me that A. Lee Stewart, Jr. had recently passed away. It was a sad moment for us.

As our conversation progressed, I showed Mrs. May some of my research that she knew nothing about. I showed her the U.S. Air Force's Project 10073 Record Card, which explained the West Virginia Monster as the Washington area meteor. I then showed Mrs. May other Project Blue Book reports, information she had never known about, and she was shocked. Even though Mrs. May claimed the government letter contained information about experimental ships, she was puzzled as to why they explained the monster as a meteor.

We discussed the illustration of the moon ship seen on the cover of *Collier's*. The illustration attached to the controversial letter. The dimensions in scale of this theoretical moon ship would in fact have been far too large for the "Flatwoods Monster." The height of this proposed "moon ship" was to be, "160 feet long and about 110 feet wide." In reference, the height of this ship at 160 feet would have been 9 feet taller than The Statue of Liberty. The base was to have "a battery of thirty rocket motors" and "topped by the sphere which houses the crew members, scientists and technicians on five floors." According to *Collier's* magazine, the moon ship vehicle would have contained a crew of twenty men.

What Kathleen May did not know about the craft pictured on the cover of *Collier's* was the scale of the illustration. Consequently, Mrs. May was unable to interpret the discrepancy in size and height between the illustration and the Monster. Had the supposed moon ship been scaled down to the size of The "Flatwoods Monster," mice would have been the appropriate- sized occupants. It is obvious that Mrs. May was intentionally misled into believing the far-fetched experimental ship explanation.

We spoke again of the controversial letter. Mrs. May ran through the story once more and said, "It was from the government and he could not open it until seven o'clock that night."

The letter said, "It was a rocket that they were building to send to the moon and there were two—[pauses] supposed to be two men in it, and they said four [ships] had come down in Braxton County that night." She was informed that three of the ships were looking for the one that landed on the Fisher Farm. Mrs. May stated, "The rest of them were looking for that one."

At this point, I ran run through a synopsis of the story, and then asked her some verifying questions.

Frank: "So this letter came to Stewart, and it came from Washington?"
Kathleen: "Uh-huh."
Frank: "And it explained everything in it?"
Kathleen: "Yeah."
Frank: "And Stewart took the letter back?"
Kathleen: "Yeah. He even took the picture."
Frank: "The picture?"
Kathleen: "He didn't give me anything."

Until Kathleen May received the letter from the government, she did not know what the monster was. While in New York for *We the People*, Mrs. May was asked if she knew what the monster was. "They asked me if I knew what it was, you know, [pauses] and Lord I didn't know, I had no idea. I know it wasn't an airplane. That's the only thing I'd seen in the sky besides a kite."

In 1952 after reading the letter, Mrs. May was convinced, it was an experimental rocket ship. It struck me as very peculiar that Stewart had taken away both the letter and the photograph.

Four years after the incident, on October 7, 1956, *The Charleston Gazette* printed the following headline: "What Happened to the Monster?"

The sub-headline read, "Braxton County Woman Feels Glowing Object Was Jet Ship Discovery in 1952 Stirred Up Nation-Wide Martian Debate." The article stated, "Flatwoods, Oct. 6 - The woman who set off a four-year debate when she saw a mysterious object near her home here said today she was convinced she didn't stumble on a craft from Mars. Mrs. Kathleen May said the 'Braxton County Monster' was nothing more than some new type governmental-owned jet or rocket plane."

I showed Kathleen May a microfilm copy of this article from my compilation of research and asked her the following question: "Have you had any change of mind over the years, or do you still think it was something from the government, or you just don't know?"

She answered, "I just don't know. Never will know, don't guess. The way things are happening now, it's hard to tell what it was."

Kathleen, concerning the letter, told me: "I never could understand why A. Lee took that, and why they sent it out to him anyway."

Then it hit me why the U.S. had sent the letter to Stewart. I believe there were actually two different letters. The letter shown to Mrs. May and the witnesses by Stewart was an informative letter from the United States. It stated that what had been seen was not a monster, but one of four Navy ships, and that one was having oil trouble. It also revealed that three of the four experimental craft were searching for the fourth ship.

This letter also contained a small amount of information about rocket fuel, information derived from the *Collier's* article. The government further stated that the metal and oil samples taken from the landing site were from one of their own experimental ships. I believe this letter was to alleviate Mrs. May's concern about the side effects of the oil and gas that the witnesses encountered.

Attached to this letter was a photograph of the moon ship that *Collier's* was planning to use on the cover of its October 18, 1952 issue. This photo reinforced the cover-up of the experimental ship explanation.

There was, it would seem, a second letter, which was nothing more than an ordinary press release concerning *Collier's* upcoming article, "Man on the Moon." This letter included the attached photo as well.

It appears to me that a switch was made with the letters, which were similar in appearance. I believe that when A. Lee Stewart, Jr. appeared on national television with Mrs. May and Eugene Lemon, he was seen by government officials.

The officials wasted no time in contacting *Collier's* to engineer a cover-up using the national media. This was a commonly accepted practice in the Cold War era, and one in which the media felt obliged to help, as a matter of national security.

In 1953, Major Donald Keyhoe stated, "Mrs. May and the Lemon boy appeared on *We the People* and retold their frightening experience. It was obvious the boys believed the monster was real, and a dozen papers and magazines sent staff writers to Sutton for new angles on the story. 'This could get out of hand,' I told Chop. 'Why doesn't the Air Force squelch it?' 'We've already said the object was a meteor,' he retorted. 'A lot of people don't believe it, and the way this has built up, its bad."

Because the government feared mass hysteria because of the statements Mrs. May had made on national television, the story had to be squelched.

When Mrs. May appeared on television and told the American public that she didn't know what the monster truly was, her story was very real, sincere, and convincing. Shortly thereafter, the media began to report this from a UFO angle.

The Washington UFO flap had only occurred a few weeks prior to the "Flatwoods Monster" incident. As tensions ran high across the United States, the American public was starting to believe that the "Flatwoods Monster" might have actually been an alien.

I believe that the U.S. government contacted Stewart, because of his recent ties to the Air Force. He was given instructions to deliver false information to Mrs. May and the other witnesses. Under the circumstances, he probably would have followed the instructions to prevent the story from escalating any further.

I think he could have rationalized any reservations he had about delivering a letter as part of a disinformation campaign. I believe both letters were mailed to him with instructions for delivery. It would not surprise me if the government had coerced or threatened Stewart had he not agreed. I believe that Mrs. May read a fabricated letter, switched by Stewart when he produced an ordinary press release to Gray Barker. By misleading a few witnesses and spreading misinformation to them, I believe the government may have prevented a nationwide panic. In 1938, the Halloween radio broadcast of "War of the Worlds" caused a nationwide panic. That radio show was broadcast only fourteen years before the "Flatwoods Monster" incident.

I am sure the decision makers in the U.S. government felt they had a valid reason for covering the truth regarding the "Flatwoods Monster" incident. Presenting the letter through Stewart left a natural door open for him to remove the letter after Mrs. May had read it. Stewart could also be on hand to gauge the reactions of the witnesses as the letter was read to them. Had the "experimental craft" letter been sent directly to Mrs. May, she would have had proof with which to question and disprove the government's official single meteor explanation. The government chose to discredit the primary adult witness, making it appear that she had misinterpreted the letter, and was perhaps unreliable.

The misinformation plan was successful; some of the best UFO investigators have been stymied by it. This is an example of a well-executed exercise in deception. However, another point had struck me as odd.

Three days after the incident, an article appeared in Time, and read in part, "The International Astronautical Federation, in Stuttgart, Germany, discussed ways and means of launching man-carrying rockets into outer space... The federation heard that long-range rockets like Hitler's V-2s can and probably will be fired to the moon or to Mars within the next ten or 20 years."

During the course of my investigation, I met Professor Harvey Wolf, a physicist who worked in the aerospace industry. His career spanned the late 1950s through the early 1970s. One project that Mr. Wolf worked on was for Lockheed Aircraft, testing re-entry vehicles. After several discussions with Mr. Wolf he agreed to be interviewed in front of a camera. During that interview, I asked Professor Wolf about the possibilities of manned space exploration in the 1950s. Wolf told me the following, "I don't know anything about the early 50s, but in the mid-50s we were beginning to talk about men in space and actually tried to figure out how to run some experiments on weightlessness."

He also stated, "At that point, none of the people I was working with were talking about putting a man on the moon or interplanetary travel beyond the science fiction aspect of it. We were interested in how one would do repairs in space. I ran an experiment with the Navy off Point Mugu in which we used underwater divers in an attempt to figure out what weightlessness does to the ability to work. We didn't have any vehicle ready for sending people up at that point, in the late 50s."

While speaking about the "Flatwoods Monster," I asked, "Harvey, these drawings are made by witnesses to this particular incident in 1952. In the aerospace program that you were involved with, or at any time, have you ever seen a craft that looked like this?"

He replied, "I've never seen a craft that looked like that. Now I don't know what the circles are [porthole eye areas]. They could be light. They could be reflected light. It could be all kinds of things. I have no idea. I can't answer that. I've never seen a missile that looked like that."

The moon ship explanation told to Mrs. May in the mysterious letter was not even remotely possible in 1952. The Air Force knew that the fireball in the sky was not a meteor nor was the monster an owl, seen by Mrs. May, perched on a tree limb in Flatwoods. Therefore, they convinced her that it was something explicable, like an experimental ship. However, there were no manned-experimental ships in 1952!

In 1952, their story seemed more believable than it does more than 50 years later. This misinformation strategy apparently worked, because Mrs. May throughout the years has believed that the monster was an experimental ship—until now.

Mrs. Kathleen May and Frank Feschino, Jr.

YESTERYEAR AND TODAY

In this book, I have outlined a logical, cohesive scenario explaining the incidents of and around the summer of 1952, including the events of September 12, 1952 to the best of my abilities. I relied on eyewitness testimonies and factual reports by sources such as our own government agencies and print media from the world over. I provided information and misinformation about the events that occurred during the summer of 1952. Yet, despite all my years of research there are still many people who do not believe in flying saucers and extraterrestrials. Well, if my accounts seem less than plausible, I offer another explanation to the events that occurred during that summer and appeared in *The Wheeling News Register* on September 16, 1952.

In an article titled "Bethany Professor Blames Imagination - Citizens 'Hypnotized Into Seeing Saucers,'" a West Virginia College Professor, Dr. J.S. V. Allen of Bethany University, when questioned about the summer of 1952 incidents, brilliantly concludes that the citizens of this nation were "hypnotized into seeing flying saucers from other planets."

Physicist Dr. Allen explained, "We are a very gullible people and our imagination can add greatly to our observations." The article adds substantial proof to Allen's theory by backing him up that all the witnesses of this and other incidents suffer from cases of flying "sorcery." He also explained many scientifically proven facts about the distance between the Earth and the nearest star and other cosmic conundrums. He also wrote about, why we are not in constant radio communications with observing aliens around our globe. The good doctor goes on to state what we all should really accept as the absolute truth…that all the witnesses of the "Flatwoods Monster" incident were simply under "hypnosis."

Apparently, the entire United States was 'hypnotized" into seeing the entire UFO flap during the summer of 1952. Furthermore, since 1952, it seems these bouts of hypnosis have not ceased. In fact, to this day, The *Associated Press* reports monthly accounts of more "hypnotized" US citizens. It seems that someone forgot to snap their fingers.

On Tuesday, January 2, 2007, I was in Connecticut and preparing for my last trip to South Glastonbury to investigate the 1952 Westover AFB jet crash. I was going over my research material, had my maps spread out and was reviewing everything throughout the day.

I took a break and sat down to read the local paper from Bridgeport, CT, *The Connecticut Post*, formerly known as the Bridgeport Post. I turned to a section in the paper, "YOUR WORLD" and started reading a column titled, "NATION/WORLD." I was surprised at the headline article at the top of this section, "UFO spotted over O'Hare." The following is the article in its entirety:

CHICAGO (AP) – Federal officials say it was probably just some weird weather phenomenon, but a group of United Airline employees swears they saw a mysterious, saucer-shaped craft hovering over O'Hare Airport last fall. The workers, some of them pilots, said the object didn't have lights and hovered over an airport terminal before shooting straight up through the clouds, according to a report in Mondays Chicago Tribune. The

Federal Aviation Administration acknowledged that a supervisor had called the control tower at O'Hare, asking if anyone had spotted a spinning disc-shaped object. But the controllers didn't see anything, and a preliminary check of radar found nothing out of the ordinary.

Next, I looked up *The Chicago Tribune*, June 1, 2007 news article about this incident. I found out the "disc-shaped object" sighted over O'Hare International Airport actually occurred on November 7, 2006. Joseph Hilkevich, the transportation reporter for the newspaper wrote an article, "In the sky! A bird? A plane? A…UFO?" He reported, "A saucerlike object hovered low over O'Hare International Airport for several minutes before bolting through the thick clouds with such intense energy that it left an eerie hole in overcast skies, said some United Airlines employees who observed the phenomenon. He gave the following details, "The sighting occurred during daylight, about 4:30 p.m., just before sunset. All the witnesses said the object was dark gray and well defined in the overcast skies. Descriptions of the size of the craft varied up to, "24 feet in diameter" and it was said the UFO, "did not display any lights." Hilkevich reported, "Some said it looked like a rotating Frisbee, while others said it did not appear to be spinning. All agreed the object made no noise and it was at a fixed positioning the sky, just below the 1,900-foot deck, until shooting off into the clouds."

Hilkevich stated, "The object was seen to suddenly accelerate straight up through the solid overcast skies, which the FAA reported had 1,900 cloud ceilings at the time. ' It was like somebody punched a hole in the sky,' said one United employee. Witnesses said they had a hard time visually tracking the object as it streaked through the dense clouds. It left behind an open hole of clear air in the cloud layer, the witnesses said, adding that the hole disappeared within a few minutes." He reporter added, "All the witnesses to the O'Hare event, who included at least several pilots, said they are certain on the discs appearance and flight characteristics that it was not an airplane, helicopter, weather balloon or any craft known to man."

The information concerning this incident sounded like a flying saucer story ripped from a newspaper headline during the summer of 1952. This UFO sighting did not surprise me. I thought, "Oh well, they're back over Chicago again." Throughout the years as I researched the history of UFOs, I was amazed at the documented UFO incidents that occurred over Chicago, Illinois including Chicago's O'Hare Airport back in 1952. As I have shown in this book, Chicago had an incredible amount of UFO sightings during that year.

When O'Hare Airport based the 4706th Defense Wing in 1952, Donald Keyhoe reported this base was frequently visited by UFOs. He wrote about this in his 1953 book, *Flying saucers from Outer Space* and plotted O'Hare Airport on his research map as being one the most frequently visited bases in the United States.

As I became aware of Chicago's history of UFO sightings, I would contact Stanton T. Friedman and we would discuss this point. Why were the UFOs reconnoitering Chicago and O'Hare Airport back in 1952? Was it because of the high amount of daily air traffic in and out of the area, the Chicago industry, or was there something else that interested the saucers? When I spoke to Friedman about the 2006 Sighting over O'Hare International Airport and knowing about the 1952 sightings, he was not surprised either. What bothers me though is why a saucer so brazenly appeared over O'Hare Airport in Chicago nearly fifty-five years later.

Joe Hilkevitch reported another interesting point about the November 7, 2006 sighting in his article. He said that United spokesperson Megan McCarty said, "There's nothing in the duty manager log, which is used to report unusual incidents." She also stated, "I checked around there's no record of anything." Hilkevitch stated, "She said United officials do not recall discussion of any such event." This is interesting because Hilkevitch interviewed several United Airline employees who saw the object. He stated, "They were interviewed by United officials and instructed to write reports and draw pictures of what they observed, and that they were advised by United officials to refrain from speaking about what they saw."

Shortly after the incident, Hilkevitch started to research the story, received the standard government runaround, and was stonewalled. Federal officials told him that they had no information about the sighting. He said, "Like United, The FAA originally told the Tribune that it had no information about the alleged UFO sighting. But the federal agency quickly reversed its position after the newspaper filed a Freedom of Information Act request." A Federal Aviation Administration spokeswoman, Elizabeth Isam Cory, came forth with some information. Hilkevich explains, "An internal FAA review of air-traffic communications tapes, a step forward complying with the Tribune request, turned up the call by the United supervisor to an FAA manager in the airport tower, Cory said." She stated, "No controllers saw the object, and a preliminary check of radar found nothing unusual." It seems that airport and government officials learned their lessons about disclosure of UFO information to the press after the twin Washington sightings in July of 1952.

Federal Aviation Administration spokeswoman, Elizabeth Isam Cory stated, "Our theory on this is that it was a weather phenomenon." She added, "That night was a perfect atmospheric condition in terms of low ceiling and a lot of airport lights. When the lights shone up into the clouds, sometimes you can see funny things. That's our take on it." I find the FAA's "weather phenomenon" theory very amusing, especially when you add the airport lights into scenario. Major General John A. Samford talked about this probable saucer explanation at the July 29, 1952 press conference in Washington D.C. Fifty-five years ago; Samford explained to the press that since 1947 the Air Force had analyzed "between a thousand and two thousand reports" concerning UFOs. He stated the following:

Out of that mass of reports that we've been able to take things which were originally unidentified and dispose of them to our satisfaction in terms of bulk where we came to the conclusion that these things were either friendly aircraft erroneously recognized or reported, hoaxes, quite a few of those, electronic or meteorological phenomenon of one sort or another, light aberrations, and many other things.

Federal officials are still using the same probable flying saucer explanations that it first used back in the summer of 1952 at Major General Samford's press conference. Another interesting point to raise that involved O'Hare Airport appeared in the Chicago Tribune newspaper on July 29, 1952. Air Force officials of the 4706 Defense Wing based at the airport gave out a public phone number to O'Hare Airport to report a UFO sighting.

The Chicago Tribune said that the telephone number was "Rodney 3- 0800." They reported that if a person called to report a UFO, "They'll ask you your name, address, approximate location of the disc, estimated altitude, speed and direction, how long it was in view and a general description." Yes, the Air Force was taking the UFO problem over the Chicago area seriously during 1952.

O'Hare Airport based the Air Force's 4706th Defense Wing of Sabre Jets in the 1950s. Their fighter jets were scrambled after UFOs during 1952 and the following high alert years of the Cold War. The Sabre jets of the 4706th also had their problems in and around the Chicago area during that time, as did the United States Navy. I found four such cases reported in the New York Times between 1952 and 1956 that involved destroyed and lost fighter jets. The first incident occurred on October 25, 1952, and appeared in *The New York Times* on the following day. This jet accident involved an O'Hare fighter jet that exploded over nearby Wisconsin. It occurred approximately 65 miles northwest of O'Hare and less than ten miles north of the Illinois border:

JET EXPLODES IN AIR, PILOT DIES

WILLIAMS BAY, Wis., Oct. (AP) – An Air Force jet plane exploded in mid-air today near a radar base three miles north of here, killing the pilot and scattering wreckage and ammunition around the area. At the base an Air Force spokesman confirmed the crash but said no information could be released until authorities arrived from O'Hare Field in Chicago.

It is interesting to note that this mid-air explosion occurred near a radar base; was the pilot of this fighter jet being vectored toward a UFO at the time the jet exploded in mid-air, killing the pilot? This jet was armed with "ammunition," at the time it exploded; was this fighter jet attempting to "shoot down" a UFO?

The next article that I found in *The New York Times* involved a destroyed O'Hare fighter jet and occurred west of Chicago. The accident occurred on October 6, 1954 and appeared in print the following day:

JET PILOT AVERTS CITY CRASH

CHICAGO, Oct. 6 (AP) – An Air Force pilot, intent on avoiding a possible tragedy, stayed with his flaming F-86-D jet tonight long enough to ride it clear of the Chicago metropolitan area. Then, he bailed out, landing uninjured in a field near Roselle, Ill., west of Chicago [Approximately 8 miles west of O'Hare]. The Air Force, which identified the pilot as First Lieut. Edward F. Schroeder, 25 years old, St. Louis, MO., said it had not learned where the plane crashed.

This mid-air accident resulted in the loss of this aircraft, but it seems strange that the Air Force was not aware of where the Sabre Jet crashed. How could the crash of a flaming jet that surely would have exploded upon impact, started a fire, made a lot of noise, and drawn attention to itself, have gone unnoticed?

The following New York Times article I found that involved a destroyed O'Hare fighter jet occurred at the airport. The accident occurred on November 27, 1954, seven weeks after the previous October 6, 1954 accident. The article appeared in print on Monday, November 29, 1954:

JET PILOT KILLED IN CRASH

CHICAGO, Nov. 28 (UP) – An Air Force pilot who took to the air in an F-86D Sabre Jet to track down an unidentified plane was killed last night when his plane exploded while returning for a landing. The victim was identified as First Lieut. Burton A. Smith, 25 years old, who lived with his wife, Barbara, in suburban Desplaines."

The article never disclosed any further information about the, "unidentified plane," that was involved in this incident. Was it a plane or actually an Unidentified Flying Object in the category of an unconventional flying aircraft? Was it just another coincidence that an Air Force fighter jet was destroyed after attempting to intercept an unidentified aircraft?

The United States Navy also had a hard time keeping track of their aircraft near Chicago in 1954. Earlier in the year on February 27, 1954, a Navy fighter jet vanished west of Chicago over Lake Michigan. While en route to NAS Glenview, approximately 10 miles north of O'Hare Airport, one of three Banshees vanished over the waters of this lake. *The New York Times* reported the story on March 1, 1952:

100 PLANES AID SEARCH

CHICAGO, Feb. 28 (AP) – More than 100 planes joined Coast Guard surface craft at daybreak today in searching a 100,000 square-mile area for a Navy Banshee jet that disappeared over Lake Michigan near Chicago yesterday. The missing plane was piloted by Ensigns Ronald J. Pingle of Pleasant Valley near Winona, Minn., the Navy announced. Ensign Pingle and two other officers piloting Banshees were on a routine training flight from Cecil Field in Florida. Their destination was Glenview Naval Air Station, a few miles northwest of Chicago. The other two landed safely.

What is interesting about this information is there was an alleged search being conducted over a "100,000 square-mile area," for a missing jet that was flying with two other jets. When the two Banshee pilots lost radio contact with the third jet that vanished over Lake Michigan, they should have known its approximate location. Moreover, the Glenview NAS should have been in radio contact with the three jets and known their approximate locations when one jet disappeared. Why was the Navy unaware of the Banshees approximate location at the time it vanished? Is it not time that hypnotized citizens woke up from their 55-year trance. Snap!

Chapter 34

THE SIX DEADLY YEARS

The New York Times reported an incident that occurred on January 28, 1952 involving an USAF F-84 jet and a UFO, over Japan. The article states, "'Disk' Seen Over Japan," and states in part, "A United States pilot saw at close range a mysterious flying disk make a pass at a [F-84] Thunder Jet…then speed away…it closed to within twenty feet." This incident occurred "in Daylight."

On July 29, 1952, The *United Press* News service released a story in response to the air forces flying saucer "shoot down" order. The president of the United States Rocket Society, Mr. Robert L. Farnsworth, sent a telegram to U.S. defense officials and urged them to restrain American armed forces from shooting at flying saucers. A very concerned Farnsworth stated the following in that telegram, "I respectfully suggest that no offensive action be taken against the objects reported as unidentified which have been sighted over our nation…should they be extraterrestrial, such action might result in the gravest consequences, as well as possibly alienating us from beings of far superior power. Friendly contact should be sought as long as possible. Robert L Farnsworth"

This information appeared in several newspapers across the United States on the following day, July 30, 1952. Another news story that appeared on Wed. July 30, was *The Louisville Courier-Journal* article that talked about Major Gen. Roger Ramey's statement made at the July 29th Pentagon press conference, "interceptor planes have raced aloft several hundred times as a report of reported sightings of unidentified flying objects." Ramey also stated, "That was just standard procedure." Just how long had the United States military been scrambling interceptor planes after "unidentified flying objects"?

In Donald Keyhoe's book, *Aliens From Space*, he made a statement about Air Force jet pursuits after UFOs, which resulted in death. He stated, "Some UFO pursuits have taken a grim toll. Several AF pilots have lost their lives while chasing these strange machines." In his 1955 book, *The Flying Saucer Conspiracy*, he reported the following information about American fighter planes shooting at saucers in the 1940s. He said:

In 1949, the Air Force told me they had been to "get" a flying saucer by any possible means. This was admitted by an Intelligence officer at the Pentagon – Major Jere Boggs. In front of General Sory Smith, Boggs told me that one Air Force pilot had fired at a saucer over New Jersey. Later on I found that fighters had fired at a UFO over Luke Field [Luke AFB, near Phoenix, Arizona] in 1945.

I used *The New York Times* as the basis of my research in searching for fighter plane accidents, disappearances, and unusual mishaps. I reviewed articles going back to post World War 2.

In the late 1940's, there were only a few military fighter plane accidents reported by *The New York Times*. One of the earliest, most famous and unusual accidents, involved the death of an F-51 Mustang pilot named Captain Thomas Mantell Jr. On January 8, 1948, the Times reported this story; "FLIER DIES CHASING A 'FLYING SAUCER.' Plane Explodes Over Kentucky as That and Near States Report Strange Object." In part, this article states, "several areas of Kentucky and adjoining states were excited today over reports of a 'flying saucer' which led to the death of one National Guard flier and fruitless chases by several other pilots.

The National Guard headquarters at Louisville said Capt. Thomas F. Mantell Jr., 25 years old, was killed late yesterday [Jan. 7] while chasing what was reported as a 'flying saucer' near Franklin, KY." It was also reported that Capt. Mantell was "an air hero during the allied invasion of Normandy" during World War 2.

A follow up article appeared in the same paper more than four years later in an article dated, "Thursday, August 21, 1952." The headline reads, "Air Force Releases Pilot's Last Message During Fatal Pursuit of Aerial 'object'." In part, it states, "The incident occurred Jan. 7, 1948, near Godman Air Force Base, Fort Knox, KY. The announcement said Capt. Thomas Mantell, 25 years old, 'lost consciousness from lack of oxygen and crashed while attempting to intercept at high altitude an 'unidentified object.'" It was also reported, "All Air Force personnel who were present in the control tower during the incident were questioned."

The statements made by these witnesses reported that Capt. Mantell sighted an unidentified object and said it was "directly ahead and above [me] and moving about half my speed…it appears metallic of tremendous size- it appears like the reflection of sunlight on an airplane canopy…it is bright and climbing away from me." During the UFOs climb, the Times reported, "that the object was moving about his same speed-around 360 miles an hour…at 15,000 feet." According to the article, "Captain Mantell then said he was going up to 20,000 feet and if he failed to close in on the object, he would abandon the chase. That was his last message. No identification of the object has been announced."

According to Edward Ruppelt, "There have been other and more "lurid 'duels of death'." How many fighter planes vanished or crashed during "lurid 'duels of death" encounters with UFOs and how many of them were covered-up by the armed forces? Even though the Air Forces official stance on flying saucers is they do not exist, Farnsworth's July 1952 "extraterrestrial" possibility seems closer to the truth than General Samford's probable "temperature inversion" statement. In reference to Farnsworth's point of view concerning the military's shoot down orders directed at flying saucers, "should they be extraterrestrial, such action might result in the gravest consequences," I firmly believe that many United States jet fighters were involved in UFO intercepts and did suffer the gravest of consequences.

I continued to search through *The New York Times* index and microfilm archives from post World War II until 1960. In his 1953 book, *Flying Saucers from Outer Space,* Donald Keyhoe said, "In the last two years, hundreds of fighters have been scrambled to intercept UFOs." Keyhoe's 1953 statement refers to an overwhelming amount of scrambles dating back to 1951. I discovered a six-year time span where 204 fighter accident incidents were reported in *The New York Times* beginning in 1951 through 1956. These were the six deadliest years during the 1950s era. Yet, the fighter aircraft accidents that I found in the Times are only a fraction of the total amount that actually occurred during those years.

For this research project, I based my statistics on major accident cases that either involved fighter planes destroyed or planes that vanished with their pilot or crews. In most incidents, the fighter accidents resulted in death, unless the flyers ejected from their aircraft. I extracted the information from each year's accidents then categorized them into different lists.

I based these fighter accident statistics on United States Air Force, Navy, and Marine Corps aircraft, which include both jets and a few propeller planes. The information that I found in *The New York Times* concerning these fighter accidents is a historical overview of incidents that this newspaper reported between 1951 and 1956…the six deadly years.

In this chapter, I will show some of the statistics that I compiled and cite examples of several mysterious fighter accidents that I found. At this time, it is not known how many fighter aircraft and aviators were lost during UFO intercept missions. I found that routine training flights and missions were said to be the most common types of missions during which fighter accidents occurred and a frequent explanation for many fighter aircraft accidents was they "ran out of gas."

The data that I compiled, according to *The New York Times* articles reveals that during these six years 229 fighter aircraft were destroyed in 204 incidents. Of the 229 fighter aircraft an amazing 192 were actually destroyed or missing over the United States. The remaining thirty-seven aircraft were destroyed throughout the world. They are listed below:

A.) Japan-12
B.) Germany-11
C.) Pacific Sea-6
D.) England-3
E.) France-2
F.) Newfoundland-2
G.) Norway-1

According to *The New York Times*, my research shows, of the reported 229 fighter aircraft destroyed during those six years, 173 were Air Force fighter aircraft, 47 were Navy fighters, and nine Marine Corps fighters were destroyed. Of the 229 fighter reported aircraft destroyed, only seven were known fighter trainers; One destroyed in 1951, none in 1952, one in 1953, one in 1954, three in 1955, and one in 1956.

The following statistics are a yearly breakdown of United States fighter aircraft that were destroyed over the, "United States," and its coastal waters, between 1951 and 1956. I have excluded the seven known fighter aircraft trainers destroyed during those years and shown the amount of USAF fighters destroyed next to the amount of fighters destroyed each year:

```
1951 - 16 Fighters   Destroyed – 10 USAF, 9 Jets and 1 Prop
1952 - 35 Fighters   Destroyed – 29 USAF, 27 Jets and 2 Props
1953 – 31 Fighters   Destroyed – 26 USAF, 26 Jets and 0 Props
1954 – 39 Fighters   Destroyed – 31 USAF, 29 Jets and 2 Props
1955 – 23 Fighters   Destroyed – 16 USAF, 14 Jets and 2 Props
1956 – 41 Fighters   Destroyed – 26 USAF, 26 Jets and 0 Props
```

Total – 186 Fighters Destroyed - 138 USAF, 131 Jets and 7 Props
Total – 192 Fighters Destroyed including 7 Trainers.

Between the years of 1951 and 1956, *The New York Times* reported 186 non-trainer fighter aircraft destroyed over the United States and its coastal waters; they were Air Force, Navy, and Marine Corps fighter aircraft. Between 1951 and 1956, *The New York Times* reported, 138 Air Force Fighter aircraft destroyed over the United States and its coastal waters; 131 were jets and 7 were propeller fighters.

The following Korean "AIR WAR" statistics appear in the book, THE UNITED STATES AIR FORCE-A TURBULENT HISTORY, by Herbert Molloy Mason, Jr.:

APPENDIX – H
THE AIR WAR IN KOREA. JULY 1, 1950 – JULY 31, 1953
Losses, USAF
Type - Air-to Air
Jet   -   83
Prop -   21
Total -   104

POINT ONE: Between 1951 and 1953, *The New York Times* reported that 62 USAF fighter jets were destroyed over the United States and its coastal waters as compared to their 83 jets lost in the "AIR WAR" during the entire Korean War.

POINT TWO: Between 1951 and 1956, *The New York Times* reported that 131 USAF fighter jets were destroyed over the United States and its coastal waters as compared to their 83 jets lost in the "AIR WAR" during the entire Korean War.

POINT THREE: Between 1951 and 1956, *The New York Times* reported the Air Force, Navy and Marine Corps had a total amount of 185 fighter aircraft, jets and props, destroyed over the United States and its coastal waters. The Air Force lost a total amount of 104 fighters, jets and props, in the "AIR WAR" during the entire Korean War.

According to *The New York Times*, 1951 through 1956 were indeed six deadly years in American aviation military history, yet these accident statistics are only a fraction of what actually occurred. My *New York Times* study reveals that during those six years of death, at least 199 aviators were killed because of these so-called fighter plane accidents. In some cases, the military did not identify the types of aircraft that were lost. Some jets carried two crewmembers, so the number flyers killed may actually be higher. I did exclude the American civilians that died on the ground. Throughout that era, and on numerous occasions, several jet fighters actually crashed into residential neighborhoods and killed or injured entire families and destroyed several homes, autos and properties.

Some incidents involved mid air collisions between fighter planes while others involved collisions between fighters and other military aircraft. I excluded the deaths of the several military men killed in non-fighter aircraft that were involved in mid-air collisions with fighters.

The following statistics are a yearly breakdown of 199 fighter aviators known to have been killed in fighter accidents between 1951 and 1956, according to *The New York Times*.

1951 - 20 men killed
1952 – 36 men killed
1953 – 30 men killed
1954 – 39 men killed
1955 – 34 men killed
1956 – 40 men killed

Of the 204 documented fighter accidents, 23 cases involved fighter pilots that were known combat war veterans. Many of these pilots were decorated World War II and Korean War heroes of the sky. Out of the 23 accident cases that involved these fighter pilots, 20 of them died during those accidents and all of them were killed in the United States or its nearby coastal waters.

Fourteen of these veteran pilots died in Air Force interceptor fighters and six died in Navy fighters. Two veteran Air Force pilots vanished with their planes; both of them disappeared in 1954.

Many of these 20 veteran pilots had received the Distinguished Flying Cross and earned numerous air medals. All of these men, who fought in foreign wars and in unfamiliar skies throughout the world, came home and died in their fighters over the skies of the United States. In honor of these brave flyers that served their country whom are forgotten by most, I have listed them below. I included the dates that these men died and some of the details of their crash or disappearance:

1.) 1951, January 28. *Captain John Gentile*, a veteran pilot, was killed on a "Routine Flight," during a crash shortly after leaving Andrews AFB in a T-33 jet. He crashed in Maryland in a suburb of Washington. Captain Gentile flew on "182 combat missions" during WWII," and received "14 bravery awards." Gentile was the "12th ranking ace," during the war and was named the, "One man Air Force."

2.) 1951, August 11. *Captain Frank Newell.* "OTIS AIR FORCE BASE MASS." The Times reported, "A much-decorated fighter pilot recently returned from the Korean War was killed today when his F-86 Sabre Jet crashed on a fog swept beach in East Sandwich."

3.) 1951, November 30. *Lieutenant John Wesley Mills,* a veteran Navy fighter pilot, was killed "on a routine training operation" in his "Skyraider" plane. The pilot crashed "after taking off from Atlantic City Naval Air Station at Ponoma." Lt. Mills "served as a fighter pilot during the war [WWII] on the aircraft carriers Saratoga and Kula Gulf. He received the Navy Cross and a commendation ribbon."

4.) 1952, February 25. *Captain Karl Wagner*, a veteran AAF pilot, also "an acceptance test pilot," was killed in a jet in the "Chino Hills" five miles south of Ponoma California. The Times reported that, "the jet plane exploded and crashed," and "was attached to the Northrop test facility of Ontario, Calif." Captain Wagner flew, "100 missions as a pilot of a P-47 Thunderbolt with the Eight AAF Corps in the European Theater in World War II."

5.) 1952, March 30. *Captain Milton Reid*, a jet fighter pilot, was killed in an "F-94 jet interceptor," when it crashed in Fort Dix, New Jersey. The Times reported, "Captain Reid recently had returned from a tour in Korea." It was also reported, "The plane, was on a training flight, had taken off from McGuire Air Force Base." It was also stated, "Air Force officials said it crashed soon after takeoff, although there was no word of any trouble from the plane." The radar operator, Captain James B. Newman, was also killed in the crash that occurred about, "six miles south" of the base.

6.) 1952, August 8. *Captain Hobart Gay, Jr.,* an Air Force fighter veteran was killed in an "unexplained crash of a F-94 all weather jet fighter…when it plunged into Vineyard Sound," near Falmouth, Massachusetts. The Times reported that, "An Otis Air Force spokesman said that Captain Gay was believed to have been trapped in the cockpit of his plane when it crashed." The pilot "completed 105 combat missions in Korea and earned the Distinguished Flying Cross and Air Medal with three Oak clusters in thirteen months, Far East duty."

7.) 1952, September 2. *First Lieutenant John Burke, Jr.,* a Westover AFB fighter pilot, was killed near the Ludlow Reservoir, at Ludlow Center, Massachusetts, located about, "five miles east of the field." The Times reported Burke was, "a veteran of 100 combat missions in Korea." Westover AFB, "officials said the cause of the crash had not been determined."

8.) 1952, October 14. *Lieutenant James Noble*, a veteran Navy fighter pilot, was killed "on a routine gunnery flight when his plane crashed into the sea twenty-eight miles north of Boca Chico Air Field."

The Navy reported Lt. Noble was, "on duty with the Navy at Key West, Fla." The Navy stated that the pilot, "served in the Pacific in World War II."

9.) 1952, October 31. *Lieutenant Eugene Bernard.* "Pilot Killed in Crash Was Korea Hero." A Navy fighter pilot and "veteran of thirty-two missions in Korea," was reportedly "killed in a crash in Pennsylvania." He was attached to The Niagara Falls NAS, in New York. Bernard had, "recently returned from the Far East." The Korean War hero had received the, "Distinguished Flying Cross," as well as an "Air Medal with six clusters."

10.) 1953, May 5. *Lieutenant Edward Hotz.* "Korea Hero Dies In Crash." A flying instructor at Perrin AFB, Sherman, Texas, "was killed in the crash of an F-86 Sabre jet during a take-off from Perrin Air Force Base." Lt. Hotz was, "decorated for thirteen months of flying F-80 Shooting Stars in Korea," and had "received the Distinguished Flying Cross."

11.) 1954, January 25. *First Lieutenant John Faris Jelke III*, a combat fighter, who "flew forty-six bombing missions in the war," vanished while he "was on a training flight from Atlanta to New Orleans." The "missing fighter plane," said to be a, "F-51 plane was last heard from when he was over Mobile, Alabama." The pilot was of the Oleomargarine family.

12.) 1954, April 5. *Colonel Councill*, a veteran pilot who "flew 130 combat missions in World War II," vanished in an F-80 Shooting Star jet. He "disappeared shortly after taking off on instruments in a heavy overcast at Farmingdale, NY… bound for his home at Langley Field, Va." The Civil Air Patrol stated that Councill "had been in trouble within five minutes after the take-off and might be down within fifty miles of the field." It was reported that the pilot had, "three hours of fuel aboard." Lt. Councill set the United States jet speed "cross-country record of 4-hours 13 minutes," on January 26, 1946. The Times reported, "It stood until last January, when another pilot broke it by a few minutes."

13.) 1954, June 12. *Lieutenant Edward Hamilton*, a Navy fighter pilot, "died when an F9F-6 Panther jet plane he was piloting crashed while taking off from El Paso, Tex." The Times reported, "He was on a flight from Atlantic City to El Toro, Calif., and had landed to refuel." In World War II Lt. Hamilton, "saw action in the Pacific…He was assigned as a fighter pilot aboard the aircraft carriers Princeton and Boxer during the Korean conflict."

14.) 1954, June 26. *Major Joseph Angyl, Jr.*, a Marine Corps fighter pilot in a Navy, "F9F-7 Grumman Cougar" was reported to have, "went into a vertical dive," from 22,000 feet over Long Island. Shortly after, "terrified onlookers at near-by Point Lookout saw the F9F-7 Grumman Cougar jet plane plunge to its doom."

Major Angyl's wing mate who was flying with him and in radio communication "saw Angyl's plane fall off in a steep dive." It was said, "When he tried to call him again he could not make contact." Lt. Angyl and his jet, "crashed at the edge of the sandbar a mile north of Jones Inlet at 11:23 A.M." It was reported that, During World War II, he was a fighter pilot in the Southwest Pacific, and flew Eighty-five combat missions."

15.) 1954, October 12. *Major George Welch,* a World War II hero at Pearl Harbor, died "of injuries suffered in parachuting from a jet aircraft that had exploded." Major Welch was killed, "while testing a super Sabre F-100," over Lancaster, California." The Times reported, "The plane exploded over Antelope Valley. Mr. Welch managed to get out of the supersonic fighter and yanked his parachute open, but he was fatally injured." In his 1955, book *The Flying Saucer Conspiracy*, Donald Keyhoe wrote, "Since the pilot had been killed, no one knew what happened. But there was evidence that the jet fighter had been torn apart by a powerful force." Keyhoe added, "For 3 months the North American Aviation Corporation had investigated the case. Now, on February 9 [1955], it was revealed that the plane encountered a mysterious force, throwing it violently to one side." *The New York Times* reported, "Mr. Welch was one of two Army Air Force pilots to get planes into the air after the Japanese struck Dec. 7, 1941. He was credited with shooting down four Japanese planes that afternoon, including the first to be downed by a United States pilot…and was credited with shooting down eighteen Japanese planes in thirty-three months of combat flying."

Major George Welch

16.) 1954, December 31. *First Lieutenant John R. Lewis.* "War Pilot Dies in Crash. An Air Force pilot who was a veteran of seventy combat missions in Korea was instantly killed when his plane crashed about one mile north of Dover Air Force Base." The fighter pilot "was making an approach to the Dover base in an F-84-F Thunderstreak jet when it suddenly crashed in flames."

17.) 1955, May 5. *Lieutenant Colonel Winifield*, "WORLD WAR II ACE DIES." A fighter pilot was killed, "when his jet fighter crashed and burned just short of the runway at Stewart Field." It was said, Colonel Brown came in under power for an emergency landing, maneuvering desperately to avoid a housing project for base personnel and their families." *The New York Times* reported, "A fighter pilot in World War II, he was credited with having downed Nazi planes, thus becoming an 'ace.'"

18.) 1955, July 27. *Lieutenant Robert Slezak*, a Navy fighter pilot, was flying, "an F-VU Cutlass fighter on a routine mission when the plane appeared to go out of control and crashed into the Pacific Ocean," near Point Mugu, California. *The New York Times* stated, "During the war he served with a fighter squadron aboard several aircraft carriers in the Pacific Theater."

19.) 1956, January 10. *Major Lonnie Moore* reported to be, "one of the leading jet aces of the Korean War was killed…in the crash of the Air Forces newest supersonic fighter, the F-101 Voodoo." The Air Force stated, "The jet plane crashed and exploded, just after it was airborne in the center of the main flying field at Eglin Air Force Base." *The New York Times* reported that Major Moore "was credited with ten enemy MIG 15's destroyed and one probably destroyed in Korea. He had total flying time of 3,570 hours and had logged 328 combat hours in World War II and Korea."

20.) 1956, October 12. *Captain Lawrence Lundberg*. "Plane Crash Kills War Hero." In Minneapolis, MN, "A jet plane crashed and burned near Wold Chamberlain…killing a pilot who had won two high medals for eight-one combat missions during World War II." Captain Lundberg "held the distinguished Flying Cross and the Air Medal."

How many of the twenty veteran fighter pilots I have shown here were involved in intercept attempts after Unidentified Flying Objects? These men all took the truth with them when they died, but how many others know the real story about American flyers that were killed during these six deadly years?

I also discovered several incidents of vanished fighter and trainer planes between 1951 and 1956 in *The New York Times*. During those six years, I found 26 cases of United States military fighter planes and trainers that disappeared without a trace, most of them jets. The USAF had the highest amount of vanished planes with 18, the Navy lost 7, and the Marine Corps lost one. Of the 26 lost fighters, 19 of them vanished over the United States and its coastal waters. *The New York Times* reported the Air Force lost three trainers: a T-6 prop plane, and two T-33 jet trainers. The Navy reported one lost trainer plane.

There were at least 40 flyers lost during the 26 vanished episodes that I found; this includes radar operators. In some cases, the military did not identify the types of aircraft that were lost. The number of lost flyers may actually be higher because some jets carried two crewmembers. In several cases when fighters and aviators were lost, there were follow-up stories. These follow-up stories would report on the status of a search or report if remains were found. There were no follow-up stories concerning the 26 vanished planes on the following list:

1.) 1951, April 8. An F-94 jet *"disappeared"* from McChord AFB, Wash., while en route to Hamilton Field, California.

2.) 1951, Nov. 20. A Navy training plane went *"missing"* over Denver, Colorado. There were "complete negative results" with "no clues" after a three-day search.

3.) 1951, Dec. 30. An F-51 fighter plane, *"vanished* while flying over Arizona" en route to El Paso, Texas, from Castle AFB, near Merced, California.

4.) 1952, Feb. 19. In Florida, a Tyndall, AFB fighter pilot and radar operator *"disappeared* while on a routine flight." The two-man crew "vanished in an F-94 jet fighter plane."

5.) 1952, July 25. In the Miami, Fl. Area, "more than 100 planes joined ground crew forces…in a search for a *missing* Marine Corps fighter jet and its pilot." The pilot was reported to have been on a "training flight."

6.) 1952, Sept. 16. During Operation Mainbrace, "a Grumman F6F fighter plane and pilot from the USS Mindoro was *lost*" off the Norway coast.

7.) 1952, Nov. 10. Off the Florida coast near Key West, "A Navy Hellcat fighter plane *disappeared* on a flight over the sea."

8.) 1953, Jan. 31. Over Madison, Wisconsin, "four F-86 Sabres on a routine flight" were involved in an incident when three jets crashed and one *disappeared*.

9.) 1953, Feb. 21. Over the area of Goose Bay, Labrador, Canada, "three USAF jet fighter planes crashed." It was reported that a fourth jet was "*missing* in Greenland."

10.) 1953, Mar. 27. At Charleston, West Virginia, an "Air Force training plane and its pilot *disappeared*." It was reported that, "Air rescue teams abandoned an organized search" for the aircraft. [T-6 aircraft].

11.) 1953, April 10. At Niagara Falls, NY, "a far flung search continued for an Air Force pilot *missing* in his fighter plane." The pilot was on a "training flight."

12.) 1953, May 5. Off the coast of Atlantic NJ, the USN reported, "3 Navy fliers *missing*" that were aboard a "Douglas Sky raider-a night attack bomber." The Navy stated, "A search by twenty-seven aircraft from daybreak to sundown…failed to find any trace of the men or plane."

13.) 1953, July 11. During joint war training exercises between the USA and Canada, "an accident marred the maneuver at San Francisco. Shortly after interceptors took to the air, a radar controlled [F-94 Starfire] jet plane with two persons aboard was reported *missing* over San Pablo Bay."

14.) 1953, Oct. 13. Near Tokyo, Japan, two F-84 Thunder jets were lost in two days over the Pacific Ocean. It was reported that, "the first F-84 *disappeared* off the western coast of Honsu…the second crashed at sea 18 miles NE of its Misawa AFB."

15.) 1954, Jan. 15. Officials at Gulfport, Mississippi, reported an "F-51 plane was last heard from when he was over Mobile, Alabama." It was said that, "Planes and ground rescue teams searched the Gulf coast" for the "*missing* fighter plane."

16.) 1954, Feb. 27. A Navy fighter plane "on a routine training flight from Cecil Field in Florida" disappeared over Lake Michigan; "2 others [jets] landed safely." The USN reported "100 planes" aided in the rescue mission while "searching a 100,000 sq. mile area for a Navy banshee jet that *disappeared.*"

17.) 1954, April 5. A USAF veteran combat flyer "disappeared shortly after taking off" over Long Island. The Air Force reported, "He had three hours of fuel aboard and was not heard from after his takeoff."

18.) 1954, June 1. A USAF F-84 Thunder Jet went "*missing…* on a flight from Goose Bay, Labrador to Barsarssuak, Greenland."

19.) 1954, Nov. 4. Over the Atlantic Ocean, 46 miles east of Cherry Point, NC, officials reported, "a Marine Corps Sky Knight jet" in search for a "*missing* jet while on a tactical mission…was reported missing."

20.) 1955, June 28. USMC officials reported, "A U.S. Marine fighter plane, searching for two [downed] Marine fliers bobbing on life rafts in the Pacific, disappeared.*"* The missing rescue jet an F-J-2 Fury, "*vanished*" in a haze while with flying with other jets of the rescue mission. He stated, "I have lost you in the haze."

21.) 1955, Sept. 21. Over Germany, a USAF T-33 jet trainer was reported, "missing with 2 men aboard." The Air Force said, "The plane *disappeared* while making a routine flight in the Wiesbaden area…The T-33 apparently became lost and ran out of fuel while over East Germany." Note: Wiesbaden is approximately 80 miles form the E. Germany border.

22.) 1955, Sept. 25. At Hampton, Virginia, the Air Force stated, three Langley AFB F-84F Thunder jets "were reported missing." Two of the Thunder jets *vanished* over Chesapeake Bay, and one vanished on a "routine navigational mission over the northeastern section of Maine."

23.) 1956, March 2. From Darrington, Washington, the Air Force reported, "two *missing* F-89
Jet interceptors and the four men they carried missing."

24.) 1956, March 8. Spokesperson in Tokyo, Japan, reported, a "jet pilot crashed in the Pacific Ocean off Okinawa…at about the same time The AF called off an air-sea search for another pilot *missing* almost 24-hours."

25.) 1956, Nov. 15. A report from Mount Clemens, Michigan, stated, "The report for a Navy plane with two men aboard *missing*…continued today with no new leads."

26.) 1956, Dec. 8. Officials in Indianapolis, Indiana reported, "twenty planes of the Indiana CAP [Civil Air Patrol] searched…for an AF T-33 trainer *missing* en route from Sioux Falls, South Dakota, to Westover AFB, Massachusetts."

Some of the most disturbing occurrences that I repeatedly found during these fighter accidents were the overwhelming amount of fighter pilots that failed to eject from their disabled jets, rode them into the ground, or water, and crashed. Based on 204 accidents from 1951 to 1956, there were 65 cases where experienced and well-trained fighter aviators failed to bail out and died. Only three of these crashes involved circumstances when it was said that a pilot chose to stay with his jet and steer it around a populated area. The following is a yearly breakdown of the 65 incidents that involved fighter pilots that failed to bail out of their disabled jets, crashed, and died:

The year 1951 - 8 incidents	The year 1954 – 18 incidents
The year 1952 -13 incidents	The year 1955 – 8 incidents
The year 1953 – 7 incidents	The year 1956 – 11 incidents

These statistics reflect at least 65 fighter pilots that died in these crashes and do not include the radar operators of two crew jets that also failed to bail out. Some of the reported incidents did not state the type of jet involved in the crash. I ask the following questions:

1. Why did these fighter pilots and radar operators fail to bail out of their disabled jets?
2. Excluding the three incidents, where it was said the pilots chose to stay with their disabled crafts, why did so many flyers fail to bail out?
3. Did the remaining 62 jets, all of various types, have canopies that malfunctioned because of faulty designs? If so, why were they not corrected over the years?
4. How many of these fighter pilots actually encountered UFOs and had their jets electrical systems neutralized, thus disabling their craft?
5. How many planes and flyers fell out of the sky because of direct UFO encounters?
6. How many of these airmen encountered an outside force and were rendered unconscious or paralyzed before they hit the ground.
7. How many flyers were dead before they hit the ground?

These questions lead into another segment of my research that I found most unusual, multiple jet accidents. These incidents involved jets that fell from the sky at about the same time and either crashed or vanished under unknown and mysterious circumstances. Between 1951 and 1956, I found twelve such episodes where between two and four jets were involved. These multiple jet accidents are as follows:

1.) 1951, Aug. 10. San Angelo, Texas. Two F-80 Shooting Star jets "crashed", one in the high plains of New Mexico and the other in West Texas, "killing both pilots."

2.) 1951, Nov. 20. Charleston, North Carolina. The "wreckage of two Navy fighter planes" was spotted from the air, "in a wooded area." It was reported, "They were of the same [jet] type and believed to be those reported missing."

3.) 1953, Jan. 31. Madison, Wisconsin. Truax Air Field. The Air Force reported, "Four F-86 Sabre Jets on a routine tactical flight from the field attempted to land but their pilots were forced to bail out." It was reported, that three of the jets were found and one jet was lost. Two of the pilots were found safe, and two of the F-86 pilots were lost.

4.) 1953, Feb. 21. Goose Bay, Labrador, Canada. Four F-84 Thunder jets from the Goose Bay AFB were involved in a mysterious accident. The Air Force reported a, "Three plane formation of F-84 Thunder jet interceptors struck the ground three miles east" of the base. Further details explained that, "All planes in the formation crashed within seconds of each other." The Air Force stated, "No trace has been found of the fourth jet, which radioed over Greenland that it had experienced engine trouble. The pilot radioed that he was getting ready to bail out."

5.) 1953, Dec. 5. Lawrenceville, Georgia. Four Air National Guard Thunder jets were involved in this most unusual multiple jet crash. It was reported, "4 Jets Crash in Formation Dive Killing Pilots in Georgia Mystery." The four jets "fell from about 11,500 feet. One of the Thunder jets struck and demolished a small-unoccupied house. The three others crashed nearby." It was reported, "Dobbins Base said all the men were experienced jet pilots and they knew of no reasons for the crashes."

6.) 1954, Jan. 11. Frankfurt, Germany. Three F-86 Sabre Jets were involved in this multiple jet crash over Germany. Two pilots bailed out safely and one pilot was said to be missing. It was reported, "Three USAF Sabre jet fighters diverted from their destination by a snowstorm, crashed within minutes of each other after running out of fuel. Two of the pilots parachuted to safety."

7.) 1955, Jan. 9. Tokyo, Japan. While on a flight from Yokata Air Base to Itazuki Air Force Base, "two USAF F-86 Sabre Jets crashed in a rice patty within 100 yards of each other…killing both pilots."

8.) 1955, June 28. Tokyo, Japan. An F3-D Sky Knight fighter with two aboard crashed into the Pacific Ocean and an FJ-2 Fury searching for it vanished with one aboard. It was reported, "3 MARINE FLIERS HUNTED IN PACIFIC- Pilot Vanishes in Search for 2 on Rafts South of Tokyo-70 Planes Sweep Sea." Details stated, "A United States Marine fighter plane, searching for two downed Marine fliers bobbing on life rafts in the Pacific, disappeared yesterday afternoon, the Navy reported." At this point, there were three missing Marine Corps fighter flyers. *The New York Times* reported yet another missing aviator, a helicopter crewman. It was reported a "fourth missing Marine was a crew member of a helicopter that crashed in the ocean on the hunt."

9.) 1955, Sept. 25. Hampton, Virginia. Three USAF F-84 Thunder streak jets from Langley AFB were all "reported missing." Two of the jets were lost over Chesapeake Bay, in Virginia, and one jet was lost over Maine. These mysterious losses occurred only, "12 hours after a wing mate was killed" in a crash at Hampton, Virginia."

10.) 1956, Jan. 27. Tokyo, Japan. The jet crashes involved more numbers and the information released about them was less. *The New York Times* released this article and it reads in its entirety, "5 U.S. JETS CRASH in FAR EAST. Tokyo, Jan. 27 (AP) - Five United States Sabre Jets crashed in the Far East today four after they ran out of fuel near Okinawa and one in Japan. The pilots escaped unhurt."

11.) 1956, March 4. Darrington, Washington. The Air Force reported that, "two F-89 [Scorpion] jet interceptors and the four men they carried," were "believed to have crashed." The Air Force believed the crashes occurred in the vicinity of, "White Mountain in the Cascades."

12.) 1956, June 24. East Sandwich, Mass. The Air Force reported that two F-94 Starfires "ran out of fuel" and crashed into the ocean. Two of the fighter flyers were reportedly rescued and a third was missing. The two jets were part of a three-jet formation from Langley Air Force Base, Va., to Otis Field. It was reported that, "Air Force officials said the three planes approached for a landing but were held off because of weather conditions. The third plane landed safely shortly after the mishap."

In reference to the, Dec. 5, 1953 incident over Lawrenceville, Georgia when four Air National Guard F-84 fighter jets all fell from the sky and crashed, I would like to point out a similar crash. In his book, *Flying Saucers On The Attack*, author Harold T. Wilkins wrote about another four-jet crash that occurred only eleven days later over England. This four-jet jet crash incident bears an uncanny similarity to the four-jet crash that occurred in Georgia on December 5, as reported in *The New York Times*. Mr. Wilkins states:

Dec. 16, 1953. A mystery of the air: Four Meteor jet planes flew into a thick fog over Waterbeach, Cambs., Eng., after taking off there. In a few minutes all the jets crashed, without collisions. Two pilots had to bale out, and one was hurt, after crash landings. These jets came, three in Cambs., one in Suffolk. The singular explanation was: "These jets ran out of fuel." (Vide January 11, infra).

In this incident, the pilots of the four Meteor jets all survived whereas the pilots of the four Thunder Jets all died. This four Meteor jet crash incident is also similar to another episode that I listed as reported by The New York Times; the Jan. 11, 1954 Frankfurt, Germany incident that involved the three F-86 Sabre Jets that crashed in Germany. Wilkins reported the following information and gave his analogy of those two cases:

January 11, 1954. Three U.S. Air Force Sabre jets were flying at night near Darmstadt, Germany, when something caused their pilots to bale out. What happened to the third pilot is unknown. (N.B. What is decidedly curious is that, here as in the exactly parallel incident recorded in the English eastern Midlands, on December 16, 1953 supra, the U.S. Air Force, like the British RAF., says that all these jets "ran out of fuel"!)

These strange multiple jet crash incidents as well as other odd jet crash incidents have been noticed by a few researchers such as Stringfield, Keyhoe and Wilkins. In these two particular cases, Harold Wilkins wrote about them back in 1954, which leads us into another year of fighter jet disasters.

The New York Times also reported five catastrophic Air Force accidents in 1954 and one in 1955, involving fighter jets that mysteriously crashed into residential neighborhoods. They are listed below:

1.) 1954, Jan. 13. Long Beach, California. F-86 Sabre Jet, "F-86 Rams Homes, 7 Die in California"
2.) 1954, July 3. Walesville, New York. F-94C Starfire, "Abandoned Jet Kills 3 in Car, 1 in House"
3.) 1954, July 8. Kansas City, Missouri. F-84F Thunder Chief, "Air Force Jet Crashes and Cuts Fiery Swath in Kansas City, Killing 4"
4.) 1954, Aug. 4. Wantagh, Long Island. F-84G Thunder jet, "JET HITS WANTAUGH; PILOT DIES, 4 HURT"
5.) 1954, Oct. 12. Clinton, Maryland. F-86 Sabre Jet, "Jet, On Fire Falls, Killing 3 in Yard"
6.) 1955, Dec. 28. Levittown, NY. F-86D Sabre Jet, "Jet Fighter Crashes and Burns in Levittown Street; No One Injured"

I have chosen some headline stories from 1951 through 1956 as a representation of the "Six Deadly Years." They are among some of the most mysterious United States military fighter aircraft accidents that I found in *The New York Times*. Following each year are monthly breakdowns of UFO reports received by Project Grudge, later named Project Blue Book, in March of 1952 [1952 Excluded].

THE YEAR: 1951

On January 29, 1951, *The New York Times* reported the following story, "Don Gentile Killed In Jet Crash; U.S. Ace in Europe Shot Down 19." In part, the article states, "ANDREWS AIR FORCE BASE, Md. Jan. 28—

Capt. John Gentile United States ace of World War II, died instantly when the jet trainer he was piloting crashed and burned. He was the war's twelfth ranking American ace in total of enemy planes destroyed on the ground. He shot down nineteen German planes and shot up six on the ground. Captain Gentile, 30 years old who lived through three years of air warfare was killed on a routine flight in a two-seat trainer, a version of the P-80 Shooting Star…An Air Force spokesman said Captain Gentile's plane crashed at 3:30 P.M. in good, clear weather. This was just twenty-five minutes after he had taken off from Andrews field." An unidentified passenger also died in the crash along with the pilot. It was reported that, "The impact sent pieces of the craft for hundreds of yards." It was said that, "The cause of the crash was not immediately determined."

The article also reported the following information about Captain Gentile:

As an American ace-he was dubbed "The One-Man Air Force" –Captain Gentile flew 182 combat missions totaling 350 combat hours. He won fourteen awards for bravery, and President Franklin D. Roosevelt once referred to him as "Captain Courageous…He also won the nickname "the Messerschmitt Killer" and once said that it was much easier for him to shoot down a flying plane than to damage one sitting on the ground. During the war, Captain Gentile had claimed up to thirty enemy planes destroyed, putting him above of Capt. Eddie Rickenbacker's World War I kill of twenty-six but several of Captain Gentile's claimed kills were not confirmed.

This article also stated, "Prince Georges County police, said Captain Gentile's plane sheared off several treetops as it swooped down and drove into the earth." It was also reported, "One of the two victims, believed to be Captain Gentile, was thrown clear of the plane. Both men were dead when fire squads from Andrews Field-two or three miles away from the accident-arrived on the scene." Why did Captain Gentile and his crewmember fail to parachute from their aircraft before it crashed? Why was the Air Force unaware of the cause of the crash? What were the circumstances that occurred prior to the crash? The pilot should have been in radio contact with his base, and at least reported a May Day distress call.

The *New York Times* also reported the following story on August 12, 1951, which was actually a triple headline article referencing three crashes. The headline states, "2 LOST JET AIRMEN ARE DEAD IN WRECK." The subtitle read, "A Third Pilot Loses His Life in Massachusetts - Two Planes Crash in Texas."

The first story states in part; "FORRESTPORT, N.Y., Aug. 11 (AP)-Two airmen, missing since Tuesday when their jet plane ran out of gas, were found dead today. It continues, "The wrecked plane and bodies were found in a swamp…Griffis Air Force Base at Rome announced that the wrecked plane and the bodies were found in a swampland." The two Griffis AFB flyers that crashed in this incident were piloting an F-94 Starfire all-weather jet fighter. I ask the following questions:

1. Did the aircraft really crash because "their jet plane ran out of gas," as the Air Force, stated?
2. The jet has a large fuel gauge in the cockpit. Why was the pilot not aware of the jet's fuel capacity?
3. Why didn't the two flyers eject from their jet when it supposedly had no fuel left?
4. Why did the two flyers opt to crash into a swamp rather than evacuate their powerless aircraft?

The second part of this article states in part, "OTIS AIR FORCE BASE, Mass., A much decorated fighter pilot recently returned from the Korean War was killed today when his Saber jet crashed on a fog swept beach."

This crash involved a Korean War combat veteran, named Captain Frank C. Newell. This "much-decorated fighter pilot" and combat war hero died when his Sabre Jet crashed on a fog-swept beach in East Sandwich, Massachusetts. I ask very simply, why did this combat fighter pilot crash and why didn't he eject from his aircraft before it hit the ground?

The third part of this triple article states in part, "SAN ANGELO, Tex., Aug. 11(AP)- Two F-80 jet planes on training flights crashed last night in [the]high plains of New Mexico and West Texas, killing both pilots." This part of the article involved two P-80 Shooting Stars that crashed on "training flights." I ask; why didn't the two pilots eject from their jets before they crashed? Why did both men choose to die instead of bailing out of their jets? Were they involved in UFO intercepts that were written off as training accidents?

During the year 1951, Project Grudge received 169 UFO reports. The following list is a monthly breakdown of the reports received by Project Grudge for 1951:

Month 1. January - 25
Month 2. February -18
Month 3. March - 13
Month 4. April - 6
Month 5. May - 5
Month 6. June - 6
Month 7. July - 10
Month 8. August - 18
Month 9. September - 16

Month 10. October - 24
Month 11. November - 16
Month 12. December – 12

THE YEAR: 1952

On January 18, 1952, two pilots were found dead in the wreckage F-94 Starfire near Dover, Delaware, the home of Dover Air Force Base. It was reported, "2 Killed in Air Force Crash." In part, the article states, "Dover, Del., Jan. 18-Two Air Force officers were found dead this afternoon in the wreckage of an F-94 all weather interceptor jet plane that crashed on a farm south of Cheswold near here. Aboard the plane, which disappeared last midnight while on a flight from the Dover Air Base, were the pilot, First Lieut. Virgil E. Plunkett…and the radar operator, Second Lieut. James H. Gifford."

This was a very mysterious incident. This jet crashed after it disappeared on a flight from Dover AFB while flying over land. The fighter pilot and Dover AFB tower men should have been in radio communication with each other. Moreover, radar controllers should have known the approximate vicinity where the jet went down, and why the jet was in trouble and going down.

1. Why was Dover AFB unaware of the jets whereabouts when it was over land and near their base?
2. Why did the F-94 "disappear" when it should have been on radar and in communication with the tower and furthermore, what caused the jet to crash?
3. Why wasn't the jet found immediately after it crashed? An F-94 jet crashing into the ground at a high speed would have certainly been noticed.
4. The jet disappeared at midnight, yet it was said the wreckage and bodies were not found until the following afternoon. Why did it take so long to find the wreckage of the jet? Was the scene covered up?
5. Why didn't the pilot and radar operator bail out of the falling jet before it crashed?
6. What type of "flight" were the airmen on when they disappeared in their Starfire at midnight?

On February 19, 1952, an F-94 Starfire jet was reported missing in an article, "Hope for 2 Lost Fliers Given Up." This article states the following information:

PANAMA CITY, Fla., Feb. 20 (UP)—Discovery of a logbook at sea led Air Force authorities today to give up hope for the lives of two officers who disappeared while on a routine flight from Tyndall Air Force Base here. The officers who vanished in an F-94 jet fighter plane at dawn yesterday were identified as First Lieut. John D. Chambers of Seattle, the pilot, and Second Lieut. George H. Elliot of Albany, Ga., radar man. The pilot's log was found floating on the Gulf five miles off shore by a crash boat today.

If we are to assume the jet crashed into the Gulf of Mexico, and the only remains found were a logbook is preposterous. It is hard to believe that the pilot's logbook was the only remaining piece of evidence found in the water after a crash; unless, the jet didn't crash in the Gulf waters and the logbook was a cover story.

1. It was said that the jet vanished; did it crash into the water, or ascend up into the sky?
2. Tyndall AFB tower should have been tracking the aircraft and been in radio contact with the jet's crew. Why were the radar operators and controllers unaware of the jet's location right before it vanished?
3. Where was the jet's wreckage? The flyers bodies were not found. Did they bail out and if they did, why were they not found...dead or alive?
4. Why was the logbook, which was supposedly found in the Gulf, the only remains?
5. Why was there no floating debris other than the alleged logbook? Was the logbook a cover story?
6. Why did Tyndall Air Force Base have such a difficult time keeping track of their jets?

7. Did the jet and flyers simply vanish on "a routine flight" or were they on a UFO intercept mission?

THE YEAR: 1953

The continuing saga of jet fighter accidents persisted into 1953 as jets continued to drop out of the skies at an alarming rate. Most noticeable were the disturbing multiple jet accidents that occurred in 1953 when several jets fell from the sky at once. On January 31, 1953, a very odd story occurred over Michigan involving four Truax AFB F-86 Sabre Jets. The headline states, "4 JET PILOTS BAIL OUT IN STORM; 2 ARE LOST. MADISON, Wis., Jan. 31 (AP)-Land, sea and air units fanned out over southern Wisconsin and northern Illinois tonight in a search for the pilots of two Air Force jet planes who bailed out of their craft in bad weather earlier tonight. The public information office at Truax Air Field here [Wisconsin] said four F-86 Sabre jets on a routine tactical flight from the field had attempted to land but their pilots were forced to bail out."

In this incident, all four F-86 pilots were said to have bailed out of their jets during an alleged "routine tactical flight." The following information was revealed:

Aircraft 1; The flight leader, Major Kemp, bailed out over the Muskego area, 60 miles east of Truax Field and was found alive.

Aircraft 2; the second jet was located in Waukesha County in the same area as the flight leaders jet, but the pilot was not found.

Aircraft 3; the pilot, Lt. Holker, bailed out south of Truax Field over Edgerton and was found alive.

Aircraft 4; the pilot of the fourth jet was not found, and the Sabre Jet was missing.

It was said that the pilots "were forced to bail out" of their jets. I ask the following questions.
1. Why were Truax Field weather officials unaware of the "bad weather," which should they should have been aware of through radar tracking? Why didn't officials recall their jets before the bad weather hit?
2. Why didn't Truax Field officials redirect their four jets around the "storm" to an alternate landing field?
3. Was "bad weather" the actual reason that the Sabre Jet pilots evacuated their aircrafts?
4. Were the pilots of these jets, really on a "routine tactical flight" when they "were forced to bail out"? The loss of two pilots and 4 jets does not seem to reflect anything routine about this "routine tactical flight."
5. Why were these particular F-86 jets up in the air during a "storm" in the first place?
6. Why were Air Force jets and pilots vanishing over America; as was the case in this story?
7. Why was the Air Force unable to keep their jets up in the sky?
8. Where these jets on a UFO scramble mission that forced them into the sky?

In the following month, another multiple jet crash occurred that also involved four Air Force jets.

On February 21, 1952, four F-84 Thunder jets that were said to be part sixteen- plane flight to Europe from Goose Bay AFB, in Labrador, Canada crashed. *The New York Times* Reported:

4 JETS CRASH IN NORTH; PILOT DIES, 1 MISSING
Special to The New York Times.

GOOSE BAY, Labrador, Feb. 22 - Three United States Air Force jet fighter planes crashed near here yesterday. A fourth is missing in Greenland…One pilot was killed and two others were injured when a three plane formation of F-84 Thunder jet interceptors struck the ground three miles east of this big Canadian air base. The fate of the fourth pilot in Greenland is unknown. The information was disclosed tonight by Canadian Air Force personnel at the Goose Bay air base.

This accident occurred at 10:30 a.m. local time, and officials gave the following information.

1. "The leader of a three plane formation bound from here to Narassuak, Greenland, discovered shortly after take-off that his auxiliary fuel tanks were not functioning properly. He turned back to Goose Bay. His two wing mates accompanied him."

2. "As the three [jets] began making a radar-controlled approach to the airport, the flight leaders fuel supply became exhausted. All planes in the formation crashed within seconds of each other."

3. "No trace has been found of the fourth jet, which radioed over Greenland that it had experienced engine trouble. The pilot reported that he was getting ready to bail out."

4. "A widespread search began yesterday over the vast reaches of Greenland for the fourth pilot. The searchers believed his aircraft had fallen over land and not in the sea. It is normal procedure to track flights of military aircraft by radar."

Also appearing in an article on the same page as this story is an update story:

AIR FORCE LACKS DETAILS

Special to The New York Times. WASHINGTON, Monday, Feb. 23—An Air Force spokesman here confirmed this morning the report that three jet planes had crashed at Goose Bay, Labrador. He said only partial information about the incident had reached the Air Force headquarters.

The exact cause of the crashes was not known but "apparently the lead airplane had engine trouble," the spokesman said, adding that it was the practice of a formation to take its bearings on a flight leader.

The formation, the spokesman continued, was bound for Europe in a routine ferrying operation. The type of F-84 jet was not disclosed. Some models, it was pointed out, are radar-equipped, which might account for the manner in which two of the planes followed the lead plane into the ground.

The three planes had not collided in mid-air, the spokesman added. The spokesperson made no mention of the fourth plane that was reportedly lost in Greenland.

1. The lead jet was the only one said to be in trouble, yet the other two jets attempted landings.
Why did the pilots of the other two F-84 jets attempt to land after following the lead plane back to the base?
2. Why did the two accompanying F-84 jet pilots follow the lead jet into the ground?
3. Was the entire story as explained by the Air Force a total fabrication; were all three jets actually damaged and therefore forced into landing attempts?
4. What happened to the fourth jet that was missing, and why was there no follow up story about it?
5. Why were Air Force jets dropping out of the skies around the world?

The outlandish story as told by Air Force officials seems to display how they were running out of excuses to explain why their jets were falling out of the sky. This Air Force base was a hotbed for UFO sightings during the early 1950s. The following UFO incidents occurred over and near Goose Bay AFB:

1. September 13, 1951. Project Blue Book "Unknown" Case 969.
2. June 17, 1952. Both Keyhoe and Ruppelt told of a UFO incident that involved a radar/visual sighting.
3. June 19, 1952. Project Blue Book "Unknown" Case 1308.
4. September 28, 1952. Goose Bay Air Intelligence Information Report dated 17 October 1952. Radar approach at Goose AFB picked up a UFO target nearby.
5. November 26, 1952. UFO eluded jet interceptors. *Canadian UFO Report*. Vol. 3, #8. Whole # 24. Summer 1976.
6. December 15, 1952. F-80 and F-94B Jet interceptors chased UFO for 25 minutes with momentary lock-on. Project Blue Book and case 104-B, Dr. Edward U. Condon.
7. May 1, 1953. Project Blue Book "Unknown" Case 2555.
8. June 22, 1953. Project Blue Book "Unknown" Case 2601

9. June 30, 1954. Project Blue Book and Case I-D, Dr. Edward U. Condon. Two BOAC Strato-Cruiser pilots saw UFOs, one reported as "jelly-fish-like." Goose Bay AFB was contacted and fighter jet scrambled.

The New York Times also reported this baffling story on December 7, 1953 in an article titled, "4 Jets Crash in Formation Dive, Killing Pilots in Georgia Mystery."

In part, this article states, "LAWRENCEVILLE, Ga., Dec. 6—Four Air National Guard Thunderjet F-84 planes, making a weekend instrument flight, crashed near this community last night. The four pilots were killed." This article also stated:

Officials at Dobbins Air Force Base at Marietta, near by, said the planes were returning from Miami and preparing to land when they fell from about 11,500 feet. One of the plummeting Thunder jets struck and demolished a small-unoccupied house. The three others crashed near by…They said there was no indication that the planes were in collision before striking the ground…the formation was starting its descent from 27,000 feet and would report again at 11,500 feet. But the fliers were not heard from again…Officials at the Dobbins Base said all the men were experienced jet pilots and they knew of no reason for the crashes. An investigation is under way."

1. What caused four "experienced jet pilots" to all crash their aircrafts?
2. Why did none of the four pilots attempt to bail out before crashing?
3. Were all four pilots unconscious or dead before they hit the ground?
4. What caused four F-84 jets to drop out of the sky all at the same time?
5. Why were the four pilots not heard from after starting their descents...were they preoccupied?

During the year 1953, Project Blue received 509 UFO reports. The following list is a monthly breakdown of the reports received by Project Blue book for 1953:

Month 1. January - 67
Month 2. February -91
Month 3. March - 23
Month 4. April - 24
Month 5. May - 25
Month 6. June - 32
Month 7. July - 41
Month 8. August - 35
Month 9. September - 22
Month 10. October - 37
Month 11. November - 35
Month 12. December – 29

THE YEAR: 1954

The year 1954 proved to be another year of fatalities in the ongoing series of extraordinary fighter accidents that occurred throughout the United States. The year started out with a catastrophic fighter jet crash that occurred over California on January 12. In an article stated as, "Special to *The New York Times*," the headline reported, "F-86 Rams Homes, 7 Die in California."

In part, it states, "LONG BEACH, Calif., Jan. 12- Seven persons died today when an F-86 Sabre jet fighter crashed out of an overcast into a heavily populated residential neighborhood in the Signal Hill Section." I have arranged the following information reported in this article, into a cohesive sequential order:

A.) "The plane was one of two Sabre Jets caught in the closing overcast while working their way toward Long Beach Municipal Air port after a flight from Williams Air Force Base near Tucson, Arizona."
B.) "The airport tower which has no radar equipment to help planes in, said that the jets circled out to sea

and tried to come in under the low clouds for a landing."
C.) "One made it. The other [jet] flying in from the north, sheared off the top of a fir tree outside of a convalescent home."
D.) "After clipping the tree, the plane ripped through a home, killing a woman and her son."
E.) "It then hit two other houses, killing one woman in each."
F.) "A second youngster was killed while playing in the street."
G.) "The pilot" was one of "six of the victims."
H.) "A seventh died of a heart attack while watching."
I.) "Three homes were demolished and a fourth partially burned. Telephone lines were torn and gas mains broken.

This was the basic series of events reported about the accident in this article. The victims killed in this crash are listed below:

1. The F-86 pilot; Major Robert A. Blair
2. Mrs. Shirley Roberts, 21 years old; her son,
3. Douglas Roberts, 18 months old, (both killed in their home)
4. Mrs. Shirley Ledbetter, 25 years old (killed in her home)
5. Mrs. Grace Miller, 63 years old (killed in her home)
6. Stephen Lois Shoup, 11 years old (killed in street)
7. Ernest G. Bailey, 72 years old (spectator, died of heart attack)

The civilians who were injured in this jet accident were:
1. Edward Ledbetter, 24 years old, critical, (husband)
2. Edward Ledbetter, 4 months old, critical, (son); It was reported that, "Thomas J. McConnell, 58, who was working near by, sprinted into the burning Ledbetter house and brought out the badly injured baby."
3. Mrs. Nancy Kinks, 18 years old; her daughter,
4. Sherry Lynn Kinks, 2 ½ years old (suffered from shock)

In the closing paragraph of this article the following information was stated, "The crash was the second in three days in a crowded Los Angeles neighborhood. On Sunday a converted B-26 twin-engined bomber fell in the Burbank district, demolishing a house and two garages and killing one man."
A follow up article about the F-86 crash also appeared on the same page as the original article:

CAUSE IS UNKNOWN
LONG BEACH, Jan. 12. (AP) - A spokesman at the airport said the control tower had been in touch with Major Blair until just before the accident. "It was just a normal conversation," he said. "We don't know what caused the crash. There was no indication that anything was wrong."
I ask the following questions:
1. What caused this Sabre Jet to crash in Long Beach?
2. Why were Air Force pilots unable to keep their jets from landing in neighborhoods and killing innocent civilians?
3. Was it pilot error that caused this jet accident, or did the jet have an unknown encounter in the air prior to its landing attempt at the Long Beach Municipal Airport?
On the following day, Edward Ledbetter, the four-month-old baby died from his injuries bringing the total casualties of the crash up to eight.

When fighter jets were not falling out of the sky in mysterious accidents they were simply disappearing. On April 6, 1952, a fighter pilot who "flew 130 fighter combat missions in World War II" vanished over Long Island, according to the *New York Times*:

JET SPEED PILOT MISSING
COLONEL VANISHES AFTER FLYING FROM LONG ISLAND IN OVERCAST

A ground-air search was started late yesterday afternoon for an Air Force jet pilot who disappeared after taking off on instruments in a heavy overcast at Farmingdale, L. I. Colonel William H. Councill, 42-year-old pilot who recently held the jet speed record from Los Angeles to New York, left the Republic Aviation Plant at 10:48 a.m. in an F-80 jet training plane bound for his home at Langley Field, Va. He had three hours of fuel aboard and was not heard from after take-off. Maj. Dan T. Brigham, air rescue officer of the New York wing of the Civil Air Patrol, said Colonel Councill apparently had been in trouble within minutes after the take-off and might be down within fifty miles from the field.

It was also stated that Colonel Councills', "cross-country record of 4 hours 13 minutes was set Jan. 26, 1946. It stood until last January, when another pilot broke it by a few minutes.

I ask; what kind of "trouble" had arisen in this incident and why was it not revealed to the press? What were the circumstances that caused this veteran jet pilot to go missing with his jet? Why didn't Colonel Councill bail out of his aircraft if he "had been in trouble?" Simply, I ask, where did this jet go?

On July 2, 1954, another catastrophic disaster occurred when an F-94C Starfire crashed into a neighborhood in the town of Walesville at about 12:30 p.m. The two-man Starfire crew bailed-out of their jet when their cockpit heated up to an unbearable temperature after being scrambled after a UFO.

In part, *The New York Times* reported:

ABANDONED JET KILLS 3 IN CAR, 1 IN HOUSE

UTICA, N.Y., July 2- A jet fighter plane returning from a quick "scramble" to investigate an unidentified plane, reported to be "friendly," crashed in flames in a crossroads hamlet today…The plane was attached to the Twenty-seventh Fighter Interceptor Squadron at near-by Griffis Air Force Base, Rome. The base said it was one of two planes ordered up on a practice scramble that turned into an actual mission. The public information officer, Major Evelyn Watkins, explained that the two planes were barely airborne on the training mission when they received radioed orders to check on an unidentified plane in the area. Major Watkins said no information was available on the unidentified plane or where it was located by the jets.

In Washington, a Pentagon spokesman said the plane was about seventy-five miles northeast of Rome on the edge of the zone covered by Griffis, when it was detected…A Griffis spokesman said the pilots had been satisfied that the plane had been "friendly" and were headed back to the base when fire broke out in the cockpit of one of the jets. The air base said the pilot and radar observer had stayed with the plane until the "last minute." A spokesman quoted Lieutenant Atkins [pilot] as reporting that he had ordered Lieutenant Coudon [radar-observer] to bail out, and then had jumped himself from about 7,000 feet.

Griffis AFB officials "said it had not determined whether an explosion occurred while the jet was in the air. Earlier, an Air Force officer said there, 'must have been an explosion.'" After the crew bailed-out, the jet fell into the small town of Walesville where, "Four persons on the ground were killed and two houses and an automobile were destroyed."

The following Air Force quote is from the official accident report section, "SUMMARY OF CIRCUMSTANCES," from the "Air Force Inspection and Safety Center at Norton AFB." It states:

As the pilot started a descent, he noted that the cockpit temperature increased abruptly. The increase in temperature caused the pilot to scan the instruments. The fire warning light was on and the pilot informed the radar observer of this fact. The fire warning light came on after the throttle was placed in "idle" so the engine was shut down and both crew members ejected successfully.

This incident has been the focus of UFO researchers for many years. A controversial point in this case concerns the onboard fire that caused the cockpit to heat up thus forcing the two flyers to bail. Did the jet actually encounter a UFO that caused it to heat up or was there a cockpit or engine fire that caused the cockpit to heat up? In reference to the jet fire, the Griffis AFB spokesman said, "Fire broke out in the cockpit of one of the planes." It was also stated, that there, "must have been an explosion."

In 1980, the "Air Force Inspection and Safety Center at Norton AFB," released a "summary sheet" of the Walesville accident to researchers Lawrence Fawcett and Barry Greenwood. These authors wrote about the "fire" aspect of the incident in their 1984 book, *CLEAR INTENT-The Government Cover up Of The UFO Experience.*

In part, this official "summary sheet," stated, "The aircraft started to descend below the clouds. During the descent, a fire warning light came on. The engine was immediately shut down; also due to the low altitude, the crew members ejected and were recovered without injury."

The authors then state, "According to the 'Unsatisfactory Report' form included in the file, the pilot, Lt. William E. Atkins, felt a sudden rise in cockpit temperature and noticed the forward fire warning light was on." Fawcett and Greenwood reported that, "The accident report on Walesville contained the following conclusions: 'Investigation of the wreckage disclosed no in-flight fire. The cause of the malfunction in the fire warning system could not be determined.'" I ask the following questions:

1. Why does the original Griffis AFB statement to the press differ from the Norton AFB documents?
2. Why was the story changed from a "fire broke out in the cockpit," to "no in-flight fire"?
3. Since there was no cockpit fire, no engine fire, and no smoke, what caused the sudden rise in temperature in the cockpit?
4. Did the fire warning light really malfunction or was this another convenient story to cover the incident?
5. Did the crew of this F-94 Starfire jet bail out prematurely or was there another outside factor that caused them to bail out?
6. Did the onboard systems in the cockpit of the jet heat up and malfunction during a UFO intercept encounter against a saucer, causing the pilots to bail out?

Later that day, two flying discs were reported over the northeast United States. Both of the sightings occurred over New Jersey, located south of Walesville, New York. The first sighting occurred over West New York at 3:00 p.m. that afternoon, two and one-half hours after the Starfire crash. The second sighting occurred over Paterson, New Jersey at 11:00 p.m. The Paterson, New Jersey Newspaper, *The Morning Call*, reported the two stories on July 3, 1952:

PHONE LINEMAN ON POLE SEES FAST FLYING DISC

John A. Caulley, of 128 South Maple Ave., Ridgewood, a telephone lineman with the New Jersey Telephone Company for 23 years has seen a lot of strange sights from his lofty perches but nothing stranger than the object that went flashing across the sky over the Hudson River, yesterday afternoon. Caulley described his experience to the Morning Call and James H. Cox, Paterson Civil Defense Disaster Control director last night. At about 3' o'clock yesterday afternoon Caully was working with another crewman on a pole at East River Drive and the Boulevard, in West New York when he spotted the strange object against the sky, that was deep blue at the time.

"It was round and disc-like in appearance and traveled at an angle to the ground in the direction of edge water and Yonkers," he said. "I saw it for eight seconds and when I moved to the other side of the pole for a better view, it disappeared behind a cloud bank." Caulley says the object appeared to be of some translucent material. Asked how fast it was traveling he estimated "so fast a jet would have a hard time trying to catch it"…
The flying disc was reported over Paterson about 11 o' clock last night by Paterson police officers.

SEEN OVER PATERSON

Patrolmen William Gibbs, Anthony Ignoffo, and Henry Fiduccia were making a patrol call to the Eastside section when they noticed a crowd standing at Madison Ave. and Market St. They stopped the patrol and alighted to learn the reason for the gathering and then in the sky saw a bright disc moving in a westerly direction.

Were the UFOs that were sighted that afternoon and evening over New Jersey connected to the Walesville crash incident earlier that day?

Damaged Air Force jets continued to fall out of the sky over the United States under mysterious circumstances. The following story appeared in an article on November 29, 1954, and involved another jet crash that occurred after an intercept scramble and once again, it involved a jet from O'Hare AFB, in Chicago.

The headline reads, "Pilot Killed In Crash." In part it states, "CHICAGO, Nov .28 (UP)-An Air Force pilot who took to the air in an F-86D Sabre Jet to track down an unidentified plane was killed last night when his plane crashed and exploded while returning for a landing. The victim was identified as First Lieut. Burton A. Smith." Was it a coincidence that fighter jets were crashing in America after attempting to intercept UFOs? It is no secret that Air Force jets were scrambled from O'Hare after flying saucers quite frequently. In this incident, the UFO was referred to as "an unidentified plane." Was 1st Lt. Burton involved in a lurid duel of death?

On December 2, 1954, an Air Force F- 86 Sabre Jet attached to the 31st Fighter Interceptor Squadron at Larson AFB crashed in a most peculiar area. *The New York Times* reported, "Crash in Atomic Area – Air Force Pilot Bails Out Over Restricted Zone at Hanford." In part, it stated, "A Sabre Jet crashed in the restricted of Hanford Atomic Works today, narrowly missing a building where plutonium for atomic bombs is produced. The pilot, Lieut. J. R. Ferguson of Claywood, N.Y. bailed out and landed uninjured." What were the circumstances that forced this fighter pilot to bail out and his crash jet into this highly dangerous area? Was this fighter interceptor pilot attempting to intercept a UFO over this restricted area or did he run out of gas?

According to *The New York Times*, 1954 and 1952 had the highest amount of fighter aircraft accident losses during that six-year period.

During the year 1954, Project Blue received 487 UFO reports. The following list is a monthly breakdown of the reports received by Project Blue book for 1954:

Month 1. January - 36
Month 2. February -20
Month 3. March - 34
Month 4. April - 34
Month 5. May - 34
Month 6. June - 51
Month 7. July - 60
Month 8. August - 43
Month 9. September - 48
Month 10. October - 51
Month 11. November - 46
Month 12. December – 30

THE YEAR: 1955

The ongoing saga of American fighter aces that died in their fighters in the United States continued into 1955. The following article appeared in *The New York Times* on May 6, 1955:

WORLD WAR II ACE KILLED
Lieut. Col. Winfield Brown Dies in Crash at Newburgh

NEWBURGH, N.Y., May 5 (AP) - Lieut. Col. Winfield H. Brown, 39 years old, was killed today when his jet fighter crashed and burned just short of the runway at Stewart Air Force Base here. He was director of operations for the two fighter squadrons based here. Colonel Brown came in under power for an emergency landing, maneuvering desperately to avoid a housing project for base personnel and their families. He was married and the father of three young children. A fighter pilot in World War II, he was credited with having downed five Nazi planes, thus becoming an "ace."

It was reported, the ace fighter pilot, was "maneuvering desperately" while trying to land his aircraft at Stewart AFB. What were the prior circumstances that caused Colonel Brown to make an "emergency landing" which resulted in a crash? Why were so many experienced fighter pilots crashing in the United States?

One of the strangest 1955 fighter accidents I reviewed involved two lost Marine Corps fighter jets. An F3-D Sky Knight fighter jet with two aboard crashed into the Pacific Ocean and an FJ-2 Fury searching for it vanished with one aboard. *The New York Times* reported the following on June 29, 1955, "3 MARINE FLIERS HUNTED IN PACIFIC- Pilot Vanishes in Search for 2 on Rafts South of Tokyo-70 Planes Sweep Sea."

In part, this article states, " TOKYO, Wednesday, June 29 (AP)-A United States Marine fighter plane, searching for two downed Marine fliers bobbing on life rafts in the Pacific, disappeared yesterday afternoon, the Navy reported. The two had been missing since Sunday night, when they either parachuted from, or ditched their twin-jet fighter after running out of fuel. Search planes from the biggest air-sea rescue armada that has been assembled in the Far East in years widened their sweeps of the sea, hoping to spot all three marine airmen. Last night, they had lost sight of one of them on a raft south of Tokyo."

The following information was given about the jet fighter that disappeared from his squadron while searching for the downed twin-jet fighter, "Lieutenant McAney's FJ-2 Fury jet fighter vanished from the other members of the flight at about 2 p.m. as they climbed to avoid clouds in the vicinity of O-shima, sixty-one sea miles south of Tokyo. ' *I have lost you in the haze*,' he reported by radio to his squadron leader. This was the last heard from him. More than seventy Navy, Marine and Air Force Planes joined in the search today…also participating were eleven ships of the United States and Canadian navies and Japanese Coast Guard."

The FJ-2 Fury fighter jet and Lieutenant McAney had simply vanished. An update report was carried on July 1, 1952. *The New York Times* reported, "WIDE HUNT PERSISTS FOR PACIFIC AIRMEN. Tokyo, Friday, July 1 (AP)…Missing Marine airman, Lieut. Alan M. McAney Jr. of Yonkers, had a radio in his emergency life raft when he disappeared Tuesday night in the search." I ask one simple question; where are Lieutenant McAney and his jet? Neither the fighter pilot nor any wreckage of the jet was ever found.

On Monday September 26, 1955, the following article appeared concerning a very bizarre series of events:

SEARCH FOR 3 PILOTS

HAMPTON, Va., Sept. 25(AP)- A widespread search was underway tonight [Sunday Sept. 25] for three Langley Air Force Base jets pilots whose F-84 Thunder Streak planes were reported missing twelve hours after a wing mate was killed in a crash in a back marsh at Hampton. Two of the missing pilots were flying over

Chesapeake Bay when contact was lost late yesterday. The third [pilot] was on a routine navigational mission over the northeastern section of Maine.

The pilot killed in the crash in Hampton, Va. on September 24, 1955, was, First Lt. James H. Henley. The three pilots who vanished were, First Lt. Peter F. Dolan, Second Lt. Harold E. Wadell, and Second Lt. Roland S. Walls. I will now raise the following questions:
1. What caused the F-84 Thunder Streak to crash in Hampton, Virginia?
2. What was the reason that First Lt. Henley did not bail out of his jet before it crashed in Hampton?
3. Why was the Air Force unaware of the whereabouts of the other three jets?
4. How did they lose three jets over the United States with radio communication capabilities and radar tracking?
5. How is it that the Air Force lost three jets over the United States yet no one noticed them going down? How did they lose track of two fighter jets over the nearby Chesapeake Bay area?
6. Why was there no wreckage or bodies found in the Chesapeake Bay and Maine incidents?
7. Why did none of the four pilots involved in these incidents attempt to bail out?
8. Did the three vanished Thunder Streak jets crash, or did they disappear in the sky?

During the year 1955, Project Blue received 545 UFO reports. The following list is a monthly breakdown of the reports received by Project Blue book for 1955:
Month 1. January - 30
Month 2. February - 34
Month 3. March - 41
Month 4. April - 33
Month 5. May - 54
Month 6. June - 48
Month 7. July - 63
Month 8. August - 68
Month 9. September - 57
Month 10. October - 55
Month 11. November - 32
Month 12. December – 25

THE YEAR: 1956

Major Keyhoe wrote a letter, dated April 3, 1956 and sent it to Virginia State Senator Harry F. Byrd in reference to the Air Force's investigation of UFOs and misleading policy. Senator Byrd forwarded this letter to the USAF. In part, it read, "Now, as a resident, property owner, and tax payer of the state of Virginia, I am requesting your assistance in ending the Air Force contradictions and secrecy. . . . Why has the Air Force hidden the 1952 Air Force Intelligence analysis of the flying saucers' 'controlled motion' and its specific conclusion that these UFOs were interplanetary space ships? . . . Why are service pilots, radar men, and other trained observers officially muzzled? . . . Why do armed Air Defense Command jets continue to chase these UFOs by standing ADC orders?"

1956 represents the last year of the six deadly years of fighter accidents that I researched in The New York Times and documented. The following multi jet accident involved three F-94 Starfire all-weather jet interceptors, two of which crashed. The New York Times Reported the following story on June 25, 1956:

TWO JET PLANES CRASH- STARFIRES RUN OUT Of FUEL – 2 Men Saved, 3d Missing

EAST SANDWICH, Mass., June 24 (UP) – Two Air Force jet Starfires ran out of fuel and crashed into the sea tonight. Two men were rescued and a third was missing. The Two planes were flying in a three-jet formation from Langley Air Force Base, Va., to Otis Field where they spun out of formation and crashed. Air Force officials said the three planes approached for a landing but were held off because of weather conditions. The third plane landed safely shortly after the mishap. The pilot and radar observer in one plane were rescued after they bailed out over the ocean. The pilot of the second plane was sought by crash boats and shore search parties.

The first point that I will raise here is in reference to, "The pilot of the second plane," who was sought by rescue parties. He was said to be the "third" flyer involved in the incident and reportedly "missing." The F-94 jet that he was piloting was a two-crew jet, yet there is no mention of the radar operator. The article mentions that, "The pilot and radar operator in one plane were rescued after they bailed out over the ocean," but does not refer to the radar operator of the other F-94 Starfire. I found this most peculiar.

Prior to the jet crashes, there were also very odd circumstances involved in this incident. It was said, the two Starfires jets, "approached for a landing but were held off because of weather conditions."

The jets then "ran out of fuel and crashed into the sea."

1. Why were these jets held off from landing at their base? They were F-94 all weather interceptors.
2. Why did the Air Force bypass the chance to land two all-weather jets?
3. Did these jets really run out of gas, or did an outside force damage them?
4. Why is there no mention of a radar operator in the other F-94 jet where the pilot was reported as missing?

In 1957, author Max Miller reported the following information in his book, *FLYING SAUCERS-FACT OR FICTION*, "As late as July 19, 1956, Civil Aeronautics Administration flight instructor Irwin Ross Vermillion confirmed a report that the Air Force has issued instructions to *"shoot down"* UFOs. (Santa Ana, Calif. Independent, July 20, 1956)." Further information states, "It is imperative," Vermillion was quoted as saying, "that the Air Force get a tangible fragment of a flying saucer, from which to detect its possible origin and construction."

Less than one week later, another U.S. news article appeared in reference to shooting down flying saucers. The Air Force was not the only game in town when it came to shooting at the saucers. The Honorable Brinsley Le Poer Trench wrote the following in his 1958 book, *The Flying Saucer Review-World Roundup of UFO Sightings and Events*:

HAVE UFOs BEEN FIRED UPON

The following reprint from the Fullerton, California, News Tribune, of July 26, 1956, is reproduced from the August-September issue of "Proceedings."

PACIFIC NAVY FLIERS ORDERED TO ENGAGE SAUCERS HONOLULU, T.H., (OCNS) [Orange County News Service, CA.]

The United States Navy will not publicly admit that it believes in flying saucers, but it has officially ordered combat-ready pilots to "shoot to kill" if saucers are encountered, OCNS has learned.

The information was first learned when Navy pilots navigating trans-Pacific routes from the United States to Hawaii were ordered in a briefing session to engage and identify "any unidentified flying objects."

If the UFO's (saucers) appeared hostile, the briefing officer told pilots of Los Alamitos Naval Air Station reserve squadron VP 771, they are to be engaged in combat.

In Honolulu, members of the squadron talked over the unique orders. It was found that the orders are not unusual. They are a standard command issued to pilots on the trans-Pacific hop.

In 1957, author Max Miller also explained the entire Navy's "shoot to kill" news story in his book, *FLYING SAUCERS-FACT OR FICTION*. He also added excerpts of the news release that were not printed in the July 26, 1952 newspaper article. Miller set the stage and explained how the story unfolded. He stated the following:

In early July 1956 Pat Michaels, news chief of KWIZ, Santa Ana California, was one of several to go on a Navy sponsored junket to Honolulu. He and other newsmen were briefed with Naval Air Reserve Squadron VP771, at Los Alamitos Naval Air Station, California. What Michaels heard was news. His account for the Orange County News Service was dispatched upon his return in mid-July.

Max Miller then quoted the following statements written by news chief Patrick Michaels for the news story.
A.) "The United States Navy will not publicly admit that it believes in flying saucers, but it has officially ordered combat-ready pilots to 'shoot to kill' if saucers are encountered."
B.) "The information was first learned when Navy pilots navigating trans-Pacific routes from the United States to Hawaii were ordered in a briefing session to engage and identify 'any unidentified flying objects.'"
C.) "If the UFOs appeared hostile, the briefing officer told pilots of Los Alamitos Naval Air Station reserve Squadron VP771, they are to be engaged in combat."
D.) "In Honolulu, members of the squadron talked over the unique orders. It was found that the orders are not unusual. They are a standard command issued to pilots on the trans-Pacific hop."
Miller then continued and wrote the following information concerning Pat Michael's story:
A.) "How do Navy pilots react to the reported 'orders?'"
B.) "How do we know our bullets will work on a 'UFO?' one pilot was quoted as asking the Orange County News Service correspondent."
C.) "'And if we do shoot,' the Navy pilot continued, that's asking them to shoot back. And we don't know what they're [going] to shoot at us!'"
Miller also quoted statements made by Pat Michaels in reference to military combat against UFOs:
A.) "Although the Air Force has publicly stated that it does not believe in the existence of saucers, extensive operational procedures, including forms of combat have been devised by various air defense commands."
B.) "Operational procedures for a UFO scramble apparently are highly classified. Most officers refused to discuss the Pentagon's plans or modes of saucer combat. However, it was learned that a concrete plan of action does exist, covering all types of saucer sightings. The plans reportedly can be swung into action within seconds."
According to this July 1956 news story, it is evident that the Navy and Air Force were under orders to scramble and intercept UFOs and engage in combat with them if deemed necessary. American combat veterans continued to die in their planes in the United States well into 1956. The following article appeared in *The New York Times* on October 14, 1956:

PLANE CRASH KILLS WAR HERO

MINNEAPOLIS, Oct. 13 (AP)- A jet plane crashed and burned near Wold Chamberlain Field late yesterday, killing a pilot who had won two high decorations for eighty-one combat missions during World War II. Capt. Lawrence C. Lundburg, 39 years old, Minneapolis, died in the crash. He held the Distinguished Flying Cross and the Air Medal.

During the year 1956, Project Blue received 670 UFO reports. The following list is a monthly breakdown of the reports received by Project Blue book for 1956:

Month 1. January - 43
Month 2. February - 46
Month 3. March - 44
Month 4. April - 39
Month 5. May - 46
Month 6. June - 43
Month 7. July - 72
Month 8. August - 123
Month 9. September - 71
Month 10. October - 53
Month 11. November - 56
Month 12. December – 34

During the "Six Deadly Years," that spanned between 1951 and 1956, the staff of Project Blue Book at ATIC received 3,881 UFO reports from the United States and around the world.

The following list consists of the months from each of those six years with the highest amount of UFO sightings reported to Project Blue Book:

Year 1951. January - 25 Reports
Year 1952. July - 536 Reports
Year 1953. February - 91 Reports
Year 1954. July - 60 Reports
Year 1955. August - 68 Reports
Year 1956 August - 123 Reports

On October 11, 1956, *The New York Times* ran a "WASHINGTON, Oct. 10" *Associated Press* story in an article titled "MILITARY ACCIDENT TOLL." This article gave the statistics of service personnel killed in "military aircraft" accidents as reported by "The Defense Department" since 1951. It was reported from 1951 until the dated October 10 news release, that there were "7,600" service personnel killed in all types of United States military aircraft. These six years were indeed, six deadly years. How many of these 7,600 fatalities occurred because of UFO intercepts written off as training costs. Is it not time that we woke up and take a further look into this matter!

The following is a top 20 list of the most UFO reports received by Project Blue Book per month between the years 1951 and 1956.

1. 536 - July 1952
2. 326 - August 1952
3. 148 - June 1952
4. 124 - September 1952
5. 123 - August 1956
6. 91 – February 1953
7. 82 – April 1952
8. 79 – May 1952
9. 72 – July 1956
10. 71 – September 1956
11. 68 – August 1955
12. 67 – January 1953
13. 63 – July 1955
14. 61 – October 1952
15. 60 – July 1954
16. 57 – September 1955
17. 56 – October 1956
18. 55 – October 1955
19. 54 – May 1955
20. 53 – October 1956

The four months that rank highest on this Blue Book top 20 list are the summer months of 1952. That year also charted six of the eight highest months on the list. There are seven months out of the top twenty months with the most received UFO sightings per month; the year 1952. The years 1955 and 1956 each had five months on the top 20 list for that six-year period but 1956 had three months in the top ten of highest months.

In Donald Keyhoe's book, *Aliens From Space*, he wrote about the Air Forces ongoing pursuits after Unidentified Flying Objects subsequent to 1956. He stated the following:

In 1957, Representative (now Senator) Lee Metcalf asked the Air Force if its pilots were still pursuing UFOs. In the reply from headquarters, Major Joe W. Kelly admitted the continued chases. "Air Force interceptors still pursue unidentified flying objects as a matter of security to this country and to determine technical aspects involved."

The UFO sightings reported to project Blue book for the year 1957, were 1,006 sightings, the third highest amount reported in Blue Book history. Edward Ruppelt stated the following in 1956, "Maybe the earth is being visited by interplanetary spaceships. Only time will tell." Fifty-one years later, I ask, how many fighter pilots and radar observers died while pursuing Unidentified Flying Objects? Only time will tell...

This story appeared on the front page of *The New York Times*, July 8, 1954 and involved the mysterious crash of an F-84F Jet.

By Stanton T. Friedman

It is clear from the previous chapters that Frank Feschino, Jr. has done an incredible job of collecting, arranging and chronicling data about the UFO events that took place during the summer of 1952. His work informs us about Project Blue Book, the press and the key players involved in the UFO problem during that era. Most importantly, Frank's persistence in researching the overwhelming amount of mysterious fighter jet accidents that occurred in 1952 and throughout the 1950s is very revealing...if not startling. As I noted in my MUFON 2005 paper, "Government UFO Lies" there was a comment by General Roger Ramey of Roswell fame, by then five years after Roswell a Major General, that planes had been scrambled hundreds of times after UFOs. It was when Frank pointed out Edward Ruppelt's statement, "There have been other and more lurid 'duels of death,'" the big picture came in to focus. So much for the notion that UFOs are not a threat to national security. There was much more going in the 1950s than meets the eye.

Then we have the Flatwoods case. On that date, there were a host of UFO sightings, close encounters, and in most of the sightings, a simple explanation was provided … meteors. The facts did not support that explanation though. Meteors don't land, they don't make sharp turns, they don't reverse course; they don't fly from city to city-following rivers and airport flight lines. When they do smash into the ground, there are often sonic booms, craters, shock waves. The fact of the matter is that there are meteor showers in September that even *Sky and Telescope* Magazine, which often listed significant meteor flights, recorded none for September 12, 1952. Furthermore, the Harvard Meteor Project that was operated between 1952 and 1954 and recorded 2401 meteor passages recorded none on September 12, 1952. The project was under the direction of Harvard Astronomer, Dr. Donald Howard Menzel, who was a well-known UFO debunker. A more detailed investigation, as reported in my book, *TOP SECRET/MAJIC*, indicated Menzel was up to his ears in highly classified activities for such government agencies as the National Security Agency, the Central Intelligence Agency, the Office of Naval Intelligence, and was a member of Operation Majestic 12. One suspects that if he could have found a meteor (or several) to explain the events of Sept. 12, he would have. One is reminded of how often Venus has been identified as the source of a UFO report even in cases when it was not visible at the time and location of the sighting.

On September 12, the press noted many reports of high-speed objects in their local area, often ignoring events in other locations and blindly accepting "meteor" even when it was clear from the witness testimony that what was observed could not have been a meteor. Obviously, there were no UFO reporters looking at the big picture for the news wire services, or apparently for Project Blue Book either. Painstakingly, Frank Feschino, Jr. did manage to piece together the Blue Book file and it was woefully inadequate.

There are aspects of the events that at first glance seem quite puzzling including the glowing varying color regions around what was observed. Now that we know how important plasma phenomena can be with regard to potential propulsion systems such as those involving magneto aerodynamics, they make more sense. We have the intriguing comments by one of the boys that even where there had been glowing regions of air, there was not high heat. The tree from behind which the "monster" emerged was not burned nor the leaves charred. Plasma is often called the fourth state of matter along with liquid, solid and gas. Most of the universe is made of plasma including the stars, the ionosphere, much of deep space. In simplest terms, everyday matter is electrically neutral. But if some electrons are separated from the atoms around which they revolve, one can create electrically conducting fluid, plasma. Fluorescent bulbs have plasmas inside them when turned on. Some plasma is relatively cool and some, such as those produced by nuclear explosions, are very hot indeed.

When the Apollo astronauts were returning from the moon, some of the command modules' energy when striking the atmosphere went in to ionizing the air around the blunt end of the system. Because it is an electrically conducting fluid, that plasma prevented radio signals from the command module from reaching the earth causing the temporary but well-known communications blackout. When we observe high-speed "shooting stars," we are actually observing the plasma created by the much smaller meteor.

The point here is that we now know that having plasma around a high-speed object moving in the atmosphere can allow one to avoid many of the problems of high-speed flight. With appropriate electric and magnetic fields, one can control lift, drag, heating, sonic boom production, and radar profile. Plasmas are produced when nose cones on Intercontinental Ballistic Missiles reenter the atmosphere. There has been a great deal of research dealing with this atmospheric plasma problem, most of it classified. If one wants the nose cone to hit a target, one must understand the effect of the ionized atmosphere on the drag (frictional slowing down) on the nose cone. One can try to change the plasma characteristics by incorporating easily ionized (broken up into ions and electrons) substances in the outer layer to fool the defense radar into mistaking a decoy for a real nose cone.

Way back in 1969 while working for McDonnell Douglas Astronautics on possible UFO propulsion schemes, I had a search done of the technical report literature produced under government contracts for the DOD and NASA. The keyword that was used was magneto aerodynamics. There were 900 references located of which 90% were classified. Powerful radar beams, microwave beams, infrared beams, charged particles from radioactive substances, can all affect the object and the plasmas around it. The new systems being used by the Lockheed F-94C in 1952 to get a radar lock-on and fire the plane's air-to-air missiles at an intruding Soviet aircraft or flying saucer would certainly have been a concern to the inhabitants of the saucers. Once they learned what the radar lock-on meant, they may have taken immediate action to destroy the aircraft on the verge of firing a missile at them. The many descriptions of glowing colored regions of gas around the objects, sound very much like manifestations of plasma phenomena and interactions with electromagnetic systems described as well as possible by people who knew nothing about such phenomena.

Dr. Stewart Way, an outstanding scientist with the Westinghouse Research Laboratory in Pittsburgh, Pennsylvania, actually supervised the building of an analogous 9' long electromagnetic submarine in 1966 at the University of California, Santa Barbara. Seawater, an electrically conducting fluid akin to ionized air, was influenced by electric and magnetic fields. There were no moving parts, but the submarine moved through the seawater. A number of years later a large Japanese company built a much larger electromagnetic ship actually using superconducting magnets to provide very strong magnetic fields while using little electrical power. Larger superconducting magnets are used in medical MRIs and in big accelerators.

I had a quiet conversation with a military radar operator who, while based in Kalispell, Montana, in the early 1950s, had the experience of being told by Canadian Air Defense people that a saucer was headed his way. A USAF interceptor in the neighborhood was vectored towards the intruder. The scenario was being watched on radar and then the interceptor disappeared. Even though they knew its direction and speed of flight and altitude, no wreckage was ever found. The radar operator told me that after that, the message went out "Do not shoot at intruding UFOs, take gun camera pictures." Many years ago, I had a quiet conversation with an individual who had worked for the National Security Agency listening post nearest to Cuba. The Soviets in the Cuban base were told in March, 1967, of an approaching UFO at 30,000 feet and moving at Mach one. Two MIG 21's were scrambled to meet the saucer heading SW towards Cuba. It did not respond to their demands to go away. The lead pilot, after describing it over the airwaves as spherical with no appendages, was told to shoot it down. His missile was armed, the radar locked on, and then suddenly the wingman shouted that the first plane had disintegrated. The UFO ascended to 90,000 feet and headed Southeast at Mach several. Certainly, the saucer could tell when the lock-on was achieved. The NSA asked for a copy of the original tape, though this was very rare, and the base was told to list the loss of the MIG as due to equipment malfunction. Attempts to obtain more information through the freedom of information act were met with strong intimidation by the FBI and the office of the USAF's Inspector General.

Unfortunately, records of all such encounters between intruding aircraft, including flying saucers, and our air defense systems are born classified and remain that way as are records of many other observations of "Uncorrelated targets" inspected by the Air Defense Command. One wonders how many of the almost completely whited-out TOP SECRET National Security Agency UFO documents (obtained through a long legal battle) dealt with observed intercepts by alien spacecraft of Earthling aircraft. I am reminded of a comment by USAF General Carroll Bolender in a memo dated October 20, 1969, and dealing with his recommendation that Project Blue Book be closed (Which it was that December). Bolender, with whom I later spoke, noted that closing Project Blue Book would get rid of a place for the public to report UFO sightings. He stated, "Moreover, reports of unidentified flying objects which could affect national security are made in accordance with JANAP (Joint Army Navy Air Force Publication) 146 or Air Force Manual 55-11 and are not part of the Blue Book System." Two paragraphs later, "However, as already stated, reports of UFOs which could affect national security would continue to be handled through the standard Air Force procedures designed for this purpose." I checked and found that Project Blue Book was not on the distribution list provided in the noted regulations.

This iceberg of data is still clearly under the water of secrecy. One wonders what it would take, starting with the extensive data compiled by Frank, to obtain the full-uncensored accident reports of events taking place more than 50 years ago. One excuse given by authorities to families seeking details of a pilot's demise is, "We want all interviewed people connected with the airplane to speak freely without fear of being sued if it turns out that a certain aircraft component had malfunctioned." Thus, the secrets of these too-close encounters are doomed to secrecy if no major press group makes the effort to cut through the secrecy.

Much less understandable is the failure of CSICOP "Investigator" Dr. Joseph Nickell to do an adequate investigation of the event. He visited the Fisher Farm, but didn't get past the first pasture and didn't see the important oak tree on the other side of the gate. Nickell didn't view the flat clearing on the mountaintop where the alleged "meteor" landed after making a slow turn over the town …without a sonic boom, without a crater, and no meteoric residue being found. In addition, Nickell didn't view the gulley where the damaged craft relocated. Moreover, he didn't talk with Mrs. May or her sons. Does anybody really believe his story of the 6-foot owl? Journalist Stewart went to the May home shortly after the event, talked to the witnesses and went onto the farm. Where the boys so frightened by this alleged owl that they became sick and Lemon threw up all night from fright though Stewart had noted a gaseous odor near the ground at the site? He thought that, while the boys had certainly been frightened, they had genuinely been ill from some substance emitted by the "monster."

In short, Nickell's investigation typified debunking at its worst, applying four major rules:
1. What the public doesn't know, I won't tell them. 2. Don't bother me with the facts my mind is made up.
3. If you can't attack the data, attack the people. 4. Do your research by proclamation; investigation is too much trouble. For shame! Any persons with first or second hand knowledge about the Flatwoods incident or those who may know of any close encounters between military aircraft and UFOs please contact me toll free, at 1-877-457-0232. Witness names won't be used without permission. Of course information will be shared with Frank Feschino, Jr. Clippings can be sent to me at PO. Box 958, Houlton, ME 04730-0958.

My email is **fsphys@rogers.com**. Web Site: http://www.stantonfriedman.com

Stanton T. Friedman

Mrs. Kathleen May and Stanton T. Friedman

Frank Feschino, Jr., Freddie May, and Stanton T. Friedman

SELECTED SOURCES

BOOKS

Ageton, Arthur A. *The Naval Officers Guide*. 4th Ed. New York: McGraw-Hill, 1951.
Air Force ROTC-Air Science II. *Applied Air Power*. ConAC Manual 50-2 Part 3. Mitchell AFB, NY: Continental Air Command, n.d.
Air Navigation for Pilots. AFM No. 51-43. Washington, D.C.: Dept. of the Air Force. 1952.
The Air Officer's Guide. 2nd ed. rev. Harrisburg, PA: The Military Publ. Co., 1951.
Aircraft Industries Assoc. The Aircraft Yearbook 1952. 34th ed. Washington, D.C.: Lincoln Press, n.d.
The Airman's Handbook. 1st ed. rev. Harrisburg, PA: The Military Publ. Co., 1950.
The Airman's Handbook. 2nd ed. rev. Harrisburg, PA: The Military Publ. Co., 1951.
The Blue Jackets Manual. 14th ed. Annapolis, MD: U.S. Naval Inst., 1950.
Casamassa, Jack V., Editor. *Jet Aircraft Power Systems*. McGraw-Hill Book Company, Inc., 1950
Condon, Edward U. Project Director *Scientific Study of Unidentified Flying Objects*. New York: Bantam Book Edition, 1969.
Davidson, Dr. Leon. *Flying Saucers: An Analysis of the Air Force Project Blue Book Special Report NO. 14*. 3rd ed. Ramsey, NJ: Ramsey-Wallace, Corp., 1966.
Filter Station Operation. AFM No. 50-13. Washington, D.C.: Dept. of the Air Force, 1952.
Good, Timothy. *Above Top Secret: The Worldwide UFO Cover-up*. New York: William Morrow, 1988.
Green, William and Cross, Ray. *The Jet Aircraft of the World*. Hanover House Edition, 1955.
Gross, Loren. *UFO's: A History 1952: June –July 20 Th*. Privately Published. Fremont, California
Gross, Loren. *UFO's: A History 1952: July 21st-July 31st*. Privately Published. Fremont, California.
Ground Observer's Guide. AFM 50-12. Washington, D.C.: Dept. of the Air Force, 1951.
Hillman, William. *Mr. President*. New York: Farrar, Strauss, & Young, 1952.
Keyhoe, Donald. *Aliens From Space*. Doubleday & Company, Inc. 1973.
Keyhoe, Donald. *The Flying Saucer Conspiracy*. Henry Holt & Co., 1955.
Keyhoe, Donald. *Flying Saucers from Outer Space*. Henry Holt & Co., 1953.
Keyhoe, Donald. *Flying Saucers- Top Secret*. Henry Holy & Co. 1960.
Mason, Jr., Herbert Molloy. *The United States Air Force-A Turbulent History*. Mason-Carter. 1976.
Miller, Max B. *Flying Saucers Fact or Fiction*. Los Angeles: Trend Books, Inc., 1957.
NASA. *The Dictionary of Technical Terms for Aerospace Use*. Washington, D.C.: U.S. Govt. Printing Office, 1965.
Povenmire, Harold. *Fireballs, Meteors and Meteorites*. Indian Harbour Beach, FL: JSB Enterprises, 1980.
Rolfe, Douglas and Dawydoff, Alexis. *Airplanes of the World*. Simon & Shuster, 1962.
Ruppelt, Edward J. *The Report on Unidentified Flying Objects*. New York: Doubleday & Co., 1956.
Stringfeld, Leonard H. *Situation Red, The UFO Siege!* Doubleday & Company, Inc. 1977
Sanderson, Ivan T. *Uninvited Visitors: A Biologist Looks at UFOs*. New York: Cowles Educ. Corp., 1967.
STARFIRE F-94C weapon data. California Division, Lockheed Airport Corporation - Burbank, California. 27 April 1953.
Tacker, Lt. Col. Lawrence J. *Flying Saucers and the US Air Force*. D. Van Nostrand Company, Inc., 1960.
Theory of instrument flying. AFM No. 51-38. Washington, DC: Dept. of the Air Force. April 1954.
The Unicorn Book of 1952: Outstanding Events of the Year. New York: Unicorn Books, Inc., 1953.
The U.S. Air Force Dictionary. Washington, D.C.: U.S. Govt. Printing Office, Air University Press, 1956.
Wilkins, Harold T. *Flying Saucers on the Attack*. New York: Citadel Press, 1954.
Wolfe, Tom. *The Right Stuff*. Rev. Ed. New York: Farrar, Strauss, Giroux, 1983.

MAGAZINES AND PERIODICALS

"Agricultural Almanac for the year 1952." Lancaster, PA: John Baers Sons, 1951.
"Almanac for the year 1952," Winston-Salem, NC: Blum's Almanac Syndicate 1951. Winston-Salem, NC. Almanac for the Year 1952. 1951.
"Astronomical Highlights of 1952," *Sky and Telescope*. (Dec. 1952): 45.
Barker, Gray. "Flatwoods W.Va. Monster, A Full Report of Investigation," *The Saucerian*. 1 no. 1. (Sept. 1953).
Barker, Gray. "The Monster and the Saucer," *FATE*. Vol. 6. (Jan. 1953): 12-17.
Birnes, William J. The Incredible Mac Magruder Story. *UFO MAGAZINE*. Vol. 21-No. 4 (June 2006).
"Conferences—The International Astronautical Federation," *Time*. no. 11 (Sept. 15, 1952): 32. "Here and There with Amateurs," Sky and Telescope. (Sept. 1952): 289.
"EQUIPMENT-Far East Pilots Praise F-94's Durability," *Aviation Week*. (July 7, 1952).
Friedman, Stanton T. and Slate, B. Ann. *UFO REPORT*. "UFO Battles The Air Force Couldn't Cover Up." Vol. 2-No. 2. (Winter 1974)
(Hamilton, C. L. "Defense of the Homeland - Taking Saucers Seriously," *Flying*. (August 1952):48 Ley, Willy. ("Man on the Moon" comp.) "Inside the Moonship," *Collier's, The National Weekly*. 130, no. 16. (Oct. 18, 1952): 56.
Keyhoe, Donald. What Radar Tells Us About Flying Saucers. *TRUE Magazine*. December 1952.
Lieb, Paul (interview with George Snitowsky). "The West Virginia Monster," *Male*. 5, no. 7. (July 1955): 39, 78-79.
Luyten, Prof. William. J. "If a Giant Meteor Hit a Modern City," *Science and Invention*. Vol. 17, no. 4. (1929): 296-297, 365.
Miller, Maxwell. "What Are The Flying Saucers?" *Mystic Magazine*, Issue NO. 11. August 1955.
Montgomery, Jack. "Report from the Readers - Circling Object," *FATE*. Vol. 6 (Feb. 1953): 108
Parrish, Wayne W., ed. "Worldwide Airline Schedules, Fares and Information,"
Official Airline Guide – An American Aviation Publication. 8. no. 12. (Sept. 1952).
Perreault, William D. "Extra Section," *American Aviation* (September 1, 1952): 42.
"Production Highlights...Lockheed F-94C Starfire," *American Aviation*. (July 7, 1952).
Sanderson, Ivan T. "Sutton Monster Real?" *Infinity*. Contained in Project Blue Book. 1 Page article.
TIME. SCIENCE. (August 11, 1952):58.
UFO Investigator, NICAP 1958. VOL. I, NO. 5.
Von Braun, Wernher Dr. ("Man on the Moon" comp.) "The Journey," *Collier's, The National Weekly*. 130. no. 16 (Oct. 18, 1952): 52-58.
Wilson, W. L., ed. *The Aircraft Flash – Official G.O.C. Magazine* 1, no. 1 (Oct. 1952).

NEWSPAPERS

"Aerial Whazzit Seen Here Friday," *The Greensboro Record*. 16 September 1952.
"Air Force Alerts Jets to Chase 'Flying Saucers' Anywhere In U.S," *United Press-(UP)*. July 29, 1952.
"Air Force Debunks 'Saucers' As Just 'Natural Phenomena,'" *The New York Times*. 30 July 1952.
"Air Force Explains 2 - Hour Delay in Chasing 'objects' Over Capital" *The New York Times*. 29 July 1952.

"AIR FORCE HERO KILLED," *The New York Times*. 3 September 1952.
"Air Force Lays Saucer Blips Here To Heat," *The New York Times*. 30 July 1952.
"AIR FORCE ORDERS 11 NEW JET TYPES," The New York Times. 14 September 1952.
"Air Force Orders Jet Pilots To Shoot Down Flying Saucers If They Refuse To Land," *The Seattle Post Intelligencer*. 29 July 1952.
"AIR FORCE PROBES FLYING SAUCERS-Four State 'Disc' Reports Unexplained," *The Greensboro Daily News*. 13 September 1952.
"Air Force's New Supersonic Jet Plane –F-94C Starfire, All-Rocket Jet Interceptor," *The New York Times*. 3 July 1952.
"Air Force Seeks Solution; Gives 'Shoot Down Order, '" WASHINGTON-INS. International News Service. 28 July 1952.
"ALERT JETS TO HUNT SAUCERS," *New York Daily News*. 29 SEPTEMBER 1952.
"An Artists Conception . . .," *Weston (W.V.) Democrat*. 26 September 1952.
"Apparso UN Mostro nel West della Virginia," *Il Giornale D'Italia*. 17 September 1952.
"Authorities Probe Flashes In Area Skies—Strange Lights Observed Over Four States," *The (Martins Ferry-Bellaire, Ohio) Times-Leader*. 13 September 1952.
"Balls of Fire In Pittsburgh: Jittery Citizens Report Planes In Flames Over Wide Area," *Wilmington (Del.) Sunday Star*. 14 September 1952.
"'Bashful Billy' Plagues Patrol," *The Wheeling Intelligencer*. 17 September 1952.
"Bethany Professor Blames Imagination – Citizens 'Hypnotized' into Seeing 'Saucers.'" *The Wheeling News Register*. 16 September 1952.
"Boogie Man Has B.O.-Monster From Space Roaming W.Va. Hills?" *The Wheeling Intelligencer*. 15 September 1952.
"Braxton County Monster," *The Braxton (W.V.) Democrat*. 18 September 1952.
"Braxton Co. Residents Faint, Become Ill after Run-In With Weird 10-Foot Monster," *The Charleston Daily Mail*. 14 September 1952.
"Braxton Folks Divided Over Visitor-'Monster May Have Been Due To Dead Tree, Meteor, Beacon," *The Charleston Daily Mail*. 15 September 1952.
"Braxton Monster Left Skid Marks Where He Landed," *The Charleston Gazette*. 15 September 1952.
"Bright Meteor Reported," *The New York Times*. 5 February 1952.
"British Society Terms 'Saucers' Strictly From Comic Books," *The Bridgeport (CT). Sunday Post*. 14 September 1952.
"BULLETIN; TAMPA-AP," *Panama City News Herald*. 14 September 1952.
"By The Way with Bill Henry," *The Los Angeles Times*. 1 August 1952.
"CAA Officials Own Story - How Radar Spotted Whatzits That Air Force Couldn't Find," *The Washington Daily News*. 23 July 1952.
"CAP To Continue Plane Search," *The Tampa Tribune*. 17 September 1952.
"Centerville, Virginia," International News Story. (INS). 22 September 1952.
"City Dust Haze Replaces Interest in Sky Objects," *Kingsport (Tenn.) Times-News*. 14 September 1952.
"'Crashing' Plane Believed Meteor," *Ohio State Journal*. 13 September 1952.
"Did It Ride Meteor?—Boys Spot Appalling Creature near Flatwoods, Link It to Fiery Objects In Skies," *The Charleston Gazette*. 14 September 1952.
"'Disk' Seen Over Japan," *The New York Times*. 28 January 1952.
"Don't Shoot Them Down, Rocket Man Says," *The Louisville Courier-Journal*. 30 July 1952.
"'Egg-Shaped' Flying Saucer Sighted Near Douglass, Kan.," *The Wichita Evening Eagle*. 16 September 1952.

"8 Residents Report 'Saucers' On Nocturnal Sweep through Sky," *The Camden Post Courier*. 6 August 1952.
"EMERGENCIES-Lost Pilot Was From Sanford, AF Reports," *The Daytona Beach Morning Journal*. 16 September 1952.
"Fiery Object Seen by Man at Clearwater," *The Wichita Evening Eagle*. 16 September 1952.
"Fiery Object Streaks across Skies of 4 States—A Meteor? Could Be," *The New Haven Register*. 13 September 1952.
"Fiery Objects Flash Across Sky in W.Va.—Many From Wheeling To Bluefield Puzzled Over Weird Spectacle," *The Charleston Daily Mail*. 13 September 1952.
"15 'Flying Saucer' Reports from N. E. Unexplained-Objects Spotted Form Holyoke, Long Meadow, Westover on List; Most of Sightings Identified," *The Springfield News*. 13 September 1952.
"Fireballs Shower City Area—Meteor Blamed As Cause Of Scare," *The Columbus (Ohio) Citizen*. 13 September 1952.
"FLAME OVER WASHINGTON," *The New York Times*. 13 September 1952.
"Flaming Object Seen at Capitol," *The Springfield (Mass.) News*. 13 September 1952.
"Flashes of Life. Green Monster with Blood-Red Face Scares Wits Out of Seven Hill Folk," *The Binghamton (N.Y.) Press*. 15 September 1952.
"Flat Rock Man Calls News To Report Flying Saucer," *The Mount Airy News*. 19 September 1952.
"Flatwoods Revisited," *The Sunday Gazette-Mail*. 6 March 1966.
"Flatwoods Visit Convinced Skeptic Saucers Are Real," *The Charleston Gazette*. 30 April 1968
"Fliers Hunt Tyndall Pair," *Panama City News Herald*. 14 September 1952.
"Flying Objects 'Invade' State; 6 Seen From Highland Park," *The Topeka Capital*. 15 September 1952.
"'Flying Saucers' Merely Light, Says Noted Harvard Scientist-Air Force Agrees With Dr. Menzel," *The Boston Globe*. 30 July 1952.
"Flying Saucers Reported in Air Force's Backyard," *The Boston Globe*. 23 July 1952.
"'Flying Saucer' Reported seen By Mrs. Blackwell," *Leaksville (N.C.) News*. 18 September 1952.
"Flying Saucers Sighted," *The New York Times*. 24 June 1952.
"Flying Saucers Still A Mystery," *The Sydney Morning Herald*. 18 July 1952.
"4 Jets Crash in Formation Dive, Killing Pilots in Georgia Mystery" *The New York Times*. 7 December 1953
"Four Mysterious Shiny Objects," *The Reporter*. 20 June 1952.
"Four States 'Bombarded by Meteor-Like Objects,'" *The Boston Globe*. 13 September 1952.
"Green Bodied, Red-Faced and Smelly. Huge 'Monster' on West Va. Hill Frightens Woman and Six Boys," *The Manchester Union Leader*. 15 September 1952.
"Hamilton Air Force Base," *Associated Press* News Story (AP). 3 August 1952.
"High Speed 'Flying Saucer' Spotted By Osborn Guard," *The Hartford Courant*. 7 September 1952.
"HXR 127-Hoyt Vandenberg," Newswire. New York. 16 June 1952.
"HUNDREDS IN STATE SEE FLYING SAUCERS," *The Indianapolis News*. 28 July 1952.
"Jet Bombers Bring 'Saucer' Reports," *The Lansing State Journal*. 28 July 1952.
"JET CRASH VICTIM FOUND TO BE HERO," *The New York Times*. 12 August 1952.
"Jet Pilot Killed In Crash" The New York Times. 29 November 1954.
"JET PLANE PILOT CHUTES TO SAFETY AT GLASTONBURY, -Royal Air Force Flier Hammers Way Out Of Cockpit." *The Bridgeport Telegram*. 6 August 1952.
"Jet Plane, Running Low On Gas, Brought In At MacDill," *The Tampa Tribune*. 17 September 1952.

"Jets Couldn't Find Them-Air Force After D.C. 'Saucers'" *The Washington Daily News*. 29 July 1952.

"Jets Fly 'Through' Target," *The New York Times*. 3 September 1952.

"Jets On 24 Hour Alert to Shoot Down Saucers," *The San Francisco Examiner*. 29 July 1952.

"Jets Ready to Chase Lights, 24-Hour Alert Ordered After Second Appearance Here," *The Washington Daily News*. 28 July 1952.

"Jets Ready to Chase Lights," *The Washington Daily News*. 28 July 1952.

"Jets Told to Shoot Down Flying Discs," *The Fall River (Mass.) Herald-News*. 29 July 1952.

"Large Meteorite Sighted In This Section," Morgantown (W.V.) *The Dominion News*. 13 September 1952.

"Last Heard From Yesterday-MacDill Searches For Pilot Down In Flight Over Gulf," *The Tampa Daily Times*. 13 September 1952.

"Laugh If You Want To- But There They Were," *The Washington Daily News*. 29 July 1952.

"LONG ISLAND JET PILOT KILLED," *The New York Times*. 28 August 1952.

"Lt. John A. Jones Is Reported Missing," *The Sanford Herald*. 15 September 1952.

"MacDill Mum on Saucers Here," *The Tampa Times*. 23 July 1952.

"Make Positive Statement," *The New York Times*. 2 August 1952.

"Many Report Thing In Sky At Reidsville," *The Greensboro Daily News*. 16 September 1952.

"Metallic Odor Indicates Meteor — Officers Shake Heads Over W.Va. Ogre Tail," *The Wheeling News-Register*. 15 September 1952.

"Meteor Seen Whizzing Across Maryland Skies," *The Charleston Gazette*. 13 September 1952.

"Meteorite Spotted In Kanawha Area," *The Charleston Gazette*. 13 September 1952.

"Meteorite Viewed By Many Residents In Early Evening," *The Greensboro Daily News*. 13 September 1952.

"Military Accident Toll" *The New York Times*. 11 October 1956

"Missing Airmen's Names Announced," *The Tampa Daily Times*. 16 September 1952.

"The Monster of Braxton County: Around A Bend They Saw A Pair Of Bulging Eyes," *The Washington Daily News*. 15 September 1952.

"Monster Still Top Subject," *The Braxton Democrat*. 25 September 1952.

"Monster Story To Be Broadcast," (Ohio) *The Times-Leader*. 17 September 1952.

"Mystery Lights Zip Through Skies Here Stirring Mild Furor," *The Wheeling Intelligencer*. 13 September 1952.

"Mystery Object Frightened His Cattle," *The Daytona Beach Morning Journal*. 16 September 1952.

"Mystery Photo, Jet Pilots' Report Added To Flying Saucer Mystery Puzzle," *The New York Times*. 28 July 1952

"Objects Seen Over Tarrytown," *The New York Times*. 29 July 1952.

"Odd Balloon Is Found In Tree," *The Daytona Beach Morning Journal*. 16 September 1952.

"Operation Skywatch Opens Monday," *The Springfield Union*. 13 July 1952.

"Ohio, Columbus," *Associated Press*. 24 July 1952. (AP).

"Pett, Saul," *Associated Press* Staff Writer. 29 July 1952. (AP).

"Pictures Record Firemen's Work," *The Glastonbury Citizen*. 8 August 1952.

"Pilot Bails Out, Lands Safely After MacDill Hears Distress Call," *The Tampa Tribune*. 13 September 1952.

"Pilot Trapped In Falling Plane," *The New York Times*. 6 August 1952.

"Pine Airmen Lost In Flight," *The Baker Democrat Herald*. 15 September 1952.

"Planes Hunt For Missing Jet Fighter," *The Tampa Sunday Tribune*. 14 September 1952.

"Planes Press Search for Jet Fighter," *Panama City News Herald*. 16 September 1952.

"Police Say Braxton Monster Product of Mass Hysteria," *The Fairmont Times*. 15 September 1952.
"Powered By Suggestion? – 'Monster' From Outer Space Arrives Here Via 'Saucer,'" *The Wheeling Intelligencer*. 16 September 1952."
"Radar Screen Picks Up Fleet Of Flying Saucers In Capital," *The New Haven Register*. 6 August 1952.
"Radar Spots 'Saucers' Over Washington Again," *The Louisville Courier Journal*. 30 July 1952.
"RAF FLIER ESCAPES DEATH IN STATE CRASH," *The New Have Register*. 6 August 1952.
"RAF Pilot Fights Clear Of Falling Jet, 'Chutes To Safety In South Glastonbury,'" *The Hartford Courant*. 6 August 1952.
"RAF Pilot Visits Glastonbury," *The Glastonbury Citizen*. 8 August 1952.
"Residents of Ohio Valley Excited as Heavenly Meteor Hurls off Bright Fragments," *The Wheeling News Register*. 13 September 1952.
"SAUCERS SIGHTED-Speedy Jets Alerted In Vain Hunt," *The Rockford Register-Republic*. 11-August 1952.
"'Saucer Suspect' Rammed by Jet; Nothing There," *The Hartford Courant*. 3 September 1952.
"Saucers Visit On West Coast," *The New York Times*. 25 July 1952.
"Scores of Baltimoreans See Meteor-Like Object in Skies," *The Baltimore Sun*. 13 September 1952
"Scores See 'Green Light Over Area,'" *The Washington Post*. 13 September 1952.
"Seven Chased By Saucer Monster Scared To Death," *The Statesville Record and Landmark*. 15 September 1952.
"'Shapeless Light' Sighted At Hydrogen Bomb Plant. *The New York Times*. 6 August 1952.
"SIGHTINGS INCREASE HERE," *The New York Times*. 30 July 1952.
"Six Armed Jets…," *The New York Times*. 25 July 1952.
"60 'Saucer' Reports Fly At Air Force in 2 Weeks," *The New York Times*. 18 July 1952.
"Sky Object Seen Here—Search Ends For Wrecked Aircraft," *The Kingsport Times-News*. 14 September 1952.
"'Something' Seen Over the City," *The Bremerton Sun*. 29 August 1952.
"Southwest's 7 Fireballs In 11 Days Called Without Parallel In History," *The New York Times*. 10 November 1951.
"Space 'Thing' 17 Feet High Has Red Face, Very Bad BO: Seven in W. Virginia Swear 'Glowing Monster' Had Green Body, Odor Made Them Ill," *The Springfield News*. 15 September 1952.
"Strange Objects in Worcester Sky," *The Lawrence Tribune*. 23 July 1952.
"Suggests No Shooting at 'Saucers,'" *The Manchester Union-Leader*. 30 July 1952.
"The Thing, 10 Feet Tall, Terrifies Party of 7," *The New York Daily News*. 15 September 1952.
"They're in the Sky Again-Radar Spots More Mystery Objects Here, Fliers Report Sighting Glowing Lights," *The Washington Post*. 28 July 1952.
"Things in Sky Here Sunday Appear Like Flying Saucers," *The Ypsillanty Press*. 28 July 1952.
"Third Time In Ten Days," *The New York Times*. 29 July 1952.
"3 MARINE FLIERS HUNTED IN PACIFIC" *The New York Times*. 29 June 1955.
"Truman To Stump Through 24 States," *The New York Times*. 13 September 1952.
"Truman Vows To Be 100 As He Gets Lifetime Pass," *The New York Times*. 13 September 1952.
"2 LOST JET AIRMEN ARE DEAD IN WRECK" *The New York Times*. 12 August 1951.
"2 In One Meteor Seen Over Ward" *The Charleston Daily Mail*. 14 September 1952.
"TWO JET PLANES CRASH" *The New York Times*. 25 June 1956.
"Unexplainable Objects Tracked By Air Force," *The Lowell Sun*. 18 July 1952.
"Unidentified Jets 'Buzz' R.I. Town," *The Boston Globe*. 13 September 1952.

"Urges USAF Not To Shoot Saucers," *The Lawrence Tribune*. 31 July 1952.
"Was Monster A Hoax? Are UFOs For Real? Hmmm A Possibility," *The Charleston Daily Mail*. 7 December 1977.
"Weather," *Panama City News-Herald*. 12 September 1952.
"The Weather," *The Tampa Morning Tribune*. 12 September 1952.
"The Weather in the Nation," *The New York Times*. 12 September 1952.
"Weather Map," *The Tampa Daily Times*. 12 September 1952.
"Well, It Was Some Ball of Fire," *The Washington Daily. News*. 13 September 1952.
"West Virginia Town Divided Over Report of Monster," *The (Martins Ferry-Bellaire, Ohio) Times-Leader*. 15 September 1952.
"What Happened To the Monster – Braxton County Woman Feels Glowing Ship Was Jet Ship – Discovery in 1952, Stirred Up Nation-Wide 'Martian' Debate," *The Charleston Gazette*. 7 October 1956.

MISCELLANEOUS

Air Force Intelligence Report. "Washington D.C. Night of July 26/27 1952."
ARTC untitled document. "Log of 26 July 1952."
ATIC-Wright Patterson AFB. *Project Blue Book*. Washington, D.C.: National Archives Microfilms, June, July, August, and September 1952.
Barker, Gray. *Letter to Major Donald Keyhoe* [USMC Retired]. 9 November 1953. Henry Holt & Co., New York.
Berliner, Donald. "*The Unexplained UFO Reports from the Files of the U.S. Air Force's Project Blue-Book UFO Investigations.*" Fund for UFO Research (1974).
Canadian UFO Report. Summer 1976. Vol. 3, # 8.
Nash, William; *Letter to Professor James E. McDonald*. 5 March 1970. University of Arizona Library, Tucson, Arizona. Special Collection Division.
Norton AFB, *Microfilm* case numbers; 52-7-27-3, 52-7-28-5, 52-9-12-4, 52-8-5-5.
Maxwell Air Force Base Historical Research Agency. *USAF Pamphlet 1993-0-738-833*.

About the Author

Stanton T. Friedman and Frank C. Feschino, Jr.

Frank C. Feschino, Jr. grew up in Connecticut. He is a graduate of the prestigious Paier School of Art in Hamden, Ct. where he studied illustration, commercial art, and photography. He was trained by several world-renowned artists including Kenneth Davies and Rudolph Zallinger, became an exceptional illustrator and earned his diploma in 1981. Feschino also studied film and video production at Phillips Jr. College in Florida where he earned an Associates Degree in 1994. As a result, Feschino honed additional communication abilities enhancing his stunning literary skills. In 1990, he became interested in UFOs when he visited a relative's farm in Braxton County West Virginia, where crop circles appeared overnight and UFO sightings were frequent. He documented these anomalies and shared his research with world-renowned crop circle enthusiast Colin Andrews.

Frank then discovered the story of the "Flatwoods Monster" incident and investigated this case for several years, becoming an authority on the event. He also applied a ceaselessly assiduous investigation into the UFO events that occurred throughout the summer of 1952, and wrote, Shoot Them Down!-The Flying Saucer Air Wars of 1952. Frank C. Feschino, Jr. has been investigating the UFO phenomena for approximately seventeen years and continues to do so, often working with Mr. Friedman. The author/Illustrator resides in central Florida.

For more information, visit: **www.flatwoodsmonster.com**

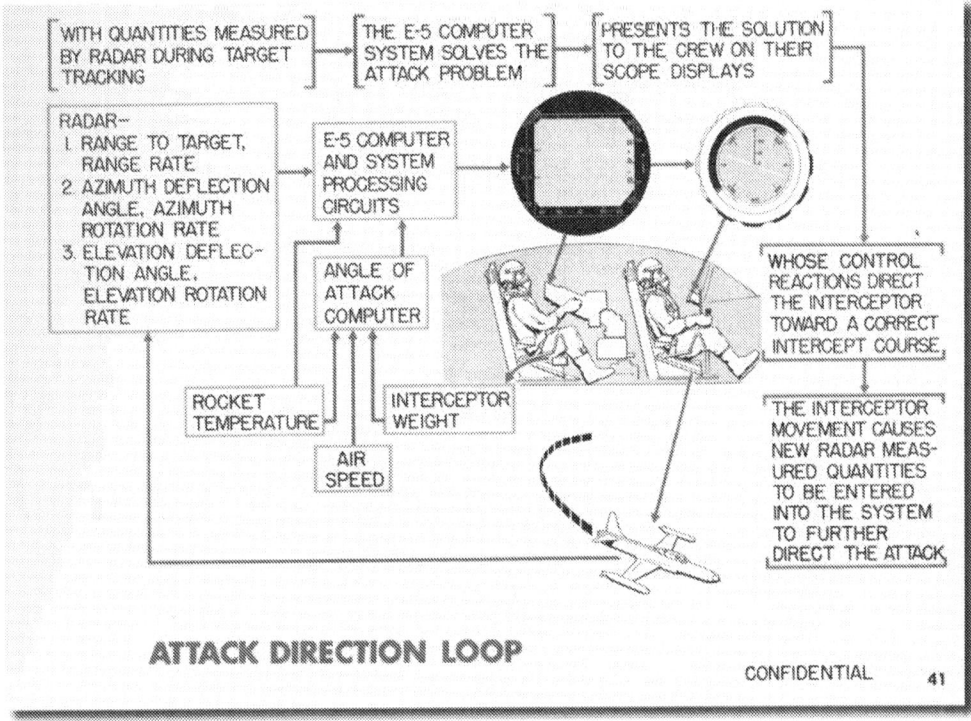

374

www.ingramcontent.com/pod-product-compliance
Ingram Content Group UK Ltd.
Pitfield, Milton Keynes, MK11 3LW, UK
UKHW051257180426
11947UKWH00020B/1754